John MacDonald

Diary of the Parnell Commission

Revised from The Daily News

John MacDonald

Diary of the Parnell Commission
Revised from The Daily News

ISBN/EAN: 9783337124533

Printed in Europe, USA, Canada, Australia, Japan

Cover: Foto ©ninafisch / pixelio.de

More available books at **www.hansebooks.com**

DIARY

OF THE

PARNELL COMMISSION

REVISED FROM "*THE DAILY NEWS*"

BY

JOHN MACDONALD, M.A.

London
T. FISHER UNWIN
PATERNOSTER SQUARE
MDCCCXC

INSCRIBED

TO

J. R. ROBINSON, Esq.,

EDITOR OF

THE DAILY NEWS.

PREFACE.

WHAT were the beginnings of the public inquiry which the Special Commission has brought to an end? When Mr. P. O'Connor was in the witness-box he told Mr. Ronan, with an amusing expression of surprise and compassion, that they were about three centuries old. For, whatever else it might be, the inquiry was an incident of the "Parnell Movement"; and Mr. Ronan, conscious that he must begin his cross-examination somehow, but feeling a little fluttered, had just asked the historian of the movement to tell him when the movement began.

Sir Henry James, in an address which even his opponents frankly admire for its ability and ingenuity, and a courtesy and considerateness that render it all the more formidable—Sir Henry James traces the origin of the inquiry to a speech of Mr. Parnell's, made during the debate on the Address, February, 1887, and warning the Government against the dangers of Coercion. But if a date must be chosen, why not make it thirty-five minutes to one of the morning of the 7th of June, 1886, when the House of Commons saw one of the most impressive scenes in its great history; when it had just reached the "parting of the ways," and each had chosen his path; and when, with an impulse characteristic of their race, the solid mass of Irish Nationalists sprang up with "three cheers for the Grand Old Man," in the hour of his defeat.[1]

The inquiry has been an expression of a general and far-reaching consequence —the re-grouping of men, in accordance with their choice between rival notions of right and duty, between rival political ideals, even between rival estimates of human nature—which has followed from that night's test, as surely as in a chemist's tube the ingredients are "precipitated" by a drop. And so, as regards Ireland, the first signs of the coming conflict manifested themselves in the February debate, of which Sir Henry James has spoken. The next came from *The Times*. On the 7th of March, 1887, appeared the first article of the famous series known as "Parnellism and Crime," the second on the 14th, the third on the 18th. And on the 22nd, Mr. Balfour answered the challenge of June, 1886, by giving notice of his Coercion Bill. *The Times* articles had prepared the way for him. For Mr. Balfour's purpose, they were worth a dozen speeches. It is hardly correct to say that they were a mere "re-hash" of forgotten accusations; for though more open to this criticism than subsequent ones, they also, like these—though in a less degree—presented the accusations with a definiteness, a systematic comprehensiveness, and a connection of detail, which were new to the public. The few well-informed persons to

---

[1] Since then I have witnessed an interesting illustration of the same characteristic, at a popular gathering. It was in a densely crowded meeting in the Rotunda, Dublin, end of 1887. Some hissing arose at the mention of Mr. Bright's name. But in an instant the sound was extinguished by a shout of protest from five thousand throats. Mr. Bright had been saying pretty hard things about the Home Rulers; but the Dublin people remembered that in other days Mr. Bright had struck many a strong blow for Ireland.

whom the articles were little more than a "re-hash" failed to make fair allowance for the ignorance of the man in the street.

Then the conflict developed itself all along the line—the Government, after a hard fight, carrying precedence for its Coercion Bill, reading the Bill, for the first time, in the beginning of April, by 361 against 253, and in three or four days more introducing the debate on the second reading; *The Times* all the while preaching from its dreadful text—"We charge that the Land League chiefs based their movement on a scheme of assassination carefully calculated and coolly applied." And London poured her Radical Clubs, Associations, and Federations of all sorts, into Hyde Park, with their endless flutter of flags, the green among them, and the emblems of the harp and the shamrock; and with British brass bands playing an Irish anthem which, borrowed by a *Times* criminal from the farewell of a convict in the dock, has since gone round the world. Fronting that long semi-circle of "pavilions," each with its orator-in-chief, Mr. Sexton, Mr. Labouchere, Mr. Hunter, Professor James Stuart, Mr. Michael Davitt, and others, there were about a quarter of a million souls, with their protest against Coercion.

The Times also took stock of this monster demonstration, and replied with a double dose of "Parnellism and Crime"—a special article on "the League at work," and a slashing leader. This was on April 12th. In another day or two appeared its report of a bitter speech of Mr. Chamberlain's at Ayr. The Irish members were goaded into fury; and on the night of the 15th there broke out the wild scene in Parliament—Colonel Saunderson, his tall figure bolt upright, his chest thrown out, shaking his fist at the Irish benches, as he called the League "a criminal conspiracy, supported by American dynamitards and murderers, with its heads in the House of Commons"; and Mr. Healy, starting up, and uttering, with all his force of hate and contempt, "liar"; and Mr. Sexton, with his "liar and coward," and threat of personal violence; and the defiant shouts from both sides of the House, "Retract," "Name," "Down with him," and all the rest of it.

So far it was, to borrow an expression of the Attorney-General's, an "open movement." But there was also an "underground movement," to borrow another. The defenders did not know, any more than the rest of the world, that the miner, patiently at work for months, was beneath their feet, ready to blow them up. It was now the morning of the 18th—last day of the debate on the second reading. And the directors of operations in Printing House Square did what any journalist would have done—any journalist, alive to his responsibilities, rejoicing in a big discovery, and naturally indisposed to incur the risk [if he refrained] of being himself blown up, as a person without patriotism and a proper sense of business. Now or never; on the morning of the 18th, *The Times* sprang its first mine: the *facsimile* letter stared London in the face, and in a few hours the Bill to coerce the alleged murder-mongers was read the second time by 370 against 269. Here is the *facsimile* letter, so called because it came first in a series of like publications:—

15/5/82.

DEAR SIR,

I am not surprised at your friend's anger, but he and you should know that to denounce the murders was the only course open to us. To do that promptly was plainly our best policy.

But you can tell him and all others concerned that though I regret the accident of Lord F Cavendish's death, I cannot refuse to admit that Burke got no more than his deserts.

You are at liberty to show him this, and others whom you can trust also, but let not my address be known. He can write to House of Commons.

Yours very truly,
CHAS. S. PARNELL.

Between the words "plainly" and "our," was an erasure of three words that appeared to be a repetition—"the only course"—of words almost immediately preceding. *The Times* explained that the "Dear Sir" was supposed to mean Patrick Egan.

Now, exclaimed *The Times*, now Messrs. Sexton and Healy, what of your "unblushing denials" of Friday night? Then, returning to the general charge, *The Times* pointed out that the accused had made no reply. Useless to pretend indifference. Either the charges against you are true, or they are not. If they are not, you should sue for "damages." But you have not done it. You have written "no letters"; not even to *The Times*, wherein the civilized world ventilates its grievances. And yet our pamphlet on "Parnellism and Crime" has been before the public for a month.

A copy of the pamphlet which I have before me bears the announcement "one hundred and twentieth thousand." The stronger expressions on its title-page are printed in red ink. In one of the corners is a mark not unlike a red thumb-mark. It is explained to be "the brand of the National League." But a leaguer might perhaps take it for the symbol of a Royal Irish constable's baton, after a charge.

Sir Henry James's speech has been an effort to prove that, even if the *facsimile* letters had been genuine they would have been chiefly interesting as illustrations or corroborations of the charges made in the three series of articles known as "Parnellism and Crime;" that the withdrawal of the letters did not matter very much. In the first article of the first series, it was said:—

> Be the ultimate goal of these men what it will, they are content to march towards it in company with murderers. Murderers provide their funds, murderers share their inmost counsels, murderers have gone forth from the League offices to set their bloody work afoot, and have presently returned to consult the "Constitutional leaders," on the advancement of the cause.

But as if that terrific charge were not enough, the article proceeded to make another, which, if true, should ultimately have led to the appearance even of Mr. Gladstone himself, and Earl Spencer, as respondents side by side with Mr. Biggar and Mr. Matt. Harris; for the article said that these were the very men "who, in the plenitude of official knowledge," made Mr. Parnell responsible for "arson, murder, and treason." The first article was entitled, "A Retrospect—Ireland"; and, in illustration of its general charge, it quoted several speeches from leading orators of the League. The second, entitled, "A Retrospect—America," reproduced certain lunatic ravings from a newspaper correspondent signing himself "Transatlantic," and a ranting speech in which Frank Byrne, then in America, advised the use, against England, of "every weapon which nature and science have furnished." The third article was headed, "The Connection between Parnellism and the Irish Murder Societies." Having declared that even "now" (March, 1887) the Parnellite "conspiracy" was controlled by dynamiters and assassins, the article proceeded:—

> We have seen how the infernal fabric rose "like an exhalation" to the sound of murderous oratory; how assassins guarded it about, and enforced the high decrees of the secret conclave within by the ballot and the knife. Of that conclave to-day, three members sit in the Imperial Parliament, four are fugitives from the law.

"Egan and Sullivan," continued the article, "ran the machine in the interests of the 'Constitutional movement,' and from this congress of Fenians, murderers, and dynamiters, the Irish National League of America arose."

After the three articles, there followed forty-three pages of notes on agrarian crimes, and the dreary record [the authenticity of which no leaguer ever denied, but the origin of which from the League was the point to be proved] ended with the following appeal for coercion:—

> Men of England! these are the foul and dastardly methods by which the National League and the Parnellites have established their terrorism over a large portion of Ireland! Will you refuse the Government the powers which will enable these cowardly miscreants to be punished, and which will give protection to the millions of honest and loyal people in Ireland?

The second reading having been passed, the House must have its moral support during the usually tedious, but occasionally exciting, committee stage. Leading articles, enforcing the general conclusion of the pamphlet, appeared in the later days of April; and on the 2nd of May, a long paper on "Mr. Dillon and Mr. P. J. Sheridan," asserting, "not only that Sheridan was simultaneously an organizer of murderous associations and the close companion of the leaders of the 'Constitutional Agitation,' but also that his personal relations with Mr. Dillon himself were of a kind which that gentleman, however convenient his memory, can hardly have succeeded in entirely forgetting."

The Times, in short, accused Mr. Dillon of wilful misstatement. And on the following night Sir Charles Lewis moved that the article should be treated as a breach of the privileges of the House of Commons. This led to a debate, in which Mr. W. H. Smith proposed the alternative of a prosecution of *The Times* for libel, and offered the accused the gratuitous aid of the Attorney-General. Mr. Dillon refused the offer. Sir Charles Lewis's motion was rejected on a division. The same fate befell Mr. Gladstone's amendment, and the subject was dismissed.

But two months had yet to pass before the Coercion Bill could become law; and in the interval the second and third series of articles were published. They contained even more serious accusations than those of the first. An article of May 13th, "Behind the Scenes in America," announced that a quarrel among the Clan-na-Gael had enabled the writer to get at his facts. "It has been possible to procure a number of important documents." What the facts and documents were, a meritorious detective, as Sir Henry James has just been calling him, was destined, as one of the most interesting witnesses in a historical trial, to set forth in greater detail. Meanwhile, the articles stated generally that in the year of the Land League the conspirators succeeded in getting the American Clan-na-Gael and the Irish parliamentary party into line. The childish gibberish of the conspirators' cipher was interpreted. "Jsfmboe" meant Ireland, and "Csjujti," British. The cipher was obtained by substituting for each letter of the alphabet the letter immediately following it. Thus the word Irish became "Jsjti," and the "D. Ps.," or district members, of the Clan-na-Gael camps were known as the "E. N."

By the 8th of July there was no more occasion for "Parnellism and Crime" articles. On that date was passed the third reading of the Coercion Bill, under which fully one-third of the Nationalist members charged by *The Times* have since been put under lock and key—several of them more than once—and with a good deal of battling against jail warders, jail barbers, and jail clothesmen.

Months passed away; neither the Irish leader nor any of his colleagues took any further notice of the accusations against them; and "Parnellism and Crime" appeared to be forgotten. But in the summer of 1888, Mr. F. H. O'Donnell, formerly a member of the party, and conceiving himself (after mature reflection) to have been included among the leading members attacked by *The Times*, prosecuted the paper for damages. From the Lord Chief Justice Mr. O'Donnell received a severe rebuke for his pains, and Mr. Ruegg, the prosecuting counsel, an unpleasant criticism on his way of conducting his case. "I cannot see anything in these articles which is a libel on Mr. O'Donnell," said Lord Coleridge: "I am really surprised that any man, having any sense of fairness, should desire for his own end, for some purpose or another, to try the cause in such a way." In the articles Mr. O'Donnell was not once mentioned. Nor was he ever regarded by the Parnellites as a leader of their party—unless his vice-chairmanship of an English branch of the League entitled him to the designation. The case was dismissed. In itself it is scarcely worth notice in this brief survey of events. But Mr. Ruegg's method of presenting it not only compelled Sir Richard Webster to reproduce and exhaustively comment upon all the "Parnellism and Crime" articles, but it also furnished him with the opportunity of startling London and the world with a long series of other *facsimile* letters, some of them more "damning" even than the first. This one, for example, read out by the Attorney-General in his address to the jury, July 4, 1888 :—

9/1/'32.

DEAR E.,
    What are these fellows waiting for ? This inaction is inexcusable ; our best men are in prison, and nothing is being done.
    Let there be an end of this hesitency. Prompt action is called for.
    You undertook to make it hot for old Foster and Co. Let us have some evidence of your power to do so.
    My health is good, thanks.
                        Yours very truly,
                                      CHAS. S. PARNELL.

"Dear E." meant Patrick Egan. In January, four months before the Phœnix Park murders, Mr. Parnell was in Kilmainham. Well might the Attorney-General say, as he solemnly read out the letter in court, "If it was signed by Mr. Parnell, I need not comment upon it." Sir Richard Webster also made the interesting announcement that the first *facsimile* letter was in *The Times*' possession for many months before publication. So also were several of the other letters, of which the following, read to the jury, are examples.
    A letter to Mr. Matt. Harris :—

24 Feb., '81.

MY DEAR FRIEND,
    Write under cover to Madame J. Rouyer, 90, Avenue de Villiers. Mr. Parnell is here, and will remain for about a week. I have spoken to him about further advances from the "A" fund ; he has no objections, and you may count upon him. All goes well. We have met Mr. O'L. and other friends who are here, and all are agreed that prompt and decisive action is called for.
                        Yours vy faithfully,
                                      P. EGAN.

"Mr. O'L." was a John O'Leary, who had been convicted of treason-felony. In February Mr. Parnell was out on parole. And the "A fund" was the "Skirmishing," or Assassination fund, started in New York by O'Donovan Rossa as far back as 1875 or 1876, and supported in one way or another by the Fords—Patrick Ford, the editor of *The Irish World*, among them.
    A letter useful for identification of handwriting, and, when Sir Charles Russell's turn came, in the ripeness of time, for comparison between certain letters produced as genuine and others alleged to be forgeries :—

PARIS, 10 June, 1881.

DEAR SIR,
    I am in receipt of your note of 8th instant, and am writing Mr. P. fully on the matter. He will doubtless communicate with you himself.
                          Yours vy truly,
                                      P. EGAN.

A letter supposed to be addressed to Brennan, agitator in Western Ireland, and also useful for the purposes above-named :—

18 June, '81.

DEAR SIR,
    Your two letters of 12th and 15th insts. are duly to hand, and I am also in receipt of communications from Mr. Parnell, informing me that he has acted upon my suggestion, and accepted the offer made by B. You had better at once proceed to Dundalk, so that there may be no time lost.
                        Yours vy faithfully,
                                      P. EGAN.

A letter to the informer Carey, who in 1883 was shot by O'Donnell. This was one of the very worst of the batch read out by Sir Richard Webster. Egan wrote, said Sir Richard, "after consultation" with his fellow-conspirators; and the getting to work meant "making it hot"—murder—for some persons already selected. By "M." was doubtless meant Joe Mullett, Phœnix Park convict :—

DEAR SIR,   25 Oct., 1881.
I have by this post sent M. two hundred pounds; he will give you what you want. When will you undertake to get to work and give us value for our money?
                                                    I am dear Sir, faithfully yrs,
Jas. Carey, Esq.   PATK. EGAN.

With reference to the foregoing letter, Sir Richard Webster observed that as soon as the informers began to speak (January, 1883), Egan fled to America, and that he had "never yet returned." Then he read the letter of January 9, 1882 [given in the above list], of which he said that "if it cost *The Times* the verdict, *The Times* would not disclose" its source. Sir Richard Webster drew attention to the fact that the letter was not initialed by the Governor of Kilmainham jail, the inference being that it was taken out secretly.

The following letter, also useful for Sir Charles Russell's subsequent comparisons between the *facsimile* letters and genuine ones, was said to have been addressed to P. J. Sheridan, who was described as going about Ireland in the guise of a priest :—

DEAR SIR,   11 May, 1882.
As I understand your letter, which reached me to-day, you cannot act as directed unless I forward you money by Monday next. Well, here is £50; more if required. Under existing circumstances, what you suggest would not be entertained.
                                                    I remain, dear Sir, yours truly,
                                                                        PATK. EGAN.

The Attorney-General next read the famous letter of "15/5/82," with which the town was startled on the morning of the 18th of March of the year before.
We shall quote only two more :—

DEAR SIR,   June 16, 1882
I am sure you will feel that I could not appear in Parliament in the face of this thing, unless I condemned it. Our position there is always difficult to maintain; it would be untenable but for the course we took. I can say no more.
                                                    Yours very truly,
                                                              CHARLES S. PARNELL.

DEAR SIR,   June 16, 1882.
I shall always be anxious to have the goodwill of your friends, but why do they impugn my motives? I could not consent to the conditions they would impose, but I accept the entire responsibility for what we have done.
                                                    Yours very truly,
                                                              CHARLES S. PARNELL.

These two letters were intended to prove that the parliamentary agitation was merely the public aspect, the peaceful, the respectable disguise of a conspiracy which in the prosecution of its purpose would not stop short of murder.
It is not altogether unamusing, in the light of subsequent events, to recall some of Sir Richard Webster's solemn injunctions to the jury : Gentlemen, it is "quite immaterial" where this letter came from. Gentlemen, we shall not tell you where we got it, never, never ; if we did, it would mean murder. All you have to decide, gentlemen, is whether this is Mr. Parnell's signature, and to do that you shall compare handwritings; gentlemen, "the question is, who wrote them, not from whom they were received." "Quite immaterial?" But the spectacle of a crowded court bursting into loud laughter, and a pre-

siding judge gravely smiling, while one of his colleagues could hardly restrain his feelings of merriment, and the other completely gave way,—all this was but a short while ahead.

After the Attorney-General's declaration that *The Times* would retract nothing, and the implied challenge in his admission that, if false, no grosser libels were ever written, Mr. Parnell took action. On the 6th of July, the day after the delivery of the verdict, Mr. Parnell, in the House of Commons, formally denied the authenticity of the letters. Next came various suggestions of an inquiry. Mr. Parnell asked for a select committee of the House. Some hot-headed members thought it would be better if Mr. Parnell were expelled. At last, it was suggested from the Treasury bench, that the inquiry should be entrusted to a Commission of Judges appointed by Act of Parliament. Mr. Parnell jumped, one might say, at the proposal. He thought, as all the world thought, that the inquiry would be limited to the question of the letters. But to the surprise of a good many even on the ministerialist side, and the disgust of the Liberals and the Nationalists, it was to be an inquiry, not only into the letters, but into ten years of Irish history. Mr. Lees, the Conservative member for Oldham, clearly thought that the public attached supreme importance to the letters. "If," he said, the Parnellites "can succeed in disproving the genuine character of the letters, they will cause a tremendous revulsion of feeling in the country." Mr. Chamberlain, agreeing with Mr. Lees, observed that "to lead the inquiry off into subsidiary and unimportant matters would be . . . fatal to the reputation of *The Times*—fatal to its success." And again, "if *The Times* fails to maintain its principal charges, I do not think much importance will be attached to the other charges. Any attempt, as it appears to all, on the part of *The Times*, to put aside those principal charges, or not to put them in the forefront, will redound to their discredit." Mr. Justin McCarthy, and Mr. Parnell, and many others in the House of Commons, and Lord Herschell in the Upper House, predicted that such a reopening of the Irish question, as was implied in the Bill, would lead the inquiry into interminable side issues on matters of merely political opinion— about which differences will and must prevail to the end of time. Mr. Parnell, in particular, warned the House that the accusers would seize the opportunity of drenching the public, so to speak, with stories of maimings, murders, and outrages of all sorts—crimes, the authenticity of which the leaguers never denied, the responsibility of which they indignantly repudiated, but the mere recital of which must tend to prejudice the public mind against them. The Bill, however, was read the second time on the 24th of July. The names of the Commissioners were added in the committee stage. Sir James Hannen, of the Probate and Divorce Division, was chosen as President of the Commission; and with him were associated Sir John Charles Day, and Sir Archibald Levin Smith. The Nationalists objected to the appointment of Mr. Justice Day, because they thought, erroneously, as it appeared, that he was an Orangeman, and because they were dissatisfied with the report signed by him in his capacity of Chairman of the Belfast Riots Commission. Mr. Justice Day's name was carried by a large majority. Finally, Mr. H. Cunynghame, a junior barrister, was appointed Secretary to the Commission.

The Commissioners met for the first time on the 17th of September, in order to arrange the order of procedure. At this sitting they directed the accusers to formulate their "particulars of the charges and allegations" against the accused, and then they adjourned to the 22nd of October. In the interval the particulars were prepared. After stating generally that, the Land, and certain other Leagues and Associations in Ireland and America formed "one connected and continuous organization" for securing "the absolute independence of Ireland as a separate nation"; and that this was to be secured partly by an "agrarian agitation" for the "impoverishment and ultimate expulsion" of the landlords, who were styled "the English garrison," the "particulars" proceeded, thus :—

The organization was actively engaged in the following matters :—
1. The promotion of and inciting to the commission of crimes, outrages, boycotting, and intimidation.
2. The collection and providing of funds to be used, or which it was known were used for the promotion of and the payment of persons engaged in the commission of crimes, outrages, boycotting, and intimidation.
3. The payment of persons who assisted in, were affected by or accidentally, or otherwise injured in the commission of such crimes, outrages, and acts of boycotting and intimidation.
4. Holding meetings and procuring to be made speeches, inciting to the commission of crimes, outrages, boycotting, and intimidation. Some of the meetings referred to, which were attended by members of Parliament, with the approximate dates and place of meeting, are given in the schedule hereto.
5. The publication and dissemination of newspaper and other literature inciting to and approving of sedition and the commission of crimes, outrages, boycotting, and intimidation, particularly the *Irish World*, the *Chicago Citizen*, the *Boston Pilot*, the *Freeman's Journal*, *United Ireland*, the *Irishman*, the *Nation*, the *Weekly News*, *Cork Daily Herald*, the *Kerry Sentinel*, the *Evening Telegraph*, the *Sligo Champion*.
6. Advocating resistance to law and the constituted authorities, and impeding the detection and punishment of crime.
7. Making payments to or for persons who were guilty, or supposed to be guilty, of the commission of crimes, outrages, and acts of boycotting and intimidation for their defence, or to enable them to escape from justice, and for the maintenance of such persons and their families.
8. It is charged and alleged that the members of Parliament mentioned in the schedule approved, and by their acts and conduct led people to believe that they approved of resistance to the law and the commission of crimes, outrages, and acts of boycotting and intimidation when committed in furtherance of the objects and resolutions of the said societies, and that persons who engaged in the commission of such crimes, outrages, and acts would receive the support and protection of the said societies and of their organization and influence.
The acts and conduct specially referred to are as follows :—
9. They attended meetings of the said societies and other meetings at various places and made speeches, and caused and procured speeches to be made, inciting to the commission of crimes, outrages, boycotting, and intimidation.
10. They were parties to, and cognizant of, the payment of moneys for the purposes above mentioned, and as testimonials or rewards to persons who had been convicted, or were notoriously guilty of crimes or outrages, or to their families.
11. With knowledge that crimes, outrages, and acts of boycotting and intimidation had followed the delivery of speeches at the meetings, they expressed no *bonâ fide* disapproval or public condemnation, but, on the contrary, continued to be leading and active members of the said societies and to subscribe to their funds.
12. With such knowledge as aforesaid they continued to be intimately associated with the officers of the same societies (many of whom fled from justice), and with notorious criminals and the agents and instruments of murder and conspiracies, and with the planners and paymasters of outrage, and with the advocates of sedition, violence, and the use of dynamite.
13. They and the said societies, with such knowledge as aforesaid, received large sums of money which were collected in America and elsewhere by criminals and persons who were known to advocate sedition, assassination, the use of dynamite, and the commission of crimes and outrages.
14. When on certain occasions they considered it politic to denounce, and did denounce, certain crimes in public they afterwards made communications to their associates and others with the intention of leading them to believe that such denunciation was not sincere.

The "particulars" next gave a long list of persons—describing them as criminals, or advocates of murder and treason—with whom the accused Members of Parliament "continued to associate." The following were the chief persons named : Frank Byrne, who admitted his connection with the Phœnix Park murders ; Patrick Egan, Land League treasurer ; Patrick Ford, Editor of *The Irish World* ; Carey, the informer ; Tynan, or "Number One," who contrived the Phœnix Park murders ; Mullett, Phœnix Park convict ; P. J. Sheridan, League organizer ; John Walsh, of Middlesborough, organizer of the Invincibles ; J. J. Breslin, of Richmond Jail, who helped Head Centre Stephens to escape ; Alexander Sullivan, of the Clan-na-Gael ; John Devoy, of the Skirmishing Fund ; O'Donovan Rossa, founder of the fund. Among the ladies named were Miss Parnell, and Miss Reynolds (now Mrs. Delahunt),

Preface. xiii

"Members of the Ladies' Land League who paid for the commission of crime."
The Members of Parliament against whom the charges were to be proved
were :—

Thomas Sexton
Joseph Gillis Biggar
Joseph Richard Cox
Jeremiah Jordan
James Christopher Flynn
William O'Brien
Dr. Charles K. D. Tanner
William J. Lane
James Gilhooly
Joseph E. Kenny
John Hooper
Charles Stewart Parnell
Maurice Healy
James Edward O'Doherty
Patrick O'Hea
Arthur O'Connor
Michael McCartan
John J. Clancy
Sir G. H. Grattan Esmonde, Bt.
Timothy D. Sullivan
Timothy Harrington
William H. K. Redmond
Henry Campbell
Patrick J. Foley
Matthew Harris
David Sheehy
John Stack
Edward Harrington
Denis Kilbride
Jeremiah D. Sheehan
James Leahy
Patrick A. Chance
Thomas Quinn

Dr. Joseph Francis Fox
Michael Conway
Luke Patrick Hayden
William Abraham
John Finucane
Francis A. O'Keefe
Justin McCarthy
Timothy M. Healy
Joseph Nolan
Thomas P. Gill
Daniel Grilly
John Deasy
John Dillon
James F. O'Brien
Patrick O'Brien
Richard Lalor
James J. O'Kelly
Andrew Commins
Edmund Leamy
P. J. O'Brien
Thomas Mayne
John O'Connor
Matthew J. Kenny
Jasper D. Pyne
Patrick Joseph Power
James Tuite
Donal Sullivan
Thomas Joseph Condon
John E. Redmond
John Barry
Garrett Mich. Byrne
Thomas P. O'Connor

Finally, the "particulars" gave a list of 310 meetings, at which the Nationalist members above mentioned delivered speeches which, according to the accusers, caused "crimes, outrages, boycotting, and intimidation." These speeches were principally delivered in Galway, Kerry, Roscommon, Tipperary, Wexford, Limerick, Mayo, Cork, Clare, and Waterford.

The first regular sitting of the Commission was held on the 22nd of October. The counsel for *The Times* were Sir Richard Webster, Q.C., M.P., Attorney-General ; Sir Henry James, Q.C., M.P. ; Mr. Murphy, Q.C. ; and Mr. W. Graham, all of the English bar: and of the Irish bar, Mr. Atkinson, Q.C., and Mr. Ronan. Sir Charles Russell, Q.C., and Mr. Asquith, M.P., appeared for Mr. Parnell ; Mr. Reid, Q.C., M.P., Mr. Lockwood, Q.C., M.P., Mr. Hart, Mr. A. O'Connor, M.P. (himself one of the accused), Mr. A. Russell (son of Sir Charles Russell), and Mr. T. Harrington, M.P. (another of the accused), appeared for the other persons charged—excepting Mr. Biggar, M.P., and Mr. Harris, who appeared in person ; and Mr. Chance, who was defended by Mr. Hammond, a solicitor. Mr. Michael Davitt also came to defend himself.

P.S.—Though written in court, or from notes taken there, the first eight articles of the following Diary did not appear in *The Daily News*. In reprinting the others, some have been shortened, and a few expanded.

LONDON,
Nov. 29, 1889.

[*See over page for Errata.*]

ERRATA.

For	Beatty	page	18	read	Beattie.
,,	Callagher	,,	62	,,	Kelleher.
,,	Charlston	,,	21	,,	Charleton.
,,	Colletty	,,	36	,,	Culloty.
,,	Coonahan	,,	53	,,	Cournihan.
,,	Courcey	,,	36	,,	Coursey.
,,	Dark green	,,	1	,,	Dark.
,,	Flannergan	,,	29	spell	Flanagan.
,,	Freeney	,,	75	,,	Freely.
,,	Heagney	,,	23	,,	Heagley.
,,	Lennard	,,	39-42	,,	Leonard.
,,	Leonard, Mike	,,	23	,,	Lennard, Matthew.
,,	Lubie	,,	121	,,	Luby.
,,	McArdell	,,	78	,,	McArdle.
,,	Macauliffe	,,	82	,,	McCall.
,,	Sandys	,,	108	,,	Sanders.
,,	Slack	,,	111	,,	Slacke.

TABLE OF CONTENTS.

FIRST DAY.

OCTOBER 22, 1888.

PAGE

The Attorney-General's opening speech declares the Land League and National League (which was the Land League under another name) to be a criminal conspiracy, with separation as its aim, and crime as one of its means.—The League only the open or public form of an organization of which Fenians and Invincibles constituted the secret executive. From 1879 leaguers in and out of Parliament delivered speeches likely to cause disturbance; as a matter of fact, outrages did follow the speeches; money was paid by the head League officials in reward of criminal acts and for the defence of persons accused of crimes; the Land League was under the control of the American physical force party; Mr. Parnell himself, as certain letters attributed to him would show, was in close association with the party of violence. During this first day, the Attorney-General quoted speeches of Mr. Matt Harris, Mr. Dillon. Clare, Mayo, Cork, Kerry, Galway were the counties to which he would confine his survey 1

SECOND DAY.

OCTOBER 23.

The Attorney-General continues his quotations of speeches delivered in Mayo, Kerry, Galway. Most of these speeches appeared to have been directed against the taking of land from which tenants had been evicted.—Land-grabbers compared to Judas Iscariot. Other epithets of the land-grabber. Mr. Harrington advising people to avoid the grabber as they would a small-pox patient.—Attorney-General says that he himself never attached a vast amount of importance to the *facsimile* letters, though *The Times* had done its utmost to satisfy itself of their genuineness 4

THIRD DAY.

OCTOBER 24.

Mr. Parnell arrives in court in time to hear the Attorney-General's account of the Phœnix Park murder.—The Attorney-General produces the *facsimile* letter of the 15th of May, 1882, and passes it on to the Commissioners.—The Attorney-General says that the very wording of the Kilmainham treaty correspondence shows that Mr. Parnell could have put down disturbance and outrage whenever he chose.—He compares crime statistics before the establishment of the League with the statistics of crime after it 5

FOURTH AND FIFTH DAYS.

OCTOBER 25 AND 26.

The Attorney-General summarizes briefly the American part of his case. He says the Land League was American in origin; attributes its paternity to Patrick Ford rather than to Mr. Davitt. Says that in Irish contemporary agitation the tenant is the victim, whereas in the agitation of the past it used to be the landlord.—Historical implication in the Attorney-General's five days' speech 6

SIXTH DAY.

OCTOBER 30.

The first witness in the Parnell Commission trial enters the box. His name Bernard O'Malley, of the Irish Constabulary. He "proves" numbers of speeches referred to by Sir Richard Webster in his opening address. He reads the speeches of which he took notes, while Sir Henry James checks him. O'Malley is unintelligible. President despairs of understanding him. Therefore Sir Henry reads while O'Malley checks. — Messrs. Biggar, Healy, and Davitt protest against extracts without context. Mr. Biggar bluntly states Sir Henry's object is to get his accusing extracts into the newspapers. Second witness appears in person of Constable Irwin 7

SEVENTH DAY.

OCTOBER 31.

A day of surprises. Captain O'Shea is "sprung upon" Sir Charles Russell, because Captain O'Shea must start for the Continent. And Captain O'Shea produces Mr. Chamberlain's Kilmainham treaty memorandum never before published. — Kilmainham treaty correspondence showing how Mr. Parnell held that without an Arrears Act Ireland could not be pacified.—"I am not expert," said Captain O'Shea; but he thinks the *facsimile* signatures to *The Times* letters are Mr. Parnell's.—Captain O'Shea says Houston and Mr. Chamberlain were his intermediaries with *The Times*.—Laughter in court when Captain O'Shea describes how he burnt all his Kilmainham documents, after a hint from Sir W. Harcourt.—Effect of the Phœnix murders on Mr. Parnell's health.—Captain O'Shea says Mr. Parnell wished to retire from political life 9

EIGHTH DAY.

NOVEMBER 1.

Most important and interesting evidence by Irwin and O'Malley, of the Irish Constabulary. Irwin thinks the only reason why police are unpopular is because they take part in evictions. Testifies to most severe distress before rise of Land League. Thinks distress led to crime. Declares that general drift of the Land League speeches was advising the people to be patient, and refrain from violence, though, he says, there were "harum-scarum" speeches at all or most meetings. Thinks secret societies were hostile to the Land League.—Mr. Davitt's *début* as a cross-examiner.—O'Malley declares the landlords were indifferent to the distress of their tenants 12

Contents. xvii

NINTH DAY.

NOVEMBER 6.

Sir Richard Webster brings before the Court a case of alleged contempt by an evening paper.—Sir Charles Russell, on the other hand, points out that *The Times* still advertises what it calls "Mr. Parnell's *facsimile* letters."—Mr. Ives, the special correspondent, *New York Herald*, states that in 1879, on a voyage to America, Mr. Parnell described the Land League as a political school for the Irish people. He says he witnessed widespread distress in Ireland during the period of the Land League.— Rafferty, a witness, assailed by fifteen moonlighters, does not attribute the attack upon him to the League.—Refusal to supply a coffin to a boycotted family 15

TENTH DAY.

NOVEMBER 7.

Still in county Galway. Constables depose to the state of the "hot" district of Woodford in the years preceding and following the foundation of the League. Mournful story of the murder of Finlay, the process-server, and of his mock funeral. A constable says that "Dr." Tully, a prominent leaguer, was in the procession.—Two other constabulary witnesses declare Galway and the West Coast not to have been badly off before the rise of the League.—But Mr. Ives, *The New York Herald* correspondent, describes the poverty and misery from 1879 to 1883 as very great.—Hideous story of the torture of sheep by moonlighters.— Bad accounts of "Scrab," a stump orator frequently quoted by *The Times* counsel 18

ELEVENTH DAY.

NOVEMBER 9.

An amusing scene with Kerrigan, a *Times* witness who can't speak English. Kerrigan witnessed the murder of Huddy, whose son appears as a witness in the box.—Mr. Botterill, a landlord, says that the League brought on the demoralization of Ireland. In cross-examination it comes out that Mr. Botterill's own tenants were in receipt of public relief, and that he contributed nothing to it.—Mike Lennard's tale about being forced by moonlighters to say his prayers in his coffin.—Tom Connair, another peasant, throws *Times* counsel into confusion by denying he ever swore to his depositions... 22

TWELFTH DAY.

NOVEMBER 9.

In reply to Mr. Lockwood, Mike Joyce says he does not attribute the mutilation of his sheep to the leaguers.—Mrs. Blake, of Connemara, describes her part of the country as it was before and after the rise of the Land League. Word combat between Mrs. Blake and Mr. Biggar—Mrs. Blake greatly amused. Mr. Lockwood and Mrs. Blake on political economy.—Mournful story of Mrs. Blake, of Loughrea, of the murder of her husband. Profound impression produced upon the Court 24

1*

xviii   *Contents.*

THIRTEENTH DAY.

NOVEMBER 13.

Still in county Galway.   Pat Kennedy defies the lawyers two full hours. He is unmanageable.   Thinks he is at present "kept by *The Times.*"— Mannion, an informer, says he never knew a moonlighter who was not a Land Leaguer.   He himself was leaguer and moonlighter.—So, according to his own account, was Flaherty, another *Times* witness. Flaherty says that eight years ago he, as a leaguer, was engaged on moonlighting expeditions, authorized by the League   27

FOURTEENTH DAY.

NOVEMBER 14.

Mike Hoarty contradicts the testimony of the informers. An ex-leaguer himself, he denies that his branch issued boycotting orders, though boycotting was "discussed" in it. He said none of his fellow-leaguers were Fenians, though he himself was. The Attorney-General goes into the history of the National League in the Woodford district   29

FIFTEENTH DAY.

NOVEMBER 16.

Lady Mountmorres. She says the tenants began to grow rude and insolent as soon as the leaguers appeared among them. Lady Mountmorres sinks down in a half-fainting state. Sir Charles Russell refrains from cross-examining her.—Scene now shifted from Galway to Kerry.—Sullivan, a Kerry bog-ranger, expected to denounce the League, rather blesses it. Says the League took his part in a quarrel. A "scene" between the Attorney-General and Mr. Harrington, when the former asked Sullivan if he had been talked to in court by any of the Messrs. Harrington.— The President sharply rebukes Mr. Harrington. Court adjourns. On resuming, the President accepts Mr. Harrington's apology   32

SIXTEENTH DAY.

NOVEMBER 20.

The Attorney-General brings a charge of gross contempt of Court by *The Kerry Sentinel,* of which the proprietor and editor is Mr. E. Harrington.—Was Culloty attacked because of his defiance of the League, or because of his immoralities?—O'Connor, a Kerry farmer, instead of condemning the League, says the League befriended him.—A series of moonlight outrages.—Extracts read by defendants' counsel showing how the chief Nationalist paper in Kerry denounced outrages.—Miss Curtin questioned as to the murder of her father in the winter of 1885   35

SEVENTEENTH DAY.

NOVEMBER 21.

Their Lordships' judgment against Mr. E. Harrington for contempt of Court in *The Kerry Sentinel.*— Miss Curtin's examination resumed. She has no reason to suppose her father's murder was instigated in any way by the League. Her brother gives similar testimony. Constabulary witnesses to the cruel and inhuman boycott of Miss Curtin's family.— Norah Fitzmaurice's mournful story of her father's murder. The cowardice and the brutish callousness manifested by people in this murder case. The *Kerry Sentinel*, chief Nationalist paper in Kerry, denounces the murder.—Land agent Mr. Leonard's pre-League well-behaved Ireland, and his impeachment of the League 38

EIGHTEENTH DAY.

NOVEMBER 22.

Mr. Leonard, agent for Lord Kenmare, reappears. His wonderful memory, and his inexhaustible black bag. He thinks the Arrears Bill a curse, as it turned honest men into rogues. Thinks that since the birth of the Land League, county Kerry has gone all wrong. Does not think much of the heroic Gordon's famous letter about the misery of the Kerry peasants. How Mr. Leonard's evidence was modified in cross-examination by Sir Charles Russell, Mr. Lockwood, Mr. Davitt, Mr. Harrington 40

NINETEENTH DAY.

NOVEMBER 23.

District-Inspector Huggins gives a dreary history of five and a half years' crime in Kerry.—Mr. Reid protests; says the outrages are not disputed; wants to know what connection they have with the case.—Tim Horan, a League Secretary, asking for money for persons implicated in outrage.—Huggins's lame answers to Mr. Reid's questions about his reasons for identifying moonlighters with leaguers.—A Kerry cattle dealer gets excited in the box. He will not undertake to blame the League for his boycott. Thinks the boycott may have been owing to trade jealousy ... 43

TWENTIETH DAY.

NOVEMBER 27.

Two members of the Irish constabulary, Gilhooly and Davis, describe the state of Castleisland district, county Kerry, since 1880.—Attribute disturbance to League initiative.—Tim Horan's letter produced.—Davis says he was informed of the existence of an "inner circle" of the League. But refuses to divulge his informants' names.—Davis cross-examined by Mr. Asquith, Mr. Reid, Mr. Davitt 45

TWENTY-FIRST DAY.

NOVEMBER 28.

More evidence suggestive of effect of family disputes in investigating crime.—Mr. John O'Connor, M.P., whom the Attorney-General calls a "long gentleman;" and his alleged riotous speeches in Cork.—Mr. Kennedy, an unmanageable witness, who contradicts his depositions before *The Times* solicitor, gives the prosecution considerable trouble 50

TWENTY-SECOND DAY.

NOVEMBER 29.

Jeremiah Sullivan, another witness unable to fix a moonlighting outrage upon him to any persons in particular, leaguers or others.—District-Inspector Crane's evidence on three districts in Kerry. Says popular demoralization began with the League. Says he found where there were secret societies that league branches coexisted with them. He attributes to terrorism the difficulty he experienced in getting information. And asserts that leaguers and moonlighters were in co-operation. Another constabulary witness, Mr. Wright, supports Mr. Crane's statement that leaguers and moonlighters co-operated. Mr. Wright and Mr. Biggar on mowing machines 54

TWENTY-THIRD DAY.

NOVEMBER 30.

Mr. Hussey's testimony about Kerry, past and present. Says that up to 1880, Kerry was as peaceful as any country in the world. Eviction was easy in the old time. He never heard the name land-grabbing before 1880. Sir Charles Russell confronts Mr. Hussey with statistics of violence in the peaceful period. Jeremiah Hegarty, who defied the boycotters for seven years, and was prepared to defy them as long again. Mr. Hegarty as a letter-writer. He is cross-examined by Mr. Davitt ... 58

TWENTY-FOURTH DAY.

DECEMBER 4.

Cornelius Kelleper whistled at because he worked for Hegarty.—A long string of inconclusive evidence.—The first priest-witness appears in the box. Canon Griffin takes the landlord, agent, and constabulary view of the issue. Says he fought the League "from the start." Admits that vast majority of the Irish priests are on the side of the League.—The informer Thomas O'Connor accuses Mr. T. Harrington of having personally instigated him to intimidate, and promised him money payment. Says he was a member of the "inner circle" of the League. Says he took part in midnight meetings. His story produces a profound impression in court 62

TWENTY-FIFTH DAY.

DECEMBER 5.

Jeremiah Hegarty's case disposed of. Dr. Tanner's description of Hegarty. —The boy-secretary Walsh and his diverse careers. Walsh gives himself an extremely bad character.—Mr. Buckley, the deaf witness, tries the vocal powers of Mr. Graham and Sir Charles Russell 66

TWENTY-SIXTH DAY.

DECEMBER 6.

Patrick Molloy first appears in court.—Burke's story of the murder of Lord Mountmorres.—He implicates the local leaguers in the crime.— Cross-examined by Sir Charles Russell, his mind becomes a blank as to places and dates. Not sure if this is the year 1888... 69

TWENTY-SEVENTH DAY.

DECEMBER 7.

Patrick Molloy tells his extraordinary story of how he "humbugged" *The Times*. Gives his counsel, the Attorney-General, immense trouble. Amusement in court. The Attorney-General tries to make out that his witness is a greater rogue than the witness will admit himself to be. Cross-examined by his own counsel, Molloy is next examined by Sir Charles Russell. Molloy shows great respect to Mr. Davitt 72

TWENTY-EIGHTH DAY.

DECEMBER 11.

Ann Gallagher says moonlighters were dressed in black clothes like policemen. —An Irish gombeen man or money lender.—"Freeing" oneself from the charge of paying the landlord's full rent. A tenant whose son was murdered for rent payment exonerates the League. Says the League denounced the murder and approved his agreement with the landlord.— But more landlord witnesses say the League demoralized Ireland.— Mysterious murder of Dillon 75

TWENTY-NINTH DAY.

DECEMBER 12.

Miss Thompson, landlords, and Captain Boycott, praise the good old times in Ireland.—Miss Thompson, however, was never called "your royal honour" by the peasants of pre-League Ireland ; she says the peasants became rude after the rise of the League—a body which had for some time previously been "brewing in the air."—*Times* counsel read endless articles and documents of sorts about speeches and outrages. Against this, Sir Charles Russell protests, wanting to know what bearing all this has upon the persons charged by *The Times*. Mr. Reid also protests. And Sir James Hannen remarks, plaintively, that life is too short for all these details put in by the prosecution. At last Sir Charles and his brethren fall upon the expedient of declining to cross-examine upon what they consider totally irrelevant evidence. Result, number of witnesses dismissed without cross-examination. Readings from old files of *Kerry Sentinel*, to which nobody listens 77

THIRTIETH DAY.

DECEMBER 13.

Police-sergeant reports a speech of Mr. Davitt's, which Mr. Davitt never delivered.—An agent-witness admits that he thought it prudent always to carry arms with him, even in the years before the League.—Informer Buckley describes his murder expeditions in association with Kerry leaguers; though at that time he himself was not a leaguer.—But he does not accuse the local league branch as an organization.—Sir Charles Russell cannot understand why Buckley tried to "escape," after he had been simply bound over on his own recognisance to keep the peace ... 81

THIRTY-FIRST DAY.

DECEMBER 14.

The Attorney-General accuses *United Ireland* of contempt of Court, and Mr. Reid, Q C., accuses Mr. Brodrick, Warden of Merton College.—The informer O'Connor is recalled by Sir Charles Russell. His memory is a blank, as regards persons, places, dates, and other essential particulars. Admits *Times* agent "forced him rather hard." Is confronted with his letter in which he wrote that he must say "queer things" to get money out of *The Times*. On the other hand, the Attorney-General reads telegrams from Dublin to O'Connor, in which O'Connor was implored by his friends to contradict all his evidence in chief.—Mr. Lockwood, Q.C., condoles with a lady witness, in fearing there's "only water" in what she is drinking from a tumbler 86

Contents.

THIRTY-SECOND DAY.

JANUARY 15, 1889.

The Irish People's William, in a thirty-five minutes' speech, protests against the conduct of *The Times* in disseminating its poison ("Parnellism and Crime") in hundreds of places day by day. Mr. Reid describes Mr. Brodrick's humour as "humour by affidavit." Mr. Brodrick's apology is accepted by the President.—Dr. Tanner's brother praises pre-League Ireland.—Another informer, named Iago, says he was paid by League to commit crimes 92

THIRTY-THIRD DAY.

JANUARY 16.

The President accepts Mr. O'Brien's explanation of his motives in publishing the *United Ireland*. In declaring, emphatically, that the Court had nothing whatever to do with politics, the President makes a warning appeal to journalists to refrain from comment calculated to embarrass their Lordships' task.—Mr. Iago, the informer, recalled, is asked by Sir Charles Russell whether he knows anybody who would believe Mr. Iago on his oath.—Another informer, Delaney, of Phœnix Park crime, appears. Says leading leaguers were associated with Invincibles, who got money from League treasurer. Delaney describes the arrangements for perpetrating the Phœnix Park murders. Admits he knew only by hearsay that leaguers were mixed up in the "hatching of the Phœnix Park business" 96

THIRTY-FOURTH DAY.

JANUARY 17.

The informer Delaney adheres to his statement that leaguers and Invincibles were in collusion.—Land agents swear to the usual proposition that the League introduced dishonesty and lawlessness into Ireland.—A mass of correspondence of Mr. M. Harris's, furnished by Dublin Castle, is found to contain nothing not known before. In one letter Mr. Brennan sympathizes with Mr. Harris in his sufferings from rheumatism 100

THIRTY-FIFTH DAY.

JANUARY 18.

More landlords' agents,—Mr. Young, Mr. Tyrrell, Mr. Powell, Mr. Verriker,—tell the old story.—Mr. Dominick O'Donnell, a Mayo landlord, drags out of her bed a woman who shams sickness. She kicks her clothes off.—Captain Plunkett's reasonings in a circle. Cross-examined by Mr. Reid, and by Mr. Davitt 102

THIRTY-SIXTH DAY.

JANUARY 22

Mr. Studdert, agent on the Vandeleur estates, repeats the general testimony of witnesses of his class,—Ireland contented, at any rate peaceful, until the advent of the League.—The first informer, from the League headquarters in Dublin, appears, Farragher his name. Says he received his post of clerk in the head office, as reward for illegal action at Mr. Davitt's

Contents. xxiii

instigation. Says he used to carry letters, with cheques, from Mr. Egan, secretary of the League, to Mullett, one of the Phœnix Park life convicts. His memory too much at fault, under Sir Charles Russell's cross-examination 105

THIRTY-SEVENTH DAY.

JANUARY 23.

Mr. Robert Sanders, landlord's son, attributes tenants' discontent to League incitement. But Sir Charles Russell shows the large reductions which the Land Court granted upon the estates which Mr. Sanders regarded as being fairly rented.—Tobin, a professed moonlighter, describes the local organization of the moonlighters with its "captains;" alleges that all the moonlighters he knew were leaguers, that he had been engaged on midnight expeditions, and that a League secretary paid him for his services. He admits to Sir Charles Russell that he had never seen any of his moonlighter friends at Land League meetings 108

THIRTY-EIGHTH DAY.

JANUARY 24.

Captain Slacke, one of *The Times'* best witnesses, finds no organization except the League, to which he can attribute crime.—Sir Charles Russell shows how great rent reductions on Captain Slacke's estates implied previous injustice to tenants: how agrarian murder ceased in Tipperary after the establishment of the League, though frequent there before the League days: how same was true of other counties. Captain Slacke, cross-examined, cannot produce proof of actual connection between crime and denunciation by the League 111

THIRTY-NINTH AND FORTIETH DAYS.

JANUARY 25 AND 29.

One day spent in reading extracts from speeches which, as the prosecution alleged, were incentives to outrage.—Mr. Hanley, a Tipperary landlord, blames the League for introducing disturbance, but, when cross-examined by Sir Charles Russell, admits that disturbance existed in Tipperary before the League.—Sir Henry James drags in Osman Digna. 114

FORTY-FIRST DAY.

JANUARY 30.

Mr. Hanley, a landlord gives evidence. Mr. Hanley keeps a battering ram 116

FORTY-SECOND DAY.

JANUARY 31.

Further evidence on the Mountmorres murder case.—Roche, whom the informer Buckley said he tried to shoot, appears as a witness. Roche corroborates the story, in some particulars. Roche's account of himself not wholly satisfactory. The Irish magistrate evidently thought the shooting business a trifling matter 117

xxiv   *Contents.*

FORTY-THIRD DAY.
FEBRUARY 1.
                                                                    PAGE
End of Captain Slacke's evidence. Mr. Davitt's arithmetic of the League.—
English and Irish constables on the work of John Walsh. Walsh's lost
bank-notes.—A little altercation between the President and Sir Charles
Russell   118

FORTY-FOURTH DAY.
FEBRUARY 5.
The Attorney-General begins the American part of his case. Le Caron,
alias Beach, enters the witness-box. Describes how he passed from the
Federal army into the Fenian force. How he acted as a spy upon his
fellow-Fenians. How the American Fenians are organized. How Devoy
passed between America and Ireland. How Le Caron took sealed
packets to Egan and O'Leary in Paris. How Le Caron has an interview
with Mr. Parnell in the House of Commons. And how Mr. Parnell gave
him a message to the American Fenian leaders   120

FORTY-FIFTH DAY.
FEBRUARY 6.
Le Caron's description of the Irish-American Conventions and their secret
committees. Le Caron on the retaliatory policy of the "United
Brethren." On Mr. O'Kelly, M.P., and John O'Connor, and the
American skirmishing fund. Members of the Royal Irish Constabulary
said to be spy members of the American United Brotherhood   123

FORTY-SIXTH DAY.
FEBRUARY 7.
Le Caron describes the schisms and rechristenings among the Irish-American
revolutionaries.—From draper boy to Adjutant-General.—Le Caron on the
secret committee at Chicago last June ; the secret committee at Boston
in August, 1884, at which force "and no compromise" were advocated.—
Le Caron gives Egan's story, first about his own escape from Ireland, and
next about Brennan's account of how Brennan himself was aided by Mr.
Sexton to escape to Paris, at the time of the Phœnix Park trials.—Says
Egan approved dynamite policy.—How Le Caron, with "credentials"
from Egan, travelled in the Southern States.—His communications with
Mr. Anderson of the Home Office   126

FORTY-SEVENTH DAY.
FEBRUARY 8.
Le Caron's relations with the Home Office.—The Irish-American Brotherhood stronger to-day than ever.—Sir Charles Russell reads Irish-American
circulars which show that the party of violence were jealous of the newly
formed "Constitutional" League.—Le Caron's enumeration of "respectable" persons among the "U. B.'s."—Le Caron cross-examined on the
management of Mr. Parnell's American tour   130

Contents.

FORTY-EIGHTH DAY.

FEBRUARY 12.

Le Caron on O'Leary and Head Centre Stephens.—On Mr. Parnell's insane notions.—Four sections among the American-Irish.—The spy's wages.—The spy votes with the majority.—Devoy's supposed letter to Le Caron, about Mr. Parnell's alleged mandate.—Mr. Parnell's last link speech.—Number One's portrait identified 133

FORTY-NINTH DAY.

FEBRUARY 13.

Mr. Mitchell, a Scoto-Irish witness, describes his struggle with Mr. Condon at Mr. Condon's shop-door.—Payment of League money to the survivors of persons sentenced for the Phœnix Park murders 137

FIFTIETH DAY.

FEBRUARY 14.

Mr. Michael Davitt's policy.—Mr. Soames appears in the witness-box.—Mr. Soames says he first saw the alleged Parnell letters at the end of 1886, and that they were submitted to the expert, Inglis, in April, 1887.—Letters were identified, not by direct inquiry into their source, but by comparison of their handwriting with that of other documents admitted to be genuine 139

FIFTY-FIRST DAY.

FEBRUARY 15.

Mr. Soames believes that neither Mr. Macdonald nor Houston knows, even now, from whom Pigott found the letters.—He says the expert evidence is enough to satisfy him of the genuineness of the letters.—Comparison of disputed with acknowledged handwriting in the witness-box.—Mr. Soames says he discovered an emissary of Egan's watching Pigott.—Mr. Macdonald cross-examined by Mr. Asquith 141

FIFTY-SECOND DAY.

FEBRUARY 19.

How Mr. Macdonald of *The Times* took things on trust.—How Mr. Macdonald refrained from inquiring about Pigott.—How the "Parnellism and Crime" writers were not asked questions.—How Houston refrained from putting questions to Pigott.—And how Houston destroyed his correspondence 143

FIFTY-THIRD DAY.

FEBRUARY 20.

Houston explains why he destroyed his correspondence with Pigott—How he refrained from investigating Pigott's story about the black bag.—He refrained from inquiring who the "people downstairs were."—He borrows from Sir Rowland Blennerhasset and Lord R. Grosvenor—who also refrained from asking questions.—Houston reproaches the editor of *The*

Pall Mall Gazette.—The Labouchere interview shakes Houston's faith. —A most important document—an alleged statement of Eugene Davis's, said to have been written at Lausanne, and given by its author to Pigott. This statement appears to be the basis on which the whole of the (alleged) forgeries rests **147**

FIFTY-FOURTH DAY.

FEBRUARY 21.

Pigott's story of the first mention of "the facsimile letter": How Pigott met "Murphy," who unearthed "the facsimile letter," and the rest. But the Paris Clan-na-Gael cannot sell without authority from America. So Pigott goes to America. Returning to Paris, he buys the first batch of compromising documents. Discovery of the second batch. And of the third batch. Payments for them. Pigott's story of his interview with Mr. Labouchere on the 24th of October; with Mr. Lewis on the 25th of October; and of his sworn declaration to Houston on the 5th of November.—Sir Charles Russell's cross-examination begins. Sir Charles asks Pigott to write some words. Pigott admits he wrote to Dr. Walsh on March 4, 1877.—Pigott begins to fall into hopeless confusion ... **150**

FIFTY-FIFTH DAY.

FEBRUARY 22.

Pigott's correspondence with the Archbishop of Dublin—saying he did not believe in the authenticity of the alleged Parnell letters, and denying that he ever had anything to do with the discovery of the *facsimile* letters.—Sir Charles Russell produces Pigott's correspondence with Egan in 1881. Pigott trying to blackmail Egan.—Sir Charles points out similarities between alleged forgeries and letters admitted to be genuine. The word "hesitency."—How Pigott tried to blackmail Mr. Forster. Mr. Wemyss Reid produces the Pigott-Forster correspondence in court.—Sir Charles Russell asking Pigott how he would forge a letter.—Laughter and excitement in court **156**

FIFTY-SIXTH DAY.

FEBRUARY 26.

The Court waits for Pigott.—The Attorney-General announces that Pigott has run away.—Sir Charles Russell's wrath—"a foul conspiracy."—The judges issue a warrant for Pigott's arrest. Sir Charles Russell announces that Pigott made a full confession of his forgeries to Mr. Labouchere and Mr. Sala on Saturday.—The President reads a communication from Pigott's housemaid. Shannon announces that Pigott has made a confession subsequently to the one made to Messrs. Labouchere and Sala. In this last of his confessions Pigott says that he forged some of the letters in the second and third batches, but that the first batch was sold to him, as described in his evidence.—Sir Charles Russell's suspicious questions to Shannon.—Mr. George Lewis's rod in pickle for Pigott.—The two constables who guarded Pigott know nothing... ... **161**

FIFTY-SEVENTH DAY.

FEBRUARY 27.

The last confession to Mr. Labouchere is received by Shannon from Pigott in Paris, and is read out in court.—The Attorney-General withdraws

Contents.

"the letters."—Sir Charles Russell's surprise at the lameness of the apology.—Mr. Parnell's first appearance in the witness-box 165

FIFTY-EIGHTH DAY.

March 1.

Mr. O'Kelly, Mr. Campbell, Mr. Davitt, Mr. McCarthy, Mr. Lewis, Mr. Labouchere, Mr. G. A. Sala, appear in the witness-box.—Sir Charles Russell asks if their lordships will draw up a special report on the forgeries.—The Attorney-General resumes the American portion of his case 169

FIFTY-NINTH DAY.

March 5.

Reasons why the President admits, in evidence, files of *The Irish World* from May, 1880, to October, 1881.—Reading of extracts from *The Irish World*, and of speeches by Mr. Gladstone, Mr. Forster, Sir William Harcourt, from Hansard.—The Attorney-General's references to the evidence of Carey the informer 172

SIXTIETH DAY.

March 6.

Reading of extracts from *The Irish World*.—Caricature of a junior and his witness.—Witnesses examined as to the doings of Messrs. Walsh, Sheridan, Fitzpatrick, and Mr. William Redmond, M.P.—An Irish-American informer says crimes were planned by leaguers 174

SIXTY-FIRST DAY.

March 7.

Irish-American Informer Colman says he was a Fenian and Land Leaguer, and associated with Land-Leaguer Macaulay in planning and attempting outrages.—But all the murderous expeditions of Colman and Macaulay prove harmless.—Informer Colman's defective memory.—Colman's story about the division of the spoil for the murder of Mr. Burke the land agent.—Untrustworthy statement that Macaulay was a leaguer.—Mr. Soames's alleged employment of ex-convict Walsh, in collecting incriminating documents.—Mr. Soames cross-examined by Mr. Lockwood 177

SIXTY-SECOND DAY.

March 12.

Timothy Coffey, another witness who has "befooled" *The Times*.—Declares that his statement to *The Times* agent was a tissue of lies from beginning to end.—Declares that his secret information to Dublin Castle was also a tissue of lies.—Sir Henry James catches Coffey tripping. People of Coffey's imagination, who have friends in the flesh.—The President commits Coffey for contempt of Court.—Coffey protests he warned Mr. Soames that he would not give evidence.—Another *Times* witness, Dominic O'Connor, believes that the Fenian Brotherhood were hostile to Mr. Parnell 180

SIXTY-THIRD DAY.

MARCH 13.

Mr. Soames relates the story of his intercourse with Timothy Coffey.—How Mr. Soames, once more, trusted to hearsay.—How Coffey's behaviour failed to arouse Mr. Soames's suspicions.—John Leavy, an informer, professes to describe the Fenian organization and the League leaders' connection with it.—Mr. Biggar and Mr. Davitt cross-examine Mr. Leavy.—Mulqueeney, another informer, attempts to connect leaguers and Invincibles.—His testimony as to the famous hundred pound cheque paid to Frank Byrne by Mr. Parnell.—Mulqueeney's relations with Captain O'Shea. End of *The Times* case.—Court adjourns for nearly three weeks 185

SIXTY-FOURTH DAY.

APRIL 2.

Sir Charles Russell begins his opening speech for the defence. Who are the accusers? Who the accused? Ireland not a Garden of Eden before 1879. Sir Charles Russell's historical references to the Ireland of the past 190

SIXTY-FIFTH DAY.

APRIL 3.

Sir Charles Russell continues his historical survey of Ireland. The testimony of the Devon Commission. The evidence, before the Commission, of Mr. Hancock, agent to Lord Lurgan. General Gordon on Kerry. Sir Charles Russell's doctrine of the division of the fruits of agricultural labour. Statistics of poverty and misery. Sir Charles Russell on the careers of Mr. O'Brien, Mr. Dillon, Mr. Parnell, Mr. Davitt 193

SIXTY-SIXTH DAY.

APRIL 4.

Sir Charles Russell's speech continued. Foundation of the Land League. Objects of the League. Mr. Parnell's appeal to the Ulster people. *The Times* blinded by animosity. Sir Charles Russell on boycotting—"let us clear our minds of cant." Sir Charles Russell on the contrast between the Attorney-General's promise and performance. The work of the Land League 197

SIXTY-SEVENTH DAY.

APRIL 9.

Sir Charles Russell's speech continued. No proof against the Ladies' Land League. The Phœnix Park murders dealing a fatal blow to Mr. Parnell's Constitutional agitation. The rise of the National League. The National party at the general election of 1885. The voice of Ireland. *The Times'* case "a rubbishy collection" of "trumpery" stories 200

SIXTY-EIGHTH DAY.

APRIL 10.

Sir Charles Russell's speech continued. The Curtin murder not even

Contents. xxix

agrarian. Nor had the League anything to do with the Fitzmaurice murder. Sir Charles Russell, Where are the proofs against the incriminated members? Against thirty of them no speeches whatever have been put in. The *Times'* heroes "Scrab" and Dr. Tully. No proof against Sheridan, Boyton, Byrne, Egan. Mr. Davitt's character. Dr. Kenny and the Tim Horan cheque. Mr. John Morley's charge of "infamy" against *The Times'* Constitutional character of Mr. Parnell's speeches in America. Le Caron's stories 204

SIXTY-NINTH DAY.

APRIL 11.

Sir Charles Russell's speech continued. Review of the American conventions. The position of Patrick Ford's paper, *The Irish World*. Le Caron's singular omissions. The Invincible conspiracy. The "recklessness" of the *facsimile* letters part of *The Times* case. Mr. Parnell's determination to unmask "the foul conspiracy." Pigott and his "tempter" ... 209

SEVENTIETH DAY.

APRIL 12.

Conclusion of Sir Charles Russell's speech. His rapid survey of *The Times* case. "Your lordships are trying the history of a ten years' revolution in Ireland." "The accused are there"—pointing to the representatives of *The Times*. "This inquiry, intended as a curse, has proved a blessing" 212

SEVENTY-FIRST DAY.

APRIL 30.

Mr. Parnell is examined by Mr. Asquith. Mr. Parnell's early history. Mr. Parnell once belonged to a secret society—the Foresters! Mr. Parnell's American tour managed by himself: Le Caron's account of it all imaginary. The "last link" speech. How the I.R.B. in Ireland opposed Mr. Parnell and the Land League. Mr. Parnell had never heard of Invincibles until after the Phœnix Park murders. Mr. Parnell and his photographs 214

SEVENTY-SECOND DAY.

MAY 1.

Mr. Parnell explains how the Tim Horan cheque must have been paid. Land League office disorganized in consequence of the imprisonment of parliamentary leaders. Patrick Ford's views not Mr. Parnell's. The funds sent to Ireland through *The Irish World*. The Attorney-General cross-examines Mr. Parnell. The Attorney-General on Mr. Parnell's relations with *The Irish World* 217

SEVENTY-THIRD DAY.

MAY 2.

The Attorney-General's cross-examination of Mr. Parnell continued. Mr. Parnell is asked about Alexander Sullivan of Chicago, and Mr. Finerty. Did John Devoy help to found the Land League? Did Mr. Parnell try

xxx   *Contents.*

	PAGE
to keep his more extreme followers in check? Mr. Parnell on Mr. William Redmond. No-rent manifestos	221

SEVENTY-FOURTH DAY.

MAY 3.

The Attorney-General's cross-examination of Mr. Parnell continued. Mr. Parnell's description of *The Irishman.* Mr. Parnell on *United Ireland.* Mr. Parnell's disapproval of physical force. Mr. Parnell on Secret Societies. His "misleading" the House of Commons 223

SEVENTY-FIFTH DAY.

MAY 7.

Mr. Parnell's explanation of his "misleading" the House of Commons. Mr. Parnell, bank-book in hand, answers questions about the expenditure of moneys. Changes in the policy of *The Irish World* 225

SEVENTY-SIXTH DAY.

MAY 8.

Re-examination of Mr. Parnell by Sir Charles Russell. Land League work—Ireland. League denunciation of outrage. The President requests Mr. Parnell to make an affidavit of all the documents in his possession, bearing on the case. Archbishop Walsh enters the witness-box. Is examined by Mr. Reid 226

SEVENTY-SEVENTH DAY.

MAY 9.

Dr. Walsh's doctrine that crime followed eviction. The League a political school for the Irish people. Dr. Walsh is cross-examined by Mr. Atkinson. Dr. Walsh's opinion of *United Ireland.* And of *The Irishman.* The Archbishop's "distinctions" in boycotting. He approved of the form of boycotting known as "exclusive dealing"; not of intimidation. Father O'Connell of Connemara. His description of Mrs. Blake ... 229

SEVENTY-EIGHTH DAY.

MAY 10.

The Bishop of Galway and three priests examined. Testimony to League condemnation of outrage. The Bishop of Galway on West of Ireland misery; and on landlord selfishness. The Bishop thinks some forms of boycotting are not incompatible with the Papal rescript 231

SEVENTY-NINTH DAY.

MAY 14.

Witnesses' descriptions of county Galway in distress. The old story about landlord selfishness. Specimens of native rhetoric. John Monaghan of Connemara breaks down, as he describes the horrors of Irish famine ... 234

EIGHTIETH DAY.

MAY 15.

Father Egan of Loughrea gives his version of the story of the murder of Mr. Blake. The true story of the "mock funeral." One of the Woodford leaders, Mr. John Roche, gives his testimony 236

EIGHTY-FIRST DAY.

MAY 16.

The examination of Mr. John Roche continued. Mr. Roche on landlord insolence. Mr. Roche boycotted by the landlords. Mr. Roche on defending one's home. Another of the Woodford leaders, Mr. Patrick Keary, appears in the witness-box. Mr. Keary on the spontaneous organization of the tenants. Mr. Keary on the "mock funeral" ... 239

EIGHTY-SECOND DAY.

MAY 17.

Father O'Donovan of Coroffin. His testimony on poverty before the League, and on landlord indifference. His knowledge of moonlighting. John Hanneffy of Galway repudiates connection between the League and crime. He contradicts a *Times* story. Father Bodkin rejects with disgust *The Times* theory that the moonlighters were the secret police of the League. Father Bodkin denounces grabbers. Father Finneran on the Attorney-General's Arcadia 241

EIGHTY-THIRD DAY.

MAY 21.

Mr. William O'Brien in the witness-box. His manner as a witness. On murders and other outrages before the rise of the League. County Tipperary before and after the rise of the League. Donegal before 1879. Peasant impression of landlord intention after the agrarian legislation of 1870. Mr. O'Brien on the wholesome result of boycotting. Mr. O'Brien on the history of *The Irishman* and *United Ireland* 243

EIGHTY-FOURTH DAY.

MAY 22.

Mr. O'Brien on the worthlessness of English Press reports on Irish affairs. The President intervenes between the Attorney-General and Mr. O'Brien. Ireland "all Greek" to the English people. Mr. O'Brien's contempt for police statistics. Objectionable paragraphs in *United Ireland*. Mr. O'Brien on the use of such words as loyal and constitutional. On the eagerness to convict Mr. Egan of complicity in the Phœnix Park crimes 245

EIGHTY-FIFTH DAY.

MAY 23.

Mr. O'Brien protests against the Attorney-General's interpretations of the "re-hashes" from other papers, which appeared in *United Ireland*. Mr. O'Brien on the Queen and the Prince of Wales. "The Woodford

xxxii *Contents.*

PAGE

spirit made England what it is." Mr. O'Brien on the changed relations between Great Britain and Ireland since 1885. Sham loyalty in Ireland. Flags and anthems in Ireland. Mr. Gladstone in court. Mr. O'Brien's distinction between English ministries and the English people. Circumstances under which an Irish rising would be justifiable. Legality in Ireland. Mr. O'Brien on the Manchester Martyrs. "Hear, hear!"— and the President's warning. Mr. T. D. Sullivan enters the witness-box. He declares that his paper, *The Nation*, has always supported Constitutional agitation. Mr. Murphy, Q.C., and Mr. Sullivan's verse. Mr. Sullivan on the "Manchester Martyrs." Mr. Sullivan considers the grabber a "moral leper" 248

EIGHTY-SIXTH DAY.

MAY 24.

Mr. Murphy again tries Mr. Sullivan's verse. Then he tries the Land League catechism. Next the news paragraphs of *The Nation*. The distinction between news and policy. Witnesses from Miltown Malbay. Mr. John Ferguson of Glasgow enters the witness-box. He knows nothing of the Land League books. Violence not in Mr. Ferguson's line 253

EIGHTY-SEVENTH DAY.

MAY 28.

Some of the missing Land League books found. The testimony of a Protestant pastor. Adjournment for the Whitsuntide holidays 255

EIGHTY-EIGHTH DAY.

MAY 29.

Examination of Mr. Biggar. Mr. Biggar contradicts some testimony given by *Times* witnesses. Mr. Biggar knows nothing of the books of the Land League. Mr. Biggar on his connection with the Fenian Brotherhood. Mr. Arthur O'Connor describes how he found the Land League offices in a state of chaos, in consequence of the imprisonment and illness of leading Parnellite members 257

EIGHTY-NINTH DAY.

MAY 30.

Mr. Arthur O'Connor's experiences of America. Mr. Arthur O'Connor's connection with the Land League office. He knows nothing about the books. Mr. O'Connor considers land-grabbers to be receivers of stolen goods. Mr. Justin McCarthy appears in the witness-box. Mr. McCarthy on Frank Byrne. Mr. McCarthy on boycotting. Mr. George Lewis knows nothing about the missing books 258

NINETIETH DAY.

MAY 31.

Mr. Arthur O'Connor on the Tim Horan cheque. Mr. Edward Harrington, M.P., examined. Mr. Harrington on Ireland before the League. On the execution of Sylvester Poff. And on the story of Herbert the process-server 260

NINETY-FIRST DAY.

JUNE 18.

Mr. E. Harrington on unjust sentences and Irish judges. He protests against unfair selection from his speeches. And complains that an Irish constabulary reporter took no note of a speech which he specially devoted to denunciation of crime. Mr. Harrington on peasant hardships. Patrick Kenny, who was censured for shaking hands with Lord Spencer. Father Godley on the boycott. D. F. O'Connor and his collection of League books. Mr. Lyne on landlord harshness 261

NINETY-SECOND DAY.

JUNE 19.

How the Central League Office in Dublin condemned the idiotic resolutions of a local branch. The landlords boycotted Mr. Lyne, grocer of Killarney. Father Lawler describes famine in Arcadian Ireland. He approves of the boycott which means avoidance. Father Harrington on the effect produced in Kerry by the Phœnix Park murders 264

NINETY-THIRD DAY.

JUNE 20.

Mr. T. P. O'Connor in the witness-box. His connection with the League; and his early political speeches. Mr. O'Connor's American tour. Cross-examined by Mr. Ronan, who grows excited over his work. Mr. Ronan's "Chinese puzzle." Father O'Connor of Firies, in Kerry, gives particulars about the Curtin murder 265

NINETY-FOURTH DAY.

JUNE 21.

Mr. Atkinson continues his cross-examination of Father O'Connor. The verb to "brazzle." The leaguers cowed by the moonlighters. Mr. Henry O'Connor, secretary of the Causeway branch of the League, paints Informer Buckley. Dr. Kenny, M.P., in the box. He gives an unflattering account of Farragher the informer 267

NINETY-FIFTH DAY.

JUNE 25.

Dr. Kenny's mistakes about Egan's visits. Dr. Kenny on Le Caron's face. Why did Dr. Kenny give a flattering testimonial to the informer Farragher? —Mr. Sexton contradicts Le Caron's story 268

NINETY-SIXTH DAY.

JUNE 26.

Mr. Sexton's qualified approval of the Fenians. Why Mr. Sexton refused to become a Fenian. Declines to give an answer.—Calls boycotting a necessary evil. Had no recollection of Le Caron.—Mr. T. Harrington on Arcadia. Denies League connection with crime 270

NINETY-SEVENTH DAY.

JUNE 27.

Father Hewson on "duty labour."—Father Kelly denies having intimidated a parishioner. But he admits that at a police siege of a tenant's house, he may have called out "to get the hot water ready." A witness contradicts the story of the informer boy Walsh 272

NINETY-EIGHTH DAY.

JUNE 28.

Five M.P.'s briefly examined.—Reference to Mr. Biggar's Hartmann speech. —An anti-coercion landlord 274

NINETY-NINTH DAY.

JULY 2.

Mr. Michael Davitt in the witness-box. Mr. Davitt on his early life, his American tour. Thinks Mr. Parnell "too conservative." Met Le Caron in America. Says Irish-Americans are content with the Home Rule solution of the Irish problem. The Forrester letter 276

ONE HUNDREDTH DAY.

JULY 3.

The Forrester incident again. The separatist principle. The Manchester martyrs. About Scrab. About grabbing. Mr. Davitt refusing to answer questions 279

ONE HUNDRED AND FIRST DAY.

JULY 4.

Mr. Davitt's cross-examination continued. Denouncing grabbing stopped crime.—The story of Mrs. Walsh, and of her son who was executed.— Mr. Davitt condemns some of Mr. Ford's expressions. His distinction between the English people and English governments 282

ONE HUNDRED AND SECOND DAY.

JULY 5.

Mr. Lowden examined by Mr. Davitt. Boycotting before the League. The Herds' League. Mr. Lowden on the unimportant character of Land League documents. Explains, indignantly, why he would give no information to the police 284

ONE HUNDRED AND THIRD DAY.

JULY 9.

Mr. John O'Connor, M.P., in the box. His early Fenianism. Refuses to tell what his relations with Mr. Devoy were. Irritation of the President. Corrupting the force 287

Contents.

ONE HUNDRED AND FOURTH DAY.
JULY 10.

Mr. John O'Connor on the Prince of Wales's tour.—A long array of witnesses. An infernal machine said to have been in court. Did Houston know anything? ... 290

ONE HUNDRED AND FIFTH DAY.
JULY 11.

Another long array of witnesses.—Mr. Condon, M.P., on O'Donovan Rossa and the Carlton Club. Mr. Condon contradicts Mitchell's story ... 292

ONE HUNDRED AND SIXTH DAY.
JULY 12.

Mr. Hogg on the loans to Mr. Houston.—Mr. Houston on Pigott, Dr. Macguire, and others. The I. L. P. U. books must only be seen by the judges.—And Sir Charles Russell says he must re-consider his position... 294

ONE HUNDRED AND SEVENTH DAY.
JULY 16.

Sir Charles Russell, Mr. Reid, Mr. Lockwood, Mr. Asquith, and all the Counsel for the defence withdraw from the case.—Mr. O'Kelly, M.P., examined by Sir Henry James.—Mr. Matt. Harris's evidence ... 297

ONE HUNDRED AND EIGHTH DAY.
JULY 17.

Mr. Harris's cross-examination continued.—He knows nothing of the League books. His early memories of eviction.—Mrs. Delahunt, of the Ladies' Land League.—Dr. Tanner in the box ... 300

ONE HUNDRED AND NINTH DAY.
JULY 18.

Mr. Harris explains why Messrs. Egan, Brennan, and himself left the Fenian body.—Dr. Tanner on "tar-capping" ... 301

ONE HUNDRED AND TENTH DAY.
JULY 23.

Mr. Parnell reappears.—Land League money.—Mr. Parnell not a man of business.—Mr. Parnell refuses to authorize inspection of the League accounts in the Paris bank ... 302

ONE HUNDRED AND ELEVENTH DAY.
JULY 24.

Mr. Moloney in the witness-box.—Mr. Miller, bank manager, appears.—Destruction of bank documents.—Phillips, the Land League clerk.—Mrs. Phillips 304

ONE HUNDRED AND TWELFTH DAY.
JULY 25.

Mr. Hardcastle's testimony about League accounts.—Court adjourns until the 24th of October 306

ONE HUNDRED AND THIRTEENTH TO ONE HUNDRED AND SEVENTEENTH DAYS, INCLUSIVE.
OCTOBER 24—OCTOBER 31.

Mr. Michael Davitt's address 307

ONE HUNDRED AND EIGHTEENTH TO ONE HUNDRED AND TWENTY-EIGHTH, AND LAST, DAY.
OCTOBER 31—NOVEMBER 22.

Sir Henry James's address 323

NOTES 349

INDEX 351

DIARY

OF THE

PARNELL COMMISSION.

FIRST DAY.

OCTOBER 22.

ON the morning of Monday, the 22nd of October, 1888, the New Law Courts presented an unfamiliar aspect. Some centuries on the way, they were here at last—the van of a multitude of Irishmen (and Irishwomen) about to assist at a unique operation of historical stock-taking.

Witnesses from every class of Irish society, the Paddy of *Punch's* shop-windows, in the flesh, in his traditional costume. He wears knee-breeches and woollen stockings. The style of his tall hat is unknown in Piccadilly. His starchless collar of blue-striped cotton falls round his lean, weather-beaten neck loosely as an æsthete's; and the swallow-tails of his baggy dress-coat of greyish brown shaggy frieze impinge upon his calves. Just as he appears at mass, or on market-days—say at Galway or archiepiscopal Tuam—while he waits, mutely, through the irresponsive hours, straw rope in hand, beside his pig.

Peasant women from the West and South. Some, alas! in the feathered hat of fashion. Others in the more picturesque head-gear, resembling the Scotch Highland *mutch*. One or two display the rich deep red of the Galway petticoat. For outer covering, some wear the heavy woollen shawl, broad striped in whitish grey, and dark brown. But the favourite garment is the long, wide, hooded cloak of deep blue. Seated, silently, with their hoods drawn over their heads, on the side benches of corridors, these peasant women look as if they were at somebody's wake.

The Irish priest, improved, apparently, since Thackeray sketched him, but still with his downcast introspective look, feels his way among the crowd.

At the corners of passages stand little groups of stalwart men, erect, brushed, polished, in dark green helmets and uniforms. Soldiers, of a sort, are they, though they have never taken the Queen's shilling. They are of the "Peeler *mor*," big police, of Celtic Ireland, in contradistinction to the "Peeler *beg*," little police—to wit, Her Majesty's troops. They are men of the Royal Irish Constabulary, the finest *gendarmerie* in the world. When they return to Ireland they will fall into the old ways of a country in military occupation. They will be seen on guard at barracks; or, rifle armed, tramping in their sounding boots on the platforms of lonely country stations, and glancing sharply into the compartments of passing trains; or on the march to storm a "fort."

There are landlords, and their agents, and district magistrates, and Crown lawyers, and inspectors and their deputies, and some of the unfortunate race of informers.

Within—in Probate Court No. 1, not an inch of standing room left by half-past ten o'clock. "Michael Davitt" is whispered over the audience, while a tall, dark-haired, dark-bearded man, with strongly-marked features nd keen frank eyes, makes his way through the crowd to the front bench in the "well" of the court. He comes to defend himself. Great need has he of defence—according to some who are present—for is he not the father of the Land League? High up in a corner sits the bard of the Nationalist Movement, Mr. T. D. Sullivan, and opposite to him Mr. T. P. O'Connor, its historiographer. Mr. O'Kelly, Mr. Healy, Mr. Justin M'Carthy, Mr. J. H. M'Carthy, Mr. Biggar, Mr. Matt. Harris enter next, and Mr. Henry Labouchere, to whom rumour attributes mysterious discoveries concerning the letters. All the lawyers, in white wigs and black gowns, are in their places, filling the first three benches. In the seats behind, and in the wings of the court, are the reporters, the writers, the artists of the London and provincial press. In the galleries, passages, and remaining seats are "the public."

Mr. Parnell arrives in court at three minutes to eleven o'clock. Shaking hands with Mr. Davitt, he has scarcely taken his seat when in comes the Manager of *The Times*, Mr. J. C. Macdonald. He and Mr. Parnell sit almost shoulder to shoulder. After a little space comes the court officer's cry of "Silence." And as the curtains are drawn aside the three judges enter, and all the lawyers and the audience rise. The President makes a low bow. Then their lordships sit down. Next the audience. And after some dry colloquial monotone about certain preliminaries, the Attorney-General rises, and the greatest political trial in English history begins. Sir Richard Webster undertakes to prove that the League was an American-Irish conspiracy, with political independence for its object, and lawless violence—including, in the last resort, assassination—as its instrument. The chief obstacle against the attainment of this independence was the "English garrison" of landlords. The best way to expel the garrison was to starve it out. And the best way to starve it out was to confiscate its rents. But the Irish peasant, with his ineradicable "land-hunger," would himself as soon starve as withhold any rent payment upon which his tenure depended. Therefore the League must coerce, by intimidation, by boycotting, by murder, all who, to escape eviction, or to occupy farms from which others had been evicted, pay rents exceeding the League limit. Whence it followed that the League conspiracy was, in the first resort, and principally, a war upon the tenants! In military phraseology, the landlord stronghold was the League's "objective" in the social war; but between it and its assailants were the multitudes of tenants who held their lands on condition of supplying the garrison, and who would gladly go on supplying, for the sake of a quiet life. If these multitudes of tenants were unanimous for non-supply, the garrison would speedily enough be starved out. But Sir Richard Webster's case was that no such unanimity existed. Wherefore, a panic must be created in the mass of the Irish peasantry—the panic of a camp wherein lurks an enemy. If an assassin is given *carte blanche* in a crowd, everyone in it stands his calculable chance of being hit. The single assassin is a host in himself: a blunderbuss on the safe side of a ditch is worth a battery. And so the success of the League meant this, and only this, said Sir Richard Webster—the success of its "underground movement," the success of the cattle-maimers, housebreakers, boycotters, murderers, who executed the secret orders of the "Open

Organization" which had its head offices in Sackville Street and its leaders in Parliament. The Land League, as known to the public, was the respectable, the "Constitutional" screen behind which the terrorists did their work.

Sir Richard Webster's detailed proof, or evidence, of the foregoing general charge may be arranged under the following heads.

Firstly, he undertook to show, from newspaper and police reports, that in and from 1879 onwards the parliamentary leaders of the League, the League organizers in the West and South of Ireland, and other officials of the League —whether of the Central Office or of the local branches—were constantly delivering speeches which were a more or less direct incentive to violence against all who refused to obey League law.

In the second place, he would show that the outrages which followed these speeches were attributable to the speeches; that, in other words, the sequence was not merely one of time, but of cause and effect. In this part of his proof he would rely to a large extent, if not principally, upon the "negative" evidence, that, as he said, the League speakers never took the trouble to denounce outrages—not even the outrages which followed their individual speeches. Thirdly, he would prove, from the League bank books and other documents, how money was paid by the Central Office in Dublin to branches throughout the country, for the remuneration of moonlighters and assassins, and of counsel and solicitors employed to defend leaguers under trial for crime. It would be proved, from documentary evidence, such as *The Times* "letters," that the collusion between the League chiefs and the local branches was maintained even when the former were in prison. In the fourth part of his speech Sir Richard Webster would prove, from the record of the expeditions of Mr. Parnell, Mr. Davitt, Mr. Dillon, and others to America, and from the story of the Irish-American Conventions held between the years 1879 and 1886, that the Irish League was under the control and in the pay of the American-Irish dynamiters. In final elaboration of his evidence Sir Richard Webster would go into the history of the rise, and progress, and management—open and secret—of the Land League; and then proceed to show how the National League, founded in 1884, was nothing else but the rechristened Land League which was suppressed in October, 1882.

Sir Richard Webster's speech, of which the foregoing was the general plan, lasted five days. The portion of Ireland surveyed by him was restricted to the five counties of Mayo, Galway, Clare, Kerry, and Cork. The Galway speeches and outrages were disposed of in the first day. As a specimen of the inflammatory oratory to which he attributed the eighteen murders which took place in Galway during the years 1880-82, Sir Richard Webster quoted the renowned "partridge" speech of Mr. M. Harris. The heroes of the Galway movement were—to judge from the frequency of the Attorney-General's allusions to them—Mr. Matt. Harris, and a certain Mr. Nally, more familiarly known as "Scrab."

And there was a dangerous agitator, Martin, who was as fond of sport as Mr. Harris himself, for he told his hearers that they ought to hunt the land-grabber as they would a mad dog. In another of his denunciatory speeches Mr. Harris compared landlords to tigers, and to that speech the Attorney-General attributed a murder which took place some twelve months afterwards. He quoted a speech of Mr. Dillon's, to the effect that "the only way to break down the power of landlordism, and to reduce rack rents, was to maintain the rule by which a man who goes and takes land and treats with the landlord is looked upon as a traitor." Mr. Parnell and Mr. Davitt seemed wholly unconcerned, Mr. Macdonald, of *The Times*, who sat within a yard of them, nodded and smiled as the Attorney-General denounced what he regarded as the villainy of the Land League. "If," exclaimed Sir Richard Webster, vigorously slapping his pile of blue books—" if Mr. Harris did not intend his speeches to lead to crimes, why did he not denounce crime? why did he not say he would have nothing to do with constituents who permitted such things in their midst?" In quoting Erse, Sir Richard nearly came to grief. He struggled with, but finally mastered somehow, the expression *thiggin dhu*, which the League orators often used in their speeches, which literally means "Do you understand?" but which, under the circumstances, he translated "Don't nail his ears to the pump."

SECOND DAY.

OCTOBER 23.

THE Attorney-General took his audience through Kerry and Mayo. As Mr. Harris was the Parliamentary hero in Galway, so Mr. Harrington was the hero in Kerry. It was Mr. Harrington who said that land-grabbers should be shunned as if they had small-pox. That was a specimen of a kind of oratory, thought the Attorney-General, of which it was "impossible to exaggerate the wickedness." He also quoted Mr. Biggar, as having said at a meeting, that "public opinion should be brought to bear" upon any who was "base enough" to take a farm from which another had been evicted. "Cut the land-grabber in every way," said a priest, "shun him," "ostracize him," he will "rot" under such a display of public opinion. The mention of Kerry moonlighting moved Sir Richard Webster once again most vehemently to accuse the League leaders of having negatively encouraged crime by refraining from denouncing it. And then he passed on to Mayo, requisitioning "Scrab" for a sporting quotation about "jackdaws and magpies," to match Mr. M. Harris's "partridges" and "Bengal tigers." It was noticeable that most of the speeches referred to by Sir Richard Webster turned upon the subject of land-grabbing. One speaker, not a Member of Parliament, declared that the "land-grabber resembled Judas Iscariot, who betrayed Christ." Another League speaker, also non-parliamentary, was reported to have said that the man who took an evicted farm was "a greater assassin than the man who fired a pistol shot." It seemed as if the strongest language came from the persons who were least responsible and most obscure. Thus "Scrab" (whose orations were so much in demand) was reported to have said that "pills" (bullets?) were inferior, as an agrarian medicine, to dynamite and gun-cotton. A collection, from Sir Richard's speech, of the epithets hurled at the head of the unhappy grabber would show how the impulsive, perfervid Celt must have laboured under the pressure of his rhetorical steam. The land-grabber was a "louse," the land-grabber was a "rapacious beast," he was a "low-life cur," a "reptile," a "putrid companion." Of the numerous speeches quoted by the Attorney-General, and advising tenants to "cut" the grabber always and everywhere—in chapel as well as in the street—we may mention Mr. Parnell's speech at Ennis, in September, 1880: "I think I heard cries of 'Shoot him!' but I think I know a better way, which will give the lost sinner a chance of repentance. You must shun him when you meet him in the streets of the town, in the fair or market-place, or even in the house of worship itself, by leaving him severely alone, by putting him into a moral Coventry, by isolating him as if he were a leper of old." But all this, whatever its value as evidence, was threadbare history. Gradually Sir Richard Webster's audience grew tired, and half the unofficial portion of it stealthily took its departure. The one lady left in the side gallery looked like patience on a monument. The President was ever on the alert. But after a time Mr. Justice Day yawned. Then he shrugged his shoulders. Then he stretched his legs. Mr. Justice Smith, dropping his pen, leant back, and seemed to fall into what is called a brown study. Some of the juniors amused themselves with sketching caricatures of their seniors. "Silence!" quoth the usher, drowsily, tapping his snuff-box, for among the lawyers, and the journalists, and the rest there arose a buzz of conversation about things in general.

As the purpose of these preliminary chapters is to indicate Sir Richard Webster's general line of argument, I need not follow him in his search after speeches and outrages throughout the remaining counties, except to say that he attributed to Land League speeches the six murders and the eighteen attempts at murder which took place in Clare in 1881-83. He touched upon the No Rent manifesto, because he regarded it as the text upon which the League organizers, the criminal agitators outside, framed their popular discourses during the imprisonment of Mr. Parnell and other leaders of the party. For a similar reason Sir Richard Webster made a passing reference to two of *The Times* "letters," one of them being an alleged letter from the Land League secretary, Mr. Egan, in Paris, to Carey in Dublin, in which the writer asked, "When will you undertake to get to work and give us value for our money?" and the other being the alleged letter of Mr. Parnell, in which the writer asked what "those fellows" were "waiting for," recommended an end to "this hesitency," spoke of making it "hot for old Forster." At this mention of a letter upon the authenticity or spuriousness of which so much depended, the Attorney-General's hearers became attentive. He must have given some of them food for reflection when, having stated that *The Times* people had instituted "every possible inquiry" into its genuineness, he remarked that for his own part he had never attached "such a vast amount of importance" to the letter.

THIRD DAY.

OCTOBER 24.

MR. PARNELL, who looked pale and ill, came in just in time to hear his supposed relationship with the Phœnix Park assassins, and his supposed authorship of the famous "*facsimile* letter" of May 15, 1882, discussed, in the frankest language, by the Attorney-General. Putting down his black bag, and putting up his coat collar (against the draughts which defy Mr. Street's architecture), Mr. Parnell turned half round, to hear himself summed up with all the Attorney-General's candour and ruthless decorum. A quiet smile stole over Mr. Parnell's face as the Attorney-General, having read out the letter of the 15th of May, 1882, handed it to the President for his lordship's inspection. Sir James Hannen, studying it carefully for a minute or two, handed it to Mr. Justice Day, who in another minute or two passed it on to Mr. Justice Smith. This little scene was watched by the two men most concerned in it—by Mr. Parnell with an expression of amused curiosity, by Mr. Macdonald, of *The Times*, with the not unnatural pride of one who had accomplished the most notable journalistic feat of the century.

The *facsimile* letter was produced in continuation of the special topic of the preceding day's business—namely, the connection of the Central League Office and its chiefs with the local branches of the "conspiracy" and the physical force party in America. Turning to the "Kilmainham treaty," Sir Richard Webster argued that its very terms implied that Mr. Parnell, if he had liked, could long ago have stopped outrage. "If," said Sir Richard Webster, "Mr. Parnell says he did do his best to put it down, I shall ask him, when he enters the witness-box, what he did before the date of the Phœnix Park murders, May 6, 1882. Captain O'Shea will testify," he continued, "that Mr. Parnell unwillingly signed the manifesto in which the murders were denounced. Captain O'Shea's testimony will also show that Mr. Parnell could have stopped outrage, treaty or no treaty. Mr. Parnell objected to doing anything that would displease the Irish-American party of violence, from which the League derived all its wealth. Why, that *facsimile* letter, in which Mr. Parnell apologized for—or explained—his signature to the manifesto, was," Sir Richard Webster maintained, "the precise kind of letter which he would have written under the circumstances." Sir Richard wound up his day's work with a reiteration of his proposition, that crime varied directly as the influence of the League. In illustration of this proposition, he said that in the whole of Ireland there were twenty murders during two and a half years ending with the establishment of the Land League, and fifty murders during the corresponding period immediately following it; that in 1883-84, the period of League inactivity under the Crimes Act, there was only one murder; but that murders increased, again, in 1885-87, when there was no Crimes Act in force.

FOURTH AND FIFTH DAYS.

OCTOBER 25 AND 26.

FIRST, the outline of the American part of *The Times* case, including American influence upon the Irish Land League, and next, a review of the history of the National League (the organization which succeeded the Land League) occupied the fourth and fifth days. On the fourth day the Archbishop of Dublin sat in the jury-box, and was, to all appearance, considerably impressed by Sir Richard Webster's account of the genesis of the Land League. Mr. Davitt, also, must have been considerably impressed; for it would seem as if the Attorney-General meant to rob him of the glory of paternity of the Land League. Anyhow, Mr. Davitt glanced quickly, now and again, at the Attorney-General, and smiled at his interpretation of Irish-American history. Up to that moment the world had been under the impression that Mr. Davitt was the father of the League. But in Sir Richard Webster's view the real father was Patrick Ford, of *The Irish World*. However, Sir Richard subsequently admitted that Mr. Michael Davitt did start the League in Ireland. Mr. Davitt went to America in 1878, and there and then arranged with Mr. Ford his plan of an organization for starving out the "English garrison" in Ireland—namely, the landlords. In the course of the evidence which he would produce the Attorney-General would show that the Irish leaders conspired with the leaders of the "American section," the members of which were advocates of communism, assassination, and other outrages of the worst sort. "It was in collusion with the American leaders," said the Attorney-General, "that the League introduced a method of illegal agitation before unknown in Ireland; for in other times the landlord used to be the victim of agrarian outrage, whereas now the victim was to be the tenant who accepted his landlord's terms." From the foundation of the League in Ireland, Sir Richard Webster passed on to the foundation of the American branch by Mr. Parnell, and Mr. Parnell's American tour in 1879-80, and an elaborate account of the American Conventions from 1880, and of the speeches made and the resolutions passed at them. As specimens of these speeches may be produced in the course of the American evidence, no further reference will be made to the subject here.

On the fifth and last day of his speech Sir Richard Webster reviewed the history of the National League. His method was the same as the one he followed in his history of Land League work; he quoted speeches, and enumerated outrages which he maintained to have been caused by them. He traversed the old ground—Kerry, Cork, Clare, Galway, and Mayo. The same old orators were run out again, in all their hot wrath, with all their ready wealth of zoological, entomological, and pathological imagery—Nally among the rest. Which Nally? "Scrab"? Or the other Nally? It mattered not, for both conspired. Long before Sir Richard Webster finished his discourse, the President asked him, in mild remonstrance, whether he did not think that, without going over another county, he had given "sufficient intimation of his line of argument." But Sir Richard plodded away—*ohne hast ohne rast*—through the leaden hours. Just on the stroke of four o'clock Sir Richard Webster aroused the attention of his hearers by announcing that in all probability witnesses would appear who themselves had taken part in murderous expeditions, and who would swear that they had been paid for their foul work in Land League money.

Not the least important kind of evidence upon which the Attorney-General relied was negative evidence. This should be constantly borne in mind by all who (to quote an expression which his principal "criminal" has made famous) would "keep a firm grip" upon the Attorney-General's argument. His argument implied—even stated—that the outrages dealt with in *The Times* case were of a kind wholly new in rural Ireland. Before 1879, the year of the foundation of the League, they were not. Nor could the Attorney-General discover anything in the social condition of the country before that date which would account for the crimes after it. In short, the Attorney-General's Ireland was a kind of Arcadia, wherein landlords and tenants were on friendly terms, wherein there were no boycottings, no moonlightings, no cattle-maimings, no war against land-grabbers—any more than thunderbolts in clear weather. In keeping with this theory of the Irish social state was Sir Richard Webster's frequent assertion that Mr. Parnell and his colleagues felt themselves bound to satisfy their American "paymasters." It was always the Irish abroad, not the Irish at home—greater Ireland, not lesser Ireland—that must be "satisfied." Necessarily, if the League agitation was a foreign manufacture.

This was the question at issue—Was, or was not, Irish outrage the harvest of a soil that had been prepared for it before ever the League came into being? Were constabulary rule and plans of campaign, Crimes Acts and League programmes, coercion and social war, "Balfourism" and "Parnellism," the variously-phased consequence of the same evil Past?

SIXTH DAY.

OCTOBER 30.

ON Tuesday, October 30th, at half-past eleven o'clock, the first witness for *The Times* entered the box. Bernard O'Malley his name was, head constable in the Irish force, in which he had served twenty-two years. One of the constabulary shorthand writers, he was now called upon to "prove" a series of Land League speeches (from 1880) delivered in the counties of Galway and Kerry. Taking a printed transcript of the speeches to be "proved," he was requested to read, while Sir Henry James, with his eye upon another copy, followed him. Away went Mr. O'Malley as fast as he could run; but his troubles began presently. Mr. O'Malley's reading was a low, indistinct mumble as of a man chewing and swallowing his words, an outlandish dialectic blur, in which stray expressions about "squalor," "misery," "cabins," were faintly distinguishable.

A good-humoured frown gathered on the President's face. "I cannot follow him at all," said his lordship, slowly shaking his head; "I cannot hear or understand what he is saying." And so Head-Constable Bernard O'Malley was pulled up. As he stopped short he smiled, as if in healthy satisfaction with his own performance.

"Supposing I read," suggested Sir Henry James, "and Mr. O'Malley checks me." Sir Henry proved to be a swifter reader even than Mr. O'Malley, but it was so easy to follow him. However, in a minute or two, three of the accused fell (metaphorically speaking) upon Sir Henry James. These three were Mr. Davitt, Mr. Biggar, and Mr. Healy, who protested against extracts without contexts, demanded every speech to be read in full, and that Mr. Bernard O'Malley should read from his shorthand notes. Mr. Biggar was very plain-spoken. Resting one hand behind his back, and waving the other, carelessly, in Sir Henry James's direction, he remarked that Sir Henry's object in reading his choice selection of extracts was to "get them into the newspapers," so that the public mind might be "prejudiced." At last the suggestion of Mr. Healy and his friends was adopted, and Mr. O'Malley was requested to read from his shorthand notes. But if at first Mr. O'Malley ran like a hare, he now crawled like a tortoise. To Mr. O'Malley's audience the prospect of a laboured deciphering of years of forgotten platform talk was appalling. "Is there much more of this?" inquired Sir James Hannen, in a tone of pathetic distress. Mr. O'Malley took it all with cheerful composure. He paused for a moment; he glanced, slowly, sideways, at the judges on the bench. Then he raised his thumb to his mouth; he damped it; and then he turned over, with easy deliberation, the pages of his too illegible manuscript.

Here are a few specimen expressions from the speeches which, according to *The Times* case, led to outrages in the counties wherein they were delivered. Brennan, in one of his speeches, declared that he did not want his hearers to give the landlords a blow or a stone, but that they might do as they liked; also that the highest form of government was a Republic, and that they might establish a Republic on Irish soil. "Scrab," of course, was quoted. Quoth "Scrab": "Why do you allow land-grabbers to live? Don't speak to them. Leave their corn and meadows uncut, and they will commit suicide without the pills."

Mr. Patrick J. Gordon, again, said he would be ready, if the occasion arose, to fight for Ireland at the bayonet point, but he recommended his hearers to try to get their rights without bloodshed. A speech of Mr. T. Harrington's invited the tenants to pledge themselves not to take an evicted farm, and not to hold any converse with any one who broke the pledge. It would seem as if some of these speakers, in the excitement and heat of the moment, and in the exuberance of their native volubility, spurted out whatever words came uppermost.

For example, one of the League orators declared, ferociously, that he cared not if half his enemies had "their throats cut before morning." "If you are put to it," said he, "sell the old cow and buy a rifle." And yet this same orator, almost in the same breath, advises his hearers to treat those enemies, the hated land-grabbers included, "with contempt, to pass them by, and not speak to them at the fair." With hardly an exception the speakers quoted were non-parliamentary members, or friends, of the League. In one of the speeches quoted by *The Times* counsel there were denunciations of cattle maiming and personal violence. The speaker was Martin O'Halloran,[1] who said, "Do not touch him [any man who took evicted land]. If you do you are enemies to the cause. I hope you will take that advice from a patriotic man, and work it prudently. Do not summon any man before God; it might not be fair." But before Mr. O'Halloran's speech was read Head Constable O'Malley left the box. The speech was "proved" by Constable Irwin, who was the second and last witness of the day. Both witnesses were requested to reappear for further evidence and cross-examination.

SEVENTH DAY.

OCTOBER 31.

SIR RICHARD WEBSTER had a surprise in store for his opponents. Instead of recalling the two witnesses of the day before, he asked permission to put Captain O'Shea into the witness-box. Sir Charles Russell objected to have a witness "sprung" upon him—especially a witness of such importance as Captain O'Shea, whom he was unprepared to cross-examine. But the Attorney-General, explaining that Captain O'Shea's immediate departure for the Continent necessitated his examination now, Captain O'Shea was called, and a whole day of most interesting testimony, including a political disclosure or two, was the result. Mr. Parnell was in his place shortly after ten o'clock—fully a quarter of an hour before the proceedings began.

The Attorney-General, after a few preliminary questions, came to the subject of the Kilmainham "treaty"—the negotiations carried on between the Liberal Ministry of the day (1881-82) and Mr. Parnell (prisoner in Kilmainham), and in which Captain O'Shea was the intermediary. The Attorney-General's purpose was to prove, from the history of the Kilmainham "treaty," the proposition upon which he had laid main stress in his opening speech—the proposition that Mr. Parnell had full knowledge of criminal acts perpetrated by his associates in the control of the League and the management of the agrarian agitation; in other words, that Mr. Parnell could at any time (even in jail) have suppressed the criminal agitation, of which, *ex hypothesi*, he and his colleagues were the authors. "It is fair to say," remarked Captain O'Shea, "that Mr. Parnell never made his own release from Kilmainham a condition of the 'treaty.'" Captain O'Shea then explained that a formal memorandum was drawn up on the subject between himself as representing Mr. Parnell, and Mr. Chamberlain on the part of the Liberal Ministry. "Will you let me see it?" asked Sir Richard Webster. Captain O'Shea, emptying his coat-pocket, produced the document, which Sir Richard now made public for the first time. "In whose handwriting is it?" said the Attorney-General. "In Mr. Chamberlain's"—at which answer Mr. Biggar laughed outright. The memorandum, dated 22nd of April, 1882, was as follows :—

72, PRINCE'S GATE, S.W.

If the Government announce a satisfactory plan for dealing with arrears, Mr. Parnell will advise the tenants to pay rents, and will denounce outrage and resistance to law, and all processes of intimidation, whether by boycotting or in any other way. No plan of dealing with arrears can be satisfactory which does not wipe them off compulsorily by a composition of one-third payable by the tenant, one-third by the State from the Church fund or some other public sources, and one-third remitted by the landlord; but so that the constitution of the tenant and the State shall not exceed one year's rent each, the balance, if any, to be liquidated by the landlords; arrears to be defined as arrears accruing up to May, 1881.

---

[1] This must be the Martin O'Halloran, carpenter, nearly Athenry, who, himself an imprisoned suspect in Kilmainham, sometimes spent an hour in teaching his fellow-prisoner, Mr. Parnell, the elements of the craft.

Of no less importance than the foregoing were two other documents, now produced in court—one a letter, dated 16th of April, 1882, from Mr. Parnell to Captain O'Shea; the other, from the same to the same, was dated from Kilmainham, 20th of April, 1882, and was the famous letter read out in the House of Commons on the 15th of May of the same year. In the 16th of April letter Mr. Parnell spoke of a "permanent settlement" of the land question as being "most desirable for everybody's sake." In the same letter Mr. Parnell expressed the opinion that "about eight millions of pounds sterling would enable three-fourths of the tenants (at or under £30 valuation) to become owners at fairly remunerative prices to the landlords. The larger class of tenants can do well enough with the Law Courts if Mr. Healy's clause be fairly amended." In the letter of the 20th of May Mr. Parnell impresses upon Captain O'Shea, through whom, as already said, the negotiations were conducted, "the absolute necessity of a settlement of the arrears question, which will leave no recurring sore connected with it behind, and which will enable us to show the smaller tenantry that they have been treated with justice and some generosity." "If," Mr. Parnell continues in the same letter—"if the arrears question be settled, ... I have every confidence—a confidence shared by my colleagues—that the exertions which we should be able to make, strenuously and unremittingly, would be effective in stopping outrages and intimidations of all kinds. . . . The accomplishment of the programme I have sketched out to you would, in my judgment, be regarded by the country as a practical settlement of the land question. ... And I believe that the Government, at the end of the session, would, from the state of the country,'feel themselves thoroughly justified in dispensing with further coercive measures."

The above quotations from the documents produced in court should be compared with the description which, in his opening speech, Sir Richard Webster gave of the character and purpose of Mr. Parnell's policy. There is an "if" running through Mr. Parnell's share in the negotiations: "If" the Government passes a satisfactory Arrears Bill, Mr. Parnell and his colleagues will do their best to put down outrage, and are confident they will be able to do it.

Mr. Parnell talked of compromise, talked not unkindly of the landlord "garrison," the starvation of which was supposed to be the purpose of the League agitation. Mr. Parnell made a passing remark on what he considered to be the natural history, so to speak, of crime in Ireland, in saying that the outrages were generally committed by the sons of small farmers whose rents were in arrears, that is to say, of the poor, struggling class for whose relief the Arrears Bill was to be introduced. In these letters and documents Mr. Parnell stated, with sufficient clearness, that without an Arrears Act he would be powerless to stop crime—the passing of an Arrears Act was an "absolute necessity." In the course of the examination, of which the "treaty" was the chief topic, Captain O'Shea said that, in Mr. Parnell's opinion, Sheridan and Boyton, who were "organizers" in the West and South, might be advantageously used to put crime down. Sir Richard Webster held that Sheridan and Boyton were criminal agitators, and that Mr. Parnell was fully aware of the fact.

Sir Richard Webster now came to the famous letter — the *facsimile* letter published in *The Times* of May 15, 1882. Captain O'Shea's demeanour, as he examined the letter, now handed to him by the Attorney-General, was watched by all present with intense curiosity. What would he say? "Whose is that signature?" Sir Richard asked him. "I am not an expert in handwriting," replied Captain O'Shea, after a long pause, looking up. "I am aware of that," replied Sir Richard, "but you can tell me whose handwriting you believe it to be." "I believe it to be Mr. Parnell's."

Wednesday] the Parnell Commission. [*Oct. 31.*

It was now Sir Charles Russell's time to cross-examine. At first (and for the reason already given) he proposed to postpone the cross-examination. But at last he went on with it, on Sir James Hannen's reminding him that he might resume it at a subsequent date, and that, in the event of Captain O'Shea not being able to reappear, the Attorney-General's examination-in-chief must stand.

Captain O'Shea described, in reply to Sir Charles Russell's questions, how in August last Mr. Joseph Chamberlain and a person named Houston were the intermediaries through whom he arranged to appear as a witness for *The Times;* how, about the date when these arrangements were going on, he dined with *The Times* editor and Sir Rowland Blennerhasset; and how, once upon a time, he stated, on the authority of a man named Mulqueeny, that some one knew of a payment of money by Mr. Parnell to Frank Byrne to enable the latter to escape arrest on a charge of complicity in the Phœnix Park murders.

"It was after that statement of Mulqueeny's," continued Sir Charles Russell, "that you were a candidate for Galway?" "Yes." "Then you did not believe those statements about Mr. Parnell at that time?" "Oh, no; certainly not."

Then there followed a long series of questions, by which Sir Charles Russell elicited some facts about the witness's breach with Mr. Parnell and the Nationalist party in 1886, and about his relations with a party of "extreme" Irish politicians, of whom Mulqueeny was one, and who were engaged in getting up a testimonial to Captain O'Shea by way of protest against his expulsion from the Parnellite party.

Sir Charles Russell pressed Captain O'Shea to answer the following question: "Did you tell any one in the winter of 1885-86 that there were in London American Fenians who were hostile to Mr. Parnell, and who held letters compromising him?" Captain O'Shea was not sure that he had said "hostile," but he admitted it was Mulqueeny who told him about the presence of the American Fenians. Then he declared that, to the best of his belief, he had never heard of the existence of compromising documents before he saw the *facsimile* of the Byrne letter in *The Times.* Passing on to the Kilmainham treaty, "Is it not a fact," asked Sir Charles, "that when you mentioned the question of release Mr. Parnell said there must be no reference to that matter at all?" "Certainly," was Captain O'Shea's reply. And he gave the same answer to the next question—"Is it not a fact that, in every attempt made to put down outrage, Mr. Parnell referred to the proposed measure of the Government—the Arrears Bill—as a means of tranquillizing the country?"

Replying, next, to Sir Charles's question as to whether he had kept any memoranda of the Kilmainham "treaty," he said that he had not. "How is that?" exclaimed Sir Charles, in surprise. Because he received a hint that, as there was a risk of a parliamentary inquiry into the "treaty," it would be as well to be reticent; and he took the precaution of destroying his memoranda. At this little revelation the curiosity of the very crowded court became extreme; and a loud burst of laughter broke forth from the audience when Captain O'Shea stated that the Minister who gave him the hint was Sir William Harcourt. As to the story that Mr. Parnell wished to visit Mr. Davitt in prison because Mr. Davitt was one of those whom it was undesirable to release at once, Captain O'Shea now gave it as his impression, founded on Mr. Parnell's words at the time, that Mr. Parnell wanted to see Mr. Davitt because he feared he would refuse to accept his release on ticket-of-leave. Next followed a string of questions about events subsequent to the Phœnix Park murders. In his replies, Captain O'Shea declared that the murders seriously affected Mr. Parnell's health and spirits, and that he (Captain O'Shea) considered them to be "a cruel blow" to Mr. Parnell's policy. "You consider that?" Sir Charles Russell repeated. "Certainly," was the answer. Captain O'Shea further said that he in person had, after the murders, taken a letter to Mr. Gladstone, from Mr. Parnell, in which Mr. Parnell offered to retire from political life. As to the *facsimile* letter (of May 15, 1882), he first saw it in *The Times*. "I did not think it was genuine," said Captain O'Shea, "but I thought the signature was." "What made you think it was not genuine?" "Well, I thought it funny that he should say, 'You may show him this, but don't tell him my address.'" "It certainly is odd," was Sir Charles Russell's remark.

Such was the substance of the testimony of the first of the principal witnesses called by *The Times* to damn Mr. Parnell. We have now to hear what the constabulary witnesses, O'Malley and Irwin, have to say on the general question, the action of the League.

EIGHTH DAY.

NOVEMBER 1.

CONSIDERING their intimate knowledge of Ireland and its people, and their long experience in the constabulary service, the testimony of Constable Irwin and Head Constable O'Malley was interesting and valuable in the highest degree. Their testimony occupied the whole of the day. Constable Irwin was a good specimen, physically, of the "Royal Irish" constable. He was tall and athletic. His manner was pleasant. His answers to Sir Charles Russell were prompt and to the point. If Mr. Irwin had a fault, it was a proneness to be too free and easy—not in a bad sense, but in a kindly, well-meant, man-and-brotherly way. Leaning his elbows on the ledge in front of him, folding his hands, and bending slightly forward, he nodded and smiled, in his pleasant way, at "Sir Char-lis" (pronouncing the name in the Irish manner). "Yes, Sir Char-lis," "Just so, Sir Char-lis," "Quite right, Sir Char-lis"—as if he was anxious to encourage the renowned Q.C. to persevere in his arduous and historic task. At last his cross-examiner became just a little irritated. "Don't call me Sir Charles." "Very well, Sir Char-lis," with a pleasant little nod, and a smile. All which amused Mr. Irwin's hearers.

Mr. Irwin knew Galway, Clare, and Kerry, in which counties he began to take shorthand reports of League meetings about nine years ago, when the League agitation was beginning. He had nothing to complain of, he said, as to the manner of the reception accorded to him at these meetings : "Sometimes I was admitted to the platform, and sometimes I was not." As to the cause of the "sore feeling" between the Irish peasants and the police, Mr. Irwin believed that the employment of the police at evictions was "certainly" one of the causes of it. "General discontent," said Mr. Irwin, "increased after 1879," and the drift of his answers was that the discontent was caused by evictions. The following questions, with their replies, will show what he meant. "Do you know that just as distress deepened, evictions increased?" "Well, I have no personal knowledge of that." And then he added : "As the people fell into arrears, of course writs were issued, and the consequence would be evictions." "And as these evictions increased, general discontent increased?" "General discontent increased since 1879." "Have outrages, in your judgment, increased in proportion to evictions?" "I have heard people who had been evicted, or who had received notices of eviction, say they did not care what became of them, or what they did." "They fell, in fact, into a state of desperation?" "Some of them." Mr. Murphy, Q.C., who was examining Mr. Irwin, on behalf of *The Times*, was trying to show that the discontent and outrages which followed the year 1879 were due to the League ("conspiracy") founded in September of that year. Sir Charles Russell, on the other hand, traced it to the general distress which, said the witness, existed in the West and South-West of Ireland during the period in question, and which was followed by evictions. It was a case of rival interpretations of contemporary Irish history. "The distress was great," said Constable Irwin, "among the smaller farmers"—the very class of persons for whom Mr. Parnell interceded from his prison in Kilmainham, and from whom came, as Mr. Parnell said, the perpetrators of the outrages which the Government were trying to suppress by Coercion and Crimes Acts. The distress began even in the year before the foundation of the League, and was especially severe in Galway, where crimes of the worst sort speedily became more numerous than anywhere in Ireland. As the witness admitted, a repetition of the great famine of 1846-48 was expected.

Having thus got the witness to admit that long before the foundation of the Land League there existed widespread distress, leading to non-payment of rent, leading, in its turn, to evictions, which in turn made the people—or, as the witness said, "some"—"desperate," Sir Charles Russell questioned him about the kind of language used by the League speakers during that period of distress and discontent. It will be remembered that, in his opening speech, the Attorney-General accused League speakers of saying nothing to dissuade the people from violence. What light could Constable Irwin throw upon that question? Constable Irwin now said, in answer to Sir Charles Russell, that among the speeches which he heard, "there were very many" in which the people were enjoined to be patient. "And did not speakers ask the people to rely upon the efforts of their leaders to secure their rights from Parliament?" "Yes; that was the general tone of many of the speeches," was the reply. Still, there were very few meetings, added the witness, at which "harum-scarum" speeches—as Sir Charles Russell called them—were not made.

As for "Scrab" Nally, whom the Attorney-General had so conspicuously honoured by quotations from his speeches, Mr. Irwin had never met him; but, said Mr. Irwin, "I know he is looked upon as a man who would say anything." He was next asked what he knew of the attitude of the League towards secret societies. "I have, certainly," said he, "heard of attempts by secret society men to break up the Land League meetings." And he knew that the counties in which disturbance was most rife in the years 1880-83, were also the counties in which secret societies had the strongest hold. Speaking of the Castleisland district of Kerry, he attributed some, at least, of the crimes perpetrated in it to young loafers and idlers who spent most of their time in watching the police.

Mr. Healy now cross-examined, and succeeded in eliciting some striking arithmetical facts. "How many speeches of *mine* have you reported?" asked Mr. Healy. "About a hundred," of which number only six were put in deposition. "How many meetings should you say were held from start to finish of the agitation?" "Perhaps tens of thousands," Mr. Irwin answered. And these meetings were open to everybody who chose to attend them. Mr. Irwin next gave a brief but suggestive account of the Irish Grand Juries, saying that they were elected by the landlords, and that it was the landlord jurors who had the power of levying rates in compensation for outrages. Mr. Irwin also declared that he had heard of such things as bogus outrages, planned for the purpose of getting "compensation" from the Grand Jurors.

Mr. Davitt then made his *début* as a cross-examiner in an English court of justice. A strong, clear, resonant, manly voice was Mr. Davitt's. "Not the slightest discourtesy" had Mr. Irwin met with at meetings at which he had taken notes of Mr. Davitt's speeches. "What did you hear me say?" In Castleisland (Kerry) "I heard you warn the people against the commission of crime." "You recollect me denouncing moonlighting very vigorously?" "Yes, I do." A brief re-examination by Mr. Murphy, Q.C., followed the cross-examination by Mr. Davitt. In this re-examination Mr. Murphy got Mr. Irwin to reassert that Kerry was "quiet" in the period immediately preceding the foundation of the Land League. The purpose of the re-examination was to saddle the League with the responsibility for the outrages which happened subsequently to its foundation. The purpose of the cross-examination by Sir Charles Russell was to show that these outrages were the fruit —sure to appear in due time—of the distress, and consequent arrears and evictions, under which the people were growing "desperate" before the Land League came into existence. As already said, the counsel for the accusers and the counsel for the accused were interpreting Irish history differently.

Mr. Bernard O'Malley's evidence coincided pretty generally with that of Mr. Irwin. O'Malley was cross-examined by Sir Charles Russell, Mr. Reid, Q.C., and Mr. Healy. In answer to Mr. Reid, he corroborated Mr. Irwin's evidence, that the speakers at League meetings generally warned the people not to commit crime—for commission of crime "would injure their cause," said the witness, quoting League speakers. "How is it," asked Sir Charles, "that you have not transcribed a speech of Father Eglinton's, delivered at a meeting some other speeches of which are put in evidence?" "I was not asked to," Mr. O'Malley answered. It turned out that Father Eglinton denounced the murder of Lord Mountmorres—"I have a distinct recollection of it," said the witness. Sir Charles Russell, in the course of his cross-examination, drew attention to another example of incomplete quotation. The example was from a speech of Mr. Brennan's.

The extract given in court was as follows: "The highest form of government is a Republic. You may establish a Republic on Irish soil." But Sir Charles Russell read out the context thus :—

If we had a Government in Ireland to-morrow which would protect the idler against the worker, I would be against them. All I see here, I think, will agree with me that the highest form of government is a Republic. Well, you may establish a Republic on Irish soil, but as long as the tillers of the soil are forced to support an idle class, a Republic would be a mockery.

Mr. O'Malley, like his fellow-witness, was asked for his opinion of "Scrab." Mr. O'Malley had a poor opinion of "Scrab." On one occasion he saw "Scrab" prevented from putting a resolution at a public meeting. "I never heard," said Mr. O'Malley, "that 'Scrab' was regarded as a sort of a lunatic; but he was looked upon as a sort of a drunkard. He was what I should call a free lance." Then Mr. O'Malley amused his audience by confessing that, on two or three occasions, he had "drinks" with this wonderful "Scrab." "It might have been at nine or ten o'clock" [at night presumably], "or it might have been any time at all"—at which Irish answers the people in court laughed. But before this part of the story was finished, Mr. O'Malley explained that he himself, as a teetotaler, drank water, though the renowned "Scrab" took something stronger.

Lastly, Mr. O'Malley gave some evidence of landlord indifference to peasant distress. When the distress of nine or ten years ago was at its height, "most of the farmers" on the Berridge property (which extends forty or fifty miles through Connemara) were, said Mr. O'Malley, kept alive by public subscription; but he never heard that the landlord had shown the smallest interest in the people's welfare, or expended a shilling for their relief.

In the earlier part of his cross-examination by Sir Charles Russell, Constable Irwin made some interesting statements about the preparation of *The Times* evidence in the first case, the case of O'Donnell *v.* Walter. Mr. Irwin had himself taken down the evidence of witnesses for *The Times*, but not, as he said, "on instructions." In "some cases," said Mr. Irwin, I gave the evidence to Mr. Horne, a Resident Magistrate for Clare and Kerry. This was done at the Inns of Court Hotel, where Captain Slack, Mr. Holden, and other Irish magistrates and police officers were living. Mr. Horne, he also said, took statements from witnesses. But he declined to say, positively, whether or not the other Irish magistrates followed Mr. Horne's example; whether they were or were not engaged in getting up evidence for *The Times*. They were writing, certainly, and witnesses were going in and out. But Mr. Irwin thought the magistrates might have been writing "their private letters." "The same kind of thing went on—on and off—perhaps for a week." "What! still at their private letters!" exclaimed Sir Charles, with a look of surprise.

NINTH DAY.

NOVEMBER 6.

To visitors in search not of a "sensation," but of insight into contemporary Ireland, to-day's proceedings must have been the most interesting of the series. Yet the morning sitting was but thinly attended. In the afternoon the court was crowded. Captain Plunkett, known in Ireland as "Plunkett Pacha," appearing among the onlookers, attracted some attention. So did Mr. Matt. Harris, M.P., who, if some of the Attorney-General's "particulars" are worthy of trust, would have liked many things worse than a day's shooting among landlords. Dr. Tanner also was among the new arrivals, squeezing himself into a corner on the solicitor's bench. Mr. Parnell, Mr. Michael Davitt, Mr. Biggar were there as usual. The day's proceedings began with a mild protest by the Attorney-General against an evening paper, which, as he said, had published statements amounting to intimidation of witnesses. He did not wish to take any definite proceedings against the paper in question, in the present stage at least ; but only to procure an expression of opinion from the bench. Sir Charles Russell then rose with a *tu quoque* sort of argument, pointing out that *The Times* was every day publishing an advertisement in which one of the letters (the genuineness of which was one of the most important questions before the Court) was described as "Mr. Parnell's facsimile letter." Sir James Hannen suggested that in future *The Times* might qualify its description of the letter with some such word as "alleged" ; and he expressed the hope that newspapers would henceforth "abstain from comments on the case at all, and leave us undisturbed in the performance of the painful duty we have undertaken."

Ten witnesses were examined during the day. The first of the ten was Mr. Ives, special correspondent of *The New York Herald*, who accompanied Mr. Parnell and Mr. Dillon to America at the end of 1879. He described how he interviewed Mr. Parnell and Mr. Dillon on board ship, and how before the results were published to all the world, both these gentlemen looked over his MS., Mr. Parnell himself making occasional corrections. Mr. Ives remembered how Mr. Parnell had spoken of the newly-founded League as a political school for the Irish people. Though at that time, said Mr. Ives, *The New York Herald* was rather more hostile than friendly to the Parnellite movement, yet that journal created an Irish relief fund, which ultimately amounted to £69,000, of which Mr. Gordon Bennett contributed £20,000. Mr. Ives also stated that in the course of his conversations with the Irish leader on board ship, Mr. Parnell declared he would have nothing to do with any illegal and unconstitutional association, such as Fenianism was. Mr. Ives also said he had travelled over Ireland in the years 1879-82, that he found acute distress, especially along the western coast—where also, he added, discontent was most acute. This was said in answer to Sir Charles Russell, who, however, postponed his full cross-examination of the witness until the following day.

Then John Rafferty, of county Galway, the first Irish peasant who has appeared at this trial, stepped into the witness-box, and from that moment until the adjournment at four o'clock, Probate Court No. 1 became a sort of Ireland in the Strand. Farmer John Rafferty, and the eight witnesses who followed him, succeeded between them in giving a vivid picture of the Ireland of the hour, and a sombre, tragic picture it was. John Rafferty, in his rough frieze coat, and with his sharp, thin, grey face, was a fair type of the Galway peasant. He was Irish in his good-humour and in his very unconventional way of expressing himself. "Bedad," said he, turning to the bench, "I never attended a meeting of the Land Laygue (League) in my life." He told how, because he occupied land from which another tenant had been evicted, he was one night—in May, 1880—assailed by fifteen men, five of whom had their faces blackened. But at this point Sir Charles Russell interposed with a question: What had all this to do with the case? Did the Attorney-General mean to bring home such offences to any of the individual M.P.'s and others charged by *The Times;* or to the Land League organization? What was the use of proving an outrage, unless it could be shown that the outrage was traceable to the leaguers? Mere proof of outrage would only prejudice the public mind. Sir James Hannen settled the dispute by suggesting, as he had done more than once before, that the Attorney-General should conduct his case in his own way, leaving it to Sir Charles Russell to disprove, by cross-examination, the connection between the Land League and the outrages.

Cross-examined by Sir Charles Russell, John Rafferty admitted he did not think the Land League had had anything to do with his maltreatment. "I don't believe," he said, "there was any League branch within a mile of the place." His face wrinkling into a broad grin, Rafferty described how the men with the blackened faces "carded" him when they pulled him out of bed. The "card," he explained, is a "wooden piece of board with a nail or two stuck in it," and the moonlighters scraped the "card" along his back. "They did not injure my wife," he added; they "only cast her about."

Rafferty was followed by Dominic Barry, a police sub-inspector of Loughrea district. Examined by Mr. Atkinson in reference to the Murty Hynes[1] case, he described how in 1880 Hynes took a farm from which a tenant named Bermingham had been evicted; how a monster meeting—of the Land League, as he emphatically averred—was held near Hynes's farm; how at last Hynes came on to the platform to intimate his willingness to surrender the farm; how three or four months after that a man named Dempsey took the farm; and how a short time subsequently Dempsey was shot on his way to church. The particular point upon which *The Times* counsel questioned this witness of theirs was his knowledge of dates. He declared stoutly that he had never heard any public denunciations of land-grabbing before the year 1879, though, as he said, some people privately condemned it. He declared that he had never even heard of the word "land-grabbing" before 1879. Up to 1879 the district had been peaceful.

The next witness was Mrs. Dempsey, the widow of the murdered man—a slight, fair-haired woman she was, who gave her evidence in a self-possessed manner, but almost inaudibly. Patrick Hughes, the next witness, stated that "torches" were lighted on the hill-tops on the night of Dempsey's funeral. He meant, perhaps, bonfires. The next witness, Mrs. Conners, was, like Mrs.

---

[1] Murty Hynes's surrender is the subject of a ballad by Mr. T. D. Sullivan, M.P., ex-Lord Mayor of Dublin, and proprietor and editor of *The Nation* newspaper.

Dempsey, the widow of a murdered tenant who had taken an "evicted" farm. She maintained somewhat vaguely, but stubbornly, that all the meetings held in the district at that period, 1880, were "Land League meetings." The neighbours, she said, would not attend her husband's funeral, and "because of the boycotting we had difficulty in procuring food."

After the peasant witnesses came the first landlord witness, Mr. Lewis, who lives within four miles of Woodford, in county Galway. Like the police sub-inspector already named, Mr. Lewis held that the district was quiet until the time of the foundation of the Land League in 1879. After that, according to his account, the people boycotted him; his mowing-machine was broken by some persons unknown, and even a Catholic priest and leaguer—Father Fahy—threatened that if he did not give his tenants the reductions they demanded his house would be blown up, and he himself killed. Mr. Lewis gave his evidence in a jerky, excitable manner. When cross-examined by Mr. Harrington he admitted that though he claimed £200 compensation for damages inflicted upon his house property and lands, he received only £30. Another Galway landlord, Mr. Lambert, examined by Mr. Atkinson, stated that until 1879 he had never known of a tenant being persecuted for taking an evicted farm.

So far all was plain sailing. But now there appeared a witness who sorely taxed the patience both of bench and counsel, though he greatly amused the audience. This was a young man named Thomas White, also of county Galway. His words ran into one another. He spoke rapidly and in a low voice, and his brogue was of the broadest. Counsel were in despair. Sharp-eyed Mr. Lockwood detected a piece of paper in Mr. White's hand. Perhaps his paper is clearer than his speech, suggested Mr. Lockwood. "Yes, it is," remarked the President, who was examining the document. However, they tried Thomas White once more. Again a total failure; examining counsel dropping his arms, and glancing round in comic despair. "Do we want an interpreter?" exclaimed Sir James Hannen, with a look of amusement and boredom. Thomas White tried it again. This time he became communicative. He rambled off into a rapid, good-natured, confidential story about his father keeping a public-house. Then Sir James Hannen appealed to the official shorthand writer, who was sitting close to Thomas White, but the stenographer's very meagre notes showed only too clearly that he also was no match for Mr. White. Then Mr. White, turning to Mr. Atkinson, began to mumble something about the (laygue) League. "Perhaps Mr. Atkinson can tell us what the witness says," insinuated Sir James Hannen, with an engaging smile. "I can't"—was the meaning of Mr. Atkinson's responsive gesture—a shrug of the shoulders. It was diverting to watch Sir James Hannen and Mr. Atkinson as, with hands to their ears, they strained after Mr. White's appallingly swift Galway brogue. At least one intelligible sentence was got out of him—that his father was boycotted for not joining the League, and that he himself was boycotted because he was the son of his father.

But he contrived to upset this intelligible declaration by another equally intelligible, that he never had been boycotted! Then Mr. Lockwood tried the written document. "Mr. Lewis," said the witness, "wrote it for me. I did not ask him to write it. He sent it to me, and told me it was my evidence." At this declaration all present naturally pricked up their ears. And there was a burst of laughter as *The Times* witness described how his evidence had been got up for him. Evidently Mr. White's listeners had come to the conclusion that the obliging Mr. Lewis was the Woodford landlord who had been examined a little while before. But Mr. Murphy, Q.C., suddenly gave the incident a fresh turn, for, after another spell of struggling with Mr. White's brogue, he elicited these two statements—that Mr. White in the first place gave Mr. Lewis the evidence which Mr. Lewis put into shape for him, and next, that the Mr. Lewis was not the Woodford landlord of the name.

The last witness produced by the Attorney-General was a Mr. Courcey, who had been in Loughrea in 1884-5-6, and who had known the process-server, Finlay, who was murdered in March of the last-named year. He described how the Woodford people to whom he applied—the clergy included—refused, on one pretence or another, to supply a coffin for Finlay's funeral; how the Woodford people refused, on the night of the murder, to give the widow fire, food, or light; and how on the following night he himself succeeded in procuring food for her. Even Finlay's own brother, the witness declared, did not accompany the body, on the day of the funeral, outside the limits of the town (Woodford). In the early part of his evidence Mr. Courcey stated that at a meeting of Leaguers held in Woodford, one of the leaders remarked that the police protectors of process-servers would soon be done away with. But now he was asked by Mr. Reid, Q.C., to explain what that meant. Mr. Courcey explained that he did not mean that the speaker threatened murder, but only that, as Home Rule was approaching, the police would be under the people's control.

TENTH DAY.

NOVEMBER 7.]

THE court resumed work punctually at half-past ten, and in less than twelve minutes three important witnesses were disposed of. These were Constables Beatty, Nally, and Gibbon. They were examined in a swift, rattling fashion by one of the Irish barristers for *The Times*, Mr. Ronan; and they gave their evidence with corresponding promptitude and brusqueness. It was a short story, but what a picture of discontented Ireland! The examination of all three turned on the assassination of the process-server, Finlay, who, as described yesterday, was murdered at Woodford in March, 1886. In a matter-of-fact, ready way Constable Beatty told how he saw Mrs. Finlay "wringing her hands" while she stood in her doorway, gazing in the direction from which some people were conveying her husband's dead body. She went to the priest's house (Father Egan's), which, we may explain, stands half way up the steep main street of Woodford. She lay down on the road. A man passing by "tried to kick her," said the constable in his gruff voice.

The next witness narrated how he escorted the coffin to Woodford all the way from Loughrea, seventeen miles off—the coffin the Woodford traders had refused to supply, even the Woodford priests refusing to interfere. All this was pitiable and tragic enough. But what followed was worse—horrible, inhuman, if the constable told the truth. The third constable, Patrick Gibbon, in a hard, bluff voice, holding himself bolt upright with a soldierly stiffness, described the mock funeral—Finlay's—of the 5th of March, 1886, two days after the murder. "A crowd of people," the funeral procession consisted of, carrying spades, headed by a brass band, bearing the coffin aloft "on pitchforks"—coffin covered with black crape, and the head of a goat sticking out of it, horns and all.

The main object of *The Times* counsel was to prove the connection between these crimes and brutalities and the Land League; and so the witness, in examination, alleged that in the mock funeral he saw "Dr. Tully," a local leader of the League, and that in a field belonging to Mr. Keary—secretary of the local branch—he saw two hundred of the processionists assembled during the evening of the mock funeral. All these events took place in what is pre-eminently known as the "hot district" of Ireland —a district of which Loughrea, Woodford, and Portumna are the centres.

Two constabulary witnesses, Welsh and Barry, the first of whom was a retired officer, and the second of whom gave part of his evidence yesterday, were closely examined by *The Times* counsel, with a view to show that in certain parts, at least, of the hot district the relations between landlords and tenants were fairly pleasant until the Land League arose, and that discontent and crime immediately followed its establishment. Constable Welsh, describing the state of Gort, a parish near Galway town, in 1879-80, declared that until 1879, the date of the foundation of the League in that locality, no disturbances had occurred, but that outrages followed after that date. He gave some account of Land League "hunts," as they were called, and which appear to have been assemblages of young men with "dogs and sticks," who amused themselves with chasing and killing hares and other game in the private "domains," or parks, of the local landlords. Welsh, however, could not say that he saw Land League men among these hunting parties, nor could he tell why the hunts were called "Land League hunts." This last admission was in reply to a question by Sir Charles Russell. After a little more fencing and various disclaimers of knowledge on the part of the witness, he further admitted that he did hear it reported in the district that rents were raised and arrears pressed for by a local landlord between the years 1872 and 1880 in revenge for the landlord's defeat at a parliamentary contest. Sir Henry James, next taking the witness in hand, got him to declare that until 1879-80 the tenants had never required police protection; and that until the same date he had not even heard the name land-grabbing. Precisely the same line of evidence was furnished by the next witness, Barry, to whom, by the way, *The Times* counsel apparently attach much importance. Barry had been stationed in the hottest part of the hot district—namely, in Loughrea—during part of 1880 and for two or three years subsequently. Drawing himself stiffly up, and twirling his moustache, Mr. Barry alleged in his most emphatic manner that Loughrea was quite a peaceful place until the League began its operations there, after which outrages began, five of them being murders, all perpetrated before 1883. It was after the advent of the Land League, said Barry, that the police force had to be largely increased in Loughrea. All the public meetings held in 1880-81, in Loughrea, said Barry, were Land League meetings, and Constable Linton, who was murdered in Church Street, Loughrea, in July, 1881, was well known as a constable whose duty it was to attend League meetings and take notes of their proceedings. Examined by Sir Henry James, Mr. Barry said that some Land Leaguers were among the Loughrea suspects who were imprisoned under the Crimes Act in 1881. One of the liveliest of *The Times* witnesses to-day was District-Inspector Bell, a smallish, youthful-looking gentleman, unlike the ordinary constabulary type. Not the least remarkable of Mr. Bell's gifts was his marvellous memory. For very nearly an hour and a half Mr. Graham plodded his way through a long list of offences—threatening letters, cattle maiming, &c., &c.—in 1880-1-2, still in Galway. Not a name, nor a locality, nor a date connected with Mr. Graham's tedious and minute narrative but Mr. Bell was ready to identify, and to give further particulars about it. Mr. Bell's testimony was in substance an agrarian history of his own district of Galway during the three years already named—a district, as he said, measuring twenty miles by six. It was a dismal monotone of cruelty and crime. The accusers hold that for these cruelties and crimes the League and its members were responsible. The accused regard these crimes as events over which they had no control, and which would have happened if an organized League had never existed. But, whichever side is right, one thing is clear—that the story of these constitutes a vivid picture of the state of the country. The number of intimidating letters and of boycotting notices quoted by Mr. Graham and promptly checked and identified by Mr. Bell was almost legion. A single specimen of a threatening letter will suffice: "My good grabber, give up your land, or if not your death will follow. Yours truly, Rory o' the Hills"—such letters being usually embellished with pictures of coffins. Many, however, of the agrarian "crimes" quoted by Mr. Graham were of the most trifling description. Mr. Graham's long lists of agrarian "crimes" were, to tell the truth, becoming tiresome. While Mr. Graham droned and plodded his way perseveringly through 1880 and 1881, and 1882, the people in court—Q.C.'s, juniors, and all, gossipped and chatted. Sir Henry James was engaged, smilingly, in conversation with Sir Charles Russell. Mr. Justice Day looked bored. But when Mr. Bell asserted the truth of a story about the cutting off of the tails of twenty horses, all present pricked up their ears. But to everybody's relief it turned out that only the hair had been cut. A shudder passed through the court when Inspector Bell, in his cool, business-like way, described how an unpopular tenant's sheep had had their wool and skin torn off their backs in such a manner that their bodies bled.

An expression of profound disgust clouded the faces of Mr. Justice Day and Sir J. Hannen—the latter frowning as the former leant over to whisper something to him. Another story about the smashing of a heifer's shoulder—the poor beast had ultimately to be killed—ended Mr. Graham's dreary record of intimidation, for 1881.

The theory of the prosecution was that these hideous crimes were caused, or encouraged, by leaguers as such. But the Father of the Land League, Mr. Michael Davitt, once declared, in a famous speech, that if his own brother were guilty of such misdeeds he would flog him at the cart's tail. Mr. Graham's list of agrarian crime for 1882 being of the same general description as his lists for the preceding years, no particular notice need be taken of it. Sir Charles Russell now took the smart deputy-inspector in hand. In the course of his story, Mr. Bell said that there were some landlords whom he knew in the county of Galway upon whose estates there were no League branches and no disorder; but, as he admitted, such landlords—he named Mr. French in particular—were indulgent landlords who had given reductions to their tenants. Sir Charles Russell's cross-examination of Mr. Bell was, therefore, designed to prove how urgently the Galway tenants at that period—as well as tenants in Mayo and Kerry—needed consideration at their landlords' hands. Crime followed the footsteps of the Land League, says one side. It followed hardship, misery, and oppression, the other side contends. All through this trial the official witnesses have generally agreed in denying the existence of exceptional distress in 1879-81. Mr. Bell airily, almost jauntily, denied that there was exceptional hardship. But when pressed by Sir Charles Russell the witness said he thought it possible there might have been forty-three thousand destitute persons in county Galway at that time! Then the Attorney-General, appearing for the first time in to-day's proceedings, endeavoured to destroy the effect of the last admission by eliciting the following answer in reply to a question. The answer—Mr. Bell's—was that the "coincidence" between the foundation of a League branch in a locality, and the outbreak of crime in that locality, was "clear undoubtedly," and he added that the payment of rent was the immediate cause of the outrages perpetrated upon the payers.

Mr. Bell left the box. Mr. Ives, special correspondent of *The New York Herald* in Ireland during the years 1879-83, was recalled. Mr. Ives's account of the state of Ireland during that period differed astonishingly from that of the police witnesses who preceded him. With a file of *The New York Herald* in front of him, Sir Charles Russell read out long extracts from Mr. Ives's despatches, describing the widespread misery in Mayo, Galway, Kerry, and especially along the Western Coast. "No language can describe the appalling condition of the people," said Mr. Ives, in one passage; "three hundred thousand people are slowly starving." There were passages also from which it appeared that as a rule the landlords were indifferent to their tenants' sufferings, and that they subscribed little or nothing to the total amount of £700,000 collected in Irish relief funds all over the world. Let the rea !er always bear in mind the purpose of this class of testimony—on the one side to prove that wherever the League appeared crime consequently followed ; on the other to prove that crime was simply the last resource of a people driven desperate—the natural result of hardship and oppression, quite apart from political leagues.

Sir Charles Russell having got this testimony as to the existence of widespread misery in 1879-80, made an onslaught upon "Scrab," with whose pet dog-like name the reader is already familiar. In his two or three days' introductory speech, the Attorney-General quoted largely from, and attributed much importance to, "Scrab's" wild speeches in the early days of the League. "Scrab" spoke wildly, no doubt, as counsel for the Parnellite members themselves admit, but they say that "Scrab" was a person whom the League leaders snubbed wherever and whenever they could. And now Mr. Ives gave his impressions of "Scrab." "Scrab," said he, was a man of no weight. "Scrab" was a drunkard. "Scrab" was "always full." "Full of whiskey?" asked Sir Charles, his head on one side. "Yes, full of whiskey," quoth Mr. Ives, with a good-humoured smile. And "Scrab" delivered his speeches—or some of them at any rate—when the meetings were over. So much for "Scrab"—whom *The Times* has immortalized.

To Mr. Ives succeeded four witnesses, the first of whom was a police officer named Charlston, who, taking up the thread of the dreary story of crime, testified to the murder of Bourke and Constable Wallace at Ardrahan, near Craughwell, county Galway—still discontented, wretched Galway—in 1882. There was one ugly touch in his description—people treading in the blood of the murdered constable. The next witness, also a constable, agreed with many of the preceding witnesses in alleging that there was no very severe distress in those years. In his district, at all events, people were, he said, generally well off. He was pretty severely handled by Mr. Lockwood, to whom he admitted that in spite of the general comfort there was a large distribution of relief. If they were well off, why did they want relief, Mr. Lockwood wanted to know.

The amusing witness was Mr. Burke, of Woodford. Mr. Burke was a short, reddish-faced young man, in roughish attire. He might have been taken for an omnibus conductor. Perhaps that was why the audience laughed when Mr. Burke, in answer to Sir James Hannen, and staring Sir James full in the face, announced that he was a "magistrhate." He was a bird of a feather with the distinguished President. Mr. Burke maintained that he was boycotted by the Woodford branch of the National League (in 1887), inasmuch as the threat of boycotting was conveyed to him by a priest, Father Egan, who was a leader of the local branch. They boycotted him, according to his own account, because he refused to go to a Petty Sessions Court for the purpose of deciding in favour of a local leaguer, Mr. John Roche, who was on his trial. "For this refusal," said Mr. Burke, "I was boycotted;" and then he described how his servants and workmen left him presumably in obedience to orders from the local leaguers. Taking a long time to think out how many people had really left his regular service, he at last rapped out "three." Then he described how nobody in Woodford would sell him food, and how nobody would shoe his horses for him. "I had my horse shod privately," and then he added, gravely and slowly, "by a blacksmith"—as if he did not wish their Lordships to imagine a tinsmith had tried it. "I was never under police protection myself," he continued, "but my house was." To the amusement of the Court, he tried, unsuccessfully, to give some coherent account of complex but wholly uninteresting family relationships between himself and the two chief persons named in his evidence, the Rev. Father Egan and Mr. John Roche. With his left elbow resting on the ledge of the witness-box, and his right hand index-finger raised, he was expatiating on this endless topic when the Court rose. Mr. Burke looked hurriedly about him, as who should say, " Where are you off to ? " Then he followed the dispersing multitude.

ELEVENTH DAY.

NOVEMBER 8.

TWENTY witnesses were examined—a good day's work. Their connected evidence was a dismal monotone of sordid, vicious spites, house-breaking, house-burning, shooting, maiming, murder. Hardly had the Court assembled when it plunged, so to speak, into a murder case—one of the ugliest in the record. This was the case of Bailiff Huddy, who was employed on the estate of Lord Ardilaun, in Mayo, in 1880, and who was murdered early in that year, shortly after he left his house, in the company of his nephew. Huddy and his nephew were murdered together. The bailiff's son now appeared in the witness-box. He saw his father and cousin start off on their day's work. " They never returned," he said, with suggestive brevity.

Then there stepped into the witness-box a man who saw them killed—they were driven against a wall, they were stoned, then shot. It took some time to get at this man's story ; for he spoke in Erse, and the Court had to employ an interpreter. The interpreter, speaking in a hard, rapid, clattering voice, was almost as unintelligible as the Erse-speaking witness. The Bench could not hear him. Counsel could not hear him. To make himself heard the interpreter moved off to the extremity of the solicitor's bench. Then it was found that he was too far away from his witness. They craned their necks, each in the other's direction, the interpreter turning his hand into an ear-trumpet, the witness doing likewise, as they bawled in their diverse tongues. Kerrigan was the Erse witness's name ; and Kerrigan almost howled when he told the Court that he had been nine months in jail, on suspicion of having murdered the two Huddys.

Mrs. Kerrigan then stepped into the box. A short, squab-figured, dumpy little woman she was, with the face of *Punch's* typical Hibernian. She wore a bright tartan shawl over her head—in the manner of Irish peasant-women. Holding a red handkerchief to her chin, she fixed her elbows on the ledge of the box, as she gave her story in a guttural Erse babble as rapid as her husband's. The *Times* counsel attached considerable importance to Mrs. Kerrigan's testimony, for she told the Court how, while her husband was in prison on charge of the murder, she used to receive money from Mrs. Keating of Galway, a leader, or leaderess of the Ladies' Land League. But at this point Sir Charles Russell promptly intervened. "We admit the receipt of the money," said he. "Yes," said Mr. Reid, Q.C., following Sir Charles; and he reminded the Court of what was a perfectly open and above-board series of transactions during the imprisonment of Mr. Forster's thousand suspects, of whom Mr. Kerrigan was only one ; there was a suspects' relief fund for food, &c., and when poor prisoners refused to avail themselves of it, the money value was handed over to their families as a grant in aid during the incarceration of the breadwinners. With this counter-hit by Mr. Reid, the Huddy case ended. Kerrigan was liberated when he divulged the names of the three murderers; he saw them do it, and he saw them hanged.

Then followed a story about a series of boycottings and incendiary outrages, all arising from rent disputes on certain estates of which Mr. Ross Mahon was in part owner, in part agent. In these cases, also, the prosecuting counsel sought to connect the boycotters and house-burners with the League. Cruce, an evicted tenant, who tried to boycott Mr. Mahon, was a leaguer, and some months after his eviction the house of the landlord and agent, Mr. Mahon, was blown up. A witness against the parties charged with the blowing-up, had his own house blown up by a Land League member, John Rafferty. At all events, Rafferty was convicted of the offence. But before counsel had done with this particular series of offences, another witness, Constable Hugh Kelly, declared that he could not tell whether Rafferty was a Land Leaguer or not. In this series of cases of outrage Constable Patrick Bolger was the chief witness. He was pretty closely examined on points which are constantly recurring in this historic trial; namely, the condition of the country, and the relations between landlords and tenants before the foundation of the Land League at the end of 1879. As we have pointed out in these articles, the constabulary witnesses have almost unanimously described these relations as peaceful. Constable Bolger was no exception to this rule. But when Sir Charles Russell pressed him, he admitted that he knew of one or two instances in which landlords had been shot at in Western Ireland even before the League was founded.

But the most interesting evidence on the above point was that of the next witness, a Galway landlord, Mr. Botterill. Like the landlord-witnesses who preceded him, Mr. Botterill dated the beginning of Ireland's woes from 1879—the year of the League. Before the League appeared there was the "best possible understanding between my tenants and myself; shortly after it appeared I and my daughter were shot at from behind a bush." "Post hoc ergo propter hoc," was the landlord's logic. "Post hoc," doubtless; but we deny the necessity of the inference, said, in effect, Sir Charles Russell. Sir Charles subjected this landlord to a long and merciless cross-examination. How jauntily the landlord declared that the tales of distress in those times were greatly exaggerated! It was quite true that the potato-crop, upon which the tenants lived, was bad; but the corn crop, with which they paid their rents, was good! Sir Charles took a pinch of snuff, and then gazed with a kindly smile at Botterill, when Mr. Botterill made that naïve declaration. And then Sir Charles pressed the landlord with a series of questions, the answers to which showed that though Mr. Botterill's tenants were so comfortably off, they were in receipt of doles from the distress funds of the period; that when they entered the Land Court they got large reductions; that Mr. Botterill himself got 20 per cent. reduction from landlords whose farms he occupied as a tenant. "Did you ever expend one farthing in assisting your tenants?" asked Sir Charles. "No," replied Mr. Botterill, with a smile; neither did Mrs. Botterill, who had lands of her own.

As regards the character and action of the National League (which succeeded the Land League), the testimony of the next witness was more direct than that of Mr. Botterill. This witness, a peasant named Heagney, was denounced last year (1887) at Portumna as a "landgrabber." But he now said that the leaders of the local branch had pronounced in his favour; that "everybody" in that quarter was a member of the National League; that "respectable" people, and not "riff-raff," were members of it; and that, to his knowledge, people joined the League of their own accord—no pressure being brought to bear upon them.

Now began the day's amusement. Mike Leonard, a steward, who, it seems, was suspected of coveting an evicted farm, and who was terribly scared in consequence, stepped into the box. He gesticulated vigorously. He turned from right to left, as if he wished everybody to hear him. He wrinkled his forehead; and his round eyes had an alarmed look, just as if he expected a repetition of his visitation of long ago. "Five hundred" men came to his place at night— "not a ha'pworth" of black or disguise of any sort on their faces; they were "clean, good-looking men, and they had arrums" (arms)—to wit, carbines—"as good as any in the Queen's possession." And they had a caffin (coffin). Here his eyes grew very round. "A big caffin," he shouted. "And they put me in it, and made me pray for my own sowl." Here Mike looked as if his hair was about to stand on end—and Mike stared hard while his audience, learned counsel and laity, broke into a fit of laughter.

After Mike prayed for his distracted "sowl," the "clean, good-looking men" left him. They only wanted to give him a hint—a pretty broad one—and they appeared to be satisfied with Mike's assurance that he did not want to grab any man's farm. Mike seemed to feel as much relief in hurrying out of the witness-box as (doubtless) he must have felt when he emerged from his coffin. He vanished in a trice.

To Mike succeeded Tom Connair. Tom was dressed in a long, baggy, swallow-tail coat of grey frieze, with brass buttons before and behind—the old-fashioned style of Irish coat, still common in Western Ireland. Into the witness-box he carried his cudgel, and his black bell-top hat, which he clapped on the ledge in front of him. In a couple of minutes Tom threw the Court into hopeless confusion. *The Times* counsel had called him to prove that he had made a deposition to the effect that the reason why his house had been burnt was that he had paid his rent against the wishes of the Land League. But now, to the astonishment of *The Times* counsel, he denied it all. "I can't answer you both at once," said Tom to the President and Mr. Murphy, Q.C., staring at them, one after the other. Nobody could find out from him what he had said, or what he had done. He could not tell whether he had joined the Land League—after the burning business. A ticket of some sort *was* given to him on *one* occasion ; but, said Tom, with a delightful frankness which completely upset the gravity of the Court, "Sure I was too intoxicated at the time to know what the ticket mint (meant)." He then let it out that it would not have been of much use even had he been sober—for he knew not how to read. In spite of protests from the bench and from counsel, Tom *would* tell his long domestic tales, and fight shy of a straight answer. Mr. Murphy gave him up in despair. So did Sir James Hannen. Nobody could make anything of him. At last Sir Charles Russell tried him, and—will it be believed?—succeeded! Sir Charles drew the admission from him, "I niver, niver said my house was burnt because I paid my rint; niver," he shouted out, clapping his fist on the bench, "as far as I can understand." When Tom had made this emphatic declaration, one of *The Times* solicitors stepped into the witness-box and stated on oath that Tom's first deposition was in direct contradiction to that which he had now delivered. Comedy and tragedy intermingle in this strange trial. Tom Connair laughs. Mrs. Lyden weeps—as she describes how her husband was dragged out of bed, "through the kitchen," out into the road, and murdered before her eyes ; how her boy screamed as he was dragged out to where his father lay dead, and how he was wounded unto death.

TWELFTH DAY.

NOVEMBER 9.

MIKE JOYCE, a tall Irish peasant, in a long loose ulster of dark-grey frieze, was the first witness. Mike told the old story—of cattle (his own cattle) mutilated, and sheep killed, as a punishment for his having taken a farm which another had "surrendered" to his landlord. In answer to Mr. Lockwood, who came in just in time to cross-examine, Joyce was unable to connect the crime with a leaguer or with anybody in particular ; and he further admitted that 1879—the year preceding that in which his cattle were mutilated—was a year of bad crops. Mike Joyce's evidence merely touched upon a subject which was discussed at great length in the examination of the next witness—Mrs. Blake, of Connemara, in county Galway.

Everybody who was in court will long remember Mrs. Blake. She is a brave, clever lady, as clever as any Q.C. in the place ; she has confounded Mr. J. G. Biggar, M.P., and brought Sir James Hannen and Sir Charles Russell into sharp collision—that for an anxious moment or two looked as if it would end in a "scene." But we are anticipating.

Mrs. Blake's estate in Connemara contained four to five thousand acres. Up to the time when the Land League agitation began, Mrs. Blake and her tenants were, so she said, on the best of terms. They went in and out of her house like friends, she knew their circumstances, she helped them when they required help. Then "the agitation came," and tenants began to withhold rent payment, not because they had no money, but because they dared not pay. With very few interruptions from Mr. Murphy, Q.C., who was examining, Mrs. Blake gave her story in a clear, connected manner, with perfect self-possession, and with a tone and gesture indicating resolution and strength of character. There were vivid touches in her story, as when she described how one tenant came secretly to pay his rent, the rent being concealed in his son's sleeve. The receipt was "sewn up the boy's sleeve," in order to prevent discovery outside. Another rent-bearing tenant had to be dragged in through the window, so that he might not be seen by Mrs. Blake's own servants. She told in great detail how some of her tenants, known to have paid her, were punished by the maiming of their cattle and the destruction of their property. As she described the condition in which she found a poor bullock, she set her lips firmly together and brought her closed right hand with a sharp pat down upon the desk.

It was in one of these emphatic moments that Mrs. Blake contrived to bring about the collision above named. She was about to describe an outrage, on second or third hand authority—that of her herd—when Sir Charles Russell, impatiently starting to his feet, protested that "evidence" of that description was inadmissible.

But the President observed that it was the herd's duty to report the outrage to his employer, and such report was certainly admissible ; besides, its value could be tested in cross-examination. But Sir Charles was implacable. He held that if such evidence was allowed to be put in, this could not be called a "judicial investigation." Sir James frowned. "That's not the proper observation to make," he said. After a pause the dispute was renewed, Sir James Hannen at last declaring, with an emphatic calmness, that "You (Sir Charles Russell) have expressed yourself in a most disrespectful manner." A minute later, and he remarked, in the same tone of quiet severity—"Somebody must have the last word, and I think it is I."

Trying to find out whether it was political "agitation," or misery, that caused these outrages on Mrs. Blake's estate, Mr. Lockwood questioned her closely as to the condition of her tenantry. There was no exceptional distress, according to Mrs. Blake's testimony. "Why," said she, with one of her resolute looks, "a cry of distress will produce distress." Mr. Lockwood, upset for a moment by the enunciation of such a doctrine, brought out his political economy. If, as you say, potatoes fetched high prices, was not that because they were scarce? But Mrs. Blake gave the testimony of her own eyes, to the effect that potatoes were not scarce. And she subsequently explained her doctrine of the distress cry in this wise—that if you can manage to get up the cry, the tradespeople will stop credit, thereby compelling the poorest to sell out their necessaries of existence. "Clever woman," the whisper went round. She was.

Then Mr. Biggar jumped up to see what *he* could do. If he could show that the Land Court reduced her rent-income a long way below the old figure, he would, he thought, prove grievous distress on her estate—in spite of her theory of distress cries. He took his plunge like a man, and the next moment looked as if he wished himself a hundred miles away. For Mrs. Blake at once entered upon a long and most interesting story—rendered somewhat fascinating by the narrator's manner—of how she anticipated the action of the Land League, and by a method so satisfactory to the tenants, that only twenty or so of the two or three hundred entered the Commissioners' Court. But while she described her method—devised by herself and conducted by herself throughout—Mr. Biggar had to stand stockstill. Instead of putting knowing questions, there he was listening to a long discourse. He was done for. "What's your income now?" he struck in at last, in sheer desperation. "Don't know." "Do you swear you don't know?" and he wagged his forefinger. The more Mr. Biggar wagged his finger and the more he challenged her to swear, the more Mrs. Blake laughed. She was mightily amused. This sort of thing went on for a minute or two. Then Mr. Biggar paused. He appeared to be tapping with his finger on Mr. Edward Harrington's cranium, as if in search of a new idea there, having exhausted his own stock. The idea came, and he rattled it forth in his rapid manner, "If you don't know whether it is above or below a thousand, can't you tell us what you think?" "I assure you I do not know," and on the battle went, Mrs. Blake laughing, Mr. Biggar white and excited, and wagging his forefinger, and challenging her to "swear."

Mrs. Blake was followed into the witness-box by her son, by one of her tenants, and by one of her herds—a stolid, healthy, garrulous, and incoherent Connemara "boy," who said he was seventy, though he would pass any day for forty. The herd warmed up to his countryman, Mr. T. Harrington, who questioned him about the condition of the district in 1879, the year of the Land League. His account of it was much less favourable than that given by his mistress; for he declared that 1878-9 was the worst year since the famine of 1847-8! He also denied that he had ever heard any of his mistress's tenants confess they could pay if they liked. On the Land League his mind was a blank.

The Times counsel next made a jump of six years—from the Land League of 1880 to the National League of 1886. At first sight it did seem as if they had unearthed a startling case of direct, immediate intimidation by the League. The charge was that the president of the National League branch near Gort, in county Galway, had accepted £15 from a tradesman who had been boycotted for hiring out his cars to the police at an eviction, and that, as a consequence, the boycott ceased. The president was the local Catholic clergyman, and the money the tradesman paid over constituted his net profit from letting his cars. But the witness's own account threw a less unfavourable light on the transaction. He was boycotted. But, said the witness, "the Catholic clergyman wholly sympathized with me. The Leaguers themselves were sorry for me," said Mr. Hughes. "I was friends with them, and particularly with Father Considine, who did not ask me for a shilling, and to whom I gave the £15 of my own accord—for the relief of the poor, or any other charitable purpose he pleased." Father Considine, he said, had not blamed him for letting his cars to the police, but had only remarked that as he (Mr. Hughes) was so well off, he might have declined to make money by giving his cars to constables who were going to turn people out of their homes.

Two or three other cases of the same general character as Mr. Hughes's came on; but they are scarcely worth notice.

The principal event of the day's proceedings was the examination of another Mrs. Blake, the widow of Mr. J. H. Blake, the ill-fated agent of Lord Clanricarde—a landlord of whom it is possible that the public may hear more before the work of the Commission is ended.

Of all the stories that have been told since the trial began, this by Mrs. J. H. Blake was perhaps the most mournful. It was impossible to listen to it without feelings of profoundest pity. Her husband was in reality sacrificed to Lord Clanricarde—in other words, Mr. Blake had warned Lord Clanricarde of the distress on his estates, and earnestly advised him to grant reductions. The landlord refused, and his agent—who was manfully doing his duty—lost his life. Such was the widow's narrative. The judges bent attentively forward —Sir James Hannen holding his hand over his eyes. The sound of a pin-fall might have been heard in the court, as Mrs. Blake, with an expression of subdued grief on her refined features (which once or twice trembled), told her story in a low, distinct voice, and in the choice English of a cultivated lady. It was a picture in words—and such a picture! "The jaunting car," starting for Loughrea, with wife, husband, and driver, passing the holiday crowds on the road; the wife, somehow, attracted by the suspicious demeanour and conduct of a boy on the highway; the shots immediately after; in two or three minutes more the husband falling dead out of the car; then the driver sinking backwards, supported by his mistress, his wounds streaming with blood; the horse still running with the fallen reins about its legs, leaving the murdered husband farther and farther behind; not a man, woman, or child among all those people on the highway answering her appeal for help in the name of God, —was it from stolid indifference, or because landlords and their agents were regarded as enemies of their kind, or was it because a great fear fell upon them also? Whatever it was, there was something appalling in that dumb avoidance of the beseeching woman in her dire need. Ireland is in the Strand; and behind the light and play of her contemporary life looms, perpetually, a dark background. Lawyers may wrangle and differ, but underneath all their differences lies this fact, which none can dispute—that Ireland is wretched, miserable, demoralized, sick unto death. This is a legal trial. It is also the *viva voce* history of a people—one of the dreariest, saddest histories in the world. And when one listens to it, one feels, with something like despair, how little Englishmen know of this mournful Ireland, which is only twelve hours' journey from London.

THIRTEENTH DAY.

NOVEMBER 13.

THE toughest work since the beginning of the trial. Pat Kennedy was called as a *Times* witness, to prove, from his personal experience, intimidation and outrage by the Land League. But *The Times* counsel had almost as much trouble with Pat Kennedy as their learned brethren for the other side had. He kept them all at it during two full hours. Not because he had so much to say, but because he would say nothing. Neither the obstinacy of a mule, nor the difficulty of getting a joke into a Scotchman, even by surgery, came up to Pat's powers of impenetrability. Mr. Atkinson, Sir Charles Russell, Mr. Lockwood, the President himself, Mr. Biggar, the Attorney-General, all tried their cunning upon this most exasperating witness. For a time, Pat's stolid obstinacy was amusing, but as the half-hours passed, it became an intolerable bore. His manners were even more trying than his taciturnity. He scowled. He darted angry glances through the corners of his eyes. He tumbled about in his box like a menagerie specimen in his cage.

But he had an advantage over the menagerie specimen, inasmuch as he could play the devil's tattoo—and he did it, with considerable perseverance and skill, on the ledge in front of him, with the four fingers and thumb of his irreverent left hand. When he was neither tumbling about, nor drumming, nor scowling, he fell into a brown study—fixedly gazing downwards for a minute or two at a time. After a spell of silence he would rap out an irascible, incoherent, totally irrelevant and evasive answer. Then he would suddenly grab his black billycock by the rim, as if he had made up his mind to leave all those chattering lawyers to find it out among themselves.

What was Mr. Patrick's grievance? He had been annoyed in one way or another—sometimes, it appeared, by a mild boycott—during most of the time from 1881 till the present date; annoyed for taking a farm from which a certain widow had been evicted. He complained that the Leaguers in their official character as Leaguers had always been urging him to give up his farm. He was a Leaguer himself; he attended League meetings; but he denied that he had received money from the police for giving them information about League assemblages. One of the hardest struggles with Patrick was Sir Charles Russell's effort to find out where he lived. At first, Patrick would not tell, because (apparently) he objected to the London population knowing it. It cost another tough struggle to find out from him how he lived. One of the many questions on this point was Mr. Lockwood's, "Who is keeping you now?" "I think *The Times*," said Patrick, after one of his long pauses.

Next came three witnesses, two of whom introduced novel and unexpected elements into the trial. The first of the two was a young Galway farmer named James Mannion. In Mr. Atkinson's hands he began tamely enough. But all at once he gave out that he was sworn a member of the Fenian Society in 1880, and that his brother leaguers of that period were Fenians—every one of them, said he. At this sudden appearance of a Fenian Land Leaguer, all present became silent and attentive. *The Times* counsel were making their first serious endeavour to connect the Land League and National League directly with secret societies, whose aim was separation, and whose instrument was murder; and here was an ex-Fenian Land Leaguer who had turned against his fellow-criminals. It was curious to hear this quiet and apparently respectable and harmless young farmer of twenty-nine describe, with perfect *sang-froid*, how, with a gang of five men, he went out one night with the deliberate intention of murdering a man who had taken a farm from which the mother (Mrs. Walsh) of one of the gang had been evicted.

Nor was "Fenian" the only title to which this young farmer confessed. He called himself a Moonlighter; and he described, with cool, matter-of-fact brevity—pretty much as one who should talk about the weather—what the Moonlighting method was. "Bedad, perhaps they bate them, perhaps they shoot them, for paying their rint or taking an evicted farm." He declared that all his Land League colleagues were, like himself, Fenians; that in his part of county Galway it was all one whether you called them Fenians or Leaguers; that Land Leaguers, in their official capacity, gave warning notices; that boycottings and outrages of all sorts, including murders, were arranged at League meetings; and that the murder above referred to—the Lyden murder—was planned at Walsh's house, where the Leaguers held their meetings. One of the young Walshes was among the six selected to commit the crime; and he was hanged for it.

Nothing could be more definite than the witness's declaration, "I never knew a Moonlighter who was not a member of the Land League." But in cross-examination by Sir C. Russell he confessed to surprising ignorance of the very A B C of Fenian history, declaring he had never heard of Fenianism before 1880. At first he had said that "Fenian" and "Leaguer" were interchangeable. Now, when pressed by Sir Charles Russell, he declined to call the priest-president of his local branch in 1880 a Fenian. After wavering for some time between conflicting statements, the witness ended by affirming that all the Leaguers he knew were Fenians.

The next witness was—by his own account—a greater unfortunate, or a worse reprobate, than Farmer Mannion. The two informers had travelled together to London, and, said this second witness, Peter Flaherty, I had "another woman along with me." (Great laughter.) Even Sir James Hannen's grave features relaxed into a smile. Mr. Flaherty was not so neatly dressed as Farmer Mannion. He was plainly, almost roughly attired; but, like Mannion, he looked as respectable as a churchwarden. Yet, without a blush, without the ghost of a shadow of a trace of shyness or awkwardness—did he admit that he went quite prepared to commit, or assist in committing, murder eight years ago at the house of a man named O'Neill; and that if he had to betray his confederates over again under the same circumstances he would do it without the slightest compunction. Flaherty said he joined the League in 1880, and he gave the names of the leading official leaguers—Ruane, Macdonald, Mulcarren, and others—the first-named of whom flits, like a sinister figure, through these criminal stories of discontented Galway, and was the most prominent figure in the outrages described by the preceding witness, Mannion.

He next joined "another society"—on which occasion, he said, he swore loyalty to the "Irish Republic." He described with great minuteness how at a meeting of Land Leaguers he had been delegated, with a number of men, to go and carry off O'Neill's cattle and sheep; and how it had been arranged at that meeting that O'Neill's herd should be shot if he interfered. All this was Land Leaguers' work—according to this informer's testimony. His examination-in-chief was conducted by Mr. Murphy, and his cross-examination by Mr. Reid, Q.C., whose cutting, contemptuous questions seemed to make but small impression upon his thick moral hide. My business, he explained tersely, was "to go moonlighting whenever I was asked to." And he further explained that he had turned against his fellow moonlighters because they unjustly accused him of the "guilt" of having warned a man whose life and property were in danger.

Yes, he exclaimed, later, he would have gone on moonlighting and murdering—by order—if one of his fellow-Leaguers had not fired at him under the misapprehension above named. This man Flaherty turned out to be as ignorant of the social history of his own part of Galway as the Moonlighter who preceded him. Whatever the "secret" society was to which he belonged, he had never heard of the "Irish Republican Brotherhood"!

Having done, for the time being, with county Galway, *The Times* counsel drew upon their trans-Atlantic resources, and produced a witness named Flanergan to prove how, in 1879 and subsequently, and under the management of the Irish president of a Land League branch at Pittsburg, money and arms were collected in America for use in Western Ireland. But as soon as he had made his statement the Court adjourned.

FOURTEENTH DAY.

NOVEMBER 14.

TO-DAY Mr. Michael Davitt displayed the gift of a quick and close cross-examiner. He operated upon the informer Flanergan, the American, who had already appeared in the box. According to Flanergan's story, a Land League official named Meaney had, in conjunction with O'Donovan Rossa and Patrick Ford, collected money from him and others—money for the purchase of arms to be conveyed secretly to Ireland. Flanergan looked very foolish as he confessed how he had misappropriated "two revolvers" that had been entrusted to him in America, for two persons in Ireland. And when sharply and severely cross-examined by Mr. Davitt as to the organization (the Hibernian Friendly Society) of which he claimed to be a member, he betrayed almost total ignorance. He knew nothing of the constitution of the society of which, said Mr. Davitt, "I am a member myself." However, he declared he had paid his weekly dollar subscription. Flanergan slipped sideways out of the witness-box, and Mike Hoarty took his place.

Mike had been a Fenian. Unlike the informers who appeared yesterday, Mike Hoarty turned out to be a singularly intelligent witness. He gave his answers promptly, clearly, and to the point. Mike Hoarty was in 1879-80 a member of the Committee of the Land League branch of his own locality, which was situated about three miles from the town of Galway; and the parish priest was president of the branch, and a young doctor was its secretary. But instead of cursing the Land League, ex-Fenian Mike rather blessed it. The only object of the League was—as far as Mike knew—to keep the tenants in "unity" for the purpose of prevailing upon the landlords to concede rent reductions. Mike declared his belief that the League Committee never passed a single resolution to boycott anybody! But the thing was talked about in an informal manner, according to Mike's testimony. Though Mike had himself been a Fenian "for four months," he did not believe that any of his fellow members on the League Committee were Fenians. And though his house had been moonlighted and fired into, he declined to connect the offence with the action of the League. He gave the Land League Committee of his parish a high character. All its members were, he said, respectable farmers. A son of Balaam, with a vengeance!! But he was not the only *Times* witness up to date, who, when put into the box, declined to curse.

Mike Hoarty also contradicted flatly the favourable accounts already given in this trial by constables and landlords, as to the prosperity of Galway in 1879-80. "Distress then?" "Indeed there was," he exclaimed, nodding emphatically and folding his arms. "It was not possible for the people to pay the rents demanded of them and live." Sir Charles Russell then read out some extracts from the official account of the Relief Funds of 1879-80; gloomy accounts they were. Was that so? asked Sir Charles. "Yes," Mike again exclaimed, nodding his head, "that's a very fair" description of the state of things.

Another point upon which Mike contradicted the landlord and constabulary witnesses was the state of the country before 1879. As the reader will remember, the police witnesses in this trial have declared that till the rise of the Land League the occupation of evicted farms attracted hardly any notice. But Mike Hoarty declared that as long as he could recollect land-grabbing was under a social ban.

Mr. Atkinson now produced a witness—Constable Creagh, who arrested the four moonlighters who attacked Mike Hoarty's house. Among these moonlighters was one whose National League membership ticket was produced. This moonlighter belonged to the "Michael Davitt" branch of the League. But nothing was elicited in the examination of this constable to show that the Land League branch was implicated in the outrage. It was only shown that an individual leaguer had been engaged in a moonlighting expedition. But what followed was more interesting. Constable Creagh—like, as already said, his fellow-constables in this inquiry—stated that, until the Land League arose in 1879, he had never heard of declarations against payment of rent, nor even of the word "land-grabbing." "Was it part of a policeman's duty to report upon crimes in his district, and send the returns to his superiors?" asked Sir Charles Russell. "Yes," replied the constable. The importance of the question and its answer speedily appeared, for Sir Charles Russell produced the Parliamentary Blue Book of Agrarian Crimes for the whole of 1879, a document which gave a list, for both divisions of Galway, of threatening letters, of house-burnings, of slaughter of stock, as punishment for payment of unabated rent—many of these offences and crimes being shown to have occurred in the early part of the year, before the League came into being, and while, according to landlord and constabulary testimony, the relations between landlord and tenant were peaceful and pleasant.

Nor did the testimony of the next witness—also a constable—fix responsibility upon the particular League branch mentioned, for the boycotting of a man who had hired out his cars to the police. The boycotting notices were issued "by order," but by whose order was not clear. However, their diction was noteworthy. The car-owner was described as a "vile wretch," and the man with whom he had dealings a "vile worm." The words "by order" appeared to have suggested a thought to Mr. Davitt, who asked the constable whether he had ever heard of "bogus notices," and of certain newspaper correspondents who had put up bogus notices of their own in order that they might have some exciting "news" for London.

The next witness, during one brief moment of his life, fancied that even a moonlighter might be a jocular person; but he soon found out his mistake, and acted accordingly. This witness was a keen-faced, dark-eyed, iron-grey, bolt upright, dapper little warrior, who, after he left the army, took service with a boycotted landlord. Armed with a gun, he went to cut his employer's grass.

At last the inevitable moonlighter came, in the dead of the night, 20th of May, 1882. At first "I thought it was a joke." But when the moonlighter fired, ex-warrior Ford took down his gun from among the rafters, followed the moonlighter, and gave him the "contints" "between the shoulders." Having told his story, Mr. Ford fired (in a metaphorical sense) a shot at the Land League: like the constables and landlords who have appeared in this trial, he maintained that until the League appeared he had never heard of "land-grabbing."

Their lordships' attention was next directed to the famous district of Woodford, and the action of the National League there since 1885. The opening statement was made by the Attorney-General. His statement was an attempt to establish a direct connection between outrages there and the speeches ma by the National League leaders—not only local leaders, such as Mr. John Roche, Mr. Pat Keary, Father Egan, Father Coen, "Doctor" Tully of the "pills" (bullets), Mr. John Sweeney; but also the parliamentary leaders, directly and by name, such as Mr. Dillon, Mr. William O'Brien, Mr. Matt Harris, and Mr. Sheehy. Mr. Michael Davitt's name was also named in the Attorney-General's list of accused.

Sir Richard Webster's first witness—an important witness—was Sub-Inspector Murphy, of the constabulary. Father Coen, it may be here explained, is parish priest and president of the Woodford branch of the National League—perhaps the most resolute and best drilled branch of the League in Ireland. Mr. Pat Keary is its secretary. The Woodford district is one of the "hottest" in Ireland.

Mr. Davitt, in cross-examining a herd from this district, made an allusion which must have added to the stock of Irish history possessed by his listeners. It was an allusion to the Secret Society of "Steel Boys"—a strange name for herds, who alone were members of it. Even the herds—according to Mr. Davitt's suggestion — were associating, in the pre-League days, against the landlord class. The Attorney-General gave brief summaries of a long series of speeches delivered by the leaders, local and parliamentary, above-named. Crimes happened subsequently to the speeches. *Post hoc, ergo propter hoc*, again Sir Richard's argument.

Then Sir Charles took the Attorney-General's witness — Sub-Inspector Murphy—in hand. At first Mr. Murphy was fairly communicative of facts tending to show that there was provocation—that is, eviction of a particularly cruel character—and that disturbances *followed* evictions. Mr. Murphy even admitted that members of the constabulary subscribed for the relief of hardly-pressed tenants. Then Mr. Murphy became much less communicative. In spite of his position and wide jurisdiction in the force, he did not know that the Land Courts were making great reductions ; he knew nothing about the Cowper Commission—a confession at which Sir Charles was greatly surprised. Sir Charles next addressing himself to a long list of agrarian offences, sent by Mr. Murphy to his superiors, Mr. Murphy made the admission that in his report he described the motives, or rather motive, partly from hearsay—*i.e.*, on the authority of his surbordinates—and that in some cases both he and his subordinates inferred the motive from what they knew of the state of the country. Here Sir Charles was specially dealing with alleged intimidation of people who had refused to join the National League. And Mr. Murphy, according to his own statement, did not remember a single case in which any of the tenants to whom he had spoken on the matter, declared that they were intimidated because they refused to join. And yet, exclaimed Sir Charles, turning to the Bench and making an expressive gesture with his hands, " he says he considers himself justified in making that report." Sir Charles Russell was at his best.

FIFTEENTH DAY.

NOVEMBER 16.

COLONEL SAUNDERSON was one of the earliest arrivals. He and Mr. Lockwood, Q.C., shook hands with a cordiality as remarkable as the warmth with which they attack each other's convictions in the House of Commons. "Shall we move the adjournment of the House at half-past one ?" suggested Mr. Lockwood, adjusting his wig. This was in allusion to the Court's usual interval for luncheon. After lounging for some time on the back benches below the gallery, the gallant colonel migrated round to the jury-box. Mr. John Dillon also appeared—for the first time since the trial began. He sat down quietly and unnoticed, at the corner of the second bench among the juniors. Punctually on the stroke of half-past ten the first witness, Farmer Kennedy, stepped into the box. A Galway man, his evidence was merely a continuation of the county history which had occupied the Court for the last few days. As a proof of connection between the Land League and intimidation, his testimony was inconclusive. It was also uninteresting. Everybody appeared bored, and a low babble of gossip began long before Mr. Kennedy was done with.

But at the name of the next witness there came a sudden hush, and all eyes were bent on the tall, pale, elegant, and sorrowful-looking lady, who ascended noiselessly into the witness-box. This was Lady Mountmorres, widow of the landlord who in September, 1880, was murdered in Galway—still this county Galway of misery and crime. Replying to Sir Henry James, Lady Mountmorres told her story, at first almost inaudibly, but with calm self-possession, how up to 1879 there had been nothing but good feeling between her husband and tenants ; how after that date, when the Land League meetings began, the tenants became rough and rude, and refused to pay rent; how her husband took out an ejectment notice against one of them, named Sweeney; how a League meeting followed, and how the murder of her husband was perpetrated several weeks after the meeting.

Then Sir Charles Russell cross-examined. The object of this cross-examination was to find out from Lady Mountmorres whether she could declare positively that besides the rent dispute there was no other cause or causes of hostility between Lord Mountmorres and his tenants — causes in existence before as well as after the time when the League meetings began. Lady Mountmorres answered that she was unaware of any—that she was unaware his conduct as a Petty Sessions magistrate had made him unpopular; and that she had not heard of any dispute between him and the people, on the ground of his alleged refusal of a long-existing right of way across his estate. Nor could she give any precise dates or localities of League meetings. She was sure that the meetings preceded the sudden and hostile change in the attitude of the tenants. There was a certain sharpness—as of rising indignation—in her quick "No," when Sir Charles Russell pressed his question about the right of way. Resolutely, but as gently as one in his position could do, Sir Charles Russell continued to insist on the question of dates. And then it was noticed that Lady Mountmorres's head drooped; her eyes half-closed; she sank into her chair in a fainting condition. It is scarcely necessary to add that both *The Times* counsel and Sir Charles Russell refrained from putting any more questions.

Lady Mountmorres's general statement concerning the cause of enmity against her husband was supported by the next witness, a police-constable, who said that as soon as the Land League was started he noticed a change in the tenants' demeanour, not only to Lord Mountmorres, but to other landlords as well. He declared, pointedly, that Lord Mountmorres became unpopular because of his known opposition to the League—an opposition which he professed in public. This general testimony, however, was considerably shaken by the cross-examination to which Sir Charles Russell, Mr. Davitt, and Mr. Lockwood subjected him. It came out that Lord Mountmorres had been under police protection months before the League was started in the district. So then, argued Sir Charles Russell, this landlord became unpopular long before he took eviction proceedings against Sweeney, which was in July, 1880. Again, in reply to Mr. Davitt, the witness stated that the people knew or believed their landlord to be in constant communication with Dublin Castle, and that this also increased his unpopularity. Finally, the witness admitted that he could not give the names of any who were members of the local branch of the League in 1879. "I was at that very meeting of which you have spoken," said Mr. Davitt. "Did you not hear me warn the people against violence?" "No," the answer was. Not much light, then, was thrown on the origin of the crime by this witness's testimony. Nor by that of Constable O'Connor, who followed him, and who was present at a meeting of the local League branch the very day after the murder. There was, said O'Connor, an attempt at hooting, in the crowd, when the murder was mentioned, but a man on the platform held up his hand deprecatingly, and said something to the effect that he (Lord Mountmorres) was "gone now."

James Bermingham, who enjoyed the double distinction of being a process-server and a tenant of an evicted farm, told a story of six years' steady boycotting from '81—a dreary interval enlivened occasionally by the destruction of his walls, by maimings of his sheep and cattle, by bullets coming through his windows—but there was in his testimony nothing that fixed responsibility upon the League. Mr. Bermingham was less interesting than his herd, Morgan, who now stepped, with a stubborn, jerky movement of his body, into the witness-box.

A very small man—with small eyes, big jaws, big Tartar cheek-bones, long, regular-Irish upper lip, and big mouth, tightly shut—was Morgan the herdsman. Because his master had eaten sour grapes, Morgan's teeth were set on edge. Less figuratively, herd Morgan was suffering for another's sins. "The bullets came in through the doore, begor"—because he worked for a patriot who served writs.

Morgan's style in the box caused the greatest merriment. "Ah-h?" he would drawl through his nose, throwing his head back and leering sideways through the corners of his small eyes, when questions were put to him. Sometimes he would peer through his half-shut little eyes for a minute at a time before condescending to reply. "Don't look so suspiciously at me," pleaded Sir Charles Russell. "Ah-h?" retorted Morgan, through his nose, "ah-h," sticking his heavy chin out. The lawyers bored and irritated Morgan with questions about his boycotting. He rapped out a short, angry assertion to the effect that he had been boycotted—but when questioned by Sir Charles Russell, he made it tolerably evident that in some instances, at least, he only fancied some shopkeepers would refuse to sell if he went to buy. "You call that boycotting," exclaimed Sir Charles in surprise. "Ah-h?" said Morgan, once more, through his nose, and sticking out his big chin, in a gesture of interrogation.

Did he know anything about the Land League, which the prosecution sought to make answerable for all these crimes? But Morgan's patience was exhausted. He snapped his lips together tight as a vice, as if he defied all the Q.C.'s in Christendom to get anything more out of him. His head went back, cocked on one side. His little eyes twinkled. After a while he relented. "I know," he rasped out as fast and contemptuously as he could—"I know nothing about anybody except what I know about my own self." "You say you have had five pounds for coming to London; did they promise you more?" "Ah-h," he snarled forth; and giving the Court to understand that he didn't care a "ha'p'orth" whether he got more or not, he dived out of his box into the crowd, and became lost to sight.

Only one other witness from Galway followed Morgan. This was a blacksmith who was boycotted for shoeing a horse belonging to the boycotted farmer, Bermingham. As far as the blacksmith's testimony went, it exonerated the Land League. The leaguers, he said, "told me at their meeting that they had nothing whatever to do with the boycott put upon me; and I believe them."

At this stage of the proceedings Sir Henry James intimated that he would now leave Galway and proceed to county Kerry. But Sir Charles Russell insisted that the case for Galway must first be finished. All that you have done, said he, is to prove the outrages; you are now bound to fix the guilt of these outrages upon the persons in your list of accused. Sir James Hannen agreed with Sir Charles, but finally ruled that *The Times* counsel should be allowed to proceed in their own way.

To the moonlighting county accordingly the inquiry was now directed. And the very first witness from moonlighting Kerry, Farmer Conway, flatly declared that the Land League not only denounced crime in general, but also the very outrage—a shot in the ankle—of which he himself was the victim. As Conway was a *Times* witness, the declaration appeared to stagger *The Times* counsel. Mr. Atkinson re-examined him, and then he made a statement to the effect that he was unaware of any such resolution by the League! So that little was gained from this witness either way.

But the Kerry man who followed Conway, a "bog ranger" named Sullivan, was much more precise. "The League even took my part in my quarrel with my tenant," declared Sullivan. The League proposed a compromise, which Sullivan accepted.

Hearing all this, the Attorney-General asked Sullivan whether any person or persons had talked to him during the luncheon half-hour (which had just ended). Had the two Mr. Harringtons seen him? In an instant Mr. T. Harrington was on his legs, warmly protesting. "An impudent suggestion on the Attorney-General's part!" exclaimed Mr. Edward Harrington. "This is irregular, and as a member of the Bar you know it!" the President interposed, sharply. It was like a "row" in the House of Commons, except that Mr. T. Harrington was in his wig and gown, and that for Mr. Speaker, or the First Lord, there was the President of the Parnell Commission. Mr. Harrington, growing more and more indignant, went on talking so loudly as to extinguish the President's voice. This Sir James Hannen could not brook; and, throwing down his pen, he declared the Court adjourned, and he retired abruptly, followed by Mr. Justice Day and Mr. Justice Smith.

Then the court was filled with a loud babble of talk and laughter. Mr. Lockwood stretched his arms and legs, gazed at the ceiling, and was hugely amused. Mr. Waddy, coming in in his wig and gown, fixed his eyes in a round stare of surprise, smiled, chuckled, and hopped and bounced about the place, whispering into his friends' ears. Mr. Harrington packed up his blue bag, as if, like the philosophic 'coon in the Yankee story, he anticipated the worst. In nine minutes the Commissioners returned. Mr. Harrington, rising at once, made a perfectly becoming apology, and so the "incident" ended. But one regrets to say that the Attorney-General made no apology to Mr. Harrington.

Net result of Sullivan's evidence—no grudge on his part (but much the reverse) against the Land League, in his portion of moonlighting Kerry. The testimony of subsequent witnesses from Kerry was less favourable to that organization—the testimony, however, being indirect. One witness declared that moonlighting was unknown in Kerry before the rise of the League. One of the most interesting of these witnesses was a white-haired, white-whiskered, big-headed, malformed, dwarfish peasant, named Reagh, whose right ear the moonlighters had cut off. He pointed to the vacant space with his left hand. With a violent emphasis which amused the audience, he replied, when asked if he was aware that the Kerry League denounced crime, that he knew nothing whatever of that body. Seven Kerry witnesses were examined before the Court rose. One of them stated that many secret societies lately existed in Kerry. And the last of them, a herd, who had been shot at for working for an unpopular landlord, made the straightforward admission that he did not believe the League was in any way concerned with the crime.

SIXTEENTH DAY.

NOVEMBER 20.

THE investigation into the squalid tragedy of county Kerry was resumed. But before the first witness of the day was called, Sir Richard Webster rose to make a formal and solemn application to their lordships. He accused *The Kerry Sentinel* of November 14th of having published an article which was at once an intimidation of witnesses and a gross contempt of court. Some of the expressions which he quoted were certainly very strong—such as that at the beginning of this trial the judges were spotless, but that they were now unable to veil their manifest prejudices. The article also spoke of their lordships as creatures of the Government and of *The Times* "conspirators." Handing in the number of *The Kerry Sentinel*, the Attorney-General remarked that its proprietor was one of the witnesses in the case—one of the Parnellite members directly charged by *The Times*—and that he was at present in court. He meant, of course, Mr. Edward Harrington, M.P., who sat, quite unconcernedly, between Mr. Biggar and Mr. Michael Davitt. The Attorney-General, in view of the gravity of the offence, requested that their lordships should take immediate proceedings. But after a brief debate between him and Mr. Reid, Q.C. (who is the counsel retained for the defence of Mr. E. Harrington under the general charge), it was agreed, with the President's consent, that further consideration of the matter should be postponed until next day; because, as Mr. Reid complained, the Attorney-General's application came upon him by surprise. The Attorney-General explained that he himself had seen *The Kerry Sentinel* only a few minutes before.

Colletty, a farmer from near Castleisland, in Kerry, the first witness called, occupied the Court for more than an hour. Besides being a small farmer, he was a sort of sub-process server and bailiff; he used to point out the defaulting tenants' houses where writs had to be served. By his own account, Colletty was not much of a hero. Afraid to live in his house, he used to sleep in and about the ditches. But at last his enemies found him; and he gave the Court a graphic and vigorous description of the night attack upon him—an attack in which the weapons (his enemies' weapons: he himself was unarmed) were a spade, a stick, and a revolver. The spade cut his head open, and the revolver shattered his leg, which had to be amputated.

In that strange country, Ireland, the constable is sometimes the undertaker; and Mr. Colletty told nothing very new when he stated that his neighbours refused to supply him with a coffin for his dead child, and that he was indebted to the police for having procured him one.

Had the League anything to do with the spading and shooting of Colletty? In reply to Sir Charles Russell, the witness admitted that in his parish there was, up to the date of the attack, no branch of the Land League, though there was one at a place six miles off. Another important statement by the witness was that he thought rents were too high all over Kerry; important because one of the objects of the cross-examinations by Sir Charles Russell and his colleagues was to show that crime and outrage were the fruits of landlord oppression, and not of what is called agitation by the Land and National Leagues.

But in this case Sir Charles tried to prove that the attack on the witness was a punishment for his (alleged) seduction of a young woman in his service, and that his assailants were the brothers or other relatives of servant-girls whom he was said to have seduced. And now Mr. Colletty waxed very wroth. He glared angrily at Sir Charles. He denounced the stories about seduction as fabrications; folding his hands over his knee, and throwing his head back, he observed with an air of profound contempt that Kerry people who were capable of murder were capable of inventing any falsehood. Colletty's testimony appeared to establish nothing very definite beyond the fact that for some people life in county Kerry has its perils—a fact of which the world is sufficiently well aware.

The next witness had a sorrowful tale to tell—the murder of her husband. Mrs. Leahy appeared to be seventy years old at least. She was dressed in deep black, with her black shawl drawn over head, hoodwise. She had a fine, rich voice. She must have been beautiful, or at least pretty, in her young days. Mr. Leahy—her husband—had taken an "evicted" grazing farm. And so the moonlighters came when the poor old couple lay asleep. Old Mr. Leahy was forced on his knees. She knelt beside him, and put her "arm round his neck." Here she paused for a moment, and the poor old lady's head drooped. The old man was shot.

Now, before Mrs. Leahy was called, Mr. Atkinson read from a Kerry paper a Land League notice denouncing Leahy as a land-grabber, advising people to have nothing to do with him, and ordering word to be sent to Land League branches. But Sir Charles Russell, to nullify the effect of this notice (the notice preceded the murder) read an extract from *The Kerry Sentinel*, in which the "revolting" crime was denounced in the strongest manner. "Fearful demon of bloodshed" was one of the *Sentinel's* expressions. Moreover, Mrs. Leahy, in answer to Sir Charles Russell, said that all her neighbours showed her the deepest sympathy in her bereavement, and that they condemned the crime.

After Mrs. Leahy left the witness-box, two constables were examined as to their knowledge of the circumstances attending her husband's death. They both said that a man named Jeremiah MacMahon, secretary of the local branch of the Land League, had been suspected of participation in the murder of Leahy, as also in other offences, such as the posting of threatening letters. One of these two witnesses, District Inspector Craig, stated that in Kerry there were many secret societies at the time of Leahy's murder.

Another witness who declined to accuse the League appeared in the person of a Kerry farmer named O'Connor, two of whose servants were threatened because, while they worked for him, he himself was boycotted. O'Connor, however, "cleared" himself, as one of these servants expressed it in the witness-box, by "not paying his rent." This notion of a way of clearing one's character greatly amused the Court. But now, when O'Connor himself stepped into the box, he declared that he never had been boycotted; that he had never received any threatening letters; that he and his friends were all members of the Land League—the president of which, the parish priest, actually took his side. O'Connor, *The Times* witness, did anything but curse the League. Had he been talked to since he came to London? If so, had he told a story different to that which he had communicated to *The Times* witness? Yes, he told the Attorney-General that he had been talked to; but he stuck to it manfully that his only desire was to give full and fair evidence, and that no money could induce him to tell his interviewers anything but the truth. Sir Charles Russell smiled as if he thought *The Times* had been "sold again."

The next witness entertained a friendly feeling even for the wretched tribe of moonlighters. He refused to give up some land. So they fired at him; "sure they only gave me a few grains of powther, which I picked out myself." He didn't think it worth while to see the police on the subject. The constable witness who testified in this man's (M'Carthy's) case was unable to connect the "powther" grains with the League; and he further admitted there were secret societies in Kerry.

There followed five other cases, all about moonlighting, all attended with shooting, some with murder. The first of these five, the murder of Farmer Hickey, was reported at the time among the Kerry people to be merely the result of a family feud, with which the League had nothing to do. Sir Charles Russell tried to elicit some definite statements on this point from Hickey's widow, but unsuccessfully. Sir Charles Russell also read out an extract from Mr. Harrington's paper, *The Kerry Sentinel*, in which the "cowardly and bloodthirsty" murder was strongly denounced; and the *Sentinel* was and is the organ of the League in Kerry.

The only clue to the authorship of the next crime, the shooting of a man named Williams, was the signature of "Captain Moonlight"—who "by God's right hand" threatened all "mean hounds" and "emergency wretches" who worked for "hellish evictors." It will be seen that the captain's style is more forcible than elegant.

Another Balaamite appeared. His name was Dowling. He had been shot by the moonlighters; but in his opinion the moonlighters were not leaguers —in fact he was a member of the League himself at that time; all his "respectable neighbours" were members. The leaguers, he added, "never gave me any annoyance for paying my rent." Sir Henry James cross-examined Mr. Dowling very severely; and yet he was Sir Henry's own witness.

The Kerry man who followed Dowling was still more emphatic in defending the Land League. He got into trouble for paying his rent. But said he, in answer to Mr. Reid, "I swear on my oath that to the best of my belief the League never had anything to do with the outrage upon me." He didn't know who his assailants were, "any more than the man in the moon."

Lastly came the inevitable tragedy; and Miss Curtin, a tall young lady of distinguished presence and manners, stepped into the witness-box to tell the story of her father's murder in the winter of 1885. Miss Curtin is one of the heroines of the social war in Ireland. In a low, soft voice—with now and then a tone of half-weariness, half-indifference—she told the whole story which shocked the English public at the time; how, when the moonlighters came, she ran upstairs for firearms; how the shots came in through the door; how she gripped one of the murderers—finally depriving him of his gun— while her brother struggled with him; how the servants obeyed her orders to go for the priest and the doctor, but how they refused to go for the police; and how the family were subjected to petty persecutions, including boycotting, and the breaking of their pew in chapel, after the funeral. Said Miss Curtin, "the curate who spoke kindly of my father at Mass was boycotted; and for twelve months after the murder the priest, president of the League, only called at our house once." At the conclusion of Miss Curtin's evidence-in-chief the Court rose.

SEVENTEENTH DAY.

NOVEMBER 21.

IN anticipation of a little "scene" over the Harrington incident, the seats below and the galleries above were crowded for some time before the Commissioners entered. On the Solicitors' Bench Mr. Edward Harrington and Mr. T. Harrington were engaged in lively but inaudible debate with Mr. Reid, who once or twice shook his head. The meaning of the head-shake appeared as soon as their lordships entered, for they had scarcely taken their seats when Mr. Reid rose to announce that as Mr. Edward Harrington had not seen fit to take his advice, he (Mr. Reid) did not consider himself in a position to say anything. Their lordships paused for a moment, as if they expected Mr. Edward Harrington to offer some explanation. Mr. Harrington said nothing. Sir James Hannen, in a low, measured tone of quiet severity, asked him if he had anything to say. Upon this Mr. Edward Harrington rose, and merely remarked that he accepted full responsibility for *The Kerry Sentinel* article. Then the Commissioners, promptly rising, adjourned. They returned in six minutes. Sir James Hannen remarked that it would be "wasting words to point out how serious was the contempt of Court." He spoke of its "personal insults," and of the bad effects that might follow if the offence should remain unpunished. The punishment pronounced by Sir James Hannen was a fine of £500.

The examination of Miss Curtin was then resumed. *The Times* counsel evidently attached great importance to this case, doing their utmost to bring the guilt of the Curtin outrage to the doors of the National League. For example, Sir Henry James was at pains to elicit the fact that some time before his murder Mr. Curtin had been asked by leaguers, or persons who presumably were leaguers, whether he had paid the unabated rent.

On the other hand, Sir Charles Russell put to Miss Curtin a series of questions, to which Miss Curtin replied that, as far as she knew, her father had no quarrel with the League; that Mr. Alfred Webb, treasurer of the central branch of the National League, sympathized with her family in their affliction, and was anxious to assist them in every way.

Miss Curtin's replies clearly showed that her knowledge of the League, its leaders, and its doings, was at that time extremely slight.

Miss Curtin's brother, who went into the witness-box when his sister left it, was much more positive and definite. He himself had been a member of the National League, and a regular attendant at its meetings. His father had been one of its vice-presidents. He had no reason to believe the League had had anything to do with the crime; and he had even read resolutions in which local branches of the National League denounced the murder in the strongest manner.

Then the evidence took another direction, when two members of the constabulary came to be examined. The first of the two, Constable Meehan, stated that Casey, one of the moonlighters implicated in the murder, was a leaguer; at all events he had seen him, with his green sash, attending League meetings. This constable also described how, after the murder, the Curtin family were hooted and insulted at chapel and elsewhere, and how, on these occasions, he had never seen man or woman interfere to protect the widow and her family from insult. And not only that, but according to the witness's evidence, the parish priest's condolences (in chapel on Sunday) were addressed not to Mr. Curtin's widow, but to the mother of the would-be murderer, Sullivan, who was shot in the attack on Mr. Curtin.

A still worse example of popular demoralization in Kerry was given in the testimony of Norah Fitzmaurice, who appeared in the witness-box a few minutes after Miss Curtin left it. Norah's father was shot by her side on the high-road at the beginning of the year. A number of cars passed, said Norah, and many people on foot, yet not one gave her the slightest help. They looked at her father's body and passed. "One of them remarked, 'He is not dead yet,' and went on." When, after her father's funeral, Norah went to chapel, most of the people rose and walked out. "They would not kneel when I knelt."

So much for the social war. But from the lawyer's view-point, her most important evidence was that in which she said that the people who left the church were headed by the National League local secretary, a man named Dowling. It was a servant of Dowling's who brought Norah's father the notice to appear before a League Court, to answer to the charge of having taken land from which Fitzmaurice's own brother had been removed. And according to Norah's testimony, a League resolution was passed in October, 1887—two or three months before the murder—in which James Fitzmaurice (her father) was described as a base and inhuman person for having "grabbed" his brother's land. Norah's story appeared to be a mixture of League politics and paltry—but spiteful—family rivalries of a kind of which there have been several examples in the course of this trial. For instance, though the notice above alluded to was in Dowling's name, it was written by the assistant-secretary, a person named Quilter, a relative of the Fitzmaurices. Quilter had some dispute with them for their occupancy of the farm. *The Times* counsel having done their best to incriminate, or bring suspicion upon the League, Mr. Asquith, on the Parnellite side, read from *The Kerry Sentinel* some passages in which the atrocious and cowardly murder of James Fitzmaurice was condemned in unmeasured terms. Sir Charles Russell quoted passages to the same effect from *United Ireland*.

There was one other important case. The first witness in it—Mr. Lennard, agent for Lord Kenmare's Kerry estates—was one to whom the Attorney-

General attached great importance. The whole of Mr. Lennard's examination-in-chief was a careful and elaborate attempt to establish "a coincidence as regards time between agrarian outrage and the League." These were the Attorney-General's words. When asked if he believed there existed any such coincidence, Mr. Lennard rapped out the word "Certainly" with a loud, aggressive emphasis that amused his audience. "Certainly," said he; and "crime was stopped by the Coercion Act from 1882 to 1885; but it broke out again after 1885, when Mr. O'Brien, and Mr. Harrington, and Mr. Healy came down to Kerry and made fearful speeches." Mr. Lennard laid terrific emphasis upon the word "fearful."

Mr. Lennard was loud, communicative, and brimful of self-confidence. He produced a long list of facts to prove the coincidence in time—Land League warnings preceding payments of rent, and payments of rent promptly followed by shooting and outrages of various kinds. But— and this was Mr. Lennard's main point—until the Land League appeared in Kerry, no tenants in Kerry ever combined against rent, ever punished any one for taking an evicted farm, ever used the word "land-grabbing." As for Mr. Lennard, he stated that for his own part he had never heard the word land-grabbing before 1885 — an extraordinary statement, to say the least. Kerry must have been a land of contentment, according to this land agent's sworn testimony, until 1881 and Mr. Parnell's No-Rent Manifesto. And the Kerry people must have been patterns of meekness, for though they were "blue with hunger" during the distress of 1879-80, they refrained from agitation against the landlords. It was Mr. Lennard's conviction that the leaguers spoiled the Kerry Paradise. There had, said Mr. Lennard, been evictions in Kerry, even before the dreadful year of leaguers — 1880-81, but not until the leaguers came did tenants barricade their houses. The Attorney-General and Mr. Lennard talked away for nearly two hours — Mr. Lennard breaking out every other half-minute into loud, and uninvited, historical comments. After so long a spell of it, his audience became tired. Just on the stroke of four he rewarded its patience. The tenant, said he, "went off to America, and he left his farm behind him." Mr. Lennard gazed slowly round about him, as if he wondered what the lawyers and the others were laughing at. He will finish at the next sitting.

EIGHTEENTH DAY.

NOVEMBER 22.

THE court was less crowded to-day than at any time since the beginning of the trial. Mr. Lennard's stores of historical and professional knowledge had but small attraction for the London public. Yet Mr. Lennard, Lord Kenmare's agent, was by far the readiest, the most intelligent, and the best informed witness who had yet appeared. His examination-in-chief occupied nearly the whole of yesterday afternoon's sitting, and nearly the whole of this morning's. Not only was Mr. Lennard ready with his answer, on any point whatever, at an instant's notice, but he was also equally prompt with corroborative documents. Rent lists, letters, Land Leaguers' tickets of membership, statistics of all descriptions, he drew, on the slightest encouragement, from a black bag— which appeared to be as inexhaustible as the pocket whence Chamisso's grey-coated personage could extract anything and everything from a telescope to a horse.

Mr. Lennard was describing, with great gusto, how his model landlord,

Lord Kenmare, had spent tens of thousands of pounds—State lent money, no doubt, as Mr. Lennard frankly acknowledged — upon land improvements, which brought the labouring class some £300 a week in wages. How much of that was spent upon the landlord's mansion? quickly asked Sir Charles. " Not a penny," was the sharp reply—Mr. Lennard drawing himself up, with a triumphant glance at Sir Charles. Mr. Lennard is a man who knows his own mind. Whatever the value of his opinions may be, they are definite, and fixed. The Arrears Bill? Why it was a curse, said Mr. Lennard, sharply; in his opinion it turned honest men into rogues. In his opinion, too, the League demoralized the very schoolchildren, and turned them into boycotters and agitators; and he illustrated this by a fluent, rapid story of a school whose five hundred children left the place *en masse*—singing " God save Ireland " —because among them were the children of one of Lord Kenmare's process-servers.

Mr. Lennard's six hours' evidence was a sermon on the one text, that the Land League and its successor, the National League, were unmitigated evils. Was it possible, the Attorney-General asked, that secret societies might have provoked the outrages on Lord Kenmare's Kerry property? " Certainly not," replied Mr. Lennard, with his characteristic readiness; the coincidence in time between the rise of the League and the astonishing change in popular demeanour and conduct was such, in Mr. Lennard's estimation, as to imply, necessarily, the relation between cause and effect.

From his well-filled black bag Mr. Lennard extracted letter after letter, in which the writers—Lord Kenmare's own tenants—suggested to Mr. Lennard, devices by which they might be enabled to pay their rents in full, while at the same time making it appear to the leaguers that they were obstinately refusing to pay without abatements. That the League was the cause of this terrorism was proved, according to Mr. Lennard's testimony, by the fact that these letters ceased during the three years 1882 to 1885, when the Crimes Act was in operation. Up to October, 1881, the witness said, I used to be on the most friendly terms with the tenants. But after that—when the League came into being—the tenants scowled at Mr. Lennard and his friends, and even set the dogs at them. That year 1881 was the *annus terribilis* of Irish history as understood by Mr. Lennard; for up to that date—to take another of Mr. Lennard's numerous illustrations—the sheriff could go over the estate and evict a defaulter without let or hindrance, and without any subsequent risk of disturbance and outrage; but after that date, said Mr. Lennard, armies of police and troops were required for evictions, and only lately he had employed " four hundred troops " in evicting a single tenant! Ever since the Plan " was sprung upon us," said the witness, things have been as in the years 1881 and 1882. All that Mr. Lennard had to say about the League would have satisfied even Mr. Balfour himself—all except one point. For he declared that in Kerry the National League was at this moment as powerful as ever. Yet Mr. Balfour, as Sir Charles Russell now reminded him, had pronounced the League dead and gone. But Mr. Lennard bluntly gave him to understand that he was in a better position than Irish constables and Secretaries to know the real state of Ireland.

One of the most important of Mr. Lennard's statistical proofs of Lord Kenmare's moderation and the Land League's violence was his list (which he picked out with lightning speed from his black bag) of evictions on the Kenmare estates since 1874. Here is the substance of it. In the years 1874-80 there were only two tenants permanently evicted, and forty-three tenants who were evicted were re-admitted as caretakers. In the years 1881-8 there had been seventeen tenants permanently evicted, and 341 re-admitted as caretakers. Allowing for the extra year in the latter period, the increase was enormous; and this increase Mr. Lennard attributed to League action.

That is to say, he maintained on oath, that he believed most of those tenants were quite able to pay, but that the League prevented them from paying. Finally he averred, solemnly and emphatically, that he never evicted a tenant whom he knew to be really impecunious. He never pressed those who were "blue with hunger" in the years 1879-80. The sum and substance of this estate agent's testimony was that—with the exception of a smallish remnant of really poor tenants, from whom he was content to receive what they were able to pay—Lord Kenmare's tenants never had any just cause for complaint.

But in the cross-examination conducted by Sir Charles Russell, Mr. Lockwood, Mr. Harrington, and Mr. Michael Davitt, the witness made many admissions which rubbed the optimistic gloss off his main story. A widow's farm, the tenant-right of which the Land Commissioners valued at £1,100, was bought up by the landlord for £10. He appeared to think, although he expressed himself with considerable hesitation, that if a tenant fell into arrears through bad harvests he was bound to find the landlord's rent from other sources than the land. The landlord's purchase of the widow's tenant-right was made at a time when there was an immense fall in prices, and when Parliament was in consequence intervening on the cultivator's behalf.

To show how badly off the people of South-western Ireland were in those years, Mr. Lockwood called the witness's attention to a tale that sounded like a voice from the grave. This was the letter which, after his return from his first visit to the Soudan, General Gordon wrote from Glengariffe, near the Kerry borders, eight years ago. In his characteristic style Gordon described the state of the people as worse than that of any other people whom he knew, and offered a thousand pounds to any landlord who would live a tenant's life in a tenant's cabin for one week.

Mr. Lennard did not attach much importance to the great Gordon's personal testimony; Mr. Lennard thought Galway and part of Clare were worse off than Kerry. Nor did Mr. Lennard appear to think over-highly of General Buller's conduct. General Buller, it will be remembered, was sent by the Government to act as district magistrate in South-western Ireland. The General, as the witness admitted, did intervene between landlords and tenants and try to stop evictions. "He brought pressure on the landlords within the law?" suggested Sir Charles Russell. "Yes, and sometimes outside the law," retorted Mr. Lennard, not once swerving from the position he maintained throughout his entire examination—the position of a stickler for legality.

Again, Mr. Lockwood tried him by quoting the case of the Duggans— tenants of Lord Kenmare. The Duggans had held their land under the Kenmare family for two hundred years. In two hundred years they had reclaimed it from sterile bog. In two hundred years they had expended thousands of pounds upon it. They were evicted at last, and the Kenmare agent admitted to Mr. Lockwood that in the two hundred years the Kenmares had not spent a single farthing upon the Duggan farm lands! Lastly, Mr. Lennard, the great stickler for legality, issued a distress warrant against Mrs. Curtin, whose daughter and son have appeared here as witnesses to the murder of their father; and it was issued although the family experienced great difficulty in making a livelihood after Mr. Curtin's murder.

It was fifteen minutes past three o'clock before Mr. Lennard was done with. At that moment the witness-box was a chaos of MSS., blue-books, and ledgers. They were scattered about to right and left of Mr. Lennard. He packed up, and did it with vigour and rapidity. It looked as if there was a cab-load. But the miraculous black bag held everything. In they all went—books, papers, and all—rammed well down by Mr. Lennard's strong right hand. My Lords the Commissioners, smiling, watched Mr. Lennard with much interest. Glancing quickly about him, and, seeing not a rag left, Mr. Lennard, the strong agent, snapped up his black bag, smiled a hard little smile of satisfaction, tripped out of his box, and vanished.

NINETEENTH DAY.

NOVEMBER 23.

ONLY two of *The Times* witnesses were produced to-day. The examination of one of them lasted from half-past ten, when the court opened, till past three. It was grave, business-like, important. The comic element—inevitable in this great trial—came in during the last half-hour of the sitting. The evidence of District-Inspector Huggins, the first witness, was taken by Sir Henry James, and was confined to Castleisland district, county Kerry, during five-and-a-half years, ending 1886. It was a long, monotonous, dreary list of threatenings by post, moonlight visits, shootings, maimings.

At an early stage in the examination Mr. Reid protested against waste of time. Not for the first occasion has Mr. Reid objected to a method of inquiry likely to prove both "interminable and ruinous." All these outrages are undoubted; what Sir Charles Russell, Mr. Reid, and the others are waiting for is the proof of the connection of these outrages with the sixty-five gentlemen directly and specifically charged by *The Times*. The hubbub of conversation which arose in court long before Sir Henry James got half-way through this list of outrages showed that none were listening to him except those who were professionally compelled.

Not even Captain Moonlight's lyrical efforts had for the audience any charm. Specimens of the captain's compositions (in prose and verse) were read by Sir Henry James. Their grammar alone should have condemned the captain to the gallows. Apart from his too obvious criminality, the captain must have been a humbug. Not only in his bloodthirsty sentences was he constantly invoking his Maker's and his Saviour's name, but also he was offering £100 reward to any one who would give him information about people who paid their rents, and £5 reward for information about people who tore down his notices. As the poet's identity was supposed to be an impenetrable secret, it was not easy to see how an informer could get at him. If ever he should get at him, he would probably have to wait for his money. However, according to Inspector Huggins's story, as given in answer to Sir Henry James's questions, it would appear that Captain Moonlight was King of Kerry. On one night his gangs visited five houses, seven on another, thirteen or fifteen on a third, and so on. He boycotted schools whose teachers were relatives of persons who had taken evicted "farms." He, or his sympathizers, murdered people on the high-road—one of these victims being Mr. Herbert, a magistrate—and the police going to the scene of the murder were hooted and laughed at.

But what had the League leaders to do with all this? In the inspector's view a good deal. For example, the secretary of the Castleisland branch, a man named Horan, appeared on behalf of the branch to defend in court a tenant who was charged with having taken forcible possession of her house. "But did you consider that to be wrong?" asked Sir Charles Russell, with an air of surprise. Mr. Huggins did. But the tenant was only charged: nothing had as yet been proved against her; could not Horan, or the organization he represented, help, with perfect propriety, the accused woman to defend herself? No; Mr. Huggins could hardly see the matter in that light, though he admitted that Horan might have interfered with perfect propriety had he been related to the accused!

Another instance in which Mr. Huggins's testimony was supposed to implicate the League was a League meeting held near the town of Castleisland, at which, though Mr. E. Harrington, M.P., and Mr. Sheehan, M.P., were both present, the most ferocious utterances were made from the platform by a local medical man, Dr. Moriarty. This Kerry physician described himself as an admirer of the Fenian Stephen, and a land-grabber as a person who should be avoided as "if he had the plague." "Let the grabber go to his grave," exclaimed the doctor from the platform, "unhonoured, unwept, unsung. Let none except his widow attend his funeral." There was a good deal more of this sort of oratory—wherein bombast and stupid brutality contended for the mastery. All this was very shocking. But now Sir Charles Russell elicited from the witness the fact that he was not sure whether Mr. Harrington was present when Dr. Moriarty spoke. Furthermore, he admitted that large numbers of "outrages" reported to the police turned out to be bogus outrages, got up—to mention one motive—for the purpose of getting compensation —or to mention another motive, for the purpose of giving the agrarian movement a bad name.

Again, Mr. Huggins's list of moonlighting outrages seemed so formidable that at first glance it would appear as if the whole district was in a murderous mood. But, in answer to Sir Charles Russell, Mr. Huggins admitted the likelihood that all the outrages were the work of one hand. Mr. Huggins also stated that the majority of the "outrages" consisted of nothing more formidable than threatening letters and notices. As to the suggestion that the murder of Mr. Herbert, magistrate and land agent, might be explained by causes unconnected with a political organization, Mr. Huggins corroborated the report that Mr. Herbert was unpopular. And he added that he heard it rumoured that Mr. Herbert on one occasion suggested that the people should be "skibbered"—a word which appears to mean anything from being "butted" with the stock of a rifle, to being run through by its bayonet.

Like the lively witness of the day before, Inspector Huggins saw League wherever crime existed. "I never heard," said he, "of any secret societies existing before those years, except," he added, with stubborn emphasis, "in connection with the Land and National Leagues."

Upon this Sir Charles Russell, who was cross-examining him, started up. "What!" said Sir Charles, sharply, "why do you say that—why give me an answer to a question I did not put to you? Do you mean to make an injurious insinuation against these two bodies?" But District-Inspector Huggins, looking a little alarmed, protested that he had no such object in view.

The secret societies topic, dropped for a little while, was taken up by Mr. Reid, Q.C., who handled the witness with great skill—eliciting from him his reasons for supposing that moonlighters and leaguers were the same persons. Whether they were the same or not, the inspector's reasons amounted to nothing more than suspicion—the worth of which he had never taken any great trouble to test. He believed that moonlighters and leaguers were identical, because until the League was started there were no outrages (a questionable proposition); because he saw, at League meetings, persons whom he supposed to be mixed up in outrages; because he had been told that a leaguer had warned an acquaintance against serving writs, under pain of having his ears lopped off.

"Is that all!" exclaimed Mr. Reid, raising his eyebrows; "are these your only reasons for saying that moonlighters and leaguers were the same?" "Yes," was the answer; and in muttering his monosyllable District-Inspector Huggins looked somewhat ruffled and nervous.

"Well," again exclaimed Mr. Reid, "you have been eight years in Cork and Kerry, and that is all you can tell us about this matter!" Mr. Reid wound up with one more question. "Beyond what you have just said, you cannot connect the League with outrage?" No, he could not. It must be recorded that Mr. Huggins also made the striking admission that the outrages in his district (Castleisland) were more numerous during the year *following* the suppression of the Land League than in the year *preceding* the suppression.

Inspector Huggins had been under examination since half-past ten o'clock; it was now twenty minutes past three; and that was all that *The Times* counsel had been able to make of his evidence!

Then came the funny man. Teahan his name was—hotel keeper and cattle dealer of Tralee. Put in a dozen words, his story was that he had been boycotted because of his dealings with a Corporation occupying evicted lands in Kerry. According to *The Times*' theory boycotting proceeded from the League. But Mr. Teahan, *The Times* witness, now announced his firm conviction that he had been boycotted from motives of private revenge. "I know it was," said Mr. Teahan, rapping his knuckles on the desk. "A few blackguards" boycotted him, and among them there was "a fellow I wouldn't give a halfpenny a year for," and another fellow who "was a man of straw, while I was a man of manes" (means). "It was all jealousy," shouted Mr. Teahan, smilingly, and with more of his knuckle-rapping—"all jealousy," because of his prosperous business, whereat he turned over from three to four hundred pounds a week. The thought of the four hundred changed Mr. Teahan's mood in a moment. "Why," he called out at the top of his voice, "I'm losing a hundred pounds by standing in this box;" and he thumped it. He glanced angrily at the Q.C.'s in general and at Mr. Reid in particular. Then the storm passed off, and he became communicative. He *would* tell the Q.C.'s how he made his money in South Africa. He *would* tell my lords how he "droove" two horses *tandem*. He smiled, threw his head back, dropped his chin on his chest, nodded, winked, placed his elbows on the desk, and again smiled knowingly, while counsel read out the correspondence between him [about that Corporation business] and the secretary of the League—of which, by the way, Mr. Teahan himself was a member. The style and demeanour of this Kerry witness may be described as good-humour intermixed with sudden explosions of wrath. He was called to curse the League; but, if he did not bless it, he at any rate exonerated it from blame. It was all private jealousy—"if I swore at all," said he, with another nod and a wink, "that's what I'd swear here." Why! bless the man, he was on his oath there all the while.

TWENTIETH DAY.

NOVEMBER 27.

ONLY two witnesses—both of them members of the Royal Irish Constabulary —were examined to-day. Castleisland was the district about which they were questioned. Like all the constabulary witnesses who preceded them, they maintained that the Land League was the cause of Irish disturbance. To support this proposition one of the two—Sergeant Gilhooly—could adduce no argument stronger than the threadbare, wearisome one—that is to say, Ireland was quiet up to 1879-80, the Land League came, and confusion followed; therefore the League caused the confusion. But Sir Charles Russell threw discredit on his first premiss.

It was the second witness, District Inspector Davis, whose evidence caused the interest, almost the excitement, of the day. His testimony was the most startling yet given before the Commission. And it was as novel as it was unexpected. But before dealing with Mr. Davis's evidence, let us indicate briefly the main drift of Mr. Gilhooly's. Examined by Sir H. James, Mr. Gilhooly described the large and rapid increments in the constabulary force subsequently to the end of 1880, the implication being, of course, that if there had been no Land League agitation, the increase would have been unnecessary. As soon as the League was established in Castleisland, said the witness, there came "a great change" over the district, crime became rampant, threatening notices and letters became common. And among the disturbers of the peace were four moonlighters who, he asserted, were leaguers. But as for the four, his only reason for supposing them to be leaguers was that he had seen them attend League meetings. That did not amount to much, because League meetings were open to the public. The question put by Sir Charles Russell in the earlier part of this witness's examination-in-chief would have been quite applicable at later stages of it. The question was, "What bearing has all this on the issues before the Commission?" and it was put with reference to the minute details about the successive police reinforcements, details which Sir Henry James drew forth with a languid persistence, as if he himself were wearied with his task. This led to great waste of time, and to "enormous" and unnecessary (on former occasions Sir Charles Russell called it ruinous) expense.

District Inspector Davis had been in Castleisland district for about seven years from the end of December, 1880. From his official position his knowledge of Kerry ought to be minute, special, and valuable. But for a long time his story, given in the form of answers to Sir Henry James, was only a minute inventory of agrarian offences committed, or at least reported, in Castleisland during the years 1881-6. Sir Henry read them out one by one—scores of them—from the Castleisland "Outrage Book" (a police document), which lay before him; and the witness authenticated each case. It would be tedious to enumerate them, or even to classify them. Enough to say that they included threatening letters and notices, injury to and destruction of farm produce, vindictive slaughter of farm stock, and one foul murder—the murder of Mr. Herbert, landlord's agent, at a spot five miles from Castleisland, on the 30th of March, 1882.

Once more, Mr. Reid, Q.C., appealed, plaintively, feelingly, to the Bench to stop all that wearisome detail. Sir James Hannen sympathized with Mr. Reid, and the result was that from the point the narrative had now reached (spring of 1883) Sir Henry James made somewhat more rapid progress, confining himself rather to typical instances than to further enumeration of individual cases.

More to the point was the District Inspector's evidence about the Land League. He knew the secretary of the Castleisland branch, Tim Horan. "This," said he, "I believe to be Tim Horan's handwriting," as he looked at a letter handed to him by Sir Henry James. The letter, dated September 30, 1881, was a request for funds for the relief of men who had been wounded in some act of violence, but whose identity was, said the writer, known only to himself and the "members of the society." The District Inspector's impression, or belief, in the authenticity of the handwriting was the only proof offered by him. This date came between two dates which were of great importance in Sir Henry James's estimation—namely, June 5, 1881, when a public meeting was held at which Mr. Herbert was named as having recently carried out an eviction and levelled the "evicted" house to the ground; and March 30, 1882, when, as said above, Mr. Herbert was murdered. *The Times* counsel showed that some months before his murder Mr. Herbert had been summoned by Mr. Horan to attend a meeting of the League branch. But when the letter was read out in court it proved to be perfectly respectful in language, and anything but dangerous or violent. Here it is :—

SIR,—I am directed to call your attention to certain statements made against you at our last meeting concerning farms held by two men. It was resolved that this meeting respectfully requests you to attend at the next meeting of the League on Saturday next, 2nd January, 1881.—Yours, TIMOTHY HORAN.

The connection which *The Times* counsel appear all along to have been striving so hard to establish was this—that the speech of June, 1881, incited the murder of March, 1882, a space of ten months intervening. Numbers of outrages speedily followed the speech of June, said Mr. Davis. He stated that from the people of the district he had never received any assistance in his search for the authors of crime. The people were afraid, said he. A new terror had risen among them: the moonlighters were unknown before 1880. Even on the very night after Mr. Herbert's death, thirteen lambs were "murdered" on his property. Mr. Davis had served thirty-five years in the force. He was intelligent. And, as he said himself, it was his duty as police inspector to know his district—to get behind the scenes of the people's life, and know more of it than other men.

The effect, therefore, was startling when, in answer to Mr. Asquith, who next examined him, Inspector Davis announced that he had discovered in the Land League a "secret inner circle," whose business it was to organize outrage, and execute orders of the larger body. He declared that this secret society carried on its evil work when the League was suppressed. On Mr. Asquith inquiring from him how he had got at this information, Mr. Davis declined to answer. Firmly, but respectfully, he refused to give his informant's names.

Then Mr. Reid tried him. Still he refused to mention names. " I must press you for it," said Mr. Reid, quietly. Why, said Mr. Reid, raising his voice, this anonymous informer, through whom the League is accused, may be "one of the greatest liars in the United Kingdom." After some consultation, the President accepted, under some reservations, Mr. Reid's claim of a right to know; but Mr. Reid nevertheless refrained from putting the question, merely reserving his right to do so when he thought fit. The informers—there were two of them—from whom Mr. Davis had derived his alleged information were, by their own account, men of the very worst type—traitors to their own friends, and organizers of crime. Here is part of the cross-examination. The "he" refers to the first of the two informants :—

Was he a member of the National or Land League?—He was a member of the Land League.
Did he profess to have taken part in the organization of crime?
Sir Henry James—I object.
The President—I think Mr. Reid is entitled to ask that question. I think he is entitled to learn to what class the person belongs.
Mr. Reid—Did this gentleman, or individual—(laughter)—convey to you that he had taken part in the "inner circle"?—He did.
Did he convey that he had himself taken part in crime?—No; he told me he had never perpetrated crime, but he admitted knowing about it. Possibly he admitted having approved of crime. He admitted having organized crime. He gave me no documents.
Have you any evidence, beyond that of the man to whom you have referred, to prove the existence of this secret circle?—I have the evidence of another man.
A man of the same class?—Yes.
And tarred with the same brush?—(laughter)—Yes. I have no other evidence save the disorganized state of the district. I have no secret or private information.
Mr. Reid—Before putting my next question, my lords, I should like to have your lordships' sanction. I want to ask if these two persons are in Ireland—if they are accessible.
The President—I have no objection. You want, I suppose, to learn whether they are available to give evidence?
Mr. Reid—Yes, my lord. (To witness)—Are they within the United Kingdom?—I believe one is.
The other is not within reach—not accessible?—No. One of the persons I never met until 1886. The statement of the first was confined to the Land League, the statement of the second to the National League.
The available person—is he the person of 1882 or of 1886?—The person of 1886.

With an expression of amused contempt Mr. Reid asked Davis whether "that was all" the evidence he had to bring forward for his statement that the League contained a "secret centre," which was engaged in organizing atrocious crimes.

We must now return to Mr. Asquith, who has hitherto taken very little part in the work of cross-examination. To-day he examined Mr. Davis to some good purpose. Mr. Davis, like other members of the constabulary, had declared that all the disturbance in his district began at the end of 1880, with the establishment of the local League branch. But he now admitted that of the condition of this district of Kerry he knew personally nothing. Mr. Asquith also elicited some extremely important facts—(from the witness, that is; in parliamentary returns they have been demonstrated *ad nauseam*)—that the larger proportion of outrages during the years under review consisted of "threatening letters," and that in some cases the people who "received" them were the people who wrote them. Also that the majority of these letters were not followed by violence of any sort; and, again, that the years when violent offences were declining were the years in which legislation was in force for securing fair rents and remission of arrears; and, moreover, that in this same disturbed county of Kerry the Bishop, Dr. Higgins, was an anti-Nationalist, who would not permit his clergy to support the League (which, according to the earnest protestations of the leaguers themselves, was an engine for the prevention of crime). Shortly before Mr. Asquith sat down the witness said that he had traced the organization of outrages to the headquarters of the League in Dublin.

Did you ever succeed in tracing any connection between the moonlighters and the Central Association in Dublin?—I saw Mr. Boyton at Castleisland, and heard him make a speech. I heard what his business was.

From whom?—From my informant.

Who was he?—I cannot give his name. I came to the conclusion that Mr. Boyton was organizing a body of the League, because the district became much worse after he was there.

You said that you searched Mr. Horan's house?—Yes. Proceedings were taken against him as the result of that search. He was convicted for keeping firearms, and fined £3. Mr. Kenny was also convicted for the same offence.

So far as you know, have either of those two gentlemen been proceeded against for any offence?—Not to my knowledge.

Mr. Horan, it will be remembered, was secretary of the Castleisland branch of the League. Mr. Kenny was, or had been, its president.

Mr. Reid having done, for the time being, with his Kerry informers, examined Mr. Davis further on the social condition of Kerry: and in answer to these questions, Mr. Davis agreed that "private malice and family quarrels were fruitful in crime." Mr. Reid next came to the question of criminal speeches. It will be remembered that *The Times* counsel alleged that the murder of Mr. Herbert in March, 1882, was instigated, or encouraged by a meeting held ten months before. And now Mr. Reid proceeded to quote from the Rev. Mr. O'Riordan's speech, wherein Mr. Herbert's name was mentioned. Here is a portion of it :—

We will not insult Mr. Herbert; we will not offer him any violence or do him any injury. The man who would do so would be the greatest enemy we have. . . . I will also ask you to tell everybody you meet that no man must do him the slightest injury, insult him, or offer him any violence, and that the man who would suggest it is the friend of Mr. Arthur Herbert and the enemy of your cause. . . Let us hear no more of these miserable outrages. They are your shame and your disgrace. Your cause does not want these things. Come out in the open daylight like men and stand together.[1]

---

[1] Other extracts from the Rev. Mr. O'Riordan's speech were read out by Sir Henry James :—

"I have a great objection to bring any man's name under censure, public or private. I will not withhold the name of a landlord here to-day. The name is Mr. William Hartley, and his agent Mr. Arthur Herbert; and I brand them here to-day as disturbers of peace and order in the land." "We are told that this landlord and his agent intend to come out here and serve these people with writs and ejectment processes. Now, I am here to-day to tell

The next document read was still more remarkable. An extract from a speech of Mr. Davitt, it was read out in open court by Mr. Davitt himself. Here are some short passages :—

> In fighting your enemy with the weapons of barbarism you are unconsciously fighting his battles. Injustice does not palliate the barbarous practices too frequently resorted to in this country. . . . The victims of injustice are not morally or otherwise justified in resorting to acts which are cruel and inhuman. The torture of dumb animals . . . is, in my opinion, a crime so brutally wicked and so blindly barbaric . . . that I would take pleasure in flogging my own brother for it. . . . I demand of you to stamp out these abominable outrages.

Mr. Davitt, addressing himself to the witness, asked if that was not a fair report of what he had said ; to which Mr. Davis replied that it was. Then Mr. Davitt put the following questions :—

> I believe that you have stated to the Town Commissioners that I had visited the district, and that I sympathized with the Curtin family ?—Yes.
> If it were suggested that I went down to aggravate the boycotting of the Curtin family you would not agree with it?—Certainly not.
> Have you ever prosecuted any members of the police for outrages?—No; but a case occurred of an outrage in connection with which a policeman was convicted for not telling the truth.
> Do you remember a case where three policemen fired into a house?—That was in the Killarney district, but I heard of it.
> Do you know that the Fenians are always supposed to be opposed to outrages?—I have had no experience on the subject, and I can't say.

Sir Charles Russell next put to District Inspector Davis a question or two :—

> You have spoken of the information you received as to the inner secret circle of the League. Do I understand you to say that you have not followed up that information by making a charge against any one?—That is correct.
> You said that Mr. Boyton came down to Castleisland?—Yes. He attended a meeting and spoke. I have no personal knowledge that he ever came to the district before or since. I however heard that he came down.
> From whom?—From the informer of 1882. I have no personal knowledge on the subject.

Mr. Davitt once more tried his skill upon the witness, asking him whether he had ever known Fenians to be moonlighters. "I do not remember," was Mr. Davis's answer, and, he added, "the persons who committed the outrages were reported to me to be Land Leaguers." There was no direct testimony, only report. Shortly after three o'clock the cross-examination of Mr. Davis was finished, and Head-Constable Gilhooly, who had appeared in the witness-box in the earlier part of the day, was recalled. His evidence scarcely requires detailed notice. But the abbreviated substance of part of it shows that distress prevailed among the tenants, and that the League contained almost all the respectable people of the district.[1]

> him if he comes into this remote district to disturb the peace, though we will not injure a hair of his head, we will make an example of him." "If Mr. Forster is just, let him raise himself above the prejudices of party, and let him apply his coercion to any one who may be about to excite disturbance, and we have a right to expect that this be applied to Mr. Herbert. Is he to be allowed, without protesting against it, to come into this district and create disorder and break up happy, though poor, homes? I say he will not." "Is Mr. Arthur Herbert to be allowed to come here to break up the homes of these poor people and cast them adrift on the mercies of the world? I say he will not. We will not insult him, or do him the smallest injury, and the man who would offer him any insult would be the greatest enemy we have. . . . I ask you all to do this ; and mark, you are the public, and if Mr. Herbert comes to serve writs and create disorder, we will, by every lawful means, endeavour to make him a remarkable man in the country. I will also ask and tell every man that you will not do him the slightest injury or offer him any violence, and, if any man does so, he is an enemy to you."
> [1] Was it not abatement they were asking for? Was there any combination against the payment of all rent?—I couldn't say. There were agrarian outrages in Castleisland from the latter end of '79. I knew there had been a very bad season in '79. I knew that the potato crop was a bad one, and it was upon that the people mainly depended for subsistence. There was a distress fund got up to which the police themselves subscribed, but I don't remember the particulars. There was a local committee for the distribution of relief in Castleisland. To that committee Mr. Roche, Archdeacon O'Connor, and Father A. Murphy belonged. When the League was established the respectable shopkeepers, and the farmers, big and small, round the place became members. There were very few exceptions.

The cross-examination of Mr. Gilhooly ended with a few questions about four men, mentioned at the beginning of his evidence, as having been tried for an attack on a police protective hut. Gilhooly had suggested that one of the four, a man named Crowley, was secretary of the local branch. He now declined to say whether Crowley was secretary or not. He admitted he did not know who was secretary. Nor, in fact, could he tell whether any one of the four men was a leaguer.

TWENTY-FIRST DAY.

NOVEMBER 28.

TWENTY-ONE witnesses, including a youth, who was put into the witness-box by mistake, or at all events prematurely, were examined to-day. The youth, who looked shy and frightened, was disposed of in almost less than a minute, for it turned out that the crime—a murder—on which he was called to give evidence, and which was committed four or five months ago, was still *sub judice*. So young Pat Horan was dismissed from the box rather brusquely, as if the responsibility for his untimely presence there rested upon him. And to Pat succeeded Mr. Tom Galvin, a farmer, who had been shot in the legs for paying his rent. That was *The Times* counsel's view of the transaction. But Tom surprised them by telling Sir Charles Russell, quite bluntly, that, after all, he did not think that was the reason. Nor was he the only *Times* witness who, in the course of the day, introduced confusion among his own side. Tom evidently suspected that a family dispute of his was at the bottom of it. He had been managing his widowed sister-in-law's farm, and it would appear that his management was interpreted by some of his relatives as "land-grabbing." It also appeared, in Sir Henry James's opinion, that Tom's story in the box contradicted his depositions elsewhere. Anyhow, it was no easy matter to extract definite statements from Tom. And before they were done with him, Tom himself manifested clear indications of impatience with his questioners. "May I go away?" said he, seizing the rim of his felt hat and picking up his blackthorn cudgel. Tom, with an expression of effusive contentment, made the remarkable announcement that he had received three hundred pounds compensation for a fusillade that left him hardly any the worse.

The examination of the third, fourth, fifth, and sixth witnesses was occupied with two separate instances of the occupation of land from which others had been evicted. The first of these witnesses was a man named Hourigan, who, having been pulled out of his house at night, was dragged "all through the yard," and made to swear upon "something like a book" not to offend again. His evidence led to no definite conclusion.

But the second case, that of Mr. Brown, who lives near Castleisland, whose house had been fired into at night, brought on an interesting discussion about League money. Yes, he had received a summons from the League about this grabbing business—a summons signed by the secretary, Mr. Tim Horan, whose name, by the way, frequently occurs in Sir Richard Webster's elaborate history of county Kerry. He had received another summons from another official leaguer, Father Murphy. Mr. Brown ignored Tim's summons, but he obeyed the priest's. But at this moment a sudden cloud of forgetfulness passed over Mr. Brown's mind. "Bedad"—to quote his frequent expletive—he had forgotten the contents of the League correspondence. After a good deal of wrestling with a defective memory, Mr. Brown announced that Father Murphy undertook to pay him fifteen pounds if he would restore the farm to Mrs. Horan. But was that League money? "Not at all," replied Brown, with energy. How then did the Rev. Leaguer propose to get the money? By "collection"—Mr. Brown explained—collection among the people. So that it would appear the whole transaction was open and above-board, and more of a charitable than a socio-political character. "Nothing was said about Land League money," Mr. Brown repeated.

Then the story took a fresh turn. The priest did not pay the £15, and Mr. Brown sued him in court, and the judge decided against Mr. Brown. One explanation of Father Murphy's refusal to pay was that the payment had been promised on certain conditions which Mr. Brown did not fulfil. That the League, as an organization, had had nothing to do with the Brown-Horan quarrel appeared to be further proved by the testimony of Serjeant O'Brien, who said that, though he had been present at the negotiations, he had not heard the League's name mentioned. Here, then, was another *Times* witness, from whom *The Times* counsel extracted little or nothing. At last, the President growing impatient at the waste of time, Mr. Brown was promptly sent about his business. But not before he gave some replies to Mr. Davitt.

The theory of the so-called prosecution, it may be repeated, is that outrages were the offspring of the Land and National Leagues. The reply of the defence is, in effect, "You don't know your Irish history; outrages are the offspring of a bad social condition which existed long before the Leagues were established, and which the Leagues have been trying to ameliorate." Hence Mr. Davitt's questions to Farmer Brown. In answer to these questions, Mr. Brown stated that he well remembered the famine years of '48-50; that there were many evictions in that period of terrible distress—evictions, because the landlords were taking advantage of their opportunity to amalgamate small farms—and that, as matter of history, evictions had always in Kerry been followed by disturbance and crime.

The seventh, eighth, and ninth witnesses were not very important. But the succeeding four gave interesting evidence. The first in this group of four was the widow of another farmer, of the name of Brown, who had been foully murdered in 1882. Mrs. Johanna Brown, her name was. Mrs. Brown's costume was of a kind never before, perhaps, seen in the Royal Courts of Justice. She was enveloped from head to foot in a wide blue-black cloak, the large hood of which was drawn well over her face. It might almost have been taken for one of those black, baggy, balloon-like garments in which, in the East, Mahommedan women wrap themselves when they visit the bazaar, or ride out on donkey-back. Nevertheless, Mrs. Johanna Brown's cloak is Western and South-Western Irish. The few peasant women who any of these mornings may be seen wandering slowly about the corridors of the Law Courts, as if they were going to some dead friend's wake, remind one of scenes at the funerals of the Lonergans, Shinnicks, Caseys, and other victims of police fusillades.

The police witnesses in the Brown case made a direct, definite charge against one of the most important of the Parnellite members. They say that Mr. John O'Connor cheered the murderers of Mrs. Brown's husband. The murderers, or supposed murderers—at all events, they were hanged for the murder—were two men named Boff and Barrett. Poor Mrs. Brown saw them run away immediately after the commission of the deed. The "long gentleman," the Attorney-General called Mr. O'Connor, bearing in mind the repeated description of him by one of the witnesses, as being very tall. Sir Richard Webster was doubtless unaware that Mr. O'Connor is known among his friends by the sobriquet of "Long John;" the coincidence between the epithets must have been accidental.

District-Inspector W. H. Rice was the first witness summoned after Mrs. Brown. He described how he was escorting from Tralee to Cork a number of prisoners, among whom were those two very men—Boff and Barrett. They were on their way to Cork prison. At a street corner in Cork he saw Mr. John O'Connor, surrounded by and addressing a large crowd. "He appeared to be their leader." "I heard him," said Mr. Rice, shouting out "Down with British law; three cheers for Boff and Barrett!" "Down with the Cork jurors!" &c., all which expressions the mob cheered. Mr. Rice, in reply to the Attorney-General, stated that he went up to Mr. O'Connor and expostulated with him. A police-sergeant, who was examined immediately after Mr. Rice, gave his evidence to the same general effect—also adding that Mr. O'Connor and his friends, seated on a car, continued their demonstrations all the way to the prison gates. Mr. Davitt, however, put a few questions to Mr. Rice, with the object of ascertaining whether he was aware that, whether rightly or wrongly, a very general impression prevailed that Boff and Barrett were innocent. Mr. Rice admitted that he was aware of the existence of such an impression; and also that he had heard that the condemned left behind them written documents asserting their innocence. The implication in Mr. Davitt's question, therefore, was that the excitement among the Cork crowd might be accounted for by the prevalence of the above-named impression.

Then came the day's amusement. It was given—at *The Times*' expense—by Maurice Kennedy, a farmer, of Inniskean, in county Kerry (still county Kerry). *Times* counsel, Parnellite counsel laboured three hours at Mr. Maurice Kennedy without getting anything out of him, without proving hardly anything about him, except that his mind was a *tabula rasa*, or that he would not though he could, or that he was a prevaricator. His good-humour was imperturbable. He was communicative to a degree; and if the lawyers had only allowed him, he would have gone on telling incoherent tales about his family affairs. One clear statement, and only one, was got out of him—that on a certain day he bought hay at a boycotted auction, and that shortly after that his horse's ear was cut off.

Mr. Kennedy joined the League, but he knew not how much entrance money he paid—whether five pounds or a shilling; he could not tell whether he had worked for an employer without being asked; he had called his fellow mortals "roosters," but had no conception of what the word meant. To all such questions as—Did you say this or that? Did you do this or that? Did you see this or that? Did you understand this or that? this perplexing witness's invariable answer was, "Well, sir, I may have," or "Well, sir, perhaps not;" anything but an out-and-out reply. And he always answered with a confiding, sympathetic air—as of a man who would do anything to oblige you; a man who warmly appreciated your thirst for knowledge. It may here be explained that "rooster" means, in the dialect of disturbed Ireland, a man who is "a landlord's turnspit." What *The Times* counsel wanted to know from him was whether the local branch of the League kept a list of "roosters," that is, of persons whom the League had resolved to boycott. As this list was alleged to be hung up in the League office, Mr. Kennedy, who was a member, ought to have seen it. But *The Times* counsel could get nothing out of him. Here is a short specimen of the examination :—

I don't know whether I saw a list of "roosters" displayed on the wall. Before I made the statement to Mr. Shannon I told him I perhaps should not understand the questions he put to me, and I very likely did not understand them. (Laughter.) Maybe I told some lies. I told Mr. Shannon that a list of boycotted people was kept at the League. Bowler and other persons were called "roosters."

Were you knocked down and beaten?—And if I was I don't remember, and I shouldn't blame the League for it.

Were you beaten?—I don't think I understand the word at all. (Laughter.)

Since making the statement to Mr. Shannon have you spoken to any one about the evidence you would give here?—No, sir ; never a word.

Sir Charles Russell—I think I ought to state at once, my lords, that, so far as we know, there is no foundation for the suggestion that the witness has made a statement to any one instructed by us.

Mr. Atkinson—There is just one more question I should like to ask.

The President—Do you expect to extract anything more from him?

Mr. Atkinson (to the witness)—Did you go to any office near the Strand the other day?—I don't know any office, sir ; but I was on the strand picking seaweed the other day.

Sir Charles Russell—And how far is the strand from your house?—About a mile, sir.

Mr. Kennedy's assurance that he had picked seaweed on the strand was received with roars of laughter.

The reader will at once see the significance of one of the above questions put to the witness: "Since making your statement to Mr. Shannon have you spoken to any one about the evidence you would give here?" *The Times* counsel were making nothing of their own witness. Mr. Shannon is one of the assistants to Mr. Soames, *The Times* solicitor. Kennedy was again pressed for an answer to the question—whether he had told Mr. Shannon who the men were whose names were put down on the League "rooster" list. All that could be learned from him was that the names mentioned "might be" on the list—an emphasis on the might.

After the luncheon hour, his own counsel—that is to say, *The Times*—renewed their attack on Mr. Kennedy.

To bring Mr. Kennedy to book, Mr. Shannon and the shorthand writer were examined about their interview with Mr. Kennedy in Mr. Soames's office. Mr. Shannon swore that he had taken down the evidence which Kennedy gave him ; and that all that he knew about him previously was the story of the horse's ear. In effect Mr. Shannon rejected the possible theory that he might have suggested to the witness subjects for evidence, upon which subjects the witness was now professing entire ignorance. Next Mr. Shannon's assistant stated what had happened. His statement, in reply to the Attorney-General, is given in a footnote.[1]

According to the assistant's statement, Kennedy knew all about the "roosters," and a great deal more. Yet on his examination in court he professed almost blank ignorance. He was not even sure whether he had been fined, or if he was fined, why.

Mr. Maurice Kennedy having disappeared, Mr. John Kennedy was placed in the witness-box. But the mind of Mr. Kennedy number two was about as complete a blank as that of Mr. Kennedy number one. Next came a blacksmith named Coonahan—a timid man, but more precise than his predecessor. He stated that he had been dismissed from his membership of the League, because he worked for a boycotted tenant. The next witness, a carter named

---

[1] I was present when Mr. Shannon questioned Kennedy, and I took down the statement. This is it (reading from his notes): "I recollect bidding for the hay at the auction. I had not seen any notices up to that time. I had been on good terms with my neighbours. After the auction the ear of my horse was cut off. . . . I attended meetings of the League before the outrage and one afterwards. I used to cart pigs from the fair to Tralee, but I lost this work. . . . The committee of the League brought a charge against me for speaking to Bowler. I worked for Justin McCarthy. They said the charge against him was his working for a boycotted man. The men who worked for McCarthy were called 'roosters.' The term signifies 'a turnspit for landlords.' About three months after the outrage I was fined 1s. 6d. for breaking a regulation of the League. After a meeting of the League I was told that Bowler was to be boycotted. I heard that a list was kept of persons who were to be boycotted. Every 'rooster' was to be boycotted. The League boycotted them. Cullinan, Shea, Justin McCarthy's son-in-law Kennedy, J. O'Donnell, T. O'Donnell, and Davis were on the list. The League devoted most of its time to boycotting roosters. On going to a meeting of the League I saw a list of roosters on the wall. After being fined I did not work for anybody on the list. I dare not. I do work for some of them now. It is since the suppression of the League that I have worked for them."

Griffin, told how he had been beaten, and even robbed, by a gang of men on the highway because he served the same "rooster," but subsequently his evidence became confused, for he admitted, rather awkwardly, that "there had been an affair between us (his assailants and himself) over a dhrop of drink." And "Begor, sir," he added subsequently, "but this dispute had nothing to do with McCarthy," for whom the "roosters" worked. Then came a police officer, who stated that the boycotting of McCarthy took place several months after the foundation of the local branch of the National League in September, 1885.

TWENTY-SECOND DAY.

NOVEMBER 29.

WE are still in Kerry. A Kerry farmer named Jeremiah Sullivan was the first witness called this morning. His story was of the ordinary type with which this Kerry investigation has made the public familiar. The purport of it was that he had paid his rent immediately after his fellow-tenants had petitioned their landlord for reduction. The usual results followed—first, moonlighters' shots at night, from which, however, he received no harm; and the morning after the shots, "Rory o' the Hills' notice," found stuck over his door—"Rory" swearing by "his God" that the man would be shot who paid his rent against "the will of the people." Sullivan's evidence established nothing except the fact of the crime.

Replying to Mr. Davitt, he stated frankly that he knew nothing as to its authorship. A question put to him by Mr. Reid elicited the interesting fact that Sullivan, though he did pay, gave the landlord less than the other tenants were ready to concede. In that case, asked Mr. Reid, why did they persecute you? Like so many of these Kerry witnesses, Sullivan betrayed almost complete ignorance of matters beyond his own patch of soil. Until he saw the moonlighters' notice he had not even heard of "Rory o' the Hills." Sullivan's case was so unimportant that the next witness, Constable Murphy, called to testify to the raid on Sullivan's house, was dismissed with one or two questions. The next witness had more information to give, but, like Sullivan, he brought no charge against the Land League—nor against any one in particular. His evidence was one of a thousand proofs and illustrations of a fact of which the public are sufficiently aware—that Kerry has for a long time been disturbed.

Pat Murphy, another witness, was a man of lucky escapes. His neighbours accused him of having grabbed a widow's farm. Accordingly, some persons unknown dragged him out of bed at night, and made him swear on his knees that he would give the widow back her land. Having got this promise, "Rory's" men might have let him alone. But they fired at him and missed. However, they snipped off part of his ear. Murphy is the second Irish farmer who has presented himself, crop-eared, before the Parnell Commission. On the next occasion his escape was still narrower. He was returning from Tralee to his home, when—this was in July, 1882—a man jumped out of a wood, fired at him from the wayside, and missed, but the shot hit one of the three "boys" who were with Murphy in the car. After this second escape, he was boycotted for years, and some of his cattle and sheep were slaughtered by "Rory's" emissaries.

Mr. Davitt cross-examined the witness. His questions were intended to find out whether the crime might be explained by causes wholly unconnected with the League—say, by private disputes and jealousies, and social conditions that had long existed. The widow's farm was the only one she had, the witness admitted. As for himself, he had a second farm, upon which he could fall back ; and he was quite aware—this also in answer to a question—that for the widow it was a choice between her home and the workhouse. Did this prove Sullivan heartless and self-seeking? But Mr. Sullivan's next observation showed that he himself was as helpless in the hands of a stronger power as the widow was in his, for he stated that the landlord had compelled him to take the widow's farm, under the threat that if he refused he would have to abandon the one he already held. Mr. Davitt's next question was suggestive. Had the widow grown-up children? Yes. And Mr. Sullivan admitted that they might naturally have found means of taking vengeance for their mother's sufferings. However, the crime was not brought home to the widow's sons any more than it was to the National League. So that Murphy's story did not appear to throw much light on the investigation.

Nor did the next case, a much more atrocious one than either of the preceding. It was that of a man named John Macauliffe, who apparently for no reason than that he had assisted his brother, a process-server, was moonlighted, and shot in the left arm, which subsequently had to be amputated. The empty sleeve of Macauliffe's rough frieze coat was tucked into his waistcoat. At the same moonlight visit, Macauliffe's brother was hurt, and his sister's head cut open. To show how these crimes were regarded by such prominent leaguers as the proprietor, editor, and chief contributor of *The Kerry Sentinel*, the principal newspaper in Kerry, Mr. Lockwood contented himself with reading out from its columns several passages strongly denouncing the outrage.

And now the Court entered upon a somewhat different line of investigation ; and one of the most important of *The Times* witnesses stepped into the box. This was District-Inspector Crane, an Englishman, and an Oxford man (by the way, only one of many men with a University education who are nowadays to be found in the Royal Irish Constabulary). Except when the comic element was present, the evidence of the Kerry men was confused, lacking in precision, and, though doubtless useful, wearisomely difficult to get at. But here was a witness who wasted no time—whose answers were prompt, pointed, unmistakable. His evidence extended over three districts of Kerry, and covered a period of seven or eight years. But the plan upon which Sir Richard Webster arranged his questions made the ready apprehension of the connection and general bearing of Mr. Crane's answers a very simple matter. Mr. Crane was required to describe the lawless condition of Kerry as he found it, to indicate what in his belief was the true explanation of the lawlessness, and then to state the grounds for his belief.

To show what the social condition was, Mr. Crane, following the Attorney-General's questions, took his three districts one after the other—Dingle district, Listowel, and Killarney. When Mr. Crane first went to Dingle—this was in 1879—he found the locality quiet. Even in 1880, when evictions took place, it had not yet been found necessary to have strong bodies of constabulary at them. The chief landlord in the Dingle district had always been, said Mr. Crane, very popular. "I never heard a word said against him." But the Land League founded its first branch there in the beginning of 1881, and then—according to Mr. Crane—the demeanour and behaviour of the people changed suddenly and completely ; and for the first time tenants under ejectment notice began to fortify their houses. To put Mr. Crane's testimony into a nutshell, it amounted to this—that upon the first local branch of the Land League there followed the first barricade and the first siege. He proceeded to describe how, simultaneously with this new agitation, the police had to be increased at different stations ; how " Land League hunts " (through the game and other preserves of unpopular landlords) came into fashion; how landlords' officials of many years standing—*e.g.*, men like Bailiff Moriarty, who had been forty years at his calling—were warned by symbolic coffins affixed to their doors; how Land Leaguers in particular and the community in general refrained from giving any assistance, any information in his endeavours to discover the authors of outrages; how crimes fell off when a new Coercion Act was put in force; how they broke out afresh in 1885, when the Act was allowed to lapse; and how he observed that wherever a Land League organization existed there also the moonlighters were sure to be.

The Attorney-General made Mr. Crane repeat this last important statement. Mr. Crane once or twice expressed the same thing in another way—he had never known any instance of a secret society existing by itself. The secret society and the open society—the League—co-existed. Why, he was asked by the Attorney-General, did the people refuse to give you any information? Was it because of terrorism? "Terrorism," was the answer, "not sympathy with crime." "I am certain of it." These last five words Mr. Crane uttered with an emphatic gesture. Two other statements completed Mr. Crane's general indictment against the League. One, that the leaguers and the moonlighters not only co-existed, but also that they were interconnected; and the other, that crimes followed breaches of the League rules. In his cross-examination by Mr. Lockwood, District-Inspector Crane admitted that he was not in a position to institute a comparison between the Kerry districts as they were before and subsequently to 1879, inasmuch as his knowledge of them did not begin before that year. Again, when challenged by Mr. Lockwood to specify individual League meetings (with names of speakers), the holding of which he could directly connect with the subsequent commission of crime, Mr. Crane was unable to name them. He could only say, generally, that League meetings—that is, official meetings and not merely open and public meetings—were regularly held; and that, although he himself was not present at them, he knew that the outrages followed. Having failed to get from Mr. Crane any direct proof that meeting and outrage had any relation to one another save the relation of sequence, Mr. Lockwood read long extracts from *The Kerry Sentinel* articles, the writer of which was understood to be Mr. Edward Harrington himself, and in which outrages were denounced as "hellish work," and their perpetrators as men possessed of a "devilish instinct." Mr. Edward Harrington, sitting on the solicitors' bench, supplied Mr. Lockwood with files of the *Sentinel*. "Cowardly, criminal, sinful, and abominable," were the adjectives with which the ultra-Nationalist Kerry paper, the *Sentinel*, wound up one of its attacks upon the moonlighters, whom Mr. Crane regarded as leaguers under another name, and for whose misdeeds he held the League responsible.

Mr. Crane's most startling statement was made in reply to Mr. Asquith, whose cross-examination of him lasted for more than half an hour.

Mr. Asquith—Do you suggest that the branches of the National League and the moonlighters are in co-operation?—I do. I say that the majority of the moonlighters are National Leaguers, but not that the majority of National Leaguers are moonlighters. The resolutions of the League were invariably carried out by the moonlighters.

The witness was then pressed as to prosecutions of moonlighters, but could not say positively that any of the men were members of the League. In one case he said the police met a party of moonlighters.

Mr. Asquith—Were they raiding for arms?—I don't know. The police met them. They were going to several farmers' houses.

How do you know that?—From private information.

Who gave you the information?—I won't tell you.

Mr. Asquith (to the President)—I suppose, my lord, that answer comes under your recent decision.

The President—Yes.

The witness—My information was that this party were going round to the farmers to compel them to join the League.

Mr. Asquith—You won't give me the name of the informant, so I don't want to know what his information was.
Witness (continuing)—From my experience I make no qualification or reserve in saying that outrages followed the proceedings of League meetings, as reported in the papers. I have seen these things over and over again, although, of course, I cannot tax my memory with the particular reports and the exact crimes which occurred after them.

The next witness was a district inspector, Mr. W. H. Wright. Like Mr. Crane, he held that until the League appeared in it, his part of Ireland had been peaceful and content; that in the years before 1879-80, the police were never at a loss to get information leading to the detection of offenders. Speaking of two to three years ago, he said that Listowel was in an extremely disturbed state at the very time that the League was exceptionally influential there. Then Mr. Wright gave a little descriptive sketch of contemporary Irish life, which must be familiar to every one who visits the country; he described how a popular leader, on horseback, would watch the police-barracks for the first signs of a march-out to an eviction; how the horseman would gallop off with the news, and warn the threatened occupier and his friends. Mr. Wright clearly thought that scouting of this description (which is done openly in Ireland at eviction times) was a serious offence. He stated that one of the scouts whom he arrested was a Mr. Murphy, Secretary to the Listowel branch of the Land League; but the particular act for which he arrested him was "blowing a horn" (another kind of danger-signal, common in Ireland). "I have that horn yet," exclaimed Mr. Wright, loudly.

Mr. Murphy was taken aback by the burst of laughter with which this interesting piece of information was received. Mr. Wright next gave a long list of agrarian offences that had taken place in his district. Did you investigate the causes? asked Sir Richard Webster. Yes, and he had found—so he said—that the causes resolved themselves into breaches of League rules about payment of rent, about occupation of "evicted" farms, and so forth. He also stated that the League prohibited farmers from substituting mowing machines for manual labour. He summed up his evidence in this statement— that the League was the only organization which he knew to have preached against land-grabbing; and that he believed the National League to be connected with the moonlighters' secret society. This testimony, a repetition of Mr. Crane's, brought out a sharp, quick question from Mr. Lockwood— "What are your grounds for that statement?" "I know the moonlighters carried out the League's behests," repeated Mr. Wright. "That is only your inference," retorted Mr. Lockwood.

For about twenty minutes Mr. Wright was closely and severely pressed by Mr. Lockwood, to give definite proofs of any one single instance of identity between the League and the Moonlighting Society.

I understand you to suggest that, in your opinion, the moonlighters who were engaged in the outrages were carrying out the behests of the Land League. Now, what grounds have you for that opinion?—Well, in the cases of these evicted farms——
What evicted farms?—I'm speaking of evicted farms generally.
But if you speak of them generally you will only give me a general opinion formed by yourself. What I want to learn is the groundwork on which your opinion rests. Give me the names and dates of outrages justifying your opinion?—Well, I can't do that. I can't refer to any particular cases; but the general question remains the same.
And so you cannot give me any better reasons for the opinion you have formed? You have made, as you must be aware, a very grave accusation, and I want to know if you can substantiate it by giving me the names and dates of particular outrages?—Well, here now (referring to his book), here is a case of a man who had taken an evicted farm, and we all know that persons who have had anything to do with evicted farms have been denounced over and over again. The man's hay was burnt on this evicted farm. Now, how was it the hay was not burnt on the adjoining farm?

To Mr. Wright Mr. Biggar put a shrewd question in reference to the subject of mowing machines. One of the witness's accusations against the League was that it prohibited the use of them. But, said Mr. Biggar, is it not the fact that the members of the League are farmers—the very persons for whom machine-mowing would be cheaper than any other form of labour? Would the farmers of the League pass a regulation against themselves?

Mr. T. Harrington and Mr. Davitt also put a few questions to Mr. Wright, the former challenging him to give specific instances.

Can you point to any specific instance in which a resolution was adopted by a branch of the National League as distinctly apart from meetings of the tenants themselves in which non-payment of rents was advised apart from the question of reduction?—I am not aware of any at the present time.

Can you point to any single instance where you heard, by information, that the National League directed moonlighting or any other kind of outrage?—Oh, no, sir.

Not even from private information—in Castleisland or any other districts—in which the National League directed outrages?—Oh, no.

Your information has been drawn altogether from the fact that the outrages had to do with agrarian questions, and that the National League had to do with agrarian questions?—Well, they followed on the regular lines of the speeches and resolutions.

It is, then, merely an inference, not founded on information?—It is an nference of my own founded on observation.

Not founded upon information?—No.

Finally, Mr. Davitt got from him the admission that he was unacquainted with the rules of the League, that he had never read them, nor taken any steps to inform himself on the subject. This concluded the examination of Mr. Wright. Of four witnesses who followed Mr. Wright, the most notable was Eugene Sheehy, a dark-complexioned man (of a Spanish type not uncommon in Kerry). He confessed that "as far as I know the League and myself have always been good friends;" so that Eugene Sheehy did not blame the League for his horse's loss of an ear. The poor horse had its ear cut off, because its owner bought boycotted hay. Eugene returned the hay. "Got your money back?" asked Sir Henry James, sympathetically. "Oh! I never paid for the hay," replied Mr. Eugene Sheehy, smiling, and—when the laughter broke out—blushing.

TWENTY-THIRD DAY.

NOVEMBER 30.

Now, then, said the Attorney-General, as he called his first witness of the day, a witness who was to describe happy Arcadia. This was Mr. Hussey, a well-known landlord and estate agent in county Kerry. His examination in chief, lasting thirty-five minutes, was practically a eulogy of Kerry and its people before the Land League appeared and spoiled (according to the witness's ideas of cause and effect) their peace. Up to the year '80 "as peaceable as any part of the world" was Mr. Hussey's regretful description of Kerry. Until then, said he, the people bore distress meekly. When crimes were committed we had no difficulty in getting evidence about them ; we could evict without difficulty ; and no one because he paid rent was punished by his neighbours. If he had to put his finger upon any date demarcating Kerry the happy from Kerry the miserable, he would select the 10th of October, 1880, the date of the first meeting of the Land League at Castleisland, at which meeting "my name was mentioned," and at which Mr. Biggar was, he said, the speaker in chief. Then the troubles of Mr. Hussey and his fellow-agents and landlords began ; and so very quickly that, "in a day or two" after Mr. Biggar's speech, Mr. Hussey himself received information which induced him to place:

himself under police protection. Mr. Hussey put his complaint in logical shape—or rather the Attorney-General led the way for him. For instance, his argument that the League must have been the cause of the new lawlessness and discontent, because in those localities where no League branch existed his relations with the tenantry remained on their old and pleasant footing, was a good illustration of what the philosophers call the method of agreement and difference. Never before, Mr. Hussey testified, at the wind-up of his examination in chief, had tenants come to him to pay their rents in secret—fearing, as he said they told him, "lest they should be shot." Never, until 1880, had he heard of moonlighters, nor of "land-grabbing" (the very name was new to him). For forty years Mr. Hussey had been, according to his own account, a popular man in the county; but in 1884 a dynamite mine was exploded close to his house, blowing its walls down, and endangering the lives of its fifteen inmates, mostly women and children.

The cross-examination of Mr. Hussey was conducted by Sir Charles Russell, Mr. Reid, Q.C., Mr. Davitt, and Mr. Biggar. The liveliest part of it was a little word combat between the witness and Mr. Biggar. The most important, as well as the most elaborate and exhaustive, was Sir Charles Russell's. The whole of this cross-examination was a most interesting and valuable chapter in Irish history, in the form of question and answer. And Sir Charles Russell was at his best—or near it. "And so then," Mr. Hussey, "you adhere to all you have said " about the state of Kerry before the rise of the League? Yes, Mr. Hussey adhered to all he said about its peacefulness and contentment.

"Very well; now let us look at the parliamentary record for Kerry in the year 1879." And then Sir Charles Russell read out, slowly, deliberately, a long list of Kerry outrages in that year—incendiary fires, threatening letters, and cattle maiming.

From these State records Sir Charles Russell also quoted passages which showed that evictions and unauthorized re-entries into "evicted" homes were not unknown in Kerry before Mr. Hussey's black year, 1880. "What say you to that?" asked Sir Charles Russell, pausing in his counter-description of Arcadian Kerry. Mr. Hussey also paused. At last he observed that he regarded the threatening notices, the incendiarisms, and such like outrages enumerated by Sir Charles, as nothing in comparison with the outrages of subsequent years. Then came Sir Charles's characteristic "Very well, very well," as if he were quite satisfied with his answer. These preliminary questions by Sir Charles Russell were meant to show that before the League ever existed there were in Kerry causes of social discontent. His next set of questions was meant to discredit a common suggestion that, for sinister purposes, the League hindered the operation of the Land Acts. Did not Mr. Hussey know that if the Nationalist leaders discouraged wholesale resort to the Courts when the Act was passed, their object was to await the result of test cases? He did not. Nor was Mr. Hussey very explicit as to the extent which "the load of arrears hanging round their necks" might have disqualified tenants from applying for "judicial rents." And he admitted that in many instances the Land Commissioners, in fixing the new rents, deprived tenants of their ancient and valuable right to turbary (free turf-fuel).

If before the League appeared the Kerry people were as prosperous and content as Mr. Hussey said (Sir Charles Russell, by the way, had already and promptly admitted their great patience), how could Mr. Hussey explain the following figures, his cross-examiner asked: In 1876 Ireland produced crops of the value of thirty-six millions. In 1879 the value fell to twenty-two millions. "Startling, is it not?" Sir Charles Russell remarked, looking up from his blue-book and addressing himself to the witness. In 1876, he continued, the potato crop was valued at twelve millions, and only at three millions in 1879. Lastly, the eviction figures were quoted, showing that in 1879 there were 3,893 evictions, or more than double the number in 1876.

"Was there anything which tenants dreaded more than eviction?" "No." "And they would make any sacrifice to escape eviction?" "Yes." But at this point Mr. Hussey threw in a qualification to this effect—that eviction was not so much dreaded now as before 1880. "Why?" "They do not dislike emigration so much;" at which assurance Sir Charles Russell smiled. Mr. Hussey next admitted that even in 1879 he "thought" the tenants of Lord Kenmare (one of the landlords whose agent he was) petitioned for rent abatement, and moreover that quite apart from the work which Lord Kenmare was providing for them in his improvement schemes, they deserved to get it. "And you know that these people hate to see their homes demolished and burnt." "Yes," was Mr. Hussey's businesslike answer, "for then they have no chance of getting back to them."

It appeared that in the summer of 1880, before any Land League branch existed in Kerry, Mr. Hussey had demolished houses in order to prevent the tenants returning to them. "Was not that cruel?" Mr. Reid asked him in his quiet way. Cruel or not, Mr. Hussey defended the act on the ground of its "necessity," because, said Mr. Hussey, there was not then as there is now a law which punished tenants for re-taking possession of the homes from which they had been evicted.

All through this examination Mr. Hussey accounted for his own unpopularity in Kerry, and for the existence of outrages there, by the interference of the Land League. But, Mr. Reid asked him, did he not think that, quite apart from the Land League, such acts as the demolition of labourers' houses were enough to make him unpopular? Mr. Hussey did not think they were. Mr. Reid gazed at him for a moment or two, and sat down.

Mr. Michael Davitt and Mr. Biggar next put a few questions to Mr. Hussey—between whom and the member for Cavan there followed a brief and lively, but not angry "scene." Mr. Hussey, probably thinking that he "had" Mr. Biggar for once in a way, made the best of his opportunity, and both gentlemen, as they went ahead with their work, grew rather red in the face, nodded at each other, and even wagged their forefingers.

Mr. Hussey's examination being now done with, the Attorney-General announced that, owing to the non-arrival of police witnesses from Ireland, he would be obliged to postpone the conclusion of his case for county Kerry. Meanwhile, he would pass on to county Cork. And Mr. Jeremiah Hegarty, a merchant and farmer, of a small place called Millstreet, was called to give his evidence.

The point in Mr. Hegarty's long and involved story—in the development of which he was constantly asking to be allowed to "explain"—was that all the worries and heavy business losses (brought on by boycotting), which he had endured for seven long years, were solely attributable to his refusal to become a member of the League. The boycott cost him two thousand a year, he said, but he had held out in spite of it, and cared for boycotters no longer. This expensive boycott appeared to have made but little impression upon Mr. Hegarty's spirits. Mr. Hegarty is stout, ruddy, robust, erect: he looks at least sixteen years younger than his age—which, to the surprise of all present, he said was fifty-six.

The League was first established in his locality in the autumn of 1880. After that a League official called upon him—presumably to invite Mr. Hegarty to join the new organization. Mr. Hegarty refused; as he repeatedly declared, in the course of his cross-examination, he would have nothing to do with it. Well, shortly after the above-named visit, said Mr. Hegarty, notices were posted all over the place, inviting people to cease dealing with him. The sanguinary rubbish contained in these notices was in the style of the mysterious "Rory o' the Hills," otherwise known as Captain Moonlight. In one notice, Hegarty was called a "leper." Another notice was dated from "Assassination Hall." And yet again, Mr. Hegarty was informed that "Captain Moonlight, Governor-General of the district for the time being, with the advice and consent of his privy councillors," would use "cold steel." Next, Mr. Hegarty observed that two men whom he had seen entering the League rooms, were keeping watch over his shop. Soon after the legal punishment of these two men Mr. Hegarty's dairy was broken into and its contents destroyed. At Divine service people even went to the extremity of boycotting Mr. Hegarty's brother-in-law—they would not sit on the same side of the chapel with him. In 1880 Hegarty was shot at, but he escaped; in 1887 he was shot at and hit on the shoulder. The League only, was the cause of all these persecutions. In all the League there was, it would appear, only one man for whom Mr. Hegarty entertained any respect, and that man was Mr. Davitt. A letter which he wrote in 1880 to Mr. Davitt, and in which he asked the Father of the Land League to interfere on his behalf, was read out in court. An admirably-written letter it was; and, withal, a great compliment to Mr. Davitt himself, for whose character the writer expressed straightforwardly, and without a trace of flattery, the warmest admiration. The letter is by far too long for reproduction here.

Mr. Reid, cross-examining the witness, looked surprised at his assurance that for the simple offence of refusing to join the League he was "twice shot at," and boycotted "all those years." Could there possibly have been any other cause or causes? To throw light upon that question was the purpose of the cross-examination, which occupied the remainder of the day's sitting, and in which Mr. Reid took the principal part, and after him Mr. Arthur O'Connor, M.P., Mr. Michael Davitt, and Mr. Biggar.

Mr. Reid—Did you ever have anything to do with evictions?—Yes. Up to 1880 I had not; but since 1880 I have been connected with the management of some properties in the neighbourhood.
Oh, I see. Did you not assist at the eviction of Lyons?—Yes. It was in February, 1886.
At the eviction of Riordan?—Yes. That was in January, 1887.
When did you first act as agent or bailiff or sub-agent or bailiff, or become in any way connected with a landlord?—I think it was in April, 1880.
Were not all evictions in Ireland a cause of dissatisfaction and discontent?—I am sorry to say they were to a large extent—that is, they have been made so.
Have you not, since its commencement, shown great hostility to the Land League?—Yes; I have always defended myself as much as I could.
Is it not the case that the National League embraces a large portion of the population in the district in which you live?—Apparently it does.
You belong to the Landlords' Defence Union, do you not?—The Defence Union, yes.
That is a body in the habit of bringing down emergency men—rightly or wrongly, I don't want to discuss it—into the district?—They have a large number of men in their employment.
Generally called emergency men?—They are called all manner of names.
They are, I suppose, rather an unpopular body among the National or Land Leaguers?—As a matter of course every one who is opposed to the Land League must be unpopular in the neighbourhood.
They cultivate evicted farms, do they not?—Yes.
You have been active in their interest for three or four years?—I was one of the executive.
And therefore you took an active part in assisting these men?—Not actively. I am sorry to say my time would not permit me to. I have exerted myself to the best I could to get people on the evicted farms protected. Of course I have been obliged to do that.
Ever since the Land League commenced—ever since 1880—is it true that you have set yourself in favour of persons who were boycotted, and who had taken evicted farms?—I have assisted them from the commencement.

After this there followed an interesting cross-examination by Mr. Davitt, who elicited from Mr. Hegarty some important admissions regarding the jealousies of his fellow-tradesmen, and the real nature of the share which the local leaguers had in boycotting him.

Mr. Davitt—You have said with some emphasis that you told me you would never join the League?—Yes.
Did I ever ask you to join, ever coerce you to join?—No.
With regard to the able letter of which you have spoken, and which you have addressed to me, did it appear in any newspaper before it reached me?—No. It was sent to *The Daily News* on the 28th of December, 1880.
Was that letter written to me in consequence of anything I had said? Had you read anything I had written or spoken about that time about any people being coerced to join the League?—I don't remember that I had, but I must have entertained a very high opinion of you at the time or I should not have written to you as I did.
I remember receiving your letter, and I thought I had replied to it. Did you get a reply?—No.
Did you hear that the local branch of the League had been reprimanded by me for their conduct towards you?—No, never. Of course your explanation now is very satisfactory.
In your letter you speak of the power of the League being used to "gratify spleen and private malice." Then you thought that trade jealousy might have had something to do with the treatment to which you were subjected?—Yes, I was strongly of that opinion.
I think you have said that the chairman of the local branch opposed some resolution that was proposed against you?—Yes.
Then officially the Land League could not have been unanimously in favour of the treatment you received?—I suppose not.

In Mr. Biggar's cross-examination of Mr. Hegarty there was one noteworthy point. Mr. Hegarty had put at £2,000 a year the income of which the boycotters had deprived him. Mr. Biggar is fond of challenging witnesses with the question, "Will you swear, will you swear?" and now he invited—rather aggressively—Mr. Hegarty to swear at what figure he had put his earnings, in his income-tax return. He meant, of course, Mr. Hegarty's income up to the year 1879. But to the inquisitorial member for Cavan Mr. Hegarty would not "swear" whether he had paid income-tax on as much as five hundred.

TWENTY-FOURTH DAY.

December 4.

THIRTEEN witnesses were examined to-day. Twelve of them were witnesses to the seven years' boycott of Mr. Hegarty. Of the twelve, four were constabulary men, and one a priest—the first of his order who has appeared before the Commission. Most of them were themselves boycotted, or moonlighted, because, as they said, they had dealings with Hegarty. One of them, named Cornelius Gallagher, described how he swore on his knees not to work for Mr. Hegarty. When he broke his promise his fellow-villagers "whistled" at him. The memory of all that hostile "whistling" seemed to haunt Cornelius in the box. Cornelius was dismissed from his box—almost hurried off—no one thinking it worth while to cross-examine him. As he dived into the crowd, with his chin on his chest, Cornelius seemed greatly relieved. To him followed Jeremiah O'Connor—a stout, prosperous farmer—seeming not the least depressed by the nature of his official calling, which was that of relieving officer. Jeremiah was waited upon by Captain Moonlight and his ruffians with the usual formalities. An easy man was Jeremiah O'Connor. He refused to get out of bed to receive the rascals. So their bullets came whistling through his door—doing no harm. Mr. Jeremiah O'Connor's ideas on the succession of the hours are quasi-poetic. When did the captain call? At night? Not at night, but "in the afternoon of the night." Mary Fitzgerald told how, because she and her family worked for Mr. Hegarty, the moonlighters tried to cut off her hair. But Miss Mary's mother defeated their attempts upon her daughter's locks, but received a wound on her forehead from one of her cowardly assailants. Old Mrs. Fitzgerald herself appeared in the box, an hour or two after her daughter. A venerable, whitehaired, good-looking, perfectly composed old lady she was. The vast hood of her black cloak almost covered her face when she entered the box. The usher tenderly assisted her to push her hood back a little, so that her aged, interesting features became visible. The other witnesses' stories are not worth mentioning. The outrages were not disputed. What Sir Charles Russell wanted his opponents to do, was to trace them to the League.

But Mr. Thomas Cahill, of the Royal Irish Constabulary, tried to prove the connection.

Mr. Cahill swore that he arrested a man Dan Connell, who had been paid twelve pounds by the Land League for moonlighting. From whom did Mr. Cahill learn that? From Connell himself. But, said Mr. Cahill, Connell did not tell me the name of the person or persons who paid him. So that, after all, Mr. Cahill's evidence was inconclusive.

The evidence of the remaining constabulary witnesses being as indecisive as Mr. Cahill's, we pass on to that of the priest—Canon Griffin, of Killarney. In so far as Canon Griffin is an anti-Nationalist, he is unlike the great majority of his fellow-priests in Ireland.

Canon Griffin is a short, thick-set, quick, intelligent, good-humoured gentleman of about sixty-three, apparently—for he was still a student in the famine years 1848-9. Canon Griffin is not exactly a typical Irish priest, either in appearance or in speech and accent.

To quote his own pugnacious expression, he has fought the League "from the start." But smilingly, and frankly, and with a pit-pat of his chubby fingers on the ledge of his box, he admitted that he was in the minority. "Thousands of them," his fellow-priests, thought differently from Canon Griffin—"thousands of them," and his reverence tossed his neat, grey head back, with an air of good-natured indifference, as who should say there was no accounting for people's tastes or convictions. Canon Griffin declared that from 1872, until the appearance of the League in Millstreet District, the people were quiet, industrious, and religious. He dwelt upon this point of religious behaviour frequently during his cross-examination. The Canon was the first witness who, besides making the League responsible for the overthrow of happy Arcadia, and the coming of the rule of lawlessness and outrage, made it answerable for religious decay. On this matter cheery, happy Canon Griffin was quite positive. Here we give a portion of Mr. Reid's cross-examination.

Are there a great many good and exemplary priests in Ireland, all over Ireland, who have been in sympathy with the League?—Thousands.
And who, no doubt, like yourself, have denounced outrage and crime?—Possibly.
You would not doubt that they did?—I have heard that they did.
I think I understood you that spleen and personal malignity had more to do with the action of the League than anything relating to the question of the land?—As far as my parish was concerned. Once it was started, persons connected with the League turned it to that purpose.
Wasn't there a good deal of distress at the time?—There was a good deal of distress, but it was stopped by the kindly aid of the different societies for relief.
I am speaking of the condition of things before the relief you have spoken of was afforded. Is it not the case that the potato crop failed?—It did. The distress round Millstreet was certainly very great.
The rents about Millstreet—were they largely reduced by the Land Commissioners when they came round?—They were reduced both by the Land Commissioners and the landlords.
You considered that reductions were necessary?—Absolutely necessary. I consider that previous to the agitation a very large portion of the land about Millstreet was entirely over-rented. I was surprised when I consulted the people that they did not complain about their rents.

The upshot, then, of Canon Griffin's evidence was that, League or no League, the people had only too much cause for discontent.

Moreover, Canon Griffin declined, in his cross-examination by Mr. Lockwood, to swear that he did not in 1878-9 denounce from the altar an agrarian agitation alleged to have prevailed in those years. "Did you do it?" he was asked. "I don't know; I can hardly remember," was his answer. Yet one of the Canon's main statements was that the Land League introduced agrarian agitation.

Nor did the Canon show to much greater advantage under his cross-examination by Mr. Davitt. Mr. Griffin had already declared his belief—smilingly, and with his air of happy, unalterable confidence—that the men who set the League a-going were people who merely wished to push themselves to the front, and make a name for themselves. Whereupon Mr. Davitt put this pertinent question—"Does not that apply not only to laymen, but also to the bishops and to the priests?" It will be remembered that the Canon had admitted that "thousands" of Irish priests sympathized with the leaguers. "You are aware, I suppose," Mr. Davitt continued, "that the Archbishop of your own archdiocese took part in the League!" "He joined it afterwards," the Canon replied. "I don't know that he took part in starting it."[1]

At the conclusion of Canon Griffin's examination the Court adjourned. But in the early part of the sitting appeared the most important witness of the day. This was Thomas O'Connor—by his own account betrayer of his fellow Land Leaguers, of his fellow National Leaguers, ex-moonlighter, and ex-member of the "Inner Circle," which two other leading witnesses before him in this trial have declared to be the secret machinery by which the criminal resolutions of the "open" League, the Constitutional League, the League known to the public, were carried into effect. But the examination of this interesting witness came between the testimony of the third witness and that of the fifth in the Hegarty case. For the sake of consecutive order we have taken all the Hegarty witnesses first, and reserved the informer's story to the last, though it was told much earlier in the day.

Thomas O'Connor is a tall, physically weak young man, with round shoulders, chest rather hollow, high cheek-bones (with a hectic colour about them), smallish, palish, oblique eyes, receding brow, and head rather full in the back part. O'Connor joined the Castleisland branch of the League in 1880. And now he described at great length and minutely how the League did its work. First, said he, the tenants used to meet and discuss what reduction they would demand from their landlord. Having agreed, they would make their demands in a body. But some went "on their own hook," whereupon the League committee would meet to discuss what to do with them. Every week, said the Informer, the leaguers met to denounce as "vile things," as persons "unfit to walk or creep on the ground," those who "went behind the backs of others"—that is, those who went to the landlords on "their own hook." He was not an official himself, but he knew Tim Horan, the secretary of the branch; Patrick Kenny, the president, and others.

Here the Attorney-General, who was examining him, paused a little. "Did you ever hear of an 'Inner Circle'?" asked Sir Richard Webster. "I did," was the reply. "Were you invited to join it?" "Yes." "Did you?" Here O'Connor hesitated; he looked a little shy and sheepish; he moved about uneasily. "I did," he said at last; "I did, in a way—some time in December, '80." Then he became bolder, readier, and more self-possessed.

[1] Canon Griffin was what his opponents call a landlord's priest. His relations with Lord Kenmare are explained in the following cross-examination by Mr. Biggar:—
From your bringing up have you not been associated with Lord Kenmare—have you not relatives in the employment of Lord Kenmare?—My brother was his physician, and when I was at Killarney I was his chaplain. Some of my relations are tenants of his. I would be very glad to be connected with Lord Kenmare in any way, because he was the best landlord in the south of Ireland.

He said that the "Inner Circle" men went by the name of "the Boys," and that the two "Boys" who first sounded him, told him it would be a fine thing for him to become a soldier of Mr. Parnell's, and get pay for doing little. "Twiss and Connor," said the witness, were the two "Boys" who introduced him to the Inner Circle; and when he was introduced, Twiss said, "Here's a fellow who is all right; we want a fellow in Hegarty's district." All the while, Tim Horan, secretary of the League, was present, and on the assurance of Twiss and his confederate, Horan replied, "All right." Such was the first part of the witness's story.

Then, the Attorney-General gently leading him on, the informer described the nature of his duties as a member of the "Inner Circle." He took part in midnight expeditions, on one occasion with thirty "Boys," who were armed with guns and revolvers, and whose business it was to reinstate an evicted tenant. For this first service he had, he said, six shillings from the secretary of the local branch. At another time he was one of a party of fifteen "Boys," also armed and commissioned to warn a landlord's tenants against paying rents above Griffith's valuation. If these people, said the informer, did not open their doors at once, we burst them open. O'Connor declared that he had taken part in ten or twelve midnight expeditions of this kind—there were many such expeditions, he added, of which no notice ever appeared in the papers.

The third part of the story touched on local electioneering for local purposes. He said he heard Mr. T. Harrington, M.P., declare that he would sooner lose £200 than that Mr. Richard Burke, a "landlord's strapper and lickplate," should be returned in place of a League candidate, at an election to a local Board of Guardians. The informer went on to say that Mr. Harrington personally ordered him and his comrades to canvass for the votes, but "not to kill" anybody, "not to hurt" anybody, but only "to frighten" voters, and not to drink—"lest we should do something foolish." And Mr. Harrington, continued the witness, told us if the League candidates were elected we might name our own price. To cut a very long story short, the League candidate did get in, but "when we reminded Mr. Harrington of his promise, he told us he had no money, and to go away, and that he was ashamed of us." But, said the witness, a few days after that a man met us and gave us seven pounds, and cautioned us not to trouble Mr. Harrington any more on the subject. The rest of Thomas O'Connor's startling story was largely occupied with details about his visit to America. He declared it was his belief that nobody could be a "Boy" unless he first was a leaguer. He stated that he received his orders from the "Captain," who was instructed by the League Committee.

The above story, told with much detail, produced a great effect. Here, at last, after the Commission had been sitting five weeks, was a definite accusation against one of the incriminated sixty-five. The informer's story was precise and circumstantial. It accused the Secretary of the National League, one of the leaders of the Parnellite party, by name, and it gave place and date. But the witness had been "sprung upon" the Court. Sir Charles Russell had had no intimation that this informer would be produced. Nor had the accused Member of Parliament, Mr. Harrington. Under the circumstances, Sir Charles Russell asked if his cross-examination of O'Connor might be postponed. Mr. Reid and Mr. Lockwood joined in the request,—which was granted, after Sir Charles Russell put a few questions, from the answers to which it appeared that O'Connor had long since been in secret communication with the police, and in correspondence with the landlord association known as "the Irish Loyal and Patriotic Union."

TWENTY-FIFTH DAY.

DECEMBER 5.

A UNIQUE story of juvenile depravity was the principal, and most interesting, event in to-day's proceedings. But before this story was told, Jeremiah Hegarty and his boycott had to be disposed of. In this last and concluding part of the Hegarty evidence, Dr. Tanner, M.P., was one of the most conspicuous persons named. Two Irish constables named Moroney and Hobbins went into the witness-box to quote some specimens of Dr. Tanner's oratory. The doctor denounced Mr. Hegarty as a "low, creeping reptile." "An infamous being," added the doctor—immediately correcting himself by saying that Mr. Jeremiah Hegarty did not deserve to be called a "being," unless it was "the lowest of creeping things—a louse."

"You picked out the plums," Sir Charles Russell remarked, when he cross-examined Mr. Moroney. "Yes," the sergeant replied, with just a touch of simplicity. Then Hobbins followed Moroney, with more illustrations of Dr. Tanner's picturesque manner; for this time, poor Jeremiah Hegarty figured as a "parasite of infamy," likewise as "a louse that fed on the rotten carrion of the landlords." How were the doctor's speeches at Millstreet taken down? Why, in long hand, and after the speeches were over. Neither of the two constabulary witnesses was a shorthand writer, and the first of the two admitted that his report of Dr. Tanner's speech was his first experiment of the kind.

Constable Hobbins having been dismissed, Mr. Atkinson proceeded to read out, in detail, a long list of threatening notices, directed at Mr. Jeremiah Hegarty. One notice threatened with powder and shot any who would buy from Mr. Hegarty. Another described Mr. Hegarty as a "pauper." Imagine calling a man a "pauper," who, while he twirls his gold watch-chain in the witness-box of Probate Court No. 1, tells Mr. Biggar and the lawyers that he cares nothing for, and is prepared to fight another seven years, the boycotters who have sliced off two thousand annually from his business profits! As Mr. Atkinson went on with his reading, the judges showed some signs of impatience. The President, in an appealing, kindly tone, asked Mr. Atkinson if it was necessary to go through "all that"? Mr. Atkinson took the hint: the remaining papers were handed in without being read; and Mr. Jeremiah Hegarty at last disappeared from the scene—to the relief of judges, lawyers, and public.

The story of the Cork County witness named Williams is interesting merely as an illustration of the inferential manner in which outrage was attributed to local branches of the League. He was shot by moonlighters. Why? Because, said he, I took an evicted farm. By whom? By the local branch of the League. Why did he think it was the League? Because, he said, the branch secretary warned him some time before of the consequences. But when Sir Charles Russell cross-examined him, Williams admitted that the secretary spoke to him in a friendly manner. In that case, suggested Sir Charles, was it not possible that the secretary, knowing the popular feeling against land-grabbing, did not mean to threaten you, but only to warn you against possible danger?

Another witness, Cornelius Regan, of Charleville, county Cork, admitted that the local branch denounced a moonlighting outrage of which he had been the victim.

The Attorney-General now "sprang upon" his opponents a boy-informer, an awkward youth, with small, restless eyes, who looked confused and frightened as he reluctantly entered the witness-box. This boy-informer came from Mayo. As soon as he began the tale of his adventures it became clear that he was well acquainted with the history of his corner of the county. Kiltimagh was the name of the place where he lived, and he told their lordships how he saw local leaguers, officials of the branch, follow a man about the shops and warn the townsfolk that the man was boycotted. James Walsh—that was the boy's name—described how committee-men of the branch were appointed to "look after" boycotted people; how he himself had written and posted up threatening notices issued by the branch committee; and how not long ago the branch warned people who did not join the Plan of Campaign. No wonder that Master James Walsh was so ready with his details. For Master Walsh was "secretary" of the Kiltimagh branch of the National League. He afterwards explained that he shared with a "joint" his load of official cares and responsibilities. Still even to be only a joint secretary of the great national organization did seem a rare distinction for a youth of his years. As he stood there in his box, the spectators watched him with amused curiosity. His cheeks and chin smooth as a cherub's, young Master Walsh might easily pass for a man just tottering on the verge of fifteen—or sixteen at the most. "Speak up, my boy," Sir Charles Russell would often call out in the course of "my boy's" examination by Sir Richard Webster. "What's your age, my boy?" said Sir Charles, in the same fatherly manner, when, rising up, and shaking his brown pocket-handkerchief, he prepared to try conclusions with Master Walsh. "Nineteen!"

Then came the revelations. Mr. Walsh informed Sir Charles Russell that he was "appointed secretary in December, 1887," and that he "gave up" the office the month after. It was not the office that retired from Mr. Walsh, but Mr. Walsh who retired from the office. Why? Mr. Walsh's answer was somewhat to the effect that it was not worth his while to keep the post. "Very well," exclaimed Sir Charles, soothingly, "very well." He paused. He looked up.

"Did the League ever make any charge against you?"—(It was now the ex-secretary's turn to pause.) "I don't remember." said he, thoughtfully.—"No charge about pilfering funds?"—"I believe there was."—"How much was it?"—"Ten shillings."—"Is it true that you took it?"—"It is true, sir."—"Did you take some money belonging to an athletic club?"—"Yes."

Were you agent to a plate-glass insurance company?—Yes.
Did you insure your mother's windows?—Yes.
Did you make out that your mother's windows were broken, and that they were made of plate-glass?—Yes.
And did you make a claim upon the company?—I did, sir.
Was your claim found to be fraudulent, and were you dismissed from your agency?—Yes.
And was your claim fraudulent?—It was.
Were you afterwards appointed agent for a life assurance company?—I was.
What company?—The Gresham.
Did you represent that a Mr. D. Smythe, the editor of *The Western People*, wanted to get his life insured for £500?—I did.
If that were true you would have been entitled to get a commission upon the premium?—Yes.
Was it true?—It was not true.
Mr. Smythe knew nothing about the matter at all?—He did not.

"Very well," Sir Charles Russell exclaimed, accenting the "very," as he resumed his seat. Mr. Walsh's demeanour, as he thus divulged some of the chief episodes in his versatile career, was noteworthy. Mr. Walsh gave his answers in a low voice, certainly; but also with a matter-of-fact, half indifferent air, as if the embezzler in question were not a person to whom Mr. Walsh bore intimate and essential relation, but a person in whom Mr. Walsh felt only a remote interest. It was pretty much as if Mr. Walsh were all the while speaking of himself not as "I," but as "he"—apostrophizing himself in the third person.

Mr. Walsh, having made a clean breast of his history, proceeded to make some disclosures of the methods by which the case for the prosecution was got up. He made them in reply to questions by Mr. Davitt.

Was any threat made to you to prosecute you if you did not give evidence?—Yes.
Who by?—The District Inspector. He said he did not know what would happen about the Insurance Company.
You took that as a threat?—Yes.
Do you know whether your mother was visited before this by a policeman?—I do not know, but she would have told me had she been.
Does your mother place any confidence in you?—She does. The Inspector asked me to tell him what I knew about the League.
Did he mention names to you?—I don't think he did. The policeman O'Connor accompanied me from Kilkiesa to the boat. I had £5 given to me in Dublin, and I saw Mr. George Bolton in Mr. Soames's office.

Cross-examined by Sir Charles Russell, young Walsh said, in reference to the message a constable had given him to call upon the deputy inspector of police, that he did not know whether deputy inspectors were in the habit of looking up witnesses for *The Times*, but that at all events they had looked *him* up.

After young Walsh came an interesting old man, Jeremiah Buckley by name. But it was difficult to get anything out of Mr. Buckley. Mr. Buckley was deaf. Nodding good-naturedly at Mr. Graham, to whom fell the duty of examining him, he remarked that if Mr. Graham expected to get information, one of the two must approach the other. Whereupon Mr. Graham clambered out of his bench up to the witness-box. Mr. Graham rested his right elbow on the ledge; Mr. Buckley both his elbows—clasping his hands, and smiling into Mr. Graham's eyes—as who should say, Now, then, shout away. Mr. Graham did shout, into Mr. Buckley's left ear. "Do you hear me?" "I live in Cark" (Cork). Mr. Graham's complexion is naturally ruddy. But it grew still ruddier under the stress of Mr. Graham's vocal exertions. While Mr. Graham shouted, Mr. Buckley communicated his replies softly. The substance of his story was that the moonlighters cut off part of his right ear because he paid his rent. They cropped it with a pair of scissors.

Having given this information, Mr. Buckley turned round his left ear for Mr. Graham's next question. "What sort of a scissors was it?" Mr. Graham shouted into the left ear, at the top of his voice. "I don't think," responded Mr. Buckley with a smile and a nod, "that they were good scissors." After this Mr. Graham climbed back into his bench, and Sir Charles Russell's turn came. Mr. Buckley came up to Sir Charles. After a while, the two gentlemen made good progress—Mr. Buckley frankly admitting that, though he himself had been satisfied with a rent reduction of 3s. in the pound, he did not consider that his poor neighbours could have got on without a more liberal allowance.

A fair type was Mr. Buckley, of the good-natured Irish peasant who does his best to put up with the hardships of life as he finds them. "I've only seven of a family," he declared. "Only seven!" "You have no other means of livelihood, except your farm?" Sir Charles called out loudly, with his mouth close to Mr. Buckley's left ear. "The divil a bit." "What's your children's food?" "Potatoes and male" (meal). Then Sir Charles, pausing as if he were taking breath for another effort, applied himself to the left ear. "I suppose you have a joint of roast every day?" "What'sh that?" returned Mr. Buckley, in a loud whisper. But the question was, what had the ear-cropping of Mr. Jeremiah Buckley to do with the league branch? And all that Mr. Buckley would say was that he had never suggested that his midnight visitors were leaguers. Nor, he added, had he ever been boycotted. Of course Sir Charles Russell's questions about the children's potatoes, &c., were put with a purpose. They were designed to show that the prevalent state of poverty in the district where Mr. Buckley lived was in itself sufficient—without any political organization such as the League—to stir up the tenantry into acts of violence against persons who went "behind their backs" to pay the landlord a rent they considered exorbitant. The Attorney-General, on the other hand, endeavoured to counteract the effect of Mr. Buckley's admissions about potatoes by asking Mr. Buckley whether he had saved any money. "No," replied Mr. Buckley, this time pretty sharply, "I don't have half enough."

TWENTY-SIXTH DAY.

DECEMBER 6.

ON the reassembling of the Court to-day the President, Sir James Hannen, announced that Patrick Molloy had been brought to London, and would —if counsel on both sides accepted the suggestion—be placed in the witness-box at once. The suggestion was promptly agreed to by the Attorney-General, and for the other side by Mr. Lockwood. Patrick Molloy has for some time been exciting curiosity. He has been described as a *Times* "dark horse"—as one who could throw strong light on past relations between the leaguers and the invincibles. On the other hand, it has been reported in Dublin that Molloy amused one of *The Times* agents with imaginary tales, which he would disavow in the witness-box. Anyhow, Molloy was served last week, in Dublin, with a subpœna; and the Commissioners' order for his arrest was issued in consequence of his refusal to obey it.

Where is Molloy? the President asked, bending over his desk. Then, through a doorway in the screen beneath the Commissioners' bench, there emerged two detectives, leading between them a young man, who carried a carpet bag and an overcoat, just as if he had arrived from, or was about to start upon, a journey. He was good-looking, and he seemed intelligent. But in addressing the President his manners were, to say the least, lacking in deference. The following conversation took place between the President and Patrick Molloy :—

What is your name?—Patrick Molloy, sir.
We have been informed that you were served with a subpœna. Is that true?—Yes.
Why did not you attend?—Because the amount of money I got was not sufficient to bring me here.
How much did you get?—Four pounds with the subpœna.
You admit that you received £4—that was amply sufficient?
It was not, under the circumstances.
The President—We are the best judges of that, and we are of opinion that £4 was enough.
Very good.
Then you ought to have attended, and not having attended, you have subjected yourself to the action of the Court, and accordingly I commit you to prison until further orders.

So young Molloy disappeared, with his brace of detectives, through the doorway in the screen, for a short sojourn in prison.

"Mike Burke!" And Mike Burke, answering to his name, shambled, with bent head, into the witness-box. At the announcement of Mike's place of residence—Ballyronan, border of Galway and Mayo—Sir Charles Russell protested. "Why are we skipping to Mayo?"—county Cork not being done with. Once or twice before Sir Charles had witnesses "sprung upon him" by the Attorney-General, and he objected to a repetition of the process. But he was overruled, and Mr. Michael Burke, ex-Land Leaguer, ex-Secret Society man, proceeded to unfold his startling and, if true, damning and diabolical tale. Here at last, by his own account, was the informer who could bring home to the leaguers of Mayo the murder of Lord Mountmorres. In his preliminary answers he stated that he had collected money for his branch of the League; that twelve or fifteen years ago in Jarrow, near Shields, he joined a secret society; that he returned seven or eight years since to Mayo, where he became a member of the League, collecting money for it, attending its meetings, and learning its secrets.

"You remember Lord Mountmorres's murder?" asked Sir Richard Webster, after a long pause, dropping his voice. Yes. And before the deed was done the leaguers held a meeting — whereat the victim's name was mentioned. Burke was there himself—at the house of Pat Carney. And he remembered the leaguers who were present—naming them. What did they say and do? Oh, it was "drawn down" that he should be done away with. "Drawn down" meant talked over. It must have been a murderous company, according to Informer Mike, for it was also "drawn down" that two other landlords should be "done away with." Informer Mike, as he stood there in his box, spoke about despatching his fellow-creatures to the other world as indifferently as if he were talking of sending something by parcel-post. "Yes," Mike went on, with a reflective nod of the head, and leaning his elbow on the ledge of his box, Lord Mountmorres was to be "done away with," but as to the others it was "disagreed on."

On the side of the high-road where Lord Mountmorres was murdered, and some hours before the murder, Mike was working on a stone wall. As he worked away, Pat Sweeney came up to him. Help us "to do away with Lord Mountmorres?" asked Pat. "I will not," replied Mike; "I have a wife and children to look after." "I might do it but for that," Mike now explained, in answer to the Attorney-General. As he said this Mike gazed fixedly at the ceiling, and tapped the desk, reflectively, with the tips of his fingers. Mike really seemed to be lost in thought—totally oblivious of the presence of my Lords Commissioners and the triple row of gentlemen in wigs.

"See any one else?" Sir Richard Webster asked, in his quiet, slow way, bringing Mike back from the clouds. Oh, yes; Pat Mulrow, another leaguer, came up to Mike while Mike worked at his stone wall. Pat Sweeney remarked to his friend Mike that he expected Lord Mountmorres would be done away with that evening. A little while after, the doomed man himself passed that way. Mike saw him—and minded his own business, thinking all the more perhaps.

His day's "job" finished, Mike trudged off to the public-house—and there he found, besides Carney (the keeper of the public-house), his fellow-leaguers, Barrett, Mulrow, Murphy, Handbury, Hennelly, and William Bourke, and Fallow and Pat Sweeney. Again, Sweeney and Carney tried to induce him to "lend a hand" in "doing away with" Lord Mountmorres. "What did you say?" asked Sir Richard. "I told Carney that I might go." They went on with their talk, and doubtless with their drink, and in about an hour's time "I missed some of them," said Mike. He could hardly have expressed it better had he been a literary artist.

In another hour they came back, and on Mulrow's hand he noticed something. Then, said Mike, we went home together, and they told me they had done away with Lord Mountmorres. Though the informer gave his answers after many reflective pauses, he yet gave them clearly and decisively enough. He was circumstantial; still retained a minute recollection of the events preceding the murder; and ran off the names of his League confederates with sufficient readiness. But when Sir Charles Russell took him in hand Informer Mike became changed. He seemed to have completely forgotten the most familiar events of his life. His answers—given out with slow deliberation—alternated between doubt and blank ignorance. He forgot the year in which he returned from North England to Ireland. "Don't know what ye mane," he growled. "What year is this?" asked Sir Charles Russell. But Mike wouldn't swear to it. It might be '87, '88, '89. "Can't swear to it," repeated Mike, taking hold of himself by his coat collar, and slowly nodding, with the air of a cautious man who did not like to commit himself.

He could not tell how long he had been in Jarrow, nor whether he had worked years or only months for the same master. "Might be months, might be years," he uttered, thoughtfully gazing once more at the ceiling. Nor could he tell the name of the secret society of which he was a member; nor did he remember his oath, if there was one; nor whether he used to know, and be known by, his fellow-members by means of signs and passwords. "Were you sworn on a book?" "I was sworn in a back yard," was the reply. Mike was growing more and more unmanageable. He would repeat Sir Charles's questions; or reply with an "Eh," or with a nasal snarl of an "m'm." In his fits of silent contemplation he would thrust out his bushy chin, stare at the ceiling, shrug his shoulders, tap with his forefingers.

"Look me in the face," exclaimed Sir Charles Russell at last, sharply; and then one saw that Mike's full face was much more unpleasant than his profile. Hitherto he had looked nobody in the face. Now, however, he gazed at Sir Charles Russell steadily. Mike had small eyes, slightly oblique; narrow, receding forehead, wide cheekbones. But the chief feature was the mouth—a short, tight, straightish slit, almost expressionless.

The informer had been, as already said, glib enough with the names of hi fellow-leaguers; but now, when Sir Charles Russell cross-examined him, he could not say who asked him to join, nor whether the meetings which he had attended, really were Land League meetings; nor even whether a League branch existed in the locality before the murder. There might have been, and there might not! But Sir Charles Russell had a long struggle with him before he got that admission from him. To the Attorney-General the informer said that Carney was secretary of the League. All he could now say was that Carney was secretary of "something." He was not even sure that all those men whose names he had given were leaguers. They might, or might not! Mike's evidence seemed to be falling to pieces. When pressed on these last questions he seemed uneasy. Then, once more, he became absorbed in the architecture of Mr. Street's masterpiece. Then he began to button his coat—taking a long time about it. "When you've done buttoning your coat, you will perhaps attend to me," exclaimed Sir Charles.

"Attend to me!" Sir Charles Russell repeated, sharply. Mike looked down, stuck his elbows on the ledge; his shoulders rose about his ears; and the obliquish eyes flashed viciously.

"Who saw you about your evidence?" Sir Charles asked. "I don't understand," said Mike, after a long pause. No answer would Mike give save "Eh"—"eh"—"m'm," as he thrust out his chin, took hold of himself by his coat collar, and became lost in thought. "Can't you answer?" the President interposed, sharply. "I don't understand what the man manes," retorted Mike, pointing, with his thumb, to Sir C. Russell. Sir Charles's questions were meant to elicit from him whether he had been nursed and primed, so to speak, for the day's work by policemen and others. But Mike would only say that he "expected" his evidence was read over to him; he could not tell whether he rehearsed his evidence yesterday or the day before. "Was it read over to you this morning?"—to which question there were three successive answers. "It might," "I think it was," "It was." But then a cloud of black, impenetrable forgetfulness instantly passed over Mike's mind, for he could not tell whether the reading took place in his lodgings.

Burke was a month in gaol on suspicion of having murdered Lord Mountmorres. Mr. Davitt now tried to get some definite information from him, but vainly. Mike Burke "might or might not" have been tried before Lord Mountmorres; he "might or might not" have sworn the dreadful Ribbon oath; the police authorities "might or might not" have talked to him about the evidence he was to give in court. Nothing more could Mr. Davitt get from him.

You saw Lord Mountmorres twice on the day he was murdered, and knew there was a vote to murder him?—I was not sure he was going to be killed.
Did you not know that his life was in danger?—It might have been.
Dit it occur to you to go and warn him?—Of what would I be going to warn him? How was I to know that it was to be done?
Do not you think that would have been a manly and Christian duty to perform?—I was at my work, and it was not likely I was going to lay aside my work for anything.
Not to warn a man in danger of murder?—I was employed by another man, and I could not leave my work before six o'clock.
You could go into a plot to murder a man, but you could not warn him?—You are too clever a man for me. I do not understand.

Informer Burke then left the box, and Mr. Atkinson returned to county Cork in search of more outrages. The most important of the outrage-witnesses for Cork was a Mr. Kelleher, who was shot at by moonlighters, because he took possession of a farm as security for a loan which the borrower was unable to pay. Mr. Kelleher declared emphatically that to the best of his belief the Land League had nothing to do with the outrage. He also admitted that compensation was refused him in court, on the ground that the whole thing was a "family quarrel." But there was in Mr. Kelleher's evidence something more interesting and important. He revised Mr. Hussey's history of Arcadia. It will be remembered that Mr. Hussey, landlord and agent, described the country during 1848 to 1879 as content and prosperous. But Mr. Kelleher was brought up on one of the estates on which Mr. Hussey was agent, and he remembered its history—how people were evicted in the horrible times of 1848-9; how people died of hunger, how people were buried without coffins. Who was responsible for these evictions?—Why, Mr. Hussey, said the witness.

TWENTY-SEVENTH DAY.

December 7.

WHEN Mr. Patrick Molloy appeared in court to-day, at twenty-five minutes to eleven o'clock, he found waiting for him—besides the Commissioners, and seniors and juniors three deep—a crowded and curious audience. The conflicting rumours about what Mr. Patrick Molloy would do—expose the leaguers, according to one account; "dish" and make sport of *The Times*, according to another—aroused interest in him. So when the usher called out for Patrick Molloy, every eye was turned to the entrance through which Mr. Patrick Molloy was composedly elbowing his way in the custody of a police-officer. Handing his coat to somebody—with the air of a grand duke attended by his valet—Mr. Molloy as composedly walked into the witness-box. He raised the sacred volume lazily to his lips, jerked it aside (a slight jerk it was, executed with a little turn of the wrist)—he slowly stuck his thumbs into his waistcoat pockets, and he gazed calmly, first at the lawyers and then at the galleries. Mr. Patrick Molloy has a lofty, square forehead, straight well-shaped nose, large eyes under level brows, nicely-rounded chin, short upper lip.

"Where do you live?" said the Attorney-General. "Well," replied Mr. Molloy, "my present address is Holloway Gaol, London." The ghost of a flicker of a smile passes over the usually rigid features of Mr. Justice Day. Then Mr. Patrick Molloy, leaning his right elbow on the ledge, crossing his legs, and assuming a picturesque attitude, directed his calm, level gaze on Mr. Attorney.

It would be difficult to say which of the two seemed the more unconcerned. The Attorney-General, after about an hour's examination of Mr. Patrick Molloy, could scarcely get anything out of him except negatives. The reader will understand at a glance the importance of this, by bearing in mind that the questions put to Mr. Molloy by the Attorney-General were merely the interrogative forms of distinct statements alleged to have been made by Mr. Molloy to *The Times* agents in Dublin. Listening to the Attorney-General's questions, one heard what purported to be the witness's own depositions to *The Times* agent—depositions read out to him for his correction and approval before their transmission from Dublin to *The Times* solicitors in London.

But here, in the witness-box, was Patrick Molloy absolutely, contemptuously denying—in his long string of negative answers—that he had said this, that, and the other thing to *The Times* agents a week or two ago in Dublin. He was charged with having said in Dublin that he was a Fenian. Here he averred that the charge was a fabrication. Nor did he know Carey the informer— "never knew the man in my life"—nor was it true that that paper (nodding at it carelessly) from which the Attorney-General was reading had been written in his presence; nor was it true that *The Times* agent read it out to him for his approval; nor did he read it himself; nor was it true that he said he had been invited to join the Invincibles some years ago; nor was it true that he knew Mr. Davitt, nor that he said he would make strange revelations about Mr. Davitt.

Molloy described in some detail how the correspondence between *The Times* agent and himself was begun by *The Times*, and how the agent paid him £11 —because "I told him I could not leave for London unless I paid two small debts." But, as Molloy now admitted, he owed no debts—though he enclosed the money in two envelopes addressed to his supposed creditors, and posted them in the presence of *The Times* agent. "You thought you were going to get over him?" said Sir Richard Webster. "I did nothing of the sort," retorted Molloy, "but I wanted to show up" how *The Times* agents were doing their work. In other words, as—according to Molloy—*The Times* agents would make him out to be a Fenian and an Invincible, and an associate of murderers, why Mr. Patrick Molloy would fool them to the top of their bent and give them a good run for their money. That was his way of putting it.

But, said Sir Richard, trying him again, did you not tell Mr. Walker, *The Times* agent, that it would be dangerous for you to come to London? "I did," replied Molloy, wrinkling his forehead, and shrugging his shoulders slightly. "Did you think it would be dangerous?" continued the Attorney-General.

"Not at a-a-all," drawled out Mr. Molloy, thrusting out his under lip, half-closing his eyes, and smiling, as if in kindly compassion at Mr. Attorney's simplicity. "But didn't you say you would be shot if you gave evidence?" "I did; but there was no danger at all. Ach!" said he, pointing carelessly with his thumb to Mr. Walker, who sat on the solicitors' bench, "that man thought I knew a lot about the Fenians, and that I could tell lots of things about Davitt and all that; they supposed I knew a great deal"—and here Mr. Patrick Molloy laughed, privately, as it were, holding his head down, balancing himself on his elbows, and slowly rubbing his palms together.

The Attorney-General now struck out another line of cross-examination. He tried to get Molloy to admit that he had been an Invincible, had known, and been actively connected with, the Phœnix Park murders. But though Molloy admitted he knew some of them more or less distantly, he denied he knew they were Invincibles. He remembered having read in the papers, early in 1883, that Farrell, one of the Phœnix Park criminals, turning informer, denounced a person named Molloy, as having been one of the gang. He also admitted that, after reading the intimation in the papers, he left for America, without giving any notice to his Dublin employer. But he denied that he thought Farrell's confession referred to him personally.

To Sir Charles Russell, who cross-examined him, Molloy said that he remained less than two years in America, that he returned "in his own name," that he had been living in Dublin ever since, "openly." Then Sir Charles invited Molloy to tell his story in his own way. Sir Charles placed his right foot on the seat, and his elbow on his knee, listened, and took a pinch or two of snuff. Young Mr. Molloy, leaning forward over his box, with his elbows on the ledge, poured forth his story—wherewith he himself seemed at times to be highly delighted.

What did Mr. Walker, *The Times* agent, say to you?—He said he knew all about me; that Mr. Davitt was a Fenian, and that so also were Dr. Kenny, M.P., Mr. John O'Connor, and Mr. Biggar. He sought information from me about them and others.

Then I may understand from your consulting your friends in this business that you were humbugging *The Times* agent?—Yes; I was humbugging him.

According to Molloy's story, it was *The Times* agent who began the game. Molloy was at the time a publisher's traveller. Mr. Walker looked over his books and "plates," admiring them, as if he meant to buy. At last Mr. Walker threw off his disguise. "I am *The Times* agent," said he; and what he wanted was, not books and plates, but information. Molloy had none to give. Come now, you have, said, in effect, the agent; I can prove you were a Fenian, a Leaguer, and an Invincible; tell me what you know about Egan, Byrne, Sheridan, Kenny, and the rest. And then it was, according to Molloy's tale, that Molloy resolved to make sport of *The Times*. Before Mr. Molloy left the box, a question or two was put to him by Mr. Davitt :—

Did you understand *The Times* agent to offer you money if you would incriminate me?—Yes.

Did he seem to care whether you swore truly or falsely?—No.

Do you believe it to be common report in Ireland that the Government and *The Times* are sending all over the country either giving to people or threatening them to induce them to give evidence against me and others?

But here the Attorney-General intervened. And the President ruled that the question was out of order. "Well, my lord," Mr. Davitt said, "that is my belief as to the game that is going on; and I considered this witness was the proper one to be asked the question." To Mr. Davitt the witness conducted himself with marked respect. The low, sweeping bow (accompanied with a smile) with which Molloy gave his answer about "incriminating" Mr. Davitt did considerable credit to Mr. Molloy's histrionic powers.

The last act in this funny piece—about the funniest since the trial began—was short. Mr. Walker, entering the witness-box, seemed somewhat embarrassed—which was natural, under the circumstances. He informed Sir Richard Webster that the person from whom he first got Molloy's name was a Mr. Houston, of the Irish Loyal and Patriotic Union. "Our time wasted," the President remarked. And so the whole case, in so far as the ingenious Molloy was for the time being concerned, fell to the ground. Molloy, from his place in the crowd, watched the collapse.

TWENTY-EIGHTH DAY.

December 11.

To-day's business ranged over Cork, Mayo, and Kerry—but principally over the second-named. As it was expected that the informer, Thomas O'Connor, would be reproduced for cross-examination, the court was full before half-past ten o'clock, in spite of the dense fog. As soon as it was seen that the informer would not be examined that day, the visitors began to leave. If excitement was the object of their visit they lost nothing—for the proceedings were the least interesting since the trial began.

"My Oh!" exclaimed Sir Henry, "I don't understand you. What do you mean by 'My Oh'?" The person addressed was a police officer from Swynford district. Mr. M'Ardell gazed in surprise at Sir Henry James. And then it was explained to the learned counsel that Mr. M'Ardell meant Mayo county. Mr. M'Ardell, a district inspector, gave an account of threatening notices which had been posted up, in 1882, throughout the locality, and in which the tenants were invited to pay no rent and to avoid the land courts. Of course, the theory of the prosecution was that these threatening notices were the work of the leaguers. But Sir Charles Russell, for the opposite side, elicited the fact that distress existed in the locality before the establishment there of the Land League. This witness also stated that at the period of the threatening notices several secret societies existed in the neighbourhood; and again, that outrages increased after the League leaders were imprisoned.

Four witnesses were called by the prosecution to give evidence as to the state of Swynford district during the early days of the League. The most interesting of the four was Ann Gallagher, daughter of a tenant who had been moonlighted for (as it was alleged) paying his rent. Like most Mayo folk, she pronounced the letter "s" as if it were "sh." So, by the way, does her excellent Archbishop, whose name was mentioned once or twice in the course of the day's proceedings. Asked what the moonlighters were like, Miss Gallagher replied that "they were dressed in black clothes, like the poleesh." The rogues who visited her were cowards, for, said she, "they gave me a few blows." As for Mr. Gallagher, her father, they "tould him to keep his rint in his pocket and to fortune his daughter." Fortuning his daughter meant giving her a dowry on her marriage. All over Ireland it is the common expression that Pat So-and-so had such-and-such a "fortune" with his wife; fortune, it is called, whether the amount be ten pounds or ten hundred.

Next followed a money-lender, or "gombeen man," as he is called in Ireland. His name was Sloyne. He, too, guilty of having paid his "rint," was dragged out of bed at night and given "a few shtrokes." A few strokes, said Mr. Sloyne, almost jauntily, as if the strokes had been administered by a lady's fan—or as if they came in the ordinary course of nature like "a few" drops of rain. In answer to Mr. Davitt, this little gombeen man stated that he charged, as yearly interest, three shillings in the pound—which, to do Mr. Sloyne justice, seems moderate for a gombeen man. Mr. Davitt's questions were intended to find out whether the visitation of the gombeen man might have been caused by harshness to a defaulting borrower, or by his refusal of acknowledgment for sums paid.

The next story, that of David Freeney, was at once a story of a tragical and brutal crime, and a repudiation—as complete as the witness could make it—of the notion that the leaguers could have had something to do with it. Freeney's offence was that he had paid his rent. He described circumstantially how he jumped into "the loft" when the moonlighters came, how they dragged his son outside, how his son escaped from them, how his son was dragged out a second time, how the ruffians fired twice, and how, when he descended from his "loft," he found his son dead on the doorstep. The language of these moonlighters and their victims has a strange significance. When the son was dragged outside by his murderers he was asked to "free himself" from the reproach of having paid more than some of his neighbours were willing to give; whereupon his mother reasoned with the murderers that it was impossible for her son to "free himself," because it was not he who had paid the money. Sir Charles Russell's cross-examination brought out the following facts: that Freeney had only done what "most" of the tenants had already done, or were ready to do—accept a certain rate of abatement; that the League had not objected to the payment of rent with the abatement—25 per cent.; that Freeney declared that the local League had even approved of the compromise. Again, the League denounced the murder; so did the Archbishop of Tuam and the clergy in all the parishes round about. Said Sir C. Russell, "Have you any reason to suppose that the Land League had anything to do with the murder of your son?" "None whatever, sir."

An atrocious murder case—the murder of a man named Dillon, for no other ascertainable cause, said his son in the witness-box, than that he had been seen attending the sheriff at evictions. This was in 1881. The son found the father lying dead by the roadside with a bullet in his head. It was a mysterious case, because, as the witness said, his father was popular in the neighbourhood up to the day of his death. Sir Charles Russell dwelt strongly on this point, with the object of showing that, as the people generally were members of the League, the leaguers, as such, could have had nothing to do with the murder. Very popular? asked Sir Charles. Yes, said the witness, and all the people about came to his "wake," and "my father's funeral was very respectable, very large." After this, there followed a long series of questions about young Dillon's father's habit of going to the neighbouring police-hut to play cards; about one of the policemen having been charged with the murder; about his father's pockets having been found empty, although it was his father's custom to carry a liberal supply of money with him. But nothing definite came of these bald, dreary, and paltry—if occasionally mournful—details.

Dillon's case being disposed of, Mr. Ronan "skipped"—as Sir Charles Russell would say—from Mayo to county Cork, and to a landlord named Mr. Thomson, whose tenants notified that they would not pay unless they got thirty per cent. reduction. This, said the agent, who was now in the box, came about in 1885, and it was the National Leaguers' doing. The leading statement in the witness's story was that after he had served writs upon the defaulters, three tenants voluntarily paid the rent, among them a Mr. O'Donnell, who soon after he paid his rent wrote to the agent requesting that he should be "noticed" again as if the amount were still due. O'Donnell's letter to the agent was read out. The writer declared that his life would be in danger if it were supposed he had paid. Then followed a batch of dull cases, the substance of which must be compressed into a few lines. They were Mayo cases—another "skip" having been made from Cork. The first was pensioner Fahy's. In July, 1881, Fahy's house was fired into, a threatening notice was stuck upon it, because he had taken land from which another had been evicted. The next witness, Moloney, had his ears bored, and his person kicked, for a similar offence. And the third witness, a landlord, named Mr. Carter, had been shot in the leg because, as he said, his tenants were displeased with his treatment of them. Like other landlords, Mr. Carter described the pre-League condition of society as one of contentment. As soon as the first League branch was established in his neighbourhood, tenants who always had been punctual stopped payment, and dissension followed between him and them.

It is the old story. Every landlord, every landlord's agent who has appeared at this trial has said the same thing. Mr. Carter's memory must have been somewhat at fault. He said at first that taking his estates all round, the Land Commissioners had made hardly any reductions on his old rents. But Mr. Reid and Mr. Lockwood quoted some startling figures—in one case a rental of twelve pounds a year having been reduced by the Court to five pounds. Moreover, before he was done with, Mr. Carter admitted that the Land Court might have reduced his rents by 20 per cent.

Lastly, Sir Henry James "skipped" from Mayo to Kerry. As a story of the ordinary relations which in disturbed Ireland subsist between landlord and tenant, Miss Thompson's account of her experiences in leaseholding, in trusteeship, in managing estates extending over thousands of acres, would perhaps be interesting to some people. The best thing in her story was its evidence of her energy and determination, and of her skill as an administrator. She dated her eight years' troubles from January, 1881, when the leaguers held their meeting at Tralee—at which meeting Mr. E. Harrington was present. Miss Thompson narrated how she had been boycotted; how wire ropes were stretched across her path in the dark, to her personal injury; how none would work for her except emergency men; how her property had been destroyed, and her cattle mutilated.

TWENTY-NINTH DAY.

DECEMBER 12.

MISS THOMPSON, whose cross-examination was adjourned yesterday at four o'clock, re-entered the witness-box, and Sir Charles Russell resumed his questions. Miss Thompson was one of the best witnesses—if not the best—who had yet appeared on *The Times* side. But it seemed difficult to understand what connection, if any, Miss Thompson's case had with the Land League.

In most of the cases brought forward by *The Times* the general argument has been somewhat as follows :—In such and such a locality the Land League came into existence at such and such a date, and then there followed a complete change in the conduct and demeanour of the tenants towards their landlords, accompanied by outrages and refusals to pay rent. But Miss Thompson's troubles began long before there existed a Land League branch anywhere in Ireland—to say nothing of Kerry, Miss Thompson's own county. Well, then, where was the connection? As the President put it, towards the end of Miss Thompson's cross-examination, "nothing comes into existence *instanter*." Whereupon the Attorney-General rose to say that it was part of their case to show that speeches, provocative of disorder, had been delivered throughout the whole of 1879, before the League came into existence, as well as after that date. But in this little discussion the Attorney-General made a curious mistake. He said that he could prove the delivery of these 1879 speeches from *United Ireland*. Sir Richard Webster was unaware, or had forgotten, that *United Ireland* was not established until long after 1879. The contention of the prosecution is that though the League did not formally come into existence before October, 1879, it existed months earlier in the speakers who were propagating the doctrines which, a few months later, were to be embodied in the published rules and principles of the League. For example, the Irishtown speech of Mr. Davitt—the Father of the League—was delivered in June, 1879.

"You were never called your royal honour?" said Sir Charles, addressing Miss Thompson. No, Miss Thompson had never been addressed in that style by her tenants—though one of the counsel present remarked that it used to be a common mode of salutation. He was right. A very curious chapter of the social history of contemporary Ireland might be unravelled if the lawyers examined the Irish peasants on their ways of showing respect to their landlords—dismounting and halting by the roadside until the great man passed; standing bareheaded, in rain or in sunshine, outside his study window, awaiting his pleasure; even kneeling before him when they came to pay their rent or ask for a little indulgence.

In so far as Miss Thompson's experience was concerned, the change in the old manners began pretty early in the year of the League. The tenants became "uncivil," said Miss Thompson: they became rude, exacting, and showed signs of a change in opinion on the subject of ownership.

Still, as Sir Charles Russell remarked, all that happened before there was any Land League anywhere. "Well," Miss Thompson exclaimed, quickly, "it (the Land League) was brewing." The expression caused some laughter. "Brewing in the air?" asked Sir Charles. "Yes," replied Miss Thompson, smiling. But if it did not occur to Miss Thompson's tenants to address her as "your royal honour," Miss Thompson was, according to her own candid account, a model "landlord." (The substantive is Sir Charles Russell's.) "Yes," "Yes," "Yes," she said, quietly, firmly, modestly to his successive questions as to whether she considered herself a good landlord, a considerate landlord. And certainly, according to the traditional Irish idea of landlord, Miss Thompson was, and is, a model landlord. Her cross-examination has clearly showed that for administrative ability, and what is called "character," Miss Thompson is perhaps the ablest "landlord" who has yet appeared as a witness for *The Times*.

However, the point at issue was not her ability, but her "goodness," "considerateness," &c., as a landlord and a manager. As regards this point she declared, in reply to Sir Charles Russell, that her tenants always had fair rents. Here Sir Charles became slightly satirical. Were her tenants always "free" agents. Yes, they were. Had Miss Thompson ever given a farthing of abatement until the Land Courts appeared on the scene? Certainly not. And Miss Thompson clearly gave Sir Charles to understand that she considered the Land Courts as meddlers and nuisances. "My tenants," said Miss Thompson, "were all better off before the agitation." After Miss Thompson said this her firm lips closed, with an expression of contempt, as if there could be no mistake whatever in her views of the League and the social history of Kerry.

Sir Charles Russell went into the figures of rent-reductions on the estates owned or managed by Miss Thompson; and the figures were—many of them —startling, for they showed that, in spite of Miss Thompson's estimation about her own "fairness," the Land Courts reduced her rents very largely. To quote a few figures, from £65 to £47; from £78 to £48; from £69 to £43; from £78 to £47; from £45 to £27. In fact, taking one of the chief estates managed by her, Miss Thompson would not be prepared to deny that the average rate of rent-reduction upon it, authorized by the Land Courts, amounted to "nearly thirty per cent." But then, in this firm and resolute lady's opinion, the Land Commission were mischievous interlopers.

"What is your profession?" asks the Attorney-General. "An Irish landlord," quoth the gentleman in the box. Mr. Attorney not only smiles, he laughs. The President is considerably amused, and the genial-looking gentleman in the box looks as if he enjoyed his little joke. When he first appeared, Mr. E. M. Richards, of county Wexford [to which we have for the moment "skipped"], was mistaken for a clergyman—because of his black broadcloth and white "choker." Mr. Richards seemed quite happy, although by his own account he found his "profession" of an Irish landlord uphill work—found it, that is, from the year 1880, the *annus terribilis* of the landowners, and constables. So that, in essentials, Mr. E. M. Richards, of county Wexford, was merely saying ditto to Miss Thompson, of county Kerry.

Up to 1880 Mr. Richards always got his rents—or "my agent did," said he. When asked how, as regards the popular manner and demeanour, he could distinguish between the good old time and the new, he stated that up to 1880 the peasantry were respectful, that they came twice a year, at stated days, punctually to pay their rents; but in December, 1880, his tenants came in a body (he had sixty tenants in all) two-and-two, many of them on horseback, with their spokesman at their head, to say that they would pay no rents higher than the Government valuation. Mr. Richards' was a fairly good picture, in words, of a peasant crowd such as may be seen anywhere, any day, in Irish country places. He described himself standing on his doorstep, watching the cavalcade of mounted labourers and farmers; and, like a good old Irish land-'lord, he told them there and then he would make no concessions to demands advanced in that new-fangled style. As in Miss Thompson's case, the days of peasant deference were gone for ever. One would like to know whether his tenants had ever called him, "Your royal honour."

But how to connect all this with the League? Well, there was the order of time; for a branch of the League now started on its career in Mr. Richards's neighbourhood. Some of his tenants told him that if they paid their rents they "would be shot like dogs," but Mr. Richards knew of no intimidating society or organization of any kind then existing, except this new-born League. Mr. Richards told a story of his being obliged to meet a tenant by appointment in a wood at night, in order to receive from him the rent due. At this stage occurred a dispute between the opposing counsel, an important expression of opinion by the President, and a friendly little "scene" between Mr. Justice Smith and Sir Charles Russell.

Sir Charles Russell, becoming impatient at the diffuse nature of the evidence, and at the sudden "skip" to Wexford, asked if the inquiry was now to extend over that county. Sir Charles appealed directly to the President, who replied as follows:—

Having been referred to upon this matter, I desire to state that I contemplate the future with alarm. We have been engaged for I know not exactly how many days on this inquiry, and we have not got to the end of any one branch of the subject; we have only entered into two of them, and there remain several others at any rate as important as the branches we have entered upon. It is impossible for us, sitting as a court of justice, to interfere, because the only ground would be that the evidence was irrelevant, and to arrive at the conclusion we must hear the whole of it together with the cross-examination. Therefore, all that I can do is to express my earnest hope that the utmost efforts will be made to compress the evidence within some limits, which have, I am bound to say, been somewhat exceeded, in some instances at any rate. Rarely, if ever, can any legal investigation be exhaustive. Life is not long enough, and we must be allowed to hope that the years of our lives may not be consumed by this inquiry.

The Attorney-General pleaded that he had always tried to compress his evidence to the utmost. "That's always the argument," retorted Sir Charles Russell. "And I assure your lordships," added Sir Charles, warmly, "that it has been a matter of great trouble and consideration among counsel on this side as to whether we are really justified in attending here and causing so much expense, to meet some of the evidence." "I think," Sir Charles added emphatically, "that the time has arrived for an expression of opinion from the Bench." Upon this, Mr. Justice Smith, leaning over his desk, remarked—

But your side has not curtailed the cross-examination, Sir Charles.
Sir Charles Russell—That inevitably follows.
Mr. Justice Smith—Pardon me. When you have a long cross-examination, the other side will follow the example.

Mr. Reid, rising quickly, protested that counsel on his side fully and freely admitted the perpetration of these outrages, that it was unnecessary to repeat them, and that "the recital of every incident and detail was done for the ake of drawing the public sympathy to the side of *The Times*;" in other words, that the purpose of all that minute recital was to associate in the public mind the idea of outrage with the idea of the League.

Then Mr. Lockwood, addressing the bench, made a similar protest on his own behalf.

Mr. Justice Smith—I don't say you. I simply remarked that when you make a long cross-examination, the other side will follow.

Sir Charles Russell—It is not that at all. We follow them. You are putting the cart before the horse.

To this Mr. Justice Smith made no reply.

Mr. Richards had his parting shot at the League. He repeated his belief that the illegal agitation in his district was caused by it. Sir Richard Webster then sat down. In the usual order of things, the cross-examination should now be made by Sir Charles Russell and his colleagues. But Sir Charles kept his seat. " I won't ask you anything," he said, throwing a careless glance at the occupant of the witness-box, and then at Mr. Justice Smith. "Nor I," said Mr. Reid.

"Nor I," said Mr. Lockwood. In the somewhat awkward silence that ensued, Mr. Richards disappeared. It was evident that Sir Charles and his colleagues had made up their minds to show, in the most unmistakable manner possible, their determination to set their adversaries a good example, and not to waste time by going over what they regarded as stale or irrelevant matter. Not only did Sir Charles and his colleagues refrain from cross-examining Mr. Richards, but they also followed the same course with respect to all the six witnesses who followed him. "Nothing to ask you—nothing to ask you," Sir Charles repeated, with a more or less marked indication of impatience. The six of them were, so to speak, run into the witness-box and then run out of it.

The most distinguished of the six was a renowned captain, who has rendered the English language some service (or disservice). We mean the gentleman who has added the verb "boycott" to the English vocabulary, and whose name is in consequence as widely known over the habitable globe as are the names of Homer, Moses, Dickens, or Parnell. Captain Boycott, late of county Mayo (we have again "skipped," as Sir Charles would say, from Wexford), is a shortish man, with a bald head, a rim of white hair, and heavy white moustache, and patriarchally rich and flowing white beard. We need not repeat his tale. Is it not written in the columns of the daily press of eight years ago? To the Attorney-General, Captain Boycott (it sounds odd to call him by his own name) made the stock deposition of landlords and landlords' agents: It was all right up to 1879 or 1880 (as the case may be); a set of men, then or afterwards, known as leaguers began to make a noise in the world, and then everything went wrong.

We need not dwell any longer on Captain Boycott's story. Witness No. 2 having made the uninteresting statement that fourteen people accused of boycotting Captain Boycott were defended by counsel who were instructed by a Land League President, was summarily displaced by witness number three, who said something about " Scrab's " (alleged) share in boycotting Captain Boycott. Then number three was run out and number four run in, and number four (who seemed to be still in a fright) told how he worked for the captain a whole week, and how, after that, a bullet came through the "doore." The fifth stated that the leaguers groaned at him because he let out his cars to the captain. And the sixth and last told an almost identical tale. As already said, Sir Charles Russell, Mr. Reid, and Mr. Lockwood would have nothing to say to any of the six.

Part of the first half of the sitting and nearly the whole of the period after luncheon were consumed in the examination of a single witness, District-Inspector Gambell, of Tralee, Kerry, whose evidence was confined to the years 1886-7. His main statement was that he had never been able to trace crime to any secret society except one—namely, the Moonlighters' Society; and that he "believed" moonlighters were leaguers under another name. "That is not the question you were asked," Sir James Hannen remarked. Did he *know* any who were at once moonlighters and leaguers? After a little fencing with the question, Mr. Gambell admitted that he was "not in a position" to make any such identification.

All that Mr. Gambell, then, could say was that he found League branches and the Moonlight Society co-existing—a fact of which all the world was already sufficiently aware. The Attorney-General's position was this—that crimes did follow Land League speeches, and that the alleged "offences" which the moonlighters punished were the very "offences" that had previously been denounced in League branches; and that often the victims of moonlighter outrages were persons who had been found fault with, by name, at League meetings. And to prove that such meetings had been held, and to show what "resolutions" had been passed at them, whole files of *The Kerry Sentinel* were produced in court, and a long time was spent by the Attorney-General and Mr. Atkinson, Q.C., in verifying them. It was a most tedious, dismal process. It was the old story over again, which we feel sure the reader would not suffer if he had the stale details presented to him here afresh. None in court, except, of course, their lordships and the distinguished lawyers immediately concerned—and perhaps here and there a conscientious journalist —paid the smallest attention to Mr. Attorney, Mr. Atkinson, Q.C., and District-Inspector Gambell.

THIRTIETH DAY

DECEMBER 13.

THE first hour and a half of to-day's sitting was occupied with the somewhat rambling examination of a police-sergeant from county Sligo, named Denis Feeley. He was called to give evidence as to the course of events in some parts of Sligo at the time of the foundation of the Land League. His story began with April, 1879, and, to a large extent, was little more than a dry catalogue of meetings, with dates, names of places, and names of speakers, spread over a long series of months. The word "catalogue" was used by the President himself, who clearly showed signs of impatience under Mr. Murphy's chronological infliction. The most important part of the police sergeant's rambling story was one in which he professed to give verbatim extracts from a speech delivered by Mr. Davitt from a hotel window in Claremorris, after Mr. Davitt's return from a popular meeting at Irishtown. The witness appeared to be quite certain that it was Mr. Davitt whose words he was reporting. "But are you quite sure it was Mr. Davitt?" Sir Charles Russell asked, as he rose to cross-examine. The police-sergeant replied that to "the best of his recollection" it was Mr. Davitt. But that was not the question; and as the police officer had just read from his note-book, utterances which he ascribed to Mr. Davitt, Sir Charles insisted upon receiving a more explicit answer. "I believe he was at the meeting," the sergeant then said, rather hesitatingly.

"Why, sir," exclaimed Sir Charles Russell, sharply, raising his voice, "have you not put into Mr. Davitt's mouth words advising the people to be united?" To this the sergeant replied that he could swear he took down those very words immediately after the meeting. But this again was an evasion of Sir Charles's question, which was repeated over and over again, with precisely the same result. At last, Sir C. Russell, turning to Mr. Davitt, who was all the while quietly sitting on the solicitors' bench, said, "There is Mr. Davitt. Is that the man you saw?" "I think so," was the answer. But to cut a long story short, it turned out that Mr. Davitt was not at the meeting where the witness fancied he saw him. Even if it had been Mr. Davitt, the expressions quoted from his imaginary oration were merely of the ordinary stamp of speeches delivered at meetings open to the public.

However, the object of the prosecution was to show that these speeches and meetings of the newly-born Land League, of which Mr. Murphy had given his long catalogue, were followed by refusal to pay rent, and by crime ; and that, except the Land League, no agency had ever been discovered to which these illegalities could by any possibility be traced.

Accordingly Mr. E. Smith, the son of Lord Sligo's agent, went into the witness-box. His story was short. One day in September, 1879, he drove out with his father to collect rents. They were fired at by four people. The shots missed. But Mr. Smith, junior, knew better how to handle his weapons, and he shot dead on the spot one of his four assailants—the fate his would-be murderer richly deserved. Now, this happened in September, 1879, and the Land League was not formally established until October, 1879 (although, as already recorded, the men who founded the Land League began these public meetings as early as April). However, Mr. Smith declared that at the time when the attempted murder took place he was unaware of the existence of a Land League branch, either in his own parish or anywhere else.

"So then," said Sir Charles Russell, "both your father and yourself were armed—was it necessary to carry arms at that time?" "We always carried arms," was the reply. "What! for how long?" "For several years; we always thought it prudent to do it." Sir Charles Russell pressed this point, for obvious reasons—because his opponents have all along been undertaking to prove that deeds of violence—such as the two Messrs. Smith had been providing against "for several years"—were unknown until the League arose, demoralizing and corrupting the population.

Mr. Smith admitted that he remembered hearing about the murder of landlords in Connaught as far back as the years 1869-71. With the view of minimizing the importance of these admissions, Sir Henry James asked Mr. Smith to show how the conduct of the people before 1879—the League year—differed from their conduct subsequently. Mr. Smith's answer was cautious and not very decided—"I think it was harder to collect rents after 1879."

Of poor old Hugh Macauliffe, who followed Mr. Smith, there is very little to be said. He was one of Mr. Smith's herds, and was persecuted for that reason only, so it was alleged. Macauliffe being deaf, and failing to understand what Mr. Murphy was saying, grabbed up his hat and made a brusque attempt to leave his box, and come close up to him. The usher stopped him, and then Macauliffe, with his elbow on the desk and his head stretched out, rattled away in broad Hibernian-English, a description of the midnight attack upon him, when the moonlighters, having replied with "Oh, nothing," to his friendly challenge of "Hullo, boys, what's up?" proceeded to point guns at him, two guns inside his cabin and nine outside. He was not cross-examined. He was promptly dismissed, and away he went, muttering to himself, as it seemed, the untold portion of his history.

Whenever Mr. J. C. Macdonald, manager of *The Times*, appears in court early at a morning sitting, one may feel sure that something unusual is about to happen. Mr. Macdonald appeared very early this morning, and not long after him, there came in James Buckley, a Kerry "labourer."

With his dark, neat attire, and white neckcloth, Mr. Buckley looked fashionable for a labourer. He was tall, and physically strong. Sir Henry James examined him; and Buckley began his very startling story with a declaration that on the 10th of November, 1880, he was sworn a member of the Fenian Brotherhood in the presence of Land Leaguers, in the Land League rendezvous, in the village of Causeway, near Tralee—county Kerry, as already said. Thomas Dea was the man who asked him to join the Brotherhood; and the two Land Leaguers in whose presence he was sworn were Tom's brother—namely, Pat Dea—and Robert Dissett. Having been initiated, the informer, according to his own story, attended many secret meetings of the Fenian Brotherhood, which meetings were held in Pat Casey's house; and there he met numbers of people who were leaguers. Casey's house was, he said, the local League branch's headquarters. The branch secretary was a man named Lynch, and he was also, according to Buckley's testimony, an active member of the Fenian organization. William Feenicks was another leaguer whom he met at these meetings, and among the rest were John McGrath, two men of the name of Harrington, Michael Lawler, and Samuel Hayes. "I attended about a dozen of these Land League meetings in the years 1880-1-2," said the witness.

Buckley, who never was a member of the Land League (though, as he said, he had often attended meetings of the League committee), had been six months in the Fenian Brotherhood when he was called upon to engage in his first murder expedition. This was in May, 1881, when meeting the man Feenicks above named, he was informed by him that an attack would be made that night on a person named Sheehy. Sheehy's supposed offence was that he took a farm from which his brother-in-law had been evicted. "Feenicks told me," said Buckley, that I must assist in the attack, and that "I was to meet the boys" at a spot three or four hundred yards from Sheehy's house. Buckley then proceeded to say that he appeared at the spot at the appointed hour, that he found there the leaguer Feenicks (before whom six months previously he had taken the Fenian oath), and that Feenicks then fired a revolver shot as a signal for the other "boys" to come up. There were eleven of us in all, said Buckley. Among them were Dick Casey (at whose house the League meetings were held), and Sam Hayes and Pat and John Harrington, and Michael Lawler, and Eugene Fitzgerald. "We all had white shirts over our clothes," said Buckley; "there was only one revolver between us, but all, except the man with the revolver, were armed with scythes and pitchforks." The gang was formed up into two companies, one commanded by Eugene Fitzgerald, the other by Feenicks. Buckley went with Fitzgerald's company, which made straight for Sheehy's door, while Fitzgerald's men broke through the windows. But, said Buckley, one of our men came round and reported that a man had escaped through a window; and believing it was Sheehy, and that he was running to the police barracks, we ran away and dispersed. "My orders," said Buckley, "were to drag Sheehy outside, tie him up, and if he refused to surrender the farm to his brother-in-law, to shoot him." This story was given with ready and abundant detail.

A year passed away, and then this interesting witness had his second opportunity of murdering a fellow-creature. This was in May, 1882; and the intended victim was a Michael Roche, whose offence appeared to be that he gave, or was suspected of giving, information to the police—information about the League, of which Roche himself had once been a member, and from which he had been expelled. As Feenicks and Pat Dea had meanwhile been in prison as suspects, the implication in Buckley's evidence was that Roche's disclosures must have led to their arrest. Anyhow, it was at Pat Dea's house that Roche's death was "arranged for," and the arrangement was that the murder should be perpetrated by Fitzgerald, Feenicks, and Buckley.

Buckley and one of his colleagues followed Roche about one day soon after the "arrangement." But they gave up the attempt. "Then," said Buckley, "as I lived next door to Roche, it was decided"—at another meeting of the conspirators—"that I should shoot him myself; and that then I should be sent away to America with the help of Land League money."

The witness also stated that his fellow-conspirators gave him a brace of revolvers and "twenty-four rounds of ammunition" wherewith to practise, so that he might be sure to hit his mark. All these minute details and a great many more were, so to speak, run off the reel without a moment's hesitation.

Informer Buckley's description of his attempt upon neighbour Roche's life was, if not picturesque, at least pictorial. One might fancy one saw Buckley driving home his cattle in the evening, hailing neighbour Roche, asking him how he was getting on; and how Roche answered that he was getting on very well, and how "Mr. Roche's head" was "turned away from me at the time"; and how then "I took out my revolver and fired," and missed. But by firing he meant pulling the trigger, and he missed for the best of reasons—that the bullet refused to go. Then, according to his own account, the informer seized Mr. Roche by the coat collar with his left hand. The trigger clicked four times—that is to say, this neighbourly assassin "fired" four times—and yet the bullets would not go off. After that it was pretty high time for Mr. Roche to provide for his personal safety, which he did by shouting out "murder" and running away.

In the course of this villainous story Buckley said that he had taken the precaution of hiding his revolver in a ditch, in order to avoid the risk of its being found in his possession at home. Well, Roche ran to the police barracks. And Buckley—according to pre-arrangement, ran to Pat Dea's house. At the judicial investigation at Tralee, it was sworn by "witnesses" that Buckley had all the while been in Dea's house (this also was pre-arranged, said Buckley). And Roche made a mistake by testifying that he heard—or "saw"—the bullets whizz past his ears—the fact being according to Buckley that the revolver missed fire. And the investigation ended in Buckley's being let off on his own recognizance.

The above story is the substance of the informer's examination-in-chief. Sir Charles Russell now rose, and questioned him on the subject of his blood-money.

Did you try to get the money to go to America?—Yes. I applied to Fitzgerald, Patrick Dea, and Feenicks.

What was said?—One of them told me I would get the money, but they would have to go to Thomas Diggins, the treasurer of the Land League, for it. In the evening of the same day I saw Fitzgerald and Feenicks, and they gave me 50s., saying that was all the money in the hands of Mr. Diggins as treasurer of the League.

Were you dissatisfied?—I was, and I told them so. Feenicks then told me that I couldn't expect to get any more, as I didn't shoot Roche. They took me to Thomas Dea, and he wrote a letter which he gave me to take to Thomas Pearce, the president of the Land League.

Did you take that letter to him?—Yes. On the following day I gave him the letter, and he read it through and retained it. He told me he would go round to some of the neighbours and collect money to aid me in my escape to America.

Then Buckley described how he went from house to house soliciting money to help him to "escape" to America. Tom Diggin's, at whose house he made his first call, gave him two shillings. Mr. Pearce contributed two more. Then the would-be murderer dunned the branch secretary, who gave him a letter of introduction to another secretary, who gave him five shillings. His collections ranged from one shilling to half-a-crown, the five shillings being a solitary example of munificence. But nothing more serious happened to this intending murderer (as he professed to be) than that he was bound over for twelve months to keep the peace.

Seeing that, according to his own account, there was no particular reason why he should make haste to escape to America, the question arose whether he had any right to keep the money.

Sir Charles Russell—After that, were you asked to return the money?—Yes. What did you say?—I told Mr. Feenicks that I thought I was entitled to the money, and as I had got it I would keep it.

How then were you treated?—I was expelled from the society (the Fenian Society). I ceased attending League meetings, and the people were less friendly with me than they were before.

Said Sir Charles, sharply and loudly, "Can you name one single person in Kerry who would believe you on your uncorroborated oath?" A dreadful question. But, quoth Buckley, "I don't understand you." After one or two repetitions Mr. Buckley candidly and calmly admitted that he "could not tell." Then he said, in reply to Sir Charles's questions, that until early last month he had had no communication whatever with any one on the subject of this trial. He voluntarily offered information, and the offer was made to the resident magistrate, Mr. Cecil Roche, by letter, through the post, and Mr. Roche, instead of replying by letter, sent Sergeant Clarke to interview the supposed ex-Fenian and would-be murderer. It was at first understood that never before had Buckley had communications with the police; but he now confessed that he had been in communication with the police in the summer of 1882—not earlier; in June, he said. His attempt on Mr. Roche's life was made in May, 1882. The police-constable with whom he was in secret communication in 1882 was Sergeant Clarke. When Sir Charles Russell asked why he put himself into communication with the police in 1882, he answered that it was because he wished to divert police suspicion from himself as a man who had tried to murder Mr. Roche; to be regarded by the police as their friend. Here the witness laughed, as if at his own cleverness.

"Don't laugh, sir," exclaimed Sir Charles Russell, sternly; "this is no laughing matter." "I wasn't laughing," Buckley retorted, coolly. As to the persons who have already been mentioned in the description, he adhered to his statement that they were leaguers. He referred to them as leaguers individually. It did not appear that he meant to say that the leaguers as a local organization—that the League as a responsible body—had anything to do with the attempted outrages. But as to the attempted outrages, "What," Sir Charles Russell asked, with a puzzled expression, "did you want to escape from?" (It will be remembered that after the Roche affair Buckley was merely bound over to keep the peace for twelve months.) "To escape for having tried to shoot Roche," was the reply.

Yet Sir Charles was anything but satisfied with the reply. "Did you mean deliberately to kill that man?" he asked. "Certainly I did," was the answer. "It was a genuine attempt at murder?" "Yes." Mr. Buckley stoutly denied that it was a bogus attempt. He also denied the truth of a story about his having broken open his mother's box to steal money from it, and of his having beaten her because he found none.

One of his statements to Mr. Reid, who cross-examined him after Sir Charles Russell sat down, caused some amusement. In 1885 Buckley was put into Holloway Gaol for having assaulted a policeman, and he assaulted the policeman in order that he might disabuse his Irish fellow-countrymen in Marylebone and elsewhere of their suspicion that he was a detective. He was warned that his throat might be cut, and in order to prove that he was an honest man and no detective, he knocked down an innocent policeman.

Sergeant Clarke, who was in court when the examination of Buckley began, and who, at Sir Charles Russell's instance, was requested to leave, was now recalled. According to Clarke's evidence, it was in October, 1882—several months after Buckley was expelled from the Society—that Buckley told him about the Sheehy affair. And yet nobody was tried for the Sheehy affair. How was that? Mr. Reid asked, in surprise. But Mr. Clarke could not tell why, except that the police authorities thought it best "to await events"— except that to refrain from prosecuting the criminals was the most "prudent" course to adopt, from the view point of a "detective's duty"—as Mr. Clarke expressed it. At four o'clock the cross-examination of Sergeant Clarke was suspended.

THIRTY-FIRST DAY.

DECEMBER 14.

FOR a few minutes before the Commissioners entered to-day, counsel and visitors in court were amusing themselves over a cartoon from *United Ireland*. The cartoon represented their lordships in process of burial under heaps of what the artist or his employers regarded as irrelevant evidence—and worse. Besides this, a copy of *United Ireland* was under the inspection of the lawyers on both sides.

No sooner had their lordships taken their seats than the Attorney-General rose to make an application that Mr. William O'Brien, editor and proprietor of the paper, should be summoned to appear next Tuesday for contempt. It had been already settled that the Commission should rise to-day (Friday) for the Christmas recess, reassembling on the 15th of January, and this sudden application for a Tuesday sitting was the reverse of pleasant.

The Attorney-General, however, held that the offence committed by *United Ireland* was so very flagrant, and its effect in intimidating witnesses so unquestionable, that proceedings should be taken against Mr. O'Brien without delay. To justify his application, Sir Richard read the whole of an article from the current number of *United Ireland*, in which article both the general character of *The Times* evidence and of certain of *The Times* witnesses was described in anything but flattering terms.

Here are some extracts from the article which Sir Richard Webster read out in court :—

> The time is come for very plain speaking on the subject of the Forgeries Commission, which has now been sitting for twenty-seven days in London without getting one inch nearer to the subject which the public understands it was specifically appointed to investigate. So far the evidence has been a meaningless parade of eight-year-old outrages, from all participation in which the victims themselves examined for the "Forger" concur in emphatically exonerating the League. The court has been cumbered with files of old newspapers, and stunned with the opinions of policemen, land-grabbers, evictors, and of one tuft-hunting Catholic clergyman (thank God there is but one in all Ireland to be found in such company) as to the condition of the country and its causes. True, the waste of time has been in some measure redeemed by an open exposure of the methods by which the "Forger" and the Government combined are desperately struggling to escape from the terrible mess in which they have landed themselves. We have no intention of waiting till the "Forger" gives leave to speak. With all respect for the Court, we do not care twopence for the opinion of the three judges specially selected, in the teeth of justly indignant Liberal protest, by the "Forger's" friends and accomplices. Assuming—and it is a large assumption in the judges' favour—that the Coercion Government which specially selected them for their partiality were deceived, their judgment is still beside the question. This is not a matter of judicial decision at all, but of intelligent public opinion.

United Ireland then proceeded to say that the public want to have the vital facts extracted from "the mass of rubbish" in which *The Times* "would hide them;" and that the vital question was whether or not the letters attributed to Mr. Parnell were forgeries. Even Mr. Chamberlain, continued *United Ireland*, admitted that if the letters were proved to be forgeries, the public would care very little for the rest of the charges and allegations.

If these letters are genuine, on the other hand, no further charge is needed to damn the character and career of the Irish leader. The Commission has now been sitting, with brief intermission, for some months, and it has never been allowed even to approach the one subject which the public regards with intensest interest, and on which Mr. Parnell has a right to claim immediate investigation and prompt decision.

Instead of going straight to the point, said *United Ireland*, *The Times* took to dirt-throwing; and then *United Ireland* quoted the boy informer Walsh as an example of a hostile witness—repeating Walsh's own confessions of his having embezzled League money, stolen money from another Irish organization, and swindled two insurance companies by which he was employed. After a sentence or two about the "hoax played off" on *The Times* by the practical joker Patrick Molloy, *United Ireland* wound up with an appeal for prompt inquiry into the real point at issue :—

We desire a cheaper, more sudden, definite, and more overwhelming exposure. The policy of vague malignity and shameless evasion must not last for ever. The country, as well as the accused, is entitled to call on the Court to compel the "Forger" to come to the point. It is about time.

As soon as the Attorney-General was done with his reading, Mr. Reid stood up to make a similar application against Mr. Brodrick, the Warden of Merton College, Oxford, on account of an extraordinary statement of his to which a correspondent has recently called attention in *The Daily News*. Mr. Reid declared that, speaking for himself personally, he would have preferred to leave all such unfair comments—whether in the Press or elsewhere—to the contempt they deserved, the contempt of all honest men. Newspapers on both sides were, Mr. Reid said, guilty of making unjustifiable comments. He denounced such comments as vulgarities, and the Warden of Merton's comments, reported by *The Times*, as the worst of them. Mr. Reid was not questioning the propriety of the Attorney-General's application ; but such an application having been made, he considered it his duty to ask that Mr. Brodrick, of Merton College, Oxford, should be summoned to appear before their lordships. The offence, Mr. Reid argued, was aggravated by the fact that the paper in which Mr. Brodrick's remarks were published, namely, *The Times*, was one of the parties in the present trial. The gist of the matter as regards Oxford was this—there was in Oxford a branch of the National League. Of this branch Mr. Henry George and Mr. Michael Davitt had been guests. And referring to this Oxonian club or branch the Warden of Merton declared that he would not be surprised if it should invite even the Whitechapel murderer—supposing he were found out.

The moment Mr. Reid uttered his expressions about unfair comments, Sir James Hannen made a sudden and emphatic interruption. Frowning and striking the desk with his hand, he exclaimed in a tone of great severity, "If it were in my power I would this instant throw up the Commission on account of these interferences. But we are here to discharge duties imposed upon us by Act of Parliament. I cannot get rid of this duty—I am tied to the stake." After a few minutes' consultation between their lordships it was decided that steps should be taken to secure the attendance of Mr. O'Brien at court tomorrow—Mr. Reid saying he felt sure that if Mr. O'Brien was within reach he would present himself without fail. Later in the day, however, intimation was received that Mr. O'Brien had left for Ireland, where he was to attend a public meeting. And as it was impossible that he could return to London by the hour appointed, it was decided, when the Court rose at four o'clock, that Mr. O'Brien's case should be heard after the Christmas recess.

Thomas O'Connor, the informer whose cross-examination was postponed some days ago, was now recalled. Looking ill and feeble, O'Connor was requested to sit down. Cross-examined by Sir Charles Russell, he repeated many of his former statements, such as that in December, 1880, he became a member of the Land League "Inner Circle." This "Inner Circle" was, as he said in his former examination, the body charged with carrying out criminal resolutions of the open body. The Castleisland branch was formed in October or November, 1880; in a week or two after that, O'Connor became an ordinary member of it; and in a week or two more, one of its secret agents, or "Boys."

O'Connor, replying to Sir Charles, was "quite sure" that until the time he became an Inner Circle "Boy" he had taken no part in outrages. His first exploit was the part he took in the reinstatement of a certain Mrs. Horan to a farm from which she had been removed.

The Land League was suppressed in October, 1881, but, in reply to Sir Charles Russell, the informer maintained that the League continued to meet all the same—secretly, of course—in the secretary's house, and the house of some other leaguer, whose name he mentioned. "Was it not the Ladies' League?" Sir Charles asked; but the witness adhered to his assertion. However, the witness was totally at a loss as to dates. And when asked when the League meeting was held after which an outrage upon a man named Cullatty followed, he could not tell. He declared that the priest, Father Callagher, was present at it, and yet he forgot where the meeting was held and when.

And now came the most interesting part of the cross-examination. In his examination-in-chief by the Attorney-General, O'Connor said that in the spring of 1881 he had met Mr. T. Harrington at a place called Curragh, near Castleisland, county Kerry, and that Mr. Harrington there and then requested O'Connor and his two confederates to procure votes by force—promising them money for their services. The election in question was an election for the local board of guardians, and, according to the informer's story, Mr. Harrington observed—in the street—that he would rather lose two hundred pounds than that the landlords' candidate Burke should beat the popular candidate McSweeney. Here, again, the informer, when questioned by Sir Charles, was greatly at a loss for dates, while as to many other details which it would have been convenient to know, his memory was at fault. Of the two men who were with him when Mr. Harrington accosted them, one had been dead for years, and the other had been abroad for years. These two men were brothers of the name of Rossnan.

Nor, again, could the informer tell Sir Charles the name of any one who had seen him and his two companions talking to Mr. Harrington in the public street.

But in a minute he corrected himself by saying he thought the landlords' candidate saw them. The informer, questioned by Sir Charles, adhered to his first statement as to what Mr. Harrington had said—namely, that they were to visit the voters at night, not to "hurt" any one, but to extort promises from them, and to abstain from drink lest they should do "something foolish." Then the informer gave some uninteresting details as to his midnight visitations, to extort votes—betraying his usual uncertainty about time. Nor was he sure about the date on which he and one of his two confederates went to Tralee to ask Mr. Harrington for their reward; nor did he remember what the place was where he found Mr. Harrington; nor could he name anyone who had seen him in the town of Tralee; nor could he remember exactly what he did with the money when he did get it—nor, at first, what kind of money it was, gold or notes; though he finally stated the money was in notes. However, he repeated his former story, that when Mr. Harrington was asked for the money, Mr. Harrington told him and his friend to be off, told them he had never promised them anything, told them he was " ashamed of them "— but assured them, at last, that somebody would be sent with the money to Castleisland.

Well, some days after the (alleged) Tralee visit somebody did appear at Castleisland, said the informer. At first he spoke as if he meant to say that the mysterious stranger came two days after the Tralee interview. But in a moment or two he said it might have been nine days after. And this mysterious stranger gave the couple £7 between them ; and O'Connor never saw the witness before or since, nor did he know anything about him, nor did the mysterious stranger ask for a receipt or acknowledgment of any sort ; nor, lastly, did O'Connor recollect where he changed his notes—perhaps, he thought, it might have been at the National Bank of Ireland.

Then came a very important part in Sir Charles Russell's cross-examination. In his statement to the Attorney-General, the witness said that in February, 1886, his brother received two letters from Mr. T. Harrington—one an official letter, on the official paper of the National League, and the other a private one, on plain paper. The official one, he said, condemned the lawlessness of Castleisland ; the private one did the reverse. According to the informer, the official one was meant to hoodwink the world ; the private one to encourage the " Boys." The informer stated that he had read them both, searched for them afterwards, and, not finding them, concluded they had been destroyed. But here the informer's memory again proved somewhat weak He could not remember whether he himself had opened the letters. He "thought" he saw them on his brother's desk, and that he had read them there. But now the letter which the witness supposed to have been destroyed was, to his great surprise, produced, and Sir Charles Russell read it.

> At the last meeting of the Organizing Committee of the League I laid before them your application on behalf of the evicted tenants Mary Russell, Mary Butler, and Mary Riordan. I regret to say that the Organizing Committee found themselves compelled to refuse grants, owing to the very disturbed and lawless state of the county of Kerry at the present time. The committee decided upon sending no grants to those districts where continual disturbances had been kept up. I don't wish you to consider that they believe the branches of the National League in any way associated with lawless outrages. They wish to save the general organization from even the suspicion of sending funds to places where outrages of this kind have been encouraged; and they regard this step as necessary for the safety and character of the organization at the present time, and have directed me to communicate their views to the secretaries who have made these applications. —Yours truly, T. HARRINGTON.

The letter was dated February 15, 1886. As for the alleged private letter, Sir Charles Russell, pausing, asked him : " Now, O'Connor, did you ever look for that at all?" emphasizing the last two words. " I did," the witness replied, after a little hesitation. And then followed answers such as these : " I won't swear I opened the letters." " I couldn't swear I did." " I can't remember if my brother gave me them." " I think I saw them on my brother's desk."

Sir Charles Russell and O'Connor gazed steadily at each other, as the former asked him whether any person or persons had requested him to say " queer things " about the Irish members. Instead of answering at once, the informer looked " hard " at his questioner. " Now, take care, O'Connor," said Sir Charles, in a low voice, leaning his elbow on his knee. Sir Charles Russell led up to this question by inquiries as to the informer's past relations with the police—eliciting from him admissions to the effect that he had in September, 1886, received £3 from a police-inspector for information, and shillings, at odd times, from another police-officer, "for a drink." But the witness denied that he either expected or desired remuneration, beyond the travelling expenses to London, for his services as a *Times* witness. His only motive was to help " banish the hell upon earth round my district," at which declaration Sir Charles Russell nodded his head approvingly.

Did Mr. Walker, one of *The Times* agents, ask him to say anything incriminating the Irish popular leaders? "No," the witness replied, "I was only asked to tell everything I knew." It was then that Sir Charles, lowering his voice, looking steadily at the witness and warning him, "Now, take care, O'Connor"—put the above-mentioned question about being requested to say "queer things."

After a little space O'Connor muttered, "Well, I understood he forced me rather hard." "Was that to fix criminality on some of the Irish members?" "I said I wanted to get out of the thing altogether." "Was Mr. Harrington the only member named by Mr. Walker?" "I think so," said O'Connor, somewhat abruptly.

"Is that your handwriting, sir?" exclaimed Sir Charles Russell—"look at the signature only; don't read the letter, sir." (O'Connor, in spite of the order not to read it, was reading it as fast as he could.) "Is that your handwriting?" "I don't know; another person might have written it." "Have you any doubt it is yours?" "It is very like it, but I am not accustomed——." "Have you any doubt, sir?" again Sir Charles exclaimed, almost angrily. And then the answer came, "I have not." "Give me the letter"—and then Sir Charles Russell read it aloud :—

LONDON, *Dec.* 3, 1888.

DEAR PAT,—I am here in London since yesterday morning. I was in Dublin two days. I have got myself summoned for *The Times*. I thought I could make a few pounds in the transaction, but I find I cannot unless I would swear quare things. I am afraid they will send me to gaol or at least give me nothing to carry me home. I would not bother with it at all, but my health was very bad when I was at home, and I thought I would take a short voyage and see the doctor at their expense—(laughter)—but, instead of that doing me any good, it has made me worse a little. I will be examined to-morrow (Tuesday), the 4th. Get some daily paper—*The Freeman*—and see how it will be on it. You need not mind replying to this, as I leave this house as soon as I am examined, which will not be longer than to-morrow (Tuesday). Whichever way it will end do not blame me for it. I thought to do some good, but I fear I cannot, but harm. Tell Martin to have 30s. out of the bank, as I fear I will have to send for the costs, if he has nothing after the fair. I am not needing it, but I am afraid I may. I will write again to-morrow night, or at furthest on Wednesday, if I am alive and at liberty.—Your unfortunate brother, THOMAS O'CONNOR.

The reading of the letter produced a great impression in court. After a moment or two's pause, the Attorney-General rose to state that the witness had received, since the date of his examination-in-chief, telegrams from his friends in Ireland, and a visit from one of his brothers named Martin. He proposed to read the telegrams. Sir Charles Russell objected on one ground, among others, that there was no proof as to who wrote the telegrams. But the President overruled him. And Sir Richard Webster read the first telegram, which was dated 7th of December, and addressed to Thomas O'Connor —"Letter received. Family and friends will die of shame. Contradict all evidence in cross-examination, and all is well. Martin left to-day to see you. Meet him. Reply." The other telegram read by the Attorney-General was received by the witness that morning. Here it is :—

"Costs will be sent to you immediately after the trial. Do as you promised me. Admit being terrified with imprisonment at their hands unless you swore to your statement. The law cannot touch you there when you tell the truth. Be cheerful. Reply immediately. Telegraph. Address Martin, care of Thomas Callagher, Ballymail, Tralee." (To the witness). —Is that the same brother who came to you?—I understand it is.

"There is one more question I wish to ask you," said Sir Richard Webster. "Are the answers you have given Sir Charles Russell to-day respecting what happened in 1880-1-2 true?" "As far as I can remember they are," was the reply, and O'Connor, very pale and bent with weakness, half-shambled half-tottered out of the witness-box.

The rest of the sitting was occupied with the examination of seven witnesses.

The general character of their evidence may be given briefly. All the depositions in chief had this in common, that they were meant to prove that the League, as the League, was directly responsible for boycotting and other forms of intimidation. The first of the seven said he had been a Land Leaguer and then a National Leaguer for years, and that in 1881-2 the chief business of the League was to pass resolutions intimidating tenants who had incurred its displeasure. He said that the people obeyed the League from fear of the consequences of refusal. But he frankly admitted to Mr. Davitt that the same people were more afraid of eviction than of the League. At the end of his cross-examination he became very impatient. "Ach," he said, "I know nothing at all, at all." In that case, said Mr. Lockwood, I need not trouble you with any questions.

Another witness, Moroney, was so voluble, that both sides appeared to be only too glad to get rid of him. He tossed his head, threw his arms about, nodded at the bench, nodded at counsel, laughed, and laughed again as he described how the moonlightersg ave him a "shtab with a bagnet" (bayonet). What did they "shtab" him for? He did not know; but they called him a "blackgyard." Mike Moroney had another fit of laughter, as if the vagueness of the charge of being a blackguard was too much for him. He would have gone on for an hour. But he was sent out of his box without any cross-examination.

Poor old Hannah Connell was amusing in a somewhat different way. She was one of the two heroines of the Milltown Malbay boycott—heroine and victim. She thought she was "fifty," but the universal opinion was that she was eighty if she was a day. She was a little, bright-eyed, red-faced woman, in a white apron, a red gown, and a dark shawl, which she wore—in Irish fashion—over her head. Her voice was an inaudible, feeble twitter; but the speed she went at! Even Sir James Hannen gave up his attempt to follow her. She became hoarse. The court officer politely handed her a tumbler, half full. She tasted, and then she put the tumbler down. They might have given her a more hospitable reception than that. At least that was the thought which crossed one's mind at the moment. Mr. Lockwood must have thought the same thing when, five minutes after, poor Mrs. Connell tried the tumbler again. "I'm afraid that's only water," quoth Mr. Lockwood.

This was too much for Sir Richard Webster. Sir Richard protested, and rather indignantly too. Whereupon Mr. Lockwood, turning round, said he was "sorry for hurting the Attorney-General's feelings." This assurance failed to soothe Sir Richard, who muttered something inaudibly. "Humbug," grumbled Mr. Lockwood, glancing sideways at the Attorney-General.

Mrs. Connell's complaint was that she had been boycotted for taking an evicted farm, so that she could buy no food anywhere. She complained grievously of the Rev. Father White, president of the League, who always told her "he knew nothing about" the boycott. Her son, who was somewhat uncertain about his age, but who, on reflection, stated that he was nineteen at the time of the Crimean war, generally corroborated his mother's story. The interesting part of this case was its testimony to the fact that the police went round the shops with Mrs. Connell in order to get up prosecutions, for boycotting, against the shopkeepers. At five minutes to four o'clock the Court rose. Sir James Hannen announced that it would meet again on the fifteenth day of the new year.

THIRTY-SECOND DAY.

JANUARY 15, 1889.

SIR CHARLES RUSSELL opened to-day's proceedings with an application for an order to the proprietor of *The Worcester Daily Times* to appear before their lordships "on the charge of contempt of Court"; the alleged contempt being the publication of an article extracts from which were read by Sir Charles, and in which certain strong statements were made in reference to Mr. Gladstone's review, in *The Nineteenth Century*, on a recently published, and now well known, life of O'Connell. These applications, said Sir James Hannen, are even more serious, distressing, and burdensome than the inquiry itself. After a hurried consultation between their lordships, the President announced that they reserved judgment.

Then Sir Richard Webster rose. But he had little to add to what he had said a month ago on Mr. William O'Brien and *United Ireland*. It was, indeed, unnecessary for him to say much; for in front of him sat the Irish people's William, ready to accept full responsibility for all that had appeared in his paper, and to defend or explain the article. And no sooner had Sir Richard resumed his place than the editor of *United Ireland* was on his feet, bolt upright, tightly buttoned, straight as a ramrod, and with his hands folded behind his back. The Court was in for a political speech. "H'sh-sh," went the round of the court, and "the public" down below and the ladies in the galleries bent forward in an attitude of expectancy. Some curious males had their palms at their ears; for Mr. O'Brien was at first inaudible—though before he reached the end of his speech his voice resounded pretty much as it does from Irish platforms and in the House of Commons. He spoke for thirty-five minutes. After a few introductory disclaimers of any intention to reflect upon their lordships' conduct of the investigation, Mr. O'Brien went straight to the point of his speech, that this was less a judicial inquiry than a parliamentary and political inquiry. "In fact," said Mr. O'Brien, in his most candid manner, "the investigation differs from one by a Parliamentary Committee simply in its being conducted by judges." That being the case, he maintained that he was fully entitled to comment in public upon what he held to be *The Times*' unfair way of conducting their part of the case. *United Ireland*, he maintained, attacked, not the Judge-Commissioners, but *The Times* counsel. Mr. O'Brien denounced in his most emphatic style *The Times*' continued publication, not merely of its pamphlet "Parnellism and Crime," but also of a separate work, embodying the Attorney General's speech and the evidence given before the Commission, and published under the title "Parnellism and Crime," just as if it were an edition or continuation of the work commonly known by that name.

I venture (said Mr. O'Brien) to bring before your lordships the hardships in which we are placed. The pamphlet entitled "Parnellism and Crime"—concerning which your lordships are solemnly inquiring whether it contains one tittle of truth—that pamphlet is being openly advertised and sold by tens of thousands in England every day. That pamphlet was originally published before these proceedings commenced. I hold in my hand, however, and shall be pleased to pass it up if your lordships will kindly look at it, a book of nearly four hundred pages which has been published by the publishers of *The Times* since these proceedings commenced. Its title is "Parnellism and Crime.—Special Commission.—Part I.," as if this were really an official message almost from the Court to the country. That book is packed with the *ex parte* statements of the Attorney-General, the chief counsel for *The Times* in this case, disseminating the most atrocious charges, 400 pages of them, against us, and disseminating them almost with the imprimatur, as it were, of the Court, as if they were matters already proved and established. So they send their poison day after day into hundreds of places, knowing that for months, or perhaps years, we shall not have the opportunity in court of counteracting their horrible allegations. These are the persons who have the audacity to come into this court and apply for punishment against me, one of the accused persons, as well as a public journalist, a man against whom the most atrocious charges are levelled. They have the audacity to ask for my punishment because I have in one leading article done my best to counteract the effect of all the frightful poison they are disseminating against us. There are other minor persons attacking us, so that wherever we go in England we see ourselves depicted in lithographed pictures as taking part in or instigating abominable crimes. But that is done by newspapers not so influential as *The Times*. Such papers hope by their insignificance to escape notice, and if they do not escape notice, but get brought into court, they will doubtless be ready to sneak out with a most sincere apology. I quote these things to show that any rigid enforcement of the law of contempt would have and must have a necessarily one-sided effect, because the representatives of the Irish people will have to remain exposed to that constant, habitual drip, drip of defamatory matter throughout England; while our mouths are to be closed if we protest against the means employed against us.

The foregoing passage was delivered by Mr. O'Brien with all his characteristic energy. In pronouncing the word "audacity" his voice grew almost hoarse with indignation, and he turned round with a gesture of scorn and contempt to where *The Times* manager and solicitors were seated, close to his friend Mr. Davitt. Holding a copy of *United Ireland* in his hand, Mr. O'Brien proceeded :

Fighting as we are against tremendous odds, are they still to carry on their defamation of us, and are we still to remain tongue-tied? I wish it to be distinctly understood that I have not for a moment claimed any right to question your lordships' rulings as to what is or is not admissible as evidence. What I do most respectfully claim in this article is that we are entitled in the fullest manner to criticise the dilatory tactics of *The Times* in reference to the substantial allegation as the result of which we are loaded with the enormous expense and worry of this Commission. I respectfully submit that we are entitled to comment on what this article calls the scandalous absence of material evidence and the still more scandalous manner in which it was supplied, and I submit to your lordships we were perfectly warranted so long as we were treated as we were by the other side, in not keeping silence and in not remaining tongue-tied as to the means they were employing against us. We court and challenge inquiry into the horrible accusations which *The Times* allege they can prove under the hand of our own leader, and we are here to meet that allegation in any tangible shape or form. But instead of having the opportunity of meeting the question whether we are a gang of secret, miserable, and dastardly conspirators; and instead of *The Times* producing the proof they said they have, and which they ought to have had before they made such terrible charges, here we are month after month incurring frightful expense, while the prosecution have not touched on the one allegation which, if true, would render the rest of the inquiry utterly superfluous, because there is not a man in the party who does not acknowledge himself to be bound by every act of our leader.

Mr. W. O'Brien declared that what the public were now told through *The Times* witnesses and counsel was not what the public wanted to hear. The public, said he, with an expression of contempt—and again turning in the direction of *The Times* manager and Sir Richard Webster—expected something very different to a summary of newspaper files extending over ten years. "If," said he, "if we did not protest against this kind of thing we should be guilty of cowardice and criminality. The article in question was merely intended to set us right and keep us right with the public"—whom the prosecution was leading away from the point at issue; that, repeated Mr. O'Brien, was the sole object of the article, and, he remarked, "it would be absurdly unnecessary for me to say that the article was not intended to sway the judgment of this Court." He continued :

There is absolutely no way of ending the period of suspense so long as our opponents are to be at liberty to circulate these abominable pamphlets against us, taking for granted in everything that they have established their case against us; while we are debarred the right of answer or comment. Looking over the article in its entirety, in substance and effect I am sorry to say I cannot find anything for which I can express honest regret, or anything which it may not be my solemn duty to repeat.

Then came the case of Mr. Brodrick, the Warden of Merton College. It was very speedily disposed of. Mr. Brodrick was in court, seated among the juniors. The Hon. A. Lyttelton appeared for him. Mr. Lyttelton read out a long affidavit the gist of which was that in his collocation of Jack the Ripper with the Irish leaders, Mr. Brodrick had only been amusing his academic audience at Oxford. In his affidavit Mr. Brodrick disclaimed all intention of saying anything in contempt of Court. In his opening remarks Mr. Lyttelton mildly ridiculed Mr. Reid for having taken Mr. Brodrick's speech so seriously. But Scotchmen, suggested Mr. Lyttelton, are serious persons. However, Mr. Reid, when his turn came to speak, repaid Mr. Lyttelton with interest. Mr. Ried—with an air of mingled surprise and compassion—expressed the hope that the Warden's speech was not an example of English humour, "humour verified by affidavit." No one would have guessed that the Warden of Merton had been talking humour, unless one had been told so. Mr. Reid, being a Scotchman, failed to detect any humour in the Warden's collocation of Jack the Ripper with Mr. Davitt. After a little wrangling between counsel, Sir James Hannen intervened. He observed briefly that after Mr. Brodrick's assurance as to the real motive and intention of his speech at Oxford, the Court would take no further notice of the case. And so Mr. Brodrick, bowing to the President, left the court.

Major Tanner, a brother of Dr. Tanner, was the first witness called. He came to prove intimidation by the League. Major Tanner is shortish and thickset, like his renowned brother. The eyes, nose, mouth, and chin also indicate the family relationship. Like the doctor, Major Tanner is prompt and decisive. But in other respects there is a startling contrast between the Major's manner and that of the M.P.—at any rate, of the M.P. when in a state of volcanic activity "in his place" in the House of Commons. Major Tanner's manner is quiet and business-like. There in the witness-box stood Major Tanner testifying against the mischief of the political organization of which his brother was a member. Major Tanner spoke from his experience as a land agent. He illustrated the greatness of the change introduced, in his estimation, by the League, by saying that whereas in the year 1879, before the League was started, the arrears on one of his estates amounted to only £3 10s., they rose to £700 in 1881, after the League was established in his district. He said, and he repeated his statement, that tenants had often asked him to wait for his rent until "they got leave from the League to pay." Evictions, he declared, had frequently had the effect of extorting payment from tenants who had previously explained they had no money.

He told a story about an interview he had in his own room with twenty-four tenants. "I asked them why they would not pay. One of them replied that when he came up that morning he saw an effigy with a placard to the effect that any tenant who paid would be killed in the same way." Tenants who had paid him had sometimes asked him in secret to prosecute them—in order to hoodwink the leaguers. Said he, a tenant who would behave politely to me when I was alone, would behave rudely when other tenants were at hand.

Major Tanner, when cross-examined by Sir Charles Russell, showed that his knowledge of his native country was somewhat limited. He applied the name "conventions" to Land League meetings assembled for the purpose of demonstrating against landlord sales of tenant interests. Once when Major Tanner wandered off into what Sir Charles regarded as irrelevant matters—and perhaps obstructive—Sir Charles impatiently interrupted him with a "Never mind that, I want to get on, Dr. Tanner." The substitution of "Doctor" for "Major" caused an explosion of laughter, in which the obstructive Major—as his cross-examiner apparently deemed him—joined, though rather reluctantly.

Though Major Tanner considered the League to be the source of the woes of Tipperary, he was obliged to admit that there had been murders in that county in 1875-6-7, and that he could not quote a single case of murder in it since 1879. The Major showed that he was not one of those who thought the Irish tenants entitled to any exceptional consideration during the starvation and misery of 1879. He had given reductions; but, as he candidly and straightforwardly admitted, he did it in order to smash the League.

The rest of the sitting was occupied with the examination of a witness from county Longford. He spelled his name Iago. This Longford witness was a short, slope-shouldered, weakish-looking man with thick red hair, little bead eyes [over which the lids often closed, leaving nothing but a narrow slit], scrubby moustache, and a scorched face. Mr. Atkinson conducted his examination-in-chief. The Longford man's story was that he had for years been a member of the League; that he was even a member of the committee of the League; that he saw the League's books; that he was present at League committee meetings, where boycottings and other outrages were officially resolved upon; that he himself had served in outrage parties commissioned by the League committee; that he had been paid for his trouble; and that he was under the impression that the money came from Dublin. One of his stories was that he assisted in intimidating tenants who had lighted bonfires in honour of a landlord whom they liked, and that the League committee arranged the business—a League committeeman firing shots among the bonfire revellers in order to frighten them. On another occasion his fellow-leaguers went disguised to fire into a house, the owner of which lodged a policeman's son. He accompanied the disguised men, and he knew that the woman into whose house the shots were fired, lost her reason in consequence of her fright. But the man's principal exploits appeared to have been in the window-breaking line. A man was secretly sentenced by the committee to have his panes smashed, because he had given testimony against the witness; and the witness had the satisfaction of being entrusted with the duty of carrying out the sentence. But according to Iago's testimony, the leaguers were guilty of worse crimes than window smashing; and he described how he had been appointed, with other leaguers, to waylay somebody. "I gave him a sthroke," said he, "he was badly wounded, and he died four days after." Gave him a "sthroke"—he told his story with an air of stupid indifference.

This supposed informer had clearly stated in his examination-in-chief that he had been a committeeman of the League. When cross-examined by Sir Charles Russell he denied this; then he corrected himself again; then he explained that at first he had only had the *entrée* to the committee rooms, and that though he had been an ordinary member for six years or more, he had been a committeeman for only six months. He was uncertain as to the exact date of his arrival in England; but he stated that he had been living nine weeks in London; he smashed windows because he had sworn to be "true to his counthree"; he hesitated when Sir Charles Russell asked him who had summoned him to London, and to whom he had given information; he hummed and hawed when asked on his oath whether he had given the police any information about any of his exploits except the window smashing; he denied that he had made any statement in London, and then he said that his statement was read over to him; he blurted out the fact that his statement was read over to him "last night." "Were you ever a member of the League at all?" exclaimed Sir Charles Russell. Yes; but unfortunately Mr. Iago had no ticket in his possession, he had written to Ireland for his ticket, and his brother replied that the ticket could not be found; but as for this letter of his brother's, why he, the ex-member, had burnt it. At ten minutes past four the cross-examination of this interesting informer was suspended.

THIRTY-THIRD DAY.

JANUARY 16.

PUNCTUALLY at half-past ten o'clock the Commissioners took their seats, and at once the President proceeded to state what decision he and his colleagues had arrived at respecting the charge of contempt of Court against Mr. William O'Brien. Sir James Hannen examined, point by point, the arguments of the speech in which Mr. O'Brien contended that the *United Ireland* article had neither brought the writer within the charge of contempt nor exceeded the limits of fair criticism. Sir James Hannen began with a flattering acknowledgment of the "becoming" manner in which Mr. O'Brien had addressed the Court. We have no reason, said Sir James, to doubt the sincerity of Mr. O'Brien's explanation, or of his claim of right as a public critic. To some extent the President endorsed Mr. O'Brien's criticism on the conduct of *The Times* in publishing pamphlets and books the very titles of which amounted to a judgment on the questions which their lordships were investigating. Again, Sir James Hannen remarked, in a kindly, sympathetic manner, that there undoubtedly was a good deal in what Mr. O'Brien had said about the political associations of this trial. But, while admitting this, Sir James Hannen observed —this time in a tone of severe emphasis—that with political issues the Commission had absolutely nothing to do. Sir James then proceeded to indicate what he considered to be the points in which the writer of the article had exceeded the limits of fair journalistic discussion. But, taking all the circumstances into view, Sir James Hannen had come to the conclusion—in which his colleagues had concurred with him—that any modified penalty to which Mr. O'Brien had rendered himself liable on account of the objectionable passages, might well be remitted. Sir James Hannen concluded his careful and comprehensive decision with an earnest appeal to public writers to refrain from everything in the shape of unfair comment on the Commission's proceedings— comments which only served to lengthen the investigation and to add to the Judges difficulties. It should be borne in mind that Mr. O'Brien is not the writer of the article in question, though he has so fully accepted responsibility for it. Mr. O'Brien, who was sitting in front of the bench, rose and bowed respectfully.

The informer Iago was then recalled, and his cross-examination was resumed by Sir C. Russell. This witness, it will be remembered, professed to be an ex-committeeman of the League, who, in his official capacity, had often been officially commissioned to perpetrate outrages. Sir Charles Russell plied Iago with questions intended to find out whether he was as great a rogue as he said he was. Iago strongly resented Sir Charles's doubts as to his rascality. As an honest man Iago claimed to be believed ; yet he perplexed his hearers sometimes. His memory appeared to be correcting itself, filling up its past gaps, amplifying itself as he proceeded with his unpleasant autobiography. He was somewhat confused in his answers to repeated questions about his committee membership. At one time he stated that his membership ended six months ago. At another he surprised his cross-examiner with the assurance, "I am *still* on the committee, your honour." Mr. Iago's audience laughed not unnaturally at this unexpected announcement. Mr. Iago wriggled about in his box, and winked his small eyes. Then there were fresh uncertainties about that letter of his which he said yesterday he had written to his brother, requesting that his card of membership should be forwarded to London. At first Mr. Iago left the impression upon his hearers that he had written to his brother direct. He now said that he asked a policeman to communicate on the subject with his brother.

Mr. Iago repeatedly excused himself for all these perplexing answers and corrections of answers by saying that he was "no scholar." Not being a scholar, he could not have written with his own hand to his brother; so he procured the assistance of some one from Mayo, whom he met in London, and whom he had never seen before. All this was done about a week ago; and the reply which Mr. Iago received from his brother, Mr. Iago burnt. Then Mr. Iago made further revelations about his past life, from which it appeared that he had been several times "run in" for assault. Again, he informed the Court that he had two-and-a-half acres of land; and in a minute or two he corrected himself by saying that the land was not his, but his brother's.

Iago stared in blank indignation at Sir Charles Russell when the latter asked him whether there was a single man in all Longford who could believe him on his oath. Then he triumphantly stated that the relieving officer of the place and three publicans would believe him. In answer to Mr. Reid, he remarked that he had turned informer because "I wanted to take my head out of the halter."

Mr. Iago slunk out of his box and disappeared. Patrick Delaney was the next name called. And after a few moments' pause "the Phoenix Park criminal" appeared—not in prison dress. Delaney is over middle height, stoutish in build, reddish-yellow haired, and with features which were more of a Russian than an Irish cast. He wore a short jacket of check-tweed, and a big white cravat about his neck. He had come, as he said, from Maryborough Prison, Queen's County, where he is "doing" his life sentence for his share in what, twice or thrice in the course of his examination, he called the Phoenix Park "business." Here he was to prove, if he could, that the leaders of the Land and National Leagues—Mr. Parnell, Mr. John O'Connor, Mr. Matt Harris, Mr. Egan, and others — were implicated up in murders and conspiracies for Irish independence; that Nationalists, Leaguers, Fenians, Invincibles were to a sufficient extent, one party under different names.

Delaney was in many ways an interesting personage as he stood erect in his box, quite composedly, with some hundred pairs of eyes fixed curiously upon him. His brother was one of those who were hanged for the Phoenix Park crime. Pat Delaney himself would have been hanged, but, as he said, in his cool, but confused, way, "I pleaded guilty, and so my sentence was changed from execution to life."

A bad career was Pat Delaney's, even before the Phoenix Park "business." " In my young days," said he, "I got five years for highway robbery." He looked not in the slightest degree abashed when he said that. By his young days he meant when he was about seventeen years old. He is now thirty-six. He looks strong and healthy. The regularity of prison discipline—regular meals, freedom from worry, steady work, and a free residence under strict sanitary supervision—have improved Pat Delaney. In health and comfort, and, really, in apparent contentment with his lot, Mr. Delaney seemed to have the advantage over millions of his poor and honest fellow-creatures who were struggling for existence outside gaol walls. It might have been noticed that Mr. Delaney had a pleasant voice, much pleasanter than his face.

The first thing Delaney did after his release from gaol in 1876 was to join the Fenians. He jumped out of gaol into the "Brotherhood." And he remained a Fenian until the time of his arrest in November, 1882. He joined the Brotherhood in Dublin, where the Fenian leaders at that time (1876) were. Patrick Egan, John Macalister, John Leary, and Donovan constituted, he said, the "Executive Council." But besides these men, there were "organizers" from America and elsewhere. All these men used to meet at the Council in Dublin, together with James and Joe Mullett, Daniel Delaney (the witness's brother), James Carey, James Elmore, and John Devoy. General Millen, the American, was, said the witness, entrusted with the duty of inspecting the secret military organization of the Fenian Brotherhood.

Having described a Fenian "centre," Delaney gave an account of the first Land League meeting held in the Rotunda, Dublin, in 1879. All the members of the Fenian circles were invited by their respective centres to be present at the meeting for the purpose of supporting the Land Leaguers. Pat Egan, who, according to Delaney, was both a Fenian and treasurer of the new Land League, was at the meeting. And so, he thought, were Mr. Biggar, Mr. Matt. Harris, Mr. Michael Davitt, and Mr. Thomas Brennan. After the meeting, continued Delaney, we Fenians received orders from our superiors (centres) not to oppose the new organization called the Land League, but to support it. The general drift of this part of Delaney's evidence was that leaguers and Fenians were either the same persons or that the League leaders were knowingly and deliberately associating themselves with the Fenian conspiracy. He made particular mention next of P. J. Sheridan, who, he declared, was both a member of the Fenian Council and a Land League organizer in the South of Ireland. The short and the long of it was, according to Delaney's statement, that the Land League and the Fenian Brotherhood were two distinct departments of one and the same organization—the League being entrusted with the duty of preparing the country for the military action which the Fenian Brotherhood would initiate and conduct.

But did Mr. Delaney know all this at first hand? No. He had only been told so by his superior officer or centre. In 1882, before the Phœnix Park murder, Delaney himself was elevated to the rank of "centre."

Next came a long string of answers, connecting leaguers, Fenians, and invincibles together. Mr. Matt. Harris, the renowned member for East Galway, to whom Delaney was "introduced" in 1876, was the Fenian "centre" for county Galway. It was Mr. Matt. Harris who swore in "Curley." He did not go the length of calling Mr. Harrison an invincible, but only a Fenian organizer. [We may explain here that by an invincible the witness meant a man sworn to assist the Irish cause by assassination ; and by a Fenian, one bound only to attain the same end by "open fighting."] "I became an invincible," said "Mr. Delaney," and he rapidly quoted a number of invincible names—James Mullett, James Carey, Daniel Delaney, Joe Brady, Mike Fagan, the two Hanlons, Pat Egan, Brennan, Sheridan, Frank Bryne, and Pat Molloy, the same witness who lately from the witness-box declared that he had only been hoaxing *The Times*.

Delaney affirmed an identity between leaguers, Fenians, and invincibles. For example, Egan the alleged invincible was Land League treasurer, and Frank Bryne was secretary of the Land League in London. As he stated at a later stage of his evidence, it was Mrs. Frank Bryne who carried the Phœnix Park weapons from London to Dublin. As for Mr. Matt. Harris, Delaney declared that he was present at a Dublin meeting, in 1879, of all the centres of the Fenian organization in Ireland. And among these invincibles was the mysterious Number One, Tynan his name was, the witness thought ; and Tynan used to go about in big spectacles : " I never saw him without his spectacles. He always went disguised ; I never saw him twice in the same dress." Who told you, he was asked, that Mr. Matt. Harris swore Curley into the Fenian brotherhood? "Curley himself," was the answer. And then he said that Sheridan [describing him as a leaguer] was one of the three Fenians who introduced the Invincible Association from America in 1881 ; that the invincibles got their money from the Land League through the hands of its treasurer, Egan ; that he himself, Mr. Delaney, had been "told off" to murder Mr. Forster ; and that he also received instructions to assist in the assassination of Mr. Burke :—

"We were told to meet at King's Bridge and assassinate a gentleman, but he didn't come." Had you any part in the Phœnix Park murders?—No. How was that?—I was not told to, and I didn't know until the murder had taken place. I was taken by force into Phœnix Park. Where were you at the time of the murder?—Close by. What were you doing?—Watching. On the ground?—Yes. What communications were made to you about the murder?—The first orders I got were to meet at King's Bridge. I was then fetched from work by Timothy Kelly and the carman Kavanagh. Where were you taken to?—To the public-house in James Street, and thence to Phœnix Park. Do you remember anything about the knives?—Yes. James Carey had the knives hidden in a dispensary he was rebuilding. He was afraid of being found out, and asked me to take them to Brady, with instructions to destroy them. Did you take them?—Yes. They were the same as Mrs. Byrne brought over. What did you do with the knives?—They were destroyed in my presence. I saw Brady break the handles, and burn them and the knives. After that, continued Delaney, " No. 1" attended a meeting at which a committee was formed. One of the meetings was attended by Byrne, who brought with him a large amount of notes and gold, which was given to the funds of the invincibles.

According to Delaney's narrative there was to be a long series of murders. Judge Lawson was to be murdered; so were Earl Spencer, and a number of policemen and detectives. And again Mr. Delaney connected all these hideous plots directly with the Land League, by saying that Byrne, who attended the secret conclave for the murder of Earl Spencer, decided at the time that nothing would be done without Mr. Egan's "orders." Finally Mr. Delaney told how Mr. Egan, the League treasurer, paid money in support of the candidature of Carey for one of the Dublin wards "in the hope that an invincible might become Lord Mayor of Dublin." At this odd announcement there was a burst of laughter in court. And then the Attorney-General wound up his examination by producing letters with Mr. Egan's alleged signature, letters forwarding, or promising, funds to Carey, and quoting Mr. Parnell's (alleged) opinion on the expenditure. The letters were handed one after the other by the Attorney-General to the witness, who, knitting his brows and staring hard at each, pronounced every signature to be Mr. Egan's. The letters were dated from Paris.

Sir Charles Russell now asked him what his motive was for giving all that information about invincibles and leaguers to the official authorities. The reply was that he did it as soon as he learned that there was a probability of his being accused of having shared in the murder of Mr. Burke. When he learned this he was in prison for the Lawson "business." There it was that he "wrote down" the "whole story from 1875 until the time of his arrest." But, he added, it was only "ten days ago" that he was asked to give information before the Commission, and he was asked by a *Times* agent, Mr. Shannon, who interviewed him in Maryborough Prison. This Mr. Shannon, he imagined, must have known about the deposition he made in gaol five years before. Only the governor of the gaol was present, said Delaney, when Mr. Shannon was taking his notes. Mr. Shannon, it seems, made him swear to the truth of his statements. "He gave me a book. I kissed it. I didn't know what it was; but it was a book of some description." Mr. Delaney's audience laughed at this revelation of Mr. Delaney's notions of the sacredness of what he was swearing by.

In his examination-in-chief Mr. Delaney had been declaring persistently that the leaguers, Fenians, and invincibles were in accord. But he looked somewhat surprised when Sir Charles Russell read out aloud the Fenian proclamation of that very period—proclamations in which the Parnellite, Constitutional, Land League party were denounced as scramblers for parliamentary place and power, and as deserters of the Irish cause. "Did you not know that, sir?" exclaimed Sir Charles Russell, in a sharp, severe tone. Mr. Delaney hesitated, but said at last that he heard there was something of the sort. As for the Rotunda meeting, he admitted that the Fenians attempted to storm the platform on which Mr. Parnell and other prominent leaguers were standing. But he added something to the effect that after the meeting the Fenians received "orders" to be friendly. However, when closely pressed by Sir Charles Russell, he admitted that he himself, personally, had received no such orders from the three centres who promulgated them. He also confessed that he had had no direct personal communication with the Fenians and leaguers whom he had been accusing all along of having hatched the Invincible conspiracy. In other words, as Sir Charles Russell put it, Delaney did not know personally that any leaguers had had anything to do with the hatching business. And Delaney learned from "others" that League money was being paid over to the plotters. "And so it comes to this," said Sir Charles, taking a long pinch, and shaking his handkerchief, "it comes to this; that you knew it by hearsay." Sir Charles next tackled him on the subject of the alleged signatures of Mr. Egan. "Are you an expert?" he asked, carelessly. No; Mr. Delaney was not an expert; but he remembered the signatures after so many years; and he identified them when he was shown them "yesterday evening" by *The Times* agent. He was able to identify them because Carey, seven or eight years ago, showed him three of Mr. Egan's letters.

THIRTY-FOURTH DAY.

JANUARY 17.

DELANEY'S cross-examination was resumed by Mr. Reid, Q.C. Mr. Reid's questions referred to what Delaney had already said about Boyton's identification of Mr. Burke for the information of the assassin Brady; and to the interview in prison between Delaney and Mr. Shannon, the Crown solicitor, who took his deposition on behalf of *The Times*. "I heard," Delaney said on the previous day, "I heard Boyton say, 'That's the man.'" Had you ever seen Boyton before? Mr. Reid now asked him. "No." Nor since? "No." "Then how did you know it was Boyton?" "Brady told me it was Boyton; and besides, I received orders to be on the spot in order to meet a man named Boyton." Brady was one of the five who were hanged for the murder.

Mr. Reid examined Delaney closely on the subject of his prison interview with Mr. Shannon. Mr. Shannon, said the witness, came to me with a letter of introduction, because I objected to giving information to people I did not know. And yet, Delaney added that he did not know who the person was who gave Mr. Shannon his letter of introduction; he had not the "slightest idea" who the introducer was. "And yet you give him information," Mr. Reid repeated. Delaney then explained it was safe to give information because none but officials would be allowed to see him in prison. Then why did you require an introductory letter? was Mr. Reid's rejoinder.

Mr. Davitt then tried Delaney, beginning with the witness's gaol conversations. "Did you talk to your warder on this matter?" No, I did not. He never talked with the warder except about the prison rules. But surely you must have known about the rules, Mr. Davitt remarked. Delaney, modifying his previous statement, explained that his friendly warder used to give him prison news—Delaney being a prisoner who works by himself. "Honestly," exclaimed Delaney, drawing himself up, "I say that the warder never spoke to me about the Commission." Nor had his wife, for, being poor, she had been unable to visit him during the last two years. And though she wrote to him regularly, she said nothing about the Commission. At this reference to his family relationships, Delaney betrayed just a passing shadow of emotion. At a later stage in the cross-examination he again showed some sign of feeling when, in reference to Carey, he exclaimed, "Yes, I was one of his dupes—to my grief."

The remainder of Mr. Davitt's cross-examination of the informer was somewhat lively. Mr. Davitt asked him whether he was aware that many people, like Mr. Isaac Butt, who had no connection whatever with Fenianism, were prominent in the meetings held in 1876-7, with the object of obtaining an amnesty for Fenian prisoners; and also whether he was not aware that such meetings were perfectly free and open to the public. "Yes," retorted Delaney, "but there were secret meetings as well, meetings to which none but Fenians were admitted, and you attended them;" and he instanced one such meeting in 1878, at which he saw Mr. Davitt. But Delaney could not remember the exact date.

"Come," said Mr. Davitt, "think, this may be a serious business for me." Still, though pressed to say when in 1878, Delaney could not answer. At last he suggested the winter of 1878. "Oh," Mr. Davitt then exclaimed, "would it surprise you if I told you that I was then in America?" However, Delaney adhered to his general statement that he had seen Mr. Davitt at that meeting, but he suggested that the year might have been 1877 instead of 1878. "You were there," said Delaney, "a fortnight after your release." Mr. Davitt then questioned him about the Rotunda meeting. "You swore yesterday," said Mr. Davitt, "that I supported Hanlon's resolution at the Rotunda meeting" (which Delaney had described as a League and Fenian meeting); "what did you mean by supporting?" The reply was indefinite at first, but eventually Delaney explained that Mr. Davitt supported Hanlon by requesting that he should be heard.

"Don't you think I was only trying to get fair play for an opponent?" Mr. Davitt continued. Delaney did not know. But if Hanlon was a Fenian and Mr. Davitt a Fenian, how could they be opponents? In order to throw light on this question, or rather on the question whether at that time Mr. Davitt was a Fenian at all, Mr. Davitt now read out in court the Hanlon resolution, which denounced "ex-political prisoners"—such as Mr. Davitt himself then was—"who, by adopting what was called constitutional agitation, were betraying the Irish cause." "Was that resolution friendly to me?" Mr. Davitt asked. After a little hesitation, Delaney answered, "They were friendly to you immediately afterwards." Whereupon Mr. Davitt pressed him, pretty severely, about "afterwards." Did Delaney know that the party of violence which Delaney was associating with the League and with Mr. Davitt, continued its attacks upon Mr. Davitt for a long time after the Rotunda meeting; that upon one occasion four men with revolvers went to his (Mr. Davitt' lodgings) to shoot him? No; Mr. Delaney was not aware of anything of the kind. Finally, as to Delaney's statement that Egan and Sheridan, and two others of their fellow invincibles, as he regarded them, had passed the word that the Fenian centres should not oppose the Land League, Delaney now said that he had not learned this from the four men directly, but from his brother (who was a Fenian centre at the time, and who was subsequently hanged for the Phœnix Park crime). Delaney smiled, and shook his head at Mr. Davitt, as he exclaimed, "Oh, yes, you were always upheld by the Fenians in 1879, 1880, 1881, 1882."

The Attorney-General's re-examination of Delaney was very brief. In one more reference to Egan, Delaney made an admiring remark about the "cleverality of his escape" from Ireland. Asked a question or two about the circumstances of the Fenian leaders eight years ago, Delaney said they were so very poor that they were obliged to "pledge their watches" in order to procure funds for sending delegates to Paris, where meetings of Fenians and leaguers were to be held. How did he know that? Why, his own brother, who was a "centre," was one of the Fenians who took his watch to the pawnbroker's. But this clue—if it was a clue—to further disclosures, real or supposed, was not followed up. When the spectators were expecting the Attorney-General to put questions about the Paris meetings, Mr. Attorney was all the while intently studying a sheet of something or other which he held in his right hand. It turned out to be a photograph. "Look at that," said the Attorney-General, "but don't remove the paper" [which covered the name], handing him the photograph. "Do you know who that is?" After a hard gaze of two or three seconds, Delaney smiled, he looked up sharply—"That's the man known as No. 1." And so the photograph of No. 1 was handed up to the Bench. The President gazed at it curiously, Mr. Justice Day raised his eyebrows, wrinkled his forehead, and just glanced at it. And then it passed on to Mr. Justice Smith, Mr. Biggar, Mr. Davitt, Mr. Reid, and the whole concourse of Seniors and Juniors. Before Delaney left the box it was arranged that he should be detained in London for some days before being sent back to Maryborough gaol.

The rest of the day was chiefly occupied in examining land agents, and in the reading of Mr. M. Harris's correspondence as a Land League organizer. Mr. Digby, agent for Lord Digby's estates in King's County, declared, like other witnesses of his class, that the League was responsible for the refusal of the tenants to pay the old rents. Another agent, Mr. Hewson, who followed him, said that before the rise of the League he had never heard of the name moonlighting. But he subsequently admitted, in cross-examination by Mr. Reid, that the thing existed years before that date.

The Harris letters were copies, supplied by Dublin Castle. Of startling disclosures of any sort they were quite destitute. They were chiefly ordinary letters from Mr. Davitt, Mr. Dillon, Mr. Brennan, "to my dear Harris," acknowledging his zeal as an organizer. Sir Richard Webster even read out a letter in which Mr. Brennan condoled with "my dear Harris" on his rheumatism. As for payments to Mr. Harris from Land League funds, all the letters showed that Mr. Harris was scrupulous in not asking for any return for his work, save his postage, travelling and stationery expenses. "As I don't know how much I have spent," said Mr. Harris, in one of his letters, "I would rather you paid me too little than too much."

THIRTY-FIFTH DAY.

JANUARY 18.

MORE land agent witnesses. The examinations, on *The Times* side, were conducted by the Attorney-General, Mr. Murphy, Mr. Atkinson, Mr. Graham; on the other side almost entirely by Mr. Reid. Mr. Asquith cross-examined once or twice, and Mr. A. O'Connor; and Mr. Davitt questioned every single witness—contriving, with his intimate knowledge of the subject, to throw some additional light on the condition of the Irish peasantry. The purpose of Mr. Davitt's questions was to show that peasant misery and landlord harshness were sufficient in themselves to account for the outrages which the Attorney-General attributed to the promptings of the League. The first of these agent-witnesses was Mr. Young, whose examination-in-chief began the day before. A question put to him by Mr. Davitt, as to whether rents levied by the London

Skinners' Company upon the tenants of their Derry estates were spent upon London entertainments, failed to elicit any noteworthy reply.

Next appeared Mr. Garrett Tyrrell, land agent, of King's County. Mr. Tyrrell led the lawyers over long walks through the various estates—four in all —of which he had charge. After Invincible Delaney's talk of the day before, Mr. Tyrrell's conversation was not exciting. Between the histories of his four estates there was a strong family resemblance.

Mr. Tyrrell's general statement was that before the establishment of the League on, or in the neighbourhood of, these estates, he had never known of combined refusals to pay rent; nor of intimidation of people who did pay; nor of any agrarian association whatever, save the League. Replying to Mr. Reid, he said that he was an honorary member of the Property Defence Association; and that "all" the tenants on one of his estates were intimidated; and the "majority" on the others. What! exclaimed Mr. Reid, as if puzzled at the notion of a whole community being intimidated by itself. "And on the other estates, the people intimidated were the majority?" "Yes." "Oh!"

Mr. Davitt got Mr. Tyrrell to admit that he had a pecuniary interest in the suppression of bodies like the League, the action of which tended to lower the rents from which he derived his percentages.

The next land agent was from Mayo, Mr. Robert Powell, of Westport. "Oh, yes," said he, answering Mr. Atkinson, "everything in Mayo was quiet up to 1879," after which (the old story) everything went wrong. He had never heard of moonlighting outrages before the year 1879. The same old story was, *mutatis mutandis*, repeated by the next witness, a Mr. Verriker.

Mr. John Barrett, of Cork, next gave his testimony. He was very brusque in his accusations against the League. A candid letter of Mr. Barrett's to Mr. Barrett's priest was read out by Mr. Atkinson. The parish priest was the president of the local branch of the League, and Mr. Barrett wrote to him deploring the use, at a League meeting, of language "too foul for publication"; accusing the branch of having discussed the propriety of assassinating the writer (Mr. Barrett); and declaring that the friendship between them both must cease, inasmuch as the president had not denounced the murderous threat. Mr. Reid extracted an unpleasant piece of information from Mr. John Barrett. It was this—that a poor tenant whom he had evicted, and whom he refused to re-admit, died of hardship and exposure, in a ditch, under the shelter of an upturned boat.

Then came Mr. Dominick O'Donnell, a Mayo landlord. He, too, told the same old story, but with interesting variations. Mr. Barrett, the previous witness, had had his effigy burnt in his presence by defiant tenants, as a punishment for the letter which he wrote to the reverend president. But Mr. Dominick O'Donnell was twice fired at—though by whom or for what reason did not appear. He escaped marvellously—once with a bullet through his coat, the next time with a bullet in his thigh. According to his own account, he must have been one of the most unpopular of Mayo landlords. For which there were several reasons. He dissented, in his capacity of magistrate, from a verdict of wilful murder which a Mayo jury gave against a police inspector who in 1881 ordered his men to fire on a crowd of defenceless people, by which firing one man was shot dead, and others, including women, wounded.

But he told another story, which doubtless accounted still more for the Mayo peasants' dislike of him. It was elicited from him by Mr. Arthur O'Connor. Well, Mr. O'Donnell, at that eviction of yours, was not the tenant's wife in bed? At this question Mr. O'Donnell jerked himself slightly upwards. "She was," replied Mr. O'Donnell, with a quick little nod. She refused to get out of bed? "Yes," replied Mr. O'Donnell, after a pause, and another little jerk. Did the sheriff pull her out? No—this time with something like an expression of *sangfroid.* The bailiffs? No. Did the police? No. By this time Mr. Dominick O'Donnell was fidgetting about rather uneasily, and he reddened, just a little, as he let the secret out : he carried her out himself. And it was at two o'clock in the afternoon. Then Mr. Arthur O'Connor, in his cold, dry way, asked Mr. Dominick O'Donnell whether it was not the fact that he carried her out "naked in presence of the bystanders." Yes; but the reason was that she "began to kick her clothes off." Had an emergency man been in the box, the story would have been less amusing; but it was comical to hear all that from a prosperous landlord, whose demeanour was as "respectable" and grave as that of a kirk elder. The observant reader will have already seen that the lady who "began to kick her clothes off" was shamming sickness. But, lest there should be any doubts on the point, Mr. Dominick O'Donnell declared, with another little nod, that he had seen her the night before "hale and hearty."

Captain Plunkett, the Irish magistrate, with whose name most newspaper readers are familiar, was the next witness. His famous message, "Don't hesitate to shoot," inspired many a hot debate in the House of Commons at the time. Captain Plunkett—whom the Irish Nationalist papers always call "Plunkett Pasha," while they designate his policemen as "Bashi Bazouks"—proved to be one of the best of *The Times* witnesses. An old constabulary hand, he stood well the cross-fire of Mr. Reid's, and Mr. Michael Davitt's, questions. Whatever the value of his evidence, as given in answer to the Attorney-General, the *method* was skilful. But of course the method was Sir Richard Webster's. Sir Richard's method was to choose two sets of districts in Kerry, one set where the League was alleged to be either non-existent or weak, and another where the League was described as strong; and then to contrast the histories of both. In the one set of three districts, where the League was weak, crime was, said Captain Plunkett, non-existent, or nearly so, during the years 1879–1883; in the four Kerry districts, where the League was strong, crime was frequent and violent. That was argument number one. Argument number two was that in the first three districts, both the people and the soil were poor, and therefore that, as crime was practically non-existent in them, the Nationalist explanation that poverty produced outrage fell to the ground. The other portion of argument number two was that the people were well off and the soil good in the four districts where, as he said, the League and crime flourished. Captain Plunkett then expressed his belief that Kerry outrages could not possibly be attributed to any secret society, except a society forming part of the Land League organization. In fact, he declined to call the moonlighters a secret society. The moonlighters are only the "Police of the League," exclaimed Captain Plunkett, with an evident air of satisfaction at the pithiness of the expression. (But this description of the moonlighters was given in reply not to the Attorney-General, but to Mr. Reid.)

Under Mr. Reid's cross-examination Captain Plunkett admitted that after all there might have been League branches in the three quiet districts simultaneously with the branches in the four disturbed districts. And then, the form, at all events, of his evidence as given to Sir Richard Webster, became unsatisfactory. It seemed as if Captain Plunkett was reasoning in a circle; thus, the League is strong in such and such a place because crime is rife; and the reason why the crime is rife is because the League is strong.

Then Mr. Reid tried another line. He invited Captain Plunkett to give any other specific reasons he had for incriminating the League. Captain Plunkett replied that crime often followed the delivery of Land League speeches; and also that informers gave him particulars about League resolutions and the outrages which followed them. As regards the first of the two reasons, Mr. Reid tried to find out whether he meant that because an outrage occurred subsequently to the delivery of a certain speech, the outrage was the intended effect of the speech. Here Captain Plunkett, hesitating, remarked that certain speeches were "calculated to produce" outrages. Then, again, Captain Plunkett did not seem quite clear as to what he himself meant by a "strong" branch of the League—whether a branch was strong because it met often, or because it had many members. Upon that point, also, his answers to Mr. Reid were too indefinite. As to his informers—of whom he had ten or twelve in a period of seven years—he told Mr. Reid that they were paid by the Irish Government for their work, and that some of them were kept in pay from year to year. Could they now be found if required to appear in the witness-box, Mr. Reid asked. Some of them possibly might, Captain Plunkett thought. Captain Plunkett was very reticent about these informers of his. Mr. Reid asked him about the informer O'Connor—the man who, in the witness-box, lately accused Mr. Harrington, and who described himself as a member of the "secret" (moonlighting) branch of the League. But Captain Plunkett, with his hands in his pockets, kept his lips shut, and his eyes fixed, smilingly, on Mr. Reid.

Then Mr. Davitt tried Captain Plunkett. Met MacDermott at Cork? "Yes," barely audible; with a little nod. Told you his business at Cork? "No; and if he had I would not tell you"; all this in a quiet, level voice. Nor did Captain Plunkett know that MacDermott was a Castle agent. Did he speak to you? No. Or you to him? No. Did he write to you? Or you to him? No. Swear you don't know MacDermott was organizing a dynamite conspiracy at New York? Captain Plunkett shook his head—just the ghost of a little shake. Standing there, steady and solid as a wall, with his hands in his pockets, and answering in his quiet, slow manner, or merely nodding, or shaking his head, in place of saying yes, or no, Captain Plunkett seemed all the more amused the more Mr. Davitt pressed him. Captain Plunkett smiled as he lazily sauntered out of his box.

THIRTY-SIXTH DAY.

JANUARY 22.

SIR HENRY JAMES's leisurely and exhaustive examination of an ex-clerk of the head office of the Land League in Dublin has been one of the most interesting episodes of the trial. There have been informers—calling themselves Fenians, Invincibles, Moonlighters—who were connected, or alleged to be connected, with local branches of the Land and National Leagues. But ex-clerk Farragher is the first informer hailing from headquarters—from the privacy of the head office itself. But before Farragher was called, Mr. Studdert, agent to Mr. Vandeleur, in county Clare, was examined on the general question of relations between landlord and tenant. This was the same agent under whom the evictions of last August carried out on the Kilrush estates. Mr. Studdert's answers generally coincided with those already given by landlord and agent witnesses. But Sir Charles Russell, in his cross-examination, elicited admissions that were not altogether flattering to the system of landlord management in county Clare. Mr. Studdert fixed at 22 per cent. the average amount of reductions granted by the Land Commissioners to tenants of Mr. Vandeleur. Sir Charles Russell quoted figures to show that in many cases the reductions had been much larger. But still more significant were the figures showing how rents had been raised by the landlord—raised, that is to say, on the tenant's own improvements. Sir Charles Russell, however, did not pursue this subject very far. Mr. Studdert also admitted that the year 1879 "was one of the worst years we ever had," and yet, that not until the end of 1881 did the landlord grant any relief to his harassed tenants. Mr. Davitt, who is an assiduous cross-examiner, and as regular and punctual in his attendance as the judges themselves, next questioned Mr. Studdert as to his knowledge of Tipperary, some estates in which were under Mr. Studdert's supervision. Like others of his class, Mr. Studdert thought that before the fatal year of the League—1879—Ireland was an Arcadia. Mr. Davitt, therefore, asked him if he had ever heard of these agrarian murders in Tipperary (giving a rapid enumeration of them), recorded to have been perpetrated between 1870 and 1879. Mr. Studdert had not heard of one of them. "Well," said Mr. Davitt, "can you tell me of a single case of agrarian murder in Tipperary since the year 1879?" Mr. Studdert could not. But then Mr. Studdert suggested that the League may have been comparatively weak in Tipperary. "Weak!" exclaimed Mr. Davitt. " Would you be surprised to learn that there have been more branches of the Land and National Leagues in Tipperary than in any other Irish county?" Mr. Studdert knew nothing about it. "But I know," was the expression on Mr. Davitt's face, as he abruptly and impatiently resumed his seat.

Farragher introduced himself as a Mayo farmer. He declared that in 1879 Mr. Michael Davitt and Mr. J. W. Walsh bribed him—for it amounted to that —not to pay the rent which, as he stated emphatically in the box, he was quite able to pay. That was when Mr. Davitt and his colleagues were founding the Land League. "I was to hold out," said Farragher, "for a twenty-five per cent. reduction; and I was promised (by Messrs. Davitt and Walsh) that if I was turned out I would be provided for." Well, Farragher was turned out. Whereupon, according to his own account, he asked for the reward of his virtue. The promised reward was a post in the Land League office. He went to Dublin. There he saw Mr. Davitt, the Father of the League, and Mr. Brennan, its Secretary. And he got nothing. I knocked about Dublin, said he, for eight or nine months, until all my money was gone. "Did you apply to Mr. Davitt in Dublin?" "I am perfectly certain I did."' At last his reward came—a clerkship in the League office at a pound a week, subsequently raised to thirty shillings. And what were Mr. Farragher's duties in the League office? He was attached to the "Law department" of the organization : that is, the department which conducted the defence of the leaguers—chiefly tenant farmers, of course—charged with breaches of the law. Through this department moneys were issued for the payment of solicitors and barristers. If there was any really criminal work hatched in Upper O'Connell Street, Mr. Farragher was in a position to know something of it, although his post in the establishment was one of the humblest. Egan, said Farragher, was the treasurer at that time, Brennan was the secretary, Dr. Kenny, M.P., was treasurer after Egan's departure for Paris. So far, the only allegation of a serious nature made by Farragher was his accusation of bribery against Mr. Davitt.

Mullett, whose name has already been mentioned in the course of the trial, was an invincible, condemned to the same life punishment which Delaney, the informer of last week, is now undergoing. Farragher now stated that on several occasions he had taken letters from Egan [in Egan's own handwriting, and containing cheques] to Mullett, at his public-house, in Dorset Street, Dublin; that Egan often visited Mullett, and associated with him in the streets.

Farragher told his story readily enough in his examination-in-chief; but his memory sadly failed him when cross-examined by Sir Charles Russell. His cross-examination may be generally described as an attempt to fix him even to a single date; but the attempt was a complete failure. Periods of a more or less approximate character, rather than specific dates, were all that could be learned from him. And his " record" was scarcely satisfactory. Charges of drunkenness and of immorality " were brought against him during his incumbency as master of Ballinrobe Workhouse, county Mayo. But, as he said, he "got out of that," though he resigned his post.

Sir Charles Russell, being anxious to find out whether Farragher had been "put up" in any way to testify against the League, asked him how it was that he came to appear before the Commission. Farragher replied that he had been summoned in consequence of an inadvertence of his own, his inadvertence being some references of his, in the course of conversation with four or five people, to his past connection with the League. But of the four ˝or five he could only identify one. Who was he? "A black man." At which answer there was a burst of laughter in court, as if the Prime Minister's phrase were here recognized. In his examination-in-chief he had stated that Mr. Parnell, Mr. Sexton, Mr. Healy, and others had been attending League Committee meetings for six months or so before the suppression of the League in October, 1881. "Do you mean to say," asked Sir Charles Russell, "that they were attending while Parliament was sitting?" He believed they did. But would he swear? No. Nor had he himself ever been present at a Committee meeting. Nor had he been very often at the public meetings. Nor could he tell in what year the Land League shifted its headquarters from Abbey Street to Upper Sackville Street. In 1880 " perhaps "; but he could not swear. How long had he been in the service of the League? He could not tell exactly; "I should say I was a year." According to his examination-in-chief, he must have been longer, for, as he was evicted in August or September of 1879, and as he received his appointment in the League office " eight or nine months" afterwards, this appointment must have dated from May or June, 1880; and he served in the League office until its suppression in October, 1881, so that he must have been about sixteen months at his post. " Will you swear you were in the League office before February, 1881?" he was asked. Yes, he would; he would say that he was in the office in the summer of 1880—which would make his full term of service about sixteen months, as already said.

Again, taxing his memory, he could not mention any date at which he had seen Egan at the League office, though " I often did see him there, twenty or thirty times at least." Egan visited the office "every time he came from Paris," but even that reminiscence could not help him to a date. Sir Charles repeated his question over and over again. " I'll try once more," said Sir Charles. " Was there ever a space of time during which you did not see Mr. Egan at the League office?" "Yes." "When?" "I can't say." Another burst of laughter, which Sir James Hannen rebuked. Farragher recollected Egan going to Paris; but could not say when. He remembered his coming back; but could not say when. He remembered Mr. Egan visiting the place after February, 1881, but could not say when, nor how often, though he suggested ten times, "perhaps." Nor could he tell at what precise dates he carried Pat Egan's letters to Invincible Mullett's public-house; nor how many letters he took. Did you take one? Yes. Two? Yes. Three? Yes. Four? Yes. Five? Yes. Six? Yes. Seven? Yes. Eight? " I can't tell you," replied Farragher, abruptly stopping short. As for these letters, Egan made no concealment whatever in giving them to him for delivery. As for the payment of money through the League, Farragher did not appear to be aware of the existence of an open and public sustenance fund for the " suspects " under Forster's Act. Nor did he seem to know what was meant by the Land Leaguers' " test cases " in disputes between landlords and tenants.

THIRTY-SEVENTH DAY.

January 23.

Sir Henry James resumed the reading of the letters, some of which the informer Farragher had declared on the preceding day to be in the handwriting of clerks of the Land League. But after a little while Sir Henry James suggested that his next batch of letters should be put in without being read. These letters were, generally, requests to the League for authority to defend prisoners charged with such offences as riot and forcible entry. And then he began to read from another batch, containing correspondence to and from the League, and "forms" of various sorts, including "guidance for organizers" of League branches. This preliminary work consumed more than an hour, after which the first witness of the day, Mr. Robert Sandys, was called.

In reply to Mr. Murphy, he gave evidence of relationship between his father and his tenants, including the tenants of other landlords for whom his father acted as agent. Mr. Sandys, now about twenty-seven years old, was at Dublin College when the Land League was beginning its operations in the districts where his father was managing his estates. Mr. Sandys was exceedingly confident in his assertions concerning the state of things before 1879-80. In 1880, soon after the League was established, Mr. Sandys's tenants asked for certain reductions. He refused. Then, said the witness, "the Land League took the matter up." "How do you know that?" Sir Charles Russell sharply interposed. Mr. Sandys, junior, described how, after that, all his father's servants left him, and how he and his brothers were in consequence obliged to labour on their father's estate. He described how tenants used to come "secretly" "long distances to pay their rents." They did it, said the witness, because they feared the League— "feared murder and outrage."

In cross-examination by Sir Charles Russell, it appeared that the following were some of the Land Court reductions of rent on the estates which, according to Mr. Sandys's evidence, were managed in a spirit of fairness—from £46 to £30, from £23 to £18, from £15 to £12, from £18 to £11. The Poor Law valuation on the £46 rent was £26; on the £23 rent, £12; and £10 on the £15 rent. Sir Charles Russell read out the figures, but Mr. Sandys was unable, just then, to check them.

And now, having shown by means of the correspondence already mentioned how the Land League branches were organized all over Ireland, the Attorney-General called for Dennis Tobin. Tobin, a dark-haired young man with a pallid complexion, sharpish features, and alert manner, described himself as a member of a moonlighting society in his native county of Limerick. He joined the moonlighters' society in 1880, and he declared that the society existed "at the present day." He rattled off his answers to Sir Richard Webster's questions, glibly, fluently, without a moment's hesitation. He spoke as one who had his eyes about him wherever he went, and upon whom not one of his exciting experiences had been lost. He incriminated the Land League right and left—associating its organizers with the secret society, for the perpetration of outrage. The man who swore him into the secret society, a man named McInery, was, said Tobin, a leaguer; "to my knowledge he established all the League branches round about." This man told me, he continued, that the "moonlighters were the support of the League; and that without them the leaguers could do no good." Tobin also gave a rapid matter-of-fact statement of the oath he took as a moonlighter—to be "true to my counthree," and to "bate down landlords and their agents;" and "if I refrained I was to suffer death."

Then Mr. Tobin proceeded to narrate how the secret department of the Land League was organized. In his district of Limerick there were three subdivisions, each with its "captain." He named the three captains—Morrissey, Conners, and Griffin, the last being a tailor. And all three of them were alive; at least he could answer for the two who were still at home, but Conners was in Australia. Of these local "captains" the chief was, he said, this same man, McInery, who swore him in; and he continued to be Captain-General until the time of his arrest as a suspect; and when he was arrested he was succeeded by another leaguer, of the name of William Mangan.

Could Mr. Tobin name any other member of the society? He could; and he named Matt Delhan, Tom Griffin, James Griffin, William Lyon, Tim Leahy, and Morris Leahy. Now, asked Sir Richard Webster, of all these moonlighters, how many would you think were leaguers? "I would say," was the answer, and here Mr. Tobin raised his eyebrows and threw out his chest, "I would say the whole were members of the League." For the sake of connection it may here be stated that Tobin himself was not a leaguer. This he stated in his cross-examination by Sir Charles Russell. So that Mr. Tobin must have been indebted to his fellow-moonlighters, who were leaguers, for his knowledge of what was said and done in the League. Delhan, one of the leaguers and moonlighters named in the foregoing list, had, he said, told him about the "resolutions" passed at League meetings for "raiding" persons whom the League disapproved. And these resolutions, Tobin added, were read at the moonlighters' secret meetings. Passing on to his further connection with associations, he said that he joined the National League in 1885 or 1886 —the Brossna branch of it, of which a man named Moriarty was secretary, and a man named Curtin, treasurer. Moriarty and Curtin are still living in Brossna, said he. T. J. Conners was secretary of another local branch, whom Mr. Tobin said he knew.

Mr. Tobin next described how the moonlighter and leaguer Delhan had supplied him with a gun and a revolver, which he kept secretly, "off and on," for six years, and how, after the end of the six years, he gave back the weapons to Captain Morrissey (one of the three local captains already named). But it did not appear that Tobin ever made any use either of gun or revolver. Still he was engaged on several criminal expeditions, the first of which was a raid on Pat Conners's cattle, at the instigation of the T. J. Conners whom he had already described as a League secretary. And this same T. J. Conners gave Griffin (Mr. Tobin's moonlighter friend) £5 to do the "job." Mr. Tobin gave an account of the scene where he and his fellow-moonlighters assembled for the purpose of "lifting" Pat Conners's cattle; how, dreading the police, who had a hut near the spot, they attempted nothing that night; how they returned the next night, and how their courage again failed them; and a third night, and how it again failed; and how the conscientious Griffin exclaimed at last that "there was five pounds gone, and we've done nothing." However, the gang made some amends to their employers, for, subsequently to the three meetings at Pat's, one of them returned and slaughtered one of Pat's cows. Some time after the above attempt at an exploit, Mr. Tobin was engaged on another expedition—against a Miss Thompson's cattle. The locality was called Knocknalough, which was one of the three moonlighting centres of which he spoke at the beginning of his evidence. At the rendezvous "I met five men and myself," remarked Mr. Tobin. Here the rascals did something for their money; they killed three cows. Then they left behind them a hatchet which they had used in the killing, and the hatchet was found by the police. How much did Mr. Tobin get for this "job"? Seven shillings and sixpence. And this money was paid to him, according to his story, by the League secretary, T. J. Conners, already named. The rest of Mr. Tobin's exploits may be briefly summed up. He was engaged in what he called a "frightening plan"—an example of which was his firing into the house of a certain James Walsh, who had supplied horses to a boycotted farmer named Pat Sullivan. Then, again, he was engaged with others in beating Dennis Connor because he worked for the Pat Conners of an earlier part of the story. At another place, he and his fellow-moonlighters stole a gun. And he would have visited somebody else, but that, said Mr. Tobin, "I got ill—I got the colic." Finally, Mr. Tobin himself was so hardly pressed that he, too, took service on an evicted farm. For this reason he was boycotted by his former colleagues, the moonlighter-leaguers, and his house was fired into. Poetic justice; he was treated as he himself would have treated James Walsh's. This was in 1887. And in the end, he and his former associates were now at loggerheads.

Although unprepared to question a witness who had been "sprung upon" him, Sir Charles Russell cross-examined. Mr. Tobin told him that he never was a Land Leaguer, and that it was the end of 1885, or the beginning of 1886, before he joined the National League. What did he know, then, of the National League branch of which he became a member? Next to nothing, as it turned out. He did not know who the president was; he could not identify the treasurer; he could only say that Moriarty took his card of membership money. Nor could he clearly identify the place where the National League met, nor say positively who the owner or occupier of the house was, except that he thought it was a man named Moore. He had only been twice at the National League office—one Sunday, when he went to pay his shilling; another Sunday, when he went for his card. Did he get his card? No. "They were out of cards," both Sundays. Tobin next confessed he had never seen any of his moonlighting friends at Land League meetings, or National League meetings; and also that he had never seen, at his moonlight trips, any of the Nationalist leaguers whom he had met on the occasion of his two only visits to the National League office. These two admissions Sir Charles Russell, after repeated questions, made sure of. All that Tobin could remember was that Moriarty occupied the chair the first Sunday and Curtin the second, and that he "never," "never" received his card of membership. Mr. Tobin pronounced his "never" with much emphasis, raising his eyebrows and gazing at the ceiling. "So then," said Sir Charles Russell, "it comes to this, that apart from what you were told by other people you had no reason for supposing that M'Inery and the other moonlighters whom you named were leaguers." Mr. Tobin admitted that that was the case. And Moriarty was regarded in the locality as a respectable man? Yes. And Curtin? Here Mr. Tobin hesitated. Perhaps he doesn't come up to your ideas of respectability? suggested Sir Charles.

Ever been in any trouble? Sir Charles inquired curiously. No; Mr. Tobin never had been. "Very well—very well. Ever in prison?" "Yes." "Oh, wasn't that trouble?" "No trouble to me," retorted Mr. Tobin, drawing himself up. What was he in prison for? For an assault on John Conners, and he was kept six weeks in gaol.

Sergeant Fawcett, R.I.C., and another witness, gave evidence about a Mr. Cronan, an active Nationalist, who had been sending in supplies of food to a large number of prisoners awaiting trial on charges of moonlighting and other crimes, and in whose company one of the witnesses had seen Mr. John O'Connor, M.P., Mr. Lane, M.P., Mr. O'Hea, M.P., Mr. Gilhooly, M.P., and Mr. T. Healy, M.P. Mr. Healy and Mr. O'Connor visited the moonlighters in prison, said the witness. Then a deputy inspector of the R.I.C., with his sword by his side, entered the box and gave evidence regarding letters and documents—including a copy of an Amended Constitution of the Irish Republican Brotherhood—which he had seized in the house of Mr. Coghlan, secretary of a local branch of the Land League in Mayo. Among the letter writers was Miss Parnell. The letters referred generally to legal processes in defence of prisoners charged with agrarian offences and crimes. Finally Captain Slack, a divisional commissioner for eight counties in Ireland, dated the beginning of the present trouble in Ireland from the year of the League, alleging that before 1879 he had never heard of moonlighting, nor of outrage upon people for paying their rent.

THIRTY-EIGHTH DAY.

JANUARY 24.

CAPTAIN SLACK'S evidence was, in some respects, the most important and interesting yet made before the Commission. To any one desirous of realizing the actual condition of the Ireland of Land and National Leagues, and moonlighter societies, and agrarian crime, this magistrate's testimony must be of the highest value.

Captain Slack's official experience began twenty years ago; and for several years he has had, as a divisional magistrate, jurisdiction over eight counties. What then is his deliberate opinion? That the Land and National Leagues are the cause of the disturbance—the social war, with its burnings, mutilations, and murders—which in his belief began with 1879-1880. He has arrived at the conclusion by a process of exhaustive reasoning, mainly. Before 1879-80 he had not even heard of land-grabbing and moonlighting; nor of punishment, by outrage, of tenants who took farms "behind the backs" of their neighbours; nor of police reinforcements for the purpose of protecting intimidated tenants: and he maintained that the amount of agrarian distress was insufficient to account for the new outbreaks of crime—crime which, he said, was new in kind. Except this new society, the Land League, said Captain Slack, there was none to which he could attribute the new disturbance and crime. Be it observed that Captain Slack insists on the newness of them— new, that is, since 1879.

In putting his argument into a more detailed form Captain Slack said he had observed: (1) That denunciatory resolutions and speeches of League branches and League orators were followed by outrages. (2) And that when crimes were perpetrated upon persons not obeying what were known to be League rules, no repudiation of these crimes followed from the League. So far, his charges against the League were inferential. But Captain Slack asserted that he had received private information of League encouragement and authorization of crime—which information had sometimes enabled him to prevent intended outrages. "You always tested your secret information?" he was asked. Always; and Captain Slack then explained, to a very attentive audience, how, for his own guidance and information, he had been collecting and classifying extracts from Nationalist newspaper reports on League meetings and League speeches. As he stood there, in his box, Captain Slack had his volumes of extracts and MS. notes, his official lists of riots, all about him, ranged very neatly. He must have been a diligent and conscientious reader of the Irish papers—to judge from the bulk of his extracts. And he had mastered them. At a hint, or a question, from the Attorney-General, down Captain Slack's hand went upon the particular cutting or MS. wanted. The divisional magistrate is a methodical man. Captain Slack is short and stout, bald—with a fringe of yellowish hair—clean shaven, ruddy; he has a good-humoured, alert look, and his movements are as lively as his eyes.

If in the pre-League period Ireland was the peaceful Arcadia which Captain

Slack (like the landlords and agents who have preceded him in court) represented it to be, how could he account for the eighty-nine Coercion Acts of the century? Was he not aware that the Governments which introduced all the Coercion Bills justified their action on the ground of the general prevalence of *agrarian* crime? After a little hesitation, Captain Slack replied that his professional experience did not begin till 1868. Then there speedily followed another admission, that the Land Act passed only two years after 1868 did not, as he thought, go "far enough" in affording relief to the Irish peasantry. Still, he considered that the Land Acts subsequently to 1880 did far more than enough. They were "gratuitous" interferences between landlord and tenant, suggested Sir Charles Russell, a description of them to which the divisional magistrate did not demur. "You are a landlord yourself," Sir Charles remarked carelessly, and he became absorbed in a list containing the names of some of Captain Slack's own tenants. There was one of Captain Slack's tenants whose poor law valuation was £23, old rent £40, and judicial rent £22—£18 struck off a rent of £40. Another tenant, whose poor law valuation was £14, paid a rent of £23, which the Land Commissioners reduced to £15, and the £23 rent had been raised from £10, the figure at which it stood in 1859. A third tenant's old rent of £5 was reduced by the Commissioners to £4. And a fourth tenant, who paid £7, succeeded on appeal to the Commissioners in getting a remission of £3. In the above statements of figures the shillings are omitted. At the end of each statement Sir Charles would look up from his paper, remove his glasses, and gaze at Captain Slack. He pronounced his "twenty-two pounds," in the first of his four statements, loudly. All the while Captain Slack stood bolt upright in his box, his arms folded, his chest thrown out, his head on one side. He did not consider that such reductions were necessary. "So you are not free from landlord feeling," remarked his cross-examiner; upon which Captain Slack retorted that he was unprejudiced on the matter.

Then came a most interesting part of the cross-examination. Asked whether he considered that, apart from agrarian crime, Ireland was as free from lawlessness as any country in the world, Captain Slack admitted, after some hesitation, that he believed it was. What, then, was the origin of this agrarian crime? Divisional Magistrate Captain Slack had already enunciated his theory and honest conviction that the League was its parent. Very well, then; Sir Charles Russell proceeded to investigate the case on the supposition that the Land League caused it. "Can you," he was challenged, "tell me a single case of agrarian murder in Tipperary since 1879?" Captain Slack plunged into MSS. and newspaper extracts. He turned over the leaves rapidly one after the other. He could not recollect any such case. "A single case in Kilkenny county?" Again Captain Slack consulted his documents, fruitlessly. And he was equally unsuccessful as regards other districts, such as Carlow and Wicklow. "And yet," exclaimed Sir Charles Russell, raising his voice, "in every parish of every one of these counties, there has been since 1879 a branch of the League." This was admitted. And in the county Tipperary alone there were one hundred and thirty branches of the League? "At least," was the reply. There, then, was an illustration, or rather a group of illustrations, of the League existing where murders were absent.

"Now take Tipperary before the League," Sir Charles Russell continued, asking Captain Slack if he recollected cases of murderous outrage, and of threatening notices long before 1879. But Captain Slack had no knowledge of them. In part of his cross-examination, as well as at its commencement, Captain Slack admitted his lack of acquaintance with the Parliamentary Bluebook literature of agrarian Ireland, and with the investigations and conclusions of Commissions—such as the Devon Commission. In the earlier part of his evidence Captain Slack expressed his belief that such agrarian outrages as did exist before 1879 arose from individual and private malice. And now Sir Charles Russell asked him whether he did not know that Commissions of Inquiry in Ireland had always reported that the peasant community, as a rule, screened agrarian crime—that, in other words, the tenants combined to conceal crime long before the League ever existed. Captain Slack replied that he did not know. Sir Charles Russell now approached the question from a third direction. There were some good years after 1870, were there not? Yes; some of them very good. And did not crime fall off during these years? Yes. And did you not see that, when the bad years returned and the rents pressed hardly, crime once more increased? Yes. And was it not the case that crime abounded most in the districts where the population was densest and the poverty greatest? That, also, Captain Slack admitted.

Sir Charles then invited Captain Slack to quote a single case in which a man had been forced to join the League. In his examination-in-chief, Captain Slack stated that the League practically became the government of whatever district it was established in; and that sometimes persons were obliged to join it. And now Captain Slack explained that he had only had private information of compulsory membership. As no names were to be mentioned this part of the subject was not pursued further. Sir Charles Russell next challenged the witness to produce a single case in which denunciation by the League had caused outrage. Captain Slack searched his inflammatory newspaper articles. At last he found an extract from *The Munster Express*, describing how a man who, in January, 1885, had put his cows to graze on an "evicted" farm was punished in October of the same year by the mutilation of his cows' tails. But it turned out that from beginning to end of the newspaper extracts there was not a word of denunciation of the cow owner. "Where is the denunciation?" Sir Charles Russell asked. But Captain Slack's reply was to the effect that the cow owner had done something which, as a matter of course, was against League policy, as indicated in League rules. On this document there was an entry in red ink to the effect that this new case "proved denunciation clearly." After a good deal of discussion over this point Captain Slack admitted that that was not the kind of document he was in search of. Could he quote any other instance? He could not, just then. And here Captain Slack explained that though he had not the required documents with him in court, he could produce them. Captain Slack had kept notes and extracts for his private use of no fewer than six hundred and fourteen League meetings, although, as already said, he could not produce at the moment even one such instance as Sir Charles Russell was asking for. Mr. Lockwood followed Sir Charles Russell with a few questions on the witness's statement that the League did not denounce crime. Mr. Lockwood referred to speeches by Mr. Parnell, Mr. John Redmond, M.P., Mr. Dwyer Gray, M.P., Mr. Arthur O'Connor, M.P., and other prominent leaguers, all condemning outrage; but Captain Slack, notwithstanding his wide journalistic reading, was unacquainted with them. If you had been acquainted with these speeches, asked Mr. Lockwood, would you have modified your opinion about the leaguers' abstention from condemning outrage! To which question Captain Slack replied with considerable hesitation and embarrassment that he would have admitted the exceptions.

With the exception of the half-hour's interval and of a few minutes devoted to the correspondence of the Ladies' Land League, the whole of the sitting from half-past twelve to four o'clock was spent in the reading of speeches delivered in Ireland years ago by the members of the Parnellite party, speeches which are public property, recorded in every newspaper. These speeches dealt generally with the principles of the League; fair rents; and peasant proprietorship, on equitable terms of purchase; and boycotting of persons who settled with their landlords on terms which the associated leaguers considered unfair.

What was the object of all that reading, Sir James Hannen asked. If it was desirable to make these speeches known to a wider public than was present in court, could it not be done in print? "I have read all these speeches through in my room," said Sir James. "I have spent days over them." And he added that if they were to be read through in full in court many days would have to be spent over the task. Could not the speeches be sent in without being read? Mr. Lockwood at once accepted the suggestion, adding that passages considered relevant should be marked. Sir Henry James, however, demurred to this proposal. Without the consent of the Attorney-General, who was not present, he could not omit the reading of his extracts. And so the reading was resumed. Mr. Lockwood read all he had to say from Mr. Biggar's speech. Then Sir Henry James followed. Next Mr. Asquith followed Sir Henry James. And so on through the slow hours. One of the most important of the speeches was Mr. Parnell's at Ennis, September 19, 1880, which was read *in extenso*. Mr. Asquith read Mr. Parnell's advice to his hearers to abstain from violence; and Sir Henry James read Mr. Parnell's observation that there was "a better way" than shooting grabbers—namely, "cutting" them, boycotting them; and then, again, Mr. Asquith read the passages in which Mr. Parnell expressed the hope that landlords and tenants might settle their differences "peacefully and quietly" while there was yet time.

THIRTY-NINTH AND FORTIETH DAYS.

JAN. 25 AND 29.

WHEN the Court rose yesterday it was agreed that before next sitting counsel on both sides should try to agree upon some plan by which the reading of the speeches delivered by the Irish members and others in Ireland since 1879 might be curtailed. When, however, the Court met to-day, Sir Henry James announced that, after consultation with the other side, he found he must proceed with the reading of those parts of the speeches which he considered to be relevant. Whereupon Mr. Reid observed that in that case he and his learned colleagues must read theirs. "Yes, I see that," the President remarked; "if one side reads extracts, the other will claim to quote passages in qualification of them. And then," he added, "have you reflected that as a matter of calculation the reading of these speeches will occupy eight or ten days?"

It would occupy some days, no doubt, Sir Henry James thought, but he expressed the hope that the reading might be got through sooner than the President anticipated. If this, continued Sir Henry James, were an ordinary inquiry, the documents would be put in without being read; but this was a public inquiry, and the speeches were important factors in *The Times* case, so that if they were not read "our tale would only be half told." This preliminary discussion ended in a prediction by Mr. Reid that in two or three days even Sir Henry's patience would give way. Then the reading began. The first speech read was one of Mr. T. Healy's, delivered in county Cork eight and a half years ago. From this speech it appeared how a veterinary surgeon had told Mr. Healy that certain cows' tails looked as if they had been cut off by a sword bayonet, and how thereupon Mr. Healy suggested "perhaps the officers at the barracks wanted to have some ox-tail soup." Mr. Parnell, Mr. Arthur O'Connor, Mr. T. M. Sullivan, Mr. John Dillon, Mr. Matt Harris, were among the Irish members whose old speeches were read. "Scrab" also flitted across the oratorical waste. One of Mr. Matt Harris's speeches aroused a little interest, for a moment or two. This was the renowned partridge speech: "If the tenant farmers of Ireland shot down the landlords as partridges were shot down in November, then Matt Harris would never say one word against them." Mr. Lockwood, for the Parnellite side, now rose to quote further statements of Mr. Harris, in explanation of the passage about partridges—Mr. Harris had in his mind's eye a picture of the ruthless exterminator, and a picture of the exterminator's victim, and what he meant by the unfortunate expression was that he would not stay the victim's hand while the oppressor's was free. There were some amusing instances of the figurative style. Thus, Mike Boyton spoke of land-grabbers as "rank weeds that were growing on the green soil that was once pressed by the blessed footsteps of St. Bridget." Throughout the day the attendance was extremely small. Even the Press seats were two-thirds empty.

The next day also, the fortieth, was spent in the reading of speeches—a dreary business, the droning monotone of which might well have sent the attenuated audience to sleep. As on the previous day, the Press seats were mostly empty. "The public" was conspicuous by its absence. The most noteworthy speeches read were some by Mr. Boyton, Mr. Dillon, Mr. Biggar, Mr. T. D. Sullivan, Mr. J. P. Gordon, in the years 1880-85. The first speech of Boyton's spoke of a land-grabber as being no less odious a person than an informer, and as a person who should be regarded as "a miserable traitor." In order to qualify the passages read by Sir Henry James, Mr. Lockwood read passages in which Boyton said that Ireland was to be regenerated, not on the battle-field, but by civilized methods, and the consent of Irishmen to live and work together. Then Sir Henry James read the speech in which Mr. Dillon was represented as having said he would show the tenants a better way than the shooting of grabbers (this in correction of a man in the crowd who called out "shoot him"). The better way was social excommunication, for which, as Mr. Dillon held, the law could not punish them. Five of Mr. Dillon's speeches were quoted, Mr. Reid citing passages in which Mr. Dillon denounced the reporting of bogus outrages intended to excite English feeling against Ireland; and in which he emphatically repudiated the assertion of the League's enemies that the movement was mixed up with crime. This tit for tat method of reading extracts was again followed in the case of Mr. T. D. Sullivan's speeches, Sir Henry James showing how Mr. Sullivan advocated such ubiquitous organization of the League as would necessitate the employment of increased police forces; and Mr. Lockwood showing how Mr. Sullivan denounced, in the strongest language, crime of every kind. A speech of P. J. Gordon's was read, but Mr. T. Harrington pointed out that when the speech was delivered Gordon was under arrest, and also that the speech was delivered from a railway carriage window, and not at a League meeting. In his rambles over eight years of Irish oratory, Sir Henry James quoted a speech in which Admiral Hewett's offer of a thousand pounds for the capture of Osman Digna was mentioned, and a comparison drawn between the Soudanese Arabs and the oppressed population of Ireland. Sir James Hannen mildly remarked that he could not see the relevancy of the Osman Digna incident. "Neither do I, my lord," exclaimed Mr. Lockwood, in his prompt, downright way.

FORTY-FIRST DAY.

JANUARY 30.

THE dreary reading of the speeches of 1885-6 occupied half the day. Among the principal speeches quoted were some by Mr. Davitt and Mr. Biggar, the former of whom advised the Clare tenants to barricade their houses, and the latter of whom was represented to have said that land-grabbers were, in his opinion, greater criminals than most who perished on the scaffold, and that the tenants, when they saw a land-grabber enter chapel, should "leave him alone in a corner by himself, for then his life would become intolerable, and he would be glad to side at last with the tenants who were fighting against impossible rents."

After the reading of the extracts was done with, Mr. W. Hanley, landlord, agent, battering-ram supervisor all in one, was called to testify to what, in his opinion, was the effect of Land League preaching on forty-two different estates with which he was connected.

Mr. Hanley lived near Thurles, in Tipperary. Up to 1879 he had been, he said, on excellent terms with his tenants; and, according to his own view of the matter, with good reason, seeing that only two years ago the Land Commissioners, instead of making reductions, made large additions to the rents of a number of tenants.

It was in 1881 that Mr. Hanley and his tenants fell out—immediately after the first Land League branch was established in his neighbourhood. His own tenants, twelve or so in number, came in a body and demanded a reduction of 20 per cent. "Many of them were much better off than I was myself," said the witness. Then he described how four of them came to him in secret to pay their rents in full. Others, he said, asked him to serve them with writs, and even to seize their cattle. He had to serve the writs himself, as nobody would do it for him. The only servant who remained with him had his house fired into. More than forty landlords, giving up the attempt to collect their rents, employed Mr. Hanley as their agent. He must have discharged his duties resolutely, for he was boycotted many years, and when necessary he superintended in person the play of the battering-ram upon the non-paying tenants' houses—"forts" as they are called all over disturbed Ireland.

Once or twice in the course of his examination-in-chief Mr. Hanley spoke of the secret visits of some of his tenants. One of them, said the witness, told him that eviction would pay him better than possession, because of what he would "make" from the League. Another tenant met him secretly in somebody's bedroom. The somebody was a publican; and after the man paid his "rint" he became conscious of a "wakeness," so that Mr. Hanley had to fortify him with brandy. But Mr. Hanley's opinion was that the man's weakness arose from fear of the leaguers.

Sir Charles Russell cross-examined Mr. Hanley. It now appeared that the tenants whose rents the Land Commissioners increased in 1887 were leaseholders. "Can you mention," asked Sir Charles Russell, "a single instance, on those forty properties, of a yearly tenant having his rent raised on going into court?" Mr. Hanley could not recollect one. Mr. Hanley then stated that many of the yearly tenants were given twenty to twenty-five and even thirty per cent. reduction, without going before the Commissioners. "I don't know," said Sir Charles Russell, "but it is attributed to you that you have a battering-ram on your premises." "I have," said Mr. Hanley. "Is that to assist in battering down the houses of tenants who are to be evicted?" "It is to save time," was the reply. "And for motives of humanity?" "Not exactly. But I may say that I attend all evictions on my property to prevent outrage." "How do you manage the battering-ram—by machinery?" "It is drawn by horses." "Do you mean to say that the Land League was the source of all the mischief?" Mr. Hanley admitted that he did not. In fact, he supposed that it began three years before the rise of the League; in the depression of 1876, or of 1877, or 1878; but he added that the people in his district did not appear to be affected by the distress of those years. He also admitted that the bulk of the people in his neighbourhood (landlords, agents, and their dependants excepted) were members of the League.

FORTY-SECOND DAY.

JANUARY 31.

THE first witness of the day was Constable Farrell. He gave some additional testimony about the murder of Lord Mountmorres, on which, it will be remembered, the informer Burke has already been examined. Constable Farrell was stationed in September, 1880, at Clonbur (near which Lord Mountmorres lived). Constable Farrell remembered that Burke the informer and Sweeney were working together on the day of the murder, and on the spot described by Burke. As for Carney's public-house, at which it was said the murderers and their confederates met before the crime, Constable Farrell stated that it was usually frequented by leaguers. On the day after the murder, said the witness, there was a Land League meeting in Clonbur market-place, and the processionists marched round Carney, carrying their banners, and also what Mr. Farrell called imitation guns.
Imitation guns? What were they? Sir Charles Russell asked the witness. Mr. Farrell explained that they were "wooden" guns, "imitation" guns, he repeated; and that there must have been forty or fifty of them in the procession. But was the procession glorifying Carney? Not necessarily, for, in reply to his cross-examiner, Mr. Farrell said that Carney was only one of a crowd round which the procession was marching. "Perhaps you might have been in the centre yourself?" Sir Charles suggested. Then followed some questions with a view to finding out whether, quite apart from the League, Lord Mountmorres had done anything to make himself unpopular. To which questions Constable Farrell replied he had heard that Lord Mountmorres had boasted of his intercourse with the "Castle," and also that Lord Mountmorres had been under police protection since August, 1879—a year, or more, before the foundation of the Clonbur branch of the Land League. Then came Mike Roche. The object of the examination of this witness, also, was to test the evidence of an informer—Buckley. Mike Roche (who after his examination-in-chief said that he had read part of Buckley's evidence) now corroborated Buckley's story about his attempt to shoot him (Roche), and about Buckley's revolver "'clicking" repeatedly, that is, missing fire. Mike Roche described himself as an ex-leaguer who had been boycotted for having paid a rent of which the League disapproved. He was an amusing example of a Kerry witness. He spoke with fearful rapidity, and in a monotonous voice, unmodulated, save for the high shrill key in which he ended every sentence. He spoke excitedly, swaying from side to side, emphasizing his periods with a sharp little nod, and, on the smallest provocation, running off into personal reminiscences and family histories. He narrated the Buckley episodes as excitedly as if the terrible Buckley were at that moment behind the witness-box with

his revolver "clicking." Mike rapped off his answers before the questions were ended—a trick against which Sir Charles Russell, when his time came to cross-examine, protested in vain. "Who brought you to London?" asked Sir Charles Russell. "A summons," was the sharp reply; and on the instant he searched his pockets. He had already undone the buttons of his waistcoat when he stopped short, on being told the thing was not wanted. "Perhaps you could show us your five pounds?" Sir Charles suggested. "No," quoth Mike; "but I'll show you my return ticket;" and he wriggled about desperately amongst his pockets. As nobody wanted to see his return ticket, Mike rushed off at full speed through a domestic tragi-comedy about a gate (the same gate of which informer Buckley had spoken long since). But Mike had one virtue. When pulled up in his gallops he came to a sudden dead-stop —always; but, then, when the chance offered away he went again. Sir Charles Russell, reading from a printed document, asked him whether it was not the fact that he had been expelled from the Land League for having given information to the police. He emphatically, indignantly denied this, insisting that he had been expelled because he had paid his rent. At the same time he admitted that there had been rumours of his having given information. He could not recollect whether Buckley had seized him when about to shoot him. [Buckley said he seized Roche by the collar.] He next confessed, rather by accident, that Buckley and himself had been at enmity long before the shooting business, and that Buckley had been twice fined by the magistrates for assaulting him. One "assault" was described as a "shove," which cost Buckley half-a-crown. "Now, on your oath," asked Sir Charles Russell, "was Buckley a leaguer?" Mike could not say that he was. By his own accounts of himself Mike could scarcely have been a flawless citizen. He was under police protection, and yet his protectors were always putting him under lock and key, on charges of inebriety. How many times? Could not tell? Twenty-eight? Didn't know. Mike looked slightly disgusted when Sir Charles Russell asked him whether Buckley might not have been shamming. "I swear on my solemn oath that Buckley did his best to shoot me dead on the shpot."

Mike was followed by a witness named Sheehy, who said that he saw Buckley with a revolver on the day on which Mike was "clicked" at. Sheehy had a poor opinion of Buckley. He would scarcely believe Buckley on his oath, and he said that Buckley was regarded as a nuisance in the neighbourhood. By the way, there was just one other detail in which Mike's story differed from informer Buckley's. Buckley said his pistol did not go off, even once. Mike now said he heard a bullet whiz past his ear; at any rate, he thought he heard one. But he allowed that it might have been an imaginary bullet. Mike ran off to the magistrate's, and the magistrate was so perplexed by Mike's variations of his story that, instead of putting the clicking Buckley under lock and key, he bound him over, as Mike said, "to keep the pace, your lordships."

FORTY-THIRD DAY.

February 1.

IN the meantime, Divisional-Magistrate Captain Slack had gone to Ireland for his private documents, from which he said he would prove causal connection between outrages and League speeches. Yesterday he re-entered the witness-box, bringing with him his papers, in folio volumes neatly covered with brown paper. A methodical man was Captain Slack. He could put his finger, at a moment's notice, upon any newspaper cutting (and his written comments upon the same). And he did it through the yawning half-hours. Except the judges, and the counsel immediately engaged, none paid the smallest attention to Captain Slack's extracts; but Captain Slack went through his work smilingly, with an expression of boundless satisfaction. To-day, he reappeared for further cross-examination.

Mr. Davitt took Captain Slack in hand, with a series of common-sense and, at the same time novel, questions in arithmetic. Captain Slack admitted that in the six counties with which he had been specially connected there must have been at least three hundred League branches. Counting the average number of speeches at these branches there must have been delivered during the years of which Captain Slack took note one hundred and forty-four thousand speeches! But as Captain Slack cited only twenty-four cases of what he regarded as crime resulting from inflammatory speeches of the League, "did not that give a very small percentage of outrages?" Mr. Davitt asked. Captain Slack after a pause replied that it did, but, he added, "I only brought forward those cases as examples. I could bring others."

Mr. Reid then asked Captain Slack if he could produce an exhaustive list of the cases upon which he relied for proof of his proposition that outrages had been caused by League speeches. To this Captain Slack replied that the production would entail "interminable" labour; it would necessitate his going through years of records, and producing witnesses to prove every incident. The discussion ended with an emphatic declaration on the part of Sir Charles Russell that as a matter of fact Captain Slack's evidence was merely a statement of outrages with the motives suggested.

And now for the first time an English police-constable stepped into the witness-box. This was Head-Constable Wilkinson, of Rochdale, who described the seizure at the Navigation Inn, Rochdale, in February, 1881, of documents in the possession of John Walsh, an organizer of the English branches of the Irish League. Among the documents seized was a green card containing, in one column, a list of English towns designated by letters of the alphabet; while a second column was headed "men," a third "short furniture," a fourth "long furniture," and another "pills." (The alleged meaning of "furniture" is firearms, and of "pills" ammunition.) Another paper found among Walsh's documents was entitled "Cash received from F. Byrne from March 13th." There were also papers containing accounts for travelling expenses and salary, and again, a copy of the rules of the Irish Republican Brotherhood.

Next came Inspector Tunbridge, of Scotland Yard, who produced a letter alleged to be John Walsh's. The letter was dated Havre, March 22, 1881, and was addressed to the Secretary of the Bank of England, informing the secretary of Walsh's loss of two ten-pound notes in Havre, and asking that payment of them should be stopped. Mr. Tunbridge proved that one of the lost notes had formerly been in Byrne's possession. Further evidence regarding the note was given by a clerk of the Pearl Insurance Office, who declared that he had seen, in a cheque-book at the office, the counterfoil of a cheque in payment for which the note had been accepted. The same witness also said that he had often seen Frank Byrne in the office with Mr. Foley, the manager, who is now a member of Parliament. Next, one or two witnesses followed each other rapidly. Sergeant Sheridan, of the Dublin police force, proved the warrant which had been issued for the arrest of Walsh, and he stated that the charge against him was that he had been accessory before the fact to the murder of Lord Frederick Cavendish and Mr. Burke. Mr. William Jackman, another police-officer, from Bradford, stated that he had seen Walsh attending meetings of the Land League and the Fenian Brotherhood in Bradford in 1881-3.

Constable Coulston, of the same town, corroborated the foregoing testimony, and then said that he had found in the house of a man named Tobin some boxes containing forty revolvers and a quantity of cartridges. The witness had frequently seen Tobin in Walsh's company. Then Mr. Withers, chief-constable of Bradford, followed with a statement to the effect that after Tobin's arrest in November, 1881, he had discovered a quantity of documents in his house. At this point Sir Charles Russell observed that Tobin was not even mentioned in the Attorney-General's "particulars," and that the man's movements were beyond the scope of the inquiry. The Attorney-General argued that Walsh and Tobin were working together "in one organization."

Sir Charles Russell—But which organization?
The Attorney-General—They are one and the same. When we have shown that Tobin was in connection with Walsh, when we have shown that there was a deposit of arms in Tobin's house, and that Walsh, a Land League organizer, was engaged in depositing arms about, we say the documents are admissible.

Sir James Hannen, however, ruled that the Attorney-General was entitled to put in the documents. On the reading of one of them, Sir Charles Russell warmly protested. Here, he said, was a letter without even a date. And were they to go back to the year 1866?

The President—I must protest against the way in which you conduct this case, Sir Charles. We have given our decision. We are not infallible; but as we have given our decision it must not be re-opened again.
Sir Charles Russell—I don't wish to re-open it. I say that we did not know of the contents of this letter until it was read, and that now it is read I am entitled to ask your lordships to consider the point again.
The President—Instead of asking us you address us in an aggressive mode that is most unbecoming.
Sir Charles Russell—I don't wish to appear unbecoming or aggressive. But I feel very strongly upon the point.

Chief-Constable Withers, continuing his evidence, stated that Tobin was in 1882 sentenced to seven years' penal servitude for treason-felony.

FORTY-FOURTH DAY.

FEBRUARY 5.

TO-DAY the Attorney-General entered upon the American part of his case. An interesting personage is Honoré Le Caron, private and subsequently major in the Northern army during the great war, and afterwards, and now—according to his own account—a high and responsible officer in the Fenian organization which still dreams of overthrowing the power of Great Britain. His name is French; but the man himself, the "Senior Guardian" of Fenian Camp No. 463 (now altered to 421), is an Englishman, whose birthplace is Colchester. My baptismal name is Thomas Miller Beach, said the major. He paused at each of his three names, pronouncing them with slow, distinct emphasis, and nodding his head as if to punctuate them. Major Le Caron is short and slightish in build; erect—like a soldier—and imperturbably cool; he has a lofty forehead, and smallish, alert eyes, which look straight. The major's is one of the boniest faces in or out of the New World,—a death's-head with a tight skin of yellow parchment. With his arms folded over his chest—like another short man, the great Napoleon—he raps out his answers, short, sharp. "Yes, yes," he says, snappishly sometimes, pronouncing it "yus."

Having risen to the rank of major in the Federal army, Major Le Caron became a member of the American Fenian organization in 1865. An Irishman named O'Neill was, it appeared, the first who made overtures of membership to Le Caron. The Colchester Englishman turned his information about his fellow Fenians to a use they were not dreaming of. The Fenians "raided" Canada twice, the second time in 1870, and, said the major, "I communicated every detail to the Canadian Government." He made this confession with an unembarrassed promptitude and candour that considerably amused his audience. "Both expeditions were lamentable failures," added the major, with a little toss of the head. Of course, for, according to Major Le Caron, the "Colonials" had a smart man in their intelligence department. Major Le Caron was, he said, in a good position to know the secrets of the Fenian organization; for he became, in the summer of 1868, one of its military organizers. An ex-major of the Federal army he became a major in the "Army of the Irish Republican Brotherhood," and his name was still on its "pay list."

About five years after the second of the "lamentable failures," the Fenian Brotherhood was, said the witness, re-organized. And Major Le Caron promptly communicated details to the English Government. "And you received instructions from the Government?" "Yus." "And you joined the re-organized body?" "Yus." The purpose of this new organization was to unite all the Fenians in America, Canada, Australia, Great Britain, Ireland—throughout the world, in fact—against England. It was a sort of watchword with this re-organized party, that England's trouble was Ireland's opportunity: the new body was to seize opportunities of siding with England's enemies. The American Clan-na-Gael Society was a section of this world-wide organization, which had its "revolutionary fund," and its "skirmishing fund," from which—to cite a single example of its method of work—Mr. O'Kelly, M.P., had drawn funds for the purpose of buying the arms which he was shipping to Ireland. In America, this organization was divided into "camps," and Major Le Caron was made senior guardian of Camp 463. At the head of the organization was a directory, the members of which were representatives from the districts. This United Brotherhood was known sometimes as the "U.B.," sometimes as the "V.C." And here the Fenian major explained the nature of the Fenian official cipher—not a very occult cipher, it would seem. The cipher was devised by substituting for each letter of the alphabet the letter immediately succeeding it. Thus "V.C." means "U.B.," the United Brotherhood. Thus, again, the word Ireland is spelled, in American Fenianese, JSFMBOE. According to the above formula, "I.R.B.," meaning Irish Republican Brotherhood, should be spelled, in Fenianese, "J.S.C."

"I still hold the position of senior Camp Guardian," said Major Le Caron, folding his arms quietly. This amused Major Le Caron's hearers, and they were still more amused when he explained that the election to Camp Guardianships were made annually, and that "yesterday" was the election day for the year 1889. Major Le Caron identified a copy of the new Fenian Constitution, which the Attorney-General handed over to him. One of its chief articles was that the independence of Ireland must be won by arms. An official and member of the "U.B." (V.C.), he knew who the active members of the V.C. were—men such as Sullivan, Finerty, Judge Moran, Hynes, Devoy, Carroll, Breslin, and others. The U.B., otherwise the V.C., had its "skirmishing" and "revolutionary" funds, and the trustees of the skirmishing fund in 1887 were Breslin, Devoy, Carroll, Reynolds, Rossa, Austin Ford, T. C. Lubie, and T. F. Burke. The purpose of the Skirmishing Fund was to strike the enemy "wherever and whenever he could be found."

Devoy, he said, visited Ireland in 1879 for the purpose of inspecting the Fenian organization there. He said that Devoy on his return to America—July, 1879—was met by delegates from all the United Brethren districts in

America, to whom he made a report of his Irish visit. A copy of this report was read by the Attorney-General, who spent twenty minutes in reading it. At this meeting of delegates, said the witness, Hynes proposed a resolution to the effect that the independence of Ireland was to be won only by force of arms. Then he told a story about Mr. O'Kelly's position in the organization: Mr. O'Kelly was one of the agents of the revolutionary directory, in the task of procuring arms and shipping them off to Ireland. "I know," repeated the major, emphatically, "that Mr. O'Kelly had money from the skirmishing fund." Again, he said, when Mr. Dillon, Miss Parnell, and Mr. Parnell visited America at that time, they were taken in hand "exclusively" by the section of the revolutionary body known as the Clan-na-Gael.

Proceeding with his story, Major Le Caron gave a series of particulars which he said were confided to him by his colleagues in the Fenian organization—Devoy, and a man named Pat Mellady. Devoy had, he said, remarked to him in 1880 that, as the Irish Land League had already received money enough for its open work, the time had come for looking after their secret, or revolutionary methods. He was told at that time by his fellow Fenian Sullivan that a man named Wheeler had invented a hand grenade which was composed of some substance far more destructive than anything yet known ; that a dozen of these grenades could be carried in a satchel ; and that the fuses were so arranged as to enable the man who fired them to make good his escape before the explosion. In 1881, the major continued, I came to Europe with two sealed packets in my possession, one for Pat Egan, and the other for John O'Leary, both of whom were at that time in Paris. John O'Leary was the accredited agent of the U.B. and the I.R.B. Pat Egan, besides being a Land Leaguer, was a Fenian Brother. So was Mr. O'Kelly, M.P. The Irish Land League and the Brotherhood were, the witness again affirmed, inter-connected ; and he himself had been a local treasurer of the League in America.

And now Major Le Caron came to the most interesting part of his very long and extraordinarily detailed and precise narrative. Introducing himself to Egan, the treasurer of the Land League in Paris, he was "cordially received" by him. He saw Egan constantly for a period of about two weeks. "I had his entire confidence," said the major ; he emphasized the adjective, and his audience, now extremely attentive, laughed a little. Egan—so ran the story—told all about his work as a Fenian Brother in Dublin. " I am a Land Leaguer to-day," said Egan, " and I shall be something else when the occasion comes. Meanwhile I cannot see why both organizations (the Land League and the Brotherhood) should not work together, the one openly, the other secretly. Parnell himself is a revolutionist to the backbone." All this the witness promptly ran off, as if he were recollecting the exact words spoken in Paris eight years ago. Then he went on to throw an entirely novel light upon Mr. Parnell himself, and to tell us something about Mr. Parnell's failure to find admission to the Fenian Brotherhood. It was Egan who told him all about it. Said Egan, the Brotherhood in Ireland was at that time in such a state of disorganization that we thought Mr. Parnell would value it all the more highly if he continued to see it only from the outside ; so the Fenians refused to have him among them. As another instance of the "entire confidence" which Egan placed in his visitor from America, Egan told him how the Fenian-leaguers, or leaguer-Fenians, had helped the Boers in their fight with England. They did it by giving Land League money to a company of Dutch officers who left Europe to assist their kith and kin in South Africa. They did it, that is to say, through Mr. Pat Egan, the Land League secretary. In Paris, also, he met Mr. John O'Connor (not the M.P.), who was at that time variously known as "Dr. Clarke" and " Dr. Kinealy," and who was engaged, under the American Fenian organizer O'Leary already named, in shipping arms to Ireland. The major spent two weeks in Paris, and two more in London, where he met Mr.

Parnell. He was introduced to Mr. Parnell in the lobby of the House of Commons, and he now described, with an accuracy really surprising, the turnings and windings of the corridors through which he followed Mr. Parnell for the purpose of an undisturbed and confidential talk. This introduction took place in April, 1881. On another occasion, in the House of Commons, he met Mr. O'Kelly, who said that the American organization should "do something" to bring itself "into line" with the League, and who described the O'Leary (named above) as "an old fossil." Then Mr. Parnell saw the major, and Mr. Parnell said to him confidentially, "You Americans furnish us with the sinews of war; if we don't act properly you can stop the supplies."

According to Le Caron, Mr. Parnell at this same interview declared that he had "ceased to believe that anything but force would bring about the redemption of Ireland; and he told me he did not see why a successful insurrectionary movement should not be inaugurated" in the country. Then Major Le Caron returned to America, where he at once put himself into communication with Breslin, who was one of the three members of the revolutionary committee, and to whom he delivered messages from Mr. Parnell, one of the messages being a request that a member of the committee, Devoy, should come over to this country to confer with the League chief. The major said that among the members of the U.B. and R.I.B. brotherhoods in America, there was a growing dissatisfaction at the "lukewarmness" of the Irish Land League." But since 1881, added the witness, there has been a perfect understanding between the American organization and the Parnellite party in Ireland. Major Le Caron's story occupied the entire day.

FORTY-FIFTH DAY.

FEBRUARY 6.

IT is easy to see that the present production of American evidence bears directly upon "the letters." One of the Attorney-General's purposes was to show that the letter of the 15th of May, 1882, was just what might have been expected under those circumstances of intimate relationship between the Clan-na-Gael and other United Brethren of America, the Republican Brotherhood of Ireland, and the Land Leaguers, which the examination of Le Caron was meant to establish.

Shortly after midday there was an inrush of visitors. A buzz of excitement passed over the assemblage as Mr. Parnell entered. The collar of his lightbrown overcoat was raised up to his ears. He carried with him a bundle of papers and a black bag. His thin, pale face wore, only too plainly, the signs of ill-health. But the eyes had lost none of their brightness. As the Irish chief came up, slowly, through the crowd, Le Caron just glanced at him, curiously.

Le Caron gave some details about the American "Conventions." In the secret sessions preceding the open meetings no members were known by their own names. They were all members of the Clan-na-Gael, and they were known by cipher names. Why was this? Le Caron was asked. Because the "dynamite campaign" was one of the questions on hand.

Major Le Caron proceeded, in answer to the Attorney-General, to give an account of the Chicago Convention of 1881. The American United Brethren and the Fenian Brotherhood in Ireland—the former of which had for it managing body the "Revolutionary Committee," and the latter the "Supreme Council"—were referred to throughout Major Le Caron's evidence as the "V.C." The president, it was said, spoke about the "strained relations" between the two associations—the American and the Irish—some of the more impatient souls in the former body being of the opinion that the Irish Fenians were too much influenced by the Land League, whose objects were not sufficiently "revolutionary." Others, again, were content to accept the Land League such as it was, considering it to be an "educational influence" in the general national movement in which all the revolutionary societies and brotherhoods were engaged.

The Attorney-General read extracts from the various departmental reports submitted to and considered at the secret convention—Le Caron, in his capacity of "senior guardian" of a United Brethren "camp," and delegate to the convention, identifying the documents, and explaining points as the Attorney-General went on with his reading. There were reports on the finance of the "U.B.," *alias* "V.C.;" on its foreign relations; on its chemical, engineering, mining business; on its military committees, and so on. One of the resolutions passed at this secret convention was, said the witness, concerned with the retaliatory measures of the united organizations. The "principle of retaliation" was recognized after a discussion in which it was argued that the principle of international arbitration, for which England had been so powerfully instrumental in procuring the adhesion of the Great Powers, must interfere with retaliatory measures, inasmuch as it was part of the "U.B." scheme to side with Powers with which England might be at war. The witness explained that this resolution was preceded by a discussion in which remarks were made about the dilatory conduct of the "Revolutionary Directory (or Committee) in America."

The Attorney-General proceeded next with details about the application of part of the "Skirmishing Fund" to the construction of what Major Le Caron called "submarine vessels." What were they? They were a kind of torpedo, said Major Le Caron, and the witness then told his circumstantial story about the two years' work of Mr. Breslin, in devising a new kind of torpedo boat, intended for the destruction of British commerce. The torpedo boat, said Major Le Caron, "turned out a failure." Examined on the details of the Skirmishing Fund accounts, which were produced in court, the witness described how some of the money was paid to Mr. O'Kelly, M.P., for the purchase of arms. Mr. O'Kelly, the witness stated, was a member of the American "U.B." (*alias* "V.C.), and the Irish "I.R.B." and Mr. John O'Connor, M.P., was, as the Attorney-General held, engaged with Mr. O'Kelly in America at that time in forwarding arms to Ireland.

At this stage, when the witness was about to quote what Mr. John O'Connor had told him about Irish-American relationships, Sir Charles Russell interfered with an objection to the effect that such second-hand information could not be regarded as evidence. The objection was, however, overruled by their lordships, and the witness then stated briefly that the sum and substance of Mr. John O'Connor's statements to him was that the home organizations and the American "U.B." understood each other sufficiently well. Amongst other persons whom Le Caron said he had met at the convention was W. M. Lomasney,—one of the men, said Le Caron, who was some years after sent on dynamite campaign business to London. It was supposed that he was blown up in the attempt to destroy London Bridge. At all events he "never returned" to America, and "the organization is now supporting his wife, children, and father."

Then Major Le Caron proceeded to tell whom he saw at the open meeting. He saw Mr. T. P. O'Connor and Mr. T. M. Healy, and he thought it was owing to the former's influence that a representative of the militant party—

a Protestant clergyman named Betts—was elected chairman in preference to a member of the moral suasion party. At any rate, he thought it was Mr. O'Connor who proposed that the objection to Mr. Betts should be withdrawn. Said the major, there were "dynamite priests," all the same, among the clericals.

Then the witness gave some account of the report of the convention, which was distributed among the local leaders of the U.B. in the early part of 1882. Major Le Caron being a " senior guardian " of a U.B. camp, received his copy of the head-quarters circular as a matter of course, and as soon as he received it he despatched it to the home Government. " All these documents, I believe," said Sir Richard Webster, "were sent home soon after you had taken a copy of them." " In every instance," was the prompt reply. " Have they been in your possession since you sent them ? " "Never."

Le Caron next gave some particulars respecting the Philadelphia Convention of April, 1883, which was attended by Pat Egan, who had arrived in America a few weeks before, and who was the ex-treasurer of the Irish Land League. The opening meeting was, as usual, preceded by a secret meeting, to which only those were admitted who were members of the Clan-na-Gael Society. At this secret meeting, said the Major, instructions were laid down for the guidance of the "skirmishing" members, and the resolution was passed to change the American branch of the Land League into the National League, a proposal which was adopted at the open meeting. The great purpose of the Philadelphia meeting was the unification, for political purposes, of the Irish race throughout the world, and the witness attended all the meetings in a double capacity, as guardian of his U.B. camp, and as a representative of the American Land League (now to become the National League). He also attended all the preliminary secret meetings. Did Egan attend the secret meetings? he was asked. He did not; but, said Le Caron, he asked me to tell him all that was said and done at these secret meetings, which I did; the result being that Egan declared that the programme (about skirmishing, and dynamite, and all the rest of it) would be "perfectly satisfactory to all Nationalists." In the report of the convention Egan was described as a personage " second only in importance to Mr. Parnell himself."

At this stage — it was half-past two o'clock — Sir Henry James took flight to "the restful world." He was comfortably asleep, his left cheek on his elbows, which rested crosswise on the desk. He must have yielded to the steady, long monotone of the Attorney-General, plodding through his convention circulars and convention speeches. Continuing his account of the other Irish visitors besides Egan, the Land League treasurer, and Brennan, the Land League secretary, whom he had seen at Philadelphia, Le Caron named Frank Byrne and Mrs. Frank Byrne. Byrne did not attend the secret meeting, but Brennan did, and, added the witness, he could not have attended unless he was a member of the United Brotherhood. Besides the Byrnes, Egan, and Brennan, there were O'Leary and P. J. Sheridan, and Wright, and Daly from Castlebar. And then the Attorney-General plunged into more U.B. circulars and speeches, and financial statements, the last of which made mention of various sums that had been sent to Mr. Egan in Paris, and to Mr. Parnell, and to Mr. Alfred Webb (one of the Dublin treasurers of the League), and to Mr. Davitt, and others. Growing tired, perhaps, of his reading, the Attorney-General took a little rest, and Sir Henry James, aroused from his slumbers, rose up, with his wig slightly awry, and had his turn at the "documents."

Sir Henry James read with astonishing speed, and nine-tenths of his hearers gossiped. Sir Henry had fifteen minutes of it. He sat down. Sir Richard got up, with another "circular"—date September, 1883—which spoke of the new epoch, the new methods, of the militant Brotherhood.

The writer of the document which Sir Richard Webster was reading invited his readers to "note with pleasure" the fate of informers and spies. Almost on the instant the longish, thin, bloodless face of Le Caron wrinkled into a smile. He flushed slightly. He moved about in his seat. He unfolded his arms—which were crossed on his breast—rested one elbow on the ledge of the witness-box, and his head on his hand.

All this while, too, another thin, pale face was directed towards Le Caron, and its pair of eyes gazed steadily upon him. The gazer was Mr. Parnell. Le Caron rose up to answer a question or two. He stated, on the authority, as he said, of the President of the U.B., that the Brotherhood had resolved to employ on desperate work, in the future, only men who had no families, and who had been carefully trained in the use of explosives; and that dangerous operations should be entrusted exclusively to the American Executive (the Revolutionary Directory), because "it had been found impossible to get the right sort of men in the home organization" (in Ireland). He also said he had learned at this Philadelphia Convention that forty members of the Royal Irish Constabulary had been sent from Ireland to America, in order to gain admission to the organization, and worm out its secrets. The rest of his evidence for the day was occupied with a description of the "split" which took place in the U.B. at the end of 1883, and of the reception accorded in January, 1884, to the two Messrs. Redmond by the American revolutionaries. Among the members of the Committee appointed to conduct the reception were, said the witness, some who were employed in a like capacity, in honour of Mr. Dillon and Mr. Parnell in 1879-80.

FORTY-SIXTH DAY.

FEBRUARY 7.

THE Attorney-General questioned Le Caron respecting the constitution of the "U.S.," and the business of the conventions. The "U.S." was one of the two revolutionary organizations into which in 1883 the "U.B.," or United Brethren Society, was split. Having split away from its parent body, this new "U.S." revolutionary society must have a brand-new "constitution" and symbols of its own. Le Caron, to whom the symbols were as simple as A B C, explained them in court. The three chief "U.S." officials (it is surprising they did not call themselves triumvirs) used for joint signatures to their circulars and confidential rescripts the figure of a triangle. The secretary and the treasurer of the U.S. had each his symbol—the former, two squares joined at the corners; the latter, a cross. On the document which the Attorney-General held in his hand, and which the major interpreted right off, there were nearly twenty of these symbols. It was passed up for the inspection of their lordships. Quite in keeping with the brethren's craze for symbols was their repeated rechristening of themselves. One year they called themselves "U.B.," another year "U.S." They grew tired of "U.S.," and they christened themselves " I.U.B." (Irish United Brethren). At last they repented them of this designation, and solemnly resolved to go back to their old name, "U.B.," the United Brethren. This they did at their convention of June, 1888. Quite in keeping with all the mysticism and symbolism and revised christenings were the grandiloquent departmental titles—"Foreign Affairs" Committees, and War Committees, and all sorts of committees, just as if the Brethren constituted a first-class Power and had a diplomatic status all over the world. This very witness, who started in life as a draper's boy in an

English country town, rose to the rank of "adjutant-general" in the army, or armies, of the Revolutionary Brotherhood. His was the second highest dignity in the revolutionary organization; and the gallant major, as he told this interesting piece of news, drew himself up, and he folded his arms, like the great Napoleon, in his pictures.

Speaking of the U.S., the Attorney-General anticipated four years of his story. Major Le Caron was present at the U.S. Convention held at Chicago last June, and there he heard a discussion about the man Lomasney, who was supposed to have been blown to pieces or drowned in the attempt to blow up London Bridge. But Sir Charles Russell, and subsequently Mr. Reid, objected to the witness's giving any indirect testimony of the kind. Mr. Reid remarked that something more solid was required than reports of vague conversations. The Attorney-General, on the other hand, contended that such evidence was useful for the purpose of showing that Mr. Parnell and his associates were knowingly in intercourse with persons engaged in getting up murderous outrages. "We do not say," argued Sir Richard, "that Mr. Parnell planned murders, but only that he was directly associated with the I.R.B. (Irish Republican Brotherhood), and that the I.R.B. and the U.B. were merely parts of one and the same organization; and that, though Mr. Parnell knew the characters of the men with whom he was associating, he did not attempt to sever his connection with them." The point was discussed for nearly half an hour between the Attorney-General and Sir Charles Russell, Sir Henry James and Mr. Reid following their respective principals. Their lordships retired to consider the subject. They returned after an interval of twenty-five minutes. Sir James Hannen then stated the decision he had arrived at.—The evidence was admissible, in as far as it referred to persons like Egan and Brennan, who were members of the I.R.B., a body which, as the President remarked, was shown in the evidence to be practically identical with the "U.B." The Attorney-General accordingly proceeded to question Major Le Caron about the Lomasney discussion at the convention of 1888, which convention—[that is, the "secret" session preceding the public meeting]—Major Le Caron attended in his capacity as high official of the revolutionary organization. This same Patrick Egan, ex-treasurer of the Irish Land League, was, said the major, present at the debate. The Lomasney question was brought up by the U.S. delegate from Detroit, who enumerated the sums which the Brethren had paid for the maintenance of Lomasney's wife, children, and father. Then, said the major, a resolution was passed directing the U.S. executive to "look after" the Lomasney family.

Having disposed of the episode of June, 1888, the Attorney-General went back to the "U.S." Convention at Boston in August, 1884. According to the usual custom, the Camp Guardians received from headquarters intimation by circular of the forthcoming convention, in which circular delegates were instructed to vote down all propositions and resolutions against the use of force in the political work of the organization, and were reminded that on this point there must be "no compromise."

Then the major entered upon an interesting part of his story. He described how he travelled from Chicago to Boston in the company of Pat Egan, ex-treasurer of the Irish Land League, and how Egan told him the circumstances of his escape from Ireland in March, 1883, almost immediately after Carey turned informer. "Egan told me," said Major Le Caron, "that within twenty minutes of the issue of the Castle warrant for his arrest," he was made fully aware of the fact. Egan, on the instant, "packed up his satchel," destroyed his "I.R.B." documents, including some letters of the informer Carey's; got his railway ticket through the help of a Belfast friend living in Dublin, caught the Belfast train by one minute, crossed to England, and took steamer from Hull to Rotterdam.

Egan, said Major Le Caron, going on with his story, told me also about the escape of Brennan, who was secretary of the Irish Land League. But here Sir Charles Russell interposed with an objection to the admission of this second-hand evidence. After a brief discussion, the Attorney-General was allowed to proceed, and Major Le Caron, who had meanwhile been requested to leave the witness-box, returned, and took up the thread of his story. Brennan told Egan, said Major Le Caron, how he and Mr. Sexton, "the present Lord Mayor of Dublin," were walking down the Strand together ; how they saw on the newspaper posters the first references to Carey's disclosures ; how they both crossed the street on the instant ; how they disappeared down a lane ; and how Mr. Sexton, taking at Charing Cross Station a ticket for Paris, proceeded with it to London Bridge Station, where he gave it to Brennan, who reached Paris that same night.

Again, on that railway run to Boston, Mr. Egan and Major Le Caron discussed the future of the organization, the former of the two declaring that the revolutionary work must be prosecuted " on the old lines "— that is, of dynamite and active hostility, on every available method, to England. Then Egan spoke of Dr. Gallagher, the Clan-na-Gael emissary, who, having been arrested in this country in the prosecution of his dynamite designs, got a life sentence for his pains. Gallagher, said Egan, was a " foolish " fellow for having disobeyed orders ; if he had only waited "twenty-four hours longer," he might have blown up the most splendid buildings in London. How was Gallagher caught ? MacDermott, another spy and informer, got the particulars of Gallagher's dynamite trip to England from Rossa, to whom Gallagher communicated them ; and MacDermott communicated them to the British Government.

But besides these organizations, which were incessantly re-christening themselves and tinkering their constitutions, there was a society called the " Irish National League of America," the counterpart of the National League in Ireland, and, like the latter, the successor of a Land League (the Land League of America). The American National League convention met in Boston, in 1884 ; and the witness stated that the " open " meeting of the convention was preceded by a secret meeting of the Clan-na-Gael, the physical force party, which, according to the witness, controlled the National League. At this National Convention he met Tynan. " Under what name was he introduced to you ? " the Attorney-General asked him. " Under his own." " Did you know who he was before this ? " " Only by reputation." " What had you heard of him ? " " I had heard of him as ' Number One.' " Here the Attorney-General produced a photograph : " Is that Number One ? " The major held the portrait at half-arm's length ; he wrinkled his brows ; he looked up with a jerk of his head : "Yes," said he ; "a very good photograph." The major stated that eleven out of thirteen of the chief officers of the American " National League " Convention were " I. R. B.'s."

Le Caron proceeded rapidly with the identification of " U. B." and " U.S." circulars, copies of which the major received, as a matter of course, from the revolutionary headquarters, and from which he promptly made copies of his own, for secret transmission to England. He explained that these revolutionary circulars, being secret documents, were read over once or twice to the assembled members of each " camp," by its "senior guardian," and then either destroyed or returned to headquarters. But whenever there were no special orders for destroying or returning them, the major transmitted them to England, thus saving himself the trouble of copying them. And that he had been doing for years. And as the Attorney-General went on enumerating them, one could see what an enormous mass of MS. copied from these secret circulars of his unsuspecting colleagues the major had all that time been supplying to the Government officials in London. The major's MSS., now reproduced in court, were neatly and carefully written. The circulars generally referred to the expediency of pushing on "active operations." One of August, 1885, gave directions for supplying headquarters with the names of officers and men fit for active service, and spoke, grandiloquently, of preparations for taking the field at a moment's notice.

At a pause in this identification of the circulars transmitted by him from America to England, the major told a story of the letters of introduction he had received from Mr. Egan to friends in the South, to which he paid a visit in November, 1885. I had previously told Egan, said Le Caron, that I was going on a tour to the South. So the unsuspecting Egan offered to give him "credentials," "knowing that I could do great service to the cause. At this observation of the major's his audience laughed outright. The major himself smiled grimly. Then the Attorney-General read the letter of introduction. "It affords me the greatest pleasure," wrote Mr. Patrick Egan, "to introduce to you my esteemed friend Dr. Le Caron, of Chicago—who has ever proved himself one of the truest friends of the Irish cause." The major smiled. His thin, yellow face rippled, so to speak, into wrinkles. Then he blushed. He appeared to appreciate the fun of the situation.

"Why did you go to the South?" the Attorney-General asked. Le Caron, making some reply (indistinctly heard) to the effect that he went to take stock of things, threw his head up, crossed his arms behind his back, and resumed his cold, hard, alert, and perfectly self-collected expression. After this amusing little episode the Attorney-General reviewed the secret revolutionary circulars of 1886, 1887, 1888, which, as already explained, were regularly transmitted to the senior guardians of camps, to be read by them once or twice in the assembled members and then destroyed : but which this loyal "Senior Guardian" copied, and promptly despatched to the Government of the country against which he had, as a Fenian official of the highest rank, sworn implacable hostility.

When Sir Charles Russell rose, the major pulled himself together, stood bolt upright, crossed his arms over his chest, and gazed at the "terrible cross-examiner." Sir Charles Russell, leaning his right elbow against the back of the bench, asked him in a careless way :

When did you first go to America?—In 1861.
What were you before you went to America?—I was first a clerk in a draper's shop in Colchester; and then in shops in London. I was after that a clerk at a bank in Paris.
What employment did you first get in America?—I joined the army, and continued in it until long after the war.
What regiment did you join?—First I joined Anderson's troop, which was reserved as a body-guard for General Anderson, and afterwards the body-guard of General Brew.
When did you leave the army?—In 1866.
When did you join the Fenian organization?—In the fall of 1865.
While you were in the army, then?—Yes.
Who invited you to join?—No one. It was not then a secret society, and any one who expressed sympathy with Ireland could join. I joined purely for the purpose of gaining all the knowledge I could of the organization.
Did you take an oath?—Yes. It was : "To fight for the cause of Ireland's independence, and the establishment of a Republic in Ireland." I also, as an officer, took a military oath of obedience.

Le Caron then explained that the organization did not become secret until 1869. "And you took that oath intending to disclose it?" asked Sir Charles. "Yus, yus," the major rapped out, with an emphatic nod of his head. Here the major began to offer an explanation. He appealed to the President to be allowed to be heard. "I never forgot that I was an English subject," he exclaimed, loudly and proudly. As he spoke the words, he threw his chest out, and his head back. He next said that before joining the Fenian Brotherhood he made arrangements for sending home his information. This meant that he had written to his father at Colchester, telling him about the projected Fenian raid into Canada, and that his father gave the information to the Member for his borough, who communicated it to the home Government. That, he said, was how his intercourse with the Government began. "And you did everything you could to find information in order to betray the Fenian confidence?" "Yus, yus," rapping out the words in his hard, dogged, prompt, cool manner. "You had no sympathy with them?" "Most emphatically, no;" and the major shook his head, and frowned with an expression of disapprobation and disgust. "I was a military spy," said he, "in the service of my country."

In 1868 he first began to correspond directly with the English Government, and since that date he had transmitted "hundreds," "thousands" of communications to London. Through his hands passed all the correspondence which led to the capture of Riel, the Canadian half-caste rebel.

These communications you speak of you have had access to?—Yes.
Where?—In this city.
Where?—My lord, am I to answer that question?
(It being decided that he must,
Major Le Caron then said) I first saw the correspondence in a bundle of documents given me by Mr. R. Anderson, and the synopsis of the case as submitted by me was prepared by myself and Mr. Houston.
Where did you first look at them?—At No. 3, Cork Street, W.
Who is Mr. Anderson?—I know him as an official of the Government.
Is Mr. Anderson an official at Scotland Yard?—I know he has been connected with the Home Office.
Then it was Mr. Anderson who entrusted you with these documents, and you took them to Cork Street, where you "culled" your evidence from them?—Yes.
And how many of the documents did you use? About one in every hundred.
And where are the other 99 per cent. of the documents?—They are still in my possession.

Before their lordships decided that the witness must answer "where," there was a lively and amusing questioning of him by process of "elimination." Was it at *The Times* office?—No. At Mr. Soames' office?— No. At the Home Office?—No. At each No the witness smiled, shook his head, and smiled again upon the great Q.C.

The "defendants," as they are called, were in high glee when the day's proceedings ended. Mr. Davitt, Mr. O'Connor, Mr. Biggar, Mr. Gill, Mr. Lockwood, Sir Charles Russell, and others formed a lively group round Mr. Parnell, who came late in the afternoon. For the first time perhaps since the Commission began its very intricate labours, the Parnellites showed a real interest in the proceedings. They looked as if at last they felt the delight of battle—felt that they were coming to close quarters. The expression of boredom vanished from their faces; and at various stages in the proceedings they even became merry. Said an eminent member of the "incriminated" sixty-five, as he was leaving the court, "This evidence will at least have one excellent effect: it will smash up secret societies in the United States."

FORTY-SEVENTH DAY.

FEBRUARY 8.

THROUGHOUT the cross-examination Sir Charles Russell addressed Le Caron by his true family name, Beach. The bundle of his letters and documents, which Beach examined in conjunction with Houston, he received in the first place from Mr. Anderson, of Scotland Yard. Asked why he went with them to Houston's house in Cork Street, he replied that a letter of introduction to Houston was given to him. This letter, he said, had no signature. And all he could remember of the letter itself was something to this effect: "I introduce to you Mr. T. Beach, who will lay the matter before you."

He next said that in August last he read something about the forthcoming Commission. "I felt," said he, "some interest in the matter, and the prosecution was making such a 'lame presentation' of the case ——." Here he was stopped by Sir Charles Russell with the remark that that was "rather hard on the Attorney-General." Beach went on with his speech, saying how he had observed that people were claiming the victory for Mr. Parnell over his adversaries. "Well," said he, "I'll cut the matter short: I wrote and said I was willing to incur every risk, and to give all the evidence I had bearing upon the case."

Mr. Beach then went on to say that for the first three years of his communication with the Government he received "not a cent" for his services. Then for twenty years had he received the pay of a patriotic spy? "I have not received as much as I have expended," was the answer. Asked whether it was to be inferred from his re-possession of his documents that the Government were assenting to his giving information, he replied that he did not understand the matter in that light. Did Mr. Anderson do it on his own account? No; "at my earnest request," said Mr. Beach. Did he know, he was then asked, that Houston was the secretary of a body called the Irish Loyal and Patriotic Union? "Not until yesterday," he answered, "was I aware of it." He also stated that when he received the bundle, Mr. Anderson told him he had "culled" out all the documents he thought would be useful; and that out of these selected documents Houston and himself had chosen thirty or forty.

Asked if the American U.B. (United Brotherhood) had a titular head, Mr. Beach explained that the head of the U.B. was the Executive, which consisted of three members, of whom Pat Egan was one. He stated that six years ago the Brotherhood contained thirty-two thousand members; that the suppression of the Land League in Ireland in 1881 gave a fresh impetus to the American Brotherhood, which he further declared was "constantly increasing," so that it was "more numerous to-day" than ever it had been. "This," he added, "I could prove from reports which I was sending to Mr. Anderson from time to time."

You mentioned yesterday something about the men Mackay, Lomasney, and Dr. Gallagher, and the work for which they were sent to London. Did you yourself take part in any of the deliberations at which these wicked plots were devised?—Yes.
And gave your advice?—I didn't think myself of sufficient importance to offer suggestions.
Did you assent to them?—I didn't make any objection.
Then you assented?—In conference—yes.
Did you know who these men were who were selected for this wicked work?—I have written many letters to England about them directly after the meetings.
Could you describe them?—Yes, for I knew them personally.
I suppose you had other persons in your pay, helping you?—Not in my pay, sir. I had friends.

The reading of U.B. circulars, which next followed, and the cross-examination of the witness as to his personal knowledge of men whom he described as being members of the revolutionary organization, were designed to find out whether or not the U.B. instead of being associated with the American branches of the Land and National Leagues, was in reality jealous of them and opposed to them—whether, in short, instead of there being a single American-Irish organization under a variety of names, there were a party of violence and a party of Constitutionalism. Here, for example, was an extract from a U.B. circular which, in his capacity of "Senior Guardian" of a U.B. "camp," Beach had received from headquarters:

Lest these organizations may at any time prove dangerous, rather than assist us in our work, we should so secure the control of their management as to disband them when it becomes necessary.

"These organizations refer to the Land League?" asked Sir Charles Russell. "Yes," said the witness. And "dangerous" meant that the newly-formed League (the circular was dated April, 1880) might cause the withdrawal of support from the secret movement? "Well," said the witness, "I am willing to put it in that way." "Why 'willing'?" exclaimed Sir Charles Russell somewhat sternly, why "willing" if the thing is true? But there were other reasons, replied Mr. Beach — for instance, the U.B. feared that the League did not go "far enough." He next stated that up to 1881 there existed in the U.B. organization some diversity of opinion as to the expediency of outrage; but he said these differences were settled by the Chicago Convention of August, 1881 — meaning the secret meeting. Asked whether he himself personally was ever under the impression that the League would prove dangerous to the U.B. organization, he answered that he was not. "Well, then," said Sir Charles Russell, "I shall read part of a circular issued before the January Convention of 1882:

It says: "A serious danger menaces us, and calls for prompt, vigorous action. What we do will depend largely on the good sense, prudence, and tact shown by the members of the V.C.[1] This danger comes from the Land League, and may, we think, be fairly attributable to the leaders of that prominent body. At the late Land League Convention a party was organized, and is now at work in that body with the object of gradually sapping the foundations of our organization, and building up a power capable of crushing out the revolutionary spirit while studiously working for Ireland."

"Do you agree with that statement?" asked Sir Charles. "Yes," was the answer; and Mr. Beach added that the U.B. endeavoured for a time to control the funds and operations of the League — to "boss the show," as Sir Charles suggested, making use of an American expression. Mr. Beach was next examined as to the statement which he had previously made, to the effect that Mr. Parnell had asked him to bring about an alliance between the Irish and American organizations.

"Now is there any circular from the V. C. to the senior guardians that has come to your knowledge in which there is, directly or indirectly, any reference to this so-called alliance or understanding?—" No."

Mr. Beach was next examined as to his impressions of the characters of some whom he named as being leading members of the U.B. Sullivan, he said, was the leading lawyer in Chicago, but he did not associate with the "aristocracy" of the place. "But he was worthy of your company?" inquired Sir Charles. "Yes, I found him useful," at which answer there was some laughter in court. As for Finnety, he was "respectable, as far as America was concerned"—apparently meaning good enough for America. And Judge Moran? Also respectable. As for Judge Prendergast, he was considered "very goodly one party and very bad" by the rival party. Laughter. Frank Agnew was also "a respectable" man. Mr. Michael Bolan was not respectable — he was expelled from the U.B. for appropriating its funds. To cut short Sir Charles Russell's long list of revolutionary U.B.'s, Mr. Beach admitted that they were all respectable men, with the exception of Mr. Michael Bolan. As to the standing of ordinary members of the U.B., Mr. Beach defined good standing as "paying up to date." "A money affair?" said Sir Charles Russell. "Yes."

In his examination-in-chief, Le Caron said that from beginning to end of Mr. Parnell's visit to America in 1880, the arrangements were "absolutely" in the hands of the U.B. He now put "substantially" for absolutely, explaining that

[1] Cipher for "U.B." United Brethren.

there was a difference between the circumstances of the eastern tour and the western tour. Mr. Beach's own personal knowledge was principally of the western tour, and in particular of Mr. Parnell's reception at three places—Cincinnati, Chicago, and St. Louis. Sir Charles Russell went through a long list of places where Mr. Parnell and Mr. Dillon were received in the course of the 1880 tour—Newark, Philadelphia, Boston, Brooklyn, Providence, &c.—and asked him if any persons in any one of these places had told him that the arrangements for the Parnell demonstrations were got up by the U.B.? "No particular individual," was Mr. Beach's reply in each case. "No—particular —individual," he repeated, pausing at each of the three words, and emphasizing them. "So that there are only three towns of which you can say, of your own knowledge, that the U.B. controlled the arrangements?" "Yes." "Was it not a fact that at each town the Mayor received the two Irish members?" "It was." "Were they U.B.'s?" "He could not tell." "Was it not true that people of the respectable classes greatly preponderated at these demonstrations?" "It was." Then he was asked if the visitors' own account—that they had been received with distinction by people of all ranks in life, and by Americans as well as Irish—was correct. And Mr. Beach admitted that it was.

Coming to the Chicago meeting, Sir Charles read out a list of persons who were on the reception committee; and Mr. Beach said that not one of them belonged to the U.B. Where, then, was the "dark conclave" that managed the whole thing? asked Sir Charles; "were you a member of it yourself?" He was not. But Mr. Beach still maintained that the U.B. did manage the Parnell demonstrations. "Three men," said he, controlled them; "they were Hynes, Finerty, and Sullivan. Finerty himself boasted that he was chairman of the Committee for arranging Mr. Parnell's western tour; and I had information as to how they were manipulating matters."—"No," Mr. Beach replied sharply, when asked by Sir Charles Russell whether he had anything more to offer in proof of his assertion that Mr. Parnell's western tour was managed by the U.B.

Sir Charles Russell next came to the conventions of the American Land League. Of the seven which he enumerated, Mr. Beach attended only three. As to the Chicago Convention of November, 1881, Mr. Beach thought there were "hardly" a thousand persons present, and that one-half of them were U.B.'s. It was at the Philadelphia Convention of 1883 that the American Land League was changed into the National League, and Sir Charles now read out to their lordships the constitution of this new body—which embraced national reform, land reform, local self-government, extension of the Parliamentary and municipal franchises, and the development of Irish industries and agriculture. From this meeting, said Mr. Beach, both O'Donovan Rossa and Finerty were "hounded out." He also declared his belief that of the thirty members present at the committee eight were U.B.'s; he could state "positively" that they were.

FORTY-EIGHTH DAY.

FEBRUARY 12.

SIR CHARLES RUSSELL'S questions about Le Caron's visit to Paris, and about the ideas of Fenians like O'Leary and Stephens, and about Mr. O'Kelly's and Mr. P. Egan's earlier association with the Irish Republican Brotherhood, were to test the theory of the prosecution, that the Brotherhood and the League were practically one and the same organization. In 1881, Mr. O'Kelly, M.P., whom he met in that year, was not a member of the I.R.B. Mr. O'Kelly had been expelled from it because, said Major Le Caron, he had joined the "open" movement. Major Le Caron had been told so. Mr. Pat Egan had resigned his membership of the I.R.B., or he had been expelled from it—Le Caron did not know which; nor could he tell when. So far there was hostility between the Brotherhood and the newly-formed "open" organization, the League. Mr. John O'Leary, whom Le Caron called "a fine old gentleman,' appeared to be an "uncompromising" enemy of the new constitutional or Parnellite movement. Of course, Mr. O'Leary's fellow Fenian, Head-Centre Stephens, was no less uncompromising. On the other hand, Le Caron did not know whether the Fenian paper of the period, the Dublin *Irishman*, was hostile to Mr. Parnell and Mr. O'Kelly.

Coming to his story of his interview with Mr. Parnell in the House of Commons, Major Le Caron repeated his former statements. He had talked to him in the lobby, and been introduced to him, "in complimentary terms," as a friend from America. At that time, he admitted, "I understood that the Fenian organization in Ireland was opposed to the Parnell movement."

"And you say," continued Sir Charles, "that Mr. Parnell complained of this opposition?" "Yes." "As a matter of fact, were the sinews of war for the home movement coming largely from America?" "Yes." And the effectiveness of the home movement, witness admitted, would be crippled, if the "sinews of war" were not forthcoming from America. Having thus got at one reason why Mr. Parnell "complained" of the opposition, Sir Charles next asked Major Le Caron whether, after his return to America, he wrote to Mr. Parnell respecting the mandate which Mr. Parnell was said to have given him to send Devoy to England, and negotiate, in America, with Sullivan, Hynes, and Dr. Carrol for peace between the American party and the open organization in Ireland. "I did not write," said Le Caron. "How was that?" Sir Charles asked, in surprise. There were two reasons; in the first place, he had not been asked to do it; in the second place, he had been instructed to write to some one else. "Who was that?" "Mr. Patrick Egan.' "Have you mentioned one word of that before?" exclaimed Sir Charles Russell, raising his voice. "No." "Why?" "Because I have never been asked."

What did you think the most important part of the conversation you had with Mr. Parnell?—To my mind, the most important matter was his view as a revolutionist.
You mean his remarks with reference to his seeing no reason why they could not inaugurate a revolutionary movement?—Yes.
Didn't you regard that as the word of an insane man?—He appeared to be sane enough.
Yes; but didn't the sentiments appear to be those of an insane man?—I had heard them before from other and as good men.

At the same time, it was Mr. Beach's personal opinion that the "sentiments" were insane. As he pronounced the words, "I did consider it an insane idea," he bowed politely, raised his eyebrows, and wrinkled his forehead.

But if Le Caron thought that in 1881 the idea of an Irish revolution was insane, he affirmed that the American Conspiracy was prospering. The last secret Convention of the V.C. was in June of last year, when Le Caron attended as a delegate. "Have you a circular of that secret Convention?" Sir Charles asked him. He had not it with him at the moment, but he would produce it; and in his business-like way Le Caron scribbled a memorandum about the circular which he was required to produce; and having done that he dropped his pen and looked up again sharply, as if he wanted to know whether Sir Charles had any more questions to ask. "Do you say this V.C. Association is flourishing?" "I say it is *very* flourishing," the Major rapped out, with a decisive little nod. And then he explained that the later progress of the V.C. dated from last June; that for some years previously to 1887 the V.C. was the prey of factions—so that in 1886 the Association was "in fragments." But in that case, what was the Major's opinion of a passage which Sir Charles read out from Mr. Bagenal's book on "The American Irish," published in 1882? The passage stated that there were three chief factions among the American-Irish; and a fourth one called the dynamite faction, which was too insignificant to deserve mention: one that had "no politics," was ignored by the leaders of the other parties, and that compelled its members to commit outrages from which, had they been left to themselves, they would have shrunk. "Would you consider that an accurate description?" "It is accurate," was the reply, "except in this single particular—that it overlooks the fact that the largest party was the U.B., though unknown to the world." Le Caron adhered to his main statement to the last, that the U.B., or party of violence, was the mainspring of the American-Irish movement.

At this stage Sir Charles Russell left the cross-examination, for a time, to Mr. Reid, Q.C. Mr. Reid questioned Le Caron concerning his financial arrangements with the English Government, which he was supplying with secret information. "My first agreement with the Home Government was," said Major Le Caron, "that I should have ample funds for my work." The specific arrangement lasted from 1868 to 1870. At what rate had he been paid all that time? "Fifty pounds a month." Some confusion arising between his statements that the fifty pounds did not cover his expenses, and yet that he "lived" upon his secret service money, Le Caron explained that besides the English service money he also received sums from the Canadian Government. During that period he must have received in all about two thousand pounds. "But," said Le Caron, emphatically, "the sums which I have received since 1872 have not repaid my expenses." "And so your utility is now at an end?" suggested Mr. Reid, raising his voice; "has anything been arranged as to your future?" "There—has—never—one—word—been—said on the future," replied the Major, stopping deliberately at each word, gazing fixedly at Mr. Reid, and bowing slowly, his arms crossed over his chest, in his favourite attitude.

Mr. Reid next questioned Le Caron about the revolutionary circulars, which, the witness stated, were "widely" distributed among the members of the physical violence party. From his statement as to the number of "Senior Guardians" in this party, it would seem that there must have been from 250 to 275 revolutionary camps in America, with a total membership of 23,000 men. "Now, said Mr. Reid, were all these 23,000 men in favour of the use of dynamite?" "Yes," replied Le Caron, brusquely. "Deliberately and knowingly?" "Yes"—pronouncing it "yus." And he mentioned several Conventions—those of 1881, '83, '85, '86—at which he had been present as a "U.B." delegate, and at the preliminary secret meetings of which he had heard the use of dynamite advocated. "And you were a delegate?" Mr. Reid asked, again in his mildest tones. "Yus." "And how did you vote?" "I—always—voted—on the side—of—the majority," returned Le Caron, in his imperturbable manner, again bowing slowly, and with his arms crossed as before. There was a burst of laughter in court. But it did not affect Le Caron. Not the ghost of a flush passed over the yellow, thin, keen features, which were as still as the features of a statue.

Mr. Lockwood followed. His cross-examination of Le Caron was extremely brief, not bringing out anything new. Mr. Lockwood, alluding to the story about Messrs. Sexton and Brennan in the Strand, at the time of the Phoenix Park trials, announced that Mr. Sexton denied that he ever had any conversation with Egan on the subject. Whereupon, Sir James Hannen observed that if the point was important, "it would have to be followed up by Mr. Sexton denying it in the witness-box." "Mr. Sexton is prepared to do so," replied Mr. Lockwood.

Finally, the Attorney-General rose to review the results of the investigation, and to hand in to the judges some fresh documents, one of them very noteworthy.

In the first place, the photograph which the witness said had been given to him by Mr. Parnell in the House of Commons was produced. It bore Mr. Parnell's own signature. The letter was supposed to be from John Devoy to the witness, and to refer to the "mandate" which Mr. Parnell was alleged to have given to Le Caron, for the purpose of bringing about an alliance between the Land League movement and the American physical force party. In producing this letter in Court, Major Le Caron explained that it was not in his possession at the time of his examination-in-chief. The letter, written in America, is given in the footnote.[1]

Major Le Caron said that the letters H., E., P., meant Hynes, Egan, and Parnell. Asked what the reference to the "kind of thing" at Buffalo meant, the Major replied that it meant attempts by the Home Rule leaders to break up the secret organization in America.

Sir Richard Webster next read a portion of Mr. Parnell's speech at Cincinnati in February, 1880, in which speech Mr. Parnell was reported to have said that—

> When we have undermined the English Government we shall have paved the way for Ireland to take her place with the nations of the earth ; and let us not forget that that is the ultimate aim of Irishmen. We shall not be satisfied until we have destroyed the last link which keeps Ireland bound to England.

That, said the learned counsel, was one of the speeches Le Caron identified. "The whole speech will be printed and handed in." Here Mr. Asquith objected that he did not admit the accuracy of the report ; upon which the Attorney-General remarked that he would show the words had never been denied. After this Sir Richard Webster went over some more of the old ground covered by the witness's examination-in-chief; and once more Le Caron declared it to be his opinion that the secret organization did succeed in "running" the open organization in America. With respect to Sullivan, one of the leaders of the secret organization, Le Caron stated, in reply to Mr. Reid, that he had once upon a time been acquitted on a charge of murder. "But not on his first trial," he added ; "it was on his second trial, and I know how." "Well ?" said Mr. Reid ; and the Major proceeded—

> Frank Agnew, the district member of my society, was sheriff of Cook's County, in whose charge the entire choice of the panel of the jurors took place. By Frank Agnew were chosen the jury, in which were men belonging to our organization. The defence raised by Sullivan was that he shot the man because of his conduct to his (Sullivan's) wife.

Pressed by Mr. Reid to say whether or not the jury was composed of members of the V.C. organization, Major Le Caron maintained that it was

---

[1] 41, Orange Street, June 24, 1881.—Dear Friend,—I am sorry I was obliged to leave here for New York last Saturday. I did not return until last night, so did not get your letter till then. It would have been sent on to me, but they thought I should return sooner. Much obliged for the information you gave me, and the interest you have taken on a matter which affects us all so closely. I have not heard from H. yet. Yesterday I received a short note from E. urging me strongly to go over, but I did not understand for what purpose until I got your explanations. I should like to go very much if I could, and if I thought my visit would produce the effect anticipated. I have, however, no authority to speak for anybody, and I could not speak for the V.C. without its authority. . . All I could do would be to tell E. and P. that I could go over on my own responsibilty—which I believe would satisfy our friends here—and make propositions that I feel morally certain would be approved of; but I would not, on any consideration, have them to pay my expenses. That would place me in a false position at once. I have asked advice, and if my friends think it a right thing to do I will start next Wednesday. They misunderstand us on the other side. We do not oppose their action in Ireland, but we cannot tolerate the kind of thing they have taken up in Buffalo.

"packed, in a sense," and that if the jurors were not V.C.'s they were at any rate favourable to Sullivan. At this point the very long examination of Major Le Caron came to an end. Bowing profoundly to their lordships, and thanking them "exceedingly for the courtesy" they had shown him, Major Le Caron tripped lightly, smilingly out of the witness-box, found a quiet corner on the solicitors' bench, right in front of their lordships, and became an interested spectator of the trial of which, for a whole week, he himself had been the hero.

After this Sir Henry James proceeded to read a long series of extracts from *The Nation* newspaper, in order to show that Mr. Davitt had "borrowed" money from the American "skirmishing fund," for the purpose of starting the Land League. The reading was very tedious, provoking at last from the President the mild remonstrance that he could "see every now and then something rising from the midst of the turbid stream." "Is it necessary to read them all?" Sir James Hannen asked. It was agreed to postpone the further reading of speeches till next day; and then—half-past three o'clock—Mr. Grove, of New Bridge Street, London, was called as a witness to identify the portrait of "Tynan," otherwise known as "Number One," whom he had once employed as a traveller. Mr. Grove gave anything but a flattering account of the future Number One's business habits and capacity.

Then a member of the Royal Irish Constabulary entered the box and identified the portrait as that of a man who used to call himself Thomson, and whom he had seen with Mr. Mat Harris. And lastly, Head Constable O'Gorman identified "Thomson," *alias* "Tynan," *alias* "Number One," as a person whom he had seen in the company of Miss Reynolds, of the Ladies' Land League, who used to go about Ireland among the peasantry.

FORTY-NINTH DAY.

FEBRUARY 13.

A MR. MITCHELL was the most interesting witness of the day. Scotch in name, he was rather more Scotch than Irish in manner and accent. Mr. Mitchell was the gentleman mentioned by Captain Slack as having been boycotted himself for having supplied boycotted people with agricultural machines. Mr. Mitchell swore the local League branch had warned him that if he persisted in this course his life might be endangered. He did persist. He lost twenty-nine head of cattle—in consequence, according to his own account.

"Where were you in March, 1883?" Sir Charles Russell asked him. "I was passing through the Bankruptcy Court," was the prompt reply—worthy of the renowned "Major" himself. There was a little laugh at Sir Charles's expense. However, he did not mind it. Nor did he mind it, when Mr. Mitchell added, somewhat hotly, "to which the parties you represent had brought me." Mr. Mitchell declared stoutly that the boycott cost him all he had in the world—four thousand pounds.

He gave a somewhat amusing story of a quarrel with Mr. Condon, M.P. Mr. Condon, M.P., now Mayor of Clonmel, carries on a butcher's business there. Boycotted though he was, Mr. Mitchell succeeded in buying some meat in Mr. Condon's shop. It was like snatching his rations out of the lion's den—almost out of the lion's jaws. It was an exploit in its way. But the lion himself was out at the time. For when Mr. Mitchell emerged with his provender, whom should he meet, almost on the threshold of the lion's den, but the lion himself! Whereupon the lion—to wit, Mr. Condon—fell upon the provender. Mr. Mitchell stuck to Mr. Condon, a tall, stout, powerfully-built man. And as the adventurous Mitchell himself is no pigmy, the tussle between the pair must have been a sight to see. Said Mr. Condon, letting Mr. Mitchell go, "If I had been in the shop, it's the knife you would have got." Such was Mr. Mitchell's story. Mr. Mitchell, who, as the reader perceives, is a person of considerable resolution, had the last shot at his opponents in the court. It being suggested that Mr. Mitchell was boycotted only because he was an Emergency man, Mr. Mitchell, glancing at Mr. Davitt, made the quick retort, "I was never boycotted properly until Mr. Davitt came to the neighbourhood." The "properly" is clearly more Irish than Scotch.

It would be tedious to record the day's speech-reading. Two of the Royal Irish Constabulary witnesses who took notes of the speeches of Mr. Boyton and Mr. Biggar admitted they could not write shorthand, one of the two candidly confessing that he took down the "worst" passages as best he could; the other, that he wrote from memory, after the speech-making.

Then Mr. Creagh, a Kerry solicitor, appeared as a witness to say that he had received from Mr. Brennan, secretary of the Land League, £60, for defending men charged with moonlighting. And Mr. Walsh, a Dublin solicitor, proved receipts signed in his presence, in October, 1883, by the relatives of men who had been sentenced for the Phœnix Park murders. Each relative of the convicted received a sum of £206 3s. 9d., and gave his or her signature on the spot. Mrs. Curley, who gave her signature was the widow of the Curley who was hanged. Thomas Hanlon was the father of the young Hanlon who was punished with a life sentence. Mrs. Fagan was the mother of another Phœnix Park convict who was hanged. Thomas Brady got his two hundred and six pounds and odd shillings and pence, and his son, too, had been hanged. And Mrs. Fitzmaurice was the wife of the carman who drove the murderers, and who was sentenced to penal servitude for life. Miss Ford, said the witness, paid the money, and she was accompanied by an American lady named Miss Doughty.

A shortish young man, with a round back, bent head, high cheek bones, half-uneasy, half-scowling look, and thick black hair, cut somewhat in "fringe" fashion over a low forehead, went into the box. His name—but nobody could make it out. Spell it! Yes; but how? "How do you spell your name?" asked Mr. Atkinson. "Faith, I don't know." Mr. Atkinson himself spelled it—Heanne. Mr. Heanne was put into the box in order to tell all he knew about people supposed to be Land League criminals in Letterfrack, co. Galway. He described how leaguers used to meet at the house of a Mrs. Walsh; he knew they were leaguers; he gave the names of some of them; and he said that the murder of a man named Lyden and the mutilation and killing of cattle were immediately preceded by League meetings in Mrs. Walsh's house. But when cross-examined by Sir Charles Russell he showed great ignorance and confusion about League matters in his parish. He did not know the priests who were respectively the president and secretary of the local branch. And though he declared that the leaguers passed "resolutions" about crimes, he did not know what a resolution meant. "Did he know what a secretary was?" "No; unless it meant a man that kept things secret?"

FIFTIETH DAY.

FEBRUARY 14.

THE day's work began with Mr. Davitt's reading of a number of passages from an interview which an American journalist had with him in New York, and which was published in *The New York World*. Portions of this interview which were reproduced in *The Nation* were read the previous day by Sir Henry James, as evidence against Mr. Davitt ; and this morning Mr. Davitt, on his part, read passages in qualification of those that had been selected by Sir Henry James. They are well worth summarising. Mr. Davitt had, as a matter of fact, declared strongly against secret associations as being unnecessary and mischievous wherever freedom of speech existed. He read his own declarations from *The World* to the effect that open organization and discussion were the only means of influencing a free public opinion. Mr. Davitt then quoted from *The World* the political programme which he submitted to this free opinion. The programme simply asked for such measures as self-government in Ireland ; an improvement of the Irish land system by the establishment of peasant proprietorship ; for a development of Irish national resources ; for improved dwellings ; and so forth. As to the story of his having "borrowed Skirmishing Fund" money to start the Land League in Ireland, Mr. Davitt explained that local committees paid the expenses of printing and of meeting-rooms : and that he himself had defrayed much of the cost from a testimonial which had been presented to him on his release from prison.

After Mr. Davitt, came the ex-Land League clerk, Farragher, who, in his previous evidence, stated that he had carried letters with cheques from Egan to Mullett, one of the Phœnix Park convicts. Farragher again stated that parcels of *The Irish World* were received regularly at the Land League offices in Dublin. Cross-examined by Sir Charles Russell, he admitted that the parcels were addressed to the Dublin correspondent of *The New York World,* Mr. Larkin ; and that he did not know whether Mr. Larkin was a Fenian. As to the dates of his conveyance of letters from Mr. Egan to Mullett, he was very hazy. He could not tell whether it was a week, a month, or a year that passed between his delivery of the first letter and his delivery of the second. Nor would he say how long he was a clerk in the Land League office, nor when he joined it.

All this while there was a buzz of conversation going on throughout the court. For the news had already leaked out that "the letters" would "spring up" before midday, and the interest in "the letters" extinguished every other. When, therefore, the Attorney-General called out the name of Mr. Joseph Soames, there was instant silence, and every eye in court was directed towards the witness-box, into which the usher, bustling ahead, was escorting the solicitor for *The Times*. The world had been waiting well-nigh four months for Mr. Soames : and there he stood at last, with his black box beside him.

But before the alleged Parnell letters were produced, more than an hour was spent in examining Mr. Soames respecting the other contents of his black box, and the steps by which he had discovered them. Mr. Soames described how he had visited Dublin repeatedly for the purpose of collecting evidence, and how, in May, 1888, in the office of Mr. Brophy, solicitor, of Dublin, he had met an ex-Land League official whom he had asked for specimens of Mr. Egan's handwriting, and who told him that he had other valuable documents in his possession, which he could produce. He did produce them, and Mr. Soames spent two hours in examining them. He took pencil copies of some of them. But the person who showed him these documents would not allow them to go out of his possession just then, though on Whit Monday, 1888, he brought them to London. Some of these documents were endorsed "J. F.," in red ink. This "J. F." was, said Mr. Soames, Mr. John Fergusson, an ex-Land League official then residing in Glasgow; for he had put himself at once into communication with Mr. Fergusson, and so was enabled to compare the handwriting of Mr. Fergusson's letters to him with the signatures he had found in Dublin.

The Attorney-General then proceeded to read a large number of the letters and documents in Mr. Soames's possession. Most of the letters contained appeals to the headquarters of the Land League for pecuniary assistance to people who had lost their employment because of their obedience to Land League rules. For example, there was a letter, bearing the endorsing signature "J. F." which authorized the payment of "ten pounds for the seven"—that is, seven labourers whom their employer, who was boycotted, turned out because they would not work for him.

At last the Attorney-General, in a tone as of indifference, and but barely audible, put the question, "When, Mr. Soames, were you consulted as to the facsimile letter of May 15, 1888?" It was at the end of 1886, the same day on which he had seen all the alleged Parnell letters, with the exception of one of June 16th. The facsimiles, nicely got up in the form of transparencies, lay on the desk before Mr. Soames, who kept his eyes on them while the Attorney-General read his copies. The gentleman who first showed Mr. Soames the alleged letters was Mr. Macdonald, the manager of *The Times*. Subsequently to the interview between Mr. Macdonald and Mr. Soames, the letters were submitted to an expert, Mr. Inglis. This was in April, 1887.

What steps had been taken to identify these alleged signatures of Mr. Parnell's before the publication in *The Times*? In answer to this question, Mr. Soames described how he had procured *bonâ fide* letters and signatures of Mr. Parnell's from the House of Commons, from Dublin, and other quarters. For example, one was an order of admission to the House addressed to Mr. Ross, one of *The Times* representatives in the House of Commons Gallery. Besides, there were *bonâ fide* letters in the handwriting of Mr. Campbell, Mr. Parnell's secretary, with Mr. Parnell's signature attached. Mr. Soames explained that he did not know—when Mr. Macdonald first showed him the letter of May 15th—in whose handwriting the body of the letter was; he had no opinion on the matter; he had no "means of judging."

Then Mr. Soames produced letters, the whole of which, signatures included, were believed to be in Mr. Parnell's handwriting; as also several summonses which had been signed by Mr. Parnell in his capacity of a justice of the peace. Mr. Soames next declared that the comparison of the documents in Mr. Macdonald's possession with the others already referred to, convinced him that the signatures of the former were in Mr. Parnell's, and the "body" of some of them in Mr. Campbell's handwriting. The Attorney-General asked Mr. Soames whether Mr. Inglis, the expert, had advised them that they were genuine? But to this question Sir Charles Russell objected, and the President ruled that it was inadmissible.

Next came an interesting piece of information. Not until after the O'Donnell trial did Mr. Macdonald tell him that the alleged Parnell letters had been received through Houston, secretary of the Irish Loyal and Patriotic Union, from Pigott, editor of the Dublin *Irishman*, the organ of the Fenians. But all payments in connection with this investigation had passed through Mr. Soames's hands. He first paid one thousand pounds to Houston, but the money was not for letters only, it was also in payment of expenses of missions to America. On three other occasions he paid Mr. Houston sums amounting to an aggregate of ten hundred and forty-two pounds, besides several smaller sums. A detective named Moser received between one and two thousand pounds for his services in America; and a Mr. Kirby had been paid two hundred and fifty pounds and his travelling expenses for a like service.

FIFTY-FIRST DAY.

FEBRUARY 15.

THE most interesting day since the trial began. The court was densely packed. Inglis, the expert in handwriting employed by *The Times*, stood near one of the doorways. Houston, from whom Mr. Macdonald, of *The Times*, received the letters, was also present. And so was the man who gave them to Houston; but the mysterious Pigott sat in an obscure corner by himself, almost unobserved. He sat there until, at Sir Charles Russell's request, he was ordered to withdraw from the court.

Mr. Soames, who was under cross-examination, had just been describing how, at the time of the introduction of the Commission Bill, Houston had released Mr. Macdonald of *The Times* from his obligation of secresy, and how Pigott had released Houston. "It was then," said Mr. Soames, "that Pigott had his first interview with me."

At this point, Sir Charles Russell requested that Pigott should withdraw. Everybody looked this way and that to see where Pigott was. It was an odd movement, this craning of necks, this peering round about—as if everybody suspected everybody else of being Pigott. Pigott slipped out almost unseen—close at the heels of the clerk to whom Mr. Soames, first jingling for a second or two in his pockets, gave a bunch of keys, wherewith to search in his office in Lincoln's-inn-fields, for certain memoranda referring to the Pigott interview and other details. Pigott having vanished into the corridors, Mr. Soames continued his story. Pigott told him simply that he found the letters in the summer of 1886. But he did not say where or from whom he got them. "And I'll tell you why I did not ask him," said Mr. Soames, in one of his frequent explanatory parentheses; "he told me at the outset he would not tell me where and from whom, and that if he ever did tell he would do it himself in the witness-box." There was not the ghost of a hint as to the source from which Pigott got the letters; all Mr. Soames knew was that Mr. Macdonald got them from Houston, and Houston from Pigott. "And I believe," said Mr. Soames, "that even now Mr. Macdonald does not know, and that Houston does not know."

And yet Mr. Soames firmly believed that the signatures were Mr. Parnell's —he believed this on the testimony of the experts and as a result of his personal comparison of the disputed signatures with letters and other documents of Mr. Parnell's which were admitted to be genuine.

Mr. Soames was equally confident as to the authenticity of the Davitt letter; for Mr. Davitt himself had copied this letter in Mr. Soames's own office, and in Mr. Lewis's presence. The likeness between the handwriting of the letter in Mr. Soames's possession and that of the copy which Mr. Davitt made of it was enough for Mr. Soames.

Next, then, about the Egan letters; and what had Mr. Soames done to satisfy himself that the letters alleged to be Egan's were authentic? Well, Mr. Soames had addresses on envelopes, signatures to photographs, &c. And Mr. Cunynghame, Secretary to the Commission, handed Mr. Soames a big bundle of Egan letters, authentic ones, from which to select two or three, said Sir Charles, and compare them with the disputed ones. Mr. Soames, in a somewhat brusque manner, said he could select all. But I only want two or three, mildly expostulated Sir Charles; and if you won't, "I suppose I must." And then followed a long interval of crumpling of leaves, h'ming and hawing, mutterings and mumblings, while the P. E.s (Pat Egan) and the little "y's" and the big "y's," the "s's," and the "r's" were compared stroke by stroke. "Look at that final 'y' in 'truly,'" remarked Mr. Soames, smiling half-pensively, and cocking his head to one side. "Anything else?" asked Sir Charles, taking a pinch of snuff, and patting his nostril with his thumb. Just look at the "Dear" in that "Dear Sir," which is the same as that in a letter of November, 1881. The same process was gone through with the Parnell letters. The r's, the l's, the n's, &c., in the acknowledged letters were compared with the same characters in the disputed ones. In the course of this leisurely operation, Mr. Soames remarked on Mr. Parnell's diverse styles of handwriting, and also on what he called Mr. Parnell's contradictory statement about his signatures. Here Mr. Parnell smiled.

It was interesting to watch Mr. Parnell's demeanour during all this investigation. Now he appeared to be lost in thought, and now he looked up with an expression of amusement when the big book from Kilmainham Goal was handed over, and the lawyers clustered about it. Mr. Parnell rose up, leant over the back of the bench, and nodded and smiled as he placed his finger on one of thirteen signatures which adorned the pages of that very commonplace-looking folio volume. If Mr. Quaritch were to advertise that volume to-morrow, there would be a run upon it. Mr. Davitt smiled as he gazed upon the old signature of his fellow "criminal." Mr. Parnell, by the way, has confuted the newsmongers. Only the night before he had been reported to be dangerously ill. The consequence was that the visitors in court did not expect him to-day. He surprised them by coming in at half-past eleven o'clock, with his yellowy-brown topcoat thrown over his left shoulder (which suffers slightly from rheumatism). Pale as he was, Mr. Parnell looked better than he did when he appeared in court eight or nine days ago; to all appearance he was on good terms with himself.

And now, all of a sudden, Sir Charles Russell put a question whereat all present pricked up their ears,—Did Pigott tell you he had a grievance against Mr. Parnell? No. Nor had Pigott said anything about his paper, *The Irishman*, which was extinguished by *United Ireland*.

Then Mr. Soames said that he had detected interviews of Mr. Lewis and Mr. Labouchere with the same mysterious Pigott. Did it not occur to Mr. Soames, as soon as he found that Pigott was in close communication with Mr. Lewis and Mr. Labouchere—did it not occur to him to press Pigott as to the source whence he derived the letters? No; not even though Mr. Soames's detectives had traced Pigott to Mr. Labouchere's house, where Mr. Parnell and Mr. Lewis also were present at the time!

Did Pigott tell you he told Mr. Lewis that he himself had forged the letters? An inarticulate murmur of surprise passed over the court.

No, replied Mr. Soames, but Pigott told me that Mr. Lewis had tried to get him to say so, and that Mr. Labouchere offered him a thousand pounds if he would go into the witness-box and swear to it.

Mr. Soames held his audience spell-bound, so to speak, as he described how Pigott himself came voluntarily to *The Times* office; how Pigott was given to understand that *The Times* would not undertake to pay him anything, but was promised that if the letters proved authentic he would not be "ruined" for his services in the witness-box; how Pigott's request for five thousand pounds reward was made, not to *The Times*, but to Houston, on the ground that Pigott could not safely live in Ireland after he gave his evidence for *The Times*; how he (Mr. Soames) had discovered an emissary of Pat Egan's; and how he watched this emissary, O'Brien, watching Pigott; and how Mr. Soames's detective ran the spy O'Brien to earth in Mr. Labouchere's house. At ten minutes to one o'clock Sir Charles Russell's cross-examination came to an end. Mr. Soames acquitted himself of his difficult task very well. Mr. Labouchere and Mr. Lewis smiled repeatedly as they heard Mr. Soames's story.

Now came the most important witness yet examined—Mr. J. C. Macdonald, manager of *The Times*. Replying to the Attorney-General, he stated that when first he received the letters he made no bargain whatever about them. All that he undertook then to do was if the letters proved to be authentic to pay Houston what Houston himself said he had expended in procuring them. Houston, he said, did not say where he got them: that was a secret, which was not divulged until after many months.

But Mr. Asquith's cross-examination was the exciting part of the business. Mr. Asquith did his work well. The main endeavour of his long stream of searching questions was to find out to what extent Mr. Macdonald had placed confidence in people who would only tell him that they had received "the letters from a person or persons whose names they would not give up," and to what extent also he had been guided in forming his opinion about the authenticity of the signatures by "internal evidence." As for the expression about "making it hot for Forster," why, exclaimed Mr. Macdonald, with an air of complete confidence, that was just the expression Mr. Parnell would have used—it was Mr. Parnell all over. He candidly admitted that he made up his mind about the authenticity of the signatures and letters "from the very beginning." He described the frequent overtures made to him before the originals were produced. He had heard that the letters were offered to Lord Hartington; but he had never heard they had been offered to *The Pall Mall Gazette* for a thousand pounds. Mr. Macdonald rather complicated matters by saying he believed that Mr. Parnell and Mr. Campbell had tried to "disguise" their handwriting. This was not the only statement of Mr. Macdonald's which was followed by a burst of laughter in court. Much merriment was caused by his statement—on Houston's authority—that the Irish leaders used three different handwritings for their letters—one for "the body," one for the signature, one for the address. But he had nothing to say to Mr. Asquith's prompt reminder that Egan's letters were written throughout in one handwriting. "No, no," the answer was, when Mr. Asquith asked whether he had taken any trouble to find out from whom Pigott got the letters. "And yet you were satisfied?" exclaimed Mr. Asquith, looking up with an expression of surprise. "Yes." "Why did you select the 18th of April for the publication of the supposed Parnell signature?" Mr. Asquith thundered out, coming down on the desk with his fist? "Why," replied Mr. Macdonald, "just because the state of affairs made it a proper occasion; because the second reading of the Coercion Bill was coming on that very night. Every journalist," said Mr. Macdonald, "must choose his opportunities."

FIFTY-SECOND DAY.

FEBRUARY 19.

THE cross-examination of Mr. Macdonald, the manager of *The Times*, was resumed by Mr. Asquith. What steps, he asked, had Mr. Macdonald taken to satisfy himself as to the authenticity of the first batch of letters which Houston brought to him at *The Times* Office in October, 1886? Why, Mr. Macdonald merely listened to Houston as he read out compromising documents. Mr. Macdonald did not read them, nor did he handle them. Nor did Houston even leave them behind for Mr. Macdonald's more leisurely perusal; he took them away with him, as if he could not trust them in the hands of the manager of *The Times*. Mr. Macdonald did not ask Houston to search for other specimens of handwriting useful for authenticating the signatures of the supposed discovery. There seemed to be a world of conviction in the little head-shake, or brief muttered "No," with which

Mr. Macdonald answered Mr. Asquith's questions as to whether he had taken this, that, or the other precaution. "*You* may be dull, slow fellow," the little head-shake seemed to say. Still, Mr. Asquith proceeded with his questions.

"Well," said he, "let us take three of the five Parnellite letters, and see if you can tell us what there is of a compromising nature in them ; " and he quoted one letter in which Mr. Parnell asked papers to be sent to him, a second in which Mr. Parnell wished some one to write to him direct, and a third in which Mr. Parnell stated his opinion that he saw no objection to the payment of a certain sum of money. " Do you think that compromising ? " asked Mr. Asquith, raising his eyebrows, and leaning back against the bench, with his hands behind him. " Yes," was the short reply, accompanied by a quiet little nod, as full of conviction and personal satisfaction as the little head-shake. After a pause, during which Mr. Asquith gazed curiously at Mr. Macdonald, Mr. Asquith put the following question, " If Mr. Houston had brought these letters only, would you have been satisfied that they were of a compromising nature ? " Again the little nod. Again the look of mild surprise on his cross-examiner's face ; and a ripple of laughter all over the court, when Mr. Macdonald, twirling his *pincenez* between his fingers and gazing for a long time absently at the ceiling, suddenly looked down, darted a look at Mr. Asquith, and remarked, with a knowing smile, " But I am not bound to tell you why that was my opinion." Then Mr. Macdonald crossed his hands behind his back, cocked his head sideways, and gazed through the corners of his eyes with a mingled air of tolerance and amusement at his questioner. Mr. Asquith tried to make him tell, but to little or no purpose. At one moment it seemed as if Mr. Macdonald were growing a little angry, as when he objected that he considered it " unfair " to press him for his reasons.

But there were two more batches of Mr. Parnell's supposed letters, and, according to Mr. Macdonald, he exhibited, with respect to these, the same thorough faith in Houston which he had exhibited with respect to the first batch. Mr. Houston did not tell him where he got the letters ; nor did Mr. Macdonald ask him where. Nor were Mr. Macdonald's suspicions aroused by the fact that no envelopes were produced with these batches. Or, rather, the absence of envelopes made Mr. Macdonald all the more suspicious of Mr. Parnell. There was an outburst of laughter when Mr. Asquith made a remark to the effect that Mr. Macdonald was strong on envelopes—Mr. Macdonald's theory being that, according to the elaborate system which the Irish leaders followed, they caused the envelopes of their " compromising " letters to be written in one hand, the " body " of the letters in a second, and the signatures in a third. Anyhow, at the mention of envelopes, a broad smile beamed all over Mr. Macdonald's face, and he gazed, again, at the ceiling. " Yes," he said, with another of his quiet little nods, " I abstained from asking Mr. Houston why the envelopes were wanting, and from whom he got the letters." " I particularly avoided the subject of origin," exclaimed Mr. Macdonald, at which admission there was another explosion of laughter. Even after he learned that Pigott was the man who supplied Houston, Mr. Macdonald refrained from making inquiries about the former's antecedents, character, and position. Of course, it may by and by turn out that Mr. Macdonald had good reasons for his confidence in Houston ; but the frequent laughter in court was clearly an expression of surprise at the apparent inexhaustibility of Mr. Macdonald's faith. Curiously enough—from the outsider's view-point, we mean—Mr. Macdonald sometimes withheld information from Mr. Soames, though he always placed such confidence in Houston. There was an alleged letter of Mr. Parnell to Pigott which Mr. Macdonald thought a proof of signature, but the existence of which he long kept secret, even from Mr. Soames.

Then Mr. Asquith passed to some of the most serious allegations in "Parnellism and Crime," with a view to ascertaining whether *The Times* had done its best to verify the letters before publishing them. And here it appeared on Mr. Macdonald's own showing that his knowledge of their source was of the vaguest and slenderest description. As for *The Times* statement about the keeping, in Palace Chambers, Westminster, of the knives employed in the Phœnix Park murders, all that Mr. Macdonald could say was that the information came from "the writer of the article," but he refused to divulge the writer's name. Here a somewhat long altercation ensued between Mr. Asquith and Mr. Macdonald, the latter refusing to give information about secrets which were the property more of the editor than of the manager of *The Times*. During the discussion Mr. Parnell entered, wrapped up in a big, brownish Inverness cape, and carrying a well-filled black bag. At last the President decided that Mr. Macdonald was bound to answer the questions put to him about the authorship of the statements and articles of the series known as "Parnellism and Crime." Mr. Macdonald, carefully looking through the article about the Phœnix Park knives, declared he did not know who wrote it. Then he said that the series was the work of several writers. All Mr. Macdonald could say was that he did not know where the writer got the information; that he did not even ask the writer where he got it; and that the writer himself offered no information on the subject!

The foregoing are fair specimens of Mr. Macdonald's general replies to questions about *The Times* authority for statements in the "Parnellism and Crime" series. He could not say what precise information, if any, *The Times* writer had before him when he said that Mr. Parnell's cheque enabled Mr. Frank Byrne to escape. There was a certain letter from which *The Times* writer might conceivably have drawn his inference; but then the letter was not "received" by *The Times* authorities before the publication of the accusation. Still, it might have been "seen" without being "received." "But was it seen?" exclaimed Mr. Asquith, in a somewhat impatient tone. "I don't know," was the reply; and there was another burst of laughter in court. The laughter was still louder when Mr. Macdonald, stating that none were "specifically" employed to write the articles of the series, threw in the remark that the articles were "written in the ordinary course of business." A few more questions of the same class concluded Mr. Asquith's cross-examination, admitted by all who heard it to be very able.

When Mr. Asquith sat down, the Attorney-General rose to re-examine; but the process was extremely brief. In a minute or two Mr. Macdonald descended smilingly from the witness-box, and sat down quietly in his accustomed seat, to all appearance thoroughly well satisfied with his performance. The Attorney-General now proposed to call the expert, Mr. Inglis; but Sir Charles Russell firmly protested, on the ground that the expert should not be heard before Houston and Pigott were questioned about the sources from which they got the letters. He declared he would not cross-examine the expert unless this course was followed. Then the Attorney-General protested. Next the President took Sir Charles's part. But Sir Richard Webster insisted on having his way, and he had it. But in less than twelve minutes, and after a brief adjournment, which he asked for—for the purpose of consulting Mr. Soames—Sir Richard Webster agreed to postpone the examination of the expert, and to call Houston. At ten minutes to one Houston entered the witness-box.

Houston appeared somewhat nervous at first, but quickly recovered his self-possession, and proved himself an intelligent witness. The substance of his story, as given in reply to the Attorney-General's questions was that he first entered into communication with Pigott at the end of 1885; that Pigott at the beginning assisted him in gathering materials for a pamphlet which he, Houston, published at that time, under the name of "Parnellism Unmasked"; that he next commissioned Pigott to find out evidence such as would connect Parnellism with crime; that he paid Pigott a pound a day and his expenses to go to Paris, Lausanne, and America, where there were supposed to be persons in possession of compromising documents; that Pigott informed him that certain important letters were kept in Paris—(in a certain house wherein Frank Byrne was said to have left them, in the hurry of his supposed flight from England); that these turned out to be the five famous letters "of Mr. Parnell" and the six "of Pat Egan"; and that during all this time he was paying Pigott's expenses out of his own pocket, or with borrowed money. He went on to say that he was obliged to borrow twelve or fifteen hundred pounds from Dr. Maguire, of Dublin; and that in his subsequent interviews with his employers of *The Times* he declared that under no circumstances would he accept any reward for himself. When he did get seventeen hundred and eighty pounds from *The Times*, the sum exactly covered all the expenses he had incurred. After the first batch there came, at considerable intervals, a second batch and a third. Not until the appointment of the Special Commission did Houston tell Mr. Macdonald that Pigott was the man from whom he got the letters.

Where did Mr. Pigott get them? That was the main question to which Sir Charles Russell addressed himself. But it turned out that Houston trusted Pigott, just as Mr. Macdonald trusted Houston. Up to December last Mr. Houston had a large number of Pigott's letters in his possession —letters which might possibly reveal the original sources from which the "incriminating" documents were derived. Well, where were they? He destroyed them all! "Deliberately?" exclaimed Sir Charles. "Yes," deliberately, was the reply. And yet Houston had shortly before been subpœnaed to appear as a witness, and he also knew that Pigott had been served with a notice on behalf of Mr. Parnell; and, moreover, the Commission had been sitting two months at the time he destroyed what might turn out to be extremely valuable proofs! Houston did not even ask Mr. Soames whether it was right to destroy the letters. "Did you heave a sigh of relief," asked Sir Charles, insinuatingly, "when Pigott told you he had destroyed *your* letters?" (Laughter.) "You destroyed your corroborative proofs," exclaimed Sir Charles, again returning to the charge. "Yes," retorted the witness, "but I wanted to destroy all clue to original sources. Besides," said he, "I was satisfied with the statutory declaration which Pigott lately made about his intercourse with Mr. Labouchere and Mr. Parnell, and with his sworn affidavit that the letters were not his forgeries." As to Sir Charles's question, whether he considered the destruction of the letters fair to Mr. Parnell, Houston replied that he did not think Mr. Parnell entitled to any consideration.

Houston glanced downwards and sideways as he said this. He tried to appear unconcerned; but he failed awkwardly. A curious exhibition of insolence and uneasiness—at which Mr. Parnell smiled.

There was just a moment of eager curiosity among the densely-packed audience when Houston said there was a man named Murphy of whom Pigott spoke in connection with the discovery of documents. Could Murphy be the missing link? No. Murphy was no longer in the land of the living, and dead men tell no tales. Another mysterious person, who was apparently in the same boat with Murphy, was a man named Colbert, but he too was dead and buried—nothing to be got out of him. "And that," exclaimed Sir Charles, "is the sum and substance of all you know about the persons, places, circumstances of these discoveries?"—Yes: that was all!

FIFTY-THIRD DAY.

FEBRUARY 20.

SIR CHARLES RUSSELL resumed his cross-examination of Mr. Houston to-day punctually at half-past ten. He plunged at once into the question of Houston's deliberate destruction—some weeks after the Commission began to sit—of all his "corroborative documents." Houston adhered to his explanation of the day before, that a determination to maintain complete secrecy, to shield Pigott's informants, and to prevent his own name from being connected with Pigott's, was his motive for destroying those proofs—including the letters which Pigott wrote to him from abroad, and in which Pigott informed him of the progress of his search for compromising documents.

"Would you just tell us in your own way," said Sir Charles, "the whole story of how you came into possession of the first batch of documents, containing the five alleged letters of Mr. Parnell?" And then, after a little fencing with his cross-examiner—such as asking him where, in point of time and place he was to begin—he narrated the story of the mysterious black bag. The black bag had been mentioned yesterday, and as a matter of fact Houston had already given the story of it; but he had to repeat the tale, and his cross-examiner was about to enter more minutely into details. As Houston proceeded with the story of the black bag, he moved about rather restlessly; his hands, clasped behind his back, were constantly twitching. The summary of the tale of the black bag is as follows: Pigott told him that he learned that certain compromising documents were left in a black bag in a room which had been occupied by Frank Byrne. This black bag was conveyed to Paris, where it was kept in the possession of certain Fenian refugees. Even when Pigott discovered the *locale* of the black bag, he found that the "open sesame" to the black bag—that was Sir Charles's expression—was not in Paris, but in America. And so the persevering Pigott must hie him forth to America, and procure from the American Fenians permission to get at the contents of the mysterious black bag. And Pigott returned, and met his employer (Mr. Houston) in Dublin, and Pigott talked about American politics—pretty much as any one might who had read that morning's papers, but as to any paticulars of Pigott's special mission, about the persons whom he had seen, about any papers he might have received from them, not a word!

"Did you take any steps to test these statements about the black bag?" Sir Charles inquired, after a long pause, wrinkling his forehead, and talking almost under his breath. No, Pigott's employer had not. But his next confession was still more astonishing; he said that for corroboration of the statements in the black bag tale, he relied generally on what he considered to be their harmony with newspaper criticisms on the Parnellite situation. But he entirely failed to answer the questions: What Press, what contemporaneous events in particular, did you rely upon? But on the first blush of it did not that tale of the black bag appear to him somewhat singular? Not altogether. This intelligent witness, brought up in a good school, the school of public affairs, refrained from making even the slightest inquiry as to where "the room" was, where the street was, how the bag had been taken to Paris. Nor did he know who searched for the black bag in Paris; all he knew was that Pigott professed to have got at its contents.

Oh, yes; there was a man in Paris, to whom Pigott had referred by name as the person supposed to be able to trace the black bag. Mr. Houston's hearers pricked up their ears when Sir Charles, leaning forward, asked who the man was, and what service he rendered. His name was Casey, and he did—nothing. Great disappointment among the audience; and perplexity in Sir Charles Russell's mind over these two facts—that the only man whom Mr. Houston remembered as having been in intercourse with Pigott was a man who confessed he knew nothing about the black bag ; and that Mr. Houston had deliberately destroyed the Pigott letters in which Pigott's colleagues in the search were mentioned by alphabetical signs. All this while Mr. Parnell sat on the front bench. The collar of his dark-brown great coat was drawn up to his ears. Mr. Parnell was absorbed in watching Mr. Houston. He gazed at him with an air of intense amusement.

Mr. Houston's faith in Pigott was as boundless as Mr. Macdonald's faith in Mr. Houston. There, for example, was the story of "the people downstairs," which Houston narrated—to the merriment of his audience. The "people downstairs" were the people who knew all about the black bag—who, we are to understand, sold the (alleged) contents thereof to Pigott, who sold them to Mr. Houston, who sold them to Mr. Macdonald of *The Times*. And "downstairs" was in Paris—in the *Hôtel des deux Mondes, Avenue de l'Opèra*, where Mr. Houston resided when he crossed over to receive the find from Pigott's hands, and pay for it on the spot. When Pigott called at the hotel to see Mr. Houston he had the five "Parnell" letters with him. But he would not part with them until he got the money—for which money "the people downstairs" were waiting. "Aye "—"aye "—"aye," Sir Charles remarked, while he tapped his snuff-box, and encouraged Houston to go on with his amazing story. "And did you go and see who were downstairs?" said the cross-examiner, taking a pinch. "No." "No?" exclaimed Sir Charles, suddenly looking up with an air of astonishment. "No." (Great laughter.) The usher scowled : he was about to shout out "Silence," but abstained.

"Did you ask who they were?" "No." More merriment—which was anything but assuaged when Mr. Houston explained—"I wished to keep myself aloof; I wanted to keep myself in ignorance of the source of the letters." This expression, or its equivalent, runs through the whole of Houston's evidence. His whole story hangs upon it. He has been saying all along that he carefully abstained from testing the worth of Pigott's researches and narratives, for the following reasons—that the names of the persons from whom Pigott got the letters were never to be divulged ; that if Mr. Houston knew nothing, why, of course, Mr. Houston could tell nothing. Mr. Houston did not even ask Pigott for a receipt for the money, £605 (£500 for "the people downstairs," and a hundred guineas for their emissary upstairs) which he paid on the spot. Nor did the emissary upstairs ever show any receipts from his friends downstairs, nor did the trustful Mr. Houston ever ask for them. "You were carefully shutting your eyes," said Sir Charles Russell, by way of summing up the strange story about "the people downstairs."

Why did Houston go to Paris ? Because of a telegram from Pigott—the meaning of which telegram was made plain to him by previous correspondence with Pigott, in which correspondence Pigott referred, by letters of the alphabet, to the people who were assisting him ; but "I purposely kept myself in ignorance as to the identity " of these persons, said Houston. And these are the proofs which Houston has destroyed in order to keep the world, as well as himself, in ignorance ! Houston was quite satisfied with Pigott's "strongly expressed " opinion that the letters were authentic. At any rate, Houston was zealous in his work ; for he not only spent his own money in collecting compromising documents which he might or might not be able to sell, but he also spent borrowed money. And here he made the interesting disclosure that Sir Rowland Blennerhasset lent him £70, and Lord Richard Grosvenor £450. The second-named amount was lent in January or February, 1886. Did the lender of the £450 know what the money was wanted for ? No ; at any rate, Mr. Houston "did not tell" the lender. "I said I wanted it for political purposes."

Having got at the alleged contents of the alleged black bag, how did Mr

Houston try to dispose of them?—Well, he consulted Lord Hartington as to what he should do with them. But Lord Hartington would offer no opinion. This appears to have been during the period when *The Times*' decision as to whether it would take the letters or not was still in suspense. But, first of all, Mr. Houston applied to the editor of *The Pall Mall Gazette*. Had he asked Mr. Stead if he could name some "Unionist" politician to whom he might dispose of the letters? Had he said that he would produce proof that Mr. John Dillon and Mr. Sexton were implicated in the Phœnix Park murders? Had he offered the letters to Mr. Stead for one thousand pounds? Had the editor of *The Pall Mall Gazette* said he had already lost so much money over another business that he could not afford to risk a thousand on Pigott's find? Mr. Houston's satirical remarks on that other business provoked a peal of laughter. The usher shouted "Silence," but he might just as well have spared his breath and his frown. Mr. Houston was severe on Mr. Stead. Glancing scornfully at the editor of *The Pall Mall Gazette*, he observed that he perceived a breach had been committed in the "honourable" understanding which journalists should observe on matters of secresy. All this the editor of *The Pall Mall Gazette* took somewhat irreverently; he laughed, as if it were capital fun. Mr. Houston can stand on his dignity, for when Sir Charles Russell, humorously improvising an imaginary letter from Pigott to Mr. Houston, began "Dear Mr. Houston," the said Mr. Houston promptly pulled up the renowned Q.C. with the correction that Pigott always addressed him as "Dear Sir." Sir Charles Russell will be more careful next time.

But though, apparently, Mr. Houston liked to keep Mr. Pigott at arm's-length, socially speaking, he gave other illustrations, besides those narrated above, of his abounding faith in him. From the mode in which he paid Pigott he had—as he admitted—no means of checking Pigott, if Pigott had put all the money into his own pocket. Well, said Sir Charles, but was not your faith somewhat shaken when you heard of Pigott's interviews with Mr. Labouchere? Here Mr. Houston blushed, but smiled pleasantly enough, when he remarked, after a pause, "Well, I must admit the Labouchere incident somewhat shook my faith," at which admission there arose another burst of laughter. But Mr. Houston has said repeatedly that his faith in Mr. Pigott was restored in consequence of the sworn declarations which Pigott had made subsequently to his interviews with Mr. Labouchere, Mr. Lewis, and Mr. Parnell. And he accepted Mr. Pigott's personal opinion as to the identity of the persons to whom the compromising letters were addressed. Mr. Pigott felt sure the letters were addressed to Egan, Byrne, Brennan; and that was enough for Mr. Houston.

But there was, after all, one letter, or alleged letter, of one of Pigott's friends which might prove useful. When cross-examined about *The Pall Mall Gazette* interview, Mr. Houston remarked that if he had really said anything about the connection of Mr. Dillon and Mr. Sexton with the Phœnix Park murder, he must have said it on the authority of a formal statement which Eugene Davis made in writing to Pigott in Lausanne, and which Pigott subsequently handed over to Houston. Produce it. This most important and interesting document was produced by the Attorney-General. But it turned out to be a copy. Sir Charles protested; where was the original? Why did the witness state in a previous part of his evidence that he had given the original to Mr. Soames? The question was becoming complicated, for Mr. Houston now said that he must have made a mistake in saying that he gave the original to Mr. Soames; but Mr. Soames himself now declared that he had the original thirteen months ago. Finally, it was arranged, after a long altercation, that Mr. Soames should institute another search for the missing original; and meanwhile the copy of the original was allowed to be read and "put in." One of Mr. Soames's clerks appeared in the box to testify that that was the very paper which he himself had copied from the Davis-Pigott original.

It was curious reading. It occupied the Attorney-General fully twelve minutes. In it Eugene Davis described how, as a Fenian, he had made, in 1881, Egan's acquaintance (on the introduction of another Fenian, Pigott himself), how Egan gave him his entire confidence; how Egan, Parnell, Brennan, Matt Harris, Biggar, &c., were all active members of the Fenian Brotherhood; how Parnell and the rest agreed that Land Leaguers and Fenians should be in ccord as to their method of warfare against England; how they agreed that, as England and Ireland were practically at war, and as Ireland was unable to cope with England in the field, the united leaguers and Fenians should have recourse to "reprisals," including assassination of officials; how after Mr. Parnell's arrest, it was agreed that Egan and the other League leaders should carry on active operations—Mr. Parnell communicating with them from Kilmainham; how Egan remonstrated angrily with Mr. Parnell for his denunciation of the Phœnix Park crime; and how Parnell explained his conduct in a letter from Kilmainham (the letter of May 15, 1882, specially known as "the *facsimile* letter"); and finally how a plot was formed to murder Mr. Gladstone and the Prince of Wales. This last statement was received in court with a loud burst of laughter. All the above details Eugene Davis (according to Pigott's story) professed to have received from Egan himself, years before Davis and Pigott met each other at Lausanne.

And now—half-past one o'clock—Mr. Houston was released from the witness-box, and in the loud hubbub which followed, the name of "Pigott" was shouted out—"Pigott," "Pigott." But Pigott was a long time in coming. He came at last in the wake of the usher, who was laboriously elbowing his way through the crowd. A short, stoutish, round-shouldered man is Pigott, with a bald, shining head, bushy white whiskers and moustache, big, somewhat irresolute mouth, big fleshy nose, and smallish eyes, far apart. "A benevolent-looking person," one spectator remarked. "Might be a church deacon," observed another.

The first portion of Pigott's evidence was mainly autobiographical. Coming to the more immediate issue, he described how first he became acquainted with Mr. Houston; how reluctant he was to undertake the search for documents, thinking it a hopeless enterprise; how at last he thought of Davis, who used to be a regular contributor to Pigott's own paper, *The Irishman*; how, in 1881, Egan, who was in Paris, wrote to him asking for Davis's address; how, in 1886, he himself (Pigott) went to see Davis at Lausanne; and how he got out of Davis the statement which we have already summarised. At this point the examination of Pigott was suspended.

FIFTY-FOURTH DAY.

February 21.

"Yes," said Pigott, almost as soon as he entered the witness-box, "I have seen in this morning's papers the reproduction of the statement which Davis made to me in Lausanne." Again replying to the Attorney-General, he said the reproduction was correct. He described very briefly the course of his negotiations with Eugene Davis in Lausanne, in January and February, 1886. At first he asked Davis if he had any details which he, Pigott, might use for publication in an anti-Parnellite pamphlet; but at the same time he said he would require Mr. Davis to put his signature to the details, by way of authenticating them. After some delay and considerable reluctance (according to Pigott's account),

Mr. Davis undertook to write the pamphlet, and Pigott got from him some notes of what the pamphlet would contain. The notes jotted down on the back of a letter were subsequently expanded into the Davis-Pigott statement read in court yesterday, and published in this morning's papers. It was during this interview with Davis in Lausanne that Davis alluded to "a letter" which he believed to be still in existence—a remarkable letter from Mr. Parnell to (it was believed) Egan, in which Mr. Parnell stated that Mr. Burke "got no more than his deserts." "This was the first time I ever heard of this compromising letter," said Pigott; and thenceforth it became the chief end of Pigott's existence to find it.

Next followed the story of Pigott's marvellous luck. Shortly after his return home from Lausanne, Pigott heard from Paris that certain Irish-Americans, who might be useful to him in his researches, had just arrived there. So he crossed over to Paris, and as he walked about the streets a man accosted him whom he once knew (though he had forgotten him) as Maurice Murphy, who said that he had just come as an emissary from the Clan-na-Gael Brotherhood in America. So Pigott told Murphy about his Lausanne adventure, and asked him whether he knew anything of that astonishing letter of Mr. Parnell's. No; Murphy never had heard about it.

Days after that the pair met again, quite accidentally, and, wonderful to relate, Murphy announced that he had discovered the compromising letter, and that the compromising letter was in a black bag, which contained four more letters of Mr. Parnell's, and six of Egan's, together with sundry newspapers, and scraps from private account books. "I'm ready to buy them," said Pigott, and under Murphy's guidance Pigott was enabled to peruse the documents. "These are they," said he, as the Attorney-General handed them over for his inspection.

As soon as he saw the signatures in Paris, Pigott "certainly believed" them to be genuine, but he could form no opinion whatever as to the penmanship of the "bodies" of the letters. Pigott rushed back to London, told the news to Houston, rushed back again to Paris, and would have clinched the bargain there and then but for an unexpected accident. The Fenians in Paris would not "sell." The Clan-na-Gael in America claimed the black bag as their property, and Pigott must cross the ocean. Which he did, with a letter of introduction from Murphy to Breslin. After eight days in America he returned with his authorization—a letter from Breslin to Murphy.

But it was several weeks before he made use of it. Mrs. Pigott's illness prevented him from going to Paris. At last he went, July 10, 1886. He had the greatest difficulty in finding Murphy, who had not given him any address. But the Fates favoured him. He met Murphy in the street. But still Murphy would not sell, without previous communication with persons unknown. Murphy saw them, or said he did, and now he was ready to strike a bargain. So Pigott telegraphed to Houston to come at once. Which Houston did; and, to cut a long story short, the bargain was concluded, and the money paid to "the people downstairs" by the emissary upstairs, as already described. But Pigott adds a detail not previously given by Houston. Pigott says, that before the letters were handed over to him, he had to give his oath to the Clan-na-Gael in Paris never to divulge the "source" from which he received them, and never, should legal proceedings be taken, to appear as a witness in a court of justice. At this there was an outburst of laughter, and Mr. Pigott himself smiled. The place where Pigott said he took the oath was a private room in a café in the Rue St. Honoré. There were five men sitting round a table. All they did was to make him "swear" on a Roman Catholic prayer book.

So much for the first batch of letters. A second batch followed, and a third. And he came upon the second by a piece of marvellous luck, such as had brought him face to face two years before, in the streets of Paris, with Murphy.

Once upon a time he had been introduced to a certain Tom Brown by a man named Hayes, living in London. And in the beginning of 1888, whom should he meet in Paris but this identical Tom? And Tom exclaimed that Pigott was the very man he had been looking for. "Because," said Tom, "I have heard you were on the look out for documents, and I have discovered some." This second batch contained three letters, two signed in Mr. Parnell's name, and dated June 16, 1882; and one in Mr. Egan's name, professing to be addressed to Carey, and dated October 25, 1881. For this batch Houston paid £500, and £50 as commission to Pigott. [Total for the first two batches, £1155, besides the travelling and incidental expenses.] And curiously enough Pigott was conducted to the café in which he had taken his first oath; and there he repeated the oath before the same five men. This took place, said Pigott, in January or February, 1888, eighteen months after the supposed purchase of the first batch. This second batch, like the first, was bought by *The Times* from Houston—and no question asked. In July, 1888, about six months after the last-named transaction, Pigott, being again in Paris, was accosted by a man whom he had never seen before, and who offered to sell him three letters. "I have heard from Mr. Brown that you are a buyer," said this new vendor. This third batch contained one letter said to be written by Mr. Davitt, one by Mr. O'Kelly, and one by Egan; this third letter, purporting to be from Mr. Egan's place of business, was known as "the bakery letter." Houston swallowed the batch from Pigott, and *The Times* swallowed it from Houston, paying £200—and asking no questions!

As to the suggestion thrown out by the other side, that Mr. Pigott might have forged all three batches, Mr. Pigott (replying to the Attorney-General) declared that there was "certainly not" the shadow of a foundation for the story. Pigott pronounced "not" with a short snort of disgust, and rammed his hands into his pockets.

Now came one of the most amusing scenes in the day's proceedings. This was the story of Pigott's interview with Mr. Parnell and Mr. Lewis, in Mr. Labouchere's house, on the 24th of October last, about three months after the sale of the last batch to *The Times*, and two days after the opening of the trial. Just a month before the interview Pigott was subpœnaed by Mr. George Lewis on behalf of Mr. Parnell. He had not yet been subpœnaed by *The Times*. After the serving of this subpœna by Mr. Lewis, Pigott, according to his own story, received an intimation that an agent from Pat Egan was waiting for him in London. Pigott went from Dublin to London. Sinclair, the alleged agent, told him he was prepared to buy any compromising documents which he (Pigott) might have in his possession, said he would give "a heavy price for them," and Sinclair also said that Mr. Labouchere was an "agent" of Pat Egan's. The alleged *pourparlers* with Sinclair ended in Pigott's writing on his own account (and, of course, without Houston's knowledge) to Mr. Labouchere, asking for an interview. Then the Attorney-General read out Mr. Labouchere's reply, in which the writer remarked that his house was the best place for the rendezvous, because it was "certainly not watched." Mr. Labouchere also suggested that Pigott should come by "the underground." When the Attorney-General finished reading Mr. Labouchere's letter of invitation, he invited Pigott to tell the rest of the story in his own way.

Said Pigott, it was Mr. Parnell who began the conversation. He declared "they had proof in their hands which would convict me of having forged the documents." And then, said Pigott, "Mr. Parnell also told me he had heard of my desire to avoid giving any evidence at all, and he asked me how I proposed to do that. I then suggested that as I had not been subpœnaed by *The Times*, my non-appearance in the witness-box might be secured by Mr. Lewis withdrawing his subpœna. But Mr. Parnell did not see how Mr. Lewis could do that." Mr. Parnell thought Pigott *must* enter the witness-box in any case.

And then, said Mr. Pigott, nodding, "Mr. Labouchere took up the running" —an expression which amused the Court.

It was now that the fun began. Judging from Pigott's story, Mr. Parnell must have been serious and stern, and Pigott could have had no difficulty in making him out. But when Mr. Labouchere "took up the running," poor Pigott became puzzled. Mr. Labouchere was "facetious." He must have thought Mr. Labouchere was making fun of him. Mr. Labouchere advised him to go straight into the witness-box and make a clean breast of the forgery. For what inducements? "Why," Mr. Labouchere said, "that I should become immensely popular in Ireland." "Mr. Labouchere also told me that the mere fact of my having swindled *The Times* would be sufficient to secure me a seat in Parliament." Here Mr. Pigott's audience broke into a roar of laughter. And next "Mr. Labouchere told me that if I chose to go to the United States he would take care that I should be received with a torchlight procession by the Fenian organization." "Of course I hardly believed Mr. Labouchere could be serious." Mr. Labouchere, sitting in his corner, joined in the merriment. For the first time since the trial began the President intervened. "I must say," said Sir James Hannen, "that whether this is true or not, it is not a fit subject for laughter."

Mr. Labouchere's advice to Pigott was as unpleasant as it was precise. He was to enter the box and swear to the forgeries; "it is a very simple matter," said Mr. Labouchere, "all you will have to do is to enter the court and take your oath, and walk out. "Besides," said Mr. Labouchere, "the Commissioners' certificate of indemnity will protect you."

Going on with his story, Pigott said that in the midst of the foregoing colloquy he was surprised by the arrival of Mr. Lewis—surprised, because he thought this was a secret meeting between the three. It occurred to Pigott that this was "a plant." And this unlooked-for stranger, Mr. Lewis, began, in his "severest manner," to charge him with having forged the letters himself, and to advise him, as Mr. Labouchere and Mr. Parnell had done, to swear to the forgery in the witness-box. When Mr. Lewis saw that his severity had no effect upon me, said Mr. Pigott, he became "conciliatory"—he even "shook hands." And then Mr. Labouchere took Pigott outside the door and offered him a thousand pounds if he would swear. But before Mr. Labouchere took him outside, Pigott himself had said something about his having asked from or having been promised by *The Times* a sum of five thousand pounds; and, said Pigott, "before Mr. Labouchere and I went outside I heard Mr. Lewis and Mr. Labouchere discussing what they should offer me." Why did they go outside? Because, according to Pigott's story, Mr. Parnell must not be told about any such monetary transaction. Pigott, according to his story, thought Mr. Labouchere's offer a handsome one. In fact, it was his impression that he led Mr. Labouchere to think that the offer was accepted. But this could not have mattered much, because as soon as they re-entered the room, Pigott—so he said—declared that he would not for any amount of money enter the witness-box to "swear to a lie." Well then, as Pigott would not swear to the forgery, and as Mr. Lewis would not withdraw his subpœna, what was to be done? Mr. Lewis had already warned him that if he did not swear to the forgery "no mercy" would be shown him, and he would be prosecuted for perjury and forgery all the same. There was another course, Mr. Lewis thought; "Let Pigott write to *The Times* and confess that he himself forged the letters; the result will be that *The Times* will withdraw the letters and allow the whole matter to drop."

Pigott then went on to describe a visit which Mr. Lewis paid him next morning, and at which Mr. Lewis offered to take his statement. Not having promised (said he) a statement, he was surprised at Mr. Lewis's request. However, he made one; and now the Attorney-General read it out in court.

In this statement Pigott was made to declare his belief that the letters were not genuine; that their publication in *The Times* alarmed him; and that he had written to Archbishop Walsh, offering to help Mr. Parnell out of his troubles. Was that in your statement, the Attorney-General asked. Pigott answered emphatically, that he had told Mr. Lewis nothing of the kind. I heard, said Pigott, that Mr. Lewis asked the Archbishop of Dublin for certain letters which I had written to his Grace, but I learned that his Grace refused. I never stated to Mr. Lewis, said Pigott, at a later stage in his examination-in-chief, that the letters were forgeries, and that I knew them to be forgeries when I bought them.

Concluding his story, Pigott said that he made on the 5th of November a complete statement to Houston, and that this statement was embodied, at Houston's instance, in a sworn declaration. "I always said I was anxious to avoid giving evidence," said Pigott, at the finish; "I had sworn secrecy, and I expected that the consequences of my breach of it would be serious."

As the Attorney-General, rearranging his gown, was slowly resuming his seat, a loud murmur of conversation broke out over the court. It stopped suddenly. Scarcely was the Attorney-General seated when Sir Charles Russell stood bolt upright. He had a clean sheet of paper in his hand. "Take that"—holding it out rapidly: and he asked Pigott to write down a few words from his dictation. It was a dramatic opening. "He has him"—a barrister whispered, turning round to the present writer. The audience saw that Sir Charles Russell was coming to the issue at once, and in the silence one might hear a pin drop.

Pigott screwed his eyeglass into his right eye, took the sheet of paper and a quill, and sat down with his round broad back to the spectators. Write—"livelihood"—"likelihood"—and your own name—"proselytism"—"Patrick Egan"—and the initials of Patrick Egan—and "hesitancy."

"Photograph them," said the Attorney-General, when the specimens of Pigott's handwriting were handed up. Then Sir Charles and Pigott looked at each other. "Do you remember having had correspondence with Mr. Parnell and Mr. Egan about the purchase of your paper, *The Irishman*?" exclaimed Sir Charles, sharply. Pigott paused. He twirled his eyeglass. He was not quite sure. But at last he recollected his correspondence with both. And his correspondence with Mr. Forster? Yes—after another pause. Ever offered any Irish Secretary any information for money? Not to the best of his belief. But at last he remembered that he had asked Sir George Trevelyan for some pecuniary aid because of the support which he (Pigott) had given to the agrarian legislation of the Government. In 1884 he gave information to Earl Spencer.

And now for his correspondence with the Archbishop. Pigott changed colour. Yes; he had written to the Archbishop; but that was under "the seal of the confessional"—an assurance which Sir Charles received with a sceptical little laugh. What was the correspondence about? "I asked his advice." About what? Was it not respecting "incriminatory matter" about Mr. Parnell and others? Pigott pondered for a minute or two. He looked down. He looked up again, with a somewhat blank expression of countenance. Yes, it was. And the matter included the letters? Yes—after another long pause. Here the Court was wrought to the highest pitch of curiosity. And this particular letter to the Archbishop was dated 4th of March, 1887, three days before the series of *The Times* articles called "Parnellism and Crime" began? Yes. And so then Pigott was aware on the 4th of March that *The Times* would, or might, print the incriminatory "letters"? No, he was not. What! was he not aware that Houston had all those letters in his possession ready to produce them, to the damage of Mr. Parnell and his associates? Again, a long pause, after which Pigott admitted he "supposed" he was. Then Sir

Charles Russell began to read from the Pigott letter (marked "private and confidential") to Dr. Walsh. Did Pigott remember the passage in which he said that proceedings were imminent which would destroy Mr. Parnell's influence in Parliament. "What were these proceedings?" "Can't say." Sir Charles stared at him. "I don't know really," pleaded Pigott, in a half-audible voice. "Was it the letters?" "Can't say; I thought it was the forthcoming articles." "What! have you not just said that you knew nothing about the articles forthcoming in *The Times*?" Pigott held his peace. "I suppose I was mistaken," he said at last.

Sir Charles proceeded with his reading. Did Pigott say in his letter to Dr. Walsh that Mr. Parnell would be accused of having "participated" in crime, and that "criminal proceedings" might follow? "I won't swear," said Pigott, after some reflection. Then Pigott admitted that if the letters were genuine they would prove Mr. Parnell's complicity in crime. And did not Pigott write to the Archbishop that he (Pigott) was in a position to prove all he said, and to "show how the designs of Mr. Parnell's opponents could be successfully combated, and finally defeated?" Yes. But how could Pigott do that if the letters were not forgeries? At this question Pigott came to a dead stop. He was utterly confused. He stammered; he declared that he could not have had the letters in his mind; that the whole thing had passed out of his recollection.

Sir Charles pressed his question. If the letters were genuine, what means would Pigott have had of saving Mr. Parnell and his associates? "I can't think." "Oh, yes; you must try." "I can't think." "You must think. Had you any qualms of conscience? All this happened only a short time ago. No qualms? Then try and remember." "I can't." "Try." "I really can't give any explanation."

Sir Charles went on with his reading. Had Pigott not asked Dr. Walsh to introduce him to some one to whom he could show how the "blow" might be avoided? Pigott could not remember. Nor could he think what he meant by the blow. "My memory is a perfect blank." Well, did he say in a "P.S." to his letter to Dr. Walsh that, had he considered the accused really guilty, he would not have troubled the Archbishop; and that he was sure, if they were tried in an *English* Court, they would be convicted?

This question was followed by a murmur of astonishment all over the court. Pigott hesitated, wrinkled his forehead, stammered, and at last declared that he must have had in his mind some other charges more serious than the letters—and that, in fact, he did not consider the letters to be so "serious" as to justify the language of the postscript. A minute or two before, Pigott declared that if the letters were genuine, they were sufficient to bring the charge of complicity in crime home to Mr. Parnell and his associates.

But what were these other terrible secrets? Pigott could not tell. Surely the letters were serious enough, said Sir Charles; they had at any rate cost two thousand pounds. "Yes, they had," Pigott replied. "I say the Archbishop has deceived me," said Pigott, moving about restlessly; "I thought he had returned me all my letters." Then he said he did not believe the Archbishop had ever sent him any reply. "Is not that the Archbishop's writing?" retorted Sir Charles. "It appears to be." "And if this other secret of yours was locked up in your own bosom, where could the danger to Mr. Parnell be?" Pigott could not tell. All he could say was that when he wrote to Dr. Walsh he must have had something in his mind "more serious" than the letters. But as to who told him this other secret, or what it was, or where he learned it, or how—Pigott's mind was a blank. "Hermetically sealed up in your bosom?" "No; it has flown out of my bosom." In the roar of laughter which followed, the day's proceedings came to an end. The judges themselves laughed. And Pigott laughed with the rest—an irresolute, meaningless, nervous laugh, while the heavy face flushed red with excitement.

FIFTY-FIFTH DAY.

FEBRUARY 22.

PIGOTT ended yesterday's part of his story with an explanation of what he meant by the seriously compromising statements against which he wished to warn Mr. Parnell through Dr. Walsh. It will be remembered that his first letter to Dr. Walsh was written three days before the publication of the " Parnellism and Crime " series was begun in *The Times.* Did Pigott mean "the letters" when he warned the Archbishop against the dangers impending over the heads of Mr. Parnell and his associates? No; it was some other secret danger of which Pigott had become aware. " Hermetically sealed up in your bosom? " as Sir Charles Russell observed when the Court arose. This, then, was the point at which to-day's proceedings began—what, if they were not "the letters," were the dangers, of which Pigott had been writing in mysterious terms to the Archbishop? "Is that your handwriting?" asked Sir Charles, sharply, plunging, without any preface, into business. Pigott stuck in his eyeglass, and looked long and curiously at the paper. "Yes," he said. This letter was Pigott's answer to the Archbishop's reply. In it Pigott said that he had only thought the impending accusations against Mr. Parnell might be forestalled by his (Pigott's) showing the accused the disgraceful means by which the documentary and personal evidence against them had been procured; at any rate it would be useful to Mr. Parnell and his friends to know beforehand the charges which were to be laid against them.

What have you to say to that? asked Sir Charles Russell, after he had read Pigott's letter. Pigott wanted to explain. And he "explained " himself, in a long, hurried, stammering narrative, which sank at last into a half-inaudible gabble difficult to catch. He "explained" that, having as a matter of fact procured the letters and given them to Houston, and knowing their compromising character, he began to grow alarmed at the prospect of their disclosure—because although it had been agreed he should never be called upon to give evidence with respect to them, he might now be forced to tell all he knew about them. He further explained that when he first received them he was given to understand that they never would be published. So, under the circumstances, he wished to leave the country, and he wanted Dr. Walsh to introduce him to Mr. Parnell, who might, perhaps, be prevailed upon to help him with money, in return for the information he could give him as to the source of the letters.

" And so it follows," said Sir Charles, " that since last night you have removed from your bosom the idea that your letter to Dr. Walsh had reference to some fearful secret not yet disclosed?" "I shall say at once," answered Pigott, "that what I wrote to Dr. Walsh was entirely unfounded. I only wrote as strongly as possible in order to make him interfere." Then Pigott had deliberately written "lies"? No, he had only written "exaggerations," though he immediately modified this correction by saying there was but little truth left in the exaggerations. These communications with Dr. Walsh were followed by two " statements," from Pigott. These statements do not appear to have furnished Dr. Walsh with any additional information; for in returning them to Pigott the Archbishop wrote that he could not see how anything contained in them would help Mr. Parnell " to expose the forger or bring the forger to justice," and that any help which fell short of that would be useless.

Poor Pigott was, so to speak, falling to pieces. He was rapidly losing what little presence of mind he had. Before Sir Charles Russell reached the end of the Dr. Walsh portion of his case, he convicted poor Pigott of three or four gross lies at least. Thus, it appeared, from one of the Archbishop's replies to

Pigott, that Pigott had assured him that he "had neither hand, act, nor part in" the publication of the alleged Parnell and Egan letters in *The Times*. And this, in spite of Pigott's own story of his journeys to Paris, and the discovery of the miraculous black bag! Pigott repeated the same disclaimer in equally strong language, in another letter to his Grace. And the disclaimer "was not true?" exclaimed Sir Charles Russell, looking at his witness curiously. "N— no," muttered Pigott, reddening, smiling awkwardly, and moving about restlessly.

Once more, in one of these later and despairing communications of his to the Archbishop, Pigott had said that he did not believe the alleged "Parnell letters" published in *The Times* were genuine; but that he thought the Egan letters were. The buyer of the contents of the black bag doubting the worth of his purchase. "Did you ever tell Houston that you had any doubts," Sir Charles asked him, sharply. "I never did," Pigott replied. Finally, Sir Charles asked him about the most interesting and famous of *The Times* letters, that particularly known as the "facsimile letter," apologizing for condemnation of the Phœnix Park murders. Of this famous letter, Pigott, as Sir Charles Russell now showed, wrote to the Archbishop—"I am not the fabricator of the published letter, as has been publicly circulated ; and I defy any one to prove that I had anything to do with it. It is another instance of one having to suffer for the sins of others." At this picture of injured innocence, as seen in the witness-box, the crowded audience laughed outright. And in denying that he had had anything to do with the notorious facsimile letter, Pigott merely repeated his falsehoods. The main point, therefore, brought out in this part of the cross-examination was that Pigott had expressly confessed to the Archbishop his disbelief in the genuineness of the letters attributed to Mr. Parnell. But in the second place, by denying that he had ever had anything to do with them, he convicted himself of falsehood. And, thirdly, the Pigott-Walsh correspondence proved that Pigott was most anxious to escape from the country.

Swiftly, pitilessly, the toils were closing round poor, dazed, wretched Pigott. Sir Charles Russell produced a correspondence which had passed between Pigott, Egan, and Mr. Parnell, in the years 1881, 1882, principally with reference to the purchase, by Mr. Parnell, of Pigott's paper *The Irishman*. Sir Charles's object was to show by comparison between passages that the correspondence of six or seven years ago formed the basis of the forgeries which appeared in *The Times* in 1887. The first of these old letters produced by Sir Charles Russell, was one which Pigott wrote on the 27th of Feb., 1881, to Mr. Egan who was then in Paris. Just as Pigott in 1887 had written to Dr. Walsh warning him against impending danger to Mr. Parnell and his cause, and offering to help both (for a consideration), so this same Pigott wrote in 1881 to Egan, giving him warning of a damaging plot against the Land League, and offering to avert the blow (for a consideration). Singular coincidence. Still more singular was an identity between expressions of the letter of Egan in 1881 and of the letter to Dr. Walsh in 1887. I have had "neither hand, act, nor part" in the Parnell letters," said Pigott in 1887. The Supreme Council of the Fenian Society has neither "hand, act, nor part" in this attempt to expose the financial mismanagement of the Land League, wrote Pigott to Egan in 1881. The story of this attempt was a strange one. Two unknown persons had called upon Mr. Pigott [so Pigott wrote to Egan] offering him five hundred pounds if he would publish in his paper *The Irishman*, a damaging statement, which they had in their possession, against the Land League. I believe their statements are false, said Pigott, in his letter to Mr. Egan; but I must have money, and if you don't give it me, the mysterious strangers will. Not receiving a prompt reply from Mr. Egan, Pigott wrote to him again, enclosing a slip of paper which he said was the written promise given him by the two strangers.

At this point Sir Charles Russell suddenly stopped. He handed the slip of paper up to Pigott in the witness-box. "Do you know the handwriting," exclaimed Sir Charles, darting a keen glance at Pigott. "No," answered Pigott, again reddening, and looking slowly up, with an awkward, helpless look, and his big, loose, weak mouth open. Then Sir Charles became ironical. What were the mysterious strangers like? Were they old, or young, or middle-aged, or tall, or short, or masked, or unmasked; and did they come in the night-time, or in the daytime; and did Pigott give them refreshments, and was it after Pigott had his own refreshments, or before? Sir Charles kept up a brisk, running fire of such questions. And Pigott answered them, recklessly, and as it were at random—looking more foolish and confused as he went on. They were middle-aged, said Pigott, and they wore no masks, and he gave them refreshments, and ——. "Come, now, Pigott," said Sir Charles, interrupting him, "is this absurd story the creation of your own brain?"

And now came the comparisons between the genuine correspondence above mentioned and the alleged forgeries. Here, for example, is one of the compromising letters published by *The Times* and alleged by the defence to be a forgery. It is dated June 18, 1881, and runs: "Dear Sir,—Your two letters of 12th and 15th inst. are duly to hand, and I am also in receipt of communications from Mr. Parnell informing me that he has acted upon my suggestion, and accepted the offer made by B. You had better at once proceed to Dundalk so that there may be no time lost.—Yours very faithfully, P. EGAN."

The letter to which it bears so startling a resemblance is the following genuine letter, dated Paris 18th June, 1881, from Egan to Pigott,—"Dear Sir, —Your two letters of 12th and 15th inst. are duly to hand, and I am also in receipt of communications from Mr. Parnell, informing me that he has acted upon my suggestion and accepted the offer made in your first letter. In fact I have before me copies, &c.—P. EGAN."

"Yes, very remarkable coincidence," muttered Pigott, in a mechanical sort of way, repeating Sir Charles's expression. And then talking wildly, "so remarkable as to be exceedingly improbable."

Another coincidence, from the Egan correspondence, genuine and alleged. One of Egan's supposed letters, published in *The Times*, runs thus, — "June 10, 1881. Dear Sir,—I am in receipt of your note of the 8th inst., and am writing Mr. Parnell fully on the matter. He will doubtless communicate with you himself.—Yours very truly, P. EGAN." The genuine letter upon which the forgery is supposed to be based runs thus, "19 May, 1881, I am in receipt of your letter of the 16th instant, and in reply shall write to Mr. Parnell as you request, and ascertain his view in regard to your proposal." To mention one other instance of coincidence from the Egan correspondence, there was a complete similarity between the beginning of the letter, in which Mr. Egan declined Pigott's overtures about the two mysterious strangers [above named] and the beginning of one of the alleged Egan letters in *The Times*. Both letters began "as I understand your letter which reached me to-day;" one letter says that "under existing circumstances what you suggest would not be entertained;" and the other, "under any circumstances I have no power to so apply any of the funds of the League."

Sir Charles next pointed out extraordinary coincidences between expressions in Mr. Parnell's genuine letters, and expressions in alleged letters of his which he declares to be forgeries. On the 16th of June, 1881, Mr. Parnell wrote from the House of Commons to Pigott in Dublin, in reference to the purchase of *The Irishman*,—" Dear Sir,—In reply to yours of this date, I am sure you will feel that I shall always be anxious to do what I can for you, but I could not consent to one of the conditions of the purchase being your constant employment on the paper. That is a matter which should have to be subject to after arrangement." Now the "compromising letter" published in *The Times* reads thus,—"June 16, 1882.—Dear Sir,—I shall always be anxious to have the goodwill of your friends, but why do they impugn my motives? I could not consent to the conditions they would impose, but I accept the entire responsibility for what we have done.—Yours very truly, CHAS. S. PARNELL."

Here there followed one or two amusing little "scenes" between Sir Charles Russell and Pigott. When Sir Charles Russell twitted him on the "anniversary use" of so many phrases, Pigott tried to laugh with the audience and failed. Then Sir Charles, leaning his back against the bench, helping himself to a pinch of snuff, and shaking his brown pocket handkerchief, asked Pigott how he would forge supposing, for the sake of argument, he wanted to. We may quote part of the dialogue :—

Would it be any help to you to have before you a letter of the man concerned?—I suppose so.
How would you use it?—Take a copy, of course.
How would you proceed to do so?—I can't say; I don't pretend to any experience of that kind.
But let us know how you would set about it?—I decline to put myself in that position at all.
Yes, but speaking theoretically?—I don't see any good in discussing the theory.
Let me suggest, now. Would you, for instance, put delicate tissue paper over the letter—would you, in fact, trace it?—I suppose so. How would *you* do it?
No; I'm asking you. Supposing you put delicate tissue paper over the genuine letter that would enable you to reproduce its character, would it not?—Yes, that is the way.
How do you know?—Well, I suppose it would be the most easy way.
How do you know? Have you tried?—No; but I suppose so.
Is Mr. Parnell's signature a difficult signature to imitate?—I do not know.
But what do you think?—It is a peculiar signature.
You mean it is a strongly marked one? Well, do you think it would be easy?—I am not competent to give an opinion. What is your opinion?
I am very anxious to have yours. Would you think it a difficult or an easy signature to imitate?—Considering its peculiarities, I should say difficult.
More difficult than a free, flowing signature?—I think so.

Next came the spelling test.

Among the words you wrote down yesterday at my request is the word "hesitancy." Is that a word you are accustomed to use?—I often have used it.
Well, you spelt it as it is not ordinarily spelt.—Yes, I fancy I made a mistake in spelling it.
What was the mistake?—I used an "a" instead of an "e"—no; I mean I——. Well, I'm not sure what the mistake was.
I'll tell you what was wrong. You spelt it with an "e" instead of an "a." H-e-s-i-t-e-n-c-y is not the recognized spelling, I think. Now, have you noticed that the writer of the body of the letter of the 9th of January, 1882, makes the same mistake?
Yes, it has often been pointed out to me. In fact I think I had, owing to this having been pointed out to me, got the mistake thoroughly into my head. But everybody spells the word wrong.

Sir Charles Russell's declaration of the identity in spelling caused the greatest excitement in Court. How could Pigott explain it away? Pigott replied that the mis-spelling in the alleged forgery had, in consequence of the public discussion on the subject, "got into" his "brain." But then, the self-same misspelling occurred in a genuine letter of Pigott's of June, 1881.

Pigott was helpless; he could only say that spelling was not his strong point.

While all these comparisons between genuine letters and alleged forgeries were in progress, Mr. Wemyss Reid, Mr. Forster's biographer was in court, engaged in selecting letters from a heap of correspondence that had passed between Mr. Forster and Pigott in 1881-2. In fact, the opening letter of the Forster-Pigott correspondence, namely Pigott's letter of June 2, 1881, had already been read. In this letter, Pigott, recounting his journalistic services to the cause of law and order in Ireland, asked for a Government subvention of fifteen hundred or a thousand pounds—a request which Mr. Forster, though expressing his approbation of Pigott's articles, refused to grant. Interrupted by the foregoing cross-examination, the inquiry into the Forster correspondence was now resumed. In a letter of the 6th of June, 1881, Pigott, regretting Mr. Forster's first refusal, asked for a loan from Mr. Forster personally. Mr. Forster made him a kindly offer of a loan of fifty or a hundred pounds, telling him he was to repay it at his convenience. Kindly Mr. Forster had said "fifty or a hundred," but his hardened applicant promptly asked for the "hundred promised." "Fifty would have suited me better than a hundred," wrote Mr. Forster, when forwarding the larger sum, and suggesting an introduction to Mr. Knowles of *The Nineteenth Century*. Pigott replied, in his modesty, that he feared his style would prove too rugged for a London magazine. And with heartfelt gratitude, he acknowledged the receipt of the hundred pounds. Pigott's gratitude by and by manifested itself in a request for fresh favours: in a letter of December 16, 1881, he described himself as utterly penniless, and asked for a Government grant to enable him to go to America ; in a letter of the 25th of December, 1881, he had the insolence to write to Mr. Forster, saying that he considered himself "badly used," because he had been "led" to entertain "hopes" of adequate reward which had not been "fulfilled."

Replying on the 26th of December, Mr. Forster said that he could not understand why Pigott considered himself unfairly treated ; that he had helped Pigott purely out of sympathy ; and that he must deny "in the strongest terms," Pigott's assertion that Pigott had been employed to write for the Government. The justice of this denial Pigott admitted in his next letter, but he added that he thought he was entitled to some recompense from Government for his services ; and that he would " loathe himself " if he " could even dream " of expecting further assistance from Mr. Forster personally. And in less than a fortnight, Pigott, loathing to trouble Mr. Forster personally, asked Mr. Forster to "induce" some of his colleagues to help him out to America and save him from destitution. Mr. Forster declined to trouble his colleagues ; but, said good Mr. Forster, " I am willing to give you myself fifty pounds to enable you to go to America ; but it must be clearly understood that is all I shall do." Pigott in reply " wanted words to express his gratitude." Pigott did not go to America : in course of time, he wrote to Mr. Forster, wondering how he could raise one hundred pounds, and whether Mr. Forster could negotiate with Messrs. Macmillan, the publishers, for the purchase, at "a reduced rate," of a book of Pigott's. In this same letter, Pigott wished to know whether Mr. Forster would see somebody "connected with *The Times*," with a view "to getting a review of my unfortunate book into the paper." To this string of cool requests Mr. Forster replied that he wished he could lend Pigott the money; but that he was unable.

Shortly after this, Pigott had an interview with Mr. Forster in London. It was in August, 1882. Mr. Forster took the precaution of " having two gentlemen in the room," as Pigott expressed. The precaution was too much for the sensitive Pigott's feelings of honour, and he complained of it in his next letter to Mr. Forster. So much hurt was Pigott at Mr. Forster's display of caution that he declared he could have no " peace of mind " until he had paid off his debts to his benefactor. " Your peace of mind has ever since been wanting," observed Sir Charles Russell. " Yes," was Pigott's reply. Said Pigott, after the laughter in Court had subsided, " it may be extremely amusing to you ; it is not amusing to me." And he might have added that it was " not amusing " to his friends from *The Times* office, who were sitting right in front of him. They took no part in the general merriment.

At last came the blackmailing letter. One day, Mr. Forster received a letter which was signed " Nemo," and which said that a plot was on foot to injure him by bribing the late proprietor of *The Irishman* [Pigott] to publish some of the Forster letters. "Nemo" suggested that it would be well for Mr. Forster to get his letters back; and that an advertisement in *The Irish Times* would secure their recovery. Sir Charles Russell asked Pigott whether he recognized any similarity between this threatening letter and the mysterious communication from the two mysterious strangers, which he, Pigott, had some time before sent to Mr. Egan in Paris. Mr. Pigott's mind was a blank.

Long before this stage was reached, the densely packed audience in court was wrought up to the highest pitch of amusement and excitement. The Court Usher had long since ceased to cry out "silence." The merriment was irrepressible, and almost continuous. The judges themselves were unable to repress their feelings. A loud, ringing roar of merriment broke forth, as Sir Charles Russell read Pigott's next letter containing an application for £200 to enable him to proceed to Sydney, and some hints as to the pressure which was brought to bear upon him to publish the Forster letters. Mr. Justice Day, bending forward, reddened, and shook, with laughter. In this letter, Pigott wrote—"I feel this is my last chance, and if that fails, only the workhouse and the grave remain." Poor Pigott looked as if he would prefer even the grave to the witness-box. He changed colour; the helpless, foolish smile flickered about the weak, heavy mouth; his hands moved about restlessly, nervously. Then came the climax—Pigott's letter to Mr. Forster, saying that he felt tempted to reveal to the world how he had been bribed by Mr. Forster to write against the interests of Ireland. The notion of Pigott's appearing in the character of injured innocence set the audience off, once more, into a fit of laughter. It was now four o'clock, and in the uproar and confusion Pigott descended from his box, smiling foolishly, as he brought down the fabric of *The Times* "letters" case in ludicrous ruin.

FIFTY-SIXTH DAY.

FEBRUARY 26.

THE court room and corridors presented a most animated spectacle, for fully half an hour before the judges arrived. The passages were thronged with people who had no chance of entrance. Within, save for the few Press seats, whose occupants had not yet arrived, there was not an inch of standing room. At times the hubbub of talk was almost deafening. Mr. Michael Davitt, coming in about ten minutes past ten o'clock, carrying a black bag, instantly attracted attention; for it was known that since Friday afternoon he had been out of the country, making inquiries into the Pigott mystery. Mr. Parnell, as he stalked in, slowly elbowing his way through the crowd, looked well satisfied. The flicker of a smile played round the corners of his eyes and thick brown moustache. Mr. Biggar beamed. Only once or twice in the course of the trial had Mr. Healy appeared; now he appeared once more. Mr. Wemyss Reid was in his place, ready to assist in further investigation of the Pigott-Forster correspondence. Mr. Jacob Bright—seen in court for the first time—stood in the crowd. In one of the Press seats to the right of the judicial bench sat Mrs. Gladstone. The crowd was denser than on any day since the trial began.

No wonder that the excitement is so great. In that dense throng there is not one who does not fully expect that Sir Charles Russell is about to extract from Pigott further statements as startling as any that he has yet made; or even that Pigott, seeing the toils closing round him, will throw the game up and make a full confession. "Silence!" exclaims the black-robed usher, throwing open the curtain behind their lordships' chairs: and the roar of talk suddenly stops. We all rise as the judges enter. The President bows. Their lordships sit down. Then we all sit. And Sir James Hannen, leaning back, folds his arms. Usher number two stands at his post, at the corner of the witness-box. After half a minute or so, Usher number two looks over his spectacles in the direction of the doorway. Then he looks at Mr. Soames. A minute passes. Sir James Hannen looks up inquiringly. He wrinkles his brow, as if he means to say, "Mr. Attorney, we are waiting." Mr. Attorney, understanding this, also wrinkles his brow, and looks round slowly, inquiringly, but to all appearance without the slightest suspicion that anything is wrong. Another minute, and still no Pigott. Then counsel begin to look anxiously at one another, and whisperings run round the court. The President, frowning a little, asks where is the witness; and after a little pause, preceded by a hurried and muttered conversation between the Attorney-General and Mr. Soames, the Attorney-General rises. His face is pale—an unusual thing for Sir Richard, and he speaks as if under a sense of pain and constraint—also an unusual thing for him. There is a strange expression of helplessness in his tone as he briefly and almost inaudibly announces that Pigott has not been seen since eleven o'clock last night.

Pigott escaped! And Mr. Parnell, Mr. Davitt, Sir C. Russell, Mr. Lockwood, Mr. Reid, Mr. Healy, Mr. Labouchere, and the rest of them gazed blankly at one another. The half-inarticulate murmur of surprise among the spectators threatened to break into uproar, but subsided—on Sir Charles Russell's prompt appeal to their lordships to issue a warrant for Pigott's immediate arrest. The almost pleading tone of Sir Richard Webster's voice contrasted strangely with the angry ring of Sir Charles Russell's, when Sir Richard, rising slowly, said that one of Mr. Soames's clerks was present who would tell all he knew about Pigott.

The clerk's all was but little. Mr. George Weir, the clerk in question, looked frightened as he felt all those hundreds of pairs of eyes fixed upon him. He could only say that he was at Anderton's Hotel (where Pigott was putting up) only twenty minutes ago; that the hotel attendant searched all over the place, and came back with the news that Pigott had not been seen since eleven o'clock last night. Mr. Soames's clerk having left the box, the President informed Sir Charles Russell that he had just given instructions for issuing a warrant of arrest. What was to be done next? The judges glanced at one another. Sir Richard Webster and his colleagues sat mute as statues. At last the President asked quietly, "Have you any other witness?" Upon this Sir Richard Webster, rising slowly, simply remarked that the unexpected non-appearance of Pigott made it necessary for him and his learned friends to consider what their future course would be, and until they settled that point they could not see their way to "recur to any other part of the case." "Is he going to throw up the case?" was the question which, in one form or another, flew about in hurried whispers all over the court. Sir Charles Russell was up in a moment, with his right arm extended. "Whatever you may do," said he, "we shall search this matter to the bottom, for we deliberately say that behind Houston and Pigott there is a foul conspiracy." And as the words "foul conspiracy" rang out sharply, indignantly, down came Sir Charles Russell's hand with a thud upon the bench.

At this point their Lordships rose to adjourn for fifteen minutes. If at the end of fifteen minutes Pigott should not be found the adjournment would be prolonged to thirty minutes. Just as the judges were retiring, Sir Charles Russell hurriedly informed them that a parcel of letters addressed to Pigott, to the care of Houston, had been received at Anderton's Hotel; and he suggested that the parcel should be sent for and placed in the possession of the Court. The adjournment, instead of lasting fifteen minutes, lasted an hour. The news having gone abroad that Pigott had run away and that the proceedings were in a state of confusion, great numbers of eager people rushed in from the other courts. In a minute or two after the judges retired, the Attorney-General and the whole body of *The Times* counsel disappeared for a time. And in Mr. Attorney's place sat Mr. Lockwood. He scribbled and scratched away at something, perhaps a caricature of Sir Richard and Mr. Murphy, Q.C., in distress. Then, in about twenty minutes, *The Times* counsel returned to their places. Mr. Soames reappeared, looking sad, weary, and bored. In Mr. Soames's wake followed Mr. Macdonald, of *The Times*. Alas! in Mr. Macdonald's face not a trace left of the self-complacence which it wore when from the witness-box he showed how, though the Parnellite lawyers were dull fellows, there was at least one man in the world who could see through conspirators' forgery tricks. The manager of *The Times* sat down submissive to the ironical Fates. And so the laughing and the talking went on. It stopped for a moment when the Clerk of the Court, Mr. Cunynghame—like somebody emerging from the under world—stuck out his head through the doorway in the screen beneath the judicial bench, and announced that the warrant for Pigott's arrest had been made out, and that the execution of it would be entrusted to Mr. Monro, conjointly with any police officer whom Sir Charles Russell might name. Mr. Lewis suggested Mr. Shore, of Scotland Yard. In another quarter of an hour the judges came in. After a few minutes' preliminary discussion, Sir Charles Russell made a wholly unexpected announcement. Last Saturday, said he, Richard Pigott, without invitation from anybody, called upon Mr. Labouchere in Mr. Labouchere's house, and there and then offered to make a full confession.

And Mr. Labouchere, Sir Charles went on, would hear nothing from Pigott except in the presence of a witness. Mr. Labouchere accordingly sent for Mr. George Augustus Sala, and Mr. Sala heard all that passed. And in the presence of Mr. Labouchere and Mr. Sala, Pigott confessed that he was the forger, and he signed a statement to that effect, but this statement Mr. Lewis returned, on Monday, to Pigott with an intimation that Mr. Parnell would have nothing to do with him directly or indirectly.

Sir Charles was asked why all this was not put in affidavit. To which he replied that, for one thing, he had come that morning prepared to resume his cross-examination of Pigott. Quick as thought Mr. Justice Smith broke in with the remark, "What, you expected to see Pigott after that confession?" But Sir Charles Russell was as prompt as Mr. Justice Smith. "Certainly, my lord," he replied, "I did expect; for Pigott was under the guardianship of a Royal Irish constable and two detectives from Scotland Yard;" and Sir Charles instantly followed this up with a request that the police officers should be placed in the box to explain how Pigott escaped from their guardianship.

It was evident that Sir Charles Russell had made up his mind to give no quarter. Meanwhile the manager of Anderton's Hotel appeared in court. As for Pigott's disappearance, all that the manager could say was that Pigott was last seen in the hotel about half-past four o'clock on Monday afternoon. Their lordships then read through certain letters, which, addressed to Pigott, reached the hotel after he left. Sir James Hannen then stated that they were private letters, and that the only thing of any consequence in them was a single "P.S." But it was a suspicious P.S. Here it is: "I done what you asked with the box. All is consumed."

The letter with the P.S. was from Pigott's housemaid in Kingstown, near Dublin. "All is consumed"—an inarticulate exclamation of surprise broke out among the audience, at this next disclosure of the destruction of evidence.

In answer to Sir Charles Russell, Mr. Soames—summoned once more into the witness-box—admitted that he had never made any inquiries into Pigott's character. Mr. Soames had had too much of other work to do—his labours on the Commission occupied him fourteen hours a day; and as for keeping an eye on Pigott, he did it after he heard that he had been in communication with Mr. Labouchere.

Have you, asked the Attorney-General, done anything directly or indirectly to help Pigott to escape?" "Most certainly not," Mr. Soames answered, as he turned to leave the box.

Then came Shannon, the Dublin solicitor who has been assisting Mr. Soames. Shannon is a tall, black-haired, pale-complexioned man, with a softish voice, and dark eyes that move slowly from side to side as if they were always on the search for something. He said that at Pigott's own request he saw Pigott at Anderton's on Saturday night; that on Saturday night Pigott made a full confession to him, a confession including the Labouchere-Sala interview; that the confession was then sent in writing, on Sunday morning, to the witness (Shannon).

In this last of his "confessions," poor, weak, despairing Pigott declared that instead of having forged all the documents (as in his confession to Messrs. Labouchere and Sala he said he had done) he had only forged two in the second batch and two in the third; that, as regards the first batch, the most important of all, containing five of Mr. Parnell's and six of Mr. Egan's, he (Pigott) had in truth got at them in the way he had described in his evidence, and that he believed the eleven letters to be genuine. Pigott, in this confession, went on to say that he feared he would be prosecuted, and that Mr. Labouchere promised him that he would not be prosecuted if he confessed to having forged all the letters; and also that Mr. Labouchere promised him the Parnellites would give two thousand pounds for the maintenance of his children. The statement ended with an abject confession that he had been drawn into forgery by penury, and with an equally abject appeal to the mercy of *The Times.* Finally, Pigott signed an affidavit to the effect that this, his last statement and confession to Shannon, was true in every particular.

"Did you consider that an affidavit lent any additional sanctity to Pigott's statement?" exclaimed Sir Charles, quickly, pointedly, as he rose up to cross-examine Shannon. Shannon, moving his dark eyes slowly from side to side, replied that he considered it did. Gazing fixedly at Shannon, and pausing for a little space, Sir Charles put the following question, in a low voice, "You notice Pigott says he fears prosecution. Did not that strike you?" And then Sir Charles pressed him; "did it not arouse a suspicion of Pigott's intention to run away?" "Were you anxious that Pigott should appear?" Sir Charles exclaimed, raising his voice to its highest pitch. "I was," replied Shannon; and then he admitted that he had neither taken any precautions against Pigott's escape, nor warned Mr. Soames. And yet Pigott feared prosecution for forgery and perjury? He might have feared prosecution by the Government, said Shannon, a remark that provoked a loud burst of laughter throughout the Court.

Shannon then declared he fully expected Pigott to appear that day, and that he was sure Pigott was still in London or near it. When did Shannon see Pigott last? Why, two hours before Pigott fled; and in that last interview between Pigott and Shannon, Pigott pressed hard for money—money wherewith to pay his hotel bill, as if there were some pressing necessity for payment. "And didn't that seem strange to you," asked Sir Charles, quietly. No. "Didn't you think he might be wanting it in order to cut?" No. "Didn't it seem singular to you that he should press you so hard?" No. "Well, well!" And then it turned out that this last interview was held, not in Anderton's Hotel nor in Shannon's rooms, but in some strange place not named before.

It was now a quarter to two o'clock. The judges rose for the usual half-hour's interval. The densely-crowded court squeezed itself out, with a loud uproar of chatter and laughter—out into the corridors. In the Strand, in front of the court buildings, multitudes of people were moving about in a great state of excitement. A loud roar of a cheer was raised in honour of somebody who did not turn out to be Mr. Parnell. The gamins in the crowd were running about shouting bogus news about the capture of Pigott. "There's Pigott," and in an instant a crowd of over a hundred and more was blocking the approach to the refreshment bar, nearly opposite the corner of Holywell Street, and peering at somebody not at all unlike Pigott, a stoutish, grey whiskered gentleman harmlessly consuming his bun.

At fifteen minutes past two the Court resumed. Mr. Lewis, going into the witness-box for a few minutes, stated that, in expectation of Pigott's appearance that day, he had procured evidence from Glasgow to show that Pigott had been a systematic forger of money bills during a long series of years, and that Pigott was a dealer in obscene books—a trade with which Pigott's journeys to Paris in search of the "black bag" might all the while have been connected. After Mr. Lewis followed Constable Callagher, of the Irish Constabulary, one of the two employed in looking after Pigott. He had very little to say. Then Sergeant Fawcett went into the box. Sergeant Fawcett was the last who saw Pigott. He saw him between three and four. He saw Pigott go upstairs (in the hotel), write a letter, and come down, and walk out streetwards and disappear. But Fawcett did not follow.

"Now, Mr. Attorney," said Sir James Hannen, after Fawcett had finished his brief story. Mr. Attorney was explaining what be would do, in the event of Pigott's reappearance. "First catch your hare," interposed the President; and Sir Richard stopped. "What we propose to do," said Sir Charles, "is to apply at once for a warrant of arrest on the charge of forgery and perjury against Pigott." The Court then adjourned. In a minute or two, with a cheering multitude behind them, Mr. Parnell, Mr. Lewis, Mr. Campbell, Mr. Davitt, Mr. Labouchere, were on their way to Bow Street police-court. There Mr. Vaughan gave Mr. George Lewis a warrant for the arrest of Pigott, on a charge of forgery and perjury.

FIFTY-SEVENTH DAY.

FEBRUARY 27.

"'PIGOTT been heard of?" was the universal question among the crowd of people who for nearly an hour before the doors were opened to-day, congregated in front of the Strand entrance. Some wondered whether Pigott might not have done away with himself. "He is too stupid," "He is too thick-skinned," "Hasn't shame enough," were specimens of the answers and comments. At last came the hurry and the scurry towards the corridors, which were speedily blocked. Of the Irish members Mr. T. Healy was the first to arrive. He and Mr. Labouchere sat together at the end of the solicitors' bench. Mr. Biggar followed, and at once became absorbed in the columns of a newspaper. Mr. Jacob Bright and Sir Charles Russell entered ten minutes before the half-hour. Mr. Sexton, who appeared in the Court for the first time three or four days ago, sat down unobserved among the Q.C.'s. Mr. Michael Davitt was all the more conspicuous by his absence, because, ever since the trial began, his attendance in court had been punctual and regular. Mr. Soames came in with the air of a man attending a funeral of dead reputations. And Mr. J. C. Macdonald, taking his seat on Mr. Soames's left, found himself side by side with his long-suffering and patient victim, now his contemptuously indifferent victor, Charles Stuart Parnell. Well, the philosopher must have remarked to himself, who observed that interesting pair, if ever there was in this puzzling Universe a case of poetic justice, surely there it is.

Mr. Parnell looked just middling well. While he quietly examined the contents of his black bag, or turned to exchange a word or two with Sir Charles Russell, his next neighbours—Mr. Macdonald and Mr. Soames—sat, with their arms folded, mute, gazing blankly in front of them. Now and again Mr. Parnell, who rose a head and shoulders above them, gazed over the crowns of their heads. He appeared to be as unconscious of the presence of Mr. Soames and Mr. Macdonald, as if Mr. Macdonald and Mr. Soames were in the moon. And, indeed, there was between Mr. Parnell and the gentlemen at his right, an interval immeasurable in miles. For want of something better to do, one took stock of the outward man of this real leader of men, whose dignified patience under charges the most foul was at last filling the minds even of his enemies with remorse. One noticed that Mr. Parnell looked a trifle younger. On further reflection one ascribed this impression to the fact that Mr. Parnell had had his hair trimmed. Idle conclusion—though not less idle than the question in everybody's mind, What of Pigott? Mr. Parnell wore a reddish brown cloak, or cape, which fell awry over his shoulders, and of which he was as careless as Sir Henry James of his silken gown.

Punctually at half-past ten o'clock their lordships entered. We all stood up. Sir James Hannen bowed gravely. Then their lordships sat down. After a few moments' pause, Sir James Hannen glanced at the Attorney-General. Whereupon Mr. Attorney rose. And he did it as if it were sorely against his will.

Sir Richard Webster merely informed the President that a letter had been received from Paris, to the address of Mr. Shannon, in Pigott's handwriting. "It has not been opened," said Sir Richard, holding out the letter, " and I desire to hand it in to your lordships at once. Immediately on the fact being known, a communication was sent to Scotland Yard by Mr. Soames, giving information. Perhaps you will look at this document." The letter was passed up to the President. Sir James Hannen, glancing rapidly over it, passed it down to Mr. Cunynghame, and asked him to read it. It was from Pigott. It contained Pigott's full confession which he made last Saturday before Mr. Labouchere and Mr. Sala, and which Mr. Lewis returned to him at once with the intimation that Mr. Parnell declined to have any further communication with him, directly or indirectly. Besides this long confession, there was one other document. It had the virtue of brevity. It was a hurried little note from Pigott to Shannon, saying that Pigott "would write again soon." This cool, easy assumption of Pigott's, that Pigott would be at liberty to write "soon," and in absolute security from the detectives much amused the audience. Pigott was writing comfortably from his Paris hotel. How did he find the money to get there? When, on Saturday, Sunday, and Monday, he dunned his colleagues for money, he declared he had not sixpence in the world.

Mr. Cunynghame read out the confession. He once or twice came to a dead stop over the Pigott manuscript. It appeared that the Pigott confession, as returned to Pigott by Mr. Lewis, reached Pigott just when he was on the point of saying good-bye to Anderton's hotel. He must have slipped it into his pocket; and as soon as he was comfortably settled in his Parisian quarters, he must have reposted it to Shannon. The confession, dated last Saturday—the day of the interview—declared that "I, Richard Pigott, am desirous of making a statement before Henry Labouchere and George Augustus Sala," and that "I make this of my own free will and without any monetary inducement, in the house of the former," and that "my object is to correct inaccuracies in the report of my evidence in *The Times*, and to make further disclosures" about the facsimile and other letters. With this preamble, this stupendous rascal entered upon his "corrections," and next upon the authorship and methods of the forgeries. First as to the corrections, as read out by Mr. Cunynghame. I told a lie, wrote Pigott, when I said that I took notes, on the spot, of conversations with Davis in Lausanne. Davis, in fact, had only given Pigott vague hearsay, from which Pigott, next day, concocted the story which he had palmed off upon *The Times*. Nor had Davis said anything about a damning letter of Mr. Parnell's (afterwards known as the facsimile letter) believed to be in the possession of a runaway Invincible living in Paris; that, at any rate, was Pigott's "opinion," as set forth in the confession which Mr. Cunynghame was now reading in Court. These were the leading "corrections."

It will be remembered that after the confession before Mr. Labouchere and Mr. Sala, Pigott made a qualifying confession to Mr. Shannon, in which he declared that he had only forged four letters in all, two in the second batch, two in the third. But in the confession made to Messrs. Labouchere and Sala, now read out by Mr. Cunynghame, Pigott averred that the first batch, the most important batch of all, the batch containing the facsimile letter, and four other letters of Mr. Parnell's, and six of Mr. Egan's, were forgeries likewise. "No one save myself was engaged in the work," says this amazing sinner. "I grieve to have to confess that I myself forged them." There was a ripple of laughter at this unbosoming of Pigott's grief. Then the forger went on to describe how, from genuine letters of Mr. Parnell's, he "picked out words and phrases to secure the proper handwriting." "I traced," said he, "some of the words by placing the letters to the window and drawing them on to a piece of tissue paper, and I thus procured the signatures."

Will those who were present in Court during the memorable Friday (last Friday) recall that very dramatic incident, when Sir Charles Russell, suddenly leaning his back against the bench, invited Pigott in a cheery, confiding way, to describe how *he* would forge a signature, supposing, just for the sake of argument, that he had to try it? " Come now, Mr. Pigott, how would you do it? Take a piece of tracing paper and lay it over a genuine letter?" and, &c. That sudden question might have upset any forger who, unlike Pigott, was not gifted with a hide of iron and front of brass. It will be remembered how Pigott flushed for a moment or two, and then recovering himself tried to turn the tables upon the terrible Q.C. by asking him how *he* would do it after he got his tracing paper. But let us proceed. According to the statement read out by Mr. Cunynghame, the "black bag" was a figment of the Pigottist fancy. Houston accepted the contents of the black bag, after a "very brief inspection," and the spoil—five hundred pounds for the mysterious owners of the black bag, and a hundred guineas for the loyal Pigott—all went into Pigott's pocket. "The second batch of letters were also written by me. I do not remember where I got Egan's letter from. . . . I had no specimens of Campbell's handwriting beyond two letters of Mr. Parnell." For this batch he got two hundred and fifty pounds—which all went into Pigott's pockets. The third batch contained a letter which Pigott imitated from a letter in pencil that Mr. Davitt once wrote to him. The "O'Kelly" letter he forged from a genuine letter which Mr. O'Kelly wrote while he was still at work on *The Irishman*. For this third batch, Mr. Houston paid two hundred pounds. It will be remembered how, in his story, as given in the witness-box, the self sacrificing Pigott stated that he had to be content with half commission for this third batch. The knave pocketed every farthing of the two hundred. It will also be remembered how, when Pigott, in his cross-examination, spoke of his poverty, Sir Charles Russell exclaimed, "What, after all that money from *The Times!*" If "all that money" meant only Pigott's "commissions," there was, certainly, but little of it. But if it meant the seventeen hundred and eighty pounds, why the starving Pigott must have been fairly well off.

The next most remarkable thing in the confession was Pigott's indignation at Houston, on account of that gentleman's "breach of faith" (in divulging Pigott's name to *The Times*). Having given vent to his grievance against Houston, and made the interesting disclosure that he told another lie when he said that he had destroyed all the letters which Houston had written to him, Pigott signed his confession in the presence of Mr. Labouchere and Mr. Sala. What of those Houston letters which were not destroyed? "I have some of them," said Pigott to Mr. Labouchere and his friend.

When Mr. Cunynghame finished his reading, there was a rather awkward pause. It seemed longer than it really was, for most people felt for the Attorney-General. The silence in Court as Sir Richard Webster stood up to address their lordships, was positively painful. In a low, deliberate, measured voice—as if he were carefully considering every word he was uttering—the Attorney-General announced that he and his learned friends had "communicated" with those for whom they appeared; that they now admitted that no one ought to attach any weight to Pigott's evidence; that, therefore, he and his learned friends "begged permission to withdraw the question of the genuineness of the letters which have been submitted to you, the authenticity of which is denied, with the full acknowledgment that the evidence does not entitle us to say that they are genuine." Here Sir Richard paused for a moment. One could hear the whisper, among the spectators, " Is that all ?" Sir Richard proceeded to say that he was requested by *The Times* to express its "sincere regret" for the publication of the letters. A fuller expression of regret will, he continued, be made by *The Times* people themselves. Sir Richard next made some remarks on Sir Charles Russell's now famous exclamation, "foul conspiracy." "I desire emphatically," said the Attorney-General, "to say that if any foul conspiracy exists, then those whom we represent have had no share in it."

Then rose Sir Charles Russell. He went straight to that very expression of the Attorney-General's which all who listened to Sir Richard Webster must have foreseen would be selected for special comment by Sir Charles Russell. "Not entitled to state that the letters were genuine," said Sir Charles, with slow emphasis. "I had hoped for a stronger statement from my learned friend." A murmur of approval throughout the Court followed that comment. "But whatever," and here Sir Charles Russell slowly raised his hand, "but whatever the course he adopts, it will in no jot alter the course which my clients will take. They will not only go themselves into the box when the proper time comes, but they will also ask your lordships whether it is true that the young man Houston, the alleged journalist and secretary of the Irish Loyal and Patriotic Union, embarked on this venture solely."

Sir Charles then asked their lordships to make a prompt declaration of their opinion about the letters, "so as to give without delay relief to one man particularly who had suffered to an extent which may be conceived, but which is difficult to describe—who has held a public position, and who has suffered the unmerited wrong of lying under this grievous accusation. I ask that he may be speedily relieved from such a gross and unfounded imputation." The "one man in particular," Mr. Parnell, was sitting in front of Sir Charles. Just before Sir Richard Webster ended his address, Mr. Parnell turned round towards Sir Charles Russell and gave him a printed document, putting his forefinger upon a particular passage. The document was a copy of the Special Commission Act, and the passage pointed out by Mr. Parnell was that which empowers their lordships, "if they think fit," to "make report from time to time." This, then, was what Sir Charles Russell had in his mind when he begged their lordships for their prompt declaration on the forged letters. Sir James Hannen replied at once. He suggested that Sir Charles should now call his witnesses, and that after their evidence was taken the Commissioners "would consider the propriety of making a special report." Thereupon Sir Charles Russell, looking down at Mr. Parnell, nodded slightly, and pronounced Mr. Parnell's name.

The next moment the tall figure of Mr. Parnell stood in the witness-box. After the extraordinary story which has gradually been unfolding itself for so many days, it is almost needless to say that Mr. Parnell's examination was little more than formal. Sir Richard Webster did not cross-examine. And as for Sir Charles Russell, he confined himself to putting a few categorical questions, repeated almost word for word, as each forged letter was, in its turn, passed on for Mr. Parnell's inspection. Behind Sir Charles Russell sat Mr. Asquith with all three batches before him. Mr. Asquith handed each letter to Sir Charles Russell, who, after glancing at it, passed it on to the witness-box. Here are some of Mr. Parnell's answers, which will give a general idea of the questions and replies:—" It is not my signature ;" " It is not like the writing of any person I know;" " I never wrote any such letter;" "This is not Mr. Campbell's writing ;" " I think this is the best imitation of Mr. Campbell's writing in the series ;" " Neither is this Mr. Egan's writing." Before giving his answers, Mr. Parnell looked over each letter deliberately. Some of his answers were given in the identical words of their respective questions, thus, " Is this your signature?"—" It is not my signature." Or, again, " Did you ever write any such letter?"—"I never wrote any such letter." But the effect of the answers lay in their tone and manner. Each word was pronounced slowly, distinctly, deliberately, in the low, gentle tone which is so distinctive of Mr. Parnell's voice. It may seem sentimental to say it—and especially when saying it respecting a man who can be the sternest of the stern, and among whose great gifts are an iron will and resolution ; but sentimental or not, there was a touch of true pathos in the scene—Mr. Parnell, with the signs of patient suffering still on his refined face, confronting—victoriously, indeed, but with an air of what remote indifference!—the men who had laboured so long to blacken his name and ruin his career. Of feeling of triumph there was, in the pale countenance and calm gaze, not a trace.

FIFTY-EIGHTH DAY.

MARCH 1.

SIR CHARLES RUSSELL'S examination of witnesses was suspended on February 27th, immediately after Mr. Parnell made his statement, and because the next three witnesses required, namely, Mr. Davitt, Mr. O'Kelly, and Mr. Campbell, were absent. These gentlemen were all in their places to-day. Mr. Labouchere was also in his accustomed corner. Mr. G. A. Sala came in shortly before half-past ten o'clock, and sat down beside Mr. Davitt ; and on the same bench sat Mr. Soames, Mr. Macdonald, Mr. Walter, jun., Mr. Houston, and Mr. Anderson, of Scotland Yard. Mr. Maurice Healy, Mr. T. Healy, Mr. Biggar, Mr. Jacob Bright, visited the court at one time or another during the day. Just after their lordships took their seats on the bench, Mr. Houston rose and asked to be allowed to make a statement. Mr. Houston seemed to be troubled. Told by the President that it was an inconvenient time for making statements, he sat down again.

Then Sir Charles Russell began to put in his witnesses. Mr. James O'Kelly, M.P., shortish, muscular, erect, resolute-looking, came first. From Hayti and the States to Carlist Spain and the Soudan, wherever there has been hot fighting and adventure, Mr. James O'Kelly has been in it. Handing him one of the letters to which his alleged signature was attached, and which was addressed to Egan, Sir Charles Russell asked if he knew anything about it. Nothing. Mr. O'Kelly looked at the thing with an air of contempt, and then walked out of his box. He had been in it only a few seconds. Then Mr. Campbell entered. As secretary to Mr. Parnell and to Mr. Egan, Mr. Campbell ought to know whether the signatures and "bodies" of the batch of letters given him for his inspection were genuine. Only in two letters of the number he was examining was the imitation even decently successful. Only two—what a bungler was Pigott. At this, that, and the other letter Mr. Campbell shook his head—an abrupt, impatient little shake. Throwing down the last of the impostures, Mr. Campbell made way for Mr. Michael Davitt.

There was a stir among the audience as Mr. Davitt walked into the box. For many reasons Mr. Davitt's personality has greatly impressed the lawyers and the laity who have seen and heard him in Probate Court No. 1. People noted the well-shaped head, the strongly-marked features—keen, dark eyes, black, thickish eyebrows, nose prominent and well formed, resolute lines about the mouth—and the mingled expression of kindliness and shrewdness. There were frankness and honesty in the strong vibrating voice. Mr. Davitt's evidence was over in a few seconds. He described how he copied one of the forged letters attributed to him, in order to show Mr. Parnell how unlike the writing of the forged letter was to his real handwriting. Pigott had spoken of his interview with Mr. Justin McCarthy; and now Mr. McCarthy declared, "I never saw Mr. Pigott in all my life, to my knowledge." Next came Mr. Lewis—very neat, wholly imperturbable, quick in his replies. Once or twice, though, he showed, in an uplifting of the brow, just a trace of boredom, whilst he narrated, once more, the story of his interview with Pigott. The details of the first interview between Mr. Lewis and Mr. Pigott are pretty well known already ; but now they were heard for the first time in court from Mr. Lewis himself. " I will tell you who forged those letters," said Mr. Lewis to Pigott, when they were alone. " You had in your possession a letter written by Mr. Egan to you." " I had not," quoth Pigott. " You had," said Mr. Lewis, "for I have your letters to Egan in my possession. You took sentences out of Mr. Egan's letter, and you did the same to Mr. Parnell's." " Mr. Parnell's ! why, I had no letters of Mr. Parnell's," says Pigott. " No! but you had though ; you had that letter of Mr. Parnell's, date 16th of June, 1881, about the sale of your paper, *The Irishman;* and not only that, but you used two of Mr. Parnell's letters of 16th of June, 1881, to produce your two forgeries of 16th of June, 1882." Swift, wide-awake Mr. George Lewis : the very first witnesses whom he subpœnaed were *The Times's* own Houston and *The Times's* own Pigott ! This announcement caused considerable amusement among Mr. Lewis's attentive audience.

Then came Mr. Labouchere. Mr. Labouchere leant his right elbow on the ledge, and waited. He wore the air of a man to whom the Pigott epic was now as a " mouthful of sand." " Tell us all about it," said Sir Charles, and Mr. Labouchere, very slowly, and very realistically, described how Pigott told him that *The Times* had offered him five thousand pounds ; how Pigott asked whether he, Mr. Labouchere, would make an offer ; how Pigott asked whether he would give a thousand pounds for the original Egan letters, upon which the forgeries had been based ; how Mr. Labouchere replied that he would buy genuine goods of that sort " over the counter " from Pigott or anybody ; how the suggestion of a thousand pounds was Pigott's, not Mr. Labouchere's ; how when Pigott called upon him a second time and Pigott said, "You'll be surprised to see me," Mr. Labouchere replied that he was not surprised at anything; and how Mr. Labouchere could hardly tell Pigott how Pigott could evade the witness-box, because, said Mr. Labouchere, "You have already perjured yourself a good deal." Mr. G. A. Sala, following Mr. Labouchere, stood in the box for half a minute, to say that Mr. Labouchere had told exactly what happened.—For Pigott's death see Notes.

Mr. Soames was then called by the Attorney-General to authenticate the various statements made to him by Pigott. Mr. Soames did not like his position, much. He was in a temper, though under the circumstances, he was obliged to consume his own smoke. It is unnecessary to repeat the substance of all the separate editions of Pigott's lies. The Attorney-General proposed the reading of these statements, because, as he said, Pigott's story to Mr. Labouchere having been heard, it was but fair that Pigott's story to Mr. Soames should also be heard. The hearing occupied a long time; and then Sir Charles Russell put a series of merciless questions, in answer to which Mr. Soames admitted that he did not know what position (besides that of Secretary to the "I.L.P.U.") Houston held; that he never even asked Houston; that he did not cross-examine Houston's statement to him about the way in which he got at the letters; that he never asked Pigott where the house was where the black bag was found; that he never asked Pigott about the names of individuals. Then Houston himself rose up, and repeated his request to be allowed to make a statement. All that Houston said was, that, as several charges had been made against him, he was ready to present himself for cross-examination and to give security for his appearance in court. "I think Mr. Houston has put it very properly," was the President's remark.

Then Sir Charles Russell asked if their lordships would now, in accordance with the powers conferred upon them by the seventh section of the Commission Act, make a special report regarding the question as to the authenticity of the letters. The Attorney-General objected that, as Sir Charles Russell had spoken of a "foul conspiracy" behind Houston and Pigott, their lordships should postpone their report until they had heard the whole of the evidence. Upon this Sir James Hannen replied that he would consider the application for the report "between this and Tuesday."

Before the half-past one adjournment, the end of the present stage of the forged letters section of the trial was reached. And then Sir Richard Webster took up the thread of his American evidence—the thread that had been dropped when "the letters" came on. It was like returning to ancient history. And no sooner did the Attorney-General sound his first notes of the old organ-grind of extract-reading than a crowd of people made for the door. The extracts were from *The Irish World;* and the purpose of the extract-reading was to identify the policy of the League with the dynamite policy of the American journal. After the Attorney-General had read for some time, Sir Henry James tried his hand at the bellows. The Q.C.'s and the juniors laughed and whispered, and some of them amused themselves with drawing comic sketches. A comic sketch by Mr. Lockwood, going the round of the benches, created some merriment. Sir Charles Russell contended, and subsequently Mr. Reid, that the Land League funds came not from *The Irish World*, but through *The Irish World;* that it was absurd to say that the leaguers, merely because they accepted the help of *The Irish World* in a certain limited form, must be held responsible for all the "ridiculous stuff," all the "maniacal" (Sir Charles Russell's adjective) rubbish which Mr. Ford chose to print in it. Was Mr. Parnell, Sir Charles asked, to refuse contributions of money sent from all parts of America, through the "conduit pipe" of *The Irish World*, merely because he disapproved of inflammatory stuff published in the paper. There is no point whatever in these extracts of yours, Sir Charles argued, "unless you can show that *The Irish World* was the adopted organ of the Land League. No proof short of that will serve your purpose."

FIFTY-NINTH DAY.*

MARCH 5.

WHEN the Court rose on Friday, the 1st of March, Sir Charles Russell, and after him Mr. Reid, argued that unless it could be proved that *The Irish World* was the organ of the Land League, the Attorney-General's reading of extracts was a mere waste of time. Sir James Hannen now decided to reject what appeared to be one of the Attorney-General's positions, namely, that the fact of the receipt of money contributions through the medium of *The Irish World* implied a unity of policy between that journal and the League. Against this position Sir Charles Russell protested most strenuously on the Friday afternoon. The Irish League, he said, did not get money "from" *The Irish World*, but only "through" *The Irish World*. The New York paper was simply the conduit pipe. The President now endorsed this view. "We think," he said, "that the mere receipt of money does not affect the recipients so as to make them responsible for articles appearing in that paper." The President went on, however, to remark that the receipt of contributions might possibly be an important link in a chain of evidence. But still, as the mere fact of the receipt only had been put in evidence, his lordship adhered to the opinion that it did not impose upon the Land League any responsibility for, or acceptance of, the politics and the opinions of *The Irish World*.

Still, Sir James Hannen ruled that *The Irish World* was admissible in evidence, and on the following grounds—one of the charges against the Irish Members and others was that they had disseminated newspapers inciting to outrage. And many constable witnesses had already given evidence to the effect that they had seized large numbers of *The Irish World* in various parts of Ireland. Moreover, a League official, named Farragher, had said in court that packets of *The Irish World* were received at and sent from the League office, and at the expense of the League. And the Secretary of the Ladies League received and distributed the paper after the suppression of the Land League. The time covered by the distribution of the paper extended, said Sir James Hannen, from May, 1880, to about October, 1881. *The Irish World* of that period would, therefore, said Sir James Hannen, be admitted. But, he added, "it remains to be seen whether *The Irish World* during that period answers to the description" of a newspaper disseminating outrage. Of course the appearance of "any isolated letter" would not suffice to establish the charge.

Then Mr. Atkinson began the reading. He read extracts from one of *The Irish World's* leading articles, which discussed the use of dynamite in Ireland's political battles. He read extracts from letters of Mr. Davitt, and speeches of Mr. Davitt and Mr. John Dillon. He read out a passage in which Mr. Davitt was made to say that *The Irish World* was "doing noble work"; that Irishmen were bound to pay deference to the views of a paper like *The Irish World;* and that, as the "sinews of war" came through *The Irish World*, the people who supplied them were entitled to tell Irishmen that they ought to adopt this, that, or the other plank for their political platform. Then Mr. Atkinson tried

---

* On Saturday the 2nd, the news of Pigott's suicide in Madrid reached London. For details see Notes.

Mr. Dillon's speeches. He quoted an American address of Mr. Dillon's, in which the speaker advocated the breaking up of the Irish Constabulary force, which for thirty years had backed up Irish landlordism. In one of the extracts read by Mr. Atkinson Mr. Davitt was alleged to have said that the New York *Irish World* ought to be distributed in Ireland.

After Mr. Atkinson had proceeded for some time with his reading, Sir Charles Russell rose to suggest that *The Times* counsel should mark the passages they intended to read, then hand them in, give time to counsel for the opposite side to consider the extracts till next morning, and meanwhile call witnesses for a different part of the case. The Attorney-General would gladly accede to this suggestion, but for the fact that the arrangements already made for calling witnesses were made on the assumption that the reading of *The Irish World* extracts should be gone on with. The President suggested that Sir Charles Russell should take note of the extracts read now, and read his own extracts next day. Sir Charles Russell and Mr. Reid thought that this plan would not save any time—as "all the ground would have to be gone over again," whereupon Sir James Hannen replied that in his "despair" he had no other plan to propose. So Mr. Atkinson returned to his extracts. While Mr. Atkinson read, counsel on the other side perused, in a leisurely way, the files of the American paper, stopping now and then to take stock of its bold, if not too artistic illustrations.

The object of these extracts from *The Irish World* was to prove that the leading leaguers were knowingly and deliberately in association with men of the very worst stamp. Suspending, for a space, the reading of *The World* extracts, Sir Richard Webster attempted to prove the same thing from references to his speech in the trial of O'Donnell *v.* Walter. He reminded the Court that the informer Carey had declared, first, that Thomas Brennan had filled in the Fenian Brotherhood the same office which he filled in the Land League—the office of secretary; secondly, that Walsh went over to Ireland from England in November, 1881, to found the party of assassination (the Invincibles); thirdly, that the Phœnix Park murders and the assaults on Judge Lawson and Mr. Field were its work; fourthly, that Walsh introduced him (Carey) to Sheridan, who was at one and the same time a "Constitutional" organizer under the Land League and an Invincible official; and, fifthly, that a woman whom he believed to be the wife of Frank Bryne (secretary of the League in Great Britain) had brought from London to Dublin the knives with which the Phœnix Park murders were perpetrated. After the Attorney-General ended this part of his reading, Mr. Atkinson produced extracts from the *United Ireland* report of Carey's trial.

The Attorney-General next turned his attention to the doings of the Land League in particular—the Land League being, in his view, only the public or open section of an organization of which the Invincibles formed the secret police. "Are you ready, Mr. Ronan?" Sir Richard asked. But Mr. Ronan was not ready. His fingers went fluttering among heaps of papers in search of the rules of the Land League. "Perhaps you might find them downstairs," suggested Mr. Attorney, with his air of inexhaustible patience. So Mr. Ronan disappeared "downstairs." And not to waste time Sir Richard thought he would meanwhile read out some of Mr. Gladstone's speeches in the House of Commons. So he produced his Hansard. A groan from the other side. But while Sir Richard read, in rushed Mr. Ronan from downstairs with the rules. Then Sir Richard dropped Hansard, and Mr. Ronan read the rules of the Land League organization. And when that was finished Sir Richard quietly resumed his Hansard, and the dismal grind went on—in spite of Sir Charles Russell's plaintive protest against this resurrection of Parliamentary debates. Sir Richard Webster replied that Mr. Gladstone's statements were made in the presence of such members as Mr. Parnell, Mr. Healy, Mr. Biggar, and

Mr. Dillon in the House of Commons. In reading his Parliamentary extracts, the Attorney-General even quoted the "Oh-ohs." When the Attorney-General got done with Mr. Gladstone, Sir Henry James took up the running. Sir Henry quoted a speech in which Mr. Forster alleged that Mr. Parnell did not take steps to stop crime. Sir Henry read with railway speed.

Mr. Lockwood then came with his modifying extracts. He showed that Mr. Parnell, in the House of Commons, had contended that the statements attributed to him were as harmless as any speeches made by Mr. Gladstone himself. Then Sir Richard produced fresh extracts to show that definite allegations were made in the House of Commons against specified Irish members by the Ministry of the day. Having done with Mr. Gladstone and Mr. Forster's speeches against the leaguers, Sir Richard quoted Sir William Harcourt's. "I must ask you," interposed the President, "to restrict yourself to statements of fact, and to spare us the oratory." Thus admonished, Sir Richard Webster confined himself to choice selections from Sir William's oratory—selections in which Sir William denounced in the very strongest terms the League and all its works—real or supposed. Long before four o'clock, the court was gradually emptying itself. The "public"—what there was of it—was getting bored with all this ancient history. Even the calling of half-a-dozen witnesses failed to arrest its attention. Not one of these witnesses was cross-examined. "We won't cross-examine," was the short, abrupt, impatient remark, which came from defending counsel, every time Mr. Murphy, or some one of his colleagues, finished their examination of a witness. The only noteworthy witness among the six was Sergeant Callagher, of the Royal Irish Constabulary, who had been employed to keep an eye on Pigott when Pigott was living in Anderton's Hotel. He testified to his discovery of a number of cases of arms sent from London to different places in Ireland in 1881, by Thomas Walsh.

SIXTIETH DAY.

MARCH 6.

COURT half empty. Mr. Atkinson, Q.C., resumed his readings from Patrick Ford's paper, *The Irish World*. Most of the reading, which occupied the first half of the day's sitting, was done by Mr. Atkinson on *The Times* side, and Mr. Asquith, on the side of the accused—that is to say, Mr. Asquith quoted the passages which were alleged to modify, or explain away, the strong extracts read by his opponent. It was a dull performance, this three hours' exchange of quotational broadsides. Before the exchange began Sir Charles Russell remarked to their lordships that, having looked through *The Irish World* files, he found there were "some wild letters," but no advocacy of crime; whereupon Sir Richard Webster retorted, blandly, that that was Sir Charles Russell's opinion. And then Mr. Atkinson began to reel off his extracts. He quoted an *Irish World* passage in which Mr. Davitt was alleged to have said, in an American speech of his, that "the hands which now dispense charity will, if necessary, dispense blows to the people of Ireland." The dispensers of charity were the subscribers to the funds transmitted to Ireland through *The Irish World*. Mr. Atkinson gave extracts from the files of August and September, 1880, from which it would appear that some of the money of the Skirmishing Fund was used for League purposes in Ireland.

Then Mr. Asquith interposed with his explanatory passages. From his file of *The Irish World* he quoted passages to show how Mr. Davitt had been condemning violence. Thus, in one of Mr. Davitt's speeches in America, Mr. Davitt was reported to have asked his audience how the Irish landlords could be abolished. " Shoot them," some one exclaimed. "No," was Mr. Davitt's comment, "let us shoot the system," for shooting Irish landlords would only bring upon Ireland the condemnation of America and the world. Then Mr. Atkinson proceeded to read a string of extracts from a wild letter writer in *The Irish World*, who signed himself "Transatlantic." "Transatlantic" in his pious moods spoke of Ireland as "God's holy isle," and in his wicked moods of the chance which another Sepoy revolt might give Irish patriots of blowing up the Empire of John Bull. Assassination paragraphs were also produced, against which Sir Charles Russell placed paragraphs from speeches by Mr. Egan, and by Mr. Parnell, Mr. Davitt, and other Irish members in America. One of the Egan passages, in reference to the Phœnix Park crime, ran thus: "We are horrified at the crime. We condemn and deplore it in the strongest manner." Again, it appeared from another extract that an American interviewer had described Mr. Parnell as "seeming very depressed," and as declaring that he considered the Phœnix Park murders to be "the most abominable, atrocious, and wanton crime that ever disgraced the annals of Ireland." Just before the luncheon interval, some amusement was caused in court by a pen-and-ink caricature, the work of Mr. Lockwood, Q.C. It was a sketch of a small boy Mike, who in the witness-box on the previous day said that he had been boycotted by other small boys, and concerning whom Mr. Lockwood uttered his barely audible remonstrance, "Let the poor boy go." " Ronan sees Mikey safely home" was the inscription on the sketch. Mr. Ronan in his wig, with his gown tucked up and his trousers rolled to his ankles, was trundling Mikey home in a perambulator!

Almost the whole of the afternoon sitting was occupied with the examination of ten witnesses called by the Attorney-General for the purpose of supplementing former evidence concerning outrages. Police-constable Ough stepped into the box merely to say that it was he who arrested the Thomas Walsh mentioned in the previous day's evidence. Then a porter at Castlereagh Station, Ireland, testified to the seizure, by the Irish police, of a case of weapons supposed to have been forwarded by Walsh from London. The third witness, also a constable, testified to the seizure of a case at Tubercurry, co. Tipperary. Then came Detective-Inspector Peel, of the London Metropolitan force, who said that having searched Walsh's premises after the arrest, he found there 277 rifles, 276 bayonets, 30 revolvers, and 9,000 rounds of ammunition. Then Mr. Loftus, a Tipperary farmer, related how a "Father Murphy" called upon him one day; how the Father turned out to be Sheridan in disguise; how he failed, at first, to recognize Sheridan; but how the dog identified him at once—a dog of which Sheridan had, once upon a time, made him a present.

Did he give you a dog?—that was one of the first questions put to the witness by the Attorney-General. Did he give you a dog?—the question amused Sir Richard's hearers. It reminded them of a stock question of Mr. Murphy's during the slow weeks of the outrage evidence: On the night of such and such a date, a great many years ago, "were you in bed?" As a rule, the witnesses looked somewhat foolish when they replied, on their oath, that they were in bed. So Mr. Loftus looked a little foolish when he admitted that Sheridan did give him a dog. Mr. Loftus described how the supposed priest asked him whether he was a member of the Fenian Brotherhood, to which Mr. Loftus replied that he was. Mr. Loftus was not sure whether Sheridan himself was a brother, but he said that, according to Sheridan's own account, Sheridan was a League organizer. And there was another man, an associate or acquaintance of Sheridan's named Fitzpatrick, whom Mr. Loftus had seen at League gatherings, and whom he supposed to be, like Sheridan, a League organizer. He also believed that Fitzpatrick, who was, or pretended to be, a commercial traveller, was a Fenian brother. But when Mr. Loftus came to be cross-examined by Sir Charles Russell he admitted that on the occasion of Sheridan's visit in disguise Sheridan said nothing about the organization of the Land League; that, in fact, Sheridan told him he had come to see about some disputed property. "As far as you know," asked Sir Charles, "had he anything to do at that time with the Land League?" "Not so far as I know," was the reply. "Now, to your knowledge was Fitzpatrick a member of the League?" "Never." "Was he to your knowledge an opponent of the Land League?" "Very much so." "And still is?" "Yes." Sir Charles Russell next asked whether the jury before which Fitzpatrick was tried on a conspiracy to murder, acquitted Fitzpatrick partly on the ground of the untrustworthiness of Delaney, who informed against him. Sir James Hannen remarking that the opinion of the Irish jury was not a matter for the consideration of the Court, Sir Charles Russell replied warmly that "he must insist on making an observation, for the purpose of showing the true character of Delaney."

The next witness, Sergeant Caulfield, of the Royal Irish Constabulary, said that he knew Sheridan and Fitzpatrick at Tubercurry, in 1880, and that at a blacksmith's forge there, at which Sheridan and others used to assemble, he unearthed, in April, 1880, a box containing ten rifles, ten bayonets, and a quantity of ammunition. As Mr. Caulfield pronounced ten in a way very common in Ireland—"tin"—his cross-examiner was puzzled about the "tin rifles." It was explained that "tin" meant a numeral, not one of the metals.

Then came another little mystery—the mystery of Mr. William Redmond, M.P. Mr. John Webb described how, as a constabulary officer, he had in January, 1882, shadowed somewhere in Kerry a person who went under the name of Mondred; how Mr. Mondred always drove out at night, with the hotel-keeper's son to show him the way; and how in the mornings he used to find copies of the No Rent manifesto dropped on the way over which Mr. Mondred had driven. At last he arrested this midnight distributor of manifestoes, and lo! Mr. Mondred turned out to be Mr. Redmond. Then he searched Mr. Redmond's luggage at the hotel, and in the luggage he found more copies of the No Rent manifesto and copies of *United Ireland* (then published in Paris), as also a pocketbook full of documents, which pocketbook he forwarded, documents and all, to the Castle. Mr. Webb said that he had lately searched for the note-book in Dublin Castle; but that he failed to find it.

Another informer and spy from America. This was a man named Coleman, who said he became a Fenian in 1866, and that some years subsequently, he was sworn a member of the reformed body, known as the Irish Republican Brotherhood, by a person named Macaulay, who was an associate of Scrab Nally's, and whom he had seen in conversation with Mr. Parnell; and who gave him (Coleman) intimation of outrages about to be perpetrated by leaguers. "This information," said Coleman, "I took care to convey at once to the police." Sir Charles Russell having objected to hearsay evidence of this sort, and having remarked that Macaulay's membership of the League was not asserted, the Attorney-General replied that he was prepared to show that Macaulay was a leaguer. Our case is, said the Attorney-General, that the leaguers did plan outrages, and that Macaulay carried out their behests.

SIXTY-FIRST DAY.

MARCH 7.

THE judges having decided that the informer Colman's testimony was admissible, Colman entered the witness-box. Colman is a shortish, thick-set man, with a sort of distorted resemblance to Mr. Thomas Sexton, Lord Mayor of Dublin, of all men in the world. The resemblance rather amused some people in the court. Colman is a "dour"-looking person—as the Scotch would say. He is dull, heavy, stolid, obstinate, and his voice is wooden. The purpose of the Attorney-General's examination was to establish, through Macaulay, the responsibility of the Land League for a series of crimes accomplished or attempted, in which Macaulay was the prime mover. Macaulay, according to the Attorney-General, was a Land Leaguer; he planned his crimes in association with Leaguers against land-grabbers and others; he and they were, to use Sir Richard's expression, "The police of the League."

There was the plot to murder a man named Wills; "And," said Colman, "I was told by Macaulay himself that he gave two revolvers to a man named Burke— a Land Leaguer and Fenian Centre—for effecting the murder." Colman was only told about it, he had not seen the transfer. Wills, however, was not shot, for Colman, by his own account, had sent warning to the police. Then there was a plot to murder George Scott, a cess-collector. "Macaulay told me about it himself," said the witness; "he came driving up to my door in a trap one night with another man named Daly, and he asked me to join them both; I promised to meet them next Thursday, and bring my double-barrelled gun for my own use, and two revolvers for them." Colman's house was a sort of arsenal for the fitting out of murderous expeditions—the gun belonged to his master, whose gamekeeper Colman was, and he had three revolvers which were the property of Macaulay. Happily, nothing came of this plot. George Scott, like Wills, was not shot. Daly, said Colman, was a leaguer; and George Scott had taken an evicted farm, and Colman himself, the associate of the would-be murderers, took care to warn the police in good time.

George had a brother James, who also was to be shot. In fact, the money was ready for payment of the murderers, £25 in all—namely, £10 from the Ladies' Land League, £10 from the Fenian Organization, and £5 from as many tenants of the neighbourhood, three at least of whom Colman asserted to be leaguers. It was a clear case, according to Colman, of murderous association between the League and the Fenians. However, nothing came of it. There was no shooting; and James escaped like the rest.

Never mind; let us shoot Richard Leonard, who has fallen out with one of our confederates. And so there is formed an elaborate plot for the murder of Leonard, of which Colman gives a very detailed account. But Leonard escapes like all the others. "On the night on which the murders were arranged," says Colman in the box, "I sent the news to the police."

Then there was Mr. Ruane, who became "unpopular" because he refused to join either the League or the Fenian Society. And so it was agreed to shoot him. But the witness in the box told the police what was coming, and Ruane was safe. Knox was another person, who was doomed merely on Macaulay's suggestion made in a public-house—"Why don't you shoot him?" But as Colman overheard this bloodthirsty suggestion, Colman was enabled to warn the police, and Knox remained unharmed. One was impressed by the dulness and the inconsequence, more than by the villainy, of this tissue of stories, as they were told by the witness, in his wooden, ponderous manner, with his arms stretched out, and his big hands sprawling over the ledge of the witness-box. To all appearance Colman would not have shown the smallest emotion, even if it had been his duty to relate that Macaulay and his associates had proscribed, not a poor dozen or so merely, but the whole country side. Colman's examination-in-chief concluded with an account of his acquaintanceship with P. W. Nally (Scrab's brother). He was introduced to Nally by Macaulay as the latter's confidential friend; and a meeting at which Nally and Macaulay and Colman were to be present was put off, because the place was swarming with detectives; and Macaulay told him how Nally received three hundred pounds for the murder of Mr. Burke, the land agent, and how Nally, having given his confederates twenty-five pounds each, kept the lion's share for himself—"a mean thing that I would not have done," as Macaulay remarked. Was it League money? Colman could not tell; all he could remember was that Macaulay had said something or other about League connection with the three hundred pounds. Such was the sum and substance of the informer's story, as told in his examination-in-chief.

The cross-examination by Sir Charles Russell was one of his severest. Colman betrayed the profoundest ignorance about the League branches in his part of Mayo, not knowing who the presidents were, nor the vice-presidents, nor the treasurers, nor the secretaries. And yet two of the branches named were in his immediate neighbourhood. "I had my own business to attend to" was his explanation of his ignorance. Sir Charles Russell asked him about his remuneration for his services as a witness. Colman promptly replied that he had quite enough money of his own. "If I get any," said he, "I shall take it; if I don't I can go without." "Do you expect any, sir?" exclaimed Sir Charles, in a sharp, loud tone. "Well, I suppose I do," replied Colman, this time rather submissively; but he declined to throw light on the next question: "Have you formed any idea in your own mind as to how much you are worth?" When asked how he came by his money, he replied "Work." When asked what work, he replied "I won't tell you." "What sort of work, sir?" repeated Sir Charles, sternly; "did you get any money from the Government for your information?" "Yes." "How much?" again very sharply. "A thousand pounds." Then he said that he had ten pounds a month for working on the Canadian Pacific Railway—doing whatever work the "boss" gave him. The thousand pounds he took with him to America. It was this money which enabled him to leave the country after he had given his evidence at the Cork trials of Macaulay and persons already named on the charge of conspiracy to murder. Sir Charles now reminded Colman that at these Cork trials he had identified certain letters written by Macaulay and Nally.

"In the face of these letters," exclaimed Sir Charles, "is it not the fact that so far from Nally and Macaulay having been supporters of the Land League, they were its enemies?" But Colman declared he believed they were not in opposition to it. Sir Charles Russell was proceeding with his reading of other letters, in which Macaulay and Nally expressed their opposition to the League, when the Attorney-General suddenly interposed with a request to be allowed to see Sir Charles's documents. "Seeing the way that *we* have been treated," retorted Sir Charles, "a more audacious request I have never heard made in a court of justice." "But I," said the President mildly, "am entitled to see the brief you have in your hand." "And if your lordships *had* seen all the brief," returned Sir Charles, "I think the witness would never have been called." "I don't think you have a right to say that," interposed Mr. Justice Smith. "Well," said Sir Charles, "if the witness was called I should be greatly disappointed." "I don't agree with your observation," was Mr. Justice Smith's rejoinder; and the little "tiff" ended. Returning to his question, Sir Charles asked witness whether he still persisted, in spite of the evidence of the Macaulay and Nally letters, in saying that these men were leaguers. Colman replied that he did, and that Macaulay himself had told him that the leaguers and Fenians were under "one cloak." Coming again to the money question, Colman said that he had £500 of his money still left—that is to say, in the form of some real property which he bought in Winnipeg, Manitoba. He also said that in America he went under a false name; but, in consideration for the man's feelings on this point, Sir Charles refrained from asking him what his assumed name was.

Then Mr. Davitt investigated Colman's past history. Had Colman been charged with theft, with illicit manufacture of spirits, with firing shots into a farmer's house? No; but he had been fined for having illicit whisky in his possession. "Did you ruin the character of a girl named Carsons?" asked Mr. Davitt. "There was some talk about it," replied Colman, in his heavy, wooden way. And the very next instant he admitted that this girl lived with him, and that his wife went away "of her own accord" to America "because of something that happened between us." The next stage in the cross-examination of Colman was the production of some of the letters which he had sent to the police, giving them information about "Fenian" and "League" plots. There was very little in them; but a remark in one of them was received in court with a burst of laughter. It was in the nature of a P.S.—"Don't be severe in my potheen case." This request was made in a letter giving intimation of the Wills plot, named in an earlier part of this article.

Francis Connor, of the Irish Constabulary, next entering the witness-box, said that both Macaulay and Nally had stated to a newspaper reporter who interviewed them at Dublin that they were members of the Land League. But when cross-examined by Mr. Reid he stated that he did not know who the reporter was, nor what newspaper he came from. Connor had known Macaulay for seven years—during which he served in Macaulay's locality—and yet he admitted that the first time he heard of Macaulay being a leaguer was at the meeting with the unknown reporter in Dublin.

At this stage the solicitor to *The Times* was called, to say what he knew of Colman. He smiled, as he ascended the witness-box. Mr. Soames first heard of Colman from Constable Preston, shortly before Christmas; and it was only seven days ago that Colman's statements were taken down. Mr. Preston told Mr. Soames that Colman was willing to come over from America at his own expense. But the most interesting part of Mr. Soames's evidence was given in reply to Mr. Lockwood's cross-examination. Mr. Lockwood wanted to know whether Mr. Soames had on behalf of *The Times* employed Thomas Walsh to collect evidence in Ireland. [This is the ex-convict who has been occasionally mentioned during the last few days, as a secret exporter of arms from London to Ireland.] And now, in answer to Mr. Lockwood, Mr. Soames admitted that he had paid from thirty to thirty-five pounds "indirectly"—that is, through a solicitor—to this same convict Walsh for travelling expenses. Where was Walsh now? Mr. Soames could not tell. He had been "spirited away," said Mr. Soames. But what had Walsh gone to Ireland for? To search for some documents that would compromise Mr. Parnell.

At this sudden allusion to more letters, which might damn Mr. Parnell and his cause, there was a low murmur of laughter throughout the court. "Did Walsh ask you for a thousand pounds?" Mr. Lockwood asked. "No," said Mr. Soames; "but he told me he had documents which would show that Mr. Parnell and Mr. O'Kelly were mixed up in the importation of arms into Ireland, and Walsh also showed me a letter signed by Mr. Parnell." "You mean *purporting* to be signed," Mr. Lockwood exclaimed in an ironical tone. But Mr. Soames was indifferent; he did not mean "purporting," he meant "signed by Mr. Parnell." And what Walsh said to Mr. Soames was that he would go to Ireland and get some more of these compromising documents, "and he said that if he procured these documents I was to satisfy myself whether they were genuine or not, after which I could arrange about terms." "Did he mention any sum?" "Yes, he mentioned five hundred pounds, but no bargain was entered into;" and then, in reply to another question of Mr. Lockwood's, Mr. Soames added, "Walsh told me it was Mr. Parnell's letter which he showed me." Then Mr. Lockwood paused. He looked hard at Mr. Soames, he bent forward, and, raising his hand and shaking it slowly, he put to Mr. Soames the following question :—" Do you recollect, Mr. Soames, that you, in this inquiry, have sworn to the signatures which were upon letters which are now withdrawn?" With that question Mr. Lockwood abruptly resumed his seat ; but Mr. Soames followed up that parting shot with the reply that he had "spoken to the best of his belief, and that he had nothing to retract."

SIXTY-SECOND DAY.

MARCH 12.

AT the last sitting of the Court, it was denied, on the part of the defence, that Macaulay ever was a member of the League. Mr. Reid now produced a file of *The Freeman's Journal*, from which he read the following sentence : "In reply to a question whether he (Macaulay) was president or secretary of any Land League branch in Mayo, he replied that he was not a member of the Land League at all." There was one other preliminary matter of importance,—Mr. Parnell's banking accounts, concerning which, evidence was given by Mr. Hardcastle, a member of a well-known firm of accountants. He stated that he had examined the Hibernian Bank accounts, but that except in a few cases there was no indication of persons from whom money was received or to whom it was paid, for the practice of the bank was merely to retain the numbers of cheques paid. The accounts showed at least one thing—that the League's appeal for public support was liberally responded to. The Land League receipts from November 16, 1879, to September 7, 1882, were £261,269, and the payments £261,276, showing an overdraft of a little over six pounds. In cross-examination by Mr. Reid, Mr. Hardcastle said that the National League had produced everything he had asked for.

And now came the lively part of the day—the evidence of Mr. Timothy Coffey! Mr. Coffey, of Limerick, bustling after the usher, entered the witness-box. He wore a heavy, reddish-grey Inverness cape, and yellow gloves. He kissed the Testament with his gloves on. But after a question or two, he threw off his heavy cape and put himself into an attitude, as if he meant business. The tone of his reply to one of the first questions put to him, even more than the manner of it, arrested attention, and it was seen that Mr. Coffey, reporter for *The Leinster Herald*, *The Cork Herald*, and other newspapers, was about to follow in the footsteps of Pigott and Molloy, by turning against the side for which he appeared as a witness. "Had he ever joined the Irish Republican Brotherhood?" Sir Henry James asked him. "Never," was the answer, given not merely with emphasis, but also with defiance. But he admitted that he had joined the Land League shortly after it was founded ; and he made a rambling explanation—unasked for—to the effect that he joined it because it was a "constitutional" body. But was he a member of the committee of his branch of the League, or only an ordinary member? To this simple question Mr. Coffey would not give a direct answer ; and so Mr. Coffey fell out with Sir Henry James, after the examination-in-chief was but barely begun. Turning suddenly round to the Bench, Coffey, with an air of cool impudence, suggested that he might be allowed to state to their lordships his own case in his own way, because, said Mr. Coffey, "I see the learned gentleman is in a difficulty." Sir Henry James took all this in good part, remarking that he, too, must be allowed "some share in the transaction." At last, after a good deal of wrangling, Coffey said that he was only an ordinary member of the Land League. "You have made a written statement?" asked Sir Henry James. "Yes," he had ; "but," added Coffey, "a statement is one thing, and evidence another." "Well, is this statement true?" Sir Henry continued, referring to the statement which the witness made to Mr. Soames in December last. "Untrue, positively untrue," exclaimed Coffey, smiling, and leaning half-way across the ledge of the witness-box, "every word of it is untrue." The audience laughed at this downright declaration. Sir James Hannen frowned. "I am surprised," his lordship began—and then, "surprised that people should laugh when a person in your position makes such a confession." Nothing abashed, Coffey retorted that if his lordship had lived in Ireland he would have understood it well enough. In plain language, Coffey's statement, made in the first place to Mr. Shannon, the Irish solicitor who assists Mr. Soames, was, according to the witness's confession now made in the box, a tissue of lies from beginning to end. "It was not I that volunteered the statement to Mr. Shannon," said the witness, "it was he who came fishing to me." "If you will read it through, you will see it's sensational," said the witness, leaning forward, and nodding confidentially at *The Times* counsel. The absurdity of the situation was too much for the gravity of Mr. Coffey's audience, lawyers and all, whom only Sir James Hannen's stern aspect prevented from breaking out into a roar of laughter. And as Mr. Shannon "came fishing" to Coffey, so Coffey, according to his present story, fooled Mr. Shannon to the top of his bent, dictated his statement to Mr. Shannon, and then signed it. "He told me," said Coffey, "that I should be handsomely remunerated, and that I should get a fine position." "My whole confession," said Coffey, putting it as pithily as possible, "was the effusion of a fertile imagination." And Mr. Coffey smiled, pulled down his waistcoat, and twisted his moustache, in the outburst of laughter which followed. Sir Henry James cross-examining his own witness was a spectacle which amused Mr. Coffey as much as any one present.

The object of Sir Henry James's cross-examination was to elicit admissions from Coffey which would show that his story, as given to the constable who first interviewed him, to Mr. Shannon next, and Mr. Soames last of all, was not the imaginative "effusion" which the witness now alleged it to be. But Coffey stuck to his new story, coolly alleging that in order to make his original story more plausible, he "purposely incriminated" two Irish members of Parliament—Messrs. Abraham and Finucane—as persons who actively assisted at a Limerick Land League meeting at which were delivered speeches that led to the perpetration of two murders. But had not Coffey given information to the police? "I have never given what you call information to the police." "No information to Constable Chalk?" Never. "No communication with him?" "Oh yes ; but not one of my communications contained a particle of truth." Then he said that all his communications with the police were made in July and August, 1882 ; and that certain direct statements which he sent to Dublin Castle (at the recommendation of the police) were all lies—all "fabrications suitable to the market." The merriment to which this unembarrassed declaration gave rise ceased at Sir James Hannen's frown of impatience.

Sir Henry James now proceeded to read the statement which the witness gave to Mr. Soames last December. In this statement Coffey, describing himself as a newspaper reporter and a member of the Limerick branch of the Land League, said that he was present at a meeting at which it was resolved that an emergency man should be "done away with"; that he was done away with by two men named Dwyer; that the League gave the Dwyers £35 to help them to escape from Ireland ; that he (Coffey) was deputed to see them out of the country, but that they were arrested all the same ; and next, because there was no evidence against them, acquitted ; and that, finally, the two Dwyers were taken care of by the Land League.

During Sir Henry James's rapid reading of Coffey's statement, Coffey himself presented a curious spectacle for contemplation. At first he looked stupidly awkward. He twirled the ends of his moustache, and put them between his teeth, grimacing as if he were trying hard to chew them. His face flushed. Then it grew palish. He lurched about, from side to side. Then, stretching out his arms splaywise over the ledge of the box, he placed his chin on his folded hands and balanced himself upon his elbow joints. In that position he gained self-possession. His half-closed eyes twinkled, and as he gazed at Sir Henry James through the corners of them he smiled slowly, he even chuckled, as if he were overcome by the humour of the situation.

"Now," said Sir Henry, looking up from his paper, "is that true?" No; it was all false, all the effusion of a fertile imagination—save the one or two statements about his profession and place of residence. All that about the Dwyers trying to get to America with League money was "a fabrication." He could not recollect if the Emergency man and the man Wheeler (there were two victims) were murdered. He could not even say if the Dwyers were arrested. But the next moment he admitted that two men were arrested. So that that part of his story was not "imagination" pure and simple. But how could he explain the fact that Dwyer was the name of the persons who actually were arrested? "Do you mean to say that that was a coincidence?"—Yes—a pure coincidence ; he imagined the names. "And you tell that to their lordships?" remarked Sir Henry James, quietly.—"Yes," answered Coffey, glancing at the Bench ; and on the instant there was a burst of laughter all over the court. His astonishing "coincidences," his inventive resource, showed that the mantle of Richard Pigott had fallen upon Timothy Coffey. Coffey's face flushed. Again he chewed his moustaches. He moved about uneasily. His smile was less confident, less impudent than before.

He was losing his self-possession, going off his guard, as appeared with swift, dramatic effect in the very next incident. "Ever heard of the Dwyers since?" said Sir Henry James. "No," and then, with a careless gesture, "nor their people either." "What! What people?" exclaimed Sir Henry James, quick as lightning. Coffey looked utterly confounded as Sir Henry James, bending forward, repeated his question, in a sharp, severe, urgent tone, quite unusual with him, "What people?" "Whose people?" "Of whom do you speak?" Alas ! Mr. Timothy Coffey, of county Limerick. Who can the people be who belong to other people who only exist in "a fertile imagination"? Coffey told Sir Henry James that if he wanted to find out who the people were he must search the county of Limerick. Then he said he did not know who the people were who left the country. His mind was in a state of confusion ; and the greater his confusion, the more impudent became his manner. Then the President interfered. "Will you endeavour to conduct yourself with decency?" said Sir James. "If you do not conduct yourself in a different manner I will commit you to prison. Be cautious ; I will not be trifled with." "Neither will I," exclaimed Coffey, drawing himself bolt upright, and facing the President. "You are consciously or unconsciously," continued Sir James Hannen, "exhibiting something which is painful to see in your character. Attend to counsel. If you do not conduct yourself properly I shall commit you to prison." "All right," said Coffey. "I don't consider it all right," said the President. "and take care you do not provoke me." "Take care of that man," exclaimed Sir James Hannen, as the Court rose for the afternoon adjournment. So Coffey was taken in charge of the court superintendent. Coffey fortified himself with a plate of soup in the witness-box, where he sat during the half-hour's interval.

At two o'clock Sir Henry James resumed his cross-examination of his own witness. Was it true—as stated in the deposition—that Mr. Finucane and Mr. Abraham had at a Land League meeting in July, 1882, supported a proposition to blow up Apjohn's house, used as an emergency residence for caretakers of evicted farms? No. It was totally untrue. And Coffey made that statement about the two gentlemen, knowing it to be untrue. And it was equally untrue that a man named Hayes had been told off to do the work. Next he stated that he did not know whether the gentlemen he had named (Mr. Abraham among them) were leaguers or not, although in his deposition he had described them as leaguers ; but he said that he had seen Mr. Abraham at League meetings more than once. Not leaguers ; "were they members of the committee?" asked Sir Henry. Coffey did not know. "What do you mean by a committee?" asked Sir Henry. Here Coffey's temper gave way. "You mean to trifle with me," said he ; "I appeal to your lordships." "I do not intend to be trifled with," exclaimed the President, sternly, "I shall deal with you when we come to the end of the examination." Then he repeated his assertion that he told a lie when in his first statement he said he had joined the Fenian Brotherhood. He had also told a lie when he said that Fenian membership cards were circulated among the leaguers. As Sir Henry James put his questions, he read out each passage from the witness's original deposition. Here is one passage—"I had one of those cards, but I destroyed it, fearing that my house would be searched." Is that true? asked Sir Henry James. It was not. The "Rev. Mr. Higgins," who at a League meeting declared that there were only two black sheep in the flock, and that they were to be boycotted, was also the creation of Coffey's imagination. The next citation, about Mr. Finucane's and Mr. Abraham's endorsing Mr. Higgins's sentiments, was also utterly baseless—"every word of it." And who is this Captain Bell whom you name in your original statement ? Bell ! why Coffey never even heard of him. "If he exists, it is only a coincidence." "As far as you know, he was not in existence then ? " " He might and might not be." " Was he in existence, sir ? " asked Sir Henry, sharply. "Well, there was a Captain Bell." Coffey gave similar answers about the other "leaguers," whom he named—McSweeney, Mulligan, and the rest. "Are these persons of your own imagination?" "Yes," was the answer, "but they might have existed as private individuals of the community." In a few seconds after this hopelessly puzzling answer, Sir Henry James sat down, and resigned Timothy Coffey into the hands of Mr. Reid. Mr. Reid plunged at once into the money question. Here is a specimen of the cross-examination :—

Have you received money from the police or from the Castle ?—I received £4 or £5 from a policeman named Doonan for my first statement.
How much money did you get to come to London ?—Well, I looked upon the first £4 as secret service money: then I got £5 with a subpœna. I next telegraphed to Mr. Soames that I could not go to London unless I got £100 to defray my expenses.
Mr. Reid—I call for that telegram.
Witness—I have a copy at my address, 44, Torrington-square.
Mr. Reid—I call for any other telegram sent by this witness to Mr. Soames.
Witness—I can produce all the correspondence that has passed between us.
Mr. Reid—Now let us pass from that. How much money did you receive ?—After that telegram I got a letter from Mr. Soames saying he could not comply with it. I held "stiff reins," and after a short time Mr. Shannon called upon me. We had a chat, and in consequence I got the sum of £50 from Mr. Shannon. He paid me in his own office, and in Bank of England notes.
What did you do with the money ?—It enabled me to see London.
Have you been staying in London since ?—Yes, and on the Monday or Tuesday after the adjournment of the Court previous to Christmas I saw Mr. Soames, and I got a sum of £40 additional. That was the day I signed the first statement. Mr. Soames paid me by cheque.
What other money did you receive ?—Since then I have received something like £20 from Mr. Soames. Also, while I was staying at my hotel, a messenger served me with a new subpœna, and gave me a guinea. That is all the money I have received.

Then, in answer to further questions from Mr. Reid, the witness began to describe how he first came across Doonan; how it was Doonan who made the first advance, telling him (Coffey) that if he gave valuable information he would be handsomely rewarded; and how he and Doonan had "a liquor" together; and how he next saw Mr. Shannon; and how Mr. Shannon told him that Mr. Soames was a "very decent fellow." Altogether Coffey had received £115 since November 8th, the date of his arrival in London and of his first introduction to metropolitan life.

Then Sir Henry James made a last attempt upon his witness, Timothy Coffey. But from Timothy Coffey Sir Henry could get nothing satisfactory; so Sir Henry sat down, after drawing from Coffey an admission that he had asked Mr. Soames the other day for more money, and that he had been refused. Coffey resembled Pigott in his love of lucre, as well as in his inventiveness and luck in coincidences. Coffey was coolly walking out of the box when the usher stopped him.

Sir James Hannen had already warned the prisoner that he would deal with him at the end of the examination. He kept his word. Sir James spoke as follows:—

We are of opinion that you have been guilty of a gross contempt of court. In the first place your manner has been insolent both to the counsel and to the Court, but I take the opportunity of stating that in our judgment you have been guilty of a still more serious contempt of court. You have avowed that you have told a long tissue of lies for the express purpose of deceiving the persons to whom you made it, and causing yourself to be brought up as a witness in order that you might then tell what you call the truth. That was a most insolent interference with the course of justice. It was foisting yourself upon the Court and taking up the time of the Court for the purpose only of befooling those who had taken your evidence and coming here with that intention. By taking up the time of the Court in that manner we have no doubt that you have been guilty of contempt of Court, and we accordingly commit you to prison for it.

The witness—If you will suspend judgment for an hour until I can send to Torrington-square for the necessary documents, I can fix the contempt of Court upon the proper shoulders.

The President—It must be proved hereafter, if it really be any mitigation.

The witness still continued to remonstrate in an excited manner.

The President—I have said all I have to say on the matter. Let him be removed.

Coffey was astounded. He became excited. "Let me have my letters from Torrington-square," said he, "and it will be seen that it is not I who am guilty of contempt of Court, but that those are guilty who put me here; I told Mr. Soames I would give no evidence." Coffey would continue his protest; but Sir James exclaimed sharply, "Let him be removed." Then Coffey became defiant. "Intimidation in its worst form," he exclaimed, as, with flushed face, he disappeared through the doorway in the screen beneath the judges' bench.

Then Mr. Soames, stepping into the box, said he had refused applications of the witness for money, and that Coffey told him he meant to emigrate. The last witness of the day was Dominic O'Connor, who said that he had been sworn in as a Fenian by P. J. Sheridan. If Dominic was called to prove friendship between Parnellites and Fenians, he proved, or at least stated, the very reverse. At the Sligo election of 1880, the members of the Brotherhood were opposed to Mr. Parnell and Mr. A. O'Connor. Mr. Parnell was "no friend" of the Brotherhood, said Dominic, replying to Mr. Reid. The Brotherhood had "no friendship" for Mr. Parnell—the feeling was "quite the other way."

SIXTY-THIRD DAY.

MARCH 13.

To-day Mr. Soames related the story of his intercourse with Timothy Coffey. A queer story of a solicitor at war with his own witness. Scarcely had their intercourse begun, when Timothy behaved like a son of the horse-leech. "Give," said Tim, when *The Times* subpœnaed him; and what he wanted Mr. Soames to give was one hundred pounds. All this, and a great deal more, came out in the letters which passed between Coffey and Mr. Soames, and which were read out in court. Coffey threatened that if he did not get his hundred pounds he would not obey his subpœna. That was by telegram. Mr. Soames retorted that their lordships could compel his appearance, but he added that if Coffey did appear, he would be no loser in a pecuniary sense. Of course, before writing in such strong terms to Coffey, Mr. Soames had satisfied himself that Coffee would prove a valuable witness. For he had already sent Mr. Shannon to Ballinasloe, and there Coffey made his "statement" to Mr. Shannon. But subsequently to his receipt of this statement, Mr. Soames had, as he thought, learned that Coffey would give additional information.

Next came, into Mr. Soames's hand, Coffey's letter of the 19th of November last. In that letter Coffey expressed his anxiety to dispel "any illusion" which Mr. Soames might entertain as to the worth of the statements which Coffey had already made to Mr. Soames's representative, Mr. Shannon, and to the police authorities. The story which he had given to Police-sergeant Chalk was "untrue;" he assured Mr. Soames that he could not help *The Times* "in the least." Whereupon Mr. Soames wrote to Coffey on the 22nd of November, saying that he was under no illusion whatever. At last, Coffey arrived in London. This was on the 17th of December, and he at once called on Mr. Soames, "without solicitation." I went over his statement with him; he had a copy of it while I read it; he signed it after he had made a few corrections, and he declared the whole statement to be true. He even told me that he was prepared to prove it in the witness-box. Then Coffey went back to Ireland. He returned to London. And then he began to have fits of indisposition. He was ill when he should have been at court, waiting to be called. Now and then Mr. Coffey would write and say he was getting better. Mr. Soames even sent his family doctor to take stock of the patient. Then Mr. Soames threatened to arrest Timothy. Timothy had his revenge. He appeared in the box and bullied Sir H. James, and defied their lordships, and behaved badly all round.

Mr. Reid then endeavoured to find out from Mr. Soames what precautions he had taken to verify the statements made to him by a witness with whom he was at war. As Coffey had said in his previous evidence, he had for a short time in 1881 been supplying the Irish Government with "information." Coffey's reports containing all this "information" were now produced in court. The authorities had given the use of them to Mr. Soames. And the reports described how "a regular organizing expedition, composed of extreme Nationalists," was at that time going about Ireland preaching sedition; how the members of the expedition were disguised as commercial travellers, how they visited fairs, and how they were cognisant of the invention of a machine for blowing up British ships.

That was a kind of information difficult to test. However, Coffey asked "the Castle" for money to assist him in watching the commercial travellers. But here was the curious point to which Mr. Reid now invited Mr. Soames's attention. In all these "reports" of Coffey's to Dublin Castle, there was not the smallest reference to the most important of the supposed revelations in Coffey's statement of the 17th of December, the revelation, namely, that Mr. Abraham, M.P., and Mr. Finucane, M.P., were at that very period supporting Land League resolutions of murder and incendiarism. It seemed to Mr. Reid that such important facts, supposing them to be facts, would have been recorded in Mr. Coffey's "confidential" reports to the Castle. It also seemed to him natural that Mr. Soames should have compared the December statement with the report. "I have not read the reports through," said Mr. Soames, with emphasis.

Mr. Reid contrives to throw a suggestion of great surprise into a favourite formula of his—"Am I to understand?" And Mr. Soames looked troubled and impatient when Mr. Reid, after a long pause, asked in his blandest, quietest manner, whether he "was to understand" that before accepting such grave accusations against members of Parliament, Mr. Soames had taken the trouble to check Coffey's statements. Mr. Soames replied that he felt quite satisfied with Irish police assurances of the trustworthiness of the December statement. Mr. Soames confessed he did not even try to find out any persons who had been present at the meeting at which Mr. Abraham was reported to have instigated murder.

Did you not think that in the case of a serious charge of murder against a man like Mr. Abraham, or any one else, it was incumbent upon you to ask for some details or some names from the man who gave the information?
Mr. Soames replied that he showed the statement to the local authorities, who believed it to be a true statement. Mr. Soames added, " I did make particular inquiries."
Of whom?—Of police authorities.
Who were they?—Gibbons and Doolan. Gibbons went through the statement word for word in my office, and said that from his own local knowledge he believed every word of it.
Did he tell you that from his local knowledge he believed Mr. Abraham had advocated murder?—He told me that he believed Mr. Abraham had been mixed up in all kinds of matters.
Now we come to the statement about Apjohn's house. He says that was blown up, and that Mr. Finucane and Mr. Abraham were present at a meeting of the League at which it was decided that outrage should be perpetrated. Did you make inquiries about that?—I told you generally of the inquiries I made.
Has any one of the inspectors or policemen, whom you have made those inquiries of, been called as a witness?—I believe Doolan has.
And has he been asked any question bearing upon this?—No. But he would have been had the counties been taken right through.

Mr. Reid having finished with Mr. Soames, Mr. Biggar put a few questions to him, from which he learned that Mr. Soames had sent an agent to P. J. Sheridan in America, and that as soon as Mr. Soames learned that Sheridan wanted "twenty thousand pounds" to come to England, Mr. Soames telegraphed to the agent to "come back." Naturally.

Then the name of John Leavy was called. Mr. Leavy was a racquet maker of Deptford. Mr. Leavy was a short, slight, slope-shouldered man, with a big, bony face, bald head, and long, grizzled, patriarchal beard. He appeared in the box in order to connect some prominent Nationalists with Fenian activity, in organizing "centres" all over Ireland, and in superintending the secret importation of arms. Leavy gave his evidence with great deliberation. He kept his hands in his pockets, and gazed at his shoe points before giving his answers. Mr. Leavy was an informer; and he claimed to have been in an excellent position to know what "the organization" was doing. He described himself as an ex-member of the Fenian Supreme Council. This body met at Dublin. Mr. O'Connor Power represented Connaught on this Supreme Council. And a Mr. Johnson, of Belfast, "represented the north." Mr. Leavy's audience laughed at this last statement, as if Mr. Leavy had meant Mr. Johnston, M.P., of Ballykilbeg. We had honorary members on our Supreme Council, continued Mr. Leavy; and among them were Pat Egan, Mr. Biggar, Charles Kickam, Mr. Innes of Preston, and Mr. John Walsh of

Middlesborough. And this Supreme Council had its president, Mr. Kickam ; its secretary, Mr. Doran of Queenstown ; and its treasurer, Mr. Patrick Egan. Leavy was a member of the Supreme Council for three or four years; and he resigned because a fellow-Fenian, James Carey, the informer, threatened one day, in the streets of Dublin, that he would take his life. He explained this enmity of Carey's by saying that he had just been opposing Carey's election to the chairmanship of the Dublin " Directory "—the Fenian body which supervised all the centres of Dublin, and received reports from them as to importation of arms. Said Leavy, Carey's appointment to the chairmanship was supported by Mr. Egan and Mr. Brennan, both officials of the Land League. Such was the substance of his story to Sir Henry James.

Cross-examined by Mr. Asquith, Leavy was unable to fix the dates of his connection with the Fenian organization, or of the supreme council meetings at which he had seen Mr. Biggar and other leading Parnellites. At one of these meetings, held at the Imperial Hotel, Dublin, and at which he had spoken to Mr. Biggar, a resolution was passed excluding members of the Parliamentary party from the supreme council. Mr. Asquith asking him whether the resolution did not imply general hostility on the part of the Fenian Brotherhood to the action of the Parliamentary party, the witness stoutly maintained that it did not—that it did not mean war to the knife between the Nationalist party and the Brotherhood as such, but only that the members of the Parliamentary party should not be given too much influence by being admitted to the membership of the supreme council.

Having answered a question or two by Mr. Asquith, the witness was taken in hand by Mr. Davitt, and next by Mr. Biggar. Leavy said that in 1881 he was imprisoned, as a suspect, in Kilmainham. " And when you came out," said Mr. Davitt, "you were prosecuted for embezzlement ? " " I was," said Leavy, after a pause. And he was convicted and sentenced to a year's imprisonment with hard labour. Leavy flushed as he admitted all this. But Leavy went on to explain that two of the directors of the company whose money he was accused of embezzling, " came to me just before the prosecution, and offered me my interest back in the contract I had with them if I would give up my opposition, and return to them." " But was that in writing ? " Mr. Davitt asked, sharply. No ; the offer was made to him verbally. Then he admitted that he had been fined five pounds by the Dublin Health Committee for carrying on an unwholesome business (or a wholesome business unwholesomely), but that to avoid paying the money he left Dublin. Then Mr. Davitt asked him if he ever carried on an illicit manufacture of whisky in Dublin, but this the witness stoutly denied. There was an amusing passage in Leavy's cross-examination by Mr. Biggar. In his examination-in-chief Leavy said that he had met Mr. Biggar, and talked to him, at the Fenian meeting at which the resolution (already described) was passed. Said Leavy now, when confronted by Mr. Biggar, " I remember your meeting me outside the room where the resolution was passed, and offering me one hundred pounds if I would have the resolution rescinded." At this declaration Mr. Biggar, who had been looking sharply and severely at Leavy, fairly burst out laughing. The people in court and the lawyers laughed also. " Do you swear that ? " said Mr. Biggar, resuming his gravity. " Yes," replied the witness, with a determined little nod. Whereupon Mr. Biggar, with a half amused, half contemptuous expression, remarked that he did not like contradicting a witness on his oath, but that he must say Mr. Leavy's little story was false.

The next witness was the most important of the day. He was the witness who professed to know about Frank Byrne, and Byrne's wife, and " Number One," and a certain parcel of knives in Byrne's possession, and about a certain famous payment of a hundred pounds to Mr. Byrne by Mr. Parnell. George Mulqueeny was this witness's name. He was a shortish, thick-set young man, with a bull-doggish, self-complacent, conceited, but not unintelligent expression. He was a Cork man, Mulqueeny. But he had been in London for the last nine years—clerk in the Victoria Docks. He had been a good many things in his day, Mulqueeny. He was a Fenian brother, sworn in London, in 1871. He was a member of the Irish League organization in London, and also secretary to the Catholic Young Men's Society of London. Mulqueeny, at a later stage of his examination, said that a sort of biography of him had been written from "the Nationalist point of view." Mulqueeny made this interesting communication with an air of self-consequence. It was amusing to observe the off-hand, patronizing way in which he acknowledged that he knew this, that, or the other Irish politician. "Yes," "Oh, yes," he would say, with a little toss up of the head and a down-thrust of his hands into his trousers' pockets. That was when he was asked about the small fry. But when the Attorney-General inquired whether he knew Mr. Parnell, Mulqueeny's manner became deferential. "I have the honour of Mr. Parnell's acquaintance," he replied, slightly bowing, but with his hands still in his pockets. Mr. Justice Smith's face slowly relaxed into a smile.

Mulqueeny knew Frank Byrne. Byrne was secretary of the London League, and his office was in Palace-chambers, Westminster. As for Mulqueeny himself, he had, in conjunction with Mr. Biggar and Mr. Frank Bryne, opened League branches in various parts of London. One in particular he remembered. It was at Tower-hill, and not only Byrne but Tynan (Number One) was with him. Mulqueeny was an important man in the organization: he was a member of the Palace-chambers Executive Committee, and remained a member until 1883. Mulqueeny gave a description of the financial state of the London League in 1881-2. The League, he said, was "very badly off" —"in a state of bankruptcy," so that we "raised money by concerts and that sort of thing." And he added that the London League, on several occasions, got help from the League in Dublin. "I remember three remittances of one hundred pounds each coming from Dublin."

Had Byrne ever showed Mulqueeny any arms? Oh, yes; revolvers; and he showed them some time before the Phœnix Park murder, but Mulqueeny could not say how long. "Did Byrne ever mention any other weapons?" he was asked. "Unfortunately he did," replied Mulqueeny with a rather theatrical solemnity, as he bent his head downwards. "He showed me a brown paper parcel in a drawer in the offices of the National League in Palace-chambers. They were knives; and Byrne said that the doctor 'had been buying some new surgical instruments.'" (This was Dr. Hamilton Williams, whom the witness had already named as one of the London leaguers.) Could Mr. Mulqueeny tell how long before the Phœnix Park murders it was that he saw the knives? He could not "fix the date." Then he said he remembered how one night Frank Byrne's brother dropped a heavy parcel upon his (Mulqueeny's) "toe"; how he then learned that the parcel contained rifles, and how he saw rifles next day in Frank's house at Peckham.

Mulqueeny next identified a letter that was handed to him in the witness-box, a letter of Frank Byrne's addressed from Paris to the executive, and containing this sentence, "Mr. McSweeney will also inform you that I received the promised check for £100 from Mr. Parnell on the day I left London."

Cross-examined by Mr. Reid, Mulqueeny called Tynan a "mystery." He would not call him a ruffian; "had I considered Tynan and Byrne to be ruffians I would not have mixed with them." "Up to December, 1882," when disclosures were made about the Phœnix Park murders, Mulqueeny thought Tynan "respectable," and he believed in Byrne until he heard that Byrne had confessed in America to his complicity in the crime. Mulqueeny next remarked that he was a little surprised when he saw the knives in Byrne's office, but that he did not consider it a suspicious circumstance. Then he admitted that even after Byrne's flight he took Byrne's effects to Paris. "Oh," exclaimed Mr. Reid in surprise, "you did not, then, consider him a criminal?" "Well," said Mulqueeny, "I had not as yet reason to suspect him; and I did not like to throw him overboard." The last words Mulqueeny uttered in a tone of high indifference. Then Mr. Asquith followed Mr. Reid. Questioned about the financial position of the London League, the witness repeated his statement that owing to its "poverty" the London branch had made applications to Dublin for money. Then Mr. Asquith asked if he remembered three letters dated 17th and 29th December, 1882, and 5th of January, 1883, and read at the League Offices, in two of which letters Frank Byrne advised an application to the Dublin League, through Mr. Parnell, for one hundred pounds, and in the third of which [that dated 5th of Jan., 1883] Mr. Byrne said that he had not received Mr. Parnell's reply, and that, owing to the want of money, the salaries of the League officials were in arrears. [Mr. Byrne sent the letters to the office because he himself was unwell at the time.] But there was a fourth letter of Mr. Byrne's, the letter dated Feb. 8, 1883, from Paris [a month after the third letter already named] in which fourth letter Mr. Byrne acknowledged the receipt of the hundred pounds from Mr. Parnell, and also enclosed a balance-sheet of accounts. "Now," said Mr. Asquith, "did you not understand that the hundred pounds were given by Mr. Parnell in reply to the repeated applications of the London League for assistance?" "That was possible," replied Mulqueeny. Asked if he looked at the balance-sheet enclosed in Mr. Byrne's Paris letter, he replied that he might have seen it; that it was "very likely" he had seen it; but he would not say whether or not he had found that Mr. Parnell's hundred pound cheque was accounted for in the enclosure. "You know Captain O'Shea?" said Mr. Asquith. "Yes," was the reply; and then he admitted that "very possibly" he might have told Captain O'Shea about the existence of that letter. "If Captain O'Shea said so I would not contradict him," the witness continued. Here is an extract from Mr. Asquith's cross-examination.

Did you tell Captain O'Shea that certain people knew that Mr. Parnell had paid for the escape of the Phœnix Park murderers?—I don't think so.
Then if Captain O'Shea says that, what he says is not correct?—I don't know.
You must know whether you made such a statement as that to Captain O'Shea.
Possibly I did, but I have no recollection of it. If Captain O'Shea says I did, then I did.
Did you tell him that this letter of Frank Byrne's had been taken away from the rooms in Palace-chambers?—I cannot say that I told him that.
Did you tell him the police had taken it away?—I don't remember.
Now tell me—did you tell Captain O'Shea that certain people knew that Mr. Parnell had paid for the escape of the Phœnix Park murderers?—Well, to my mind he did.
Did what?—Paid for the escape of Byrne.
How?—By the £100.
And do you now suggest that this £100 was paid by Mr. Parnell to Byrne to enable him to escape from justice?—I suggest that the money was sent to Byrne, and that he used it to go to America.
In other words, that Byrne misappropriated the money?—Probably that is so.
That Mr. Parnell having sent him £100 for the Land League purposes, he bolted to Paris, and thence to America?—Well, I don't know. Possibly that is correct.
Was that what you meant when you told Captain O'Shea that certain people knew that Mr. Parnell had paid for the escape of the Phœnix Park murderers?—I don't think I told him anything of the kind.
If you made that statement to Captain O'Shea, had you any foundation for it other than that this £100 had been, as you believed, misappropriated by Byrne?—I can't say.
Have you any other ground for the statement now?—I had nothing else in my mind but Byrne's letter.

The remaining questions put to Mulqueeny were of minor importance. In a few minutes, and after a long pause—during which everybody must have guessed what was coming—Sir Henry James rose. He said—

My Lords—In the absence of my learned friend the Attorney-General, I have to say that these are the witnesses that we are now in a position to place before your lordships in support of the case we have had to present to you on behalf of our clients.

And so the case for *The Times* closed at seventeen minutes past three o'clock.

The rest of the day's business was merely formal. The President announced that he was not prepared to issue an interim report on the forged letters case. Sir Charles Russell briefly sketched the line of defence which he would follow in replying to *The Times* case. Excepting Mr. Dillon, against whom nothing of any consequence was alleged, all the Members against whom any evidence had been given, would appear in the witness-box. He would also meet every instance in which the Central Office of the League had been charged with criminality; and every instance of alleged evidence against local branches. But to answer the charges against members of the League, in their private, individual capacity, would, said Sir Charles Russell, necessitate his calling 367 witnesses from Mayo alone. He would therefore have to consider how he could present his case, without putting in such an enormous mass of evidence. For this reason he asked for an adjournment till Tuesday, 2nd of April. In granting Sir Charles Russell's request for an adjournment, the President intimated that he would issue an order for the release from prison of Mr. W. O'Brien, M.P., and Mr. Edward Harrington, M.P., to enable them to appear before the Commission.

SIXTY-FOURTH DAY.

APRIL 2.

PRECISELY at half-past ten o'clock Sir Charles Russell opened his case for the defence. He was to lift the veil which the Attorney-General had dropped over pre-Land League Ireland. He was to show how landlord greed and tenant misery produced their baleful crop of disturbance and crime years and generations before the Nationalist party and the Land and National Leagues came into being.

The accused, whose story we shall soon hear, laugh to scorn the notion that Ireland has been fairly painted by the sixteen district inspectors, and the ninety-eight subordinate members of the constabulary, by the landlords and landlords' agents, by the eighteen informers—most of them the sorriest specimens of humanity—who were among the three hundred and forty odd witnesses examined on behalf of *The Times*. As Sir Charles Russell pointedly remarked at the beginning of his speech, only one priest—one member of the class of Irishmen whose knowledge of the lives and circumstances of their fellow-countrymen is the most complete and intimate—has been called by *The Times* counsel.

Besides these witnesses, said Sir Charles Russell, there have been five experts—" Captain O'Shea, and the informer Delaney, and I am afraid I must add Mr. Soames and Mr. Macdonald; and the fifth, Mr. Inglis, called and sworn, but, fortunately for Mr. Inglis's reputation, not examined." The ironical implication in the words "fortunately not examined" was not lost upon Sir Charles's audience.

The audience, if that is the right word, was not uncomfortably large—not so large as during the memorable days when the costly fabric of the "letters" case was tumbling into ludicrous ruin about the ears of the dealer in obscene photographs who was its solitary support, yet who made his employers believe that it would last for ever. Among the earliest visitors who arrived in court was Mrs. Gladstone, who found a seat near the jury-box, well in front of Sir Charles Russell. Mr. Biggar, Mr. Davitt, and Mr. Parnell were in their usual places on the solicitors' bench. Sir Charles Russell himself arrived early. In front of him was a heap of books on Ireland—Lecky's, Froude's and others—of which he made good use during his five-and-a-half hours' speech; also a basket containing the notes of his speech.

This first day's instalment of his speech may be divided under the following headings:—Who are the accused? Who are the accusers? What is the accusation? How has *The Times* conducted its case? What have been the predisposing causes of crime—what is the testimony, on that point, of two centuries of Irish history? The accused were eighty-five members of the total number of 103 whom Ireland returned to Parliament, although, for some reason unknown to him, the accusers chose to name only sixty-five. History, said Sir Charles Russell, presents no parallel to this preponderating force of representative opinion (as embodied in the Nationalist party): "some of its members may be more or less indiscreet," but the eighty-five members "are solid." In accusing this party, continued Sir Charles Russell, the opposite party are attempting to do what Edmund Burke declared could never be successfully done; they are attempting to indict a whole nation.

With a contemptuous reference to the absurdity of attacking a "great social revolution" (such as the Irish movement of 1879-1889) as if it were "an Old Bailey" case, Sir Charles passed on to his second question, Who are the accusers? The answer, as given by the questioner himself, was the reverse of complimentary to the accusers—"a company, a co-partnership, or a syndicate, I don't know which, called by the public *The Times*; a syndicate which in the whole course of its existence had been consistent in at least one thing, unrelenting hostility to the Irish people and their cause." And as an illustration of their undying hostility, Sir Charles quoted *The Times*' condemnation of Lord Mulgrave for having invited "that rancorous and foul-mouthed ruffian O'Connell" to dinner, that same O'Connell whom even "the principal Irish minister" now claims as "a supporter of his policy." In the same vein *The Times* rejoiced over the depopulation of Ireland caused by the famine: "The Irish are gone at last, gone with a vengeance." Sir Charles quoted the words. And the emigrants were likened to rats leaving an empty vessel for one with a full cargo. "There have been," said Sir Charles, "transient gleams of statesmanship in the columns of *The Times*, but these have been counterbalanced by its insolence—rendered more intolerable by its condescending insolence." There was a sharp, indignant ring in these last words. "But," he added, "we have this consolation; it is the fate of *The Times* to help every cause which it has opposed."

Coming to the next head—What are the accusations? Sir Charles enumerated them: That the Nationalist agitation depended on a paid system of murder and outrage; that the Nationalist organization assisted murderers and other criminals to escape from justice; that the Nationalist denunciation of crime was false and hypocritical. But if the people who make these charges are serious, asked Sir Charles Russell, why have the accused not been tried at the Old Bailey long ago? Then Sir Charles Russell gave a humorous description of the conduct of *The Times*' case. For many weeks, Lincoln's-inn-fields, Mr. Soames's official headquarters, resembled an Irish police and military station getting ready for an eviction expedition; "on these benches," here Sir Charles waved his hand, "on these benches Mr. Soames's deputy-inspectors, and police magistrates and constables, have been as thick as leaves in Vallombrosa; and we have had magistrates taking evidence for *The Times*, and Irish policemen personally conducting witnesses; and spies have been doing *The Times* work; and the gaols of the kingdom have been scoured to see whether from the refuse within their walls some might be found to testify against the accused." Here came in one of those striking and pathetic passages in which Sir Charles Russell's speech abounded. With a touch of pathos, he called up before the mind's eye a picture of some wretched life-long prisoner, tempted by some vague prospect of reunion with wife and children, to find for himself a loophole of release in an incriminating tale. Then Sir Charles, continuing his calm, merciless criticism of the tactics of his opponents, complained of the manner in which witnesses had been sprung upon him. And he declared emphatically that the purpose, the unavowed purpose, of the heterogeneous, unmethodical mass of criminal history brought out by the Attorney-General was to prejudice the minds of the people of England. What else, he asked, could have been the object of recounting the mournful stories of Lady Mountmorres, of Mrs. Blake, of the Curtin family?

Worst of all was the Attorney-General's great sin of omission. In his introductory speech the Attorney-General "gave us no clue" to the state of things out of which grew the Ireland of 1879. The Attorney-General spoke of the Ireland of 1879 as if it had come down "from the firmament," as if "her career began in 1879"; as if before 1879 Ireland " were a Garden of Eden"; as if before 1879 "Ireland were a country of patriarchal relations between landlords and tenants, the landlords looking down upon their tenants with paternal regard, and tenants looking up with eyes full of reverential gratitude."

In the delivery of this and similar passages Sir Charles Russell was at his best. His satirical description of the Edenic Ireland of Sir Richard Webster was keenly appreciated. Not once, but many a time, while he showed what the real Ireland was, as distinguished from the imaginary Ireland of her enemies—the real Ireland of alternating hope and despair, of grateful hearts, of patience and long-suffering and generous forgiveness—did his voice tremble and falter with emotion. Proceeding to make visible what this Ireland was over which the Attorney-General had drawn the veil—what the soil was out of which the crop of discontent, disturbance, and crime inevitably and naturally grew—he quoted extracts from Lecky and Froude and Goldwin Smith, the general drift of which was that Irish crime and discontent were caused by the combined action of past restrictive legislation against Irish trade and agriculture, the penal code, the uncontrolled powers of the landlords, and the general misgovernment of the country. The cattle maiming which the accusers attributed to the agitation of the last ten years, existed in the beginning of the eighteenth century. He showed how the Whiteboys' secret society was directed against the landgrabbers, whose name, say *The Times* witnesses, was not heard of before 1879. The records of the middle portion of the eighteenth century proved that Ireland was not the Eden of Sir Richard Webster—that high rents and confiscation of improvements led to crimes of exactly the same nature as those which *The Times* counsel attributed solely to the Land and National Leagues. In those days, said Sir Charles, house burning and death were the penalty of land-grabbing. The Whiteboys already named, the Steel Boys, the Oak Boys, the Levellers, were all secret societies of the eighteenth century, and they were the natural and inevitable results of landlord greed and cruelty and agrarian misery.

Even the sturdy Presbyterians of Ulster suffered then as much as the Western and Southern Celts suffer now. They left Ireland and fought on the American side in the War of Independence. Sir Charles Russell showed how crime diminished whenever the Irish people saw ground for hope in remedial legislation. The years 1780 to 1806 afforded a case in point. From 1806 to 1820 was a period of relapse into despair, and the mournful round of crime began again. Lastly, Sir Charles Russell illustrated his explanation of the genesis of Irish disturbance and crime by extracts from Sir George Cornewall Lewis, and from the interesting reports of the House of Commons Committee in 1852. In that year, just as in 1889, the official witnesses—such as police constables, magistrates, inspectors, landlords, land agents—all agreed in testifying to the effect that the discontent and crime were not owing to agrarian causes, and that Ireland could be put right again by a strong dose of coercive law. And sixty years ago as well as now—as the Committee investigations proved—bailiffs were beaten, and herds on evicted farms were murdered; and the peasantry sympathized with law-breakers, and subscriptions were got up for prisoners accused of crime; and the law-breakers were labouring-men and the younger sons of small farmers; and the outrages were most frequent where ejectments were most frequent.

SIXTY-FIFTH DAY.

April 3

Sir Charles Russell resumed his address with a brief recapitulation of his general argument of yesterday, that distress and crime had in the past history of Ireland accompanied each other like substance and shadow. Where distress was greatest, crime prevailed most. As regards the year 1879, he illustrated this proposition by the public records of what were then called the distressed districts," in Galway, Mayo, Kerry, Cork, Clare. As to the evil system of agrarian tenure which was mainly, at least, responsible for the misery which prompted the tenantry to commit crime, Sir C. Russell named a long list of high authorities who, either before the Act of Union or after it, wrote in strong condemnation of it. The condemnation, said Sir Charles, is unanimous. "I challenge you," he exclaimed, turning round to where sat *The Times* counsel, "I challenge you to produce a single writer of authority who has ever defended that system." Authoritative writers, differing in political creed, as well in their callings in life, had denounced this system—which, in his address of Tuesday, Sir Charles Russell had described as a system for the good of the few at the expense of the many. Dean Swift condemned the landlord system of Ireland. Bishop Berkeley denounced it. And Lord Townshend. And of course Arthur Young, the greatest authority among them all. And so did Lord Clare, whose words, by the way, recall General Gordon's description of the peasantry of Kerry. What Lord Clare said was that, speaking from his intimate acquaintance with the province of Munster, he believed it was impossible to find "greater human misery" anywhere than existed there. The peasantry, said Lord Clare, are "ground to powder by their relentless landlords." So much for authorities before the Act of Union. As to those after the Union, Sir Charles Russell quoted, besides some writers of books, the numerous Parliamentary Reports in 1819, 1823, &c., as also Poor Law Commission Reports, and the Devon and other Commissions.

The Devon Commission, of which Sir Charles gave a clear and rapid sketch, was, like all Commissions of the same class, a landlords' Commission, inasmuch as its leading members belonged to the landlord class. And yet, in spite of the natural bias of these members, their reports, as submitted to Parliament, threw a black, mournful shadow upon the land which the Attorney-General's land agent and constabulary witnesses had, with astonishing unanimity, been describing as the home of sunny peace and kindly feeling between landlord and tenant until the leaguers arose to spoil it all. The Devon Commissioners, 1843-5, saw that social disorder was inevitable under a continuance of the Irish land system. The Devon report declared that where tenant rights were respected, crime was at a minimum, or non-existent. A striking proof of this was quoted by Sir Charles Russell from the testimony of one of the most valuable witnesses examined before the Devon Commission, namely, Mr. Hancock, agent to Lord Lurgan. Mr. Hancock pointed out that the Ulster districts in which disturbance existed were precisely those districts in which the ancient tenant right of the province was violated by the landlords. It was Mr. Hancock who declared that if a rising should occur in Ulster, in defence of peasant rights, there was not enough force at the Horse Guards to put it down. Twenty-five years later, when Mr. Gladstone's first Land Bill was in progress, and with the advantage of his quarter of a century's additional experience, Mr. Hancock repeated the same general testimony which he had given before the Devon Commission. Sir Charles Russell incidentally drew attention to another cause, besides respect to tenant right, of the general immunity of Ulster from disturbance. Ulster was a manufacturing province, so that labourers removed from the soil were enabled to find there means of subsistence. Given an absence of manufactures and of tenant right, Ulster would have been as harassed by disturbance and crime as Mayo, Clare, or Kerry. Instead of Acts passed for the relief of the peasants, Acts were passed for the relief of landlords, such as the Encumbered Estates Act of 1848, which only served to make over Irish lands to mere jobbers, whose sole object was to wring out of their tenants the largest returns upon the money they had invested. An Act of twenty-eight years ago—a time when the spirit of Irish politics was at its lowest—served chiefly to improve the landlord's powers of ejectment. It granted facilities for "ejectment, purely and simply for non-payment of rent." There was nothing like that in English law, said Sir Charles Russell. As for the Act of 1870, it did to some extent generalize the Ulster system; but it made no provision against arbitrary increase of rent, and as it excluded leaseholders from its benefits, it tempted the landlords to force leaseholds upon their tenantry. Referring again to the Hancock testimony, Sir Charles Russell pointed out once more the coincidence between the statistics of poverty, ejectment, and crime. Quoting from the official reports before him, Sir Charles Russell sketched the condition of Ireland ten years ago, just when the League was beginning its work. He quoted from the truly appalling testimony given by Mr. Fox to the Mansion House Relief Committee. And he read out Gordon's description of Kerry, as contained in that great man's letter published in *The Times*. All this is old, it may be said. It is old, and it is unredressed.—scenes of wretchedness such as those over the recital of which Sir Charles Russell could hardly restrain his feelings, are still occurring in Ireland at this very hour.

In denouncing the landlord greed, which in Sir Charles Russell's view led to the sad condition of things which made it necessary for the tenants to combine under the Nationalist leaders in self-defence, Sir Charles Russell repudiated with his utmost emphasis and scorn the extreme landlord doctrine of the sacredness of contract. "For that species of sacredness I care nothing," exclaimed Sir Charles Russell. What was "economic rent?" It was the share of the surplus produce which the landlord should take *after* the labourer and the cultivator had received the full reward of their toil. Three parties were, in the present dispensation of things, interested in this question, the labourer, the tiller, the landlord. If one of these three classes had "to go to the wall," who was the last who should go? In Sir Charles's opinion, it was the labourer. But in practice the labourer and the tiller were the first to go; the landlord was the last to suffer; and the result was that the Irish peasantry were the worst housed, worst fed, and worst clothed population in the civilized world.

No one who has heard Sir Charles Russell will call statistics uninteresting. It depends upon how they are treated; and in Sir Charles Russell's hands they are made to tell, vividly and irrefragably, their sad, damning tale. Two most striking characteristics of this speech are its condensation of a vast amount of knowledge, and the presentation of it in a manner so clear and rapid as to enable those who listen to it to seize the scope and significance of it with ease. To complete his sketch of what the Ireland was out of which the Land League grew, Sir Charles Russell showed, from Government statistics, the tremendous fall in the annual crop of potatoes and cereals during the years 1876-7-8-9. In that period of four years the potato yield dwindled down to about one quarter; and the potato crop was, and is, as every one knows, the main food of the bulk of the Irish people, and the only food of multitudes among them. Turning to the cereal crop statistics, Sir Charles showed that here also an enormous fall had taken place; in those four years the annual value of the crop fell from thirty-six to twenty-two millions. Next, he showed how the area under cultivation was falling off in each of those years by hundreds of thousands of acres. In 1879, too, the loss upon the amount of wages earned by Irish reapers and other labourers habitually crossing over to England for the harvest season amounted to two hundred and fifty thousand pounds for the province of Connaught alone. And the death rate was running up, reaching its maximum in 1880, the first full year of the Land League.

What did the Irish Secretary of the day, Mr. Lowther, reply to the Irish request for an extension of the Ulster tenant right to Ireland generally? Why, that such a measure would be "pure and undiluted communism." The Government would do nothing. And once more was witnessed the spectacle of a "mendicant" Ireland, as Sir Charles expressed it, with a tremor in his voice—Ireland subsisting miserably on Mansion House and American doles, while the live stock of her peasantry was sold for rent.

Mr. Forster, Mr. Lowther's successor, had compassion upon the Irish. And the Compensation for Disturbance Bill—a Land League measure, at the moderation of which even extreme Tories of to-day might well feel surprise—was thrown out by the Lords in one of the largest assemblage of Peers ever witnessed. But though the Irish peasantry received no help, their landlords, as Sir Charles Russell now proceeded to describe briefly, did; they had State money lent to them free of interest for the first two years—money upon which some of them contrived to extort four or five per cent. from their tenants. Was it strange, asked Sir Charles Russell, that the Irish leaders should have felt alarmed at the prospect of the rivival of the old, the too familiar, scenes of famine horrors? Ireland an Eden before the year of the League? If so, what of the showers of ejectment notices at that critical period, 1879-80? Sir Charles had tried to discover the numbers of ejectment notices at that period, by references to entries made by the Irish clerks of the peace. For whenever an Irish landlord was about to eject, warning was given to the workhouse authorities, so that room might be prepared for the castaways. Well, Sir Russell had discovered that the Ulster notices were in 1880 twice as numerous as their annual average from 1853 to 1878; the Connaught ones more than twice; the Munster ones more than twice; and the Leinster notices, 1,363 in 1880, as against 912 for the twenty-five years' average. Sir Charles Russell next showed how the increase manifested itself in special localities, such as Galway, Mayo, Clare, Kerry, East and West Cork. Here, then, said Sir Charles, was a state of intense distress; and also an acknowledgment by the Government of the day that relief was necessary.

The landlords did nothing—but eject. His voice ringing with indignation, Sir Charles Russell asked what would have happened in England, if the like spectacle of peasant hardship and landlord cruelty and greed had been witnessed within her borders. Property has its duties as well as its rights; but Sir Charles Russell carried the development of Drummond's famous dictum another step forward, by declaring that "Property has no rights inconsistent with the good of the people." The Irish leaders in 1879-80 were driven to take action; their new movement was "justifiable," was necessary "before God and man." As to its human justification, look at the Statute Book; look at its successive Acts from 1880 to 1887, Acts which "owe their existence to the men who, at the instance of *The Times*, have been held up to public obloquy and public odium as criminals and accomplices in criminality before the law." The parts of the speech of which the foregoing sentences are the baldest summary were delivered with splendid effect.

"Who are the men" who did it? What were they? What their motives? Did they come together under the cover of a "pretended movement to redress a pretended grievance?" "This is the question which you, my lords, have to decide. For this," Sir Charles continued, "is not an inquiry into crimes incidental to the movement. The charge is that these men carefully calculated and applied a system of murder." Sir Charles Russell, in giving a preliminary answer to his question, selected seven men, differing widely in their early history and pre-occupations and advantages or disadvantages. The seven were Mr. Biggar, Mr. Egan, Mr. William O'Brien, Mr. Dillon, Mr. Davitt, Mr. Sexton, Mr. Parnell. A man of ability and resolution, Mr. Biggar was in those critical times engaged in business. Mr. Egan was a man of great capacity against whom—whatever his American career might have been—not a scintilla of proof of crime had been brought in the course of this trial. Both Mr. Biggar and Mr. Egan had joined the Fenian organization, from which they were expelled when they joined Mr. Butt's Home Rule association. Mr. Sexton was a literary man, whose early career in the Irish movement corresponded with that of Mr. Biggar. Mr. William O'Brien and Mr. Dillon had joined no association, secret or open, before they joined the League. Mr. O'Brien was a journalist, Mr. Dillon a medical student. Their conduct might not have been always discreet, but their purpose was unselfish and honest. They were enthusiasts. "My lords," said Sir Charles Russell, pausing for a moment or two, "there is room in the world for more enthusiasts." The modern world was not so free from "dulness, selfishness, materialism," that it could afford to dispense with men who raised it above its vulgar level.

Then there was Michael Davitt, the peasant's son, who had none of the early advantages which had been the lot of his countrymen already named. Michael Davitt's earliest memories were of a day when, a child of five years old, he saw his mother weep, when the evictors came and seized the old home, and threw its contents out upon the roadside. His next memory was that of his mother turning away with him from the workhouse door in her anger and grief when the warders refused her admission except on the condition of separation from her child. All this time Mr. Davitt was sitting in front of Sir Charles Russell, his head bent, and resting on his one hand—the left. To this simple, pathetic recital of Mr. Davitt's early history the Court listened in deep silence. It created a profound impression. From the workhouse door, through the convicts' yard, to the foundation of the National Land League of Ireland; from the obscurity of a Mayo cabin to renown, and respect, all over the English-speaking world—such has been Michael Davitt's lot. Sir Charles Russell had just spoken of the dulness of our English everyday life. Whatever else the lives of these Irish leaders may have been, they have not been commonplace.

SIXTY-SIXTH DAY.

APRIL 4.

HAVING yesterday shown what the economic and social conditions were that rendered a popular combination "justifiable" and "necessary" "before God and man," Sir Charles Russell to-day resumed his address with an account of the foundation of the Land League. The League was founded on the 21st October, 1879, and suppressed in October, 1881. Mr. Parnell, said Sir Charles, was reluctant to join it. Mr. Parnell was by "temperament, by mental character, a Parliamentarian." Mr. Parnell, said Sir Charles, lays no claim to the kind of eloquence that moves multitudes, but he has discernment, resolution, self-control, and prudence. At last, however, Mr. Parnell consented to accept the presidentship of the League, the inaugural meeting of which was held in a place famous in the story of the Nationalist movement—the Imperial Hotel, Upper Sackville-street (or as it is now called O'Connell-street), Dublin.

To show the aim and purpose of the new League, Sir Charles Russell read out its constitution, its rules, as also a number of public addresses distributed over Ireland by the League leaders at and after its foundation. The first of these manifestoes was the "appeal" to the Irish people. This interesting document (read out by Mr. Asquith) declared that the land system of Ireland existed only for the benefit of the few. It directed attention to the prosperity of countries where the cultivators, unlike the peasants of Ireland, had rights. It repudiated the notion that the peasant proprietorship which the League would fight for meant confiscation. It invited the six hundred thousand peasants of Ireland to associate for the purpose of arresting the evil which had banished millions of workers from their native land. As for the specific rules which local branches of the League were to enforce, their main object was to prevent land-grabbing"—that is to say, to prevent, by fair means, tenants from occupying lands from which others had been evicted for non-payment of rack-rents. The prevention was to be secured simply by getting as many as possible of the tenants to become members of the League, and by expelling any members guilty of land-grabbing or of violation of any rule devised by the League for the common good. The connection of boycotting with the operations of the League branches was discussed by Sir Charles Russell in a later portion of his speech.

Another of the popular appeals was that of date 5th November, 1879, signed by Mr. Parnell and his fellow-officials, and addressed to the tenant-farmers as a class, pointing out to them the circumstances—such as American competition—under which the purchase of their farms was becoming easier for them. One of the most remarkable of these manifestoes of the League was that specially addressed to the occupiers of that very province of Ulster between which and the South and West there have been such persistent attempts to sow discord. This Land League document, read out by Mr. Arthur Russell, spoke of the Ulster people as men who once upon a time had led the van of Irish progress; it invited the Ulster people, as "countrymen and brothers," to work for the common good of Ireland; it repelled the charges of sectarian and religious bigotry which in some quarters had been made against the Catholic west and south; it challenged proof of a single instance of religious jealousy on the part of the Catholic community; and in proof of freedom from all such unworthy feeling, it drew the attention of the Ulster men to the fact that in the west and south of Ireland Catholic candidates for representative office who were indifferent to the popular cause were passed over for Protestants who were friends to it.

Was this League, with its "free and open programme," and its public appeals, "a criminal conspiracy?" Sir Charles Russell asked. If it was, it was unlike any other criminal conspiracy he had ever heard of. Catholic bishops and priests—intimately acquainted with the people—supported this new League from the very first; and, with very few exceptions, the body of the episcopate and clergy joined it after the rejection of the Compensation for Disturbance Bill. As to crimes incidental to the movement, why, even in England itself no great popular movement had ever taken place—and he instanced Free Trade, and the workmen's movement for right of free combination—without "the incidents of disturbance and crime." If popular leaders, in Ireland or anywhere else, were to be deterred by the prospect of incidental violence from efforts after social amelioration, there would be no such thing as social amelioration at all; there would be "no crusades against despotism." Sir Charles Russell illustrated this position by reference to Sir James Macintosh's criticism on Burke. As for the people who, in Ireland or America, contributed to the funds of the League, or otherwise befriended the movement, Mr. Parnell simply proceeded upon the principle of excluding no one, of refusing the help of no one, who freely and honestly offered his support. When invoking popular aid, "was Mr. Parnell to ask for a certificate of previous political conduct" from every one who responded to his invitation? Was he to refuse contributions without such certificate? Did the Irish landlords refuse the American dollars sent to rack-rented peasants by their children and relations in America?

You have heard, said Sir Charles Russell, you have heard from the spy Le Caron some statements about an unconstitutional movement of Irish in America; but how puny is that movement in comparison with that of which Mr. Parnell has been the head. "It is not always that the merits of a man are recognized in the day in which he lives. The motives are misconstrued, the aims are misrepresented; and within the last few days we have had a notable example of what one may call the posthumous gratitude of a nation, when by the grave of one of the greatest men of this generation has ascended the loudest and the shrillest 'keen' of mourning from the men who spent their lives in denouncing the whole character, in vilifying the motives, and doing all they could—but puny were their efforts—to bring disgrace and infamy upon his head.". And Sir Charles went on to say that he had no doubt the day would come—was coming rapidly—when Mr. Parnell would be recognized as a statesman who in striving for the good of Ireland had rendered "true and loyal service to England." The passage was one of the most eloquent in the whole of to-day's delivery, and the style of the delivery was worthy of the substance.

Returning for a few moments to the public appeals and manifestoes of the National Leaguers, Sir Charles Russell quoted the League programme of April, 1880, offering to the landlords terms of purchase, which, Sir Charles Russell declared, they would only be too glad to accept now if they had the chance. The landlords then missed an opportunity, said Sir Charles, which they were not likely to get again; and he drew attention to the fact that, though the other leaders of the League appended their signatures to the document, Mr. Davitt withheld his. Mr. Davitt, Sir Charles explained, thought the terms offered to the landlords were too favourable, and events had proved that Mr. Davitt was right. How comes it, exclaimed Sir Charles Russell, raising his voice to its highest pitch, and turning round to where the Attorney-General sat, "How comes it that such documents have not been presented before your lordships, if this case is to be fairly presented in a broad, in a just, and in a statesmanlike fashion? How is it that all these documents come, I think I may say, as a revelation upon your lordships? My lords, nothing but blind animosity, the judgments of men distorted by prejudice, carried away by a desire and impulse to blacken the characters of political opponents, can account for the way in which the Attorney-General has been imperfectly instructed in presenting this case. I think it is a grave matter. I must say it is a grave scandal." The court rang with Sir Charles Russell's impassioned voice, as he denounced this "grave scandal."

Next followed the passages about boycotting. Those who heard them will long remember them. "Boycotting?" Then a pause—during which Sir Charles takes out his snuff-coloured pocket-handkerchief. "Boycotting?" He drops his voice. "My lords—let us clear our minds of cant." "Boycotting has existed in all ages and countries." What is it? Why, a "focussing of the opinion of the community in condemnation of the conduct of some members of that community." It may be criminal, or justifiable, according to its methods of working. "Is there no boycotting at the Bar?" "No boycotting in the Church?" "No boycotting in politics? or in trade? What is meant by sending a man to Coventry?"

Then he instanced the successful boycott of a Cape governor—refusal to sell, refusal to supply him with horses—until his Excellency yielded to the colonists' demand that a convict ship about to land her cargo of criminal offscourings should be ordered to make off with it elsewhither. This was a justifiable boycott; the only sort of boycott which Sir Charles would condemn, was the boycott of intimidation and violence. And as to the League's denunciation of land-grabbing and boycotting of land-grabbers, why landgrabbing was simply one of the forms of landlord oppression against which the tenants combined. The combination must either denounce grabbing or cease to exist.

To show from another point of view what the real character of the Land League was, Sir Charles Russell quoted denunciations which the Irish Republican Brotherhood launched against Mr. Parnell, Mr. Davitt, and other members of the open and constitutional body, the Land League. Sir Charles Russell concluded this part of his address—the foundation of the Land League—by declaring emphatically that, as far as the case had already gone, there had been produced against the accused not a single proof of complicity in crime which, if the trial were an ordinary criminal one, would justify their lordships in submitting the matter to a jury. It is a most remarkable and striking fact, continued Sir Charles, that every informer who has sworn to participation with leaguers in the commission of crime was himself a member of some secret society.

The Attorney-General, exclaimed Sir Charles, undertook to prove that sums of thirty, forty, fifty pounds were paid down by Mr. Biggar, Mr. Brennan, and other officers of the League, to the actual perpetrators of crimes. Where was the proof? Sir Charles asked. Where was the Attorney-General's authority for that statement? "Who was the informer, who the convict, who told that lie?" But then the Attorney-General explained that he did not mean to say that Mr. Biggar and the others were directly cognisant of crimes committed, or about to be committed. "What a contemptible case, what a wretched thing of shreds and patches has the Attorney-General presented to your lordships. Will no explanation be given of these statements? No apology be made for them? They are directed against his colleagues in Parliament, whose reputation is as dear to them as the Attorney-General's is to him. Such statements should not be made recklessly by any member of the Bar, whether he be the highest or the lowest." The passages summarized in the preceding sentences were delivered in Sir Charles Russell's most emphatic style. He pointed to where *The Times* counsel sat. He turned round to the Attorney-General, who leaning back in his seat, next bent forward, leant back again, and finally scribbled something with his quill.

Sir Charles Russell now came to the next division of his subject—the

League's work. The work of the League, said Sir Charles, was twofold—relief and organization. The League spent £50,000 in relief during the famine of eight or nine years ago. Mr. Davitt was then the head of the League. In 1881 Mr. Davitt went to America. On his return he issued a circular, which was distributed throughout the length and breadth of Ireland. In that circular, while exhorting the tenants to stand firm, he urged them to abstain from violence, he characterized threatening letters as being "stupidly unnecessary" and "criminal," he declared that persons resorting to such means of influencing landlords were unworthy of League membership, and he expressed his inability to believe that members of the League could possibly be identified with the crimes reported from all quarters of Ireland.

Now, exclaimed Sir Charles Russell, though this League circular was distributed all over Ireland, the Attorney-General never referred to it. On the contrary, the Attorney-General had said that none of the League leaders had denounced outrages. To illustrate his position that the Land League was an organization of order and peace, Sir Charles Russell showed how disturbance and crime followed its suppression. The disturbing effect of the No-Rent Manifesto was as nothing in comparison with that produced by the imprisonment of the trusted leaders of the people. If the No-Rent Manifesto was "an unconstitutional blow," it was dealt against "an unconstitutional blow." But, in fact, said Sir Charles, considering what the occupation of land meant to an Irish peasant, "I do not believe that any organization could prevent the payment of rent, if the people had it to pay."

The work of the League, said Sir Charles Russell, has been described by accusers as criminal; but if that is the correct account, is it not strange that in an organization extending over most of Ireland, and with every facility for conducting its search, *The Times* has been able to find only one League letter purporting to connect, directly, the Land League organization with crime—the letter of a local official, who, however, is not in the land of the living? Then Sir Charles went on to describe, somewhat humorously—though still in his serious vein—how the Royal Irish Constabulary searched over the length and breadth of the land for incriminatory documents, and found nothing really relevant to the point at issue before their lordships. Sir Charles Russell concluded with a statement of the Land League objections to the Land Bill of 1881, and a description of the League's policy of "test cases" before the Land Commission, as a method of saving the tenants the heavy costs involved in an application to the Courts, and of saving both tenants and Courts much valuable time.

SIXTY-SEVENTH DAY.

April 9.

In spite of the attractions of Sir Charles Russell's eloquence, the attendance in court to-day, when their lordships entered at half-past ten o'clock, was unusually small. Sir Charles Russell resumed his speech with a summary of what had gone before. He had endeavoured to show that the action of the Irish Parliamentary leaders had been entirely constitutional, entirely influenced by the desire for social peace and improvement. That had been the great ambition of the Land League. But besides the Land League usually known by that name, there was a smaller body, the Ladies' Land League, formed shortly before the suppression, in 1881, of the larger body, and dissolved, by itself, in August, 1882, soon after Mr. Parnell's release from Kilmainham.

But for a particular observation of the Attorney-General's, Sir Charles would have passed over the subject of the Ladies' Land League without any notice whatever. This Sir Charles said with a tone of downright contempt in his voice at the treatment which the League had received in Sir Richard's opening speech. Sir Charles took a single illustration, namely, the Attorney-General's words about Miss Reynolds, "whose career will be traced, whose course through the country would be traced by the deeds which followed her agitation." Having read out these words, Sir Charles Russell paused; he gazed for a moment at Sir Richard Webster, and then looked at the judges. Here, he said, we have a picture of a lady wading through blood, leaving bloody footsteps behind her. "Where," he exclaimed almost fiercely, "where, I ask, is the proof of all this to be found? Where is the justification for this statement? Not one iota of evidence have we had in proof of this imputation made in the Attorney-General's statement." With this expression of flat contradiction and challenge, Sir Charles Russell dismissed contemptuously this branch of the Attorney-General's statement, and passed on to the Kilmainham episode of the Parnell movement, and Captain O'Shea's relations with Mr. Parnell and others.

Mr. Parnell and his colleagues, said Sir Charles, do not deny that they advised the tenants to combine; do not deny that they did not "differentiate" between poor tenants and tenants who were well off. Their hope was that the well-to-do and strong would combine for the sake of the poor and the weak. When the Arrears Bill was first discussed, Mr. Parnell had predicted that if some such measure was not passed disturbances would ensue among the poorer tenants. As a matter of fact, the Government in 1882 followed the advice of Mr. Parnell and passed an Arrears Bill—they were guided by the man whom his enemies regarded as an arch-conspirator, and more or less indirect dabbler in crime. But before Mr. Parnell's advice was adopted the state of Ireland was perilous in the extreme. One thousand men, many of them popular leaders, were in prison as suspects. There was a growing dread, shared by Mr. Parnell, who also was in gaol, that a great outburst of crime might take place. Members of the Government were feeling alarmed. And at last Captain O'Shea appeared as intermediary between them and Mr. Parnell. Sir Charles gave briefly the drift of the conversations between Mr. Parnell and Captain O'Shea, and of Mr. Parnell's earnest advice—"Drop coercion, pass an Arrears Bill, and don't trouble about our release, for that will come in good time." Captain O'Shea, said Sir Charles, was mistaken when he said that Mr. Parnell requested that some of his fellow-prisoners should be detained for a little while after his own release. Mr. Parnell's own account of the transaction differed from Captain O'Shea's.

Sir Charles Russell next referred to Captain O'Shea's assurance as to the frame of mind in which he found Mr. Parnell—a state of mind in which rancour had no part, but only an earnest desire for the peaceful settlement of the land question. At last, in the early part of May, 1882, Mr. Parnell was released. Mr. Davitt was released a few days later. Mr. Parnell's recommendations had, as already said, been accepted by the Government. The substitution of Lord Spencer and Lord F. Cavendish for Lord Cowper and Mr. Forster seemed to be the triumph of the constitutional policy of the Irish leaders. Lord Spencer and Lord F. Cavendish "went to Ireland bearing the olive branch in their hands, the first time it had been borne since there were Lord-Lieutenants in Ireland." "They were received with acclamations." "There was no hollow pretence" in the popular joy. The Irish people fully "recognized" the nature of the change that was taking place. Then came the Phœnix Park murders. "The most malignant enemy of Ireland could not have struck a more malignant blow." And these men, Mr. Parnell and his colleagues, whose policy was at last becoming victorious, had to bear the "hardship" of accusations against them of complicity in a foul and dastardly crime; the hardship of "public obloquy and opprobrium as hypocrites when they raised their voices in condemnation of those dastardly deeds." His contrast between the Parnellite position before the crime and after it—between the seemingly certain fulfilment of Mr. Parnell's policy of conciliation, and the shattering of his hopes by the atrocious and stupid murders of Phoenix Park—was effective in the extreme.

Recalling how Mr. Parnell, his health suffering from the shock, almost "yielded to despair," and to a determination to retire from politics, Sir Charles Russell came to the Phoenix Park manifesto, signed by Mr. Parnell and others. The manifesto was read out by Mr. Reid. "It is said," continued Sir Charles, that Mr. Parnell "signed this manifesto unwillingly. What authority has the Attorney-General for that statement? How does the Attorney-General know it?" And, then, Sir Charles Russell went on to pay some tribute of respect and admiration for the attitude which the English Press (with one exception) preserved during the excitement of the Phoenix Park murders. To the spirit of justice shown by the English Press towards Mr. Parnell and his colleagues at that critical time, it was, Sir Charles thought, due that the public mind was not dangerously excited against the Irish party. Sir Charles concluded his remarks on this period—the period between the suppression of the Land League and the rise of the National League—by showing how the passing of the Arrears Bill was followed by a large diminution in the number of the worst species of crimes.

The next part of Sir Charles Russell's speech dealt with the National League, founded in October, 1882, the rules and constitution of which were now read out in court. National self-government, extension of the franchise (Parliamentary and municipal), and the development of Irish agriculture and industry,—these were the main objects of the National League. The land question was to be settled by peasant proprietorship—the peasants to buy their holdings at a fair price, by the help of a State loan, repayable with interest in sixty-three years. The National League programme also included popular representation on the Irish Boards, the abolition of the Lord Lieutenantship, the improvement of labourers' dwellings, &c.|

But the Irish people, in whose interests all this was to be accomplished, were themselves insufficiently represented. Up to 1885 the proportion of Irish voters to the Irish population was ludicrously small as contrasted with the state of the popular representation in England. Sir Charles Russell quoted some striking figures in illustration of this. He had an object in all this. It had been said that the Irish people were terrorized by a small minority—the Nationalists, of whom the Parnellite party were the leaders. Sir Charles now showed, from the figures of the general election of 1885, how the Irish people, having attained to full and free Parliamentary power and responsibility, chose as their representatives, by tremendous majorities of thousands against hundreds, those same Parnellite tyrants. The Irish elections of 1885 were the expression of the free opinion of the majority of the Irish people. Does this, exclaimed Sir Charles Russell, afford the clue to Lord Carnarvon's policy of conciliation; and to the policy of a greater man than Lord Carnarvon?

The humaner and juster policy began in 1881 with land legislation, which, if carried out in full, would have changed the course of Irish history; it would have made the political question all the more easy of solution. As it was, the Irish party had done great service to their country. It is, exclaimed Sir Charles, because of their energetic service for Ireland's good that they are arraigned before your lordships. They may have done foolish things; they may have not always done the right thing at the moment, but they have vindicated themselves before the world. And to show how their conduct in the land agitation had been justified, he quoted the average annual reductions granted by the Land Courts since 1881—showing how the tremendous reduction in 1886-7 was necessitated by a fall in agricultural prices. Even good landlords, said Sir Charles, quoting figures, have been forced to give these great reductions —what of the bad ones?

The next topic was the Attorney-General's evidence connecting the perpetration of crime, and the payment of crime, with the League. The Attorney-General had named sixty-one persons (here Sir Charles read out the list) who had been "named" or denounced by the League, and who in consequence of that denunciation had been, according to Sir Richard Webster, subjected to intimidation and outrage of various sorts. But, said Sir Charles, in all the sixty-one, not one single case has been proved to be an instance of such connection. Sir Charles argued, generally, that only a sequence had been proved, not a consequence; that, in short, the Attorney-General's argument had been "after this, therefore, because of this." But there was not a single proof of the relationship of cause and effect.

Sir Charles intimated that he would call witnesses to disprove the Attorney-General's case—to prove that the League exercised a pacifying, moderating effect on the tenants. Meanwhile he rapidly surveyed the evidence given by such witnesses as Captains Plunkett and Slack. The former, when pressed in cross-examination to give his reasons for saddling the League with the responsibility for crime, could give none except his personal suspicions, and hearsay. Captain Plunkett argued that because the League was strong in this, that, or the other district, therefore crime was frequent; and that crime was frequent in the district because the League was strong. Considering that all Governments had been hostile to the League, was it not marvellous, Sir Charles asked, that they had never been able to get at incriminating details of the kind given by the informer Colman to Captain Plunkett? It is also a curious fact, continued Sir Charles, that the informers by whom Captain Plunkett and others were guided were in all cases members of secret societies.

As for Captain Slack, continued Sir Charles, his unrivalled experience extended over eight counties, yet, as evidence establishing a causal relationship between the League and crime, his evidence was "trumpery in the highest degree"; it was "a mere rubbishy collection" of stories. Sir Charles further illustrated his position by somewhat detailed references to the Attorney-General's evidence for Cork, Kerry, Mayo, Galway, Clare. The Hegarty boycott was bad, said Sir Charles—he would not defend it; but he showed that the president of the League branch was opposed to it, and held that, from the circumstances of the case, the Hegarty boycott would have happened if the League had never existed. More crimes of violence, including murder, had taken place in Galway than in any other county; but Galway has been in a state of exceptional distress. Confining himself to murders, Sir Charles himself selected one case, that of Luke Dillon. He pointed out that the man had been in the habit of carrying large sums of money with him, and that, on the other hand, Sir Richard Webster had not produced a tittle of evidence to connect the man's fate with the action of the League. As for the murder of Lord Mountmorres, Sir Charles intimated that he would produce witnesses who would show what manner of life he had led. The murder, said Sir Charles, was due to conduct on the part of Lord Mountmorres "over which I would willingly draw the veil;" it had nothing to do with agrarian or League disputes. In not a single case, repeated Sir Charles, has murder or complicity in it been brought home to the League, or to any single one of the persons who are charged. And he instanced the numerous cases in which the Attorney-General's own witnesses expressed their belief that the League had had nothing whatever to do with the crimes which it was sought to bring home to them.

SIXTY-EIGHTH DAY.

APRIL 10.

THE Curtin case and the Fitzmaurice case were the two chief instances which Sir Charles Russell selected to-day in his review of the evidence by which the Attorney-General sought to make the Land and National Leagues responsible for murder and outrage. Now, asked Sir Charles Russell, what is the true story of this sad case of the Curtins? Why, Sir Charles exclaimed, "the Curtin murder is not even included in the official police records of agrarian crime. If I am wrong, correct me," remarked Sir Charles Russell, turning round to the Attorney-General. But Sir Charles Russell proceeded on his way uncontradicted. The murder of Mr. Curtin had nothing whatever to do with the agrarian question, said Sir Charles. Mr. Curtin had no quarrel with the League. He was even a vice-president of the League. All that was known about the Curtin tragedy was, said Sir Charles Russell, the following : On one occasion a gang of moonlighters visited Mr. Curtin's house for arms. In November, 1885, the visit was repeated—probably by the same gang. Sir Charles thought young Mr. Curtin was the first to begin firing. He shot one of the moonlighters, who fired in return, killing Mr. Curtin, the father. Now, continued Sir Charles Russell, the president of the local branch of the League endeavoured to protect the Curtin family from the cruel boycott to which they were subjected. Mr. Davitt went from Dublin on the same errand. Mr. O'Connor, M.P., did likewise; and on the Sunday following the murder, the Rev. Father Murphy, a local priest, denounced the crime from the altar. And all the local branches of the League round about passed strong resolutions in denunciation of it. Such, said Sir Charles Russell, is the sum and substance of the Curtin story.

Coming to the Fitzmaurice story, Sir Charles Russell maintained that it afforded no more evidence of complicity on the part of the League than the Curtin story. James Fitzmaurice, the victim, had grabbed land from which his brother was evicted. This brother's name was Edmund. And Edmund, being homeless, found refuge in the house of a friend named Costelloe. After that Costelloe was "processed" by the land agent, Mr. Hussey—not, as the people in the neighbourhood believed, for non-payment of rent, but because he had shown some humanity to a sufferer. Sir Charles contended that the circumstances of that agrarian dispute were precisely of the kind to inflame the tenantry against the person whom they held responsible for them, namely, the landgrabber James Fitzmaurice.

Sir Charles next denied that the Land League paid for the defence of the prisoners accused of the murder; he pointed out that neither of the two, Hayes and Moriarty, who were hanged for this murder, was a leaguer; and that some of the witnesses attributed the murder, not to League action, but to family disputes. In describing the treatment of Costelloe, Sir Charles took the opportunity of showing what a heinous offence it was, in the eyes of landlords and agents, for a tenant to assist his evicted neighbour. He narrated the story of a child of ten years of age, to whom a woman had twice refused shelter (from fear of the landlord), and who next morning was found dead on her doorstep.

I have now gone over ten years' history of four counties, said Sir Charles Russell, and have shown that distress and crime have been interconnected. He cited, finally, the example of the district between Woodford and Loughrea, the most fruitful of crime in Ireland ; and why the most fruitful ? Sir Charles answered this by referring first to Chief Baron Palles's remark to the effect that Lord Clanricarde took a different view of right and duty to that entertained by the rest of mankind ; and next to the Chief Secretary's refusal to give Lord Clanricarde the military and police assistance to which he was entitled by the letter of the law.

Sir Charles next came to the evidence against the accused members, and the five others who were not members, namely, Messrs Sheridan, Byrne, Boyton, Brennan, and Egan. Of the sixty-five accused members Sir Charles first named twenty-eight, and asked their lordships whether they had in their minds any recollection of a single tittle of proof against them. Reading some more names, Sir Charles Russell declared that if this were an ordinary criminal trial the so-called evidence against these men would be regarded with utter contempt. Making a passing reference to Mr. Redmond's offence, he showed that it consisted in distribution of No-Rent Manifesto circulars. (In a later part of his speech, Sir Charles Russell reminded their lordships that "No-Rent" never was a part of the Land League policy; and that the manifesto was meant as a temporary expedient.) Much of the Attorney-General's case, continued Sir Charles Russell, consisted in the reading of speeches, some good, some bad, some indifferent, some—but proportionally a very small number—highly condemnable. But, said Sir Charles Russell, of the sixty-five members, there are thirty against whom no speeches whatever have been put in. Of the speeches that had been put in, he could not recall one which would be judicially regarded as an incentive to outrage. There were "Scrab Nally's" speeches. "Scrab" was not a member of Parliament. "Scrab," Sir Charles exclaimed, after one of his little pauses, "yes, *The Times* has made a hero of Scrab, and your lordships will learn by-and-by what Scrab's true position was." "Doctor" Tully was another intemperate orator and non-Parliamentary personage, of whom *The Times* had made much. That man's speeches, Sir Charles observed, were like "Scrab's," capable of an evil interpretation;" but he did not know of any offence which had been charged against Tully, except the delivery of a foolish speech. *The Times*, said Sir Charles Russell, has put in four hundred speeches in all; and out of these four hundred, only two speeches were delivered during the period when crime was at its worst — namely, from October, 1881, to the end of 1882—and of the two, only one was an Irish member's.

Having made that point about the two speeches, or one speech, Sir Charles proceeded to give a rapid survey of the Attorney-General's evidence against the five non-members already named. And first of Sheridan. He was accused, as a Land Leaguer, of having organized outrages in Western Ireland. "Give me one item of proof," exclaimed Sir Charles. "I say there is none." It is insinuated that Mr. Parnell in Kilmainham thought that Sheridan, who had got up outrages, could be used to put them down. I say, again, repeated Sir Charles, that for this statement there is "not an item of proof." The proof, derived from an informer's story, that bayonets and other arms were found in a smithy which Sheridan sometimes visited, Sir Charles dismissed with contempt. I should like to know the grounds, remarked Sir Charles, on which the informer Delaney declared that Sheridan was an Invincible. And he made a brief comment, significant more perhaps in its tone than in its substance, of the contrast between Delaney's directness of statement in his examination-in-chief—statements as of facts within his own knowledge—and his collapse under cross-examination. Apart from Delaney's story, there was, Sir Charles Russell said, no evidence that Mr. Sheridan had ever had anything to do with crime. As to Byrne, Sir Charles said that more would have to be said about him in relation to Mr. Parnell. But meanwhile he would observe that the accusations against Byrne were based on statements said to have been made by him in America, and upon the dock clerk Mulqueeny's story about knives found in Byrne's office in Westminster.

There was "no shadow" of evidence that Boyton was implicated in crime. As for Le Caron's story about Egan's story of Brennan's story about Mr.

Sexton, why Mr. Sexton would have something to say in the witness-box. And Sir Charles passed on to the evidence against Mr. Egan, which, he said, rested on the story of the messenger or clerk, of the Dublin Land League office, named Farragher, who said that he carried letters from Egan to Mullett, but who was "vague in his dates." The men who knew Egan best will not fear to answer for him before your lordships, said Sir Charles Russell; and he remarked that the American Government, at all events, thought sufficiently highly of him to appoint him its Minister in Chili. Had it not been for the "rotten foundation" of *The Times*' letters, exclaimed Sir Charles Russell in a tone of mingled anger and contempt, there would have been no case against Mr. Parnell and Mr. Egan.

Of Mr. Davitt, Sir Charles said that he would at the proper time speak for himself. But Sir Charles observed that Mr. Davitt had always openly avowed what he had done, and he spoke of his "straightforward," "manly" conduct in the cause which he believed to be just. Mr. Davitt has shown "enormous moral courage," said Sir Charles; he separated himself from the Fenian body in order to initiate constitutional methods, and he did it at the risk of his life.

As for Mr. J. O'Kelly, M.P., he will tell you himself, continued Sir Charles Russell, how he separated himself from the Fenian organization. With the exception of the fact that he occupied a high position in the Fenian Brotherhood, "there is not one tittle of evidence against him." As for Mr. E. Harrington, M.P., "I have seen nothing in his paper, *The Kerry Sentinel*, of which he need feel ashamed." Paying next a high tribute to Mr. Dillon's integrity and honesty, Sir Charles remarked, with a somewhat comically helpless gesture, "I don't know what is the evidence against him." As for the following five members, Mr. Maurice Healy, Mr. Lane, Mr. Deasy, Mr. P. O'Hea, and Mr. Gilhooly, the evidence against them was "childish and ridiculous."

Next he came to the charge against Dr. Kenny, M.P. There, Sir Charles said, was the only fact that in any way went to show that the League's central office in Dublin was implicated, directly or indirectly, with crime, or with any payments, real or supposed, in connection with crime. Sir Charles was referring to the letter which Horan, secretary of the Castleisland branch of the Land League, wrote to Dr. Kenny, requesting money for men who had been hurt in some illegal adventure. Dr. Kenny did send a cheque, "presumably in answer to that letter." Sir Charles Russell would not mitigate the importance of that letter; but, he said, it must be remembered that the cheque was sent when the League was in an extremely disorganized condition; and he added that Mr. Kenny himself and Mr. Sexton and Arthur O'Connor would go into the witness-box and tell their lordships that to their knowledge no League money was ever paid for the commission of crime or for the shielding of persons engaged in it. The very terms of the application to Dr. Kenny, said Sir Charles Russell, implied that this was the case, otherwise the money would have been asked for "as a matter of course." Mr. Biggar, said Sir Charles Russell, appears for himself. He will tell your lordships how and why, like Mr. Egan, he was expelled from the Fenian Brotherhood. Mr. T. M. Healy, also, would appear in person. "No man is better qualified to defend himself."

And now Sir Charles came to one of the most effective passages in his speech—his endorsement of Mr. John Morley's charge of "infamy" against *The Times*. It came about in his reference to *The Times*' evidence against Mr. Redmond. "What is the evidence?" Sir Charles said, dropping his voice, and turning round to Mr. Asquith. At this expression of perplexity, Sir Charles's audience—the "public" portion of it at all events—laughed. Then he turned round again, slowly, facing the judges. "I have no notion what the evidence is," said he, with a shake of his head. And then, all of a sudden he dropped, so to speak, upon the Manchester incident. Mr.

Redmond, when on his way to a meeting at Manchester, heard the news of the murder of Lord Frederick Cavendish. He announced it at the meeting. He expressed his horror of it, and in his dismay at the foul deed he caused the meeting to be adjourned. Next morning *The Times* declared that, though Mr. Redmond had expressed his feelings about the murder of Lord F. Cavendish, he did not say a word about the murder of Mr. Burke. But Mr. Redmond knew nothing about Mr. Burke's death. The terrible news came upon him by surprise, and he was under the impression that Lord Frederick was the only victim. This explanation Mr. Redmond forwarded without delay to *The Times*. *The Times* refused to insert it. Then Mr. Redmond made the explanation in the House of Commons. It was reported in the Parliamentary columns of the morning papers. But from *The Times* Parliamentary report the explanation was "deliberately omitted."

Here Sir Charles Russell stopped. He gazed for a moment or two at the spot where sat the manager of *The Times*. He began to say something. He stammered. One could hear a pin fall in the silence. But controlling himself, he uttered in a low voice the words which a distinguished statesman had made current—"nothing short of infamous."

After this judgment upon the conduct of *The Times*, Sir Charles Russell briefly alluded to the charges against Mr. Matt. Harris, Mr. T. Harrington, and Mr. T. D. Sullivan. As for the celebrated "partridge speech" of Mr. Harris, Mr. Harris himself, at the conclusion of his meeting, apologized for the words he used and explained what he really meant by them. It was untrue to say that Mr. Parnell was on the platform when Mr. Harris spoke. Then, turning to Mr. Harrington's case and the story told about him by the informer O'Connor, Sir Charles intimated that he would like to put the informer into the box again, so as to learn from him all the circumstances under which he confessed to the priest that his evidence in Court was a lie. Sir Charles read out the letter in which O'Connor told his brother that he "expected to make a few pounds over the transaction"; but that he could not unless he swore "queer things." I am afraid, said Sir Charles, that a good many persons have been making a few pounds out of *The Times* in that way. Sir Charles Russell then spoke about Mr. T. D. Sullivan, M.P., and of the universal respect in which he is held in Ireland. He himself, said Sir Charles, will describe to your lordships the career of his paper, *The Nation*, which opposed Fenianism, and which, in consequence, was abused by *The Irishman*, the paper belonging to "that wretched man Pigott" (another of those who made a few pounds by *The Times*). Against Mr. Sullivan, said Sir Charles Russell, there is "not a single tittle of evidence from beginning to end."

Having thus rapidly surveyed the charges against the Irish members, Sir Charles Russell addressed himself to the American section of his speech. In two or three introductory passages of great eloquence and pathos, Sir Charles dwelt upon the forced emigration of the Irish people, and of the now declining feeling of hatred of the American Irish against this country, as the fruit of "the misunderstanding, misgovernment, misrule of the past." Of the sixty or seventy millions of people in the States fifteen millions were of the Irish race. And the secret of their old feeling of bitterness might be understood from one of the first sights that met a stranger's eye as he landed on American soil.

"On the hill-side above New York," said Sir Charles Russell, "the emigrant's attention is drawn to a collection of huts, as miserable as any to be seen in Galway or Mayo. What are they? What is their history? What purpose have they served? My lords, they have served as squatting refuges for the wretched creatures who have been landed on the hospitable shores —for they have been hospitable shores to the Irish race—of America, but who, without the means to eke out their existence, have been compelled to seek refuge, until they could find employment, in these wretched homes."

There survive to this day, said Sir Charles, sad stories of the fate of Irish

208 Wednesday] *Diary of* [April 10.

emigrants in the New York hospitals, some wards of which were named after the landlords whose evicted tenants the patients had been—named after them in memory of the misery and the deaths of which these wards had been the scene.

In a passing allusion to the careers of the American Irish, Sir Charles quoted the declaration of the illustrious General Sheridan, of the Secession War, to the effect that if he lived in Ireland he would be a Fenian. The old spirit of the American Irish was evidenced in the fact that the American Fenian organization once upon a time counted two hundred and thirty thousand men. That has dwindled down to the small fraction of the Clan-na-Gael, and, said Sir Charles Russell, it is the boast of Mr. Parnell and Mr. Davitt that they have done this. Sir Charles then proceeded to relate how Mr. Davitt, when in prison, thought out his scheme of substituting constitutional agitation for violence, and how he preached his ideas in America in 1878, after his release from prison. Then Mr. Asquith read the declaration in which Mr. Parnell, previous to his first American journey, impressed upon his Irish fellow-countrymen the truth that their hope lay in co-operation with the English democracy, the English people. What is the central idea of this declaration? asked Sir Charles, after Mr. Asquith had done with his reading. Is it not a disclaimer of recourse to force? Is it not that between the peoples of England and Ireland there never has been enmity, but that it is English Governments that have been responsible for misrule? Mr. Parnell's policy, exclaimed Sir Charles, has borne fruit; the English people and the Irish people have been drawn together.

In America, said Sir Charles, Mr. Parnell delivered sixty speeches, and of these sixty *The Times* has cited only one, the famous "last link" speech. Yet, said Sir Charles, that expression does not occur in the reports of the newspapers of Cincinnati, where the speech was delivered. Mr. Parnell believes *The World* misreported him. But even if he had used the words, said Sir Charles, it is not Mr. Parnell's political opinions that your lordships have to decide upon. The result of Mr. Davitt and Mr. Parnell's tour was, said Sir Charles, the foundation of the American Land League. He read out its constitution—the suppression of rack-renting, creation of peasant proprietorship, organization of Irish tenant farmers.

Coming to Le Caron's story, Sir Charles treated with scorn the spy's account of the influence of the Clan-na-Gael, "the mere rump" of the old Fenian party. It certainly tried to "capture" Mr. Parnell's "open movement," but "it failed." However, Le Caron, "or Beach," showed this much, that the doings of the Clan-na-Gael caused Mr. Parnell endless difficulties in his endeavours to secure the triumph of open and constitutional methods. Then Sir Charles showed of what little use Le Caron was, even as a spy. "He was by no means the important person he claimed to be;" he had completely failed to give forewarning of such dynamite enterprises as those in which Gallagher and others were engaged.

Le Caron's interview with Mr. Parnell in the House of Commons? Why, Mr. Parnell, who would tell his own story in the witness-box, had not the smallest recollection of it. Mr. Parnell did not even remember having seen Le Caron. But Mr. Parnell admitted that Le Caron, "or Beach," might have been introduced to him as an American visitor, and that he—Mr. Parnell—might have expressed regret at the hostile tactics of the American Fenians. Mr. Parnell's whole career, said Sir Charles, has been against violence, against all revolution of the physical sort. As for Le Caron's story that Mr. Parnell had given him a commission to bring about an alliance between the revolutionary party and the constitutional party in America, and to send Devoy, or Sullivan, or any one over to Ireland, Mr. Parnell denied it point blank. He denied that he ever had any communication with these men or ever saw them.

"Le Caron!" exclaimed Sir C. Russell, "He is a living lie," who has subsisted by the betrayal of his friends.

At this stage Sir Charles made two of the best points in his great speech. At the very time, said Sir Charles, that Le Caron was supposed to be in communication with Mr. Parnell, the attitude of the Government was one of stern hostility to Mr. Parnell and his colleagues. The Ministry would have been only too glad to be put in possession of proofs of Mr. Parnell's complicity with the physical force emissaries from America. "Why did not Le Caron follow it up? Why did he not draw Mr. Parnell on?" Why did he not inform the Government whose spy he was? It was a damning admission that he did none of these things. Once more, Le Caron saw Mr. Parnell in May, 1881. By August, 1881, after Le Caron had returned to America, the "alliance" which he had been commissioned to effect was brought about. And shortly after that, this spy Le Caron wrote one of his "long-winded, secret circulars" about the secret Convention at which, as he now says, the "alliance" had been resolved upon. Yet, exclaimed Sir Charles Russell, this circular is "utterly and absolutely silent" on "this one cardinal point" of the Parnell alliance with the American party of physical force.

SIXTY-NINTH DAY.

APRIL 11.

SIR CHARLES RUSSELL to-day made further reference to Le Caron's statement that the "alliance" between Mr. Parnell and the American party of violence was effected at an American secret Convention in August, 1881. This meant that it was Mr. Parnell who allied himself with the physical force men—that the latter thenceforth "pulled the wires." But if such an "alliance" had been effected, what signs of its existence did the subsequent Conventions (of 1881-2-3-4-6) show? Sir Charles's answer was, in effect, that not even the shadow of any such sign existed; that the whole story of these conventions —as shown in the spy Le Caron's, "or Beach's," "long-winded secret circulars" to the English Government—demonstrated the very reverse of an alliance.

In spite of the great detail into which Sir Charles Russell entered, his rapid review of these successive annual Conventions was clear in the extreme. Beginning with the Chicago Convention of December, 1881, Sir Charles Russell quoted the instructions given to the United Brotherhood members as a proof that the open party and the secret party were still at war. At the next Convention, that at Washington, in the spring of 1882, resolutions were passed in support of Mr. Parnell's constitutional policy; the "Irish people seek no vengeance," was one of the expressions used in one of the resolutions, which also enjoined upon the Irish people the duty of abstaining from violence. The President of the Convention had nothing whatever to do with the "U. B." (United Brotherhood). And this same President also took the chair at the Chicago meeting. Moreover the Washington meeting was held at the time when Mr. Parnell and about one thousand others were still in prison as "suspects."

The next Convention was that of Philadelphia, April, 1883. Sir Charles Russell read out Mr. Davitt's reply to the invitation to attend this Convention —a very remarkable reply from a man whom Le Caron had described as being (together with Mr. Parnell) in alliance with the "U. B.," or party of violence. This reply, it should be explained, was sent from prison, where Mr. Davitt, by reason of a speech of his, was kept under lock and key; and some of his friends were apprehensive lest, partly in consequence of this arrest, some violent speeches might be delivered at the forthcoming meeting. That was why, in his reply, Mr. Davitt said there need be no fear of violent language at Philadelphia, and spoke contemptuously of the few who called themselves dynamitards. A dynamite war, continued Mr. Davitt in his reply, would be a war against the English democracy; it would arm public opinion against us; it would alienate from us the sympathy of all nations; and when "you hear of dynamiters in New York, you can take it for granted they don't represent us."

As to the report that Patrick Ford had joined the U. B., Mr. Davitt, in the same reply, said that he could hardly believe that Ford had "abandoned reason for Rossa." Is it not, exclaimed Sir Charles, the sheerest absurdity to suggest that the man who wrote that, and the party of whom he was a leader, were in "alliance" with the U. B.? And almost contemporaneously with this letter, continued Sir Charles, Mr. Parnell was in the House of Commons denouncing the party of violence. At this Philadelphia Convention, said Sir Charles Russell, there were eleven hundred delegates, only thirty or forty of whom belonged to the extreme party. At this time also, *The Irish World* was hostile to the Constitutional, or Parnellite movement.

Speaking yesterday, Sir Charles Russell was careful to point out that long before this date *The Irish World* ceased to be the medium through which contributions reached Ireland from America. Rossa, Boyton, Sheridan, and Byrne were at this Convention, but only "as spectators." Rossa was at the time "utterly discredited" by the constitutional organization in America. And Mr. Parnell himself telegraphed to the Convention expressing the hope that it would "frame its platform" in such a way as to justify the Irish party in accepting contributions from America. Passing over the Boston Convention of August, 1884, the story of which showed how powerless the "U. B.'s" were in comparison with the Constitutional party, Sir Charles Russell came to the Chicago Convention of August, 1886. Mr. Gladstone's Bill, said Sir Charles, had been defeated. Surely that Convention, then, afforded an opportunity to the U. B.'s to ridicule all such trumpery schemes for Home Rule. But what happened at this Convention? A vote of confidence in the wisdom of Mr. Parnell and of thanks to Mr. Gladstone and the English democracy. At this stage Sir Charles reverted, for a moment, to the extraordinary fact (upon which he had dwelt the preceding day) that Le Caron "or Beach," spy though he was, took no steps to inform the Government of his alleged talk with Mr. Parnell about an "alliance"; took no steps to "draw Mr. Parnell on"; made not the slightest allusion in his subsequent "long-winded" secret communications to this supposed alliance. But, said Sir Charles, the most crushing argument against Beach's story "is the history which I have just given your lordships of these American conventions." The Beach despatches relating to these conventions not only were silent on the subject of the alliance, but they also proved the unsuccessful effort of the U. B. to control the constitutional organization.

The above concluded the American portion of Sir Charles Russell's address. Now he came to the Invincible conspiracy and the forged letters. He treated them together, because, as he said, but for the forged letters Mr. Egan and the others would never have been accused of association with the conspiracy. The authority for including Egan, Brennan, and Boyton among the Invincibles was the testimony of the three informers, Mulqueeny, Delaney, and Farragher, and of Le Caron, who spoke only on hearsay. Sir Charles Russell showed how extremely small an acquaintance the informers had with the Invincibles, how "vague" their story was. Five men, said Sir Charles, were executed for the Phœnix Park murders. Many more—and he named them—were sentenced to long-term, or life, imprisonments. How came it that Delaney was the only Invincible among them whom *The Times* produced? "Because," exclaimed Sir Charles, "criminals though they were, they would not add perjury to their crimes." How was it that not one of these convicts, still living, had said anything to implicate the leaders of the constitutional movement? All that even Carey the informer, whose life had been a career of hypocrisy, could say was that the money the conspirators were alleged to have received came, according to one report, from America, according to others, from the Land League.

Then Sir Charles Russell passed on to the "letters." A more merciless criticism than his description and denunciation of the conduct of *The Times* has, perhaps, never been heard in a court of justice. One almost pitied the accusers as they sat under the lash. "Such recklessness," "I might almost say such criminal negligence," "persisted in rancorously"—with these, and like expressions, the court rang. "And even when the letters were discredited," thundered out Sir Charles, turning sharply upon *The Times* counsel, "even then they did not make that generous disclaimer, that absolute and complete withdrawal which would have been the act of common justice and common charity."

Merely because Mr. Parnell was "inactive," some "people were inclined to believe in the genuineness of the letters. They did not know Mr. Parnell. What Mr. Parnell cared for was the unmasking of the foul plot that led to the manufacture of the letters. "It will be your lordships' function to aid him; or, if it be not, he will pursue his task perseveringly, unrelentingly, until he exposes this foul conspiracy." As for Pigott—poor Pigott!—he could not be "accused of bringing voluntarily his spurious wares to the market." But he was in desperate straits for money, and his children were in want. "Then"— a pause,—"came the tempter"; and at the word Sir Charles, with his right hand stretched out, pointed at Houston, who, sitting in his corner seat near *The Times* people, changed colour, and looked as if he were trying to swallow a lump in his throat. Houston's conduct in destroying his Pigott correspondence was "that of a man knowing he was engaged in an infamous fraud." All *The Times* people "seemed to have lost their heads except Mr. Buckle, the editor," who passed Houston on to Mr. Macdonald. Then Mr. Macdonald came in for his share of description—Mr. Macdonald was a man who "swallowed wholesale, in spite of improbability," every story which told against the Irish members. *The Times* took no warning even from Houston's precaution not to guarantee the authenticity of the wares he was offering for "sale or return"—another of Sir Charles's cutting expressions. In the middle of last year *The Times* people knew that the alleged letters came from Pigott; and from October last they were aware of Pigott's interview with Mr. Labouchere and others, and of accusations made against Pigott to the effect that he was the forger; yet they took no pains to inquire how Pigott came by the letters. Then Sir Charles retold, with a grave humour, Pigott's legend of the black bag, and of Pigott's being accosted in Paris by "Murphy," whom he did not know, and by "Tom Brown," whom he did not know, and of Pigott's taking an oath, "on his knees," before other people whom he did not know. But mark the oath. Pigott was not to divulge names before a court of justice. Why that reference to a judicial inquiry? asked Sir Charles Russell. Pigott's last letter from Paris was, Sir Charles held, an indication that Shannon knew of Pigott's intention to run away. And the Pigott telegram, signed Rowland Ponsonby, from Madrid, was in his estimation a proof of pre-arrangement. The letters case having broken down, the accusers, Sir Charles said, might have withdrawn from their general case, which, in fact, was destroyed through its sheer extravagance. They had then their opportunity of showing they were not "filling the role of pertinacious, rancorous opponents." "But no, the vials of wrath must be poured out to the last dregs upon the head of the Irish party."

SEVENTIETH DAY.

APRIL 12.

BEGINNING at half-past ten o'clock, Sir Charles Russell ended at half-past twelve his speech for the accused, the greatest and most impressive speech ever delivered on the subject of Ireland. The subject, of which the style has been in every way worthy, has raised this speech entirely beyond and above the ordinary forensic sphere. The history of English law and justice offers no parallel to Sir Charles Russell's task, whether we regard the unique character of his position or the greatness of the cause committed to him. His task is the defence of a nation. The advocate has become merged in the patriot and the statesman.

Sir Charles Russell began with a rapid survey of the charges made by *The Times* against the Irish leaders. The first of them was that the Irish leaders had based their movement on crime, not stopping short even at the line of murder. Had not the accusers spoken of the enforcement of the high decrees of secret conclaves with the bullet and the knife? Yesterday, said Sir Charles Russell, when dealing with the letters, "I felt that I was flogging a dead horse." But "take those letters away, and what becomes of the accusers' evidence?" Among the alleged members of the supposed murderous "conclave" were Messrs. Sheridan, Egan, Brennan, against whom no proof whatever had been produced. Mr. Brennan, for example, was, as Sir Charles Russell again repeated, imprisoned in May, 1881, nearly six months before the supposed formation of the murderous society (the "Invincibles" of Phœnix Park), and he was released on the 16th of June, 1882, after the murder. Making a passing reference to the Attorney-General's conduct of *The Times* case, Sir Charles remarked, with a wave of his hand, that even Le Caron himself, in his "disgust" with the manner of the prosecution, came forward to put *The Times* people straight. The second of the charges, continued Sir Charles, was that the Irish leaders took no steps, either by word or act, to stop outrage: to which Sir Charles replied by reference to the general counter-testimony given in his speech during the last two or three days. Constable O'Malley, the police reporter, one of *The Times*' own witnesses, had attended hundreds of Nationalist meetings; and his testimony was that the presidents, or chairmen, generally condemned lawlessness. As to the third charge, that if condemnations of outrage were made they were hypocritical, Sir Charles Russell cited against *The Times* the evidence of their own witness, Mr. O'Shea.

The fourth charge was that no cause save League agitation could possibly, could conceivably be alleged in explanation of the disturbances and crimes since 1879. Sir Charles Russell's reply to this charge—his lifting of the veil which the Attorney-General dropped over pre-Land League Ireland—was in many respects the most important part of his speech. It contained a history of the Ireland of the Nineteenth Century—a history the clearest, the most consecutive, and compact. As for the fifth charge, habitual payment of Land League funds for outrage, there was not, said Sir Charles, glancing at his arguments of the preceding days, a tittle of evidence. Summing up what he had formerly said about the sixth charge—that Mr. Parnell was aware that Sheridan was organizing outrage in the West, Sir Charles passed on to the seventh—that the Invincibles were a branch of the Land League. The forged Egan and Carey letters were, said Sir Charles Russell, the only ground for this accusation. We pass over the eighth, which was, that Mr. Parnell knew of the Invincible plots, which the Attorney-General said he did not mean to advance, but which, Sir Charles argued, was implied in *The Times* case. The ninth and last was that Mr. Parnell had sent Byrne a hundred pounds to enable him to escape from justice. Here, again, Sir Charles summed up rapidly, lucidly, what he had previously said on that matter, showing how the payment was one of the ordinary open, "straightforward, and thoroughly innocent transactions" between the richer League in Dublin and the poorer, and often impecunious League in London.

Having thus rapidly surveyed the nine charges to which his six days' speech had been an answer, Sir Charles Russell came to his peroration. "Your lordships," said he, "are trying the history of a ten years' revolution in Ireland," and "you are trying it at a moment when, by the legal process of the Queen's Courts" (the Land Commission Courts) "the Irish people are gathering the fruits of that revolution." And here he paused for a moment to pronounce a generous eulogy on the principal actors in that revolution. "They have done marvellous work—marvellous in the face of the difficulties they have had to contend against." When these leaders began their work, ten short years ago, the Irish peasant stood tremblingly before the landlord, agent, bailiff; to-day "he stands erect, and becomes a free citizen in a free country." In ten years, Irish secret organizations have given place to "constitutional means of redress." despair to buoyant hope, distrust of England to feelings of friendship, and—in England itself—indifference to Ireland, to heartfelt interest in her fate. "I have come, my lords, to the end." Slowly and with frequent pauses, and in tones that would have hardly been audible but for the deep stillness, Sir Charles spoke under strong emotion. He stopped when he spoke of the land of his birth; and again when he said that in defending Ireland he was serving the best interests of the country, England, where his laborious life has been passed. Once, and once only, his voice rang out, loudly, almost fiercely, and that was when, turning suddenly round, he exclaimed, "to-day the position is changed; *We* are the accusers;" and then, pointing to the representatives and counsel of *The Times*, "the accused are there."

Here are the last sentences of the speech. The reader will note the skilful touch in the word repay:—

"I have spoken not merely as an advocate. I have spoken for the land of my birth; but I feel, I profoundly feel, that I have been speaking to, for, and in the best interests of England, of the country where my years of laborious life have been passed, and where I have received kindness, consideration, and regard, which I should be glad to make some attempt to repay. My lord, my colleagues and myself have had a responsible duty, we have had to defend not merely the leaders of the nation but the nation of Ireland itself. We have had to defend the leaders of the nation whom it was sought to crush, to defend the nation whose hopes it was sought to cast down, to dash to the ground. This inquiry, intended as a curse, has proved a blessing. Designed, prominently designed to ruin one man, it has been his vindication. In opening this case I said that we represented the accused. My lords, I claim leave to say that to-day the positions are reversed—we are the accusers—the accused are there (pointing to the representatives of *The Times*). My lords, I hope this inquiry at its present stage and in its future development will serve more even than as a vindication—that it will remove painful misconceptions as to the character, the actions, the motives, the aims of the Irish people and of the leaders of the Irish people; that it will set earnest minds—and, thank God, there are many earnest and honest minds in this land—thinking for themselves on the question; that it will remove grievous misconceptions and hasten the day of true union, of real reconciliation between the people of Ireland and the people of Great Britain, and that there will be dispelled, and dispelled for ever, the cloud, the weighty cloud, that has rested on the history of a noble race, and dimmed the glory of a mighty empire."

"A great speech worthy of a great occasion," were the words of a message which Sir James Hannen, dashing off on a piece of paper, passed down to the speaker.

SEVENTY-FIRST DAY.

APRIL 30.

AT three minutes past the half-hour, Mr. Asquith, rising, called out, "Mr. Parnell." This was a surprise to the spectators, who expected that Sir Charles Russell would conduct the examination-in-chief. However, the honours of the day fell to the cross-examiner of *The Times* manager, and Sir Charles Russell sat quietly following his distinguished junior's performance. Mr. Parnell looked fairly well, as he stood up in the witness-box. He certainly was in good spirits. During the five-and-a-half hours' questioning Mr. Parnell remained on his feet, not showing the slightest symptom of fatigue. In that time he gave a clear, connected, and interesting sketch of his career, from his birth, only forty-three years ago, to the foundation of the National League at the end of 1882.

Heir to a name famous in Irish history, and to a high social position, Mr. Parnell, escaped from college, might have stepped at once into some prominent place in Irish politics. The country life of Avondale had a greater attraction for him. He did not trouble himself about parliamentary matters. He took some share in the local affairs of his county, Wicklow ; and, for the rest, he read Irish history, and kept an outlook, at a pleasant distance, upon the brawling world of politics. But in those quiet Avondale days, from about 1868 to 1874, the political ideas of the future leader of the Irish party and people were taking definite form and shape—crystallizing themselves. He was enthusiastic enough to cherish an ideal, and his political ideal was that of Gavan Duffy and the men of '48.

The first great political event which determined the future of Mr. Parnell's political career was the Ballot Act of 1872. Here at last were the means of the liberation of the Irish peasant from his ancient thraldom under the landlord. No longer need the Irish peasants allow themselves to be "driven to the poll like sheep"; no longer shall the landlord have it in his power to rack-rent, drive forth into the world the tenant who dares exercise his rights of a free citizen. "Driven to the poll like sheep"—Mr. Parnell pronounced the words with some emphasis. Mr. Parnell, replying to Mr. Asquith's questions, passed rapidly over the history of his first connection with Mr. Butt's Home Rule League, one of the members of which was Mr. Patrick Egan, of whose honesty and ability I, said Mr. Parnell, formed "a high opinion."

In 1875-6, and in Parliament, Mr. Parnell still occupied what the Americans call a "back seat." But, as usual, he was watching the course of affairs. And he told the Court, in his quiet, mater-of-fact, unimpassioned manner, what he thought of Isaac Butt's followers ; most were "lukewarm," others were "ready to take office at the first chance." After a string of questions about Mr. Parnell's connection with the Dublin Amnesty Association and other matters, Mr. Asquith paused, as if he had something important to say. "Now, Mr. Parnell, were you ever a member of a secret society?" Mr. Parnell also paused. Deep silence in the court. "Yes," said Mr. Parnell, and he paused again, exciting much curiosity. "I belonged to the Foresters' Society," quoth Mr. Parnell; and Mr. Parnell's audience laughed outright. The President smiled. So did Mr. Justice Day. "As for another secret society, the 'I.R.B.,' I never joined it," said Mr. Parnell, "and I was never asked." Mr. Asquith "put in" a list of the Irish measures which the Home Rule Leaguers, otherwise the Buttites, endeavoured, unsuccessfully, to pass through Parliament. Mr. Asquith's object in putting in these documents was to demonstrate the constitutional character of the Irish movement from its beginning. Mr. Parnell described very briefly the origin of the Parnellite party, paying a high compliment to the "sterling character" and "straightforwardness" and the patriotism of Mr. Biggar, one of the two or three who were its first members. He described how he gave a new direction to the work of Irish members in the House of Commons by plunging with them into Imperial questions; and how humane reforms in prison discipline and army and navy discipline were the results. Next he narrated how in the years 1877-8-9 he began to study hungry and ragged Ireland with his own eyes—away west in Mayo. "I travelled through miles of the finest land without seeing a house or meeting a human being," said Mr. Parnell, but I found a congested population on the poorest lands. But, added Mr. Parnell, when we proposed remedial legislation the Irish Secretary of the day, Mr. Lowther, "pooh-poohed the whole thing." According to Mr. Parnell's brief account of the foundation of the Land League, he was at first disinclined to join Mr. Davitt in the enterprise, for this reason, among others, that he rather disapproved of any course of action which might render the leaders of the movement responsible for "every foolish act of the local branches." Next Mr. Parnell entered into the details of his American trip. He went to America in 1879 with Mr. Dillon, to collect money for the distressed districts, which, as already said, he visited in person.

Here Mr. Parnell entered upon a very interesting part of his story, flatly contradicting Assistant-Adjutant-General Le Caron at every step. It is utterly untrue, said Mr. Parnell, that as soon as I reached New York I called upon Patrick Ford. "I have never met him in my life," said Mr. Parnell, smiling. Was it true, as Le Caron said, that Mr. Parnell's tour was entirely in the hands of the Clan-na-Gael? "False," said Mr. Parnell, in his quiet way; "my tour was in nobody's hands." Mr. Parnell's story of his tour was, in some passages, amusing. There was no organization at all, said Mr. Parnell, "we had to complain of the want of it;" and he described how in their geographical ignorance Mr. Dillon and himself often passed by large towns where they might have spoken to advantage. On one occasion, owing to want of organization and of help, Mr. Parnell and his companion had to retrace their steps over a journey of a thousand miles the day after a meeting.

Here Mr. Parnell produced a map to show how erratic, in consequence of the lack of co-operation from the Americans—revolutionary or otherwise—had been his trips over the American continent. According to Le Caron's statement the tour was carefully "bossed" from beginning to end. According to Mr. Parnell's interesting narrative, the tour was an unaided, un-"bossed," higgledy-piggledy (to quote an expression of Sir Charles Russell's) peregrination. We went "by instinct," said Mr. Parnell. The Cincinnati "last link" speech? The Attorney-General said that if Mr. Parnell had not delivered that speech, Mr. Parnell would not have been listened to in America. But Mr. Parnell, standing in the witness-box, declared that he had addressed forty meetings before he delivered the Cincinnati address. In the second place, Mr. Parnell declared he had no recollection whatever of the "last link" expression. "I don't believe I used it. It was unlike anything I ever said or thought. I could not find the expression in *The Cincinnati Gazette*, the newspaper of the very place where the speech was delivered. The expression only appeared in *The Irish World*, in New York, a thousand miles away, and at the meeting *The Irish World* had no reporter." The words, said Mr. Parnell, repeating himself, "are entirely opposed to anything I ever said or thought; if I did use them, they must have been largely qualified by other matter."

Mr. Asquith asked Mr. Parnell about a circular telegram which he sent from Montreal to New York, inviting people to meet him there on his return journey to Europe. Mr. Ford in transmitting the telegram to various parts in America wrote about the "glittering banner of the party," and about "keeping the ball rolling." But all that, said Mr. Parnell, with a smile, looking at the Ford telegram, which professed to be a copy of the Parnell original, is "journalistic padding." The Conference which met in New York on Mr. Parnell's invitation was the origin of the American branch of the Land League. "There is no truth whatever," said Mr. Parnell, "in the statement that I left our interests in the hands of Patrick Ford." He next described how he collected sixty thousand pounds in America for the relief of Irish distress. "All the proceeds from my own meetings," he continued, went without an exception, to the relief of the distress of which the Government of the day took no notice. Half a million pounds were collected in America and Australia, and elsewhere for relief, to which, said Mr. Parnell, you may add half a million from relatives in private remittances to their friends in Ireland. At last the Government moved in the matter, but too late, and more in the interest of the landlords than of the peasants.

Then came a portion of Mr. Parnell's evidence, directly contradicting *The Times* accusation that the League was in association with Fenians and other physical-force people at home. He described how he and his friends were attacked by the I.R.B.'s in Wexford in the general election of 1880, and again at the Rotunda meeting in Dublin, April 30, 1880. The Rotunda platform was stormed by the Fenian party. Mr. Parnell explained what Mr. Davitt intended by asking the Rotunda meeting to give one of the Fenian speakers a hearing. It was because the speaker in question undertook to go away quietly if he were allowed to speak. According to the prosecution, Mr. Davitt's action was evidence of collusion with the party of violence.

Coming to the troubled times of 1880-2, Mr. Parnell recalled to mind how Mr. Davitt, returning from America (end of 1880) drew his attention to the increase of crime in the poverty-stricken districts, and how the League issued a circular (produced in court) warning the peasants against the commission of outrage. Mr. Davitt's imprisonment in that period, Mr. Parnell described as a grave mistake. Here Mr. Parnell stopped and paid his warm, generous tribute of admiration to Mr. Davitt. "He was the one man," said Mr. Parnell, "whose history and antecedents gave him the claim and the power to control his countrymen." One might have noticed that there was a tremor in Mr. Parnell's voice as he spoke about his friend and fellow-patriot. He glanced for an instant at the spot where Mr. Davitt was sitting.

Mr. Davitt's imprisonment was not the only misfortune that befel the party. All the principal leaders of the movement were put in prison. One result of this was disorganization in the offices of the Land League. The clerks, said Mr. Parnell, did what they liked. There was no responsible head over them. That, said Mr. Parnell, accounted for the unsatisfactory condition of the League books during a period of the League's existence. As for his own imprisonment in Kilmainham, one notable thing he did there was the issue of the No Rent manifesto. This subject led to an examination of Mr. Parnell's alleged communications with the party of violence while he was still a prisoner. It was "utterly untrue" to say he was visited by Eugene Davis in the disguise of a priest, or that he sent out instructions for co-operation with the I.R.B., or that any correspondence passed between him and Egan planning assassination, and payment for the same.

All the charges about sanctioning outrage in Ireland and plotting the death of Mr. Forster and a number of prominent officials, Mr. Parnell repudiated with a few simple words, more expressive of indifference than of contempt. He said he had never even heard of the Invincibles before the Phœnix Park trials of 1883. It was "quite a mistake" to allege that he had advised the retention of Mr. Davitt in prison at the time of the release of the suspects. And Mr. O'Shea was, he said, wrong in stating that he had advised the continued confinement of Mr. Brennan. He contradicted Mr. O'Shea's story that he, Mr. Parnell, adopted the Phœnix Park manifesto, because it was necessary to flatter Mr. Davitt's vanity. "I regarded the Phœnix Park murder," said Mr. Parnell, impressively, "as the greatest possible calamity which could befall our movement." He expressed the opinion that the murderers were, possibly, Americans. Mr. Parnell also contradicted Mr. O'Shea's story of his asking for police protection. "I never had police protection," Mr. Parnell remarked. He shook his head, by way of saying he knew nothing about the letter in which Mr. Burke was said to have got no more than his deserts. But it is unnecessary to pursue this subject. Enough to say that Mr. Parnell denied the construction put by the prosecution upon the Byrne cheque, and that he explained why he sent it. Le Caron's stories were answered in the same way. Mr. Parnell could neither recollect the name nor the appearance of Major Le Caron. "Entirely imaginary. . . . I never said nor thought it, even in the worst period of coercion," said Mr. Parnell, when asked whether he told Le Caron that he had ceased to believe in any cure but force. "Never sent a message by him to America," "never thought of such a thing." "It was not my habit to give my photograph away," he said, in reply to other questions. But, said Mr. Parnell, "I think this is my genuine signature." He explained that people often sent him his photograph with a request that he might return it with his signature attached. All this while, Le Caron was in court.

SEVENTY-SECOND DAY.

MAY 1.

"THIS was quite a revelation to me ; I would on no account have sanctioned such a payment," was Mr. Parnell's answer to Mr. Asquith's question about Mr. Timothy Horan's letter to the central office of the Land League in Dublin in September, 1881. Tim Horan was secretary of the Castleisland branch of the Land League, and it was stated in the earlier part of the trial that he applied to Dublin for money wherewith to pay men engaged in an illegal transaction, and got it. In his opening speech Sir Charles Russell explained this payment from the central office in Dublin by saying that during the period in question the central office was in a state of disorganization in consequence of the imprisonment of the chief leaders and the absence of others of them in Paris. In consequence of the arrests there were frequent changes in the central office staff. Mr. Parnell made a similar explanation in his earlier evidence. The payment, he said, must have been made during the illness of Mr. Sexton, who was acting as secretary. And to-day Mr. Parnell declared that Mr. Egan could not have been responsible for the payment, because Mr. Egan was at the time in Paris. In further reference to this subject of League money, Mr. Parnell said that, as far as he knew, none of it was devoted to the "Spread the Light" mission of *The Irish World* in Ireland. "I would not have permitted it." Nor was Mr. Parnell aware that any copies of *The Irish World* were posted from the Land League Dublin office for distribution in Ireland. "*The Irish World* had a fund of its own ;" and as for its correspondent in Ireland, he was not a member of the Land League, he even "attacked us, and called us opprobrious names." If, added Mr. Parnell, there was any posting of copies of *The Irish World* from the League office, it must have been during the period of disorganization, when, as he formerly remarked, there was no responsible supervision, and the clerks did what they liked. One other statement of Mr. Parnell's about *The Irish World* is that after May, 1882, no money was sent through that journal to the League in Ireland, "so far as I knew. And in February, 1883, I said, during a debate in the House of Commons, that Patrick Ford's aims and hopes were not mine." As to other Irish Americans with whom—as at the Conventions of Philadelphia, Buffalo, and other places—the League leaders had communication, Mr. Parnell stated that, as far as he knew, no prominent member of the Land and National Leagues in America ever was a dynamiter. As for O'Donovan Rossa, said Mr. Parnell, his influence ceased as soon as the Constitutional movement began in America. But before that, Rossa undoubtedly did possess influence—dating from the Irish Fenian period (1865), and owing to what he himself had suffered for what he deemed to be his country's service.

Mr. Asquith now came to the last section of his examination-in-chief, that concerned with the various "funds" collected in America, and published in *The Irish World*. The Mitchell fund, collected for the widow of one of the most distinguished of the '48 men? Mr. Parnell knew nothing of it. Nor of the "Skirmishing Fund"—except that it came to a close even before the Land League was founded. Nor of the "Spread the Light Fund," except that its object was to stimulate the circulation of *The Irish World* in Ireland. One half of the Land League fund did come through *The Irish World*, said Mr. Parnell; some of the Constitutional party in America objected to transmission through that paper, but, said Mr. Parnell, "I did not feel at liberty to refuse. His object was to associate Irishmen all over the world in the Constitutional movement. About the O'Donnell defence and the martyrs' testimonial funds he knew nothing. And now, said Mr. Asquith, for the whole of this movement from its beginning in 1879 to the present day, have you to the best of your ability honestly endeavoured to conduct it within Constitutional lines and within the limits of the law? Here is Mr. Parnell's reply: "I can say that I have honestly endeavoured to conduct it within the limits of the Constitution and the law, and have endeavoured to keep it free from crime. I will, however, make this exception with regard to the technical offences with which we were charged in Dublin at the State trials of 1880. We were charged with inciting the tenants not to pay their rents, and if that be an offence against the law we admit it; and if the same thing came over again we should do the same thing again."

At twenty-five minutes past eleven o'clock Mr. Asquith ended his examination-in-chief. The Attorney-General was up in an instant. Until four o'clock (except during the usual half-hour's interval) he displayed an energy, a warmth, a liveliness, and occasionally a (little) temper that were in striking contrast with his manner during his previous conduct of *The Times'* case. There was just one other contrast equally striking, and that was Mr. Parnell's imperturbable coolness during Sir Richard Webster's performance. The warmer and more impatient grew Sir Richard, the more blandly, smilingly, deliberately did Mr. Parnell give his replies. It looked as if Sir Richard Webster, smarting under the *fiasco* of the letters, had made up his mind to punish Mr. Parnell somehow.

Sir Richard Webster came to close quarters at once by asking Mr. Parnell—with reference to one of his statements in his examination-in-chief—whether he seriously meant to say that he had never heard of the Clan-na-Gael as a "murder club" until he heard Le Caron's story about them. That is "absolutely" true, said Mr. Parnell, with a smile. And it was "perfectly" new to him (another smile) that the Clan-na-Gael programme contained a "dynamite" policy. How would Mr. Parnell explain the paragraph in the very first number of *United Ireland*, August 13, 1881 (nearly eight years before the advent of Le Caron) in which "the scattered Clan-na-Gael" threatened a death-sentence against every evicting landlord? The paragraph was Rossa's "warning to landlords," extracted from *The Irish World;* and *United Ireland*, just then established, was the organ of Mr. Parnell and the League. "I never saw that paragraph," said Mr. Parnell, "I knew nothing of it;" and then, in his quiet way, he pointed out that the expression "scattered Clan-na-Gael" meant simply the "scattered Irish race"—another expression in *The World* extract, and not a definitely constituted association. [Clan-na-Gael means, in English, "children," or race, of the "Gael," or Celts.]

Then the Attorney-General tried Mr. Parnell from another direction. Mr. Parnell had said that from May, 1882, *The Irish World* became hostile to Mr. Parnell's policy. Was that so? Yes: *The World* became hostile at the time of Mr. Parnell's release from Kilmainham, and because of his withdrawal of the No-Rent Manifesto. But in that case, how, Sir Richard asked sharply, could Mr. Parnell account for the fact that the Irish League continued to receive funds from *The World* long subsequently to May, 1882. Sir Richard planted his palms on his hips, and paused for a reply. The reply came, in the usual way, slowly, and with one of Mr. Parnell's pleasant smiles. Such payments must have come from remote branches of the American League, which branches were unaware of the change in *The World's* policy; the contributions came "filtering" in as before, and Mr. Ford, as a matter of course, must have sent them on to Ireland. "Old sums in hand" must have been coming in, said Mr. Parnell, "but the policy was changed all the same."

Sir Richard again returned to the charge. Could Mr. Parnell quote a single article of *The Irish World*, a single expression which justified his statement that *The Irish World* became opposed to him after May, 1882. Not having the advantage of the Attorney-General's knowledge of *The Irish World*, quoth Mr. Parnell, he could not give any quotations right off; but, doubtless, he would be able to discover some in the files of the paper. Here Sir Richard Webster warmed up, and from that moment, for an hour or two, most of the cross examination was a sort of single combat around these two points—challenge to Mr. Parnell to produce articles or expressions in *The Irish World* showing the alleged hostility to him from May, 1882; and challenge to say whether or not the League continued to receive from 1882 to 1886, thousands of pounds from *The World* for its Parliamentary fund. Sir Richard Webster pounded away in the style of an Old Bailey practitioner. Mr. Parnell maintained his composure. "It is a surprise to me," said Mr. Parnell, if there have been any such receipts, *The Irish World* did not collect anything for the Irish Parliamentary party. The question and answer were repeated, the Attorney-General challenging Mr. Parnell to swear, and Mr. Parnell simply replying that he knew nothing of an *Irish World* Parliamentary fund. The chief statement which Sir Richard Webster took as the base, so to speak, of his attack on Mr. Parnell was Mr. Parnell's declaration in the House of Commons in 1886 that for the past five years *The Irish World* was hostile to his policy. Sir Richard was always challenging Mr. Parnell to produce his proofs, and Mr. Parnell repeated as persistently his answer that, not being a regular reader of *The Irish World*, he did not carry the details of its articles in his head, but that, with a little time to look up old files, he would be sure to unearth a good many.

Then Sir Richard Webster tried to confute Mr. Parnell out of the mouth of Mr. Davitt—who, by the way, appeared to be considerably amused at the course the cross-examination was taking. In October, 1885, Mr. Davitt published in *The Irish World* itself an article in which he praised the "unparalleled services" of *The World* to the Irish Land League, and declared that "the first inspiration of the movement and most of its financial strength came from *The World*." What of that? asked the Attorney-General. Mr. Parnell replied that he did not agree with Mr. Davitt's estimate of *The Irish World*, and that the "chief inspiration came from the Irish people themselves." But warm and brusque—angry, sometimes—as was the Attorney-General, he only once made use of a harsh expression. "Untrue" was the word. He said he would produce articles and extracts from *The Irish World* which would show Mr. Parnell's statement (that *The World* was hostile to him since May, 1882) to be "untrue." But in other parts of his cross-examination, Sir Richard Webster made use of the less ambiguous adjective "incorrect," or its equivalent. To show the incorrectness, he read articles of *The Irish World* in support of the Messrs. Redmond, when they were on a political tour in America. While the reading was going on Mr. Reid rose to say that Mr. Redmond denied the accuracy of *The Irish World* reports.

Then Sir Richard returned to his contributions. Was Mr. Parnell aware that since May, 1882, the writer known as " Transatlantic " of *The Irish World* had contributed a pound to the Parliamentary fund? No, it was new to Mr. Parnell; but, remarked Mr. Parnell with a smile, "I am glad to hear he did." At this there was a little burst of laughter in court, which did not improve the Attorney-General's temper. And what about a contribution from *The Irish World* (50 dollars) in 1885? Mr. Parnell explained that that must have been a personal contribution from Mr. Ford himself, in his satisfaction at the overthrow of the Liberal Government in 1885, and the prospect of the concession of Home Rule by the Tories. Several times during his cross-examination Mr. Parnell said that in 1885-6 Mr. Ford's policy of hostility began to change again into one of friendliness. The Attorney-General, leaving America and Patrick Ford, returned to Ireland and the Fenians. He questioned Mr. Parnell about the "landlord garrison" whose expulsion was to be the first step to Irish independence. Mr. Parnell said that when he spoke of driving out the landlords he only meant landlordism—the system, not individuals. The landlords, said Mr. Parnell, are popularly known in Ireland as the English "garrison." I never wished, he repeated, for more than Parliamentary independence. And all the stories about a coalition between the open and secret organizations for the purpose of effecting independence were "absolutely untrue." In his replies to Mr. Asquith Mr. Parnell mentioned the Enniscorthy and Rotunda meetings as instances of Fenian hostility to the open movement. But now Sir Richard Webster challenged Mr. Parnell to name any other instances showing opposition between Leaguers and Fenians. Mr. Parnell replied that he mentioned those two because he himself had personal experience of them; and that on inquiry he would be able to find other instances. Besides, he said, the stronger the League grew the fewer became the physical-force party's opportunities to create disturbance.

After this there followed, and lasted until four o'clock, when the Court adjourned, a fusillade of questions over the whole field—questions about trips to America, trips to Ireland, Mr. Davitt's speeches, Scrab's speeches. Sir Richard severely cross-examined Mr. Parnell about his alleged meeting with a mysterious Fenian at Queenstown, when Mr. Parnell was starting on his American tour. Nothing definite came of it. Nor did Mr. Parnell remember anything whatever about a supposed meeting between him and Mr. Davitt and an American Fenian, at which the plan of the future Land League was laid down. Nor could Mr. Parnell tell whom Mr. Davitt saw in America. He saw "hundreds"—"thousands" of people, perhaps. The audience laughed and Sir Richard grew angry.

Mr. Davitt never discussed the plans of his American tour with me, said Mr. Parnell. Had Mr. Parnell ever repudiated "Scrab's" "utterances"? Never heard much about "Scrab's" utterances, said Mr. Parnell, smiling. "Scrab" tried to get in at the tail-end of meetings, and nobody attended to him. "I had something more important to do than to watch Scrab," quoth Mr. Parnell. Mr. Parnell gave the same answer in respect of the orations of a certain Malachi Sullivan. Mr. Parnell made very light of Malachi. Then the Attorney-General read a fearfully long manifesto signed by American Fenians whom Mr. Parnell met in America—not knowing them to be Fenians.

Mr. Asquith here mildly asked whether it was necessary to read all that. "I was thinking the same," remarked the President. And again the audience laughed. But Sir Richard solemnly said he must read it. Now, Mr. Parnell, will you say you have never seen that manifesto? " Never seen or heard of it," says Mr. Parnell, with an expression of surprise. Again the spectators laughed. The President smiled. Then came a story of the American, Mike Kennedy, who, at one of Mr. Parnell's meetings in the States, handed him "five dollars for bread and twenty for lead." "Was not that expression repeated all over Ireland, as an argument for physical force?" exclaimed Sir Richard, with tremendous emphasis. "Yes; by your side," retorted Mr. Parnell, bowing. "What do you mean?" "The Tory party in Ireland."

SEVENTY-THIRD DAY.

MAY 2.

ARE you quite sure, the Attorney-General asked Mr. Parnell, on resuming his cross-examination, that you did not know before 1885 that Mr. Joseph Nolan was a member of the "extreme," or physical-force party? Mr. Parnell was sure of it; he first heard of Mr. Nolan's Fenianism at the time of the appointment of the Select Committee to inquire into the admission of strangers into the House of Commons. Then Mr. Parnell was questioned about Alexander Sullivan. It was from the spy Beach, or Le Caron, that Mr. Parnell first heard that Sullivan was a member of the Clan-na-Gael Society. In other words, he could not have known it during his American tour, when Sullivan made arrangements for some of Mr. Parnell's meetings. Moreover, said Mr. Parnell, it was not true that Sullivan accompanied Mr. Parnell and Mr. Dillon over the States; "we arranged our own meetings;" but Sullivan may have arranged three or four meetings in the north-west. Condon, one of the American Irish who organized the Parnell reception at Washington, was said to be a member of the Clan-na-Gael; but whether he was or not Mr. Parnell did not know. As for Mr. Finerty, Mr. Parnell described him as a violent person and "a notorious dynamite orator." This Mr. Finerty was an organizer of the Parnell demonstration at Chicago. And now Sir Richard Webster pounced upon Mr. Parnell. If that was Mr. Parnell's opinion, why did he write to Finerty congratulating him upon his election to Congress, and describing it as a great boon to the Irish cause? Mr. Parnell answered, in his quiet way, that he wrote the letter in December, 1882, before he was aware of the facts which led him in February, 1883, to denounce Ford and with him all dynamiters, in his speech in the House of Commons.

The Attorney-General wanted to know if it was true that John Devoy was associated with Mr. Davitt in establishing the Land League. Mr. Parnell never knew that he was. If Devoy had been associated with the heads of the League, the fact would have been awkward for the League, for Devoy was accused of threatening a member of the Cabinet. And now it appeared that, having heard of the plot, Mr. Parnell telegraphed to America, "You are reported to have sent a threatening telegram to the Home Secretary. If true, action most censurable; if untrue, cable contradiction." It was Sir Charles Russell who suddenly produced this telegram in Court—the Attorney-General rather warmly objecting, but intimating that he would reserve his "action on that cable."

The Attorney-General now came to a more interesting subject—Mr. Parnell's sins of omission, as the prosecution regards them. Had Mr. Parnell kept his followers in check, and condemned outrages and inflammatory speeches and newspaper articles? Yes, said Mr. Parnell, in his easy manner, he had remonstrated with his M.P.'s when their discretion failed to keep pace with their tongues. There was Mr. William Redmond, for example; and Mr. Parnell pointed in a careless way, and with a good-natured smile, to Mr. Redmond, who sat on the front bench, much interested in hearing himself summed up by his chief. "I looked upon Mr. Redmond as being a very enthusiastic, sincere young man—perhaps rash." Here Mr. Parnell, stroking his beard, and fumbling about among his papers, proceeded to observe, in a sort of soliloquy which greatly amused his audience, that "it was hard to put old heads on young shoulders, but that that was a fault which time usually remedied if people lived long enough." Over the smiling face of Mr. Redmond there passed the blush of ingenuous youth.

So much for checking intemperate speech. What about outrages? "Did you ever in Ireland denounce outrage?" exclaimed the Attorney-General, folding his arms and leaning his back against the bench. "Yes, certainly," replied Mr. Parnell; and Mr. Parnell, producing a pamphlet (a collection of his speeches), from his black bag, looked up the denunciatory passages. He read extracts from speeches at Bala, Swynford, Castlereagh, New Ross, and other places in the year 1879 and subsequently. His hearers were admonished to act "within the law and the Constitution;" "above all, to abstain from acts of violence, and to remember the teachings of Mr. Davitt;" to remember that "the land movement was peaceful and constitutional."

Having done with his extracts, Mr. Parnell remarked that had he been then aware (latter end of 1880) that crime was so largely on the increase he would have spoken much more strongly against outrage. Though Mr. Parnell returned from America in March or April of 1880, it was the month of September before he crossed over to Ireland. And it was Mr. Davitt who told him how outrages had been increasing. In one of the speeches he delivered at this time in Ireland Mr. Parnell drew a picture of what the state of distressed Ireland would then probably be if, as in the case of the famishing Ireland of 1846, there was no organization of the tenants: outrages and evictions would be much more numerous. Mr. Parnell claimed for the League of 1879-80-81 the credit of two great services to Ireland—prevention of the assassination of landlords, and prevention of evictions. In this part of his cross-examination Mr. Parnell produced the manifesto which in February, 1881, the Irish members issued against crime: "Fellow-countrymen,—We adjure you to maintain the noble attitude that has already secured your ultimate victory. Reject every attempt to lead you to conflict, disorder, or crime."

At this stage Sir Richard Webster's most combative form of challenge— the "Now, sir," with the admonitory, rapid shake of the forefinger, and the somewhat excited manner—became frequent, and all the more noticeable because of its contrast with Mr. Parnell's imperturbable calm. Had not Mr. Parnell planned a No-Rent manifesto long before his arrest? No. But Patrick Ford declared that the manifesto was ready months before Mr. Parnell's arrest? If so, Mr. Ford said what was untrue. But Mr. Egan distributed a manifesto all over Ireland at the end of 1881? The Attorney-General read it out. "A very condemnable manifesto," said Mr. Parnell; "but I was in prison when Mr. Egan issued it, and my colleagues and I sent Mr. Egan instructions to withdraw it, which I believe he did." Mr. Parnell admitted that he did not condemn it on his release, but, he said, by that time the matter had blown over. But there were other publications in which Mr. Parnell was interested—articles in *United Ireland* and in *The Irishman*. The Attorney-General read out many extracts from the early numbers of *United Ireland*, and Mr. Parnell admitted that they were too strong, and that if he had been the writer he would have expressed himself differently. In several of these extracts Mr. Parnell indicated the parts he did approve. For example, "the destruction of Irish landlordism;" he himself desired the destruction of Irish landlordism, meaning the establishment of a peasant proprietary at fair terms for the landlords. But then there was *The Irishman*. And Sir Richard Webster read out a very long series of extracts of a more or less violent character, some of them extremely violent. One of these extracts called Carey, the informer, "a hypocrite and cunning coward," and Brady, one of the Phœnix Park murderers, "a sincere, lionhearted enthusiast." "Do you approve of that?" Sir Richard asked. "I do not," was the answer. "Exaggerated," "I don't think that that is a proper article," "undoubtedly violent," "highly objectionable," were some of Mr. Parnell's comments on the Attorney-General's extracts from *The Irishman*. But Mr. Parnell was a shareholder of this very *Irishman*? Yes, but *The Irishman*, which lasted only a short time after the establishment of *United Ireland*, was, said Mr. Parnell, a paper which, "though disreputable, was mischievous to our cause; had I known that such and such articles were appearing in it, I would have asked its editor to alter the tone; we let it die a natural death. We bought *The Irishman* for the simple reason that we wished to terminate Mr. Pigott's journalistic career in Ireland." As Mr. Parnell said this, he bowed slightly and smiled at Mr. Attorney.

SEVENTY-FOURTH DAY.

MAY 3.

MORE extracts from *The Irishman*, followed by the Attorney-General's stock question—What do you think of that, Mr. Parnell? And Mr. Parnell's reply, "reprehensible," "unjustifiable," or some equivalent word. As Mr. Parnell repeatedly explained, with just an indication of boredom and in a variety of ways, *The Irishman* was a paper to which he did not attach any importance. He caused some amusement by remarking that he regarded *The Irishman* as "a *damnosa hereditas*" from poor Pigott. Two corrections which he wished to make in his evidence of the preceding day showed how little knowledge he had of *The Irishman* and its articles. In his evidence of the previous day, he stated that *The Irishman* died a natural death in about a year after the establishment of *United Ireland*. But since four o'clock of Thursday afternoon Mr. Parnell learned that *The Irishman* survived for a couple of years longer. Again, in his evidence of Thursday Mr. Parnell said that Mr. W. O'Brien was the editor. But in the interval Mr. Davitt pointed out to him his mistake: Mr. James O'Connor was the editor. Said Mr. Parnell, *The Irishman* was kept going solely for the purpose of giving O'Connor something to do: and once upon a time Mr. Parnell requested that the "*damnosa hereditas*" should receive its *coup de grace*. "I assure you," said Mr. Parnell, addressing the Attorney-General, who was very severe, "I assure you I knew nothing about the policy of *The Irishman* at that or any other time. I suggested that it should stop when we had organized *United Ireland*. . . . I assumed my wishes had been carried out. I did not attach importance to it at any time."

The Attorney-General asked him if it was not the case that in *United Ireland*, which was the organ of the League, there appeared paragraphs of the same stamp as those of the paper (*The Irishman*) which he repudiated. I must compare the files, replied, in effect, Mr. Parnell. However, Mr. Parnell admitted at once that there did appear in *United Ireland* articles "stronger than he approved." Whereupon the Attorney-General wanted to know why he did not control or separate himself from, or repudiate Mr. W. O'Brien and his works. The general drift of Mr. Parnell's answers under this head was pretty much the same as that of his answers on the same subject the day before —when he said that all the members of the Land League did not think alike. Both Mr. Dillon and Mr. O'Brien, for example, held more advanced views than Mr. Parnell himself did. As for "publicly repudiating" the *United Ireland* articles, Mr. Parnell explained—or, rather, remonstrated—that that was not his way of dealing with his colleagues. Mr. Parnell declared that he considered he did quite enough when he privately remonstrated against extravagant expressions, and showed by his own public utterances that any such expressions did not represent his own personal views.

And do you then disapprove of the use of physical force in support of the aims of the Irish party? asked Sir Richard Webster. "Most undoubtedly," answered Mr. Parnell, with great deliberation, "I have always disapproved of it from the first time I entered public life. I have always thought that physical force was useless and criminal. If the constitutional movement fail— of which there is no present prospect—I should have to consider whether I should not quit public life." But were Mr. Dillon's speeches always constitutional? Had Mr. Parnell made himself acquainted with Mr. Dillon's speeches? "I have never made a practice of reading anybody's speeches," quoth Mr. Parnell, smiling, "except my own"—an answer which was received with a burst of laughter throughout the court. However, said Mr. Parnell, "I have on several occasions taken grave exception to things which Mr. Dillon said, and have remonstrated with him." Among the other Leaguers about whose utterances the Attorney-General questioned Mr. Parnell was Mr. Redpath. Mr. Parnell admitted at once that Mr. Redpath did deliver violent speeches. "Some of them," said Mr. Parnell, were violent and reprehensible, but they were limited in number.

In the afternoon portion of the sitting Mr. Parnell was questioned principally about his views of the relationship between crime and secret associations, and about the disappearance of the League books. If, as the Attorney-General said, Mr. Parnell held that secret societies caused crime, why did he in the debates of 1881 allege as an argument against the passing of the Coercion Act that secret societies no longer existed? Because, Mr. Parnell replied, he wanted to defeat the Bill; "I was trying to mislead the House so as to cut away the ground from the feet of" the Government. "I believed," said Mr. Parnell, after another question or two, that the League did put down secret societies, but I exaggerated." The Leaguers, he added, could put down the secret societies by influencing the class of discontented small tenant farmers from which the societies were recruited. As for the missing books of the League, he had been unable to trace them. Egan, he believed, had some in America, but he thought they were unimportant. Mr. Parnell had asked Dr. Kenny, Mr. Campbell, and Mr. Harrington about them, but they could give him no information. But he had not inquired from Mr. A. O'Connor, Phillips, or Moloney. Mr. Moloney was the person in whose possession the books were believed to have been last seen. "We attribute great importance to the production of these books," said the President; and Mr. Parnell said he would renew his endeavours to find them. Nor, said Mr. Parnell, was there any trace of what had become of the letter-books, the cheque-books, and counterfoils.

Tuesday]   *the Parnell Commission.*   [*May* 7.   225

SEVENTY-FIFTH DAY.

MAY 7.

AFTER the staggering effect which Mr. Parnell's frank and famous declaration of last Friday produced in the minds of many excellent people, it was generally expected that to-day's proceedings would open with an explanation by Mr. Parnell of what he really meant to convey. The explanation was made as soon as he entered the witness-box. What he said on Friday was that, in the debate of February, 1881, he deliberately used a misleading argument when he maintained that the secret societies which the proposed Coercion Bill would put down, did not exist. That is to say, not having the context of an eight-year-old speech in his mind when the Attorney-General quoted the passage about the non-existence of secret societies, Mr. Parnell, on the spur of the moment, made that extremely candid admission. But since Friday afternoon Mr. Parnell looked over the February speech; he discovered what the particular secret societies were which he then alleged to be no longer in existence—they were, as he now explained to the judges, the Ribbon Societies, which, as a matter of fact, had been crumbling away for some years before 1881. " At the date of the February speech they were," added Mr. Parnell, "practically non-existent. That was a fairly accurate representation of the state of existing affairs, so far as I knew them, and not a misleading statement made either intentionally or otherwise." "You must take the context of my speech," said Mr. Parnell, at a later stage of his cross-examination by the Attorney-General, "I was comparing the state of Ireland in 1881 (as regards secret societies) with its state years before." On Friday afternoon Mr. Parnell said, and he repeated it yesterday, that in 1881 he expected a fresh devolopment of secret organization, as a result of Coercion. A further reference to this matter will be found in its proper place—in Sir Charles Russell's re-examination.

The misunderstanding having thus been cleared up, the Attorney-General returned to the subject of payments from League funds—one of the most noteworthy of which was the payment of 100 guineas for the defence of a number of people accused at the Cork Assizes, in 1881, of moonlighting. Speaking generally of such applications of League funds, Mr. Parnell said he would approve of them if he thought that the law was "strained unduly," or that the accused were innocent; and he mentioned a particular case in which, after his release from Kilmainham, he paid out of his own pocket for the defence of a man whom he believed to be innocent and who finally was acquitted.

This led to a long series of questions about Mr. Parnell's cheque payments, Mr. Parnell answering them bank-book in hand and with a bundle or two of counterfoils and returned cheques beside him. The payments were to Mr. Biggar, Mr. T. P. O'Connor, the Messrs. Redmond, Mr. Boyton, Mr. W. O'Brien, and a great many others whom it is needless to enumerate. The hundred-pound cheque to Mr. Boyton was to enable him, after his release from Kilmainham, to furnish his house in London, Mr. Boyton being "in distress" at the time. It was a gift from Mr. Parnell—not a farthing of it from Land League funds. It now appeared that Mr. Parnell paid away, for the open public work of the League, hundreds upon hundreds of pounds, thousands even, from his own private means, when the League funds were low. "I paid that;" "it has never been returned to me;" "it had nothing to do with League funds"—Mr. Parnell was .constantly saying in reply to Sir Richard Webster. It may be said, in passing, that the inquiry into these financial transactions threw a most interesting and pleasant light upon the personal relations between the leader of the Irish party and those connected with him.

Next followed a series of questions about the relations between him and certain

16

persons outside the Parliamentary organization, more particularly Mr. Egan and Mr. Patrick Ford. "I have never heard," said Mr. Parnell, "that Mr. Egan joined the Clan-na-Gael; had he done so I should have regretted it." And then, he added, with that simple frankness which impresses his audience as much as his imperturbable calmness, "but I would have considered it natural," under the circumstances of the time, such as the suppression of the League. As for certain speeches which Ford attributed to Mr. Parnell, and which Sir Richard Webster now read out in Court, Mr. Parnell declared, bluntly, that Ford always "twisted" his speeches, "designedly," and put ideas into them which their author never meant to convey. There was one speech in particular, the warlike, sanguinary passages in which Mr. Parnell declared to be the work of the reporter's imagination.

The Attorney-General's cross-examination ended at ten minutes past one. Sir Charles Russell's re-examination, which immediately followed, turned exclusively upon Mr. Parnell's relations with *The Irish World*. The Attorney-General had cited comparatively recent receipts from *The Irish World*, in disproof of Sir Charles's former statement that the contributions through the medium of *The Irish World* ceased in May, 1882. And Mr. Parnell, replying to Sir Charles Russell, now proceeded to explain. The contributions from May to October, 1882, through *The Irish World*, were those which continued to be received from remote parts of America until the donors became aware of Ford's hostility to Mr. Parnell. When, in consequence of the Parnellite victories at the end of 1885, Ford reverted to his old policy of friendship, *The World* became, once more, the medium of contributions to the League funds; the first acknowledgment of a contribution was on the 26th of December, 1885. In the interval—summer of 1882 to end of 1885—Ford was steadily assailing Mr. Parnell and his party. The Attorney-General had maintained that Mr. Ford and the Parnell party were associated. And now, for nearly two hours, Sir Charles Russell read *Irish World* articles, in which Mr. Parnell's policy was described as "Parliamentary tomfoolery," "Parliamentary farce," and Mr. Parnell's followers as persons without "brains" or "patriotism." Ford furiously attacked the Arrears Bill, which Mr. Parnell was so anxious to carry through. And he denounced Mr. Parnell's policy of a peasant proprietary— "my settled policy," said Mr. Parnell, and "now the settled policy of the State." "Without the Arrears Bill," said Mr. Parnell, "any attempt to put down crime would have been useless," and he took the opportunity of emphasising the explanation which he made at the beginning of the day's proceedings. He explained that though Ribbonism and Fenianism had ceased to exist as organizations by the year 1881, there were isolated groups which, if an Arrears Act was not passed, would be sure to be recruited by young men from the very class of farmers which the Act was intended to pacify and benefit. Mr. Parnell stated that at one time the American branch of the Irish Land League contained a million and a half members. Ford's attacks, said Mr. Parnell, weakened the League for a while; but in time those who had withdrawn from the League "came round again," and Patrick Ford with them.

SEVENTY-SIXTH DAY.

MAY 8.

SAID Mr. Parnell, "not counting those at unimportant places, I delivered about sixty speeches in the course of my American tour; and of the sixty only four or five have been put in by the Attorney-General." Of the three hundred set speeches delivered by him in Great Britain and Ireland from the beginning of the agitation until now the proportion selected by the prosecution was still smaller. The very first speech he delivered in America—which was in Madison Square, New York—struck the keynote of all the speeches that followed. In that speech Mr. Parnell said that not one cent of the money collected during his tour would be devoted to the purpose of encouraging armed resistance in Ireland. He said this because he understood that a great many of his fellow-countrymen in America favoured, not recourse to constitutional agitation, but appeal to force. Mr. Parnell was next asked by Sir Charles Russell what he had to say about Le Caron's description of the members and chairmen of the reception committees. Le Caron, it will be remembered, thought that this, that, or the other committeeman was perhaps respectable enough "for America." Mr. Parnell, whose turn now it was to speak, thought the men who received him were "respectable" enough for any society. At any rate, they kept their "gig." They turned out in their coaches to do honour to their visitor. City Corporations offered him their hospitalities. Generals in the great war, ex-Governors of States, ex-Ministers to European courts, local legislators, men of science, men of letters, University professors—in short, representatives of all the intelligent and "respectable" classes of America were found upon the Parnell reception committees, or otherwise engaged in according him a public welcome. In some towns the militia marched and paraded, and in Chicago Mr. Parnell received the freedom of the city. Was it true that the chairmen of these committees were members of the Clan-na-Gael? The only ones whom Mr. Parnell believed to be members of the society were Mr. Condon and Dr. Carroll.

This ended the American part of Sir Charles Russell's re-examination, and Mr. Parnell was asked some questions about League work and expenditure, and bookkeeping in Ireland. On his return from America, it was arranged between him and Mr. Davitt that Mr. Davitt should proceed to the West to denounce the outrages which, as Mr. Parnell learned from his friend, were on the increase. Here Sir Charles Russell read out numerous extracts from speeches of Mr. Davitt's, in which outrage was strongly condemned. But, as Mr. Parnell here explained, mere denunciation of crime would have been fruitless among a people situated as the Irish peasantry then were; and he and his fellow-leaguers relied less upon denunciatory speeches than upon proselytism, so to speak, from secret association to the ranks of the open association, the Land League. And, added Mr. Parnell, we always did our best to get the local Catholic clergy and other influential people to take the lead in this open movement. All the Parnellite party worked openly and above board. "My firm belief," said Mr. Parnell, "is that no member of our party who formerly was a member of the Fenian Brotherhood ever re-entered the society after he joined our ranks."

Of the opposition which at that time, end of 1880, he experienced from the physical-force party, he gave a curious and amusing instance from Blarney, in Cork. On his way from Blarney to Killarney he was stopped by the physical-force men, who carried revolvers. A fight followed between them and Mr. Parnell's friends, and the latter were allowed to continue their march only when they surrendered "two hostages" to the enemy. At this part of the story our old friend " Scrab's " name was re-introduced. After he was told about Scrab's conduct at League meetings, Mr. Parnell gave instructions that he should not be allowed to speak at them, whereupon the flow of Scrab's oratory ceased. Scrab's figure has been flitting across the scene since October. Perhaps we have seen the last of him.

Then there followed some questions about cheques, bank-books, League cash-books, letters, &c. "Your lordships," said Mr. Parnell, "are perfectly welcome to any letter I have ever written or ever received." He explained the nature of certain payments which in his cross-examination by the Attorney-General he could not at the moment account for. Among them was a five-pound cheque payment, about which Sir Richard Webster made inquiries the day before. In the interval Mr. Parnell found out all about it. "My subscription to the Wicklow harriers," said Mr. Parnell. The President smiled, and the Court laughed.

Sir Charles Russell having finished his re-examination, Sir Richard Webster rose to put a few more questions which in the interval had suggested themselves to him. Mr. Parnell had spoken about the constitutional character of his American speeches, and about anti-outrage speeches in Ireland. What about a speech which, as was reported, he delivered in Liverpool shortly before he started on his American tour, and in which he said that one hundred thousand swords would leap out of their scabbards to defend Irish independence? Mr. Parnell remembered nothing about the swords and scabbards. Nor did he know anything about the alleged Fenian antecedents of certain persons who seemed to be his prominent supporters at the Liverpool meeting. Of one such person he remarked that the only warlike accounts he had ever heard of him were about his experiences in the Franco-German war. This, and a similar answer about the warlike qualities of some one else, rather irritated Sir Richard Webster. Not satisfied with Mr. Parnell's evidence regarding the monetary transactions of the League, the Attorney-General suggested that a sworn affidavit should be taken of all financial documents, pass-books, cheque-books, &c., in Mr. Parnell's possession, and bearing upon this investigation. Sir James Hannen preferred that these documents should first be examined by the Clerk of the Commission, in conjunction with Mr. Asquith, representing the defendants, and Mr. Graham, representing the prosecution. Mr. Parnell, while complaining that the Attorney-General had selected only a very few instances which appeared to suit his purpose, expressed his readiness to answer any question about any payment whatsoever. Sir Charles Russell promptly backed up Mr. Parnell, and remarked upon the "injustice" of the Attorney-General's procedure. To this criticism the President warmly objected. Sir Charles, as warmly, replied that he would maintain his opinion that Mr. Parnell should there and then be allowed to do as he wished—to "explain the whole matter." "I submit, in fairness, it ought to be done," said Sir Charles. "We think it ought not to be done now, but at a more convenient period," retorted the President, sharply. The further consideration of this point was postponed, the President once more remarking that Mr. Parnell should make an affidavit of all the documents in his possession.

Then Archbishop Walsh entered the witness-box. He was examined by Mr. Reid, Q.C. But Mr. Reid had not proceeded far when the President intervened. Mr. Reid's questions were designed to elicit the Archbishop's opinion on the question as to whether such an organization as the Land League was required under the circumstances of the time in Ireland. As the Archbishop said, his very position in the Church, his relations with the clergy—who were at the head of the movement all over Ireland—necessitated his acquiring full information, and forming careful opinions on the subject. Sir Henry James objected that the Archbishop's opinion was not what the Court wanted, but the Archbishop's knowledge of facts upon which to base his opinion. Mr. Reid retorted that the landlords and agents who had appeared as witnesses for *The Times* were allowed, and even invited, to state their opinions as to the results of League agitation. And he quoted, as cases in point, the evidence of Mr. Leonard, and the evidence of Captain Slack. Mr. Lockwood pressed the same argument, adding that a witness of the authority of Archbishop Walsh should have the same liberty of stating a general opinion in reply to a general question, which had been enjoyed by the landlord and agent witnesses. Mr. Biggar also struck in, "I have been from the beginning a constant student of these proceedings, and have observed that similar evidence has been given by the hirelings of the Government." "I cannot allow such an expression as that," remarked Sir James Hannen. "Then I will say officials," returned Mr. Biggar. "I maintain that if such evidence as this is not allowed on our side, the whole inquiry will be a farce." "Well, you have not assisted us," remarked the President, quietly. Their lordships adjourned for a few moments to consider the case. On returning, the President decided that his Grace's opinion—without preliminary facts stated in court, on his Grace's own knowledge—was inadmissible as evidence. But the matter was, Mr. Reid declared, of such serious import to the defence, that, in consequence of their lordships' decision, he must ask for an adjournment in order that he might consult with his colleagues and reconsider his position. The court, therefore, was adjourned at half-past three o'clock.

SEVENTY-SEVENTH DAY.

MAY 9.

THE cause of outrages, the influence of the League, the ethics of boycotting (a slippery subject even for the subtlest priest), were the themes of Mr. Reid's examination and Mr. Atkinson's cross-examination of Dr. Walsh, Archbishop of Dublin. The theory of the prosecution is that crime followed the foundation of the League, as naturally as the fruit its seed. That's not it, says the Archbishop; crime was the offspring of eviction—and eviction, according to the theory of the defence, was the penalty of inability to pay rack-rent.

Did the League denounce crime? It did, said the Archbishop. He was very positive on this point. And what was more, the League did succeed in putting crime down. "I think so, decidedly," said Dr. Walsh. Dr. Walsh credited the League with the new interest which eight or nine years ago the Irish peasantry began to feel in Parliamentary politics. At the beginning of this period, said the Archbishop, the people were generally indifferent—they seemed to have lost all hope in constitutional action. But the League changed all that—such, at any rate, was the Archbishop's belief. He had known only one instance, in his diocese, in which a local branch of the League acted, he would not say criminally, but foolishly, and perhaps dangerously. This was the Clondalkin branch, in the suburbs of Dublin; and its offence consisted in a proposal to publish a "black list"—that is to say, a list of persons who were not members of the League. This was at the end of September, 1885. Dr. Walsh immediately communicated the news to Mr. T. Harrington, and, said Dr. Walsh, the matter was no less promptly taken up at headquarters—in "O'Connell Street." O'Connell Street is the patriotic name for Sackville Street—which one renowned traveller, at least, has called the finest street in Europe. When you hear a Dublin "boy," or any other Irish "boy"—lay or ecclesiastic—say O'Connell Street instead of Sackville Street, you put him down for a Nationalist of the Nationalists.

The foregoing was the substance of Dr. Walsh's answers to Mr. Reid. And now Mr. Atkinson tried what he could make of his Grace. The Archbishop's impressions about secret societies corresponded with Mr. Parnell's. But did the League act as constitutionally as the Archbishop alleged? Did not the League "prohibit" the peasantry going into the Land Courts created under the Land Act of 1881? The League "advised" them, replied Dr. Walsh, with a polite little bow, and proceeded to say that events proved the wisdom of the advice. What about the strong rhetoric of *United Ireland* and *The Irishman*? Was it constitutional? The Archbishop declared frankly, just as Mr. Parnell had done before him, that there were things in *United Ireland* which he did not approve. The Archbishop did not like its "intemperate personal attacks;" but, said he, "I do not read *United Ireland* regularly." As for poor Pigott's old paper, *The Irishman*, he was surprised to learn from Mr. Parnell's evidence that *The Irishman* survived so long as it did. "Approve of its articles?" Mr. Atkinson asked. "Approve! Oh, no!" exclaimed his Grace, sharply; "they were abominable. The teaching of *The Irishman* was at variance with the teaching of the League."

Did his Grace approve of boycotting persons who took evicted farms? Here Mr. Atkinson entered upon the delicate—at a later stage in his cross-examination he called it the "metaphysical"—part of the agrarian question. The Archbishop was ready with his distinctions. "Eviction? What sort of an eviction do you mean, Mr. Atkinson? a just one or an unjust one? And "boycotting"—what sort of boycotting?" "Come, come, your Grace; I mean what's commonly called boycotting." "But many things are commonly called boycotting in Ireland," quoth his Grace. If Mr. Atkinson meant by boycotting a form of intimidation, then his Grace was strongly against boycotting. He would ever condemn it. But boycotting without intimidation— boycotting as a form of "exclusive dealing"—was another thing. And then the Archbishop introduced a distinction even as to exclusive dealing. To sum up several answers on this head, his view was that the boycotting, without intimidation, say of persons who profited by "unjust" evictions, was not a crime, but a means of preventing crime.

Father O'Connell, who followed Dr. Walsh in the box, had for years been parish priest in one of the poorest districts of Connemara. He came from Letterfrack, county Galway, and many of his parishioners lived on the estate of Mrs. Blake, of Connemara, the clever witness who gave her evidence in the earlier part of this trial. Father O'Connell sketched rapidly, and with quite sufficient vividness, an Irish "interior" in his poverty-stricken parish— the wretched cabin, the food of potatoes or of boiled seaweed—"a slow poison," he called it—even the "sacks" in which the family slept, without any other covering. Father O'Connell had anything but a flattering account to give of clever, energetic Mrs. Blake. Help her tenants in their distress at the time they were kept alive by famine funds? No, "quite the contrary." What did he mean by "quite the contrary?" asked Mr. Lockwood, who was examining him. "Why," said Father O'Connell, "she used (1878–1882) to take a third of their kelp which they fished out from the sea." (Here he described how the Connemara folk dragged in their seaweed.) Not until October, 1880, was a branch of the Land League established in that quarter of Connemara, and Father O'Connell thought it was then high time to establish one, because he was "perfectly certain" that many of Mrs. Blake's tenants were unable to pay their rents. It was Father O'Connell himself who drew up the tenants' memorial.

In the earlier part of the trial it was stated by a *Times* witness that the League branch used to meet in the house of Mrs. Walsh, the mother of the young man who was executed on a charge of having murdered a man named Lyden. This Father O'Connell emphatically denied. "The story was absolutely false." As he showed, in his cross-examination by Sir Henry James, this branch of the League had little more than a nominal existence— "it never even met." As to the other persons who were tried on the charge of conspiracy to murder, Father O'Connell either denied that they were Leaguers or said he knew nothing of the matter. As he had already said, the branch was little more than nominal. This was more fully explained in the cross-examination by Sir Henry James. To him Father O'Connell described how the Lyden murder was denounced by Father McAndrew, president of the branch, and how he himself had denounced from the altar another murder, that of a man named Cavanagh. He could not account for the murders. All he could say was that the crimes were sincerely condemned by his parishioners. "There was not among them the slightest sympathy with the murderers;" on the contrary, "they were extremely shocked."

Then Father Considine, of Ardrahan, county Galway, gave a like testimony as to the effect produced in his parish by the murder of the land agent, Mr. Burke, which murder, he said, was perpetrated in June, 1882, after the suppression of the Land League, and six months before the foundation of the National League. Father Considine described how "I said mass for Mr. Burke's soul"—the ordinary Sunday mass—before the whole congregation; how immediately after service a public meeting was held "in the house of God" to express public detestation of the crime. Another glimpse of Irish life.

SEVENTY-EIGHTH DAY.

MAY 10.

SEVEN witnesses, including one bishop and three priests, were examined and cross-examined. The first of the seven was Father Considine, of county Galway, in the course of whose examination-in-chief the Court adjourned yesterday. The main interest in Father Considine's examination was centred in the Hughes incident. Hughes, it may be remembered, was a *Times* witness who, it was expected, would testify that the League branch of which Father Considine was President (the Ardrahan branch) had released him from a boycott, "for a consideration," and that the proposal of such conditional release was made by Father Considine himself. Hughes, however, when put into the witness-box, declared that Father Considine did not ask him for anything; that, in fact, the offer was a voluntary one on Mr. Hughes's own part. So that the cross-examination to-day of Father Considine was to a large extent a scrutiny by *The Times* counsel of the credibility of one of their former witnesses. Mr. Reid's examination of Father Considine lasted only a few minutes. "Mr. Hughes," said the witness, "came to me of his own accord, and asked me to intercede with the Leaguers to release him from his boycott, and I promised him I would do my best. It was then," said Father Considine, "that he offered to give up the money he had made by letting out his cars for eviction work" (the action for which he was boycotted), and it was only when this voluntary offer was made that the witness suggested to his repentant visitor what he might do with the money.

Father Considine repeated this account of the matter in his cross-examination by Mr. Murphy. Mr. Hughes, he said, voluntarily made the offer, in order, as Mr. Hughes himself expressed it, to signify the sincerity of his regret for having let out his cars for any such purpose; besides, Mr. Hughes wished to "stand well with the people." Then Mr. Murphy turned to Father Considine's own oratory as a League politician, and to the ethics of the boycott. Father Considine had declared that people in his parish never were pressed to join the League. Mr. Murphy quoted a strong extract from a speech of Father Considine's, in which extract people who refused to join were consigned to the "cold, deep damnation of disgrace." Mr. Murphy threw himself into an attitude expressive of horror, and asked Mr. Considine what he thought of such rhetoric.

There were several questions to the same effect, and as many answers—the gist of which appeared to be that the bite was not meant to be as bad as the bark. Father Considine further observed that in later years he made use of less intemperate language. Whereupon Mr. Murphy produced some of Father Considine's later expressions about grabbers being amongst the worst of their kind, and about men who kept aloof from the League being as condemnable even as landlords themselves. "Strong," Father Considine admitted, but he meant it only "for moral suasion." Did he consider boycotting moral? It depended on the kind of boycotting. I would "avoid" the grabber, said Father Considine—avoid him because of his avarice, but "I would not starve him." "What! have you not heard of funerals being boycotted?" Mr. Murphy exclaimed. But Father Considine had no personal knowledge of funeral boycotting in his parish. Like the Archbishop of Dublin, who was examined the day before, Father Considine approved only of the "negative" boycott; when it meant intimidation, he would have none of it; and as for the form of boycott which meant deprivation of the necessaries of life, he considered it "wicked and sinful." "So," exclaimed Mr. Murphy, "you draw a distinction between intimidation and making things disagreeable." "I think there is a distinction," was the emphatic reply. Finally, Father Considine was asked some questions about the murder of Mr. Burke, near Loughrea. He replied that the constable told a falsehood who, in the earlier portion of the trial, said that people on the roadside deliberately trod upon the blood of the murdered man.

The murder of Mr. Burke and his companion, Corporal Wallis, was the principal theme of the examination of the next two witnesses, the first of whom was Stephen Tarpey, of Ballyglass, county Galway. He was examined by Mr. Hart. Stephen Tarpey was returning from mass when he heard the news that a murder had just been committed at a spot about two miles distant. He went to the spot at once, saw some people about, but saw nobody behave in the inhuman manner described by the policeman, nor did he hear any "jeering." And the Sunday following, said Mr. Tarpey, the murder was denounced by Father Considine from the altar; and at an open meeting, which was held in the chapel immediately after mass, a resolution was passed, expressing the hope that the perpetrators of the crime might be brought to justice.

This corresponded with Father Considine's own statement of the day before. It should be said that Mr. Tarpey was a member of the League. Mr. Tarpey was pounced upon in cross-examination by Sir Henry James, for having said that he arrived at the spot in about a quarter of an hour after the murder was committed. How did he know that the murder was committed a quarter of an hour before? for Tarpey was coming away from Mass at the time. Evidently Mr. Tarpey, who was a slow, somewhat shy witness, was only speaking in a vague way about the impression left upon his mind by informants whom he met on the road. I remained an hour on the spot, said this witness; and I did not see anybody treading in the blood. The next witness, Patrick Joyce, assisted the police in carrying the bodies. He was several hours about the spot, and at one time there were between thirty and forty people there; but he saw no signs of unseemly behaviour. The murders, he added, caused "sadness and regret" in the locality.

Mr. T. Harrington, M.P., examined the next witness, Mr. Patrick Cawley, of Craughwell, a dreary poverty-stricken little village in Galway—between Loughrea and Athenry. In order to show their lordships what the distress in the district was in 1879-80—distress, on the defence theory, leading through eviction to crime—Mr. Harrington questioned the witness about the famine contributions received by him, as Land League treasurer, from a great many quarters. Mr. Cawley is at the present time secretary of the local branch of the National League. In all his experience he had not known, he said, that a single penny had been spent in getting up outrage. There never was a suggestion of crime among the local leaguers; "they would not listen" to any such thing, said the witness, firmly. Had there been no League, said he, in reply to a question by Mr. Reid, outrage would have been more frequent.

Then came Dr. McCormack, Bishop of Galway. Mr. Lockwood examined him. The bishop described what he had seen of the hardship and misery of peasant life in Western Ireland. There was not the smallest exaggeration in it. Rather the reverse. He mentioned, briefly, how bog-land was reclaimed by the peasants without any help from the landlords, the largest of whom, Lord Dillon, has "always been an absentee." This absentee landlord has about four thousand five hundred tenants in county Mayo. Distress, said the bishop, went on increasing until 1879–80, when, but for the establishment of the Land League, clearances and outrages would have followed as in the time of the great famine, thirty-five years before. In spite of the distress in 1879–80, said the bishop, the landlords gave their tenants no help whatever.

All these details were given, in answer to Mr. Lockwood, in order to show that, independently of the Land League, there existed a state of things out of which disturbance and crime would naturally spring. Between the years 1879 and 1882 Dr. McCormack was consulted by Mr. Lowther (the Irish Secretary) and Lord Spencer; both of whom he assured that the League, by organizing the open expression of discontent, had been instrumental in destroying secret —in other words, criminal—societies. But what about the League and boycotting, asked Mr. Atkinson, referring the Bishop of Galway to the Pope's own rescript against what is "commonly called boycotting" in Ireland. What was the meaning of it? The bishop, to judge from his manner, must have thought that the best man to answer that question was the Pope himself. But as the Pope could not be put into the witness-box, the bishop made the best of it. He thought "negative" boycotting was not incompatible with the rescript— the boycotting, which meant shunning a person guilty of injustice. In the bishop's opinion there may be justifiable boycotting, as there may be unjustifiable eviction. His Holiness's rescript was clearly against intimidation, the bishop thought.

Would he approve of boycotting—even "negative" boycotting—in the House of God?—No. But upon this subject of boycotting, Mr. Reid, when the next witness came on, made the general statement, that counsel and witnesses for the defence did not deny that, within certain limits, the practice had been advocated by the local League branches. Intimidation and outrage were, said Mr. Reid, the limits. Father Fahy, of Gort, in Galway, was in the box when Mr. Reid made that observation. Father Fahy flatly contradicted the story which had been told about him by a *Times* witness early in the trial— namely, that he had endeavoured to procure the removal from the country of a young man who was prosecuting several people charged with outrage. Father Maloney, who followed Father Fahy, hailed from Kinvara, at the head of Galway Bay. As president of the local branch of the Land League seven years ago, and of the National branch now, Father Maloney declared that all his respectable parishioners were members of the organization, and that he did not believe any of them—directly or indirectly—connived at crime of any kind whatever.

SEVENTY-NINTH DAY.

MAY 14.

FATHER MALONEY, the Galway priest, reappearing in the witness-box, was cross-examined by Sir Henry James, principally about the books kept by the Land and National League branches of which he has been president. Father Maloney frankly admitted that he had presided, in the autumn of 1885, at a National League meeting at which a resolution was passed disapproving the conduct of a man named Thomas Conolly, in giving information to an evicting landlord. In about two years and a half after that, Conolly was shot at. But, said Father Maloney, the attempt on Conolly's life was made outside our district. According to Father Maloney's account of the matter, the bark of the local League branch was always worse than its bite; its strong "resolutions"—and some of them were very strong—were a letting-off of rhetorical steam.

Among strongly-worded resolutions recorded in *The Tuam News* was one to the effect that "We condemn the dirty, selfish, ignorant, unprincipled scoundrels," &c. Sir Henry James appeared to be shocked at the fact that Father Maloney, a priest and a man of education, should have presided at a meeting in which resolutions of that kind were passed. Nevertheless Father Maloney in the witness-box quietly remarked that the persons called dirty, selfish, ignorant, &c., had been guilty of the conduct of which they were accused. The really significant part of Father Maloney's answer was that in which he said: "We perhaps thought we did our duty by merely passing the resolution." The meeting appeared to have let off its steam, and to have taken no further steps against the "dirty" and "ignorant" "scoundrels." Finally Father Maloney declared he would not approve of boycotting which proceeded to the extremity of withholding the necessaries of life.

Mr. John Kennedy, Town Councillor of Loughrea, was the next witness. He came from a "hot" district—wherein seven murders were perpetrated within a period of fourteen months during the disturbed years 1880-2. But of the seven murders there was only one of which Mr. Kennedy had anything to say—and even that was extremely little. This was the murder of Sergeant Linton, near the police barracks, in the town of Loughrea. Living, as he had done, for thirty years in Loughrea, Mr. Kennedy could think of no reason for attributing the murder to agrarian causes. The police-sergeant, he said, was an over-officious person, who was always spying about shops—especially the spirit shops, on Sundays—and he pursued his espionage in disguise; and the persons who were tried for his murder were a grocery and spirit seller and his wife, who were both acquitted.

The next witness was much more interesting. He threw some unpleasant light upon the Arcadia of the prosecution. The great distress in 1879-80, in and about Tuam, reminded him of the distress of 1850, when the people were dying of hunger. I was the relieving officer at that time in Tuam district, said this witness, Bartholomew Canavan; and he described how, on one occasion, he "met" two dead bodies on the road; and how, on another, he was present at the inquest on the bodies of two children, who, having left the workhouse, took refuge in a barn, where they died of starvation, and where their remains were partly eaten by rats. Coming to a later period, relieving officer Canavan told how a Tuam landlord, named Botteril, began raising his rents previously to the later period of scarcity, 1879-80, and the rise of the Land League. Here are a few illustrative figures:

ORIGINAL RENTS.	RAISED TO.
£ s. d.	£ s. d.
11 18 1	17 0 0
6 14 11	11 0 0
7 0 1	11 7 0
1 8 2	2 7 3
1 5 0	2 17 0
1 0 0	2 0 0
7 4 0	18 0 0
6 12 0	12 0 0
7 3 0	15 0 0

Mr. Arthur O'Connor, who was examining Mr. Canavan, said that the average increase was about 60 per cent. What had this landlord done to improve the holdings which he rack-rented at this terrific rate? Nothing, was the witness's answer. Botteril's tenants were among the poorest in the district; and when the hard times of 1879-80 came, they were all on relief—all, " with the exception of one."

Mr. Canavan was president of the Land League branch, which was founded in August, 1880; and when the National League branch was founded he became its secretary. So Mr. Canavan claimed to know what he was talking about. He said there was no truth whatever in the story told by a *Times* witness that the landlord Botteril was summoned before a League court to explain his conduct. He could not possibly have been summoned—for the best of reasons, which was that the branch never held a court. Moreover, Mr. Canavan declared that he himself took this rack-renting landlord's part against a herd whom he dismissed. Our branch connected with crime? Never! exclaimed Mr. Canavan, emphatically. We expelled some of our members who broke the rules, said Mr. Canavan; but that was all. And now Mr. Canavan produced his books, Land League books, and National League books—the first of their kind produced in court. The books when examined were found to contain minutes of meetings—including resolutions against offending Leaguers—and entries of expenditure on furniture, rent, printing, delegations to Dublin, &c. There were entries about certain poor people who pawned their clothes to pay their rent. Some of the resolutions against people who failed to stand fast by their fellow-leaguers in their contest with the landlord were very amusing. Some of these backsliders were described as " vultures flying about the parish in search of small pieces of pasture land and gobbling it up with tiger-like ferocity." This specimen of the rhetoric of rural Ireland greatly amused Mr. Canavan's audience. The President himself, as he took a note of it, laughed outright. The passage was read out, not by counsel for the prosecution, but by Sir Charles Russell, who fully enjoyed the fun of the thing.

But the prosecuting lawyers had their turn in due course. Mr. Atkinson unearthed a passage in which certain weak-kneed leaguers were denounced as "rotten limbs" that ought to be cut off, and another passage in which the particular person abused first as a vulture, and next as a tiger, was disposed of as a "snail" who had "drawn in his horns."

The next witness, Mr. Edward Jennings, a secretary of the Land League of Clonbur, had been subpœnaed by *The Times*, evidently for the purpose of giving evidence about the murder of Lord Mountmorres. But *The Times* counsel never called him, though he was in attendance for about five weeks. Mr. Jennings, now appearing as a Parnellite witness, ridiculed the notion that the League encouraged crime; he rather thought the League put crime down. " We had no boycotting," he continued ; " and with the only case of it of which I was accused I had no more to do than your lordship on the bench." This to the President. Before he left the box he gave some description of the great distress which began in his district shortly before the Land League branch was founded in it.

Lastly, there entered the witness-box Mr. John Monaghan, farmer, of Oughterard, in Connemara. A stout, ruddy-faced, white-headed, frank and honest-looking farmer, of sixty-five, was Mr. John Monaghan. His service in the witness-box was to lift the veil which *The Times* witnesses had dropped over pre-League Ireland. He gave us a mournful picture of the Arcadia of the landlords and their agents. He quoted instances from the good old times, when if a man failed to pay his rent by three o'clock on rent-day he was fined twelve shillings; or had his rent raised if he sheltered evicted tenants. Martin Molloy's rent was raised from £5 to £7 10s. for that very reason. Mike Troon suffered still more heavily for his humanity. The President was so impressed with these statements that he stopped the witness for a moment, and asked for details. Did he remember the great famine? Of course. Tell us what you saw, said Mr. T. Harrington, who was examining him. And forthwith Mr. Monaghan proceeded to describe the Arcadia, in which, according to the landlords and their agents, no causes of crime and outrage existed before the advent of the League. He said that he saw " Bianconi's " cars upset by corpses lying on the road. Then he went on to describe a dead mother and her child. Mr. Monaghan faltered. His voice grew husky. Then he stopped. " The old man is crying," some one whispered. " The old man " told the judges how the child sought nourishment from its dead mother's breast; and how they put "the mother and the baby in one coffin." " I myself," said Mr. Monaghan, "brought thirty dead bodies to the grave in bags." To most people in Probate Court No. 1 it must have been a new experience to see " the old man crying " over a story of Irish famine. But they may often see it nowadays—at eviction time, when the carpenters are laying the foundations of a League "hut," and the old parish priest, giving his blessing to the undertaking, makes allusion to the past. People thought, said Mr. Monaghan, that what happened more than thirty years before might happen again in 1880.

EIGHTIETH DAY.

MAY 15.

YESTERDAY'S investigation was confined to the country round about Woodford and Loughrea—the Clanricarde region it might be called; the "hot" district of Ireland. More than half the day was occupied with the examination and cross-examination of Father Egan, parish priest of Dunivy, near Loughrea. Father Egan, a man apparently of about thirty-five years of age, is a good specimen of the younger race of Irish priests, who are as active in politics as they are in the cure of souls. Father Egan began by describing the distressed condition of the Woodford-Loughrea region in 1879-80, when, a newly-appointed curate, he began to take an active interest in politics. According to Father Egan's testimony, the state of Loughrea at that time must have been about as bad as that which the preceding witness, Mr. Monaghan, alleged to have existed during the same period in Connemara. Among Father Egan's first experiences as a curate were some visits to starving dying patients, whom he found half naked. But for the relief funds which were started, said Father Egan, numbers of people would have died of hunger. There were many relief funds. There was the fund of eight or nine thousand pounds collected by Dr. Duggan, the venerable Bishop of Clonfert, who, but for weak health, would have been in London to give evidence before the Commission. Most of that money went, said Father Egan, to the relief of the tenants of a landlord of whom the British public have already heard more than enough—Lord Clanricarde. There was the Duchess of Marlborough's Fund, distributed by the landlords. Thirdly, there was the poor law relief. Fourthly, there were the American and other foreign remittances, upon which many a poor family depended, in the last resort, for rent payments to the Clanricardes and for escape from the last and worst of indignities—refuge in the workhouse.

Father Egan was president of the Loughrea Branch of the Land League, and, in subsequent years, treasurer of the Woodford Branch of the National League. It was during his residence in Loughrea that Mr. Blake, Lord Clanricarde's agent, was murdered. And now Father Egan was invited to give his version of the story which Mrs. Blake had given months before in the witness-box. It will be remembered that Mrs. Blake gave anything but a pleasant account of Father Egan's conduct on the day of the murder—June 29, 1882. Father Egan's description differed widely from Mrs. Blake's. He described how he, in company with his younger brother and a Mr. Bowes, was driving into Loughrea from a distant parish ; how a runaway horse and cart came dashing down the road after them ; how Mr. Bowes jumped off to stop it ; how Father Egan, leaving his own car in charge of his younger brother, followed Mr. Bowes ; how he found Ruane, Mr. Blake's driver, in a dying state ; how he instantly gave him absolution ; and how then, at Mrs. Blake's request, he went further up the road "as quickly as possible," and found the body of Mr. Blake. " We heard no shots," said Father Egan ; and we had "no idea of what had happened." According to Mrs. Blake's story, Father Egan was quite indifferent—did nothing. " There is not the slightest foundation," continued Father Egan, " for the statement that I showed no sympathy for Mrs. Blake." He said that he called more than once at the hotel to which Mrs. Blake was conveyed after her husband's murder, and that on several occasions Mrs. Blake's sister and Mrs. Blake herself thanked him for his services. Finally, on the following Sunday, Father Egan and other priests, as well as Dr. Duggan, bishop of the diocese, denounced the murder.

Mr. Atkinson's cross-examination of Father Egan lasted fully two hours. It was principally occupied with the story of the process-server Finlay, who was murdered at Woodford in the summer of 1886. The Finlay murder story, as told long ago by one of *The Times* witnesses, Sergeant Coursey, is one of the most dismal, brutal, and disgusting yet heard before the Commission. It is the story of the "mock funeral," of boycotting the widow, of heaping insults upon her, of priestly refusal to assist the widow in procuring a coffin for her husband's remains. Of this story, except to a certain extent the last part of it, Father Egan gave a very different version to the police-sergeant's. " Every trumpery " incident, said Father Egan, was exaggerated into a tale of insult against Finlay's widow. As for the " mock funeral," Father Egan did not believe any such thing ever took place; at any rate, he was absent from the parish at the time it was alleged to have happened. It is quite true, said Father Egan, that Finlay's widow went about the Woodford streets cursing me and other leading people of the place, and that must have had something to do with the boycott to which she was subjected ; but she afterwards expressed her regret to me for what she had done, and now she regards me as her best friend. But the particular point on which Mr. Atkinson concentrated his strength was the coffin story. Sergeant Coursey did call upon Father Egan and Father Coen to assist him in procuring a coffin ; and as certainly the two priests refused. But Father Egan explained that the police-sergeant must have known better than he did himself where he could get what he wanted. As for the police story that Mr. Keary, the League treasurer, refused to supply one, Father Egan explained that Mr. Keary was neither a carpenter nor an undertaker, and that a coffin was more easily procurable in the neighbouring towns of Portumna and Loughrea, respectively ten and seven miles distant.

"Did you suggest that course to Sergeant Coursey?" Mr. Atkinson asked. Father Egan was not quite sure, but he thought he did. At the same time, he admitted that if the sergeant had addressed him and Father Coen in "a more becoming manner," they might have been more helpful to him. This admission gave Mr. Atkinson an opportunity—of which he made the best—to come down upon Father Egan with a string of ironical, denunciatory questions about the rival claims of "offended dignity" and Christian duty—in this case the duty of a priest. Father Egan stood Mr. Atkinson's thunder with composure, repeating his statement that he did not think the sergeant would experience any difficulty in procuring a coffin, and that he really thought the sergeant's request was meant as a "trap." Then as to his non-attendance at Finlay's funeral, Father Egan explained that this was owing to mis-information regarding the time at which the interment was to take place. But for that accident, either he or Father Coen would have been in attendance. Finally, as to his share in the Clanricarde evictions of 1886, Father Egan declared frankly that he was all along in favour of passive resistance—as by barricading—but that he was from first to last opposed to the active defence of fortified houses by the young men of the neighbourhood.

In the evidence of the next witness, Mr. McInerney, a solicitor, there was one statement which bore directly upon the history of the Loughrea-Woodford district. Mr. McInerney, who had been engaged in contesting (on the part of the ratepayers) a number of claims of compensation for malicious injury, said that the claim in the case of Sergeant Linton (murdered at Loughrea) was refused on the ground that the crime was unconnected with agrarian disputes. Then came another of the leaders of the "Woodford movement," as it is called in Western Ireland—Mr. John Roche. He was questioned about "Doctor" Tully's "pills," and the Woodford "Tenants' Defence Association," and the Finlay mock funeral. The "Doctor" was a boatbuilder, who owed his nickname of "Doctor" to his habit of calling boycotting, and anti-landlord combination, medicine. It was an utterly false story, said Mr. Roche, that the "Doctor" spoke of "leaden pills." "He was the most harmless and inoffensive man I ever came across," said Mr. Roche. "The Tenants' Defence Association," of which Mr. Roche was chairman, was, said he, a means of averting eviction and of preventing crime. The Association was, in fact, the precursor of the Plan of Campaign. Mr. Roche's account of its rise and progress corresponded with that given in one of *The Daily News* letters from Ireland in the autumn of 1887. "Our whole object," said Mr. Roche, "was to bring about a compromise between landlords and tenants;" and he pointed out that of the dozen or so estates, round Woodford, the only ones upon which disturbances had occurred were the three whose landlords refused to negotiate with their tenants. One of the three was Lord Clanricarde, and Mr. Roche now made it known that this landlord had just declined the suggestion of his tenants to follow the Vandeleur example of arbitration. As for the Finlay "mock funeral," the whole story was, according to Mr. Roche, a mere invention. The alleged funeral procession was, he said, only a crowd of people who were helping persons about to be evicted, and who were displaying a board, or boards, decorated with a goat's head, and inscribed "Down with the landlords." The demonstration "had nothing to do" with the Finlay funeral.

EIGHTY-FIRST DAY.

May 16.

Two of the Woodford Nationalists and the parish priest of Miltown-Malbay, in county Clare, were examined. Preoccupied by the electioneering contests at the end of 1885, the National League declined to give its active support to the Woodford combination against the landlords, though it was ready to grant relief in individual cases of hardship. So the Woodford men took the conduct of the land war into their own hands, and in two or three weeks' time their newly-formed association collected one thousand pounds. The Woodford association was, like the combination known as the " Plan," an extreme section of the Nationalist party, and to both of them the central office of the National League maintained a neutral attitude. It is the boast of the Woodford Union men that their movement was the spontaneous work of the general body of the tenants. However that may be, there can be no doubt about the energy and determination of its leaders. Mr. John Roche, miller, of Woodford, and chairman of the Association, and Mr. Patrick Keary, merchant, of Woodford, and secretary, who both appeared yesterday, are excellent specimens of the Woodford type of Nationalist.

The object of the Attorney-General's cross-questioning of Mr. Roche was to prove an artificial origin of the Woodford agitation. If the Government valuation of the Woodford property of Lord Clanricarde (to select one landlord) was so much higher than the rental ; if up to November, 1885 (when the Tenants' Association was founded), the tenants paid their rents so regularly that there were scarcely any arrears, how could it be said that the tenants were forced to combine in self-defence against landlord oppression ? Mr. Roche promptly replied that the Government valuation covered the landlord's own "demesne," and that it was a mistake to suppose that up to 1885 there were no serious arrears of rent. At a later stage of his cross-examination he declared that some of the rent deficits must have extended over periods varying from two to three or four years. And when challenged to say whether a single tenant on Lord Clanricarde's Woodford estates signed the 1886 memorial in demand of a reduction of 25 per cent., Mr. Roche asserted that it was signed by every tenant named in a list which the Attorney-General had a little while before read out.

Mr. Roche remembered the tenants' procession to landlord Lewis's house in December, 1885, when Mr. Roche himself and Father Egan and other prominent men accompanied it. And he frankly admitted that strong speeches were made outside Mr. Lewis's gate. But that was quite natural, thought Mr. Roche, considering that our offered compromise was received "in an insolent manner," and that, in fact, Mr. Lewis's "door was slammed in our faces." Next the Attorney-General asked him what he had to say in defence of the wild oratory of some of his associates—of " Doctor " Tully of the " pills," for example. Mr. Roche declared that he had never heard that Tully had spoken of " leaden pills ; " that " pills " did not mean leaden pills ; that the " Doctor's " " medicine " was only another name for boycotting, or for the hot water which the defenders of Irish " forts " squirted out upon their besiegers. In short, the " Doctor's " rhetoric was, in Mr. Roche's estimation, as harmless as the boat-builder Tully himself, whom he characterized the day before as the most inoffensive person he had ever come across.

As for boycotting, Mr. Roche denied that in Woodford there was any boycotting, save censure, or expulsion of members who broke the rules of the association. Why, Mr. Roche considered himself to be the best boycotted man in Woodford, for the local landlords would " rather send to Timbuctoo than buy a pennyworth of stuff from me." And he was positive that any one of the sixteen boycotted persons named by Sir Richard Webster would have found no difficulty whatever in buying goods in Woodford. He knew as a fact that Pat Conroy, one of the persons supposed to be boycotted, was all the while a regular customer of Mr. Patrick Keary's.

In the next place the Attorney-General questioned Mr. Roche about his share in the siege operations at Saunders's "fort"—the scene of the most exciting contests in the Woodford eviction campaign. As Mr. Roche explained further on, Saunders was a man who, after his first eviction, went to Australia, and who, returning to Ireland in better circumstances than when he left it, built a new house (the future "fort") at his own expense and with his own hands. Did Mr. Roche cheer the defenders? "It would not be me if I did not," quickly replied Mr. Roche. And was that constitutional? "I will tell you what it is," Mr. Roche exclaimed, turning alternately to the bench and the prosecuting counsel, "When a man—as did his forefathers before him—has spent a lifetime in building his house, without ever getting a penny from any one to help him, I believe that when a landlord comes and tries to deprive him of that house, and to throw him out on the roadside without a shelter for him and his family, and without the prospect of compensation, I consider a man is justified in resisting him." "That is your idea of passive resistance?" "It is what I call defending my home."

"Throwing out hot water appears to be funny to you, Mr. Roche?" But if it was, Mr. Roche took his fun seriously. "No, sir," said he, striking the ledge of the witness-box, "not to me; nor to you, if you had seen those people as I have. It may be to some of our English friends who have never seen them, as I have seen them, in their misery and distress." Mr. Roche's story contained the inevitable tragedy. Among the twenty defenders of Saunders's "fort" was young Tom Larkin, a mere boy, who for his share in the work was sentenced to eighteen months' imprisonment in Kilkenny gaol. There he died of hardship. Mr. Roche could scarcely control his emotion as he described the fate of young Larkin. "The unfortunate boy was lying dead when we went to see him; he was so disfigured that his own father failed to recognize him, and the cell in which he lay was no larger than this box."

The cross-examination of Mr. Roche concluded with Mr. Reid's production of the correspondence between Sir Michael Hicks-Beach and Lord Clanricarde. Mr. Reid's object was to show that the Irish Secretary's warning to the landlord was in itself a justification of the tenants' discontent. But as soon as Mr. Patrick Keary took Mr. Roche's place in the box, Mr. Atkinson tried to get him to admit that "this business"—the Woodford agitation—was "got up" by Father Egan, Mr. Roche, and one or two others. Mr. Atkinson always has his eye upon Father Egan. The quietude of Woodford until his Reverence came on the scene in August, 1885, has become a formula with Mr. Atkinson: the reverend firebrand appeared, and then the conflagration began. Mr. Keary, however, stoutly maintained that it was the tenants who of their own accord started the demand for rent reductions. Mr. Keary endorsed Mr. Roche's story about the mock funeral. Mr. Keary caused a laugh at Sir Richard Webster's expense by telling him that the alleged mock funeral of the process-server Finlay took place two months after the murder, instead of in two days, as Sir Richard appeared to think. Nor was it true that the mock coffin was laid beside Finlay's grave. The mock funeral, said Mr. Keary, was only a procession of young men who went to gather the crops upon a farm about to be "evicted."

Mr. Keary saw the procession pass up the street, and the inscription upon the deal box or coffin, which the young men carried on their shoulders, was "Down with landlordism." Was it true that Police-sergeant Coursey wanted to buy wood from him for Finlay's coffin? No. The sergeant asked for a coffin, not for wood, and Mr. Keary did not sell coffins—they could be had "ready-made" in Portumna or Loughrea. Why did he not offer to sell the wood? Because it was not his habit to make offers to his customers. Did he assist in boycotting the police? Certainly; and he did it because the police behaved brutally at evictions. Would he have boycotted a certain Sergeant Murphy, even to the extent of refusing to sell him and his child the necessaries of life? Yes, replied Mr. Keary, sharply; and then he explained that in his shop he did not sell necessaries of life. Replying to Mr. Lockwood, he declared he had never even heard of such a thing as boycotting the food of children. "I have an abhorrence of crime in every shape and form," Mr. Keary said as he left the box; adding that the Tenants' Association had been successful in keeping Woodford parish free of outrage.

Father White, who next went into the box, entirely contradicted the most important portions of the boycotting tale of Mrs. Connell, one of *The Times* witnesses. But his evidence was suspended at four o'clock.

EIGHTY-SECOND DAY.

MAY 17.

THE cross-examination of Father White having been concluded, the Rev. Michael O'Donovan, parish priest of Corrofin, in county Clare, gave evidence about Tulla district, of a Land League branch of which he was president. Speaking of the influence of Moonlighting societies in the days before the foundation of the Land League, "I myself," said he, "have had threatening letters from these moonlighters, and I have seen several other notices of the same description." Father O'Donovan, not only as a priest, but also as a Land Leaguer, denounced these secret outrages. Mr. Lockwood's questions to him on this point were intended to demonstrate this hostility between the Land League—the Open Association—and the secret body of which "Captain Moonlight" was the head; some of the most exciting evidence given before the Commission having on the other hand affirmed collusion between moonlighters and leaguers.

Taking Major Moloney's estates as an illustration, Father O'Donovan described the state of the tenantry in the years before the foundation of the League, and subsequently to it, as one of "miserable poverty." Of the hundred or so tenants, said the witness, only six were able to pay their rents. And, as a consequence, twenty-five of them were evicted in February, 1882. The tenants, according to Father O'Donovan's story, had for many years been growing poorer and poorer—ever since 1870, when rents were raised on the estate. Whatever improvements had been effected on the tenants' holdings were the work of the tenants themselves. Yet in the years of distress the landlords, said Father O'Donovan, did "nothing whatsoever" to relieve the people. In contradiction of the theory of the prosecution, Father O'Donovan declared that landgrabbers were the objects of intimidation and outrage long before the Land League existed. "A man who took an evicted farm would be regarded as an enemy of the tenantry." But, Father O'Donovan added, "the League always denounced crime."

If it did, how could he account for the fact that agrarian crime reached its maximum during the existence of the Land League? So it was put by Sir Henry James, who, the instant he rose to cross-examine Father O'Donovan, plunged into the statistics of outrage. *Post hoc*, certainly, according to Sir Henry's figures, which showed that the number of outrages rose from five in

1877 to two hundred and thirteen in 1881, and two hundred and seven in 1882. But not, in the witness's view, *propter hoc*. Father O'Donovan, who was a somewhat slow witness, said something or other about the inclusion of such minor offences as threatening letters in the criminal statistics. Sir Henry James took the statistics for the whole of Clare, whereas Father O'Donovan was speaking only of a single parish.

By the way, Sir Henry James's cross-examination of this witness was a good specimen of his tact. In his most exacting moods, Sir Henry James is considerate, forbearing, deferential, no matter who the "subject" may be upon whom he is operating—rough, garrulous peasant from Kerry, or smooth, precise bishop from Dublin or Galway. In which respect, his style of cross-examination is in not unwelcome contrast with the loud, bullying manner of some who might be named. But to return to Father O'Donovan. In spite of Sir Henry James's cross-questioning, he adhered to his statement that the moonlighters were in existence before the Land League, and opposed to it. In fact, the Reverend Father appeared to know so much about "Captain Moonlight" and his crew, that Sir Henry James expressed a polite surprise that Father O'Donovan took no steps to put the rascals under lock and key. In his slow, half-embarrassed, fatherly manner, Mr. O'Donovan assured Sir Henry James that he had often expostulated with the young men whom he suspected—and to such good effect that one of them at least fled the country. "Could you not stop it?" "No, I could not." The good priest did his best. He told Mr. Lockwood that he denounced their misdeeds "forty Sundays running." He had no definite proofs to bring against them. His explanation of moonlighting coincided, in the main, with that of Mr. Parnell and others—it was the work of sons of small farmers of the poorer class.

The next witness, Father John Hanneffy, of Riverside, county Galway, was even more emphatic than Father O'Donovan in repudiating all connection between the Land League and crime. Riverside was the residence of Peter Dempsey, in celebration of whose murder bonfires blazed on the hill-tops. So it was said in *The Times* evidence, earlier in the trial. Father Hanneffy contradicted the story. There were no bonfires, nor was Dempsey boycotted for taking the farm from which (as a matter of fact) somebody had been evicted. Nor was Mrs. Dempsey boycotted after her husband's murder. There was no truth whatever in the suggestion that the local branch of the League had anything to do with the crime. In fact, Dempsey's brother was a member of the Land League at the time of the murder, and secretary of the local branch of the National League now.

Witness number four, Patrick Keogh, of Kiltullagh—again county Galway—also flatly contradicted *The Times* evidence about another murdered man, James Connor. The fifth witness was the parish priest of Mullagh, near Loughrea. President first of the Land League, and next of the National League, he ought to know something about both. Father Bodkin has a temper of his own, and there was a note of anger and disgust in his rejection of *The Times* proposition, that the moonlighters were the "secret police" of the League. Contemptuously, too, he denied the story that at a certain meeting of the League a landgrabber named Kennedy had been warned that some day his two dogs would eat him up. Father Bodkin, however, admitted that the League had condemned Kennedy's conduct; but "he was not interfered with," said Father Bodkin. His conduct was condemned, said Father Bodkin, early in 1881. "He took from a rack-renting landlord, who raised his rent every time he got a new tenant, a farm that was occupied by a poor widow with five children. The widow and her children are thrown on the world to this day." Before he left the witness-box Father Bodkin spoke pretty strongly against the grabbers, who used to get their neighbours evicted by paying higher rents. Mr. John Nolan, from Ballynoonan, Galway, was the next witness. He was detained only a minute or two. The substance of his testimony was that the Land League, instead of causing crime, prevented it.

The seventh and last witness of the day was Father Finneran, parish priest, from near Ballinasloe, Galway. Examined by Mr. Lockwood, he described the wretched condition in which he found the peasantry on the estates of Mrs. Blake, of Connemara, in the year 1870. Speaking of another estate in the same quarter of Ireland, at the same period, he told one of those mournful stories with which the Court is already only too familiar—a story of a man named Gannon, who with his sick wife and five children were turned out on the roadside in December. After the eviction the priest was sent for, to administer the last rites of her religion to the dying woman. He found the family outside their old home, and the children, crying, trying to re-enter it. At this point the President interfered. Why go back to the year 1870? After a pause Mr. Lockwood, drawing himself up, replied that his object was to refute a supposition which pervaded *The Times* case since the trial began, the supposition that up to the foundation of the Land League, landlords and tenants lived on the friendliest terms; to show that causes of agrarian war were at work before the League ever appeared. Mr. Lockwood uttered every word of his appeal (of which the foregoing is the substance) slowly and deliberately. Perhaps those present in court might have felt somewhat expectant when Mr. Lockwood quietly remarked that he hoped their lordships, before restricting the scope of his inquiry, would "think what they were doing." A candid way of putting it. *The Times* counsel, urged Mr. Lockwood, had reiterated their theory of a peaceful Ireland in the pre-League days. Therefore he wished to be allowed to enter into details which would prove its groundlessness. Sir James Hannen remonstrated that evidence of such details, from a period so remote, might prolong the trial for ten years. But still Mr. Lockwood claimed his right to show what the state of mind among the tenants was, when outrages began, and how it was produced. Take your own course, replied Sir James Hannen, in effect; but he reiterated his opinion that Mr. Lockwood was going too far afield.

EIGHTY-THIRD DAY.

MAY 21.

FATHER FINNERAN, who concluded his evidence, corroborated the too familiar story of landlord indifference to tenant hardship. Though there was nothing new in what he said, he was about the best of the clerical witnesses. Speaking of Mrs. Blake, of Connemara, he said that her estates, when she assumed the management of them, were heavily mortgaged; and this he appeared to suggest, accounted, partly at least, for their rack-rents.

Mr. William O'Brien—his name called out by Mr. Reid—was the next witness after Father Finneran. As he stood up in the witness-box he looked somewhat less weak than he did when he arrived in court in charge of his warders from an Irish gaol two or three weeks ago. But the President requested him to be seated. And then he began the story of his life, with his tours all over Ireland, as a newspaper correspondent. An admirable witness is Mr. William O'Brien, the best and the most interesting—though of course not the most "sensational," for there Le Caron and Pigott beat him hollow—who has yet appeared before the Commission. His prompt, precise answers were the graphic record of a keen observer of unique experience and untiring industry, to whom even his enemies do not deny the virtues of sincerity, patriotism, and courageous self-sacrifice. "The intelligent foreigner," paying a visit to the court might well feel puzzled at learning that the invalid-like witness seated in the box was one of the two or three most loved leaders of the Irish people, and a gaol-bird whose imprisonments had been so numerous that he might be excused if he had lost count of them.

As regards the vexed question between accusers and accused—whether the rise of the Land League was followed by outrages of a kind wholly new in the history of Ireland, Mr. O'Brien's evidence was by far the most definite yet given before the Commission. Murders? Take the series of them which was perpetrated in Tipperary during the eight or nine years preceding the foundation of the Land League. No one was ever brought to trial for the murder of the landlord, Captain Baker, 1871, whose inquest Mr. W. O'Brien described at the time. In those days it was possible for a murderer to kill his victim in broad daylight, coolly walk out unmeddled with into the street, and live among his townsfolk for years unaccused. No one was ever punished for the terrible murder of Tracey—1871 or 1872—whose offence was supposed to be land-grabbing. Mr. O'Brien mentioned other cases of agrarian murder, the perpetrators of which were never brought to justice.

Is it true, asked Mr. Reid, that fourteen agrarian murders were committed in Tipperary in the ten years before the foundation of the Land League? Mr. O'Brien would not undertake to say what the exact number was. He would only speak of instances which came under his personal observation; and passing to other forms of outrage, he mentioned instances in which land agents escaped attempted assassination, and were put under police protection. Then followed the argumentative comparison. Such was Tipperary *before* the Land League; but in Tipperary *after* the Land League, "I have not been able to find a single case of agrarian murder." And again, Tipperary is the county where the League organization has been "strongest"; but before the League, the Tipperary tenants had "no organization of any kind."

Was it true that fortified houses were unheard of before the League? No; and Mr. O'Brien mentioned an instance in which the defending tenants loop-holed the walls of their house and shot a policeman dead. And there were threatening notices then as now. The only difference, said Mr. O'Brien, was that before the League the notices were signed by "Rory o' the Hills," and by "Captain Moonlight" after it. Leaving Tipperary, Mr. O'Brien gave some vivid description of what he saw about Mitchelstown, county Cork. He described how the peasants on the Galtee hills, by carrying soil and manure on their backs from the valleys below, created the farms upon which they were rack-rented. As a consequence, or alleged consequence, the landlord's agent was shot at. That was on the Buckley estate, which formerly was included in the Kingston estate. Since the rise of the League, said Mr. O'Brien, the agrarian disputes on the Kingston estate have been unaccompanied by slaughter—save the shooting of people by the constabulary in Mitchelstown Square. What struck Mr. O'Brien most in his visit to the Galtees in the years before the League, was the combined wretchedness and industry of the peasants.

He passed on to Donegal, and the murder of Lord Leitrim and his clerk in 1876. They were killed in broad daylight. And no one was "made amenable." Then Mayo and Galway during the distress of 1879. "Oh, it was horrible." "It was appalling." "There seemed to be no way out of it." "And the landlords ridiculed the notion of distress, and did nothing." "Absentee landlords, with an aggregate rent-roll of one hundred thousand a year, would not reduce their rents one penny." And the general opinion among the peasantry was that the famine of 1846 "would come back." As Mr. O'Brien described all this, his face flushed; and there was in his voice just a note of the fierce wrath which often blazes forth when he is "on the stump." Once or twice only, in the course of his evidence, did his indignation get the better of him.

Seated in the box, with his legs crossed, and his papers about him, he talked exactly as he does with some solitary visitor in his sky-high garret, Imperial Hotel, Sackville Street (we beg pardon, Upper O'Connell Street), Dublin. He answered Mr. Reid in a conversational, reflective way, as if he were unconscious of the presence of anybody except Mr. Reid, speaking all the while with the graphic force of one before whose eyes were passing the scenes he was describing. The sudden impulsive "Oh, it was horrible," was a good example of this manner.

Mr. O'Brien came to the time of the Land League. What would have happened had there been no League? Mr. Reid asked. "There is nothing more certain in history," replied Mr. O'Brien, "than that there would have been wholesale famine and a civil war." "It was the universal impression" among the tenants, he continued, that the landlords were trying "to break up the land legislation of 1870." But for the Land League the million of money which saved the Western Irish from death would never have been raised. And, said Mr. O'Brien, the police were actually evicting in Clare Island at the very time when the coast population was " literally and absolutely starving " on shell-fish and sea-weed (as in the island of Innishark).

Mr. O'Brien stated, emphatically, that to his knowledge the young men about Lough Mask were at that time contemplating an attack on the troops. Mr. O'Brien is nothing if not outspoken. And he declared, with all the earnestness at his command, that in a country like Ireland there was nothing like boycotting for keeping down outrage. By boycotting he meant an expression of organized public sentiment and opinion, without admixture of intimidation. The boycott, by preventing grabbing, prevented eviction—which he considered to be the source of outrage. In the most matter-of-fact manner he quoted the criminal history of Mayo, Kilkenny, West Meath, Wexford, as "arithmetical" proof of his position, that "the boycott is the peacemaker of Ireland."

Lastly, Mr. Reid came to the history of *The Irishman* and *United Ireland*. Mr. O'Brien's audience laughed loudly as he declared that at the time of its death, in 1885, *The Irishman* had a circulation of only some twelve hundred copies per week, and that about half of them were sold by Messrs. W. H. Smith and Sons. As we knew *The Irishman* was doomed, said Mr. O'Brien, and as we did not like to displease the section of extreme Nationalists, we preferred to let the paper die its natural death. Speaking of that section, our object, said Mr. O'Brien, was to conciliate all parties; and he regarded Mr. Parnell's conciliation—his attempt to bring over the extremists to constitutional agitation—as the strongest point in his policy. As to the organ of the League, *United Ireland*, one interesting fact in its history was that sixteen members of its staff (including the editor, two acting editors, the sub-editor, and others) had been under lock and key in Kilmainham. The afternoon sitting was chiefly occupied in reading extracts from *The Irishman* and *United Ireland*, for the purpose of showing that certain incriminatory passages quoted by the accusers were only extracts from other papers, and also of showing how *United Ireland* was for years protesting against the assumption, common in the English press, that the policy of the League was identical with the policy of the party of violence.

EIGHTY-FOURTH DAY.

MAY 22.

"It is absolutely untrue," said Mr. O'Brien, "that the National League has encouraged outrage; its secretary, Mr. Harrington, has suppressed local branches because they were guilty of strong language ; and for the last four or five years the central office of the League in Dublin has promptly called public meetings in any locality from which news has been received of danger of outrage." In order to show how entirely the mass of the American-Irish supporters of the National League were in favour of constitutionalism, Mr. O'Brien gave a brief and telling description of the great meeting which he attended at Chicago in 1886, at which fifteen thousand people were present, and at which a unanimously "loyal and hearty support of Mr. Gladstone's policy" was voted. This was the meeting at which both Mr. Davitt and Mr. O'Brien repudiated the physical force policy of the well-known Irish-American, Mr. Finerty, who made a speech on the same occasion, and who found himself in a minority of one. Before he went to America Mr. O'Brien knew nothing of Finerty, beyond what he had read in the London papers. "And I should be sorry," said he, "to believe anything the London newspapers said in their estimate of the character of Irishmen." Mr. O'Brien is nothing if not straightforward. To sum up his evidence about his American tour—all over America he was welcomed by men of the highest position ; an ex-Speaker of the United States Senate presided at one of his meetings ; he received the freedom of the City of Boston ; and he refused a public reception in New York, when he discovered that physical force men were engaged in organizing it.

At two or three minutes to eleven o'clock, the Attorney-General rose to cross-examine. His first few questions referred to *United Ireland.* During his imprisonment in Kilmainham, 1881-2, Mr. O'Brien knew little of the paper. In fact, *United Ireland* being "suppressed," led a sort of nomadic life, printed in some English town "to-day, and hundreds of miles off next week."

And so, continued the Attorney-General, your position is that from 1879 till now your policy has been constitutional. Neither in writing, nor in speech, nor in action, nor in thought, had he, replied Mr. O'Brien, been anything but constitutional. Later, however, he made one exception. At Mitchelstown, in 1887, just on the eve of the passing of an Act which would relieve the tenants, but which for that very reason the landlord was doing his utmost to discount, Mr. O'Brien did advise the tenants to stick to their holdings. So there were no evictions, said Mr. O'Brien, and "nobody was a penny the worse." Half the day was spent in a dialectical battle between the Attorney-General and Mr. O'Brien, over the latter's assertion of his constitutionalism. The Attorney-General, by trying to show up Mr. O'Brien as a supporter of boycotting and other forms of illegality, was doing his best to destroy his claim. But Mr. O'Brien was as ready with his "destinctions," as any ecclesiastic—say like Dr. Walsh—trained in the logic of the schools. What kind of boycotting do you mean, Mr. Attorney? What we in Ireland call boycotting is what you in the West End call "blackballing." Moreover, Mr. Attorney, we in Ireland distinguish between "criminality" and "illegality." The people in Ireland have no love for criminality, but as for illegality, meaning an attitude towards law as law—the letter of the law—why, exclaimed Mr. O'Brien, "illegality is bred in us." This downright frank declaration elicited some not unsympathetic laughter, which was renewed on Mr. O'Brien's remarking that for years the very existence of the Irish people was "illegal."

The Woodford people were given to illegalities ; and, as Mr. O'Brien said later, it was "the Woodford spirit that made England what it is." That was one for England, and neatly put. And if boycotting destroyed a man's business, well, what of that? Supposing the person boycotted was a man who had earned his money by usury, and who made use of the profits he got out of his neighbours to overbid some one or other of them for his poor holding on the very first opportunity? The boycott, which meant social avoidance, and excluded intimidation, was, in Mr. O'Brien's opinion, the only weapon left to the Irish peasantry. Mr. O'Brien was dead against intimidation, against violence, in whatever form, "against brutality of all sorts." The boycott, as thus restricted and defined was, Mr. O'Brien repeated, the only weapon which the peasants could turn against grabbers and landlords. It was their only plan of retaliation. "À la guerre, comme à la guerre!" exclaimed Mr. O'Brien. The Attorney-General instantly seized upon the expression. Ah! and that is your idea of constitutional action, Mr. O'Brien? Mr. O'Brien warmly protested. "I am sure," said he, turning to the Bench, "that no one listening to me could say that, using the words in a figurative sense, I should be regarded as applying them to actual warfare." "No, certainly not," remarked the President, "I did not take it as meaning that."

Mr. O'Brien's demeanour at this time must have struck most of his audience. It was one of weariness and hopelessness. "All Greek," said he, "to you English people; we understand in Ireland what boycotting is, you don't." And when the Attorney-General quoted police statistics to show how crime and the League were like substance and shadow, Mr. O'Brien, with an expression of contemptuous impatience, remarked that he did not "care a rush for police statistics." The only police statistics which were trustworthy were those of murder; because murder could not be hidden; but as for other outrages, "they were made to increase or decrease according to the requirements of the Government." And as for cattle maiming and firing into houses, Mr. O'Brien believed that landgrabbers often "got up" these outrages in order to get police protection and money compensation.

Said the Attorney-General, crime was, in 1880, more frequent in Munster than in Ulster—though in that year the League was supposed to be strongest in the former and weakest in the latter province.

"At such a crisis," replied Mr. O'Brien, "no human power could prevent crime. But I do say the League prevented crime which might have occurred. I, however, attach no importance to police returns." "What the police call crime, we look upon as the very best thing a citizen can do. For instance, the police included in their crime returns such charges as those of speech-making against the Messrs. Harrington, for which they were sent to jail."

These speeches were delivered in Kerry, the county to which Sir Redvers Buller was sent in order to put down moonlighting. The General, said Mr. O'Brien, "was sent to curse, and remained to pray." And then came one of those half-soliloquies to which Mr. O'Brien often gives expression. One of these was the "all Greek" expression named above. And now came another: if the members of that Court knew Ireland as he knew it, the inquiry before their Lordships would be "materially curtailed." In a moment of seriousness and sudden inspiration, even Mr. Coffey, the trifler and the prevaricator, said the same thing.

At the Attorney-General's next criticism Mr. O'Brien's patience gave way. What of the "armed resistance" offered by the Woodford tenants during the eviction campaign? "Armed resistance," exclaimed Mr. O'Brien, angrily; "the description is perfectly monstrous." The resistance of "hot water"— against the arms of constabulary and police. It was resistance of the most "trumpery character." Did you in any of your speeches, Mr. O'Brien, call upon the people to assist the Government in detecting crime? "No, I did not," was Mr. O'Brien's reply, with the same expression of impatience and annoyance. "To do that would be to acknowledge a state of things which they absolutely denied existed. It would be interpreted as an admission that the country was steeped in blood, whereas, with regard to the vast area of the country that was absolutely and totally a falsehood. Besides, no means existed by which the people could co-operate with the police."

The rest of the cross-examination for the day was chiefly occupied with questions about *The Irishman* and *United Ireland*. A column headed "Incidents of the Campaign" appeared to the Attorney-General to imply that the acts of violence recorded in it were part of the Plan, had the approval of the leaders of the Plan. Mr. O'Brien explained that they were simply news paragraphs. But, said he, some of them are very objectionable—the paragraph, for instance, which said that perhaps the threatened blowing up of a certain police-barracks "had been postponed." Mr. O'Brien suggested that the paragraph might have been a "comment on a *canard*." Of these paragraphs Mr. O'Brien himself knew nothing at the time, for he was in prison when they were published. Notwithstanding the publication of these "incidents," Mr. O'Brien strenuously maintained that neither in speech nor in writing had he advocated unconstitutional methods of agitation. But with his usual perfect candour he objected to the ordinary use of such words as loyal, and constitutional : loyalty, said he, " has two meanings, force and affection. Force I bowed to, both in my paper and elsewhere ; of affection I had none, and never pretended I had until 1885." Only two more questions need particular notice. Why did Mr. Egan escape from Ireland? Because he knew that if the smallest particle of evidence could be got up against him [in connection with the Phœnix Park murders] his life would not be worth twenty-four hours' purchase. Mr. O'Brien believed there was a "desperate anxiety" on the part of certain police officers in Ireland to connect Mr. Egan with the murders. The second question was about Dan Curley, one of those sentenced to death for the Park crimes. In *United Ireland* appeared this letter :—

"Dear Sir,—Now the strangling commission is over, and honest Dan Curley is killed off, I enclose 10s. for his widow."

"Very reprehensible," said Mr. O'Brien ; but the letter was inserted when Mr. O'Brien was in Kilmainham—when, consequently, he had no control over the paper.

EIGHTY-FIFTH DAY.

MAY 23.

NOT a single line of argument was overlooked by which Mr. O'Brien's claim of constitutionalism for his policy might be overthrown. On resuming his cross-examination, the Attorney-General sought to find in Mr. O'Brien's "exchanges" a proof of Mr. O'Brien's sympathy—if not worse—with policies of outrage. Among the papers which were received at Mr. O'Brien's office in exchange for *United Ireland* were *The Boston Pilot*, *The Chicago Citizen*, *The New York World*. *The Chicago Citizen* was the organ of Mr. Finerty, whom the prosecution have alleged to be a dynamiter, but whom Mr. O'Brien most strenuously affirms to be a respected, honourable American-Irishman, who used to believe (if he does not believe it still) that it was useless for Ireland to hope for redress from England save through insurrection. As for Mr. Patrick Ford's *Irish World*, it ceased to be sent to the office of *United Ireland* some time in 1882, and as for the "strong" paragraphs which were printed in *United Ireland*, and to which the Attorney-General had taken such strong objection, why, said Mr. O'Brien, they were merely "re-hashes" from other newspapers, put in as news in the ordinary journalistic way. In these news paragraphs, said Mr. O'Brien, I myself "did not take any interest." He had quite enough to do in writing the leading articles for his paper and in attending to his Parliamentary business, and his political journeys over Ireland. In reference to this matter of extracts from the American papers, Mr. O'Brien declared over and over again that quantities of them were reproductions, "re-hashes" from the London newspapers. On this point Mr. O'Brien made some very emphatic and indignant criticisms. It was the prominence given by the London newspapers to sensational stories about American-Irish dynamitards that did more than anything else to advertise them and encourage them. In Mr. O'Brien's candid estimation, his brother journalists of London were doing more mischief than a host of O'Donovan Rossas.

"Yes, I wrote that," Mr. O'Brien replied, in his prompt, downright way, when the Attorney-General quoted a passage from an old article referring to the toast of the Queen at a banquet to Mr. Parnell,—"An old lady who was only known in Ireland by her scarcely decently disguised hatred of the Irish people, and the inordinate amount of her salary." Was that constitutional? Sir Richard Webster asked, in his most solemn manner. "I think," replied Mr. O'Brien, "that it was perfectly constitutional to criticize the conduct of the sovereign; I think that in the condition in which Ireland then was I was perfectly justified in writing in these terms." The calm air of sincere conviction in which Mr. O'Brien uttered these words was perhaps more impressive than the Attorney-General's solemnity. Sir Richard drew himself up. He repeated the words, "Scarcely—veiled—hatred," pausing at each, and then pausing for a reply. "It is strong language," Mr. O'Brien replied, "but my words expressed the universal belief in Ireland." With the utmost composure Mr. O'Brien said he would write the same words again under the same circumstances; but, said he, the circumstances have changed.

Here, in fact, Mr. O'Brien touched upon the argument that has run through his evidence from first to last. In the earlier part of his evidence he put his whole argument in a nutshell when he said "the Woodford spirit made England what it is." He expressed the same idea to-day when he said that agitations which would be "legally criminal" in England were morally justifiable in Ireland—anything but "morally disgraceful"—provided that they were kept free from intimidation. Mr. O'Brien's meaning was fully illustrated and made perfectly clear when the Attorney-General came to Mr. O'Brien's articles on the Prince of Wales's visit to Ireland. Could Mr. O'Brien reconcile these articles with his claim to constitutional character as a politician? Yes, Mr. O'Brien could. And he proceeded to draw a distinction between constitutional, "in a certain narrow view of it," and constitutional in the broad English sense. Mr. O'Brien justified his opposition to the ceremonial of the Prince's reception, because the Prince of Wales's visit was regarded in Ireland as "a party move." The Prince's visit was used (not by the Prince personally) as a sort of counter-demonstration to the national movement. "When," continued Mr. O'Brien, "*The Times* made use of the Prince's visit to declare that Parnellism was upset by it, we felt bound, we thought it was a matter of desperate necessity, to protest; and in the broad spirit of English freedom we were right." "I would not write these articles *now*," repeated Mr. O'Brien; for, as he had already said, the relations between England and Ireland had been changed in the interval.

In one of the articles under discussion, and quoted by the Attorney-General, Mr. O'Brien had said that the chairman of the Kingstown Commissioners, the gentleman by whose casting vote the public reception was accorded to the Prince of Wales, would, when he came to seek re-election, be hunted by his constituents from public life. "And he has been," said Mr. O'Brien, when Sir Richard read the passage. "You mean that as a joke?" remarked the Attorney-General. "No, sir," replied Mr. O'Brien, sharply, and with a ring of indignation in his voice; "I only state it as a fact. Everybody in Ireland knew what would happen at the next election of the Kingstown Commissioners. These demonstrations of 'sham loyalty' were only deluding the English people." They "misrepresented the true position of Ireland." It was therefore "terribly necessary that we should expose them. As for the Prince of Wales personally, I never said a word against his character." Mr. O'Brien declared that if his Royal Highness had only "passed through Ireland" in his private character, he would not have written as he did; but that he considered the visit as "a counter-force" to the Nationalist movement, and its purpose to persuade the English people that the Nationalist feeling was "a bogus feeling." "Yes," exclaimed Mr. O'Brien again, "I say that in the large sense of constitutionalism our action was constitutional, and that we followed English example."

Mr. O'Brien adopted the same line of argument when the Attorney-General cross-examined him on his journalistic opposition to the display of English flags, and to the "hated notes" of the National Anthem. As for the flags, they were, in Ireland, said Mr. O'Brien, emblems of party factions; there was not a "shred of honest loyalty" in the exhibition of them. And then as for the "National Anthem," it used to be in Ireland, a party tune, like "The Boyne Water." But that was in the past; since the "revolution" in Irish feeling which the last two or three years had witnessed, the "National Anthem" was regarded differently. "Ah," said Mr. O'Brien, slowly shaking his head, and putting on, for once, an expression of ironical humour, "since 1885, 'God save the Queen' has lost its charms for our opponents." This satirical stroke was quite appreciated by Mr. O'Brien's densely packed and attentive audience.

Just at the moment when Mr. O'Brien was explaining the political aspect from which the Nationalists regarded the Prince's visit, Mr. Gladstone made his appearance, for the first time since the beginning of the trial. Conducted by Sir Charles Russell, he entered the court through the doorway in the screen below the judicial bench. He sat down among the lawyers, beside Mr. Lockwood, and in a moment, with his hand at his ear, and his elbow on the bench, he was absorbed in the cross-examination. On the opposite side of the court, to the Judges' left, sat, among a crowd of visitors, Mrs. Gladstone, busily taking notes. A few minutes before somebody in court had passed up to her a little bouquet of flowers. Mr. Gladstone's arrival was luckily timed. For in this cross-examination there was, unavoidably, a good deal of political, as distinguished from legal, reference; and he heard passages which must naturally have interested him.

For throughout the whole course of Mr. O'Brien's evidence—evidence most profoundly impressive, whatever "side" one may choose to take in regard to it—runs the distinction between English Governments and the English people. For example, when the Attorney-General, quoting an article of Mr. O'Brien's on the destruction of the English power, was leading up to the Prince's visit, Mr. O'Brien frankly declared, "No; I don't approve of that article now." He considered himself justified in writing it in November, 1884, before the year of the "revolution" in Irish feeling; but he would not write it now. "I tell you," said Mr. O'Brien, "that we always distinguished between English Governments and the English democracy." "'England' meant for us, in those times, one class of people." Then the Attorney-General questioned him about a speech delivered some months later in Phoenix Park. Yes, Mr. O'Brien had used strong expressions. But he was smarting under a sense of indignation at his expulsion from the House of Commons. And if Ireland had been strong enough to rebel then against her misrule, he would have been the first to risk his life for her. "If ever there was a right of rebellion that right was with our people then, but as there was not the remotest chance of success, the attempt would have been insanity and criminality." "Did not such language tend to inflame the people?" asked the Attorney-General. "The stronger the language I used the greater was the relief to the people," replied Mr. O'Brien; "just as I believe the stronger the language we used against the landlords the less the risk of outrage against them. The denunciation of them served as a lightning conductor — taking off the excessive feeling against the landlords, just as the conductor acted on the electricity in the air." And then, in his most earnest manner, Mr. O'Brien, clenching his hand and striking the desk with it, reminded the Attorney-General that in the same speech he had declared that there were even in the House from which he had been expelled men for whom the Irish people felt a deep regard, most of all "for Mr. Gladstone, whose kindliness and tenderness for Ireland were like drops in an ocean of prejudice."

Once more, Sir Richard Webster turned to the question of Irish hostility to "England," by quoting *United Ireland* articles about the Afghans, the Boers, and the Soudanese. "We sympathized with these peoples," said Mr. O'Brien, "because they were fighting against odds for what they considered to be justice." And then Mr. O'Brien repeated what he had often said before about the revolution in Irish feeling, and the "hope" of Ireland in the "English people."

At this stage again, Mr. O'Brien made one of those many professions of his, which strike even his opponents by their magnificent frankness and intense sincerity. "If," said he—"if by any misfortune—which God forbid—it became perfectly clear that the English people would give no satisfaction to the national aspirations of Ireland, then, beyond all manner of doubt, I think still, if a rational chance offered, it would be justifiable to take it."

But, as he repeatedly said, in effect, in the course of his evidence, for English Cabinets there had been substituted the English people; and the consequence was, a revolution in Irish feeling. He gave an illustration of this revolution, from the Irish-American meeting at Chicago in 1886, which Mr. O'Brien himself attended. In that American journey Mr. O'Brien appealed, as he expressed it, to the whole Irish race. And the Chicago demonstration was an endorsement of the new Anglo-Irish policy, as "a triumph of Mr. Gladstone's policy." Mr. O'Brien's speech at Chicago was made before fifteen thousand men, who received Mr. Gladstone's name with as much enthusiasm as if the demonstration were taking place in England.

The other points in Mr. O'Brien's evidence may be rapidly passed over. Had he advised tenants to barricade their houses? Certainly. He had advised them to offer the utmost amount of passive resistance. "But," said Mr. O'Brien, "in that very speech which you are quoting I advised the tenants to shun crime as they would poison." In those barricadings, said Mr. O'Brien, "the suffering has been all on one side, I am sorry to say." But if Mr. O'Brien had advised the people to shun crime, had he not also, in the Saunders barricading case, advised the jury to acquit the accused, even before the trial began? Was not that doing the very thing of which Mr. O'Brien himself accused the Castle — bringing undue influence to bear upon jurors? Mr. O'Brien at once explained how in trials of that description juries are packed. "I said," he continued, "that the defenders were not guilty of *crime.*" "My advice was moral advice, not legal advice." "I hold conscience to be higher than legality." "Law has not the same meaning in Ireland that it has in a freely governed country like England."

The same idea pervaded Mr. O'Brien's remarks on another topic, which suddenly sprang up, on an incidental allusion of the Attorney-General's, and which created considerable excitement in court. Sir Richard Webster made a passing reference to the "three murderers, Allen, Larkin, and O'Brien." Quick as lightning, Mr. O'Brien repudiated the word murderers. The three "Manchester Martyrs" were not murderers. They were only trying to rescue their fellow-countrymen from the prison-van; they fired into the lock, for the purpose of breaking open the van-door, and Sergeant Brett was accidentally shot.

"Hear, hear!" exclaimed some one, in a low voice, from the well of the court. The Attorney-General protested. "A most unbecoming expression," said the President, "and if I knew who used it, I should order him to leave the court, whoever he might be; and let me observe with regard to this that I fully understand Mr. O'Brien's statement in the matter. He says that what these men did under the circumstances doesn't warrant the ordinary appellation of murder. Well, I am not going to discuss that with him now. I need only remind him, and every one else, that in this court at least it must be regarded as murder. The prisoners were tried and found guilty of murder."

The person who "used it" was Mr. Michael Davitt. And the person who on behalf of the Treasury prosecuted the three men to their death, was the Mr. James Hannen, who in the course of years was destined to sit in judgment on the Irish Nationalists.

A striking contrast between the man who had just walked out of the box and the man who now entered it. Mr. O'Brien, with only thirty-seven years of life; haggard, bent, careworn, fragile, with his expression of intense earnestness; "Murty Hynes," white-haired, white-bearded, and sixty-two or three, straight as a ramrod, hearty in manner, and brimful of happy humour and animal spirits. As regards temperament, two different types of Irishmen. But both exactly alike in conviction, and in their totally unembarrassed, frank, downright, fearless style of saying their say.

Mr. T. D. Sullivan, M.P., ex-Lord Mayor of Dublin, is often called "Murty Hynes," after his famous ballad. "T. D." is the bard of the Nationalists. Mr. Sullivan was examined by Mr. Reid. He described himself as member of Parliament for the "College-green" division of Dublin, and as editor and proprietor of *The Nation*, and as an opponent from the beginning of his career of all "impracticable" schemes, such as Fenianism, for the regeneration of Ireland. He showed how he had all along supported the constitutional movements in Ireland, as against physical force projects. Of Mr. Martin's Home Rule party, then of Mr. Butt's, lastly of Mr. Parnell's, Mr. Sullivan had been an adherent. He had never even heard that the Land and National Leagues, of which he was a member, had encouraged outrage. His paper, *The Nation*, had denounced outrage in every shape and form. More than an hour was occupied by Mr. Reid in quoting, from *The Nation*, extracts in which mutilation was unsparingly denounced, and dynamite notions ridiculed.

Mr. Murphy now rose to cross-examine. If Mr. Sullivan was opposed to deeds of violence, why had he celebrated, in verse, the shooting of a policeman by Captain Mackay? Had he celebrated it? Mr. Sullivan shook his head. He smiled benignly upon Mr. Murphy. Knew nothing about any such "song." Mr. Murphy tried again. Well, Mr. Sullivan, did you write anything? Mr. Sullivan again shook his head. He could not recollect. Then Mr. Murphy looked puzzled. He had made some mistake. "Well, let us try something else," quoth Mr. Murphy. "No, no," said "T. D. S.," in his bright, hearty way, "let us dispose of this first." An outburst of laughter, wherein Mr. Murphy did not join.

"But you did write a song, Mr. Sullivan, in praise of a man who gave up an evicted farm?" This was the famous ballad of "Murty Hynes." Mr. Sullivan bowed. "I have not seen it." said the President, with a kindly smile. Well, Mr. Sullivan had a copy of his poems (bound in the national colour, green), which was at Sir James's disposal. It would have been interesting to hear Mr. Murphy read out that popular ballad in court. At his pleasant "At Homes" in the Dublin Mansion House, my lord the Mayor often sang "Murty Hynes," for the delectation of his guests. Mr. Sullivan has a splendid voice, and his rendering of the Irish brogue is inimitably humorous. Mr. Murphy next mentioned Mr. Sullivan's "God Save Ireland," a song founded on the story of the Manchester trials, and since become the anthem of the Irish race all over the world. What of that song, Mr. Sullivan? "I shall say nothing to throw dishonour on the memory of those men," was the answer. "They acted a foolish but a brave part." Forgetful of the President's warning, given when Mr. O'Brien was under cross-examination, some one called out, Hear, hear! "There are," said Mr. Sullivan, "legal crimes which in Ireland, under the circumstances of the times, could not be called moral crimes." Of course he was questioned about boycotting and intimidation. Upon which he generally replied that he had over and over again said he would not hurt a hair of the grabber's head. "I would give him bread if he wanted it." But for all that "I consider the grabber a moral leper; it is he who has created rack rent?" For a long time Mr. Murphy pounded away, heavily, perseveringly, with questions about the Land League books. "Why did you not ask about them, Mr. Sullivan?" "Oh, why did I not ask about a thousand other things?" replied Mr. Sullivan. "Did you ever help the authorities to detect crime, Mr. Sullivan?" "Help? How? What do you mean? Give the police information? Why, I had none to give."

EIGHTY-SIXTH DAY.

MAY 24.

MR. MURPHY renewed his bombardment of Mr. T. D. Sullivan. Mr. Murphy, Q.C., had in the interval been studying "Green Leaves," and Mr. Murphy thought he had caught the poet. Listen to this, Mr. Sacer Vates of Nationalism—

> Here's to West Meath,
> Where a tyrant cannot breathe.

What of that melodious couplet? "Nonsense, man" (Mr. Sullivan waving his hand), "Why, that's poetry." And Mr. Sullivan raised his brows, and shrugged his shoulders, as if he thought (but didn't like to say) that it was no use arguing with the literal-minded Murphy. But it must mean something, quoth Murphy, looking a little troubled. Well, yes; and the verses were only the bardic way of saying that the "grabber" (the Ishmael of Ireland) had no footing in West Meath. The bard and the lawyer gazed at each other— Apollo and Rhadamanthus seeing each his side of the shield. The poet regarded the lawyer in amused pity. Then it turned out that Mr. Murphy made a mistake in his quotation. What he should have said was—

> Where a tyrant scarce can breathe.

But as the lawyer's is the most unpoetic of callings, Mr. Murphy still failed to see it, and remained unconvinced when Mr. Sullivan informed him that he had toasted (in tuneful numbers) all the counties of Ireland, and found in "breathe" a handy rhyme for Meath.

Then Mr. Murphy tried the Catechism, the Land League Catechism only— though, as the reading proceeded, it aroused some dismal reminiscences of another catechism. Mr. Murphy reeled off his catechism at irreverent speed, showing what was the chief end of (Nationalist) man, what the deserts, both now and in the future, of the grabbing sinner. Mr. Murphy droned away like a curate in a hurry. And the congregation yawned.

Having done with verse and the Catechism, Mr. Murphy tried journalism. As editor and proprietor of *The Nation*, Mr. Sullivan had been accustomed to print a weekly column under the title "Incidents of the Campaign." The incidents included cases of boycotting and of other forms of intimidation. Did Mr. Sullivan approve of such incidents? Mr. Sullivan stared at Murphy in astonishment. These "incidents" were cuttings from other newspapers. And they were inserted simply as news. "We are bound to publish news," said Mr. Sullivan, thumping the desk. But that would not satisfy Mr. Murphy, who again asked, " Did you mean to glorify evil news?" "Glorification had nothing to do with it," was the answer; the incidents were inserted as news. But there was a leading article which Mr. Murphy fixed upon. In that leader, an article of *The Times*, denouncing dynamitards as fiends was treated in a scoffing spirit. But Mr. Sullivan explained that *The Nation* writer was not scoffing at his *Times* brother for denouncing dynamiters, but because he was doing it hypocritically—coming down heavily upon the Irish—or American-Irish—offender, while letting the Continental offender down easily. "I regard dynamiters," said Mr. Sullivan, "as criminals of the deepest dye. And as for fiends, no man is a fiend," exclaimed Mr. Sullivan, loudly and sharply. At this generous expression about human nature, Mr. Justice Day laughed, and laughed again until he grew red in the face. He laughed almost as heartily as he did when Sir Charles Russell was reading out Mr. Pigott's applications to Mr. Forster for fresh loans.

After Mr. Sullivan there followed three witnesses from Miltown Malbay in county Clare. They were examined respecting *The Times* evidence on the murder of Mike Moroney, and the intimidation of James Connell. On both counts they contradicted *The Times* witnesses. The first of the three, Father Stewart, was of opinion that the murder of Moroney was not of agrarian origin. He thought it was the result of a private feud. The second witness, Mike Killeen, secretary of the local branch of the Land League, denied that he had summoned Connell to attend a League Court. And the third witness, James Clancy, who was at one time president of the branch, denied that he had ever threatened Connell with the boycott for refusing to become a member. Clancy himself was evicted in 1881. "What have you been doing since?" asked Sir Henry James. Oh, nothing; only "knocking about"; but the National League had been giving him twenty-three shillings a week for the support of his family, and he lived in one of the League cottages. Clancy's rent was sixty-five pounds a year when he was evicted. He answered cheerfully and pleasantly all along. But he nearly broke down, he stammered fiercely, when he came to describe how the buildings which he himself had put up were destroyed and carted off by the landlord, and how his children had suffered.

Lastly came Mr. John Ferguson of Glasgow, whose name and initials have often been heard of in the course of the trial. His examination-in-chief—in which he declared that if Parnellism had not been constitutional he would have had nothing to do with it—occupied only a couple of minutes. But his cross-examination filled part of the forenoon and the whole of the afternoon. Yet this cross-examination was the most dismally dull and fruitless in the whole course of this trial. The utmost it did was to give Mr. John Ferguson an opportunity of proclaiming himself a disciple of John Stuart Mill and Mr. Herbert Spencer. The great point at issue in the cross-examination was to find out from Mr. Ferguson what had become of the missing Land League books. And Mr. John Ferguson knew absolutely nothing. He was bombarded with questions—principally about the Tim Horan letter—Tim being secretary of the Castleisland branch of the Land League, and the letter being a request to the Central League office for money to be paid to certain men who had been hurt in some mysterious fray, and about whom, said the letter, nobody, except the doctor and the society, knew anything. The letter bore Mr. Ferguson's initials, but Mr. Ferguson had forgotten all about it, and he declared that the very date of the endorsement showed that the letter must have been received when the League was about to be suppressed, and when therefore its concluding business was done in a hurry. Besides, said he, the letter was an application for medical relief, which, speaking personally, he would not refuse to give to a criminal, supposing he had it to give.

The letter from local secretary Tim Horan was the solitary proof—if it be a proof—even of indirect support, by the Dublin office, of physical violence and intimidation. One of the four who had been engaged in the adventure lost the use of an eye, another was wounded in the body, but what the affair was in which the men were engaged, neither counsel nor the prosecution could tell. From beginning of his career, Mr. Ferguson had been opposed to violence in any shape or form. "That's not in my line," he replied, when asked if he knew anything of the story that the League money had been spent in sending Dutch officers to South Africa, to help the Boers against the English, "I would rather send the Boers arguments." Instead of spilling blood, he would "spread the light," by writing and lecturing. Mr. Ferguson was organizing Home Rule branches throughout the United Kingdom six years before the foundation of the Irish Land League. And when the time came, he helped Mr. Davitt to found the Land League. A Republican in politics, he helped Sir Charles Dilke once upon a time to "spread the light" of republicanism in Glasgow.

EIGHTY-SEVENTH DAY.
MAY 28.

MR. REID began by giving the Court a pleasant surprise. Some of the lost books of the Land League had been found. And Mr. Reid had them in court—even the cash-book, as Mr. Reid blandly intimated, in reply to a prompt and anxious question put by Mr. Justice Smith. The disappearance of these books had long been the subject of unfriendly speculation—unfriendly to the accused. The absence of the League books was one of the negative grounds on which the Attorney-General based his charge of criminality against the League. It was a somewhat comical element of the situation that the books had been in the possession of a gentleman, Mr. Moloney, whom *The Times* itself subpœnaed.

Mr. Reid having merely alluded to this, Sir Henry James rose to express his desire that the motives of *The Times* counsel should not be misunderstood. Mr. Maloney was subpœnaed in order that he might identify handwriting; and "it is not to be supposed," added Sir Henry James, "that we knew there were books in his possession, or that they could be procured through him."

Then began the examination of the first of nine witnesses. All the nine were from county Cork. The first eight were questioned about outrages. They declared that the League systematically denounced them. The first of the nine, Mr. Mackay, a journalist, who had attended large numbers of League meetings, declared that these denunciations were so much a matter of fact that reporters thought it not worth while to record them. O'Connell's warning that "he who commits crime gives strength to the enemy" became, said this witness, a hackneyed expression at League meetings. Similar testimony was given by Canon Shinkwin, of Bantry, League President, who stated that he would have had nothing to do with any League which encouraged crime in any way ; by Father Malley, the parish priest of Drimoleague, who strongly and wholly contradicted the murder story of a *Times* witness ; by the Protestant rector of Drinagh, who turned out to be the funny witness of the day ; by

Father Morissey, of Ballinteer, who declared that the League branches in his neighbourhood proposed to unite for the purpose of bringing criminals to justice ; by Canon Ryan, of Aghada ; by Father Murphy, of Skull ; and by Mr. Edward Raycroft, League official of the same parish. Mr. Healy's evidence referred principally to the character of Irish jury trials. The main position sought to be established by Mr. Reid and his colleagues was that landlord selfishness provoked the crimes which the League was successful in preventing. Canon Shinkwin's evidence ended with a very interesting piece of statistics, quoted by Mr. Reid, and showing how outrages and evictions increased simultaneously from 1877 to 1882. If the figures for outrages alone were given, some people might conclude that the new organization, the League, was responsible for the increase.

The Rev. Mr. Anderson was the first Irish Protestant pastor who appeared before the Commission. Unlike most Protestant clergymen in Ireland, he is a National leaguer. He is even a member of the League Committee. He was elected to the post by Catholics. No religious jealousy? "Oh, no "—with great emphasis on the "no"—"Catholics often came to consult me." "Always on good terms with the Catholics," exclaimed the rector, smiling and striking his palms together. " Landgrabbing ?" Why, Mr. Anderson once upon a time advertised a forthcoming sermon of his on " The Sin of Landgrabbing." And the result was one of the biggest congregations he ever had in his life ; the Catholics came in crowds. Here the worthy rector laughed heartily, and bent as he laughed.

Boycotting ? Nonsense. There was a feeble sort of a boycott, now and again. Why, the only decent boycott in the whole of Balinteer was the boycott to which he himself was subjected. Here he laughed again, threw his head up, next stared at his boots, laughed again in the greatest good humour. How boycotted ? Oh ! here you are ; and he produced a pinkish-yellow paper, showing how the landlords, because of his League principles, cut down their contribution to his stipend. The courageous rector did not seem to mind it in the least. Again he became merry. His wonderful knack of changing all in an instant his laughing face into one of fixed solemnity was comical in the extreme. He might have made his fortune by it in a less sacred profession. " Here's a funny thing," said he ; " Colonel Chute boycotted me by decreasing my stipend, and then his tenants came to me to ask me to lend them money to pay his rent." Here Mr. Anderson fairly gave way. He laughed until his face grew red. He looked up and down, and round about. Everybody laughed. In the twinkling of an eye Mr. Anderson's features became grave. He stuffed his papers into his pockets, and walked off.

During the examination of the next witness an interesting conversation arose between the President and counsel about the Whitsuntide holidays and the probable duration of the trial. Mr. Reid asked for an adjournment from next Friday to the 18th of June. The Attorney-General did not object ; nor did the President, except that he first wanted to know when the case for the defence was likely to end. Mr. Reid hinted that that depended upon his friend the enemy—to wit, the cross-examiners. Did Mr. Reid think that it would end before the long vacation (August 12th) ? Mr. Reid certainly thought it would ; in fact, he thought it would be done with " early in July." Whereupon the President remarked that he gladly granted the adjournment asked for. Half-an-hour or three-quarters of an hour later, when Sir Henry James was cross-examining at some length, Mr. Reid repented him of what he said about "early in July." He started up and withdrew his half promise. Mr. Justice Day smiled. So did a good many other people who were present.

EIGHTY-EIGHTH DAY.

MAY 29.

MR. MAURICE HEALY, Mr. Biggar, and Mr. Arthur O'Connor were examined to-day; the first-named for only a few minutes, in conclusion of his evidence of the preceding day. Mr. Joseph Biggar, with his elbows on the ledge of his box, talked for four hours. He and Sir Henry James got on very well together—the reason perhaps being that they are good-humoured personages both. One could not help speculating what would have happened if the renowned member for Cavan had been subjected to the knock-down, method of the Attorney-General. But Mr. Reid's turn came before Sir Henry James's; and to Mr. Reid Mr. Joseph Biggar described how he was an Isaac Buttite in 1871, and a Fenian (and a Supreme Councillor of Fenians) in 1875-6; and how in 1877 he was expelled from the Fenian Brotherhood because he voted against a resolution of theirs condemning reliance upon Parliamentary action instead of upon physical force.

Mr. Biggar flatly contradicted one or two stories which had been told about him by witnesses for the prosecution. There was the story of the informer Leavy, who said that Mr. Biggar offered him a bribe of one hundred pounds for his vote in the explusion business. "Not the slightest foundation" for it, said Mr. Biggar. Nor was it true that, at the great meeting in the Rotunda, he seconded a resolution against the definite adoption of constitutional agitation—that is, against Parliamentary action—for one reason among others, that such a resolution was not even moved. As for the Land League, he said, very emphatically, that at the time of its establishment, some "combination" of the kind was "indispensable." He knew not, nor believed, that the League had ever caused, or connived at, outrage. As for the "Invincibles," not until long after the Phœnix Park crime did he even hear the name of them. Sir Richard Webster, in his opening speech, had said that League emissaries had received from Mr. Biggar, who was one of the treasurers of the Land League, sums of money for the planning and execution of outrages. "Not the slightest foundation" for that story either, answered Mr. Biggar. His examination by Mr. Reid lasted only twenty minutes.

Sir Henry James's cross-examination was a sort of free-and-easy colloquial swamp, spreading out in all directions and ending nowhere in particular. As treasurer of the Land League, Mr. Biggar ought to know about the League's cash-books, ledgers, letter books. But that was only Sir Henry James's way of looking at it. Mr. Biggar knew nothing whatever about them, nor took any trouble to know. Mr. Biggar was only an ornamental treasurer—a sleeping partner in an office of which the active partner was Mr. Egan. But Mr. Egan, being for the moment in the United States, could give no help to Sir Henry James. Mr. Biggar did not even know whether Mr. Egan before leaving for America made over to any one the charge of the League funds in his possession, nor was Sir Henry James successful in identifying Mr. Biggar's Fenian oath. The Fenian oath which Sir Henry read out in court was not the one Mr. Biggar swore to. And what the precise terms of the real oath were Mr. Biggar could not recollect. He could only say that they were less grandiloquent than Sir Henry James's.

As the aim of the Fenians was to bring about an armed insurrection, and as the subscriptions of the brethren were supposed to be devoted to the purchase of arms, Sir Henry thought he could catch the member for Cavan by getting him to say what his subscription was. Subscription? Mr. Biggar never paid any. Nor was he ever asked for one.

Mr. Biggar, as he now explained, became a member of the brotherhood with the intention, as he expressed it, of checkmating the more violent among them, and of converting them to the constitutional movement. He was a proselytizer. In the long run, the brethren invited this easy-going Fenian—this unsatisfactory revolutionist—to resign. He preferred to fight them, so they turned him out, and Mr. Biggar had had nothing to do with them from that day to this.

Several of Mr. Biggar's speeches were quoted—or supposed to be quoted, for Mr. Biggar repeatedly called in question the accuracy of the reports in the Irish papers. In one of these speeches, delivered at a banquet given to Mr. Parnell in Cork, Mr. Biggar was reported to have said that if the constitutional agitation failed, Ireland would produce another Hartmann—of the type of the man who attempted the Czar's life. Without admitting the accuracy of the report Mr. Biggar said he could only have meant that, under certain circumstances, the Irish people might be driven into outrage. Mr. Biggar was extremely frank on the subject of boycotting. Mr. Biggar would boycott any one who "deserved" it, even to the extent of depriving him of the necessaries of life, and of cutting him in chapel; he would draw the line only at physical violence.

Mr. Arthur O'Connor was examined after Mr. Biggar. He described briefly how he went to Dublin to supervise, for a few days, the Land League office, the business of which had fallen into utter confusion in consequence of the imprisonment of its chiefs, and the absence, through illness, of Mr. Sexton. He found "hundreds of letters" unanswered, and the books in a state of chaos. It was when the office was in that condition that the application from Tim Horan (repeatedly alluded to in previous evidence) arrived, and was granted. But Mr. O'Connor remembered nothing whatever of the transaction.

EIGHTY-NINTH DAY.

MAY 30.

ON resuming his examination of Mr. Arthur O'Connor, Mr. Lockwood began with America, and in the course of a few minutes Mr. O'Connor summed up his experiences of twenty-seven States. Mr. O'Connor's American tour was made in 1887, Sir T. Esmonde accompanying him. They went to thank the Americans for their kindly help in the past, and to ask for its continuance. Mr. O'Connor's American experiences were a repetition of Mr. Parnell's. Everywhere he and his friends were most warmly received by the best—intellectually and socially—in the States, by State Governors, Judges of the Supreme Court, members of the learned professions. At one of the great receptions accorded to the two visitors, the gentleman now President of the United States was in the chair. And the future President there and then declared that "every honest man would rather be William O'Brien in Tullamore Gaol than the Lord-Lieutenant in Dublin Castle. This little story of Mr. Arthur O'Connor's was all the more interesting because President Harrison had just turned one of *The Times* "criminals," Mr. Patrick Egan, into United States Minister to Chili. It is needless to add that Mr. O'Connor declared that he had nothing to do with secret societies in the course of his American tour. It is equally needless to quote any of the extracts which Mr. Lockwood read from Mr. O'Connor's speeches by way of showing how entirely open and constitutional Mr. O'Connor's business in America was. It was an odd circumstance, brought out by Mr. Lockwood, that Mr. O'Connor was a member of a Royal Commission appointed by a Tory Ministry, at the very time when, in common with most of the Irish party, he lay under a charge of criminal association.

Mr. O'Connor was cross-examined by Mr. Atkinson—principally, of course, about the League books, and in particular about the Timothy Horan letter. Mr. O'Connor took a good deal of trouble to get Mr. Atkinson to understand that his supervision of the Land League business was strictly confined to the short period succeeding the date at which he took charge of it; and that this restriction was necessitated by his absolute inability to overtake the arrears, and restore order into the confusion which he found in the League offices. Mr. O'Connor had no previous experience of the Land League work; and of its books, or what became of them, or who had charge of them, he knew nothing. Nor had he any knowledge of the Tim Horan letter. As the letter was addressed, not to the League Secretary, but to a head clerk by name, he doubted very much whether the letter was ever passed through the League register.

Mr. O'Connor having expressed his belief that some of the League books were seized at the time by the authorities (presumably the Castle) and retained by them ever since, the President promptly directed that inquiries should be made to ascertain whether that was the fact. And then it looked as if Mr. Atkinson had discovered a mare's nest. "Just examine that cash-book of the Land League, Mr. O'Connor. You see it extends over a period of weeks and months; and yet it looks as if it had been written right off. Isn't the ink the same all through, Mr. O'Connor?" Mr. O'Connor replied that it was black ink all through. "Yes; but from the same bottle, Mr. O'Connor?" The book was passed up for the President's inspection. The President did not appear to see anything suspicious in it. He merely thought it looked as if it had been written by "the same clerk." In plain English Mr. Atkinson was suggesting the notion of forgery. Glancing at *The Times* people, Mr. O'Connor remarked, with a dry little smile, that he was "not an expert."

Mr. Atkinson then turned off to a different subject, Mr. O'Connor's speeches about grabbers, and Mr. O'Connor's notions of boycotting. Mr. O'Connor frankly informed him that he still regarded the grabber as "a receiver of stolen goods," and that if a boycott should drive the grabber into the workhouse which sheltered his victims, it would serve the grabber right. At the end, Mr. Atkinson asked Mr. O'Connor if in one of his speeches he thanked God for a bad harvest! The answer was a quiet but indignant "Never." Unsophisticated persons may fail to see why Mr. O'Connor should thank God for a bad harvest. Bad harvests meant no rents for landlords. Paddy cutting off his nose to spite his face. Before he left the witness-box Mr. O'Connor stated that of the hundreds of speeches which he had delivered, only one was put in by *The Times*. That solitary speech was supposed by *The Times* to have caused a murder perpetrated four years after its delivery.

Next came Mr. Justin McCarthy, Vice-President of the Irish Parliamentary party. As Mr. McCarthy never held any office in the Land League, and as he had nothing to do with the details of management of the National League, it followed that counsel on either side had little or nothing of much consequence to ask him. Still, the performance must be gone through—for was he not one of the incriminated sixty-five? People must have been amused to hear questions—put with all the gravity in the world—as to whether Mr. Justin McCarthy was mixed up in bloodthirsty conspiracies. Being President of the English branch of the National League, Mr. McCarthy was, of course, in frequent communication with its secretary, Mr. Frank Byrne. "I found him," said Mr. McCarthy, "a straightforward, business man." "I never heard or saw a word from him that would lead me to suspect he had anything to do with the Phœnix Park murders." Mr. Murphy tried Mr. McCarthy on the subject of boycotting. Would it be right to boycott a herd, with his family of six children, merely because the herd worked for a farmer who occupied an "evicted farm?" Yes, "that might be necessary and right"—

meaning in the case of a farm "evicted" for non-payment of unjust rent. In his re-examination by Mr. Reid, Mr. McCarthy found his opportunity to remind the Court that landlord eviction of a man with six children was at least as harsh a measure as the tenants' boycotting of him.

After Mr. McCarthy came Mr. George Lewis, to say what he knew about the League books. All he knew was that he had put into Court every single Land League book and document in his possession; and that he had invited Mr. Soames to come to his office and inspect all he had, but that Mr. Soames never came. He was asked by the Attorney-General why he had not inquired after this, that, and the other League book; why he had not followed the movements of this, that, and the other Lady Land Leaguer. It looked as if Sir Richard Webster was asking Mr. Lewis why he had not assisted Mr. Soames in getting up *The Times* case.

NINETIETH DAY.

MAY 31.

THE net result of the cross-examination of Mr. Arthur O'Connor to-day was to absolve the League of all except a merely technical responsibility for the famous "moonlighting letter." Probably we have heard the last of this letter, to which *The Times* people have attributed such great importance—and naturally, for the letter was the one proof which they had discovered, in nine years' League history, of any participation, direct and indirect, by the central office of the Land and National Leagues in outrage. There is in one of the central office books before the Commission a record of the payment of money, for the relief of "labourers," to Mr. T. Horan, secretary of the Castleisland Branch in county Cork. The theory of the cross-examining counsel was that this payment for "labourers" was in response to Horan's appeal for relief to the men who had been wounded in a secret expedition. In looking through the books in the witness-box Mr. Arthur O'Connor, who is sharp at accounts, gave reasons for believing that the "labourers'" grant was in reply to another application—that there were two different transactions. The truth then would appear to be that the labourers' relief had been authorized by the League Committee, and that for the medical grant to the men wounded in the midnight affray Mr. Quin, a clerk in the League Office, was personally responsible. For more than half-an-hour Mr. Atkinson laboured, and belaboured, this authorization of the secret grant—with the object of finding out whether Mr. O'Connor knew anything of the transaction. All that Mr. O'Connor would do was to repeat, over and over, that he knew absolutely nothing. "I understand," said Sir James Hannen, "that as far as you personally are concerned, you never saw this letter at all." "I am perfectly sure I never did," Mr. O'Connor replied; "if I had, I would have sent back a reply that the Land League funds were not to be used for such purposes. It was a most improper application."

After Mr. Arthur O'Connor came Mr. Edward Harrington, member for West Kerry. There was a laugh when Mr. Harrington said he resided in Kerry "when permitted." But it was not always a laughing matter to Mr. Harrington; for he alluded to his imprisonments, from one of which he had but lately been released in order to enable him to appear before the Commission. Since his arrival in London, Mr. Harrington's hair has grown a little. Mr. Harrington has endured his prison hardships fairly well; so has Mr.

Condon, M.P., who has arrived within the last day or two. But as for Mr. John O'Connor, many who knew him well failed to recognize him. His appearance shocked them. He looked fifteen years older.

Mr. Edward Harrington made an excellent witness. He showed the most astonishingly comprehensive and minute acquaintance with the history and condition of Kerry. The Land League had been a whole year in existence before a branch of it was founded in Mr. Harrington's locality—Tralee. Mr. Harrington believed that the establishment of local branches in Kerry was necessitated by the rapidly increasing rate at which the landlords were evicting their tenants. In the county of Kerry there were only seventy evictions in 1879; but there were one hundred and eighty-one in 1880, and the numbers increased largely in succeeding years. It was these evictions which, in Mr. Harrington's view, led to riots and outrages, which the police endeavoured to suppress by capturing crowds at haphazard. He knew of one instance in which a man, detained thirteen months in prison without trial, was eventually discharged for want of evidence. The natural result was complete mistrust in law and justice in Kerry.

Mr. Murphy tried hard, and long, to overthrow Mr. Harrington's statistics, but without success. Mr. Murphy next tried to prove that at least one murderer was in the pay of the League. This was Sylvester Poff—of whom Mr. Harrington spoke as follows: "I don't believe there's a man in Kerry who thinks this day that there was anything against that man. On my oath, I solemnly believe he was as innocent as any man in this court." "Were you present at his trial?" Mr. Murphy asked. "I was present at his examination before the magistrate, but not at his trial—if you can call it a trial." "But," Mr. Harrington continued, "I have sufficient facts to account for what I say, and I invite you to examine me on them." The condemned man, said Mr. Harrington, was not a member of the League; and whatever pecuniary assistance he had must have been given him only because he was an evicted tenant, or because he was one among many "suspects," for the maintenance of whose families the League was raising public subscriptions.

Mr. Harrington threw some strange light upon a story told in court by process-server Herbert, a *Times* witness. This man Herbert said he had been shot at. But, said Mr. Harrington, he did not tell their lordships that at the time he was supposed to have been attacked he had a revolver in his pocket, and that several holes were found in his coat-tails. Mr. Harrington believed that in fumbling for his revolver the weapon must have gone off accidentally, wounding Herbert in the wrist, and that Herbert invented the story of the murderous assault upon him. Mr. Harrington was put in prison just at the time when he was investigating the Herbert story. As to boycotting, there was too little of it in Kerry, said Mr. Harrington. Had there been more boycotting there would have been fewer outrages. The day's evidence ended with Mr. Harrington's citation of instances in which the League, and he himself individually, had not only denounced outrages, but done their utmost to assist the authorities in finding out the perpetrators.

NINETY-FIRST DAY.

JUNE 18.

AFTER eighteen days' silence, Mr. Murphy's cross-examination of Mr. Edward Harrington was resumed this morning without preface, without preliminary flourish of any sort, bluntly, baldly, abruptly, like an organ-grinder's tune, at the point where it abruptly broke off. Mr. Murphy, Q.C., is a steady, patient hand at the bellows. For two hours he led Mr. Harrington the old dance to the old grind. The number of visitors to the court was unusually small. In the side gallery sat the wife of Mr. Alexander Sullivan, of Chicago. The *Times* counsel were in full strength. On the Nationalist side, Mr. Reid, Q.C., was the leading advocate present.

In order to show that Mr. E. Harrington, in Kerry, was not an upholder of justice, Mr. Murphy quoted some extracts from *The Kerry Sentinel* (Mr. Harrington's paper), in which sentences passed upon certain agrarian offenders were vigorously denounced. Mr. Harrington, in the witness-box, declared that the sentences were a violation of justice. Other people charged, said Mr. Harrington, escaped the punishment due to their crimes—and they escaped it because they paid the landlords' rents. Here Sir James Hannen interposed with the remark that no part of his duty caused a judge so much anxiety as the meting out of sentences; and he asked Mr. E. Harrington whether he still felt it right to characterize the action of Judge Lawson in the terms which he had applied to it six or seven years ago. With the utmost deliberation, and without the slightest pause or embarrassment, Mr. Harrington replied that he would "not hesitate to write the same words again under the same circumstances."

Then Mr. Murphy approached him from another direction. At the time of the Phœnix Park trials, a Dublin correspondent wrote to *The Sentinel* a letter in which informers like Delaney were described as "craven cowards" and "as kindly helping to expedite matters by pleading guilty," and at which more reticent witnesses at the trials were called "noble exceptions." Mr. Harrington expressed his belief that the writer of the letter had no sympathy whatever with the murderers; but he added, frankly and unreservedly, that he did not approve of the correspondent's language, and that had he seen it beforehand it would not have been admitted into the columns of *The Sentinel*. But again, with the utmost frankness, Mr. Harrington said that he accepted full responsibility for whatever appeared in his paper.

Not satisfied with Mr. Harrington's unreserved admissions, Mr. Murphy pressed him with this unpleasant question, "Are you not ashamed of it?" (the Dublin letter). Sir James Hannen interfered at once, remarking that such questions were "superfluous," and calculated to "give the witness pain." There was an angry flash in Mr. Harrington's eyes at the moment when the President interfered. But in a minute or two more there came about a little collision between Mr. Harrington and the President himself. Mr. Murphy, turning off to another part of the inquiry, was questioning Mr. Harrington about his own speeches, when the latter suddenly and warmly protested against the unfair manner in which "the Government," for the purposes of the Commission, had selected speeches which might damage the Nationalist cause, and carefully ignored speeches, such as his own, in which outrages were denounced in the strongest terms. "The Government have nothing to do with this inquiry," exclaimed Sir James Hannen, sharply, "the witnesses are ordinary witnesses." "But I am not able to discriminate, my lord," said Mr. Harrington. "You should," was the President's answer. "I will not allow such allusions to be made to the Government." This was an interesting part of the cross-examination; for Mr. Harrington reiterated his statement respectfully, but in his most emphatic manner, that the police shorthand reporters were incapable of taking shorthand reports; that their reports were merely summaries of what they read in the papers. Mr. Harrington strongly protested that one of *The Times* constabulary witnesses, Huggins, though present during its delivery, made no report whatever of a speech in which he, Mr. Harrington, inveighed for nearly an hour against perpetrators of outrage. The cross-examination of Mr. Harrington ended with a candid statement of his respecting his defiance of evictors; and with an explanation of "a threatening notice" for which he had been sentenced to six months' imprisonment. As to the first, Mr. Harrington told the Court that he had repeatedly "kicked open" the doors of houses from which poor women and children had been driven out by the bailiffs. "I made them re-enter," said Mr. Harrington. "I found them by the roadside in the cold of November and December; and many of the women were suckling their infants. Some of these farms were worth only two pounds a year, but the houses upon them, built by the evicted tenants themselves, were worth twenty." As to the "threatening notice" published or reproduced in *The Sentinel* (by a misapprehension, as Mr. Harrington said), the witness maintained that the very terms of it showed that it was only a practical joke; for the "notice," though warning people who refused to become members of an "Invincible" branch about to be formed, stated publicly and plainly where and when the inaugural meeting of this criminal society would be held.

All the day's witnesses were from Kerry. The next witness, Patrick Kenny, of Castleisland, enjoyed the distinction of having been "censured" by his fellow-leaguers for having shaken hands with Earl Spencer, Lord-Lieutenant of Ireland. Mr. Kenny, president of the Castleisland Land and National League branches was, of course, cross-examined with especial reference to the famous Tim Horan letter and the books of the Castleisland branch. He told his cross-examiner, Mr. Atkinson, that he knew nothing of the letter, nothing of the mysterious expedition for which League money was said to have been paid—nothing save what he had read in the reports of the evidence given before the Commission. He knew nothing about one of Horan's friends having lost an eye, or about another having been wounded in the leg. But all that "might" have happened, said Mr. Kenny, airily. Mr. Kenny's "might's" and "may be's" rather exasperated Mr. Atkinson. President, though he was, Mr. Kenny knew nothing of the branch books, nothing about subscriptions, nothing about correspondence with Dublin. But of course there "might" have been correspondence and fully-kept account books. It was not his business to trouble himself about such things. Nor did Mr. Kenny appear to consider it to be his duty to act the part of rogue-catcher for the Irish Government. Mr. Kenny could not say positively whether he had ever seen the book kept by Tim Horan. But of course "I might" have seen it, remarked Mr. Kenny, turning to their lordships, who were tired of him.

Mr. Kenny was succeeded in the box by a Kerry priest, Father Godley, who drew the boycotting line at refusal to supply necessaries of life, but who also maintained that the sufferings of boycotted people who took "evicted" farms were not greater than those of people who had been turned out. He told his examiner (Mr. Arthur Russell) that from the altar, and in private, he had always denounced outrage. Next came D. F. O'Connor, secretary of the Abbeydorney branch. He had with him a black pormanteau, containing League books and other documents, from which he was prepared to show how the League had persistently been denouncing crime. Some extracts from these documents were read. The last witness was Mr. Lyne, of Killarney, who described how at a public meeting he heard Mr. Davitt make his cart-tail speech, and Mr. Healy propose the formation of a vigilance committee for the discovery of outragemongers. Among several instances of hardship, Mr. Lyne mentioned the deaths from exposure of children who were ill of scarlet fever before they were evicted. As for the murder of D. Leahy (mentioned in the evidence, and attributed by the prosecution to the influence of the League), Mr. Lyne said that Leahy was universally popular, that the regret for his death was general, and that almost all the leaguers of the district attended his funeral.

NINETY-SECOND DAY.

JUNE 19.

COUNTING O'Connor, who was recalled for a few minutes, and Mr. Lyne, of Killarney, whose examination was resumed, seven witnesses gave their testimony to-day. They were all from county Kerry. The joke of the day was the joint work of Sir Henry James and John Greany, a Kerry man, with a vast, wild stock of hair about his face, and a broad brogue. Sir Henry asked him where the address of a certain leaguer was to be found. "He's in eternity," quoth Mr. Greany. "Is he going to be called?" inquired Sir Henry, suavely. Mr. Greany stared. It turned out that Sir Henry James thought Greany said that the missing man was " in Italy "—which is less vague than " Eternity." Mr. Greany, a strenuous witness, maintained that his part of Kerry, at any rate, was all the better for the League, which persistently denounced crime.

When O'Connor was recalled, Sir Richard Webster read some extracts from League books produced by the witness the day before, from which it appeared that O'Connor had once sent a kind of circular letter to the League branches, advising them to forbid people from hiring threshing-machines from farmers who were not members of the League. The Attorney-General appeared pretty well satisfied with this instance of an attempt to increase membership by intimidation. But Mr. Reid read a letter from Mr. T. Harrington, secretary of the Central League office, in which the attempt was roundly denounced as "idiotic," and the offending branch advised to close its doors if it could not help the national cause in any other way than by passing such "stupid" resolutions. There could be no mistake about the meaning of the message from Dublin.

After this prompt and successful countermove by Mr. Reid, Mr. Lyne, the Killarney merchant was questioned. Examined by Mr. Davitt, Mr. Lyne said he attributed crime to landlord injustice. He did not complain of it, but as a matter of fact the landlords and their people deprived Mr. Lyne of their custom as soon as he began to take an active part in League work.

A good witness was Father Lawler, parish priest of Killoughlin. He scouted the landlord and landlord's agent theory of a pre-League Arcadia. There were outrages before 1879; he named the victims of some of them. And before 1879 landlords confiscated their tenants' improvements. And in the year before the foundation of the League the whole of his parish population, save twelve farmers, were in receipt of relief—to which the landlords contributed nothing. Combination was, for the tenants, said Father Lawler, an absolute necessity; and the League supplied the means. It was his firm belief that the League saved the tenants, and that it largely reduced crime. He was frank on the subject of boycotting. Of course the leaguers sat "in court" over agrarian disputes; and when a man refused to surrender a farm from which his predecessor had been unjustly evicted, why the leaguers took Mr. Parnell's advice: they "avoided" him—as Sir Charles Russell would say, they sent him to Coventry. In that Father Lawler saw nothing wrong.

The next witness was a priest, Father Daniel Harrington, president of the Listowel Catholic Seminary. He corroborated the preceding witness's testimony to the effect that the League prevented wholesale clearances of tenants, and caused a diminution in crime. Speaking of the Phœnix Park murders, he said that when the news reached Listowel, the town went into mourning and the school children marched through the streets with crape on their arms. It was Father Harrington's opinion that police agents sometimes manufactured outrages. He mentioned one such offender, by name Cullinane. "Where is he?" asked Mr. Atkinson. "The Government knows best about that," was the answer. "Did you ever exhort your people to try and bring criminals to justice?" Mr. Atkinson continued. "I might as well," replied Father Harrington, "ask them to capture Jack the Ripper." Good—though the Ripper was not then in existence.

Next, Mr. John Shea, proprietor of a hotel at Glenbeigh, described how completely free of crime the place was during the terrible evictions of 1887. This he attributed to the influence of the League. Of John Greany, of Knocknagoshen, we have already spoken. The last witness, Thomas J. O'Connor, of Knocknagoshen, contradicted the story of a *Times* witness named Tobin, that he, O'Connor, had offered Tobin five pounds if he would "lift" somebody's cattle.

NINETY-THIRD DAY.

JUNE 20.

SINCE the previous sitting Sir Henry James had looked over the League books produced in court by O'Connor of Knocknagoshen. Among them he discovered a quaint resolution by the local branch—a resolution condemning those who "had issued threatening notices against and poisoned the hens of Mary O'Sullivan." Most of the resolutions condemned outrages as the work of low fellows, unworthy to be called Irishmen. In fact, it was not quite clear to outsiders why Sir Henry James read out these resolutions; they might as appropriately have been quoted by counsel for the defence. However, before eleven o'clock Sir Henry James was done with the Knocknagoshen League records, and to O'Connor of Knocknagoshen succeeded O'Connor of the Scotland division of Liverpool.

"T. P." was examined by Mr. Lockwood. Having given brief particulars about his birthplace—picturesque Athlone—about his beginnings in journalism, twenty-two years ago, and about his election for Galway and for Liverpool, Mr. T. P. O'Connor said that from what he remembered of the time, secret societies existed in the Athlone region during his boyhood. Ribbonism, secret association for the commission of crime, was the subject of common talk there in 1866-7. Before the foundation of the Land League in 1879, said Mr. O'Connor, the Irish tenants were unprotected against rack-rent and eviction. Combination was necessary, and organization; and as a matter of fact, Mr. O'Connor himself it was who suggested the formation of the Land League organizing body, of which so much has been heard in the course of the present trial.

To show what was the complexion of Mr. T. P. O'Connor's Land League politics, Mr. Lockwood read out one of Mr. O'Connor's speeches, which was delivered in September, 1880, and which advocated the extension, with fair compensation to landlords, of peasant proprietorship in Ireland, partly on the ground that such extension would promote social stability and security. When Mr. Parnell was in the witness-box he described Mr. T. P. O'Connor as one of the moderate members of the party; and the speech quoted by Mr. Lockwood answered to the description.

Continuing the story of his career, Mr. O'Connor said he had opposed "tooth and nail" the Coercion Act of 1881. He spoke contemptuously of this Act, saying it was based on statistics of crime which included such offences as upsetting a beehive and spilling a barrel of tar. From this subject Mr. Lockwood passed to Mr. O'Connor's American tour of 1881-2. Like Mr. Parnell (and to quote Mr. Cook), Mr. O'Connor personally conducted his own tour; no Clan-na-Gael managers, nor any other managers, had any control over it. And like Mr. Parnell, Mr. O'Connor had to complain of the lack of organized help during his tour in the States. In the whole of this tour Mr. O'Connor only once heard discussion about a dynamite policy. This was in the course of talk with Finerty, who " said something to the effect that any means were justifiable for the obtaining of what the Irish wanted." " I strongly denounced " that view, said Mr. O'Connor.

Coming to Mr. Parnell's payment of one hundred pounds to Frank Bryne, Mr. O'Connor said he had no distinct recollection of that particular payment, but that it was a perfectly ordinary transaction between the Dublin League. which had money to spare, and the London League, which was too often impecunious. But this explanation of what *The Times* alleged to be a murder-grant is now so well known that we need not repeat it. The examination-in-chief ended with an emphatic declaration by Mr. O'Connor that the effect of the Parnell movement was to substitute constitutional agitation for violence, and open combination for secret association. " Have you ever," said Mr. Lockwood, " lent any countenance to crime or outrage?" " I have never," replied Mr. O'Connor, " heard it suggested that I had."

Mr. Ronan jumped up to cross-examine. He began with the Parnell movement, of which Mr. O'Connor had just spoken. " Tell me," said Mr. Ronan, excitedly, " the beginning, not of the Land League or of the National League, but of the Parnell movement." A wide question, and as vague as it was wide. It amused Mr. Ronan's hearers. " What do you mean?" said Mr. O'Connor, almost under his breath, and raising his eyebrows. " I should say," exclaimed Mr. O'Connor at last, " that the Parnell movement began three centuries ago." Mr. Ronan looked troubled, and the Court laughed. Than Mr. Ronan dived into a pile of books—a book by Mrs. Alexander Sullivan, of Chicago, to which Mr. O'Connor wrote a preface ; a book by John Devoy ; and Mr. T. P. O'Connor's own book on the Parnell movement. Mr. Ronan thought that because Mr. O'Connor wrote a preface to Mrs. Sullivan's book, he would fix certain heavy responsibilities upon him, and he thought he could prove from the book that the Parnell movement was an American birth of the year 1878. But coming to details, Mr. O'Connor assigned the birth of the Parnell movement to 1879 and Irishtown. The more Mr. Ronan searched among his books for proofs of his American theory, the more excited he became. He plunged through his extracts nervously, noisily, hurriedly, here, there, and everywhere, until at last the President remarked, with an air of comic despair, that the whole thing was growing like a " Chinese puzzle." Mr. Ronan went at " T. P." like a barking terrier at a taciturn, good-natured mastiff. He was making hard efforts to wring something treasonable out of Mr. O'Connor's American speeches. Had Mr. O'Connor said that British rule in Ireland was without legal and moral sanction ? " Certainly," said Mr. O'Connor, " British rule in Ireland, being against the wishes of the Irish people, was without moral sanction ; it might be legal because every Government was *de facto* legal." And he added, in a quiet, easy way, that the present Government in Ireland was exactly in the above position.

Next Mr. Ronan tried, but unsuccessfully, to get Mr. O'Connor to admit that there was an encouragement to murder in a passage of one of his American speeches, in which he said he would not like to be an insurance agent for a man who took an evicted farm, adding (what Mr. Ronan omitted to quote) that that was a horrible and savage state of things, produced by misrule. Next Mr. Ronan plied him with questions about moonlighting. " I know nothing about it," said Mr. O'Connor. " The moonlighters did not make me their father-confessor. You ought to know more about them than I do, for you have lived more in Ireland." Twice or thrice the President interfered to say he could not see the point of Mr. Ronan's questions. It was altogether a rambling, incoherent, futile piece of cross-examination.

Father O'Connor, parish priest of Firies, county Kerry, now entered the witness-box. In the Curtin evidence, it was said of Father O'Connor that he neglected to visit the Curtin family on the occasion of Mr. Curtin's murder, and to denounce the crime from the altar; but that he expressed, from the altar, sympathy with Mrs. Sullivan, the mother of one of Mr. Curtin's murderers. Father O'Connor now explained that the parish services were divided between himself and his curate, that on the Sunday after the murder he was officiating in the remoter part of the parish, but that his curate, who was officiating in the chapel which the Curtins attended, denounced the crime from the altar. As for the sympathy with Mrs. Sullivan, he gave particular expression to it, he said, because the poor woman had lost her reason in consequence of her son's fate. The cross-examination of this witness was interrupted at four o'clock.

NINETY-FOURTH DAY.

JUNE 21.

THE greater portion of the forenoon sitting was occupied by the fruitless attempt of Mr. Atkinson, Q.C., to saddle Father O'Connor and the leaguers of Firies with some, at least, of the responsibility for the persecution of the Curtin family. Counsel and witness wrangled for a while over the meaning of the word "brazzle." A "brazzle" is the mark which farmers put on sheep they buy at a sale. And Father O'Connor, president of the local branch of the League, was reported to have said in one of his speeches that landgrabbers ought to be brazzled so that the community might know them. The literal-minded Mr. Atkinson appeared to be trying to get the worthy Father to confess that he meant an actual visible mark. Now, the worthy Father's temper is none of the meekest, and it was rapidly approaching explosive point as he explained that he used "brazzle" as a figure for censure. But Mr. Atkinson laboured away at the verb to brazzle, until at last the President interfered, saying that the witness had made his meaning clear. From Father O'Connor's story, the leaguers of the district must have stood in abject fear of the moonlighters. And the "parishioners" must have been demoralized, for he said that hundreds of them used to meet in the yard of the chapel, and hoot the Curtin family on their way to worship (this, too, after the murder of the father). Father O'Connor said that the League was afraid to pass a resolution condemning the murderers, because the proposer's life would be in danger. That, at any rate, showed hostility between the League and the party of outrage. Father O'Connor was the least satisfactory of the priest witnesses. It was not pleasant to hear him say that he refrained from visiting the Curtins, for these two reasons among others—that he thought they received him coldly; that he feared the Curtins might expect too much from him! One of his answers may have conveyed to his hearers a meaning different to what he intended. When asked if the Curtin family were in a state of great affliction after the father's murder, Father O'Connor replied with an abrupt, "Why not?" Some people in court appeared surprised and shocked. But the "why not" was merely a very common Irish equivalent for "it was natural that they should." Father O'Connor appeared, however, to have openly condemned the boycott when it took the form of what he called sacrilege—that is, boycotting the Curtins in chapel, or breaking their pew. His reverence did not seem to have any lively conception of such a thing as "sacrilege" against human nature outside the chapel door. Breaking a pew appealed to his superstitious terrors. Father O'Connor, like the crowds of witnesses for the defence, who preceded him, denied the charge of League complicity in outrage. But his narrowness, and hardness, and a certain stamp of mechanical sacerdotalism about the man, must have repelled most people who listened to him.

Mr. Foley, one of the members for county Galway, was called when Father O'Connor left the box. He was to be examined in reference to the Frank Bryne cheque of one hundred pounds, but his examination was postponed because certain documents required were not in court.

Father Lawler, who had already been examined, was recalled, but his additional evidence contained nothing of any special importance.

Mr. Henry O'Connor, secretary of the Causeway branch of the League, near Tralee, showed from the books of the branch that some outragemongers, whom *The Times* alleged to have been members of it, never had joined it. He told a ghastly little story of a process-server who, finding the tenant dead, placed the eviction notice upon the man's body. He described Informer Buckley, *Times* witness, as the worst character in Kerry. At this point Mr. Reid handed in a list of outrages in proof of Mr. T. P. O'Connor's assertion about the prevalence of agrarian crime during a long series of years preceding the rise of the Land League.

Dr. Kenny, M.P., next entered the witness-box, to answer questions about the books of the Land League, of which he was a treasurer from February to October, 1881. He remembered nothing about the Tim Horan letter. But he signed the Tim Horan cheque, just as he would sign any other cheque brought to him for his signature—he signed it as a matter of course. As said in preceding evidence, the League office was in a state of chaos when Dr. Kenny assumed temporary and nominal charge of it; and he was unacquainted with details. As for the books of the League, Dr. Kenny surmised that Mr. Egan must necessarily have had some of them with him in Paris, in order to enable him to transact League business. It will be remembered that the informer Farragher stated that he had conveyed letters from Egan, in the Dublin office, to Mullett, at his public-house, in the summer of 1881. Dr. Kenny said this was impossible because Egan was all the while in Paris. According to Dr. Kenny, Farragher, the Land League office servant, was a liar and perjurer. Replying to Mr. Davitt, Dr. Kenny said that Farragher was dismissed from the League office on suspicion of stealing stamps.

NINETY-FIFTH DAY.

JUNE 25.

FOR nearly two hours the Attorney-General and Dr. Kenny, M.P., disputed about Mr. Patrick Egan. Dr. Kenny said positively that Mr. Egan had not visited Dublin from the month of February, 1881, when Egan left Dublin for Paris, until long after the suppression of the Land League, which suppression was effected on the 18th or 19th of October, 1881. But the Attorney-General had found abundant evidence of Mr. Egan's presence in Dublin, early in October, 1881. What could Dr. Kenny mean by his stubborn denials? Sir Richard Webster laboured this point with the assiduity of one unveiling some terrific plot. Mr. Egan's name was among the list of visitors to Kilmainham early in October, 1881. But Dr. Kenny cared nothing for that; the entry might have been a hoax—patriotic Irishmen have often hoaxed the "peelers" before and since. The Attorney-General quoted long reports of several meetings of the League Committee in Dublin early in October, 1881, reports four or five columns long, written by the *Freeman* and *Express* reporters, and giving the very words which Mr. Egan uttered at these meetings. But Dr. Kenny was unshaken. He stoutly maintained that Mr. Egan was not present at these meetings. Mr. Reid, in order to put an end to the wrangle, rose to say that Dr. Kenny was under a misapprehension, and that he himself was instructed to say that Mr. Egan was in Dublin early in October. "Won't believe it," quoth the doctor, sticking his hands into his pockets. Mr. Parnell himself, in his evidence, had said that Mr. Egan paid a visit to Dublin early in October. But Dr. Kenny could not help that either. Of course, the position was quite clear. As the President and Mr. Reid observed, Dr. Kenny was somehow labouring under a misapprehension; and, as they did not observe (though they may have thought it) Dr. Kenny had a good share of obstinacy in his nature.

Next Mr. Attorney pressed the doctor upon his alleged relations with Le Caron, and this supplied the incident of the day. Le Caron, according to his own story, was entertained by Dr. and Mrs. Kenny in Dublin; they took him about and showed him the lions of the city; and he drove on a "jaunting car" with Dr. Kenny to Kilmainham. Dr. Kenny had no recollection of the jaunting car; "I don't believe I showed him the sights of Dublin." He had no recollection of taking a message from Boyton, who was in Kilmainham, to Le Caron, who was to take it with him to Boyton's friends in America. "I may have seen Le Caron," said Dr. Kenny, "but I have no recollection." "Is Le Caron here?" Sir Richard Webster inquired. A movement among the crowd in the doorway, and in a moment Major Le Caron, *alias* Dr. Beach, ex-spy, ex-deputy adjutant-general of the armies of the United Brethren stood before the Dublin doctor. It was interesting to observe the pair. The adjutant-general, a short man, looked up smilingly. The doctor, all the taller in his box, looked down curiously, as if he were examining some "specimen" in a museum. The doctor gazed, and gazed, and paused. The doctor threw down his pen. He put his hands into his pockets. He wrinkled his forehead. Said he, "I would never let a man with a face like that enter my house." The adjutant-general reddened—and vanished. "What's wrong with the face?" growled Mr. Attorney, with his palms on his hips. "It speaks for itself," answered the doctor. "As what?" "As that of a man I would not choose for a friend." "As what?" "The face," exclaimed the doctor, rather loudly, "is as false as a man ever wore." The President frowned.

Sir Richard and Dr. Kenny next wrangled about some postage stamps. Last Friday Dr. Kenny said that Informer Farragher had been dismissed in September or October, 1881, on suspicion of stealing the office stamps. Sir Richard Webster now produced a document showing that Farragher had received on the 15th of October, three days before the suppression of the Central League office where Farragher was employed, so much wages for overtime. Sir Richard now wanted to know if the dismissal took place in the brief period between the 15th and 18th or 19th. But after so many years Dr. Kenny had forgotten the precise details of the Farragher episode. And now came Mr. Attorney's crushing question—"In March, 1888, Dr. Kenny, did you not give Farragher a testimonial?" Yes, a testimonial in which he called Farragher a "conscientious," and "hard-working" man. This admission caused much amusement in court, but Dr. Kenny explained that after so many years he forgot all about the stamp episode, and, added the doctor, "I was not positive as to his identity." The rest of Dr. Kenny's cross-examination was a long, laborious, and fruitless effort to get information about the missing books of the Land League. Dr. Kenny thought the most valuable of the books—the grant book, as it was called, being a record of grants of money made by the central office—might possibly be in the possession of Mr. Moloney. He laughed at the statement, calling it absurd, that "seventeen hundredweight of Land League books" were removed from the Dublin office. He could give no details as to the alleged conveyance of the books to Liverpool, and to Palace Chambers, Westminster. Nor did he know anything whatever about the time or place of Mr. Egan's disappearance from Ireland. Nor had he had any communication with the practical joker Molloy before Molloy's interview with *The Times* agents in Dublin. "Molloy told me," said the doctor, "that *The Times* agents promised him money if he would say anything." And, added Dr. Kenny, frankly—glancing at *The Times* people who were in court—" I believe it; for I have been told that Mrs. Mullet was promised money, and her husband his release, if they would give evidence for *The Times*."

To Dr. Kenny followed Mr. Sexton, M.P., Lord Mayor of Dublin. Mr. Sexton had no information to give the Attorney-General about the Land League accounts and books. "I have delivered hundreds of speeches," said Mr. Sexton, replying to Mr. Reid, "and in them I incessantly denounced outrage." Mr. Reid asked him about Le Caron's romantic story of Brennan's escape through the narrow side street in the Strand with Mr. Sexton's own help. "From beginning to end," said Mr. Sexton, in his quiet way, "the story is an absolute fabrication."

NINETY-SIXTH DAY.

JUNE 26.

FOR about two hours the Attorney-General laboured hard to extort some admission from Mr. Sexton which would convict him of active sympathy with Fenians, Clan-na-Gael folk, and physical force people generally. He questioned him about his associates in Dublin, and the people whom he met in America; and about the "Spread the Light" operations of *The Irish World*. As regards the Fenians, Mr. Sexton frankly stated that he sympathized with some of them personally, though he did not approve of their method of righting the wrongs of Ireland. He felt for some of them the respect which he would feel for any men who underwent self-sacrifice for a cause which they honestly believed to be right. The plainness, promptitude, and straightforwardness of Mr. Sexton's answers impressed the Attorney-General, who treated him all along with a courtesy and considerateness which, if the truth must be told, Sir Richard has not always extended to the principal witnesses for the defence.

Sir Richard Webster appeared to think it a suspicious circumstance that Mr. Sexton contributed to a fund (now long forgotten) which was raised for Head-Centre Stephens. Mr. Sexton explained that he subscribed out of compassion for the Stephens' family, who were in a state of destitution "in a foreign capital" (Brussels). Then the Attorney-General abruptly asked Mr. Sexton whether, in 1878 or 1879, he had refused to join the Fenians because of his disapproval of the Fenian oath. Mr. Sexton replied that he refused to become a Fenian because he could not bring himself to promise to obey the secret orders of men of whom he knew nothing.

"Who asked you to join, Mr. Sexton?" "I refuse to say who," was the reply; and then followed a little "scene" which, at one moment, looked as if it might become serious. Sir Richard Webster pressed—politely—for his answer. Mr. Sexton as politely stuck to his refusal. The President mildly ruled that the Attorney-General was entitled to put his question. Whereupon Mr. Sexton rapidly uttered the following decisive little speech—" Rather than disclose the name of any man who by my disclosure would be brought into a position subjecting himself to the penalties of the law, I would incur any of the penalties the Court has the power to inflict on me." This certainly sounded somewhat precipitate. So that Sir James Hannen observed—"You need not make any such remarks, Mr. Sexton ; I must say that I see no plausible ground for your taking any such objection. If there were I should take such steps as I thought necessary to prevent what you anticipate. Therefore, I see no ground why the question should not be answered."

Thus encouraged, Sir Richard Webster tried Mr. Sexton once more—" I must ask you to give me the name of the person." Mr. Sexton replied that it was some one whose name had not even been mentioned in connection with the trial, and, said he, " I decline to answer." Upon this Mr. Lockwood rose to say that Mr. Sexton was there to meet accusations against himself. " A witness is here," the President interposed, sharply, " not to give what information he thinks fit, but to give evidence," and he intimated that the course which Mr. Sexton proposed to follow " must tend to diminish the value of the case presented."

Once more the Attorney-General put his question to Mr. Sexton, who replied that the disclosure of the name would not help the proceedings in the slightest degree ; " if," said he, " I disclosed the name I should despise myself all my life afterwards." " To treat our ruling thus," said the President, " is not to treat the Court with respect." " Having myself refused to join the Brotherhood," Mr. Sexton replied, " and knowing nothing of their secrets, I respectfully submit, especially after what I have said as to the immateriality of the disclosure, that I should not be asked to say." " You are not the judge," returned the President. One thing was clear—that Mr. Sexton had made up his mind to withhold the name. But the incident came to a sudden end by Sir Richard Webster's intimation that " though reserving " his right, he " would not press the question further now."

Sir Richard Webster turned to another subject, boycotting, which Mr. Sexton readily enough admitted to be "a necessary evil." He said that not only would he himself disapprove of a boycott extending to "the necessaries of life," but that he had never known an extreme case of that description. Boycotting within certain limits he considered to be " the lawful weapon of the people." Mr. Sexton was equally candid in declaring that he certainly would have disapproved of the distribution of the "Spread the Light" numbers of *The Irish World* from and at the expense of the Dublin League ; but that he did not believe *The Irish World* was circulated in any such way—*The Irish World* had a distribution fund of its own. Mr. Sexton was questioned at considerable length respecting his American tour. But the only questions of any general interest were those of which Le Caron, *alias* Dr. Beach, was the subject. He might have met Le Caron in America, but he had no recollection. " But, in one of your American speeches, did you not say," the Attorney-General asked, " that you had met in Boston a Frenchman who was following in the track of liberty and working for Ireland's freedom ? " Who could that " Frenchman " have been unless it was Le Caron (a French name), Le Caron, *alias* Beach, of Colchester, Deputy Adjutant-General of the armies of the U.B.? It might, said Mr. Sexton, have been a " French Canadian ;" it might even have been Beach himself; but if it was, Mr. Sexton had forgotten all about him. Would Mr. Sexton like to look upon Le Caron (who was sitting in a quiet corner in court) ? No ; Mr. Sexton looked upon Le Caron's face yesterday, and had no desire to see it again. Re-examined by Mr. Lockwood, Mr. Sexton said that the Foresters' was the only "secret society" of which he had ever been a member. " A convivial society," Mr. Lockwood threw in, as Mr. Sexton left the box.

Next came Mr. T. Harrington, M.P. for one of the divisions of Dublin, ex-proprietor and editor of *The Kerry Sentinel*, and secretary of the National League since its foundation. Mr. Harrington's evidence began with a brief description of the Irish Arcadia of *The Times* landlord witnesses, a description based upon what he had seen when ten years ago he travelled as a newspaper correspondent through the starving western and south-western regions. In this happy Arcadia the peasants lived on turnips—when they could get them. "I have delivered hundreds of speeches," said Mr. Harrington, "and among them all you cannot produce a single one which, if fully reported, will not be found to contain condemnation of outrage."

Not the least interesting part of his story was his answer about the informer O'Connor, who, it will be remembered, swore that Mr. Harrington had once given him money for promising to intimidate voters at a local election. "The informer's statement," said Mr. Harrington, "is, as far as I am concerned, an absolute fabrication from beginning to end. I never saw the man until he appeared here."

As for the assertion of the prosecution that League funds were used for criminal purposes, Mr. Harrington repudiated it with indignation and scorn. He declared that he had not only reprimanded local branches which were overstepping the line of legality, but that he had also suppressed several, and letters were put in by Mr. Reid in proof of this statement of Mr. Harrington's. Mr. Murphy's cross-examination of Mr. Harrington was tedious. But once or twice it grew lively. Mr. Murphy was asking Mr. Harrington why he had opposed a certain claim of compensation for destruction of a certain Kerry farmer's property. The reason was that there were doubts as to the alleged origin of the damage ; and, added Mr. Harrington, "if you were a ratepayer in the place, you would not like to be saddled with a heavier levy than was necessary." Mr. Harrington spoke angrily. "You must restrain yourself, Mr. Harrington," said the President, "and not indulge in personal observations." Mr. Justice Smith also interfered, and both the President and Mr. Justice Smith reminded him of the distinction between counsel and witness. A little later Mr. Harrington declared to Mr. Murphy that he would not be "shut up."

NINETY-SEVENTH DAY.

JUNE 27.

MR. REID produced a number of witnesses from county Mayo, which he described as the cradle of the Land League. He produced them in order that they might prove the existence of landlord oppression during the years before the League, and, inferentially, the necessity for combination on the part of the tenants.

The first of these Mayo witnesses was Father Hewson, parish priest of Belmullet. To illustrate the condition of his parish, he gave details of the "duty labour" exacted by landlord Bingham, one of *The Times* witnesses. "Duty labour" was merely another name for what is known as *corvée* labour ; and landlord Bingham exacted twelve days of it yearly from each of his tenants, or its equivalent in cash—half-a-crown a day.

Mr. Atkinson, in his cross-examination, called this labour a form of rent, which the President admitted it to be, qualifying it, however, as objectionable. But to return to the examination-in-chief, which was conducted by Mr. Reid, Father Hewson said that the *corvée* labour was exacted during the periods of the spring and autumn when the tenants' attention to their work on their own holdings was most needed. The tenants, said Father Hewson, were very poor, yet they were the sole creators of improvements on their farms. In the month in which the Land League was suppressed (October, 1881) landlord Bingham was fired at. Continuing his description of Mayo landlords, Father Hewson mentioned landlord Carter, who was shot at within a fortnight after he had evicted some families. Was landgrabbing unpopular before the League? Father Hewson said that it was, adding that his parishioners, who were an Erse-speaking people, did not know it by that name, but in their own language as *saintough*—covetousness, "one of the seven deadly sins," observed the reverend Father.—[The Celtic peasant of Ireland and the Celtic "crofter" of Scotland have the same name for the same "deadly sin;" but there is this difference, that landgrabbing has never been known among the Scotch Celts, nor its accompaniments, moonlighting, murder, maiming, or agrarian outrage of any kind].

Cross-examined by Mr. Atkinson, Father Hewson said he did not believe that Bingham was fired at. He shared the popular impression in Belmullet that the supposed shooting was the accidental work of Bingham's own pistol. The good Father raised a laugh by saying that "duty labour" meant that "a man must leave his own tillage work, carry his breakfast in his stomach, get his dinner—a bad one—from the landlord, and go home supperless." "I shouldn't object to his carrying his breakfast in his stomach," remarked Mr. Atkinson. "The best place for it, I should think," said the President. No doubt. But when an Erse-speaking Irishman says he "carries his breakfast in his stomach," he does not necessarily mean that he has any breakfast to digest. He may mean, and often does, that his stomach is breakfasting upon itself.

Mr. Atkinson, in his cross-examinations, attaches great importance to certain negative evidence which he often succeeds in eliciting. His stock question is, In the ten, fifteen, or twenty years (as the case may be), preceding the foundation of the Land League, can you name a single instance in which a man was outraged for taking a farm from which another man had been evicted? Father Hewson could recollect no individual case in his parish in the twenty years before the rise of the Land League. What Father Hewson claimed to have established was that the provocation to outrage, the landlord greed and oppression, existed; and that the Land League taught the people to combine in self-defence.

The general testimony as to the wretched condition of Mayo before the foundation of the League, and as to extortions by the landlords, were confirmed by the next witness, also a priest, Father Kelly of Moygarna. Speaking of a Miss Knox's estate, Father Kelly said that her tenants would have been unable to live but for the Mansion House Relief Fund.

Father Kelly was severely cross-examined by Sir Richard Webster. Father Kelly confessed he once refused to interfere on behalf of a man named Mike Brown, whom his neighbours were annoying in various ways. That a minister of religion should refuse to interfere in the cause of peace and goodwill among men shocked the Christian Mr. Attorney exceedingly. However, the hardened "P. P." had something to say for himself. Mike Brown, said Father Kelly, was guilty of sin in forcing up rents and driving the people from the country. *Saintough*, covetousness, "one of the seven deadly sins," over again! The worthy Father appeared to think it would serve Miky Brown right if he received hotter punishment than being "jeered at" by small boys.

The Attorney-General next sought to prove that Father Kelly had tried to intimidate people from giving evidence for *The Times*, and that Father Kelly had gone on the war-path, organizing the defence of the tenants' forts, and defeating the bailiffs and police. Father Kelly stoutly denied the intimidation charge; but, after a long struggle, he made several important admissions—or confessions—under the second head. Hard as his work was, the Attorney-General got through it in good humour. He was much more polite and man-and-brotherly to his reverence than he was to Mr. Parnell. Bit by bit Father Kelly admitted that on the morning of the attempted evictions, he left four or five men drawn up in front of Dunleavy's house, and four or five more at MacAndrew's, and that when the enemy (to wit, the bailiffs and the police) came up, they thought it discreet to give both forts the go-by. "Did you," said Sir Richard, "hear anybody call out 'Get the hot water ready?'" "No." Did you hear anybody say, "Don't do it?" "No." And then Sir Richard paused. He leant forward over the bench. He lowered his voice—"Did you yourself, Father Kelly, call out, 'Get the hot water ready?'" Father Kelly's eyes became round as Giotto's "O," as he answered, "I may have." There was a burst of laughter in court, and Mr. Attorney drew himself up with a triumphant gesture. And Mr. Justice Day must have been shocked by the reply. He was leaning forward, listening with all his might. At the Father's answer he started back, he thrust his hands into his pockets, he frowned, he shook his head, he muttered—but his words were inaudible. At a later stage in the proceedings Father Kelly maintained that if he did call out, "Get the hot water ready," he must have meant it jocularly. Sir Richard was happy for once.

Mr. Waldron, of Ballyhaunis, was the next witness. Secretary to the local branch of the Land League, he said that the two murders, about which he was being examined, were perpetrated after the suppression of the branch; and that the League was always opposed to outrage of all sorts. In a social sense, the only notable thing in Mr. Waldron's evidence was his statement that neither he, nor any one else, took any steps to inquire into the cause of the murder of two men who, according to his own account, were popular in the neighbourhood, and whose funerals were largely attended—Mr. Waldron himself attending both.

Then came Charles Burke, "small farmer," of Kiltimagh. He was called to contradict the story given by *The Times* witness, the boy Walsh, who, it will be remembered, swindled the Kiltimagh branch of which he was joint secretary, and some insurance company for which he was agent. Mr. Burke emphatically denied Walsh's story that he (Burke) and members of the League were associated with him in planning outrages.

The Rev. Father McHale, from near Crossmolina, testified to extortionate renting before 1879. Up to 1879, said he, "I had no sympathy for popular movements, but what I saw of the people's misery convinced me that a tenants' combination was necessary."

NINETY-EIGHTH DAY.

JUNE 28.

MR. REID passed nine of his witnesses through the witness-box. Five of them were members charged. They were Dr. Commins, member for South Roscommon; Mr. J. F. X. O'Brien; Mr. Donald Sullivan, one of the members for Meath; Mr. Clancy, one of the Dublin members; Mr. Power, one of the members for Waterford. But before the members were called, Mr. Thomas Harrington, of *The Freeman*, was examined. Mr. Harrington, who had attended large numbers of the Land League meetings, produced extracts from reports of them, showing how speakers habitually declared that only the enemies of the National cause would profit by outrage, and that what the Irish peasantry wanted was fair rent, or purchase on fair terms.

Sir Henry James cross-examined Mr. Harrington with special reference to a banquet speech of Mr. Biggar's, in which (as was reported) Mr. Biggar intimated that if the rulers of Ireland did not mend their ways, Ireland might perhaps bring forth avengers of the Russian Hartmann type. Mr. Harrington said he did not hear Mr. Biggar make use of any such expression, that Mr. Biggar was indistinctly heard, and that he believed the reporters were misinformed by somebody who professed to have heard what Mr. Biggar really did say.

After Mr. Harrington came Dr. Commins, M.P. Dr. Commins quietly remarked that he believed he was charged with something or other, but did not know what. As nobody seemed to know why he was charged, Dr. Commins was speedily done with. Dr. Commins it was who gave Frank Byrne his first lift in the world. He regarded Byrne as an "exemplary young man," and he was "astounded" when he heard it said that Byrne in America confessed to having been implicated in the Phœnix Park murders. Said Dr. Commins, "I have been a member of the executive committees of the Land and National Leagues, and I ought to know their secrets if they had any."

"In 1867 were you not sentenced to be hanged, drawn, and quartered?" Mr. Reid asked, in the gentlest of voices. The lady spectators, in particular, fixed their eyes curiously upon the gentleman to whom this unusual question was addressed. It was Mr. J. F. Xavier O'Brien, M.P. "Just so," replied Mr. O'Brien. "For high treason, I believe?" "Yes." Mr. O'Brien upon whom this terrific—and ludicrous—sentence was passed twenty-two years ago, is under middle height, neat in person, cool, mild, and precise in manner. He wears a long, thick, whitey-gray beard, and a nicely-trimmed whitey-gray wig, primly parted in the middle. His evidence was over in a couple of minutes, and the only notable incident in his cross-examination by Sir Henry James was his point-blank refusal to divulge anything upon which his Fenian oath bound him to secrecy. Sir Henry did not press him. Sir Henry appeared to be rather pleased than otherwise to release Mr. O'Brien. There was nothing to ask him about. As Mr. Xavier O'Brien himself remarked, in his matter-of-fact, dispassionate way, "I am one of the charged, to my surprise."

Mr. Sullivan, of Meath, is the brother of the lyrical "T. D."—to whom he bears some traces of resemblance, in outward manner. His examination and cross-examination, purely formal, sleepy ceremonies, lasted only a minute or two.

After Mr. Sullivan came Mr. Clancy, M.P., one of the best business men among the Irish party. Sir Henry James questioned Mr. Clancy as to whether he knew this, that, or the other person, supposed to be a member of the physical force party. Mr. Clancy's repeated "No"—"No"—"No"—"No" at first bored people. Then it amused them, as it began to be whispered about that Sir Henry was confounding the gentleman in the box with another Clancy, a sub-sheriff, or something of the sort, in Dublin! Somebody was at sea. But it did not matter a straw. Mr. Clancy, with a little yawn, walked out of his box, and Sir Henry promptly sat down, with the air of a man tired of his performance.

The seventh witness, Patrick Scanlon, a Kerry man, testified, like the second witness, Martin Fitzpatrick, of Robeen, Mayo, to popular discontent caused by landlord oppression in the years before the Land League.

Then Mr. Power, landlord though he was, declared that he thought the No-Rent Manifesto quite justifiable.

And lastly, Mr. Vincent Scully, a Tipperary landlord, and magistrate and deputy-lieutenant of the county, said he resigned his position as a magistrate for two reasons—because there were so many Coercion Acts; and because he "would not sit" as a political dispenser of justice.

NINETY-NINTH DAY.

JULY 2.

IN anticipation of Mr. Davitt's appearance the court was crowded. Mr. Davitt is one of those who "appear in person." But as soon as the judges took their seats Sir Charles Russell intimated that he had been asked by Mr. Davitt to examine him. This Sir Charles Russell proceeded to do, and the result was a review, lasting till three o'clock, of Mr. Davitt's career. People in court seemed surprised to hear from Mr. Davitt that he was only "turned forty-one." The extraordinary contrasts in Mr. Davitt's life were brought out, or suggested, in the rapid, light manner characteristic of Sir Charles Russell's cross-examinations. Evicting bailiffs, the old home set on fire, workhouse officials refusing admittance to the Davitt family because the mother would not be separated from her child—these were Mr. Davitt's earliest memories of his forty-one years; the contrast, visible in the witness-box, was the father of the Land League, one of the three chief actors in the ten years of Irish history—the Irish "revolution," as Sir Charles Russell called it—upon which their lordships were sitting in judgment. Though there was a tone of indifference in his resonant manly voice, the colour fled from his face as he recalled that little scene at the workhouse.

"We were very poor," Mr. Davitt said, as he described how, shortly after their eviction from their home in Mayo, the Davitt family came to live in Lancashire. Haslingden, the name of the place was, and there Michael Davitt, at the age of nine, was put to work in a mill. "One day I was kicked across the floor and told to do work which a lad of eighteen would ordinarily do; and when I was at that work I lost my arm." His parents were "Nationalists;" no wonder, perhaps. And they even encouraged him to enter the Fenian Brotherhood, which also was natural. And he entered it, at the age of seventeen. Then came the Chester Castle raid, and young Davitt's voluntary share in it; his services to the Brotherhood in forwarding arms to Ireland; and, finally, his sentence at the Old Bailey, in July, 1870, to fifteen years' penal servitude on a charge of treason felony. On the 19th of December, 1877, he was released on ticket-of-leave. "Immediately on my release," said Mr. Davitt, "I rejoined the Fenian Brotherhood;" and then he explained his object in doing so—to win over as many of the Brotherhood as he could to an open and constitutional agitation, "because I had made up my mind that secret conspiracies were of no use." In 1878 he lectured in America "in favour of an open movement;" and at a Boston meeting held in December of that year he set forth his views on a new kind of agrarian agitation in Ireland. "Mr. Parnell," said Mr. Davitt, "had nothing to do with my American tour; I went to see my poor old mother."

Returning to Ireland in 1879, Mr. Davitt began to put his ideas on open constitutional agitation into practice. And he chose his native Mayo, where his father and mother and himself were burnt out of their home twenty-six years before. The first of the meetings which led to the foundation of the Land League was held at Irishtown on the 20th of April, 1879. The small farmers of Western Ireland contributed towards the expenses of these meetings. Mr. Davitt himself gave the proceeds of his lecturing tours through Great

Britain and the United States. Mr. Davitt went to his work with a will; he was impelled by what he saw in the West of the abject "misery and poverty" of the tenants and their "slavishness" to the landlords. All this time, Mr. Parnell, the arch-revolutionist of *The Times*, was holding aloof from the Land League movement. "I think Mr. Parnell is too conservative altogether on the agrarian question," said Mr. Davitt, during a brief pause in his examination At last, in August, 1879, the Land League of Mayo was established at the Castlebar Convention; and finally the National organization, the Land League of Ireland, was founded in Dublin on the 22nd of October. It was at this second period that Mr. Parnell fell in with the movement. It required much persuasion to bring him round. And now he was appointed president of the new organization.

At this stage of the examination Mr. Asquith read out the rules and principles of the new League. Formulated generally at the Castlebar Convention, they were sufficiently conservative for Mr. Parnell's acceptance, their governing idea being that, as the landlord system was the curse of Ireland and the cause of her demoralization, that system should be superseded by peasant proprietorship on fair terms to the landlords. Then Mr. Davitt proceeding on his second journey across the Atlantic, entered upon his task of organizing the League's American branch, the rules and principles of which, read out by Mr. Asquith, corresponded to those of the Irish organization. He attended meetings of the Clan-na-Gael, a society which, said Mr. Davitt, was "no more a murder club than the Carlton is a murder club." Mr. Davitt was Major Le Caron's guest at Braidwood. And he spoke at a meeting which, as he thought, was organized by Le Caron. At these meetings Mr. Davitt condemned violence. "Shoot the landlords," exclaimed some one at one of these demonstrations. "No," was Mr. Davitt's rejoinder, "shoot the system," this "robber system," as he described it in the same passage of his speech. "I have conscientiously believed all my life," said Mr. Davitt, replying to Sir Charles Russell, "that landlordism is the source of crime in Ireland."

Mr. Davitt spoke in the highest terms of Mr. Alexander Sullivan and Mr. Patrick Ford, saying of the latter that he was misunderstood in England, and of the former that he was a man "incapable of doing anything dishonourable." He admitted that Ford had once upon a time gone over to the dynamite party; but, he added, Mr. Ford has since joined the constitutional side. Here Mr. Davitt made a notable declaration. "Do not think," he said, "that I am opposed on principle to the use of physical force." And he maintained that, under certain circumstances, the use of physical force would be justifiable—"if Ireland had the chance, for God knows she has had sufficient cause." But was there an alternative to this physical force? There was; and Mr. Davitt, in his description of the Chicago Convention of 1886, showed what it was. The mere mention of the date suggested it. At that great Convention there were twelve hundred delegates, many of them formerly strong advocates for the separation of Ireland from Great Britain. But what Mr. Davitt, to his surprise, saw at that Convention was the universal acceptance of the Home Rule alternative to separation. The Chicago Convention voted confidence in Mr. Gladstone and thanks to the democracy of England. "I have not the slightest doubt," said Mr. Davitt, that the Chicago resolutions "represented the feelings of the Irish race in America."

Before making this interesting statement Mr. Davitt spoke of the effect which the Phœnix Park murders produced on Mr. Parnell. "I never saw him in such a state of prostration. He was utterly broken down. When he told me he was thinking of resigning, I said to him that the reasons were stronger than ever why he should remain at the head of the Irish people." As an instance of Mr. Parnell's Conservatism—besides that already given—Mr. Davitt mentioned the fact that after the Phœnix Park murders Mr. Parnell was opposed to the establishment of a new political organization in Ireland.

Cross-examined by the Attorney-General, Mr. Davitt said that he became a "Centre" soon after he joined the Fenian body; and soon after that again organizing secretary for England and Scotland, with about one hundred "circles" under his supervision. Sir Richard Webster suddenly asked him if "rotten sheep" was a Fenian expression. It would mean traitor or a useless fellow, said Mr. Davitt, adding that he himself had used it in a letter. Was that letter addressed to Forrester, Sir Richard Webster asked. Mr. Davitt refused to answer. This was the letter, already referred to in Sir Charles Russell's examination-in-chief, partly upon the strength of which Mr. Davitt was sentenced at the Old Bailey. At that trial it was interpreted as an incitement to murder. In his examination-in-chief, Mr. Davitt stated that the letter was intended to prevent murder. And now Mr. Davitt claimed to be allowed to make a further explanation to the Court. He said that the letter in question was his reply to one written to him by a fellow-Fenian, a hot-headed young man of eighteen, who had made up his mind to take the life of a member of the Brotherhood, whom he believed to be a traitor. "My letter," said Mr. Davitt, frankly, "was criminally foolish." He was only twenty years old when he wrote it. But, as he repeated, its somewhat elaborate instructions to the would-be assassin were a device for gaining time. Mr. Davitt advised the young man to communicate with "Jem" and "Fitz," cipher names of two members of the Fenian Supreme Council; but in the meantime he took the precaution to warn "Jem," and "Fitz," of his correspondent's intentions. No murder was committed; and Mr. Davitt believed that he had been instrumental in preventing a crime. Yet, at the Old Bailey, Mr. Davitt's letter was regarded as a proof of the writer's complicity in a plot to murder. Mr. Davitt refused to tell the Attorney-General who "Jem" and "Fitz" were. The President then asked Mr. Davitt if he had given that explanation at the Old Bailey trial. Mr. Davitt had not; if I had, said Mr. Davitt, "I would have betrayed the young man who trusted in me." "He is in America. I appeal to him from this witness-box to come forward and give me the necessary permission." "I have borne this stigma for twenty years, and imprisonment as well. I hope the man for whom I have borne this will now do me justice and tell the truth."

Here is the text of Mr. Davitt's letter to the would-be assassin:—

My dear Friend,—I have just returned from Dundee, which place I have left all right. Your letter of Monday I have read. I have no doubt but that your account is correct. In reference to the other affair, I hope you won't take any part in it whatever—I mean in the carrying of it out. If it is decided upon, and you receive Jem's and through him Fitz's consent, *let it be done by all means;* but one thing you must remember, and that is that you are of too much value to our family to be spared, even at the risk of allowing a "rotten sheep" to exist among the flock. You must know that if anything happened to you the toil and trouble of the last six months will have been almost in vain. Whoever is employed don't let him use the "pen" we are and have been selling. Get another for the purpose—a common one. I hope and trust when I return to Man—— I may not hear that every man, woman, and child know all about it ere it occur.

Pen meant revolver; flock meant the Fenian party; and the rotten sheep were the traitors.

While the cross-examination went on, Mrs. Alexander Sullivan, of Chicago, sat in the ladies' gallery. She had the satisfaction of hearing Mr. Davitt's praise of her husband—all the more welcome, no doubt, because of the world-wide speculation on the Cronin murder. Egan, Mr. Davitt held in high esteem. He first made Mr. Egan's friendship in 1877; "and I am proud to say that that intimacy continues to the present hour. He was one of the most respected merchants in Dublin; a man of the highest character and honour, who, though an advanced Nationalist, had numerous friends among the classes who differed entirely from him." No amount of personal regard ever prevents Mr. Davitt from saying what he believes to be truth about a friend. Thus he considers Mr. Parnell a Tory in agrarian policy, and he says it. And in his references to Mr. Parnell, he sometimes gives the public an interesting glimpse of the inner history of the Irish movement. For example, Mr. Davitt is a land nationalizer. To substitute for a handful of big landlords half a million small ones, will never, he believes, settle the Irish question. Mr. Parnell, on the other hand, holds out, as he always has done, for a peasant proprietary.

ONE HUNDREDTH DAY.

JULY 3.

SIR RICHARD WEBSTER resumed the subject. He wanted to know if Forrester was a Fenian, and Mr. Davitt refused to tell him. He dwelt for some time on the curious defence put up by Mr. Davitt's counsel at the trial. Sir Richard Webster wished to show that there was an incompatibility between the spirit in which Mr. Davitt refrained from betraying even the would-be assassin who had wronged him, and the spirit of his counsel's defence of him at the Old Bailey. Mr. Davitt's counsel said that Mr. Davitt's exportation of arms had no connection whatever with the Fenian conspiracy, but was intended to enable the landlords to arm themselves against outragemongers! There certainly was an immense difference between the spirit of that plea and the chivalrous spirit which prompted Mr. Davitt to undergo penal servitude rather than expose a fellow-Fenian. But Mr. Davitt was ready with his explanation. "I knew nothing," said Mr. Davitt, "of the line my counsel would take in defence until his speech was delivered. I am not the man to resort to subterfuge, even to save myself from penal servitude."

Then the Attorney-General turned his attention to a question which, in one form or another, was repeated a score of times in the course of the day's cross-examination—the question of Mr. Davitt's opinion, after the year 1879, on the alternative of physical force. In his evidence-in-chief Mr. Davitt had said that immediately on his first release from prison he re-entered the Irish Republican Brotherhood, with the express purpose of winning over its members to constitutionalism. This statement, and Mr. Davitt's repeated assertion that even now he was not opposed, "in principle," to the use of physical force, appeared —according to the Attorney-General's repeated cross-questionings—to be irreconcileable. But, in the first place, what Mr. Davitt tried to wean the Fenians from was reliance upon force secretly organized—secret conspiracy, in a word. In the second place, though he accepted the "principle" of physical force, he "knew there was no chance." Thirdly, since the end of 1885, Mr. Davitt had come to recognize another alternative, for which, he believed, there was a chance. This other alternative was the Gladstonian solution of Home Rule. "On principle," said Mr. Davitt, "I am personally in favour of separation between Great Britain and Ireland ; but I am ready, if the Home Rule experiment is tried, to give it loyal support. I believe, if Home Rule had a fair trial, the cry for separation would die out." He said this with an emphatic gesture. Mr. Davitt's position was perfectly clear. He explained it with downright frankness and sincerity.

In quoting his remarks on the Home Rule plan, we have, for the sake of connection, anticipated the course of the cross-examination. We now return to its earlier portions. Having done with the Old Bailey trial, Sir Richard

Webster questioned Mr. Davitt about his views on the Clerkenwell Prison affair; on the Manchester prison-van attack; and about the characters and antecedents of the people—Messrs. Biggar, Egan, Parnell, Dillon, Carey (the future informer), and others—who arranged for a complimentary dinner to him on his release from Portland Prison. As to the first, he said he entirely disapproved of any attempt that would imperil the lives of innocent people. As to the rescuers of the police-van, "I have lauded the men," said Mr. Davitt, "and will as long as I live;" and he remarked that he himself would gladly have joined in the enterprise had he been "ordered." Mr. Davitt was alluding to Mr. Bright's opinion on the Manchester rescue case, when Sir Richard Webster stopped him with another question about the Fenians and their friends who gave him a public reception, on his release. "Why," exclaimed Mr. Davitt, "every man in Ireland worth his salt was at that time a Fenian."

At this stage in the proceedings Mr. William O'Brien entered the court and sat down on the solicitors' bench, looking none the worse for his last Irish adventure. Shortly after three o'clock Mr. Parnell arrived; he left before the Court rose.

The Attorney-General persevered in his attempt to show that Mr. Davitt was the same unregenerate conspirator after 1878 that he was before it. Mr. Davitt replied with his unvarying candour. Speaking of nine or ten years ago, my idea was, said Mr. Davitt, that the land question should "be used as the stepping-stone to independence, that we should treat the landlords as the English garrison—which they are." But then, quickly added Mr. Davitt, smiling upon Sir Richard, "the land programme of the Nationalists is now the land programme of the Tory party." Sir Richard Webster dived into his bundles of papers.

But while Mr. Davitt was, according to his own account, definitely engaged in the open constitutional movement, was he associating with people who were secretly engaged in importing arms, and directing or inspecting secret military preparations in Ireland? He was questioned about Mr. O'Kelly's alleged employment as Arms Agent for the Fenian Brotherhood; about the purpose of General Millen's visit to Ireland ten years ago; and about John Devoy's visit to Dublin at the same period.

To most of these questions Mr. Davitt replied that he must refuse to divulge information upon which he was bound in honour to maintain secrecy. As for Mr. O'Kelly, and some others about whose antecedents and alleged share in Fenian meetings Mr. Davitt was questioned, he remarked that he must refer Mr. Attorney to those gentlemen themselves. But as for Mr. Matt. Harris, Mr. Davitt said at once that he was a member of the Fenian Supreme Council; "I have his leave to say so," Mr. Davitt explained. But as for other members, "it would be cowardly and dishonourable in me to hold these up to ruin in violation of my pledged word." "Will you say," asked Sir Richard Webster, "that Mr. James O'Kelly did not act with you in distributing arms before your imprisonment?" "I do not;" Mr. Attorney must question Mr. O'Kelly on that matter.

The Attorney-General then wandered off once more into the United States, offering interpretations of Mr. Davitt's speeches there, which interpretations Mr. Davitt generally accepted. In fact, Mr. Davitt's ideas about Irish landlordism as the curse of Ireland, and about landlords as "the garrison" never changed. "I am a Republican in principle," he remarked in the course of his replies on this general topic.

Among the characters, good, bad, and indifferent, about whom Mr. Davitt was questioned were James Daly, of Castlebar, and "Scrab" Nally. James Daly had, according to Le Caron's evidence, gone as a Fenian delegate to America; but according to Mr. Davitt's statement, he had never been in

America in any capacity. Daly had not in him the stuff out of which conspirators were made, Mr. Davitt thought. During earlier stages of the trial the Attorney-General had endeavoured to saddle the leaguers with the responsibility for Scrab's wild oratory. Mr. Davitt now said that as far as he himself was concerned, he had given orders that Scrab should not be allowed to speak from his (Mr. Davitt's) platforms. Scrab, said Mr. Davitt, was a person upon whom Nature had not wasted any discretion, and who "could no more keep a secret than a sieve could hold water."

In the afternoon sitting, the Attorney-General asked Mr. Davitt if he approved of a letter in which Boyd O'Reilly spoke of Joe Brady as "righting the robber's wrong," and as deserving the respect of Irish patriots all over the world. "I no more approve of that letter than I approve of the leading article in *The Times* justifying the attempt to assassinate the Emperor of the French." This article was one of three from *The Times*, which at the beginning of the day's cross-examination Mr. Davitt wished to be read. After a string of uninteresting questions about more or less foolish manifestoes from America, Mr. Davitt was cross-examined about his connection with *The Irish World*. Mr. Davitt condemned "Transatlantic's" letters in *The World*, but he did not hesitate to circulate the paper among the Irish tenantry, said he, because he thought they would be benefited by the journal's tone of independence and its views on the nationalization of the land. In distributing *The World* Mr. Davitt had not spent a penny of the Land League's money. Mr. Davitt was at that time the correspondent of *The World*. Mr. Quinn and Mr. Brennan before him were correspondents of *The Irish World*, and, he said, if they distributed the paper—in other words "spread the light"—they did it as the correspondents of the paper, not as secretaries of the League.

At last Sir Richard Webster wandered back again to Ireland. What were Mr. Davitt's views on landgrabbing? Grabbing is "stealing," was Mr. Davitt's answer, meaning that the people thought grabbing morally wrong, though it was "not a crime according to the law." Shortly before four o'clock the Attorney-General thought he discovered a dangerous speech of Mr. Davitt's, delivered in Kansas City. But Mr. Lockwood pointed out that in the context Mr. Davitt said that in the struggle with England the Irish must appeal to reason, justice, and common sense. "Yes," said Mr. Davitt, turning to Sir Richard Webster, "it was only a war of ideas, and I have yet to learn that a war of ideas is inconsistent with the British Constitution." The cross-examination, though dull and incoherent, was the cause of a display of humour by a gentleman who is a clever caricaturist and a clever lawyer in one. This artist, Mr. Lockwood, Q.C., drew an amusing caricature of the Shah leading Mr. Attorney to Persia in the character of a missionary. The pen and ink portrait of the King of Kings was excellent. Behind the King of Kings, and led by a rope which the Shah carried over his shoulder, Mr. Attorney followed, in knee breeches, and with a clerical coat instead of his silk gown. The work of art was passed quietly round to the general amusement.

Half a dozen times in the course of his cross-examination to-day did Mr. Davitt decline to answer the Attorney-General. On the second occasion, when Mr. Davitt refused to name members of the Fenian Supreme Council, the President interposed, severely. Said he, "If the witness refuses to answer you had better go on, and after you get through and we see how far you have got, we shall see whether it will be necessary to take any steps." However, in spite of that ominous hint nothing more was said on the subject. Mr. Davitt next declined to tell Sir Richard Webster why General Millen came to Ireland from America. "To inspect the military efficiency of the Fenian Brotherhood?" the Attorney-General suggested. Perhaps—or perhaps not; nothing more could Mr. Attorney learn from Mr. Davitt. Then there was Dr. Carroll's visit. If there was nothing wrong in Dr. Carroll's mission argued the Attorney-General, why will you not tell us what he came to Ireland for? Oh, replied Mr. Davitt, promptly, "there are many things morally innocent which are illegal in Ireland." Some interesting illustrations of Mr. Davitt's downright frankness came out in his replies to Sir Richard Webster's questions about his tour through Western Ireland in 1879. If Mr. Davitt did see Fenian leaders during his tour, what about it? Was it not his purpose to win men of all ways of thinking over to the Parnell movement? Mr. Davitt did not know that arms were being distributed at that time. But Mr. Davitt very plainly gave Sir Richard Webster to understand that if he had known, he would not have interfered. Had not all free men the right to carry arms? If England ruled Ireland justly, why should she object to the Irish possessing arms? Why should the peasantry be disarmed, while the landlords and their agents had the right to carry rifles and revolvers?

ONE HUNDRED AND FIRST DAY.

JULY 4.

THE Attorney-General resumed his cross-examination of Mr. Davitt to-day by asking him about his connection with the Ladies' Land League and what he knew of its books and its funds. Mr. Davitt explained that except in having made the suggestion he had had little or no share in the establishment of the society. Nor did he know what had become of a book of the society's called, after the famous monastic record, "the Book of Kells." The society's book was a sort of Domesday Book, in which evictions were recorded, and rents of holdings and landlord and tenant relations generally over the whole of Ireland.

Giving up his fruitless inquiry into this subject, the Attorney-General plunged into landgrabbing. "You denounced grabbers as traitors," exclaimed the Attorney-General. Yes; Mr. Davitt acknowledged that he had often denounced them in strong language, but he quickly explained it was the system he denounced. "I don't believe I ever mentioned an individual grabber's name; if I did I am sorry for it." Sir Richard Webster then quoted Mr. Davitt's support of a resolution passed in October, 1884, at a meeting at Maryborough, and in which grabbing was denounced as "treason to the cause of Ireland," as "a gross outrage on the people," and as a "legal robbery." Mr. Davitt denied that in the form in which he put it, his approval of the Maryborough resolution was an incentive to outrage. Neither had he named any offender, nor was it shown that any person suffered in consequence of his speech. He reiterated his belief that the condemnation of grabbing stopped crime.

From grabbing to boycotting was a natural transition, and the typical boycotting case which the Attorney-General produced was that of Mr. Hegarty, whose story occupied so much of the time of the Court during the earlier stages of the trial. Though believing that Mr. Hegarty's story of his boycott was inaccurate, Mr. Davitt wrote, in Mr. Hegarty's behalf, to the president, or some other official of the boycotting branch.

Though Mr. Davitt was at that date, and for a short period in charge of the Land League office, he had "nothing to do" with the League funds except when money passed through his hands for the payment of the clerks. Then the Attorney-General tried another line of attack. When Mr. Davitt visited the Western Counties in 1880, did he search out the Fenian county "centres?" Mr. Davitt had no recollection of any such special search; but Mr. Davitt observed that in his mission as an organizer, and as a proselytizer of extreme politicians to the open and constitutional movement, he never avoided any man, whatever his politics might be. What was the Fenian "black list?" the Attorney-General inquired. Only the list of members who had been expelled from the order by reason of their misconduct—such as misappropriation of funds, or for their bad character generally.

And now there followed a most striking and impressive incident in the day's cross-examination. The Attorney-General put the simple question—simple almost in the unfavourable sense—whether the detection of criminals was not the best way to prevent crime. Obviously it was. Well, then, did Mr. Davitt remember the Widow Walsh case, as it was called? "Yes," said Mr. Davitt. "Mrs. Walsh wrote to me saying that her boy was innocent of the charge of murder upon which he was tried, and that they both knew who the murderer was, and that he had escaped to America." "I have not Mrs. Walsh's letter," said Mr. Davitt; "I must have destroyed it with thousands of other letters." Young Walsh was tried in August, 1882, and in a letter to *The Irish World* in November of the same year Mr. Davitt gave some particulars about him. Young Walsh was fifteen years old. When her boy was in prison, Widow Walsh heard that attempts were being made to induce him to divulge the murderer's name. She visited him, and begged him to remain firm. Young Walsh died on the scaffold. What did Mr. Davitt think of it? "If that woman sacrificed her son rather than make an informer of him, I say it was a noble action." A low murmur passed over the audience; but whether of admiration, or horror, or pity—well, which of the three would the reader prefer it to be? Mr. Davitt's face grew pallid, and there were "tears in his voice" as he spoke.

"I," said Mr. Davitt, "have suffered nine years' penal servitude" for conduct like young Walsh's. "You say," continued the Attorney-General, after a pause—"you say that Mrs. Walsh's was a noble action." "Yes," said Mr. Davitt, "on account of the horror the Irish peasantry have of the name of 'Informer.'" "Why did you not communicate with the authorities?" was the Attorney-General's next question. "Never!" exclaimed Mr. Davitt, in a tone now of fierceness; "I say the authorities are the criminals of Ireland. Communicate with them? not as long as I live." One could see that Mr. Davitt's eyes were filling. For a few moments, and for the first time since his examination began, he almost lost his self-control. "Observe," continued Sir Richard Webster, "this poor boy died protesting his innocence." "Ah," Mr. Davitt replied, with an expression of profound sadness, "many have done that in Ireland." Having as it were projected upon his commonplace London background this sudden vision of a fragment of the life of this strange Ireland, the Attorney-General passed on to the story of the "Manchester martyrs," in respect of whom Mr. Davitt said, in his Walsh episode vein, that "the heroism of self-sacrifice is something to be worshipped in mankind." Being on the topic of violence, Sir Richard Webster alluded to violence against landlords, upon which Mr. Davitt remarked : "I have never preached against landlords individually; they are only the accidents of a bad system; against that system I shall preach as long as I live."

Once more the Attorney-General wandered off to America. What of Mr. Davitt's acquaintance, Finerty? "I rebuked him," said Mr. Davitt, "whenever, in my presence, he advocated the use of dynamite." He merely thought that Finerty had been embittered by memories of Irish wrong, but that his oratorical bark was worse than his bite. Sir Richard Webster next tried whether under a fresh bombardment of questions Mr. Davitt would abide by his high estimate of Patrick Ford's character. Mr. Davitt repeatedly said that he must speak of Ford as he found him. Ford had assured him three years ago that he had given up dynamite politics for ever, and Mr. Davitt was only too glad to have the assurance. In politics, as in religion, said Mr.

Davitt, we ought to judge charitably of men's past. Several of Mr. Ford's expressions Mr. Davitt unhesitatingly condemned as "stupid," "reprehensible," "criminal," but he adhered to his statement that Mr. Ford had changed his politics, and that he was in reality an excellent man.

Mr. Davitt was still more ready to condemn "Transatlantic's" wild effusions, which unfortunately for Ford's character as a Christian and a philanthropist (Mr. Davitt's description of him) found admission into *The Irish World*. In September, 1886, Sir Richard exclaimed, Mr. Ford said that he stood by all he had written on dynamite; how could Mr. Davitt reconcile that with his estimate of Mr. Ford? Why, answered Mr. Davitt, "he meant what I would mean if I said that I stood by my Fenian record. That would not mean that I am a Fenian now, or intend to be. The considerations under which I became a Fenian are not applicable now." But at the end of the cross-examination some very pointed questions were put to Mr. Davitt about his extremely strong speeches at Bodyke in June, 1887. "I was excited," said Mr. Davitt, "I was labouring under strong feeling. I don't like going to evictions, because they excite me. I say it is an outrage upon civilization to pull down houses built by the tenants themselves, because a few pounds are owing to an absentee landlord."

"I will put a question to you," said Sir Charles Russell, rising to re-examine—a question which the Attorney-General has not asked you, though you have been two days under examination. You are charged with complicity in the Phœnix Park murders. Is there any truth in that?" "None whatever." Then Mr. Davitt had an opportunity of further explaining certain circumstances of his Old Bailey trial. He could not at that trial fully account for his letter to the would-be assassin, without implicating, not only his correspondent, but also the two Fenian superiors who were spoken of in the letter by their cipher names of "Fitz" and "Jem." "The day will come," said Mr. Davitt, looking away from Sir Charles Russell, "when these two men will corroborate me, and when the man who wronged me will do me justice." Mr. Davitt earnestly repeated what he had written to his two superiors, warning them of their fellow-member's intentions; and, Mr. Davitt added, the murder did not happen.

Then returning to the subject of his prison life, Mr. Davitt said he passed much of it in thinking out plans of constitutional agitation, which he should put into execution when he was released. Speaking of the English people, he said that the English people, not being in possession of the franchise in those times, could not be held responsible for the misgovernment of Ireland. The League, he said, has destroyed secret societies, and led the Irish people to see that the plan of Home Rule would satisfy their aspirations. "I know the vast majority of Irish-Americans are in favour of Mr. Parnell's Home Rule policy." In 1880 the dynamite policy men were numerous in America; but in 1886, the year of the Home Rule Bill, any one who at the Chicago Convention "would have proposed dynamite would have been howled down."

ONE HUNDRED AND SECOND DAY.

JULY 5.

A NEW development of the trial to-day. Mr. Michael Davitt called a witness of his own, instead of being re-examined as a witness himself. The points upon which it was supposed he would be re-examined by Sir Charles Russell will be dealt with by Mr. Davitt in his own concluding speech. Mr. Davitt's witness was Mr. J. J. Lowden, Irish barrister, Irish landlord, Irish tenant, Irish Nationalist, all in one. He was an excellent witness—as downright and candid as his examiner—and he succeeded in thoroughly interesting his hearers. He began by showing up Irish landlords who hurried off abroad as soon as they "raised the wind," and who either came back when their money was spent, or sent their bailiffs to turn out tenants who would not or could not pay. Did the landlords whom he knew ever subscribe to relief funds? "Not a shilling."

This led to the subject of distress, upon which Mr. Davitt produced some striking evidence from *The Times*. Even Mr. Lowden, who is anything but a lover of *The Times*, remarked with amusing emphasis, that "*The Times* was truthful on *that* subject anyhow." The evidence consisted of a number of articles, republished by *The Times* as recently as 1880, but originally written in the years of the great famine, and exposing those "aristocratic mendicants" (the landlords) as heartless persons who not only did not contribute to the relief of distress, but who would be glad if their tenants could subsist on the potato stalks while they themselves appropriated the "roots." And as the landlords and their friends, continued Mr. Lowden, contrived to "nullify" the agrarian legislation which began with the Liberal Act of 1870, there was nothing left for the tenants to do but to combine, which they did in the Land League of 1879. This led to a series of questions about the meetings which preceded the foundation of the League, and whose perfectly moderate legal and constitutional resolutions were supported on the spot by men like Mr. M. Harris, Mr. Egan, Mr. Brennan. "Had the Fenians anything to do with the Irishtown and Castlebar meetings?" Mr. Lowden replied that they had not; though "perhaps" there may have been individual Fenians present. "Nor," he added, "had there come any money from America in support of the meetings which led to the formal establishment of the League."

As to the connection between crime and outrage, Mr. Lowden made the common-sense remark that "most decidedly" there was nothing more likely to tempt a man into outrage than the destruction of his home and the eviction of his family. Boycotting? There was boycotting even before the League days; the landlords were adepts at it. "I was myself socially ostracized by them; they obstructed my professional advancement. The landlords tried to destroy every one who was opposed to them." Mr. Lowden said quite enough to prove that the landlords were not in touch with the people. "Was Dublin Castle in touch with the people?" Mr. Davitt asked, smilingly. "What! it's not in touch with civilization." In the burst of laughter which greeted this bad account of Dublin Castle Mr. Lowden leant over his box, and nodded, as if to punctuate his sentence. Mr. Lowden did not join in the merriment. The mention of Dublin Castle opened the floodgates of his wrath.

Mr. Davitt then led his lively witness over the topic of outrages. In the first place, the perpetration of outrages could not have been encouraged by the League; for, as Mr. Lowden put it, "outrages were injurious to the League, and blackened its character." During the existence of the League in Mayo, several murders were perpetrated in the county: there was the murder of Lord Mountmorres, the Feerick murder, the Lyden murder, and in the neighbouring county of Galway there was the murder of the Huddys. But he held that Lord Mountmorres was murdered because he "eked out his wretched income as a landlord" by doing spy's work for the Castle, and taking bribes; that Feerick was murdered because he was a "drunken bully"; that, in a word, the murders were the work of a secret society which was at enmity with the Land League, and which was known as the "Herds' League," a society which was especially strong in the wild region known as the Joyce country, the scene of several of the murders. The Herds' League, said Mr.

Lowden, was "purely and simply a murderers' organization." This Herds' League attacked the property of Land Leaguers—like Mike O'Neil and Pat O'Neil, whose sheep and cattle the "Herds" threw over the cliffs. "I swear," exclaimed Mr. Lowden, "that Head-constable Whelehan had these Herds' Leaguers committing outrages, and it was while he was at that work that he lost his life."

Sir Henry James now rose to cross-examine. Before he came to his most interesting questions he spent much time in asking Mr. Lowden about the persons described by Mr. Davitt as the "Nationalists" who got up the Mayo meetings before the foundation of the League; why the Archbishop of Tuam wrote a letter in which he opposed the new agitation; whether it was a fact that in twelve or fifteen months the League collected eighty or ninety thousand pounds all of which, except twenty thousand had been spent in local expenses; who the organizers and auditors of the League were; and what had become of the League books. As to the first point, Mr. Lowden held that Nationalists did not mean Fenians. As to the second, he averred positively, that a Nationalist like the Archbishop would never have written such a letter; that it was written (on vague instructions from the Archbishop, who was ninety years old and in his dotage) by the Archbishop's nephew, who was a Tory; and that he himself (Mr. Lowden) wrote to the papers at the time, saying what he now said in the witness-box. As to the third point, Mr. Lowden was positive that the alleged amount of contribution was grossly exaggerated, and that the rule directing the transmission to Dublin of 75 per cent. of the contributions was of later origin. Before he came to the question of the League books, Mr. Lowden suddenly looked at the clock. It was on the stroke of half-past one. "Lunch time," quoth Mr. Lowden, with a nod. "The only clear piece of evidence I have had from you yet," said Sir Henry James.

At two o'clock the cross-examination was resumed. Some time before half-past one Mr. Lowden apologized for his "sore voice." Now his voice was in better condition. He declared he knew nothing about the Land League books. Nor did he see how the executive could know, for the executive were "all in gaol." "I was never consulted about the removal of the books," said Mr. Lowden, and "I have never made any inquiries about them." Then he volunteered the interesting remark that, executive officer of the Land League as he was, he never "came across a Land League document that was of any great importance." "Has anybody else" attempted to find the books, the President asked. Mr. Justice Smith promptly joined in the President's question. Mr. Lockwood replied that whatever documents had been discovered were produced. Sir James Hannen said that he wanted to know into whose hands the books passed when they were taken from the League offices.

And then Sir Henry James addressed himself to the subject of the Herds' League. "When did you first hear of it?" he asked. "In 1880 or 1881." But if Mr. Lowden knew so much about the Herds' League, and its headquarters, did he try to bring its members to justice? No. And yet the Land League was against crime; "Why did you not try to bring the Herds to justice?" "I take my solemn oath," Mr. Lowden replied vehemently, "that the police knew the Herds' League as well as I did;" and he repeated what he had already said about men like Whelehan and Tracey. "I took no steps whatever," Mr. Lowden replied, in answer to another question; and he added that to have communicated with the police would have made him unpopular, because "between the people and the police there was no sympathy." Turning to his cross-examiner Mr. Lowden said, "I tell you, Sir Henry James, that we understand these things differently in Ireland to what you do in England. It was no business of mine to give information."

Mr. Lowden, in short, was doing, only less impressively, what Mr. Davitt did the day before—he was raising the curtain over a fragment of the life of contemporary Ireland, a life as strange and unintelligible to the people of London as if it were life in another planet. Sir Henry tried him again. "If you had information of a kind that would probably lead to the detection of a criminal, would you give that information to the police?" Mr. Lowden paused for a long time. At last he replied, "I would give the information to the Press—but to go privately to the police, and give them the information would be to rank myself among all the scoundrels and ruffians my country has produced." Mr. Lowden's blood was up. He struck the desk with his fist as he exclaimed, "Help those police who serve as spies and who stab women in the back!" He was alluding to a savage bayonet-and-bâton charge by the police in Mayo some years ago. In answer to an insinuating question by Sir Henry James as to whether his League colleagues would act as he did, Mr. Lowden flatly declined to speak in their name. He then observed that what the Irish peasantry objected to was, not the detection of crime, but giving assistance to the police. He strenuously maintained that, although he had not given information to the police, he had risked his life in denouncing outrages, and that his denunciations materially contributed to the break-up of the Herds' League.

ONE HUNDRED AND THIRD DAY.

JULY 9.

FOUR of the Parliamentary members "charged" were examined to-day. First came Mr. Garrett Byrne, M.P. for Wicklow. It was difficult to find out what Mr. Byrne was charged with. But from the multitude of his speeches of the last ten years two were "put in" to prove his bad character as a politician. One of the speeches was described as having been delivered in Waterford, and now it turned out that Mr. Byrne had, as he expressed it, "never been in the county of Waterford up to this moment."

Then came Mr. Jeremiah Jordan, member for West Clare. Of his speeches also, only two were "put in," though, like his predecessor in the box, he had delivered a multitude of them. From Mr. Jordan his cross-examiner could learn little or nothing. The third witness, Mr. Thomas Mayne, member for Mid-Tipperary, was confronted with several specimens of his own picturesque rhetoric. Mr. Mayne is prompt, precise, definite, resolute; and he looks it. Did he in one of his speeches liken landgrabbing unto leprosy and cholera— whose victims must be shunned? Why not? though he did not, at the moment, recollect the figurative expression. Mr. Mayne argued the point with Sir Henry James. Said he, if people do have cholera or leprosy, surely the sensible plan is to steer clear of them. And when people contracted the moral disease of grabbing, they ought to be isolated. That was all he meant. Boycotting was, as Mr. Mayne brusquely defined it, "the science of severely letting a man alone." "Would you," asked Sir Henry James, "boycott a man to the extent of depriving him of the necessaries of life?" He would. Mr. Mayne boldly went as far as his logic carried him: "If the boycotted man wants necessaries, he knows on what conditions he can have them." He must, said Mr. Mayne in effect, take the risks if he attempts to break down the tenants' combination for self-defence. But, in answer to Mr. Reid, the member for Mid-Tipperary said he had never known an instance of boycotting carried to such extremities.

The next witness, Mr. John O'Connor, member for South Tipperary, occupied the Court for the rest of the day—some five hours. He was one of the most interesting witnesses who had yet appeared for the defence. He was only fifteen when he became a Fenian—a tender age for a political career, secret or open. He took the Fenian oath in 1866. His conversion (to use Mr. O'Connor's own expression) to Mr. Parnell's constitutionalism took place ten years ago. But the change had been coming over him many months before he either heard or saw the future Nationalist leader. It was begun by the letters of John Devoy, who advised the Fenian youth of Ireland to emerge from their "rat-holes of conspiracy" and take part in the national life of their country— meaning the open agitation.

After that, said Mr. O'Connor, I read the speeches of Mr. Davitt, now released from Dartmoor, where, like a beast of burden, he was made to work with a horse-collar round his neck. Mr. O'Connor's "conversion" was completed by Mr. Parnell's speeches at Cork in 1880, and Mr. Parnell's election for Cork, in spite of the disadvantages under which he laboured at the moment. Once converted Mr. O'Connor entered into his new work with a will. He founded a branch of the Land League in Cork. Arrested as a suspect in July, 1881, and released in June, 1882, he founded, upon the ruins of the Land League, the Labour League of Ireland, which soon became merged in the National League, Mr. O'Connor entering the new association as a member of its executive council.

Mr. Lockwood, examining Mr. O'Connor, questioned him minutely about the story of his doings in Cork in 1886, as told by Sergeant Faussett, one of *The Times* constabulary witnesses. Mr. O'Connor's version of the affair differed widely from that presented by the prosecution. He did not accompany the moonlighter prisoners, as the prosecution said he did ; he came upon them unexpectedly at Cork railway station. " I saw Dr. Brosnan among them ; he was handcuffed to another prisoner ; I went and shook hands with him, and told him to 'cheer up,' and that has been made a charge against me." When the crowd in the streets cheered for the Kerry moonlighters, Mr. O'Connor gave them a counter-cheer "for a fair trial." "I did not say down with British law, but give us British law. I did not say down with the Cork juries, but down with packed juries." Nor did Mr. O'Connor stop his car before the house of a Cork juror, in order to intimidate him, but only to wait for the Mayor of Cork, who lived near the juror in question. " I always," said Mr. O'Connor, " denounced crime." As soon as he heard of the murder of Mr. Curtin he left Cork on a visit to the bereaved family.

Now came the cross-examination, conducted by Mr. Atkinson. Hardly had Mr. Atkinson begun when Mr. O'Connor stopped him with one of those frequent refusals to give information which provoked several remonstrances and significant warnings from Sir J. Hannen in the course of the morning and afternoon. Mr. O'Connor refused to tell from whom he received the Fenian oath. But he admitted with the utmost frankness that he distributed arms, and that every man who could pay for a rifle got one. Mr. O'Connor took his cross-examiner completely by surprise when he said that he first met Mr. John Devoy in 1874, and in America, " where I was on a Fenian mission." What was Mr. O'Connor's business with John Devoy, Mr. Atkinson asked, with much curiosity. With a smile, Mr. John O'Connor refused to say more than that he met John Devoy there in 1874. " I do indeed object to tell you my business with John Devoy."

Here Sir James Hannen, frowning ominously for some time, sharply interrupted the cross-examination. Said the President : " The excuses which are made are not for a moment tenable in a court of justice. The illegal oath of an illegal association not to give evidence is, of course, not to be recognized. My brothers and I have a delicate task to perform, and I do not propose at present to take the measures which are in my power. All I will do at present is to point out to this gentleman and to others who may be in the same position, that they must necessarily have an unfortunate influence on our judgment when we find that at every point we are obstructed in the inquiry we are bound to pursue by these refusals to give evidence."

Mr. Atkinson then tried to learn from him the business on which he had had interviews with Mr. John Devoy in Ireland, in 1879. Sir Henry James also contended that it was of the utmost importance to know "the circumstances under which Devoy came to Ireland in 1879 to assist in the organization of the Land League." But Mr. O'Connor surprised Sir James and his colleagues by telling them that John Devoy came for a very different purpose—came to dissuade him from joining the Land League. Yet it was John Devoy's letters which, according to Mr. O'Connor's own account, began the process of his conversion to the open agitation. But John Devoy in Ireland was trying to wean Mr. John O'Connor from the open agitation. How was that? Mr. John O'Connor could not tell precisely. Perhaps Mr. Devoy had changed his mind. Then an idea flashed upon Mr. Atkinson. Were these apparently irreconcilable actions of John Devoy a proof of *The Times* contention that the secret association (the party of physical force) and the open movement—Fenianism and Parnellism—were merely different aspects of one and the same thing? When John Devoy advised the Fenian youth to come out of their "rat-holes of conspiracy, and enter municipal and other forms of local politics," did that mean that a man should remain a Fenian and still enter municipal life? That was Mr. Atkinson's question, repeated over and over again, with the object of suggesting, if not proving, that the open or Parnellite movement had never yet separated itself from the secret conspiracy.

The President, irritated at Mr. O'Connor's steady refusal to give information about details, and tired, perhaps, of Mr. Atkinson's repetitions, remarked that "we have sufficient to infer from if the witness ['this man,' as he once called him] will not give direct answers." Upon this, Mr. O'Connor became indignant. "With every respect to the Court, I am giving direct answers upon matters I know of. There is no equivocation about me. I have told you of matters to which I will *not* speak, but of those which I can I will." While he said this, Mr. John O'Connor nodded and clenched his fist, as if he had made up his mind that no power on earth should extract from him information he swore to keep secret.

Even before this incident the President and the witness came into collision on this same question of a respect for a Fenian oath. "I have too much regard for my own obligation," Mr. O'Connor had just said. "Are you a Protestant or a Roman Catholic?" the President inquired, in a tone of severity. "A Catholic, my lord." "And do you mean to assert that your Church justifies your refusal to give evidence on the ground that you have taken an illegal oath?" "Well, I have never studied the theological aspect of the case." "Nor the moral?" "No. But I know what my own code of honour is, and I mean to adhere to it."

After a short pause Sir James leant back in his chair, and allowed the cross-examination to proceed. Replying to further questions of Mr. Atkinson, Mr. John O'Connor stated that he had not formally separated himself from the Fenian body, but that he had "gradually dropped out of the organization." And it was true that at a meeting at Bantry in 1880 he had declared against the chairman's resolution condemning the revolutionary movement. Why, having joined the open movement, did Mr. O'Connor do that? Because, Mr. O'Connor explained, the chairman's speech would do more harm than good; "there were in the neighbourhood many influential Fenians less friendly to the open movement than I was, and it would be a mistake to arouse their jealousy and enmity."

The Judges were more irritated with Mr. John O'Connor than with any other principal witness on the Parnellite side. His reticence on matters about which his Fenian oath bound him to secrecy annoyed them. His speeches and some of his accusations against the "Castle" authorities shocked them. Mr. Justice Day smiled, however, when Mr. O'Connor, confronted with one of his own speeches, said he must have expressed himself "figuratively" when he spoke of "shouldering a rifle" in Ireland's cause. What, Mr. Atkinson wanted to know, did Mr. O'Connor mean by saying he would not advise his hearers to nail the grabber's ears to the pump? Did Mr. O'Connor ever say it? Mr. O'Connor could not recollect. "But I dare say I did say it," remarked Mr. O'Connor. But surely these were words which, if a man uttered them, he must remember. "I do *not* remember them," sharply retorted Mr. O'Connor; and, turning to the President, he remarked that it would be "unreasonable" to expect him to recollect individual expressions ten years after.

In a minute or two more Mr. O'Connor damaged his cause by his candour. Advice which once upon a time Mr. O'Connor had given to the Irish police to throw up the service rather than perform certain duties was treated by Mr. Atkinson as if it were an attempt to "corrupt the force." "My desire was to disaffect the force," said Mr. O'Connor. "Was that a way to put down crime?" retorted Mr. Atkinson. "I did more to put down crime than the Irish police ever did," was Mr. O'Connor's answer. But the portion of his evidence which appeared to produce the most unfavourable impression upon the Bench was that in which he accused—"not the Lord-Lieutenant," as he said—but the local officials in Castleisland district, of permitting Poff and Barrett [two alleged moonlighters] to perish on the gallows, knowing them to be innocent, and knowing who the real criminals were. But when pressed for his authority for such a statement Mr. O'Connor could only say that every man in Kerry assured him of its truth. "And that is all the evidence you have," Sir James Hannen remarked, "for making these serious charges." "If the authorities knew who the culprits were," said Mr. Justice Smith, "why did they not hang them?" And when Mr. O'Connor, defending his hearsay evidence, argued that hearsay was his only ground for believing in the existence of Australia, the President abruptly and contemptuously characterized the argument as "ridiculous." "It is a shocking charge," exclaimed the President, "and it ought not to be made except on evidence."

ONE HUNDRED AND FOURTH DAY.

July 10.

PROCEEDINGS began to-day with Mr. Lockwood's application for the temporary release of Dr. Tanner from prison, in order that he might attend as a witness. The application was granted under the usual conditions, and then Mr. Atkinson cross-examined Mr. John O'Connor tediously and minutely on certain expenditures made by him during the interval between the suppression of the Land League and the rise of its successor. The total in question—three hundred and forty-three pounds—included small sums the history of which Mr. Atkinson appeared to think Mr. O'Connor should have kept in perfect recollection. All that Mr. O'Connor could tell him was that a hundred pounds was spent on registration, and the rest in paying the travelling expenses of organizers and lecturers.

Then Mr. Atkinson questioned him about his past speeches, notably a Cork speech of 1880, in which Mr. O'Connor was represented as having advised his hearers to "make" the government of Ireland by the English "impossible."

In looking through that speech a short time ago in his cell in Tullamore, Mr. O'Connor marked some passages whose authenticity he thought doubtful. "Make" was one of the doubtful expressions about which "I made a point of interrogation in my own mind," said Mr. O'Connor, much to the amusement of the Bench and the Q.C.'s. What he had really meant was that his countrymen should expose the failure of the English administration of Ireland. Once or twice Mr. O'Connor more than hinted that only a constabulary reporter would have reproduced his speeches so badly.

What Mr. O'Connor had to say about his speech on the Prince of Wales's visit was very interesting. His account of the matter coincided with Mr. William O'Brien's. At first Mr. O'Connor and others advised the Irish people to "preserve towards the Prince of Wales a respectful neutrality." But the Nationalists' indignation was aroused when two London journals described the reception as a triumphant reply to "the challenge thrown down by the Separatists." Mr. O'Connor and his friends prepared an address to the Prince protesting against the misrepresentations of *The Times* (one of the two papers mentioned), and showing the Prince of Wales what the reasons were for Irish disloyalty and disaffection. The deputation that went to present the address at Mallow station was, said Mr. O'Connor, bludgeoned and driven off by the police. In one of his last answers to Mr. Lockwood, Mr. O'Connor declared he did not consider himself morally bound by the Coercion Act (under which he is still a prisoner). He declared that the Irish constabulary were at this moment more hated than ever they had been; and he remarked that Mr. Atkinson had not yet replied to his challenge to produce a single instance of crime following as a consequence from any speech of his.

Mr. Daniel Crilly, M.P., of *The Nation* newspaper, and member for North Mayo, was the next witness. He stated that he had constantly been denouncing crime. His examination and cross-examination occupied only a minute or two. When Mr. Crilly left the box Mr. Lockwood rose to announce that he would now introduce, from places outside the five counties of Galway, Mayo, Clare, Kerry, and Cork witnesses of good social position, who, from their own personal experience, would testify to the peaceful spirit and beneficial influence of the League. Here they are in the order in which they appeared in the box : Mr. Gallagher, Poor Law Guardian of Strabane ; Mr. O'Hagan, Chairman of Commissioners, from county Monaghan ; Mr. Ryan, Mayor of Cork ; Mr. O'Keefe, Mayor of Limerick ; Mr. Toole, Mayor of Waterford; Mr. Coyle, Mayor of Kilkenny ; Mr. Devereux, Mayor of Wexford ; Mr. Conolly, Mayor of Sligo ; Mr. Meehan, Chairman of Maryborough Commissioners ; Mr. William Adams, Chairman of Tullamore Commissioners ; Mr. Delahunt, of Wexford.

All these men, occupying prominent positions in their respective communities, agreed in testifying to the "respectability" of the membership of the League, and to its great services in discouraging and repressing outrage and crime.

The incident of the day was Mr. Davitt's application for summoning before the Court the editor of a London evening paper in which had appeared a paragraph describing alleged precautions for protecting the Court against dynamiters. Sir James Hannen quietly ridiculed the story about the bogus dynamite machines said to have been deposited in or about the court. For his own part, Sir James Hannen was not a bit afraid of being blown up ; he regarded the whole thing as a "silly hoax." The President, however, failed to soothe Mr. Davitt, who maintained that there was an attempt somewhere to bring discredit upon the defence. Mr. Davitt at last exclaimed that he "broadly accused Le Caron of having brought the machines, with the sanction of Houston." As Mr. Davitt said this, he turned round and pointed to Mr. Houston's accustomed seat. "You have no right to say that, Mr. Davitt, without direct evidence," Mr. Justice Smith remarked, quietly. Sir James Hannen only observed that he regretted Mr. Davitt's departure from his usual "demeanour." "My lord," replied Mr. Davitt, "I feel very strongly about it." "Yes, I know that is so."

ONE HUNDRED AND FIFTH DAY.

JULY 11.

If the trial has been prolonged, it is hardly the fault of the "defence," as it is called. To-day, fourteen Nationalist witnesses were disposed of. Mr. Reid, Q.C., has so rigidly excluded all evidence which he did not regard as strictly relevant, and the witnesses have been produced in such rapid succession, that the Court must have been prepared for his welcome announcement of the approaching end of the Nationalist case. Mr. Reid informed the judges that only two or three witnesses remained to be examined.

Mr. Meehan, chairman of the Maryborough Town Commissioners, re-appeared to answer some questions by Sir Henry James, on entries and resolutions contained in the minute book of the Maryborough branch of the League. Several of the resolutions were directed against the occupation of evicted farms, and spoke of the expulsion of "traitors" from League membership. Traitors was merely another word for grabbers, and the "penalty" threatened in the minute was nothing—meant expulsion only. Would members of the League be allowed to deal with other members who had been expelled? Sir Henry James asked. That, according to Mr. Meehan's answers, might depend upon circumstances. In a word, Mr. Meehan's account of the League in Maryborough corresponded generally with what other witnesses had said regarding branches in other parts of Ireland.

The next witness was Mr. Foley, M.P. He had been examined before—about a hundred pound cheque of Mr. Egan's, payable to Mr. Frank Byrne. He had produced the cheque in court, but without its counterfoil. Now he came provided with it. The cheque was crossed, and Mr. Foley took it in exchange for an open one of his own, made payable to Mr. Frank Byrne. He understood the money was for Land League purposes, and he had cashed several cheques of the same description for Mr. Byrne. Mr. George Shrubsole, Mr. Foley's clerk, entered the witness-box to corroborate Mr. Foley's statement.

Mr. Ryan, the Mayor of Cork, who had appeared the day before, was the next witness. His cross-examination, resumed by Mr. Atkinson, turned principally on the attitude of the Cork leaguers towards crime perpetrated in outside localities. Mr. Ryan's fellow-leaguers had denounced the Phoenix Park murders. Why did they decline to take part with the neighbouring League branch of Buttyvant in an attempt to bring some outragemongers to justice? That was in February, 1881. Mr. Ryan was not quite sure, at this distance of time, what his reasons were for declining ; but probably he thought that the Government might be left to do their own police work. Some of the next witness's answers bore directly upon this matter. The witness was Mr. Flood, chairman of the Longford Town Commissioners. In his answers to Mr. Davitt and Mr. Reid he declared that the people would not give information to police authorities, whom they regarded as their enemies. "There is no sympathy between the people and the police—who are the servants of the landlords."

Mr. John Hammond, of the Carlow Town Commission, showed that in his part of Ireland immunity from crime co-existed with immunity from eviction.

Then there followed Mr. Foley, of the Nenagh Town Commission (county Tipperary), who said that the Nenagh National League branch contained all the "respectability" of the place, and whose examination and cross-examination scarcely occupied sixty seconds. Then there followed Mr. Robinson, of the Kingstown Commission, who said that most of the League funds were spent on parliamentary, municipal, and poor law registration ; Mr. Robert Sweeney, Town Commissioner from county Donegal, who said his fellow-leaguers sometimes were useful as arbitrators between landlords and tenants ; and Mr. Hughes, of Belfast, who testified to the value of the League, as an instrument of political education.

And now came the principal witness of the day, Mr. Thomas Condon, member for East Tipperary. One of his first answers was characteristic of Ireland. He informed the Court with a smile that he had just learned of his re-election as Mayor of Clonmel. Mr. Condon is still a prisoner under the Coercion Act, and six weeks of his time have yet to expire. Mr. Condon was once upon a time an out-and-out Fenian. But long ago he came to the conclusion that Fenianism was used up, and that the sensible thing to do was to go in for the Nationalist movement. Replying to Mr. Davitt, Mr. Condon said that Tipperary was troubled with agrarian outrages ten years before the rise of the Land League. Mr. Condon raised a laugh by saying he was told that the Carlton Club had contributed £250 towards O'Donovan Rossa's electioneering expenses at Tipperary in 1869 ! Sir James Hannen at once interfered. "Stories of that kind," said he, "should not be dragged in. Such statements should not be made without some foundation of fact." Sir James thought the story absurd. Mr. Condon replied with the utmost coolness, that had he known he was to be questioned on the matter, he would have been able to produce his proofs. "Reserve your statement," the President replied, "until you are in a position to prove it." Mr. Condon next observed that of all the speeches he had delivered not one was "put in" against him by the prosecution. Yet, as he remarked, he was put into prison for having been present at a meeting whereat was delivered a speech that he not only did not deliver, but did not even hear ! This was the speech in which Mr. Healy said that though the ratepayers had to find a thousand pounds for Constable Leahy's injuries, received at the Mitchelstown massacres, they would have had to pay nothing if Constable Leahy had been killed outright.

Mr. Condon quickly disposed of the story formerly told in the box by *The Times* witness, Mitchell. Mitchell said that, being under the boycott, he bought some meat in Mr. Condon's shop ; that having made his purchase, he was met by Mr. Condon outside ; and that Mr. Condon told him if he had been in the shop at the time, customer Mitchell would have got "the knife," in place of provisions. "Not a shadow of foundation for the story," said Mr. Condon. "I never knew the man, I don't know him, I never saw him until lately when he was pointed out to me in London." Nor, according to Mr. Condon's account, could his shop assistant have threatened Mitchell, for the assistant was a Protestant and an anti-Nationalist, and more likely to befriend Mitchell than to boycott him.

The testimony of some more of *The Times* witnesses was flatly contradicted by T. Berrane, Joseph Kelly, and John M'Carthy. Berrane denied that Macaulay, convicted of sharing in the Crossmolina conspiracy, was a member of the League. Mr. Berrane was secretary of the branch. His evidence was corroborated by Mr. Kelly, president of the branch. A jovial witness was Mr. Kelly. He must be a general merchant, for, as Sir Henry James, interpreting Mr. Kelly's brogue, repeated to the President, "he can clothe any one of us from the cradle to the grave." Lastly, Mr. M'Carthy, League branch president, declared that neither he nor anybody in county Longford would believe *The Times* witness Iago on his oath; and that there was no truth whatever in Iago's story that the League branch had resolved to shoot a man named Scanlon for having taken an evicted farm.

ONE HUNDRED AND SIXTH DAY.

JULY 12.

THE court to-day presented a spectacle somewhat unusual of late. Counsel on both sides were present in full strength; and Sir Richard Webster and Sir Charles Russell were in their places early. Mr. Parnell, who seldom appears in court, was among the first to arrive. As soon as the judges took their seats, Sir Charles Russell requested that Mr. Soames should be instructed to produce a list of his payments to witnesses, and also his communications with agents in Ireland and America. The Attorney-General mildly remarked that he did not "see" on what grounds Sir Charles Russell based his application. With the rejoinder that Sir Richard Webster would see presently, Sir Charles Russell called out the name of Mr. John Mather Hogg, merchant, Dublin, who thereupon entered the witness-box.

Mr. Hogg, a member of the General Committee of the Irish Loyal and Patriotic Union, was examined as to his knowledge of the financial management of the Union. The object was partly to ascertain whether the Union was the source from which the purchase-money of the Piggott letters was in the first place obtained, and, if so, by what channels the money reached the purchaser—in other words, the forger. Sir Charles Russell's questions recalled the livelier scenes of the trial, when he announced that no effort would be spared to unearth the "foul conspiracy" behind Pigott and Houston. It turned out that Houston during his negotiations with Pigott had borrowed sums of money from Mr. Hogg. But, as Mr. Hogg now explained in the witness-box, Mr. Hogg knew absolutely nothing, before the autumn of 1887, of the transactions between Pigott and Houston. Mr. Hogg added that although he had lived in Dublin all his life, he had not known anything, good or bad, about Pigott. Mr. Hogg was not a member of the finance committee of the Union; but, like Mr. T. W. Russell, he was authorized to sign its cheques. He had no recollection of the payment of Union money to the Dr. Macguire who lent Houston £850. As for the money which he himself lent Houston, it was not Union money, but his own, and he understood that Houston required it for purposes wholly unconnected with Union business— for purely private purposes.

First of all, on the 30th of April, 1886, he lent him sixty pounds, which was repaid within a fortnight. A little later Houston—then, as he still is, secretary of the Union—asked him for a loan of three hundred. According to his own fluent story, as given in the witness-box, Mr. Mather Hogg must have been a little staggered at this request. Mr. Hogg asked for a day or two to think it over. He did think it over; and then, said Mr. Mather Hogg, what do you want all that money for? Oh, for purely private reasons. Not for Stock Exchange speculations? asked Mr. Hogg. No; Mr. Houston had never in his life tried his hand at Stock Exchange business. These assurances satisfied Mr. Hogg, and in a day or two Houston was told that he might have the money. Houston borrowed from him, in all, three hundred and ten pounds, mostly repaid. In an earlier part of his examination by Sir Charles Russell, Mr. Hogg said that the Union paid a small sum to Sir Rowland Blennerhasset for his travelling expenses. "I have no questions to ask," said the Attorney-General, when Sir Charles Russell sat down.

Sir Charles Russell then called on Mr. Soames. Sir Charles Russell's questions to him were intended to find out how Mr. Soames came to know Le Caron; how Pigott came to be employed in visiting (on *The Times* behalf) convicts in prison; how the "Castle" authorities procured documents for *The Times*; and how the convict witnesses were brought over to England. Mr. Soames first heard of Le Caron through Mr. Macdonald, at the end of 1888. And in consequence of Le Caron's having lost his post as Government spy, Mr. Anderson of the Home Office had been told that Le Caron should not be allowed to want so long as his present employers had money.

Mr. Soames then left the box, and Mr. Houston entered it. Some of Mr. Houston's dates were noteworthy—the I.L.P.U. was founded, and Mr. Houston first came to know Pigott, and "Parnellism Unmasked" was published in the summer of 1885, just when the hubbub of the great political struggle of the autumn was beginning to be heard throughout the constituencies. "Parnellism Unmasked," Pigott's pamphlet, became in Mr. Houston's hands "Parnellism" simply; and in the fulness of time, "Parnellism" blossomed, in the pages of a London journal, into "Parnellism and Crime." The Union paid Pigott sixty pounds for his "Parnellism Unmasked." Mr. Houston could not recollect who introduced him to Mr. Pigott but he thought it must have been one of the politicians associated with him during the 1885 election—possibly Lord R. Grosvenor.

Lord Richard Grosvenor, of the I.L.P.U. (the London branch of which was founded in 1886), was one of those from whom, during his transactions with Mr. Pigott, Mr. Houston borrowed money. Sir Rowland Blennerhasset was another. Professor Macguire was a third. Said Mr. Houston, "I told Professor Macguire what I wanted the money for." Sir Charles Russell appeared to think it strange that so poor a man as Dr. Macguire should have had so much money to lend. Mr. Houston thought that Dr. Macguire was well off, "and I think so still." "I repaid him in 1887." And yet Dr. Macguire died poor? Yes, Mr. Houston admitted that; adding that he was "surprised," and that he could not understand where the doctor's money "could have gone." Sir Charles Russell then asked whether there was anything to show that Dr. Macguire had paid money to the Union? Not the "slightest trace" of such a thing, said the Union Secretary. Did Dr. Macguire keep a banking account? Yes. At any rate, Dr. Macguire told Mr. Houston that he had money in a bank at Galway. But he advanced the loan to Mr. Houston, not by cheque, but in bank-notes. Here Mr. Houston produced a cheque for £100, paid to Eugene Davis through Mr. Pigott. Sir Charles Russell carefully studied this interesting receipt of Davis's. Then, looking up, "Do you really think, Mr. Houston," said he, "that this is not Mr. Pigott's handwriting?" In an off-hand way and with a smile, Mr. Houston remarked that he did not need to look. But "look," repeated Sir Charles Russell. Houston looked carelessly, smilingly, as if, in his good nature, he wished to humour his examiner. Mr. Houston was satisfied that the handwriting was not the departed Pigott's.

At last Sir Charles Russell reached the point at which he was all the while aiming. Let us probe this business to the bottom by a scrutiny of the I.L.P.U. books. Houston was ready with his answer. Turning round to the judges, he informed them that he was instructed to say that the Union books were at their lordships' disposal, but that the committee objected to having them placed "in the hands of our political opponents." "I quite appreciate the force of that objection," retorted Sir Charles, on the instant. The Court laughed, and a "hear, hear," was barely audible in the back seats below the main gallery.

Sir Charles Russell based his application on the "suspicion" that the Union was Pigott's paymaster, and Dr. Macguire the medium through which the money was passed; and also on the proposition that "various agencies, all working to the same end, had been placed at the disposal of those representing *The Times*." To this application the President objected, first on the ground that it involved charges against persons not before the Court, and secondly, that the only question with which the Court was concerned was the truth or falsehood of the charges. Upon this Sir Charles Russell turned round to Mr. Asquith, who promptly rose to address the judges. The Act imposes upon your lordships, said Mr. Asquith, the duty of "inquiring into and reporting on" the charges. "Yes, whether they are true or false," Mr. Justice Smith interposed. But Mr. Asquith held that the judges were bound to do more than that :—

"The Act imposes upon your lordships the duty of inquiring into and reporting not only into the truth and falsehood of these charges and allegations, but as to the circumstances under which they were put forward, and as to their genesis, their origin, and growth. This is material from the point of view of enabling your lordships' to understand and appreciate the evidence that has been brought before you. Even if your lordships' sole duty is to inquire into the charges, it is material to consider whence they proceeded, by what men they were put forward, and by what means they were engendered."

Then the Attorney-General spoke. Repeating Mr. Houston's objection, he intimated that there would be no objection to letting Mr. Cunynghame inspect the books. But Sir Charles Russell would not be satisfied with any such partial concession. And then Sir James Hannen gave his decision :—

"We are of opinion that the inspection ought not to be granted. The Commission which is given to us, is to inquire into these charges; we can attach no other meaning than that we are to inquire into their truth or falsehood. Any evidence to this purpose we should admit and have admitted. The examination which has taken place to-day has been to a great extent beyond what in strictness, would, we think, be admissible. Even if it should be proved that the money of the Loyal and Patriotic Union had been paid for the purpose of putting before the public these statements which are now complained of, still the only question we have to determine is whether or not these charges are true or false. We therefore reject the application."

The words were hardly out of the President's mouth when Mr. Parnell turned round and handed a paper to Sir Charles Russell. Sir Charles, rising, intimated respectfully to the Court that in consequence of the President's ruling he must "consider his position." "Very well," said the President, abruptly. After an awkward pause, Sir Richard Webster put a question to Mr. Houston, who was still standing in the witness-box. Was there any truth in what Mr. Davitt said yesterday about Mr. Houston's connection with the dynamite hoax. "Not the slightest" was Mr. Houston's answer. "Have you contributed articles to *The Evening News and Post* during the past month?" asked Mr. Davitt, suddenly starting up. "I decline to answer." In another minute Mr. Parnell with his black bag in one hand, and his overcoat across his elbow, walked out of court. Mr. Davitt, putting up his papers, and looking as if he meant good-bye, followed him. Lastly, and after a decorous interval, Sir Charles Russell quietly disappeared. In a few minutes more, the rumour was spread along the Strand that Sir Charles Russell and his client had "withdrawn" from the case.

ONE HUNDRED AND SEVENTH DAY.

JULY 16.

TO-DAY, long before half-past ten o'clock, the Court was densely crowded. The "defendants" were in greater strength than almost at any time since the beginning of the trial. But there was one conspicuous figure missing—Mr. Davitt. Otherwise the Nationalists were well represented. Mr. T. D. Sullivan and Mr. Biggar sat on the Solicitors' Bench, the latter smiling and nodding, laughing, and generally conducting himself as if he expected some entertainment on the appearance of their lordships. Mr. Sullivan, also, was in high glee. Dr. Tanner, looking none the worse for his imprisonment, dressed with scrupulous neatness, and wearing a shamrock in his button-hole, talked away with Mr. O'Kelly, whose military appearance and bearing struck everybody. The two Tipperary "boys," Mr. Condon and Mr. John O'Connor, sat together, somewhat silently. They were still in captivity—putting up at Holloway Gaol, when they were not attending court. But the London captivity of Irish members brought from their Irish gaols to give evidence before the Commission was not too severe, as was evident from Mr. William O'Brien's perplexity one day as he strolled about the court "on the search for my keeper." Besides the foregoing there were Dr. Fitzgerald, Mr. Haydon, Mr. P. J. O'Brien, Mr. Byrne, Mr. Justin Huntly M'Carthy, and last, though not least, Mr. Matt. Harris, silent, in a "brown study," with his white hair, and wan, grey face bearing traces of illness.

When Sir Charles Russell came in without Mr. Parnell, people jumped to the conclusion that Mr. Parnell had definitely "withdrawn." When, in a minute or two, Mr. Parnell did appear, they jumped to the conclusion that he had "thought better of it." But there was Sir Charles Russell, putting their doubts at rest, for the Judges had scarcely entered when Sir Charles was up and addressing them. Speaking slowly, in a low voice and with every mark of reverence, Sir Charles announced that, though the course he was about to take had been resolved upon on Friday, he thought it more respectful to their lordships to wait until this morning. Mr. Parnell's instructions to him were in writing; there could be "no mistaking their meaning," said Sir Charles; they were peremptory, and, to cut a very short address still shorter, "we"—Sir Charles and Mr. Asquith—"no longer appear in this case."

The President, polite, precise, unmoved, leant slightly forward, as he expressed regret for the loss of the learned counsel's assistance, and then he added, just a little stiffly, that Mr. Parnell nevertheless remained "subject to the jurisdiction of this Court." Sir Charles was about to say something when Mr. Parnell quickly rose to his feet, whereupon Sir Charles Russell and Mr. Asquith, gathering up their papers, left their seats, elbowed their way through the crowd, and disappeared. Mr. Justice Smith's eyes twinkled; he smiled. Mr. Justice Day stared at the retreating figures, with a hard, stony stare expressive of intense disapproval. The President's face was less easy to read. After the pause caused by the withdrawal of Sir Charles Russell, Mr. Parnell began. He reminded the Judges of the amount of evidence which he had given, and of the time which he had spent in court since the "explosion" of the letters case. He requested that their lordships should either release him from further attendance or enable him this week to undergo the Attorney-General's deferred cross-examination on certain cheque books. The Attorney-General promised to do his best to oblige Mr. Parnell.

Even the spectators must have felt a certain awkwardness of the situation. Q.C.'s, who are, perhaps, somewhat hardened persons, must have felt it. Mr. Reid rose with the demeanour of a man performing a duty he would cheerfully avoid. For he, too, had received his "instructions": he must withdraw. But as for his client Mr. O'Kelly, he would appear for himself; "he will give any information your lordships may desire." On this well-meant assurance, Sir James Hannen struck in, coldly and with dignity, "You are in the unfortunate position, Mr. Reid, of representing the witness while no longer counsel." Mr. Reid sat down in silence. Then Mr. Lockwood rose up. Sir Henry James had just asked "what about Mr. Matt. Harris?" and Mr. Lockwood wished to speak for Mr. Matt. Harris, and others. But Mr. Lockwood spoke as if he did not at all like the position he was in. He, too, Mr. Lockwood, had received his instructions. He, too, must withdraw. But Mr. Harris and Dr. Tanner would appear for themselves. And then, as if to encourage their lordships, "I may say, on behalf of all those for whom we have appeared, they will treat with the utmost respect any summons from this Court." This was very kind of Mr. Lockwood; and the President followed him up sharply, thus—"I have already observed that nothing is changed in any respect except that we shall no longer have the assistance of counsel in the case. In every other respect the position is as it was. They are bound to present themselves before the Court if they have any information to give, just as it was before."

When the President ceased speaking, there was a general movement on the Nationalist benches. Mr. Reid rose. Next Mr. Lockwood. Then the juniors. And away they went,—slowly making their way through the crowd, —lawyers, M.P.'s, and all, and the tall figure of Mr. Parnell, with a top-coat over the left arm, and a hand-bag in the right hand, bringing up the rear. A quiet smile passed over his thin, refined features. Decorous, matter-of-fact, brief as it was—it occupied no more than three minutes—this was one of the most interesting scenes in Court since the opening of the Commission. After the Nationalists left, with a multitude of spectators behind them, the Court presented a singularly lop-sided appearance—the Nationalist halves of the lawyers' benches being completely deserted, *The Times* portion being full.

Another awkward pause. Mr. O'Kelly, Mr. Matt. Harris, Dr. Tanner, sat on the Solicitors' Bench, stock still. They were ready to be examined, but who was to do it? At last, Sir James Hannen mentioned Mr. O'Kelly's name. Mr. O'Kelly rose, and in his strong, hearty, frank voice expressed his readiness to answer any questions which might be put to him. Sir James bowed. Mr. O'Kelly strode to the witness-box, entered it, took the oath, and then submitted to the examination—that should have been a cross-examination—by Sir Henry James. With his erect, stout figure, in close-fitting, buttoned-up frock coat, his fierce moustache, keen, frank, steady grey eyes, prompt, downright address—but respectful, withal, as of a man who respects himself—Mr. O'Kelly looked every inch a soldier. He exactly realized the description given of him, as soldier and journalist, in Mr. T. P. O'Connor's graphic narratives.

Mr. O'Kelly was a first-rate witness. He gave the fullest and frankest details of his membership of the Fenian Brotherhood up to the year 1879-80, when he entered the National movement, since which he has had no intercourse with the society. When in America he was a member of the Clan-na-Gael. In America, in 1879, said Mr. O'Kelly, there was a general belief that Ireland was about to be visited by a famine: in which case, the physical force party in America had resolved upon fighting. And Mr. O'Kelly came over from America, to Ireland, ready to fight for the peasants against their landlords, in the event of famine outbreak. He came, as he expressed it, to "organize" Ireland for insurrection. All this, Mr. O'Kelly declared with the utmost frankness. "Whatever you want to know about myself personally, I will tell you," and Mr. O'Kelly was keeping his word. He was equally frank in his account of his career up to 1870, nine years before his organizing mission to Ireland. In that earlier period, he had, as a Fenian, been active in importing arms into

Ireland. "There's no concealment about it," Mr. O'Kelly remarked, with a laugh, turning his keen, grey eyes on Sir Henry James. Sir Henry was reading long extracts from Fenian letters addressed to Mr. O'Kelly in his Fenian days, letters often in enigmatic language, which Mr. O'Kelly readily explained to his cross-examiner. Mr. O'Kelly smiled, and smiled again, as these long-forgotten letters reminded him of his times of old romance, of his hot, indiscreetly patriotic youth. When he came to " organize " Ireland, for the purpose above mentioned, Mr. O'Kelly brought American money with him. But it was not " Skirmishing Fund Money," said Mr. O'Kelly ; that fund was Rossa's. And when it appeared that there was to be no famine, and therefore no chance of a peasant insurrection, Mr. O'Kelly returned the money to America. But there was another reason why Mr. O'Kelly returned the money. The new leaders of the Irish people were going in for Parliamentary action ; and in 1880 Mr. O'Kelly joined the Parnellites. " You say you supported Mr. Parnell," Sir Henry James remarked. Here is Mr. O'Kelly's reply :—

" Yes, I found that most people in Ireland were inclined to support him, and that there was a strong impression and hope that they could obtain their objects without conspiracy or fighting. I rather sympathized with that view, and so joined the League."

Mr. O'Kelly gave this answer with telling effect. It was meant as an affirmation and endorsement of Mr. Parnell's great claim—and defence—that the Parnell movement converted conspiracy into constitutionalism.

Mr. O'Kelly then left the box and Mr. Matt. Harris entered it. Mr. Harris looked extremely weak. Yet, notwithstanding the President's kind request that he should sit down, he preferred to stand. He gave his evidence with that air of weary familiarity so often observable in the testimony of the Nationalist witnesses—the weariness of men who, though themselves conscious of intimate knowledge and thorough insight, yet seem to feel a despair of making other people understand Ireland. Mr. Harris was as outspoken, in his own tired way, as Mr. O'Kelly was. He had been a Fenian for fifteen years, from 1865. Egan and Sheridan were Fenians like himself. And they imported arms ; and almost every farmer in Ireland who could afford to buy a weapon possessed one. He made no concealment whatever about the fact. Mr. Harris admitted. in his frank way, that at first he did not care much for the Land League. It embraced only a single class, the farming class, and its main object was social. But Mr. Harris preferred an organization that was political and social. With characteristic honesty, Mr. Harris confessed that he thought the farmers a rather " selfish " class—who would care little for national interests, if once their own sectional interests were sufficiently provided for. In his simple, direct way too, Mr. Harris defended secret societies—conditionally. Whether they were good, or bad, was, said Mr. Harris, a question that depended on the circumstances under which they existed, and on the manner in which they were conducted. He admitted, with equal candour, that he sometimes had used indiscreet language, as when he, once upon a time, wrote of Mr. Davitt's "caterwauling" about the Phœnix Park murders and his "canting about cruelty to animals." He made use of that language, said Mr. Harris, at a time of bitter controversy with Mr. Davitt, and when he thought that Mr. Davitt was raising a somewhat insincere clamour about both. " I said at the time, that I hated murder and cruelty as much as he did." Still, as Mr. Harris now admitted, such language was dangerous.

ONE HUNDRED AND EIGHTH DAY.

JULY 17.

TO-DAY Sir Henry James resumed his cross-examination of Mr. Matthew Harris. He began with questions about the Land League books and accounts, but Mr. Harris could tell him nothing. Any documents Mr. Harris may have had he must have destroyed long ago. Nor did Sir Henry James elicit any information of a compromising character from . acknowledged motives in visiting America in 1883, and his occasional intercourse there with Mr. Egan and Mr. Ford. Mr. Harris explained that his chief inducement in visiting America was to make some money by lecturing. Not only could Mr. Harris not give Sir Henry James any information about the League books, but he knew nobody who could. "Is there any reason," asked Sir Henry James, "why Mr. J. P. Quinn should not appear as a witness?" Mr. Harris knew not of any. Mr. Moloney was said to be the person in whose possession the Land League books were last seen. Was there any reason why he should not appear? Mr. Harris knew of none, except that Mr. Moloney had private and domestic troubles of his own. But there was Mr. Campbell, M.P., private secretary to Mr. Parnell. Mr. Campbell had been engaged in the removal of the Land League books from Dublin. Why should not Mr. Campbell appear as a witness? "I don't know," was Mr. Harris's answer; "he ought to have some information on these subjects." Then Sir Henry James came to Mr. Harris's speeches, reading from them several extracts. Mr. Harris defended his strong language by saying that he spoke under the influence of strong feeling; that the objectionable expressions would not be taken literally by those who heard them; that exceptional means, strong language among them, were required to arouse a peasantry so abjectly demoralized as the peasantry of Ireland then were. In putting before the President a typical case, showing the terrible provocations to which Irish tenants had at all times been subjected, Mr. Harris nearly broke down, for he was describing an eviction effected two days after his father's death on his father's farm. Upon this farm of his father's, five hundred pounds had been spent in improvements. There was, said Mr. Harris, a law higher than mere legality—rather than see his wife and children turned out of the home which he himself had made for them he would stand in its doorway, gun in hand, and "shoot down all the landlords in Ireland, one after the other."

As Mr. Harris uttered these words, he drew himself up, his voice quivered and his eyes flashed. Before he uttered them, he had just been explaining his famous "partridge speech." When he said he would under certain circumstances shoot down landlords like partridges in September, he was, he said, speaking only in a figurative sense, as people sometimes do when they say a man ought to be hanged; and when he did use the words, he had in his mind's eye scenes such as those in which he and his family had been the victims. Strong language was, he held, naturally provoked by the circumstances. His feelings overcame him when he advised combination against a certain "man-eating tiger" of a landlord. And if all said about Mrs. Blake of Connemara was true, he would not hesitate to call her a "she devil."

In some respects Mr. Harris's evidence was more impressive than any that had preceded it. Mr. Harris is—as all who know him are aware—a man of gentle nature, honest, sincere; a man who hates violence and cruelty as much as any man in Ireland. This only rendered his intemperate utterances all the more noteworthy. Sir James Hannen appeared, somehow, to be more impressed by him—touched by him, one might venture to say—than by almost any other witness. Sir James bent forward, listening to him most attentively, as he told the story—breaking down in the recital—of the old eviction.

Next came the first lady witness on the side of the defence. The lady was Mrs. Delahunt, formerly Mrs. Kenny, whom Sir Richard Webster had, in his speech, called by her maiden name. For having taken this liberty with her name, Mrs. Delahunt administered a severe rebuke to Mr. Attorney. Mr. Attorney had made a dreadful charge against Mrs. Delahunt—"outrage had followed in her footsteps." "It was I," exclaimed Mrs. Delahunt pointedly, "that followed in the footsteps of outrage"—meaning, apparently, that her mission was to repair the damage done by landlord selfishness, particularly the evictions, which she described as the worst kind of crime in Ireland, as "legalized murder!" Now that Mrs. Delahunt and Mr. Attorney were face to face, would Mr. Attorney be good enough to substantiate his accusation? Accordingly Sir Richard Webster asked Mrs. Delahunt if she approved of certain speeches made in her hearing by members of the Ladies' Land League —of such expressions, for example, as "Warning the wavering." Mrs. Delahunt replied, generally, "that the Ladies' Land League never threatened anybody." The Attorney-General made much of the fact that Mrs. Delahunt was imprisoned three weeks for her League work in Southern Ireland; and of the story that the windows of the police district-inspector were smashed the night after Mrs. Delahunt was sentenced. Sir Richard Webster questioned Mrs. Delahunt about crime statistics in Kerry before and after her visit to the county, but she could give him no information, could not tell him whether his figures were right or wrong.

Mrs. Delahunt visited America four or five years ago; and in New York she was introduced to Mr. Patrick Ford; but she refused, without permission, to say by whom. Of the accounts of the Ladies' Land League Mrs. Delahunt knew absolutely nothing—"Probably in the waste-paper basket," remarked Mrs. Delahunt, with a glance of scorn which, one fears, was thrown away upon the Attorney-General. "Where's the waste-paper basket?" was the problem which seemed to fill Mr. Attorney's first and best thoughts, to the exclusion of all other considerations. If glances of lady's scorn could have upset any man's equanimity, the Attorney-General ought to have been in a complete state of demoralization, long before Mrs. Delahunt left the witness-box. But Sir Richard Webster can stand a good deal.

When Mr. Attorney was done with the witness, or the witness was done with Mr. Attorney—whichever it was—Sir James Hannen called upon Dr. Tanner. The renowned doctor, tastefully dressed, wearing a shamrock in his buttonhole, smiling sunnily, and looking all the better for his gaol life since May last, entered the box. "Happy to give you any information I have "— and in a moment Dr. Tanner was on the topic of boycotting. The Cork "classes" boycotted Dr. Tanner, ruined his practice as soon as he became a Nationalist politician. If the classes boycotted, why not the masses? What's sauce for the goose is sauce for the gander, was the doctrine Dr. Tanner preached from public platforms. All this, and a great deal more, Dr. Tanner detailed with perfect urbanity and the utmost good humour. But about "grabbers," quoth Mr. Murphy. Had he called them "vultures," "noisome beasts," and other picturesque names? Dr. Tanner would not answer for the exact expressions; but, said he, with another of his polite bows, "I have denounced grabbers to the best of my ability."

ONE HUNDRED AND NINTH DAY.

July 18.

Mr. M. Harris returned for a few moments to the witness-box, in order to make a statement in reference to the Messrs. Egan and Brennan severance of their connection with the Fenian organization. Mr. Harris's active connection ceased in 1880. The withdrawal of Mr. Egan and Brennan, preceded that of Mr. Harris, and was owing to the same cause—their decision to join the open movement.

Dr. Tanner then appeared, and his cross-examination was resumed by Mr. Murphy. The subject of it was Dr. Tanner's public oratory. "Did you," Mr. Murphy asked, "ever advise the people to boycott every man, woman, and child who did not support the League?" Dr. Tanner denied that he had ever said any such thing. "I hope I had too much common sense to talk of boycotting children," he added. He must have been inaccurately reported, Dr. Tanner thought. Nor had he any recollection of having in his speech compared the evictor to a hawk or a carrion crow, and the grabber to a vulture feeding upon dead carrion. All that Dr. Tanner would say was that he advocated boycotting to the best of his ability. He did recollect having called Mr. Hegarty, of Mill-street, a "creeping louse:" the hostility between him and Mr. Hegarty had reference to electioneering business, and not to agrarian disputes.

But in spite of the strong denunciations of evictors and grabbers, Dr. Tanner had always condemned outrage. From his place in the witness-box he challenged Mr. Murphy to produce a single instance of outrage following, as an effect, from any one of his speeches. Mr. Murphy suggested such a connection between a speech in which Dr. Tanner advised the young women of Ireland to avoid the police, and the tar-capping of a Miss Murphy—on the alleged ground that she had spoken to a constable. "I condemned that outrage as a most infamous thing," Dr. Tanner said, alluding generally to public speeches in which he had done so.

Like so many others among the principal witnesses on the Irish side, Dr. Tanner frankly acknowledged that in the event of the failure of the Constitutional movement, he would gladly try the alternative of physical force. When Mr. Murphy sat down, Dr. Tanner proceeded to read from his own speeches some extracts in proof of his statement that he had always condemned intimidation and outrage. The reading lasted only a few minutes.

There was a pause when Dr. Tanner left the witness-box. "We have exhausted the list of witnesses," said the President, looking at Mr. Lewis, who then rose to say that so far as he was aware there were no more to be called. This was at a quarter to twelve. Nine months from the beginning of the trial, Dr. Tanner closed the list of witnesses for the accused.

ONE HUNDRED AND TENTH DAY.

JULY 23.

YESTERDAY the court was crowded, in anticipation of Mr. Parnell's reappearance in the witness-box. The proceedings began by Mr. Parnell's correcting a former impression of Sir Henry James's that certain letters of Mr. Parnell's had not been disclosed to *The Times* counsel until Mr. M. Harris produced them the other day in court. Having frankly and politely admitted his error, Sir Henry James addressed himself to the reading of a number of letters and documents handed in by Mr. Harris. One of these was a letter from Mr. Harris to "the Irish patriot, Kickham." Enough to say of this letter that its sentiments and ideas were just the same as those to which Mr. Harris had already given expression in his straightforward and impressive evidence in the witness-box. As to the second production, one may venture to say that the reading thereof did credit to Sir Henry James, and that the writing thereof said much for Mr. M. Harris's religio-poetic temperament. Putting its mere politics aside for the moment, this interesting production really showed Mr. M. Harris in a new and pleasant light. It was Mr. Harris's funeral oration on John O'Mohoney, a Fenian of the olden time, for whose self-sacrificing character Mr. Harris felt a warm admiration. This oration was never spoken. It was only written. The "peelers" seized it, and by a whimsical kind of poetic justice its delivery was reserved for Probate Court No. 1 and the elocutionary powers of Sir Henry James. And Sir Henry, resting his left elbow on the ledge behind him, read the funeral oration most feelingly.

Then Mr. Parnell, looking even more pale and worn-out than usual, went into the witness-box. As to the question which had just been raised by Sir Richard Webster, Mr. Parnell remarked that Mr. Lewis had long ago been instructed to subpœna Mr. Moloney, the only person in this country, besides the Parliamentary members, who was likely to know anything at all about the missing accounts. Then the Attorney-General plunged into the interminable topic of League money; and he went to his work in his old and too unpleasantly aggressive manner. However, he refrained from the finger-shaking, loud style of his earlier cross-examination. He wanted to know who were the trustees of the League funds kept eight years ago (and still kept) in Paris. Mr. Parnell said they were, besides himself, Mr. Justin McCarthy, and Mr. Biggar. The Attorney-General appeared to think it a suspicious circumstance that Mr. Parnell did not on the instant mention Mr. Egan's name. Of course Mr. Egan was a trustee; "and he may be so still for all I know," added Mr. Parnell. Even on that point Mr. Parnell was not in a position to give any precise information. As Mr. Parnell observed at a later stage of his cross-examination, Mr. Egan was at present American Minister to Chili. Nor could Mr. Parnell tell the Attorney-General the amount of the Paris bonds of which he and Mr. Egan and the others were co-trustees. Mr. Parnell could not even tell within ten thousand pounds.

"But "—and here the Attorney-General lowered his voice to a pitch expressive of profound surprise—" but, Mr. Parnell, you are a man of business." "I am not," quoth Mr. Parnell, "and never was." Mr. Parnell made this candid confession about himself with an air, half of resignation, half of boredom, which much amused his hearers. He made them laugh again in his reply to Mr. Attorney's question whether he had taken any steps to find out the Ladies' Land League books. "Not the slightest, and I don't intend to." As to the missing books of the Land League, Mr. Parnell now expressed his opinion that the earlier books, or some of them, might be in Mr. Egan's possession; that is, that Mr. Egan might have taken them with him in February, 1881, when—in consequence of Mr. Forster's Coercion Act—he left Dublin for Paris; and that he might have carried them with him from Paris to America.

Why had not Mr. Parnell suggested that explanation long ago? Over this point Sir R. Webster laboured for a considerable time. Mr. Parnell replied that the explanation was suggested to him by his reading of the evidence of the financial expert whom the Attorney-General's side had appointed to examine the books that had been submitted to the Court. "Last night," said Mr. Parnell, "I came finally to the conclusion that the books must be in Mr. Egan's possession;" and here he produced two papers that had been drawn up for him on the subject by Mr. T. Harrington, and which appeared to him to settle the point. The papers were passed up to the Judges.

And now the Attorney-General perhaps thought that Mr. Parnell had seriously commited himself. He produced a balance-sheet from Mr. Egan in Paris, and Mr. Egan's accompanying letter saying that the accounts were incomplete because certain books were in Dublin. "Let me see that letter," said Mr. Parnell. Mr. Attorney would rather not; he would read it. But Mr. Parnell must see it. And he did see it. "As I thought it would," remarked Mr. Parnell, quietly, "the sentence about the books being in Dublin refers to the books of the Relief Fund, which I never suggested had been taken to Paris by Mr. Egan. The point could be settled, the President observed, by the production of the balance-sheet. Mr. Parnell had not the balance-sheet. It was "whisked off by a reporter, at the time," and "I have not seen it since." But the balance-sheet could be seen in the Dublin papers. The Attorney-General belaboured Mr. Parnell with questions as to whether he had written to Mr. Egan about the missing books, or tried to get Mr. Henry Labouchere's help, or to arouse Mr. George Lewis's zeal. But Mr. Parnell had only arrived at his conclusion "last night," and Mr. Egan was in Chili, and Mr. Lewis was scarcely an "expert" in Irish politics; while as for Mr. Labouchere, "his interest in the Commission ceased when the forgeries were shown up."

Mr. Parnell's cross-examination ended with a series of questions about the sustenance fund, raised for the benefit of the imprisoned suspects and their families in 1881-1882. The Attorney-General's purpose was to find out if Leaguers only received allowances, and if Invincibles had their share. Mr. Parnell explained that all prisoners put in under the Act received the benefit of the fund, whether they were Leaguers or non-Leaguers; there was no mystery about it, for the Ladies' Land League cheques were sent to the governors of gaols, who saw after the distribution of the money; even Mr. Parnell himself had his allowance, at first fifteen shillings a week, and next a pound. The spectators laughed at this little revelation of prison life. Sometimes, said Mr. Parnell, a prisoner preferred to take the ordinary prison fare, in which case his share of the money would be sent to his family.

About a quarter-past one o'clock the Attorney-General put his last question —When did the first remittances come from America? This was Mr. Parnell's reply—"The great stimulus to the American payments came in 1885, when we helped Lord Salisbury to turn out Mr. Gladstone's Government." The Attorney General sat down.

And now there followed a brief and most interesting little scene. The President, leaning forward, asked Mr. Parnell if he would authorize Messrs. Monro, the Paris bankers, to submit the League funds and accounts in their keeping to inspection. "No"; Mr. Parnell spoke in a low, deliberate voice, "neither friend nor foe" should become aware of the resources at the disposal of the League. Only a few days before there was another little scene, not unlike this one: Houston's refusal (on the part of the I.L.P.U.) to show books that would disclose "to our political opponents" the secrets of the Union. "Very well," said Sir James Hannen, after Mr. Parnell had given his quiet, resolute, but respectful answer, "you will use your own discretion."

ONE HUNDRED AND ELEVENTH DAY.

JULY 24.

AT last the long expected Mr. Moloney appeared in the witness-box. Those who expected from Mr. Moloney some interesting revelations about the missing documents of the Land Leagu must have been disappointed. Mr. Moloney said he knew absolutely nothing of any League books save the four already before the Court. Mr. Moloney had had only the slightest connection with the official work of the Land League. In fact he did not become an officer of the League until October, 1881, the month of the suppression, when the League had been two years in existence. When the League was suppressed, the office furniture of the Central Branch and a quantity of "No Rent" manifestoes—but no other books or documents whatever—were removed to Mr. Moloney's house. The four books now before the Commission were, he repeated, all the Land League books he had ever had in his possession. And he corrected a mistake which Mr. Parnell made in his cross-examination the day before. In 1882, Mr. Moloney, having after his bankruptcy left Ireland, gave orders for the destruction of all League books and documents found in his house. That was Mr. Parnell's statement. But Mr. Moloney said that Mr. Parnell must have been misinformed. He had given no such orders.

"Is it not a fact," asked Sir Henry James, "that on the suppression of the League Mrs. Moloney went to the houses of different clerks and collected various books and documents?" "I don't believe she ever did," was Mr. Moloney's answer. Questioned by Mr. Sexton, Mr. Moloney said that in compliance with his subpœna by *The Times* he had attended the court regularly for six months; that the Attorney-General might have called upon him at any time; that at any time during those six months he was ready to produce his four books, if only he had been asked for them; and that Mr. Soames had not yet paid him his expenses. "Do you believe," Mr. Sexton asked, "that any of the money that passed through your hands was ever used for any but a legitimate purpose?" "So far as I know, it was not." "Or was any money ever paid by you out of League funds for the commission of or as a reward to those who had committed crime?" "No; it was not. I should never sanction such a proceeding."

When Mr. Moloney left the witness-box, Mr. Miller, manager of the Charing Cross branch of the National Bank, re-entered it. On the preceding day he had stated that a large quantity of bank papers and documents, including some of the League's, were burnt in the early part of the present year, and that it was the custom of the bank so to dispose, at stated periods, of such portions of their accumulated material as it was unnecessary to preserve.

Here Mr. Biggar got up. He reminded Mr. Miller of the existence of a rumour that the destruction of the bank documents in January last had been instigated by the "parties charged." Was there any truth in it? "Not the least shadow of a foundation." Then Mr. Tyrrell, one of the bank assistants, was called. And Mr. Tyrrell said that he received in December last his instructions to destroy the surplus documents. He also stated that he had received particular instructions not to destroy anything likely to be required for the purposes of the Commission. "You do not seem," Sir James Hannen quietly remarked, "you do not seem to have observed the caution given to you." This observation of the President's was caused by Mr. Tyrrell's explanation that he had destroyed nothing of later date than the year 1886. Then came Phillips, the ex-Land League clerk, who had supplied *The Times* with some of its documentary evidence. The President asked what Phillips was called for. The Attorney-General replied that he was called in order to disprove Sir Charles Russell's assertion that Phillips had stolen some of the League books, and to show that there were other books at the League offices besides those produced in court.

Phillips had been employed by an accountants' firm in Dublin for five years before October, 1881, when Mr. Arthur O'Connor got him to take the League books in hand. He said that on the suppression of the League, Moloney gave him a list of documents which he was to receive from four League clerks, named Farragher (the informer who has already appeared in court), Pearson, Tighe, and O'Donoghue. This list he recovered a short time ago. Phillips was imprisoned as a suspect at the end of November, 1881. At the time of his arrest he had a considerable number of documents in his house, but most of them escaped the eyes of the detective who called to search for them. Replying to Mr. Sexton, he said that no one connected with the League had ever suggested to him to destroy any of these papers.

Mrs. Phillips appeared after her husband. She said that the League documents just mentioned by him were taken away by Mrs. Moloney and two other visitors. "They took away two large sackfuls." "I helped to pack them up," she added, "and I have not seen them since." The last witness of the day was Mr. Hardcastle, who gave a long account of the results of his examination of the four books. According to his statement, a sum of upwards of ninety-three thousand pounds remained unaccounted for.

ONE HUNDRED AND TWELFTH DAY.

JULY 25.

MOST of to-day's sitting—which lasted only an hour and a half—was occupied by Mr. Hardcastle's disquisition on book-keeping. The details would be wholly uninteresting to the public. Enough to say that Mr. Hardcastle was quite satisfied with the fulness of the National League accounts to which he had free access; and that, when he spoke of sums "unaccounted" for in the Land League books, he meant that certain entries were missing. In other words, by "unaccounted" he did not necessarily mean "misappropriated."

Much more interesting than the book-keeping details was the statement of the results of the examination of Mr. Parnell's correspondence. This examination of a correspondence, extending over many years, was conducted by Mr. Campbell, M.P., Mr. Arthur O'Connor, M.P., Mr. Graham, and Mr. Asquith—not Sir Charles Russell's junior, but Mr. Asquith of *The Times* side. These four gentlemen had examined between three and four thousand letters of Mr. Parnell's. There were nearly eleven hundred letters belonging to the year 1884, but of that large number only forty-two were put aside as having some connection, more or less remote, with the League. The great bulk of the correspondence was trivial in the highest degree, consisting of small bills, requests for autographs and photographs, begging letters, &c.

Then the Attorney-General came to documents of another sort. He "put in" an exhaustive—and exhausting—statistical statement of agrarian crime before and after the great year 1879. The mass of material now before the Judges must be terrific. The Attorney-General having "put in" his statistics, Mr. Sexton rose, and in the gentlest, most suave manner, remarked that his Parliamentary experience had taught him how such Ministerial figures were used to damage the National cause.

Then Mr. Sexton, who, by the way, has proved himself an excellent cross-examiner, put Mr. Soames into the witness-box. Mr. Soames once more! Would Mr. Soames now fulfil his promise and say how much money *The Times* had spent in paying witnesses. Mr. Soames made no such promise, said the Attorney-General. He did, retorted Mr. Biggar. Mr. Soames protested, mildly, against making any statement of the kind, unless he was allowed to give explanations. Without such explanation people might wonder why so much was expended upon the witness Leavy, for example. At first Leavy was paid very little; but as soon as Mr. Soames learned that Leavy's life "was threatened," *The Times* had to provide liberally for him. Mr. Soames could not tell even within ten thousand pounds how much he had spent upon his witnesses.

"In the ordinary course of events," said the President when Mr. Soames left the box, " the persons charged would sum up. Do you desire to address the Court, Mr. Sexton?" Mr. Sexton replied that neither he nor his colleagues had had any idea that the case " would reach this stage to-day." He would like to have an opportunity of consulting with them.

Sir Henry James spoke next. He said the Attorney-General had requested him to reply on behalf of *The Times*. He now applied to their Lordships for an adjournment until after the long vacation. In that case, observed Mr. Sexton, I and those with whom I act will of course be allowed to reserve our right of summing up our evidence. The President having granted Sir Henry James's request, and intimated that additional evidence might be admitted on special application to the Judges, the Court adjourned until the 24th of October.

ONE HUNDRED AND THIRTEENTH DAY.

OCTOBER 24.

THIS morning, one year and two days after its opening, the Commission resumed its inquiry. The number of visitors was much larger than during the days immediately preceding the rising of the Court for the long vacation. The reason was that Sir Henry James was expected to begin his reply —a performance which in all probability will prove more attractive than Sir Richard Webster's opening address. But in the place of Sir Henry James we had Mr. Biggar. He rose from his corner on the solicitors' bench at twenty minutes to eleven, and he finished his speech in a quarter of an hour. He began with a sharp attack on the Attorney-General, who sat in his usual place beside Sir Henry James. Mr. Biggar thought that Sir Richard Webster in his rambling case had confused a simple issue as successfully as any prosecuting lawyer in Ireland could have done. He complimented Sir Richard on the feat, as a feat. Mr. Biggar also expressed some not unnatural satisfaction at the heavy costs which Sir Richard and Mr. Soames had heaped upon *The Times*. Then he wagged his finger at Sir Richard, and wanted to know why Sir Richard Webster had not apologised to those of the accused sixty-four against whom no evidence whatever was even attempted to be brought in the course of the trial. He finished off with some candid remarks on land agents and landlords. Land agent Leonard, said Mr. Biggar, was honest, though harsh. Mr. Leonard had admitted that in the League year the peasants were "blue with hunger," and that they hated the grabber. But the other agents and landlords, said Mr. Biggar, contradicted all that ; they drew their picture of Arcadia. They " swore it in the most unblushing manner ; " the whole gang of them " committed wilful and deliberate perjury." " Under these circumstances," said Mr. Biggar, " I think the Commission ought to report that no evidence of a substantial nature has been brought against me and the other defendants." Mr. Biggar's wrath was aroused. He did not argue the point. He was angry. He would waste no words. He said what he had to say, and then sat down. If a speech of the Attorney-General's is the longest line between two points, Mr. Biggar's is the shortest.

Then Mr. Davitt rose up. His written speech lay before him on a despatch box. He began by saying that he appeared that day, as he had done all along, on his own behalf alone. Possibly, too, in appearing at that stage of the inquiry, he might " run counter " to the Irish opinion which had endorsed the withdrawal of Mr. Parnell and his colleagues. " But," said he, " I feel impelled by a sense of loyalty to the cardinal principles of truth and justice, to stand here and defend, as well as I can, the name and character and cause of the peasantry of Ireland." Further on, in his speech, he remarked that his task was the "heaviest ever undertaken by a layman in a court of justice." But if so, Mr. Davitt is of all men the most competent. For the Land League, upon which their lordships are sitting in judgment, is the offspring of the thoughts which, as Mr. Davitt expressed it, "lightened the burden of my penal servitude." The whole passage is worth quoting. Here it is :—

> The Land League, which is here on its trial, is largely, if not entirely, the offspring of thoughts and resolutions which whiled away many a dreary and tedious hour in political captivity, which lightened the burden of my penal servitude, and brought solace to me to some extent for the loss of liberty, of home, and of friends. The idea of the Land League recalls more than even this to justify my present position before your Lordships. The conception of some such movement did more than give to my thoughts a congenial occupation while in the companionship of the thieves of Dartmoor Prison. It represented the triumph of what was forgiving over what was revengeful in my Celtic temperament. There is in every man, whether Celt or Saxon, a living, constant combat between what is good and what is in its nature evil, and when a man found himself in prison at the age of twenty-two, bereft of everything that endeared him to life, and surrounded by every condition of existence that could excite and keep alive passion and resentment, it was a hard and unequal struggle to conquer the spirit of hate and revenge.

Mr. Davitt then proceeded to say that he believed as firmly, in Dartmoor prison, as on the last of the hundreds of platforms from which he had spoken, that a movement such as the Land League would secure justice for Ireland,. and put an end to the animosities between the two countries. It was said that crime had accompanied the League, added Mr. Davitt ; but it was only the crime inevitably associated with all popular movements against injustice, crime arising as naturally as fruit from seed. "I don't indict nature," he continued : "but I repudiate *The Times* charges, that are repugnant to my nature, and to the Irish race as to any race on earth." In bringing these charges against the Irish leaders, said Mr. Davitt, the prosecution overlooked all the natural "incentives to disorder ;" all the social and political conditions whence the disorder sprang. His defence was that the Land League was a *bonâ fide* constitutional organization, that its work had been and still was beneficial ; and he would show that the crimes were attributable to the system which the League tried to overthrow. But as to the charges against himself personally, what were they? He was charged with being a Fenian convict. Well, he had been a Fenian, like most of the young men of Ireland in the 1867 to 1879 period, and he declared that, under the circumstances of twenty years ago, he would become a Fenian again. But why were they Fenians? Because Fenianism, in the days when no open political combination existed, was a necessity of the situation, a natural and inevitable social growth. To put it another way, Fenianism was simply one of the many Irish movements, justified by their fruits in Imperial legislation. All these risings, said Mr. Davitt, were "justified by subsequent reforms " ; as the dangerous agitation subsequent to 1810 was justified by Catholic Emancipation. He described Fenianism in yet another way as the offspring of the '48 movement, which itself was arrested by the great famine. Then he quoted Lord John Russell, Mr. Goldwin Smith, Lord Derby, who lamented the fate under which Ireland never received justice except as a concession to illegal agitation. "This," said Mr. Davitt, "is my justification for my connection with Fenianism." Then followed an extremely effective and dexterous passage, in which Mr. Davitt reminded the Court that he had learned his lessons in political liberty, not in Ireland, but in England, where he had spent two-thirds of his life. He asked whether the sympathy which free England extended to Italy, to the oppressed all over the world, was to be withheld from the Ireland so close to her own shores?

Mr. Davitt next came to Delaney's evidence. Delaney had accused him of having attended, in 1878, amnesty meetings which were in reality Fenian meetings; of having associated with Curley, who was hanged for the Phœnix Park murders; and of having helped Fenians to attack a Land League meeting in Dublin, in April, 1880. All these statements, Mr. Davitt, repeating his former sworn testimony, described as the "deliberate perjury of an informer," who has recently asked the Government for the reward of his services in giving evidence. Mr. Davitt showed, from the newspaper reports of the time, and from mass petitions to the Queen, that the amnesty movement was public, and not merely sectional and Fenian. As for the secret Fenian meeting which he was alleged to have attended just before the Rotunda meeting, Mr. Davitt repeated his former testimony that he had never even heard of such a meeting until the informer and ex-Invincible Delancy spoke of it in the witness-box.

Then Mr. Davitt came to the story of the Forrester letter. It will be remembered that the letter written by Mr. Davitt and found upon young Forrester, was the "evidence" which decided Mr. Davitt's fate at the Old Bailey trial; and that Mr. Davitt, rather than become an informer, by divulging the circumstances under which the letter was written, accepted the bitter alternative of penal servitude for fifteen years. It will also be remembered that, when in the witness-box, Mr. Davitt solemnly declared to their lordships that the Forrester letter, instead of prompting murder, had the effect which he meant it to have—the prevention of murder. He repeated the statement now. And then came an impressive passage, delivered with touching earnestness. It was as follows:—

I have done what I have never done before in the course of a chequered and somewhat unfortunate existence—I have made an appeal to a man in a personal matter. I have appealed from that witness-box to the man who was alone responsible for the guilt which that letter frustrated, the man who would have stood in my place in the Old Bailey dock nineteen years ago if I had not kept silence through feelings of delicacy and honour. I have asked that man from his safe asylum in America to release me from the silence which I considered that moral obligations imposed upon me, but I have appealed in vain, and the man has not had the courage to confess that nineteen years ago he had been saved by me from staining his hands with the blood of an innocent comrade. In the *Liverpool Courier* of January 7, 1870, there is a report of the proceedings before the stipendiary magistrate, Mr. Mansfield, on the occasion when Forrester, upon whom the letter was found, was admitted to bail. During those proceedings, as will be seen from the report, not even an allusion was made to the letter found upon Forrester, although it had, of course, attracted the attention of the magistrate when the accused was previously bound over. If the police in Liverpool had any real suspicion that the letter was the expression of a design to take human life, it is not conceivable that they would ever have acted as they did at the time. Long before "Parnellism and Crime" was written, this unhappy incident was quoted against me in *The Times*, and the people of these countries were made to believe that I had deliberately, when in the Fenian organization, written a letter encouraging or authorizing the assassination of an individual. I wish to assert that there is nothing more foreign to my nature than the idea of assassination. It is as repugnant to me as it is to the whole of the Irish race throughout the world, and I will repeat what I said in the witness-box under all the solemnity of an oath, that that letter, boyish and foolish as it might be in its terms, was in reality written to prevent a lad of seventeen from carrying out a wicked plot against an associate. No harm was ever done to any human being in consequence of that letter; no man was ever injured through it; and yet because of it I have been held up to the world as the accomplice of assassins.

Then he turned to the American part of his story. "All ancient history," some may call it. But it is unfortunately too new to the vast majority of people in this country. Besides, some of it was a striking answer to the allegation of the prosecution, that the Land League funds came from the Clan-na-Gael. It will be interesting to see how Sir Henry James meets Mr. Davitt's account of the sources of the Land League funds.

But in all that Mr. Davitt said to-day about the American share in the agitation, he had one great object in view—to point out the influences that aroused and kept fiercely alive the sentiment of Irish-American hatred of England. What were the natural causes which, as he said, the prosecution had from first to last ignored? He reminded the prosecution that the first Anti-English Society ever formed by the Irish in America was "The Friendly Sons of St. Patrick Society," Philadelphia, 1771. He told them that its founders were evicted emigrants from Ulster. He told them that Irishmen were as numerous as Englishmen in the War of Independence; that twelve of George Washington's generals were members of the St. Patrick Society, and that among the signatories to the declaration of American independence were nine Irishmen. "America was lost through the Irish emigrants," said Mr. Davitt, quoting from the Irish Parliamentary debates of 1784.

What that migration was—the great migration which began with the famine —Mr. Davitt illustrated by statistics of disease and death. He quoted from medical journals and historical works of note, the frightful rates of mortality among the emigrant ships of forty-two years. One example will show the general character of the statistics given—of 1,476 passengers on board the *Virginius*, 276 died at sea. "Coffin ships," the emigrant vessels were called. And from the American shore to Ontario and beyond, the path of the emigration was "an unbroken chain of graves." All this, Mr. Davitt continued, explained the American-Irish hatred of England. And then Mr. Davitt told the following story:—

I remember calling, in 1878, upon the late General Sheridan, who died Commander-in-Chief of the United States army. He was at that time commanding the division of the West, and he had his headquarters in Chicago. I asked him, among others things, how many men of Irish blood in the United States would, in the event of a war with England, join the American army. His answer was that inside of forty-eight hours after war had been declared a million men of Irish blood would leap to arms. And that was the distinguished soldier and citizen of the American Republic who once declared that if he had been born in Ireland he would have been a Fenian.

Among the numerous other illustrations which Mr. Davitt gave of the origin of this hatred was the following, from the history of O'Donovan Rossa, the founder of the Skirmishing Fund:—

If any one will inquire in the town of Skibbereen, in county Cork, what Rossa was thirty years ago, he will learn that he was a genial, kind-hearted, and open-handed young man of unblemished character and undoubted respectability. He had been an eye-witness of the famine horrors. He joined the Fenian movement in after years, was tried for it, and sentenced to penal servitude for life. He had told the story of his prison experience, and that story related that on one occasion for twenty-eight days he was so manacled that he was obliged to get down on his knees at meal-times and lap up his porridge like a dog.

Mr. Davitt ended this day's instalment of his speech with an account of the sources of the Land League funds. "Not a particle of truth," said he, "is there in the allegation that they came from the Clan-na-Gael for the purpose of crime and outrage." The first subscription ever received was at the end of 1879; the subscribers described themselves as "friends of Ireland," who "wished to encourage and assist Mr. Parnell and his friends in the work they have undertaken, and to prove that we in America are not unmindful of their exertions on behalf of the rack-rented people at home." Mr. Davitt said he did not deny that hundreds of people subscribed because they were actuated by revengeful feelings; but he maintained, first, that the letter already quoted was a fair indication of the general spirit of the contributors, and Americans of all nationalities—Germans, Frenchmen, Englishmen, as well as Irishmen—contributed to the League funds.

ONE HUNDRED AND FOURTEENTH DAY.

OCTOBER 25.

MR. DAVITT is interesting his hearers. The more he says, the more certain it seems that he is supplying Sir Henry James with fresh food for reflection. It is hard to believe that the speech Sir Henry James will deliver will be the same as that which he would have delivered had Mr. Davitt fulfilled the general expectation that he would not speak at all.

The prosecuting counsel, who follow him closely, held for a minute or two what looked like a council of war when at half-past one o'clock the Court rose for the half-hour's interval. There was at least one famous visitor present—Beach, the spy. Sitting in a corner, close to the doorway, he was repeatedly exchanging nods and smiles with Houston. For a time Beach appeared to be rather amused than otherwise at the hard things Mr. Davitt, in his downright way, was saying about him; but his face became rigid, and a scowl settled upon it, when Mr. Davitt, turning sharply round and darting a glance at him, suggested the possibility of Beach's being another Pigott. This was in reference to the "U.B." secret circulars transmitted by Beach to the Home Office, and all—as Mr. Davitt believed—in Beach's handwriting.

Mr. Davitt read the local resolutions and documents of various sorts from societies and individual contributors, which showed how the American supporters of the new Irish movement were actuated, not by political hatred, but by sympathy with the rack-rented tenants, and how they regarded with "detestation" and "abhorrence" the Phœnix Park murders. In all that quantity of evidence there was not, Mr. Davitt declared, the smallest justification for the theory of the prosecution, that the American funds for the Irish League were "stained with blood." The overwhelming majority of the contributors were, Mr. Davitt maintained, thoroughly in favour of the new Irish constitutional movement, as opposed to the less conciliatory policy which at that time was Patrick Ford's. This led Mr. Davitt into a description of Mr. Ford's attitude towards Mr. Parnell's Parliamentary method. He showed how Ford repudiated the notion that *The Irish World* was the organ of the League; how he did it as vigorously as Mr. Parnell himself; how Mr. Ford contemptuously characterised Mr. Parnell's reliance upon the Parliamentary method as an "absurdity"; how he called the Home Rule idea an "illusion," and pointed to the suspension of the Irish members as another warning that they must not expect justice at Westminster.

Mr. Davitt then came to the third charge against himself—that he had associated with criminals in America, and that he had brought about an alliance between the Clan-na-Gael and the open association in Ireland and America. For "the first part of the accusation against me," said Mr. Davitt, "there is no proof except Le Caron's statement in 1878, at Chicago, he saw me associating with Colonel Clingen, supposed to be a Clan-na-Gael member." Not that Mr. Davitt meant to admit that meeting and talking with Clan-na-Gael people was in itself condemnable. As he said in a later part of his address, he would associate with the Clan-na-Gael, even as he had done before, in order, if he could, to argue them into a better frame of mind. I had no authority, said Mr. Davitt, from Mr. Parnell or anybody else, to found any alliance. As for the second part of the accusation, Mr. Davitt said it was in contradiction with some other statements of Beach's. Beach dated the origin of the alliance from his alleged talk with Mr. Parnell in the House of Commons, but at that time Mr. Davitt was, as he reminded the Court, in Portland prison.

In 1878 Mr. Davitt went to America on his own responsibility, and even without the knowledge of Mr. Parnell. He had no introductions. Mr. James O'Kelly, then on the staff of *The New York Herald*, was the only man he called upon when he landed at New York. He was the only person he knew. He did not even know John Devoy, whom he then met. The only thing he knew of him was the signature which Devoy had scratched on the door of Mr. Davitt's cell in Millbank prison; for, said Mr. Davitt, "he preceded me along the dreary path of penal servitude." As to Devoy's "new departure" (dynamite *plus* the open movement), which was the subject of Devoy's famous telegram from America to Mr. Parnell, Mr. Davitt knew nothing at the time. That telegram, addressed to Mr. Kickham, who was expected to lay it before Mr. Parnell, was alleged to be the basis of the supposed alliance between Parnellism and Dynamitism. But, in the first place, Mr. Davitt was at the time a thousand miles from the place (New York) where the message was drawn up; in the second place, Mr. Kickham, being a consistent revolutionist, refused to submit the proposal to Mr. Parnell, whose policy he disapproved of. Mr. Parnell himself, said Mr. Davitt, never even received the proposals; and Mr. Davitt himself condemned them as soon as he heard of them.

Mr. Davitt's own "new departure" was something entirely different to that of Mr. Beach's alleged revelations; and it was set forth in the very first speech which he delivered in America, the speech of which all his subsequent addresses in the United States were more or less detailed reproductions. Self-government for Ireland; immediate improvement of the land system, leading to peasant proprietorship on terms fair to the landlord; encouragement of Irish industries; reform of popular education—that was Mr. Davitt's "new departure," and parts of it, he added, have already been adopted by the Imperial Legislature. Was there dynamite in that programme? Mr. Davitt exclaimed; his "new departure" was, he alleged, the first peaceful and constitutional programme ever set before the American Irish. He invited the Irish race throughout the New World to adopt it. He made no distinctions. "I would," he again exclaimed, "attend to-morrow any meeting, however violent, and stand up for common sense." And Mr. Davitt claimed that the "new departure" preached by him, and organized by himself and Mr. Parnell, had won the overwhelming majority of the Irish in America to constitutionalism, and to the policy of federal union with England in place of separation.

Mr. Davitt rejected with contempt and scorn the allegation of the prosecution that the dynamite faction controlled the open movement. He said that *The Times*' second line of attack had failed as completely as its first—the publication of the forged letters. And then Mr. Davitt said something about the letters, which arrested the attention of everybody present. He reminded the Court how in the O'Donnell trial the Attorney-General had said that *The Times*, knowing what an informer's fate meant, would not divulge the name of one of the "several" persons from whom the letters had been received. "Several," Mr. Davitt repeated; "this was said by her Majesty's Attorney-General for England at a time when it was actually within the knowledge of Houston and his co-conspirators in *The Times* office that Pigott was the forger; for it has come to my knowledge, through Pigott's servant, that he confessed to her ——" But here Sir James Hannen quickly interrupted him. Said the President: "I cannot have any statement of that kind." "Very well, my lord," was Mr. Davitt's reply, "it will have to be proved elsewhere."

Then Mr. Davitt returned to the American part of his address. He gave interesting personal descriptions of the leading Irish-Americans whom he met, and who have been named in the course of the evidence—Mr. M'Cafferty, Mr. Collins, Mr. J. Mooney, Mr. Alex. Sullivan, Mr. Patrick Egan, Mr. John Fitzgerald (present president of the Irish National League of America), Mr. John Finerty, Mr. John Boyd O'Reilly, Mr. Brennan. The prosecution had said that when the informers had begun to tell of the Phœnix Park murders Mr. Egan took to flight. But Mr. Davitt showed that Mr. Egan was so horrified at the news of the murders that he resolved there and then to retire from political life and leave for the States. He quoted *The Daily News* Paris correspondent's letter of April 20, 1887, which was reproduced in *The Times* of the following day, and in which were given the particulars of Mr. Egan's reception of the terrible message in Paris, where he was living at the time. The *Daily News* letter is given below.

Finerty's views certainly were extreme, said Mr. Davitt; but Finerty was refused a hearing at the Philadelphia Convention of 1883 because of his known preference for violent methods. But Finerty, said Mr. Davitt, "is no empty-headed fellow; he is able and honourable; his methods are not mine, but he is as ready as any one else to make sacrifices for a cause he believes to be just." Of the Hon. P. A. Collins, President of the first Land League Convention in America, Mr. Davitt spoke in terms of high praise. Mr. Collins, he said, was a Conservative, and no attempt had been made to connect him with revolutionary societies. As for Mr. A. Sullivan, whose name was again before the world, Mr. Davitt did not believe that the American clergy would have supported him as they did had he been a member of the Clan-na-Gael: and he added that Mr. Sullivan certainly did not owe his election to the presidentship to any violent opinions he might have entertained. With Egan Mr. Davitt's intimacy had been, as he described it, close and affectionate; he said that Mr. Egan's character and career could bear the closest scrutiny. Mr. Fitzgerald, who had raised himself from the position of a poor Irish labourer to that of one of the wealthiest and most influential men in Nebraska, was, Mr. Davitt said, known as "honest John Fitzgerald." As for Mr. Brennan, Mr. Davitt pronounced him incapable of any base transaction. And Mr. Davitt pointed out, as a singular fact, that in 1884, Delaney—who was then examined in the Sligo conspiracy case—did not associate the name of Egan, or of Brennan, with the Invincibles. Yet Delaney had done so before their Lordships.

Mr. Davitt then passed on to the topic of the League Conventions in America. There was nothing, said Mr. Davitt, to bear out the story of secret conclaves of assassination directing the open meetings of these Conventions, except Beach's "bundles" of documents. Beach, like Pigott, exclaimed Davitt, "has produced documents which he declares to be authentic. I believe these documents are in his handwriting. It was on the evidence of these documents, backed by the oath of a man of the infamous profession of a spy, who acknowledged in the witness-box having perjured himself repeatedly, that *The Times* relied for proof that the Land League and Clan-na-Gael was one and the same organization, and that the dynamite explosions were carried out under the auspices of that organization." Every eye in court was at that moment turned upon Le Caron (Beach), who sat in his corner, with, as already said, a scowl on his face.

Against the "ridiculous ciphers" quoted by Beach, and Beach's secret circulars to the Home Office, Mr. Davitt placed the records of seven Conventions of the American League, Mr. Parnell's speeches, and the numerous resolutions, instructions, circulars of all sorts which Mr. Davitt himself had distributed in his capacity of central secretary for the American organization. Of all that mass of documentary matter *The Times*, in Mr. Davitt's estimation, knew nothing. And did *The Times* know anything of the bye-laws which were adopted by the branches of the organization all over America, and about which there was no concealment? At that very time, said Mr. Davitt, "I was a guest in Beach's house; I had a cold; he gave me some medicine; and I believe the medicine did me good." Here the President smiled. Mr. Davitt spoke to Beach unreservedly in those Braidwood days, and Beach kept nothing secret from Mr. Davitt. How was it that Mr. Davitt was not accused by him? Curiously enough, Mr. Beach presided over a Braidwood meeting at which Mr. Davitt delivered an unexceptionably constitutional address. Little did Mr. Davitt think under what circumstances the man who gave him the bolus would meet him again.

The following are the passages quoted by *The Times* from *The Daily News'* Paris letter referred to above :—

The French papers reflect the excitement which the Parnell affair causes in England. Perhaps it may not be amiss for me to describe how Egan, whose name has been mixed up in the matter, received the news of the Phœnix Park murders. I sought, entirely for journalistic purposes, to make Egan's acquaintance while he was here, and got to know him very well, as he happened to live near me, and I had frequent opportunities of meeting him in the tramcars, public gardens, and other places. It happened that I saw him at the moment he heard of the Phœnix Park murders. It was at the Madeleine Station of the tramway leading to the Avenue de Villers, where he resided. I was going in that direction and Egan was coming from it. He stepped out of the car and went to a kiosk to buy an evening paper, and then sat down on a bench hard by to read it. When he opened and looked at it the paper fell from his hand, and he became quite corpse-like. I had not, as he had not seen me, intended to accost him, but when I perceived his state I was under the impression that he was dying, and went to see what was the matter, so as to call assistance were it wanted. For perhaps five minutes he could not speak, and kept staring in a fixed way, looking more dead than alive. I questioned him at last, and he pointed to the paper *La France*, and said, "Look at that." I picked it up, and read of the Phœnix Park affair. Egan's words, when he was able to speak, were, "What an awful calamity ; Cavendish was the best of the whole lot. Poor Cavendish ; poor Lord Frederick." Later on he conversed a good deal. His feeling was that what had happened would damage the cause he had at heart. He was terrified at the savagery of the act. About ten days later I met him again in the street, and he told me he thought of going off to some western part of America, where peace and quietness were to be obtained. Egan was, it appeared to me, the very contrary of reckless or unscrupulous, and struck me as a man of gentle disposition and by no means strong nerve.

ONE HUNDRED AND FIFTEENTH DAY.

OCTOBER 29.

CONTINUING his vindication of the American Leaguers, Mr. Davitt argued to the general effect that the spirit of their Conventions was fairly indicated in the words of the Hon. P. A. Collins, President of the Convention at Washington, 12th and 13th April, 1882, that "we in America shall go as far as the people of Ireland, and no faster ; " that "we" in America "are followers, not leaders ;" that if "I (the speaker) judge the Irish people rightly, they seek justice, and not vengeance." These words, said Mr. Davitt, together with the many speeches of which they formed, as it were, the text, were uttered a few weeks before the horrible crime of Phœnix Park.

Mr. Davitt next illustrated his position by reference to the Astor House Conference, New York, in the summer of 1882, at which Conference, said the author of "Parnellism and Crime," the Fords, Walsh, and other notorious Extremists were present. Mr. Davitt observed that the "Flanagan or Pigott" of "Parnellism and Crime" had said that he associated at this Conference with murderers and assassins ; but that "on this occasion" he did denounce murder. Mr. Davitt maintained that in putting the emphasis on the word "this," he was fairly interpreting the intention of the Pigott, or Flanagan, who wrote "Parnellism and Crime." Well, said Mr. Davitt, turning round to where *The Times* people sat, "there is nothing more disgracefully suggestive to be found in that liar's and forger's catechism, ' Parnellism and Crime.'" Mr. Davitt's own speech, and the New York Mayor's speech at this very Conference were, Mr. Davitt maintained, a sufficient refutation of "Pigott or Flanagan." Mr. Davitt's speech had for its basis the proposition "the attainment, by moral and justifiable means, of free land, free labour, free government for Ireland " ; while, he added, the Mayor of New York's speech was a denunciation of the Phœnix Park murder as "a crime against humanity and the civilization of the age." Mr. Davitt made some contemptuous references to the conduct of the

"Pigott or Flanagan" of the articles in suppressing the names of those present at the meeting who were not known to be in sympathy with the physical force party, and in recording the names of the two or three who were.

The next serious misrepresentation of which he accused the writer or writers of "Parnellism and Crime" was the statement that Mr. Egan was the originator of the "Martyrs' Fund," a fund, as the articles described it, for the encouragement of assassination. But Mr. Davitt pointed out that the Egan in question was not Mr. Patrick Egan, but Mr. P. B. Egan. The "Martyrs' Fund," said Mr. Davitt, "no more encouraged murder than the Discharged Prisoners' Aid Fund encouraged burglary." Here Sir James Hannen threw in the remark that contributors to the last-named fund "do not call the discharged prisoners martyrs." Upon which Mr. Davitt merely repeated what he had already said about the true character of the American fund. As for the Egan misstatement, Mr. Davitt fully acknowledged that Sir Richard Webster "frankly withdrew the charge, and apologized." It was a serious charge; for it also stated that Egan was present at a celebration—an "inhuman feast," as *The Times* writer called it—in honour of the memory of the murderer Joe Brady. This was the "feast" at which a purse was presented to Mrs. Byrne, who was said to have carried the knives to Ireland. As "Egan" was reported to have been present at the feast, it was concluded that the "Martyrs' Fund" was an assassination fund. But while Mr. Davitt acknowledged Sir Richard Webster's courtesy, he refused to believe that the misstatement in *The Times* was otherwise than wilful and deliberate. By the omission of the initials "P. B.," said Mr. Davitt, the "whole civilized world" was led to believe that the Egan present at the "inhuman feast" was the colleague of Mr. Parnell and Mr. Davitt in the Irish National Land League. Finally, on this point, Mr. Davitt flatly contradicted the story that the feasters, or any of them, were members of the great Chicago Convention of August, 1886. And he read out the resolutions of the Convention—expressing approval of Mr. Parnell's Parliamentary policy, and thanks to the British democracy and to Mr. Gladstone, and enjoining upon the Irish people the exercise of self-restraint under whatever provocation.

"I do not deny," said Mr. Davitt, that there must have been among the members of these Conventions persons of extreme views—Clan-na-Gael people, as well as Leaguers pure and simple. But even the Clan-na-Gael people present were there, said Mr. Davitt, not as Clan-na-Gaels, but as supporters of the Parliamentary policy of the Irish National League. "In no single instance," said Mr. Davitt, "has any one been appointed to office at these conventions, unless as a supporter of Mr. Parnell's policy." "You must judge these conventions," said Mr. Davitt, "by their corporate action," authorized by "overwhelming majorities." "Would you call the House of Commons a masonic institution," asked Mr. Davitt, "because there may be a hundred Freemasons in it?" "Do the opinions of Dr. Tanner, Mr. Bradlaugh, and Mr. Conybeare, affect the sound Conservatism of the Attorney-General?" The Clan-na-Gael Society, said Mr. Davitt, existed legally, openly in the United States, and men known to be members of it were also—as in the case of Mr. Finerty and Mr. Haynes—members of State Legislatures. That being the case, why, Mr. Davitt asked, should Mr. Parnell in America take it upon him to exclude such men from an organization intended to embrace the Irish race?

The Attorney-General, said Mr. Davitt, "has fought at long range;" he did not come to close quarters; there were in America 2,000 branches of the Irish League, yet from these 2,000 branches, continued Mr. Davitt, not a single incriminating document, resolution, or act had been put in evidence by the Attorney-General. "I now ask your lordships," said Mr. Davitt, "whether you think that in face of these facts you can think the Clan-na-Gael and the American Land League were the same?" And if Sir Henry James, Mr. Davitt continued, maintains their identity, he must explain away the following facts:

the solemn oath of Mr. Parnell and Mr. Davitt that no such union or identity ever existed: *The Times'* failure to produce a particle of proof of such union, save the forged letters; that neither Mr. Parnell nor Mr. Sexton, nor any of their envoys, or colleagues, from the Irish or American leagues, ever attended a Clan meeting; that neither Mr. Parnell nor Mr. Dillon, when in America, were present at any Clan-na-Gael Council; that in Beach's bundles of secret circulars and correspondence there was not a single scrap of paper from the Leagues, or from Mr. Parnell, or from Mr. Davitt himself to the Clan-na-Gael Society, while in these very bundles of Beach's there were intimations of Land League hostility to the Clan, and instructions to Clan-na-Gael members to try and "capture" the Land League; and that Beach failed to cite "a single word or act" of Mr. Davitt's from 1878 to 1886 which would go to prove Mr. Davitt's alleged efforts to bring about the "alliance." And why had Beach left it to Mr. Davitt to inform their lordships that he (Mr. Davitt) had visited Clan-na-Gael camps?

"The Clan-na-Gael are commonly called a murder club," Mr. Davitt continued. "But," he said, "there is no evidence that it is so. I do not believe the Clan-na-Gael to be a murder club. If I did believe so, I would not have associated with its members." "America," he added, "would not have suffered the existence of 'a murder club' against a friendly Power;" and, in fact, the Clan-na-Gael Society was "not, properly speaking, a secret society, it was as well known as the Foresters, and it had its feasts and excursions" like other brotherhoods not criminal. It is a "revolutionary" club, said Mr. Davitt, but not a "murder club." And, continued Mr. Davitt, just as there had been no union between the Clan-na-Gael and the Land League in America, so there had been no union between the Land League and the Irish Republican Brotherhood in Ireland. Beach, added Mr. Davitt, has produced the "damning proof" of Mr. Parnell's photograph, "but that only shows that Mr. Parnell may have been more liberal with his photograph to strangers (such as Mr. Beach, who said he received one) than to his own colleagues, not one of whom has ever been favoured in that manner." Mr. Davitt's summing up of the American part of his defence was a most skilful and impressive performance.

Mr. Davitt now came to the Irish portion of his address—the origin of the Land League. *The Times* calls the League a Separatist conspiracy dating from 1879. Mr. Davitt undertook to show that it grew naturally out of the condition of the Irish people, and that its beginnings were far earlier than 1879. One of the main causes of the Land League was, said Mr. Davitt, the frustration of the efforts, during the period from 1850 to 1879, of the representatives of the Irish people to improve the agrarian law and custom. To illustrate this, Mr. Davitt proposed to give a rapid review of the legislative failures of the period. But Sir James Hannen intervened with the objection that the Court could not properly sit in judgment on Parliamentary legislation, and that it was constituted to try a single issue, whether the parties accused did or did not attempt to accomplish their ends in an unconstitutional manner. Sir James Hannen did not wish to stop Mr. Davitt, but only to put it to him—whether he considered such a review essential to his case. Mr. Davitt frankly acknowledging the President's unfailing courtesy and kindness, and refraining from taking advantage of Sir James's implied permission to him to follow his own course, readily suppressed that portion of his address—"confiscated it, as he expressed it afterwards.

Putting then legislation aside, Mr. Davitt turned to other beginnings of the Land League. Mr. Davitt observed that he must "rob himself" of the distinction of being the "Father of the Land League;" "I was only," said Mr. Davitt, "giving voice to the opinions of other men who came long before me." Among these men, said he, were the founders of the Tenants' League, Mr. Isaac Butt and his colleagues. The Tenants' League, or, to give it its full name,

"The Tenants' Defence Association," was established nearly forty years ago. Mr. Parnell was a member of it. So was Mr. Matt. Harris, and others who subsequently formed the Land League. The speeches at the Tenants' and the speeches of the Land League were, said Mr. Davitt, identical in scheme and spirit. The Tenants' Association, founded nearly forty years ago, really began the education of the Irish people. And if any proofs were required to show that the Tenants' Association was a necessity, there were, said Mr. Davitt, the remarkable articles published by *The Times* during the period of the great famine, and reprinted by *The Times* in 1880, when a second famine seemed imminent. And certainly they were very strong articles, those in which *The Times* of the day denounced the cruel selfishness of the landlord class, and vividly pictured the misery of their rack-rented tenants. "The starving mother with her dead child on her shoulder, and the rich landlord keeping his pocket shut," were a spectacle that aroused the indignation and disgust of *The Times* in days gone by. It was in such scenes that Mr. Davitt himself first drew the breath of life—those were the scenes which first filled his childish mind, and of which he retained the indelible memory. Mr. Davitt paused a little and then spoke as follows:

> I remember, although I was only a child, we were evicted in Mayo shortly after the great famine, and the house in which I was born was burnt down by the agent of the landlord, assisted by the agents of the law. That was not a circumstance that would cause me to be a very warm supporter of the landlord, or for the law as it stood. I remember, though I was only a child, we went to the workhouse a few miles away, and were refused admission because my mother would not submit to certain conditions imposed on those who seek those homes of degradation. In our English home I have listened to my mother's stories of the great famine, and remember hearing from her an account of how three hundred people were buried during that time—were thrown uncoffined into one pit in the corner of the workhouse yard. So great an impression did that make upon me that, twenty-five years afterwards, when I visited the place, I went straight to that very spot. My lords, my experience was the experience of the others of my class.

There was a dead silence in court as Mr. Davitt slowly, and with his strong, unfaltering voice—but with his face paling—told his mournful story. A unique instance of growth—from the homeless child, turned away from the workhouse, to the mature man whom the Irish people all over the world revere, and whom his misfortunes have educated into the advocate instead of the avenger of his race.

Well, continued Mr. Davitt, the foregoing facts justified the Land League in the attitude it took up in 1879—that the peasants must feed their children first and pay the landlords next. No more, if the League could help it, would the peasants die of famine while the wealth they produced was exported to pay rack-rent on lands which they themselves and not the landlords had reclaimed and improved. It was said, observed Mr. Davitt, that the clearances would improve the condition of the tenants who were left, but the tenants who were left were as badly off as those who had been removed by famine and emigration. The Act of 1870, said Mr. Davitt, did no good, for it prevented neither rack-rent nor eviction. That was part of the natural history of the Land League; but against these facts of history the prosecution had, said Mr. Davitt, little to advance except a few extracts and wild speeches from " Scrab " Nallys, whom everybody laughed at, and the "curiosities from that phonetic museum known as the Royal Irish constable's notebook."

In his description of the Chicago Convention of August, 1886, Mr. Davitt pointed out that Beach and the author of " Parnellism and Crime " contradicted each other in their accounts of its origin. Beach said that the business of the Convention was arranged at a preliminary sessions of which Finerty was the ruling spirit. The author of " Parnellism and Crime " had said that its programme was arranged by the feasters—Byrne, Hamilton, Williams, &c.—of the Joe Brady anniversary. Said Mr. Davitt, none of those men were present at

Chicago, save the two Fords, who did not even speak at the Convention. The Convention, added Mr. Davitt, contained 1,027 members, and only one of them—Mr. Finerty—voted against the resolutions in support of the Parnellite, or Constitutional movement.

ONE HUNDRED AND SIXTEENTH DAY.

October 30.

MR. DAVITT began his day's work with a citation of Sir Richard Webster's compendious description of the Land League, as "a scheme of assassination, carefully calculated and coolly applied." It is meant, said Mr. Davitt, "that Mr. Parnell and myself and others deliberately selected our instruments and sent them about the country to help us by means of assassination." On the previous day Mr. Davitt had remarked that if that was the character of the Land League, "no such stupid body of men ever existed" as the League leaders; for they were all along taking the very means best calculated to defeat their criminal purpose.

Following up this line of argument, he now asked their lordships how that theory of the prosecution could be reconciled with the programme of the Mayo Land League (a body which in two months was expanded into the National Land League of Ireland), and with the programme set forth by Mr. Parnell himself at the great meeting of the Land League in the spring of 1880—a programme which Mr. Davitt himself "considered too liberal to the landlords," inasmuch as it offered them the purchase of their lands at twenty years. That was how the League leaders were then trying to drive out the "English garrison," as the landlords are called, in Ireland. Take these programmes of the League, take all its official documents, if you wish to know what were the objects of the League. "Why, the very plans which are now entertained by the Government for the settlement of the Irish question are the very plans which we Leaguers were advocating ten years ago. I wonder whether the landlords would now object to be murdered—to use the objectionable word applied to the League—by twenty years' purchase of their estates." Successive Governments, Mr. Davitt argued, had borrowed their plans from the Land League programme. The Compensation for Disturbance Bill was an instance in point; the Lords threw it out, and crimes broke out afresh.

Next Mr. Davitt came to the second general charge against the Land League—that it did nothing to stop outrage—and he quoted the Attorney-General's statement that (as far as he knew) there did not exist a single League speech in denunciation of outrage. Logically, as he remarked, he might content himself with the production of one solitary speech; but, he said, "I propose to bury the Attorney-General's charge so deeply in counter proofs that Sir Henry James will require microscopic aid to find it again, and shall show that the Attorney-General was deliberately misled by those who employed him." The Attorney-General's charge was refuted by two of the very first witnesses who appeared for *The Times*, Constables O'Malley and Irwin. These witnesses took down the speeches of "Scrab," a sort of half-witted "wild man," at whom everybody laughed, while his (Mr. Davitt's) own speeches denouncing outrage were carefully ignored. "I was a less eminent person than 'Scrab,'" said Mr. Davitt. In the same way the Constabulary reporter ignored the speech in which Father Eglington denounced the murder of Lord Mountmorres, although he took down the utterances of "Scrab" and his friend Gordon. "There could be no grosser injustice than *The Times'* suppression of the conciliatory speeches invariably made at League meetings, by the League leaders and the local clergy."

To complete his proof against this, one of the most serious charges made by *The Times*, Mr. Davitt now proposed to read speeches delivered by himself and the Land League leaders over a series of years, and throughout Great Britain and Ireland, and even in parts of America. "I regret to have to talk so long," he said, "but, with the exception of the forged letters' charge, this is the most serious accusation made against my colleagues and myself; and I must ask your lordships' permission to deal with it in the completest way."

Sir James Hannen, remarking that this would amount to the introduction of new evidence, hoped that Mr. Davitt would make his extract readings as short as possible. But the Attorney-General was rather alarmed at this sudden prospect of a reopening of this gigantic case. He objected that the production of this fresh evidence might necessitate the calling of more witnesses; at any rate, he would have to verify Mr. Davitt's extracts and examine their contexts. The President endorsed Sir Richard Webster's opinion so far as to say that the time for producing fresh evidence was past. Then the three judges consulted for a few minutes. At last Sir James Hannen announced their decision —that notwithstanding the irregularity of Mr. Davitt's request, and in view of the vast importance of the issues, they were anxious to give him the fullest scope. Mr. Davitt heartily thanking their lordships for their indulgence, offered to save time by simply putting in the dates of the speeches and the names of the places where they were delivered, so that the judges and counsel for the prosecution might satisfy themselves as to the truth of his general description of them. But Sir James Hannen preferred to hear them all. So Mr. Davitt began with his reading. Sir Richard Webster, with a pile of *The Freeman's Journal* before him, found the task of following so tedious and difficult that Mr. Davitt gave up the attempt. "It will take a week at that rate," he remarked; and thereupon he waived his right to go through his colleagues' speeches, and he confined himself to his own. We need not accompany Mr. Davitt over his speech-making in America. We will only say that the extracts read by him, strong as they were, were not directed against landlords, but against the landlord system. "Not one solitary speech denouncing crime," said the Attorney-General. "Why there are hundreds, thousands of them," retorted Mr. Davitt. He maintained that no League leader had ever said anything stronger than Mr. Bright's observation to the effect that if Ireland were a thousand miles off, and the landlords and tenants left face to face, the tenants would soon settle their differences. "If the Government believed *The Times* charges, why have we not been criminally prosecuted? I can't understand why I am here."

Having done with the Land League, Mr. Davitt gave a brief account of the Ladies' Land League, which, he said, was conducted on the same lines as the larger institution. It was he who first proposed the foundation of the Ladies' Land League; Mr. Parnell did not like it at all; but Mr. Davitt often calls Mr. Parnell "a regular Tory." "I am also charged," said Mr. Davitt, "with encouraging boycotting." But he held that the kind of boycotting which he defended had existed in all ages and countries; and he quoted a curious and striking instance from a "Blackwood" article of the year 1832, in which article all good Tories were enjoined to take away their custom from all traders, and to boycott all manufacturers who supported the Reform Bill. At the very lowest estimate one hundred thousand speeches must have been delivered at League meetings during the eight years following 1878. Sixty-nine persons were "named" in these one hundred thousand speeches, and sixty of the sixty-nine remained uninterfered with.

Mr. Davitt arrived at his calculation of the number of speeches by halving the actual number (2,000) of Land League branches, and assigning to each branch one meeting a month instead of one a fortnight, and one speech to each branch in place of a string of speeches. He made the same deduction of 50 per cent. from the number of central office meetings and open-air assemblages. As then, only nine persons had been assailed in eight years, it followed that there was only the 10,690th part of an outrage for each year. Of the nine persons assailed three were killed. When I say "three only," observed Mr. Davitt, "I do not wish to minimize criminality," "but I say these figures are an unanswerable reply to the Attorney-General's statement that 'the Land League rose like an exhalation to the sound of murderous oratory, and was guarded about by assassins who enforced its high decrees by the bullet and the knife.'"

Another statistical point of Mr. Davitt's was—that of the twenty-six murders perpetrated during the eight years (principally, as will be seen, of persons not named at League meetings), nineteen were committed in 1881-2, during two-thirds of which time no League existed. To prove that outrages increased with evictions, Mr. Davitt quoted figures showing that in the eight years before the League 24,111 persons were evicted, and 1,981 agrarian outrages committed; but that in the eight years after the foundation of the League the number of evicted rose to 133,679, and of agrarian crimes to 14,956. For the first time since his appearance before the Commission, Mr. Davitt broke down: he was describing Irish evictions, and his feelings overcame him.

Mr. Davitt was lifting the curtain over the Irish Arcadia of the prosecution. The constable witnesses, the agents, and the landlords had declared in the witness-box that before 1879 no tenants took the precaution of paying their rents at night, or perpetrated outrages upon grabbers. He now carried the war into the enemy's camp. He read extracts from *The Times* of 1854, showing that tenants sometimes did pay at night, and that an "anti-rent campaign" was a thing not unknown in those days, and that outrages were perpetrated upon grabbers — though the word grabber was not then known. At that period also, said Mr. Davitt, reading his extracts, men went about at night to intimidate people from paying the landlords. "County Tipperary at that period occupied the position which county Kerry holds in ours." And Captain Moonlight was known in Arcadia; only he was called "Captain Starlight." This was the most interesting part of the extracts. A very curious letter was read from the "Captain Starlight" of thirty-five years ago, a letter in which the Captain warned somebody that twelve men had drawn lots to kill him, that the lot fell upon the undersigned; but that the undersigned gave him timely notice to vacate his farm, "otherwise you will be accessory to your own death." So that according to Mr. Davitt's documentary proofs, the Arcadia of the land agents and the R.I.C.'s was not always happy.

ONE HUNDRED AND SEVENTEENTH DAY.

OCTOBER 31.

"THREE exquisite scoundrels," Mr. Davitt called them—the informers Farragher and Delaney and the forger Pigott. The first-named, observed Mr. Davitt, said he had been in confidential employment in the Land League office, yet he had not been able to produce a single proof of payment of Land League money for criminal purposes. Here Mr. Davitt dwelt— as he did the day before—on the striking fact that only one such proof had been found in the whole known history of the Land League, with its hundreds of branches and multitudes of members scattered all over Ireland. But even this solitary payment was made on the personal authority of a Land League clerk, the League itself being at that time in a state of demoralization, in consequence of the imprisonment of its leading members and officials. Farragher had admitted that he had been charged with drunkenness and immorality of various sorts. This was by the Guardians of Ballinrobe, in the workhouse of which Farragher was master. The Guardians dismissed him; but Farragher did not appeal to the Local Government Board. Farragher's own account of the way in which he had been led to give evidence was, Mr. Davitt maintained, untrustworthy. According to Farragher's story, he was subpœnaed in consequence of what he had said to five or six persons in Ballinrobe; but in reply to Sir Charles Russell, Farragher said he knew only one man of the five or six, "and this he said," remarked Mr. Davitt, "of a place near which he was born, in which place he was then master of a workhouse, in a Mayo village of two thousand or three thousand people, where everybody knew who everybody else was. He actually swore that he could not give the date of his own eviction."

The Attorney-General had said that the Land League agents used to get sums of twenty or thirty pounds from Mr. Biggar, or some other official, for criminal purposes. How was it that the informer Farragher, who swore he had been employed in the League office from May, 1880, to October, 1881, had been unable to produce a single proof of such use of League funds? The very fact that Farragher was unable to substantiate the Attorney-General's charges was, Mr. Davitt argued, a demonstration of their falsity. Land League books were missing, but was it suggested that the League leaders having prophetic knowledge of the present Commission, destroyed the documents that would establish the proof of Pigott's statements?

Another charge against us, said Mr. Davitt, is that the Invincibles were a branch of the Land League, paid by Mr. Egan. But for this charge there was no proof except the statements of the Invincible convict and informer Delaney and the forger Pigott. Mr. Davitt regarded it as absurd that Pigott's "bogus interview" with Eugene Davis should be accorded greater respect than the acknowledged character of Egan and of Brennan. This same Delaney had been taken out of gaol in order to give evidence against P. N. Fitzgerald at the Dublin trial of 1884; "but the jury was so scandalized at Delaney's perjuries that it added a resolution to its verdict of acquittal stating that Delaney was unworthy of belief, even on his oath." Mr. Davitt then recalled Delaney's own story, that Shannon, one of *The Times* agents, introduced himself to him in prison as a Crown solicitor in order to get from him, on his oath, evidence against the accused. He added: "In justice to Delaney, however, I ought to say that within the past few weeks he has addressed a letter——" But here Sir Richard Webster hastily interrupted him. "No, Mr. Davitt, you have no right to make such a statement." "Evidently," replied Mr. Davitt, "the Attorney-General knows all about it, as he objects to what I was going to say before I said it." "I objected to your referring to statements not in evidence," Sir Richard Webster explained.

Mr. Davitt passed on to another of *The Times* charges against the League, that Mr. Parnell was intimate with the Invincibles before the Phœnix Park murders, and that he apologized to them for his condemnation of the murders. For this accusation, Mr. Davitt held, there was only the word of the forger, whose pamphlets and bogus interview formed the basis of "Parnellism and Crime." "We are asked to believe that *The Times* knew nothing of Pigott before his appearance in the box. *O! sancta simplicitas!* it is known who subscribed the money which Houston gave to Pigott, and as surely as your lordships tolerate my address here to-day, so surely shall the names, the donations, and the dates they gave them on, be made public before long; and those who did it will have to take the consequences before the world."

When the forgeries were at last admitted, said Mr. Davitt, the tone adopted by *The Times* was "characteristically mean." There was no "manly apology" to Mr. Parnell or Mr. Egan or the others who were libelled. *The Times's* expression of regret merely meant, "We regret deeply that we have failed to convict you of forgery, and therefore we apologize." But was it true that *The Times* knew nothing of Pigott? By way of answering this question, Mr. Davitt read articles from *The Times* of 1871, in which this same Pigott was denounced for his sympathy with assassination. There was a murmur of laughter in court when Mr. Davitt declared that in that remote period Pigott charged *The Times* with having forged "a malicious libel" against him! Well, poor Pigott had his revenge—in 1886-9.

The remaining charges, about the knives in Palace Chambers and the Byrne cheque, Mr. Davitt passed over rapidly. He then came to two pathetic incidents of the Phœnix Park murders. His hearers listened to them in deep silence. Among the hundreds of cards left at Lady Frederick Cavendish's house, by sympathisers, on the day after the murders, was Mr. A. M. Sullivan's. Mr. Sullivan expected no recognition of his visit. Next morning he received from Lady Frederick a note thanking him for his sympathy and assuring him that she did not lay her husband's murder at the door of the Irish people. The other incident was the following :—When the Phœnix Park murderers were in prison, awaiting execution, a Sister of Mercy visited them daily. She paid particular attention to Joe Brady. She took a message from him to his mother on the morning of his execution. Joe Brady never knew that his visitor was the sister of the man whom he killed in Phœnix Park—Mr. Burke.

Mr. Davitt now came to the close of his speech. He thanked their lordships for their fairness to him personally—he had felt it from the beginning; he regretted his want of legal training; he knew that the people of Ireland thought as he did, that no matter how bitter their memories of misgovernment might have been, these memories would die out under the influence of the awakening goodwill of the English nation. However unskilful in a technical sense his conduct of his case might have been, he had at least refrained from using the venal talents of the forger, and from tempting convicts with the prospect of liberty. Here are some passages from the peroration of Mr. Davitt's speech :—

"This is, if I may say so without presumption, as serious and momentous a duty as any judge in England has ever been called upon to perform. The tradition of your lordships' exalted position, exalted as it is above the play of political passion or the influence of fear, will call—and I am sure will not call in vain—for the exercise by this Court of the great qualities of trained ability, calmness, discriminating judgment, and courage which are the proud boast of the judicial Bench of England. Whether or not the test of cold indiscriminating law can alone decide an issue in which political passion has played so great a part, and whether the heated language of platform oratory or the sometimes crude attempts at political reform are to be weighed in the balance of legal scales, which have never, in England at least, been made to test political action, or whether the test is to lie with the amalgam of law in its highest attributes and of calm reason and consideration of the men and motives of the Land League, which is accused, and of *The Times*, which has made these charges; as a layman I am unable to forecast; but, be that as it may, if the decision be only based upon truth and guided by the simple monitor of common sense, I, on my own behalf and on that of the Land League and the peasantry of Ireland, hopefully, confidently, and fearlessly will say, ' Let justice be done, though the heavens fall.' "

As Mr. Davitt sat down there was a burst of applause, with which, quite irregular though it was, neither the President nor the court officers interfered. "It was not necessary for you, Mr. Davitt," said Sir James Hannen, bending forward, "to plead your want of legal knowledge, for you have put your argument with great force and ability, and we are obliged to you for having given us the assistance which has been withheld by others."

At this compliment by the President the applause was renewed. Mr. Davitt rose and bowed respectfully to their lordships.

At a few minutes before one o'clock Sir Henry James rose to reply. He came to close quarters almost at once. He began by answering the preliminary questions in Sir Charles Russell's speech, Who are the accusers? who are the accused? when were the accusations made? The accusers, said Sir Henry, are not people who have been, as Sir Charles Russell described them, consistent only in one thing—hostility to the Irish people. *The Times* supported the Irish people in Catholic emancipation, in their demand for an extended franchise, for disestablishment, for agrarian reform. *The Times* supported the cause of the Irish nation, said Sir Henry James; and that brought him to the answer to the second question—that the accused were, not the Irish people, but only a body of agitators. *The Times*, said Sir Henry James, has not made an indictment against a nation, but against a particular combination of men. As for the third question, his answer was that the accusations began to be made in February, 1887, when in the debate on the Address Mr. Parnell said the Government would have to choose between the League and the Invincibles.

"That speech" (said Sir Henry James) "was made in the month of February, 1887, and in the first article that has been the subject of the inquiry in 'O'Donnell v. Walter,' the first article of those which constitute the publication called 'Parnellism and Crime,' a reference is made to that saying of Mr. Parnell's; and it was for the purpose of demonstrating if the alternatives were as Mr. Parnell stated them to be, what would be the fate of that country if, the Invincibles being put on one side, there should remain one alternative and one only—the League, as the *de facto* and absolute government of Ireland. That was the time, my lords, when the accusations were made."

"It is said that these charges are stale," but the "proofs" of these charges have never before been "collected and arranged," "linked together," for the public information. Sir Henry James next proceeded to argue that the four causes to which Sir Charles Russell traced Irish discontent were either irrelevant or obsolete. The four causes were restriction of trade, the penal code, landlord power, and mistrust of the Government. But, said Sir Henry, the first two causes disappeared long ago; while as for the third, improved agrarian law (coupled with emigration, or diminution of the population) has made the Irish people more prosperous than at any period of their history. Doubtless there was discontent, and that very discontent Mr. Davitt made use of when, in 1877, he emerged from prison an unconverted Fenian, to accomplish the purpose of his life—separation between Great Britain and Ireland. Sir Henry James drew a vivid picture of Mr. Davitt planning, during the "dark, dreary years" of his imprisonment, his future career. As soon as Mr. Davitt came out of prison he rejoined the Fenian Brotherhood, and became a member of their Supreme Council. Sir Henry James contended that Mr. Davitt's purpose was unchanged, only the means were changed, or rather extended—to Fenianism Mr. Davitt added the Peasant Movement.

There was the Irish famine of 1846; and Sir Henry James admitted its effects as a cause of political and social disturbance. But he argued that even the great famine was more of a blessing than a curse to the Ireland of to-day—economically considered. He contended that in his description of Irish misery Sir Charles Russell had gone for his facts to the last century; and he traced Sir Charles's quotation, "the worst clad, worst fed, and worst housed population upon the face of the civilized globe," to Lord Chesterfield; and "therefore," said Sir Henry, "they must have been spoken a hundred years ago." The causes of Irish distress did not arise to any considerable extent from landlord oppression, but from over-population in the eighteenth century, coupled with the sudden cessation, at the end of the Napoleonic wars, of the demand for Irish agricultural products. The small corn-growing crofts were then amalgamated into pasture-lands. Therefore, when the famine came, the over-dense population of small cultivators died of hunger. By the year 1881 three-fourths of the old population of about eight millions disappeared—all the better, economically, for the survivors, thought Sir Henry, quoting the following passage from Dr. Grimshaw's history :—

Possibly we might have advanced faster than we have done; but when we consider the mighty collapse that took place at the commencement of the past half-century, which began in the days of the great famine of 1846, 1847, and 1848, it may be that Ireland has advanced more rapidly, and recovered from a condition of almost total wreck, more completely than any other country would have done, or ever has done.

In short, the Land Act of 1870, imperfect though it was, had removed the political grievances of Ireland; and any revolutionary appeal to the peasants must be made on social considerations and to their individual, and class, selfishness. The man who made this appeal was Mr. Davitt, who, having been in prison for so many years before 1878-9, could not have known the happy state of things brought about in Ireland since the Land Act of 1870. Sir Henry James's remarks on Mr. Davitt, at this stage of his address, are worth quoting :—

"Some of us here have sat in close contact with Mr. Davitt. Your lordships will have observed the quickness with which he has appreciated your rulings. I am sure that there is not one amongst my learned friends who is not grateful to him for the courteous bearing which he has observed towards us, and for the assistance which he has rendered us, his great knowledge of this case having enabled him to do so more than once. We have here gained some insight into that strange quickness of intelligence, that instinctive power which must have made him a paramount figure in any negotiations with the Irish peasantry, an agent almost invincible when contending with men of a lower degree of intelligence. I think there are few men who have been in contact with Mr. Davitt who would not feel it a repugnant task to trace to him conduct involving bad motives or errors of judgment. But the facts of the case stand before your lordships, and Mr. Davitt's conduct must be judged by you."

As already said, Sir Henry James pointed to the fact that Mr. Davitt, as soon as he was released from Dartmoor, rejoined the Fenian Brotherhood. He quoted the Old Bailey letter, which we reproduce here, and to which reference is made in Mr. Davitt's cross-examination. This letter, written to a fellow-Fenian in 1869, was found upon Forrester, at Forrester's arrest, and produced at the Old Bailey trial :—

"Dear Friend,—I have just returned from Dundee, which place I have left all right. Your letter of Monday I have just read. I have no doubt but what the account is correct. In reference to the other affair, I hope you won't take any part in it whatever—I mean in the carrying of it out. If it is decided upon and you receive *Jem's*, and through him *Fitz's* consent, let it be done by all means; but one thing you must remember, and that is that you are of too much importance to our family to be spared, even at the risk of allowing a rotten sheep to exist among the flock. You must know that if anything happened to you the toil and trouble of the last six months will have been almost in vain. Whoever is employed don't let him use the pen we are and have been selling; get another for the purpose, a common one. I hope and trust when I return to *Man* I may not hear that every man, woman, and child know all about it ere it occurred."

While willing to accept Mr. Davitt's explanation that he wrote the letter, in order,—through the device of delay—to prevent murder, Sir Henry James quoted it as proof of the character of the organization which Mr. Davitt rejoined.

ONE HUNDRED AND EIGHTEENTH DAY.

NOVEMBER 1.

LIKE the speaker who preceded him, Sir Henry James thoroughly interests his hearers. But his lay audience is larger than any which listened to Mr. Davitt. To judge from the appearance of the court to-day, the crowds which came, expecting to hear an exceedingly able speech, were in no wise disappointed. As Sir Henry James said, in the opening part of his address, it was not the charges themselves which were new, but the linking together of the chain of proof. It was the general opinion that in this linking operation Sir Henry James displayed great dexterity. Anyhow, he succeeded in imparting considerable freshness to a tale eleven years old, one year and ten days of which have been spent in telling it in Probate Court Number One. The proposition which he is doing his best to prove is that the Land League was the offspring of treason—not of the social conditions enumerated by Sir Charles Russell and Mr. Davitt. In the first day's instalment of his address, he maintained that Mr. Davitt's aim had been the same after his imprisonment as before it. To-day he endeavoured to show what the means were to which Mr. Davitt had recourse. Mr. Davitt himself had admitted, said Sir Henry James, that he went to America in 1878, immediately after his release from prison, with a purpose.

The men with whom Mr. Davitt associated in America were the men from whose combination the Land League sprang. These men were the trustees of the " Skirmishing " Fund ; and a letter copied into *The Freeman* of November, 1879, and signed by Trustees Carroll, Luby, Breslin, Devoy, and one of the Fords, said that the object of the Skirmishers was to strike a blow against England wherever and whenever an opportunity offered itself—such a blow, for example, as the laying of London in ashes. Mr. Davitt, Sir Henry James argued, must have known what this fund was, and who its trustees were, when he went to America. John Devoy, he continued, joined the new Land League movement only because it was a " step towards the overthrow of the English dominion." The Land League platform was the only one on which the various Irish and Irish-American parties—agrarian revolutionists and political revolutionists—could meet.

The plan was, said Sir Henry James, quoting Mr. Lalor, a revolutionist of 1848, to link repeal to some other question, like a tender to its engine. This, he maintained, was what Mr. Davitt was doing in his American lectures ; and a lecture which Mr. Davitt delivered at Brooklyn in October, 1878, proved, added Sir Henry James, that the idea of an alliance between the physical force party in America and Mr. Parnell's Parliamentary party at home was " already present in Mr. Davitt's mind." For only a few days before the delivery of this speech the famous cablegram, correctly quoted by Le Caron, had been sent to Mr. Parnell by Dr. Carroll, Breslin, Devoy, General Millen, and other trustees of the Skirmishing Fund. " I accept Mr. Davitt's explanation," said Sir Henry James, " that this cablegram was retained by Mr. Kickham and not shown to Mr. Parnell ; but "—and here Sir Henry James assumed his most emphatic manner both in voice and gesture—" I look upon it as the result of Mr. Davitt's intercourse with the revolutionists, who would not have sent it unless they knew Mr. Davitt's views." The cablegram, said Sir Henry James, recommended, among other measures, the substitution of independence for federation, and agrarian agitation on the basis of peasant proprietorship.

Again, in the month of December, 1878, another lecture by Mr. Davitt, and a letter from Devoy in *The Freeman*, were, in Sir Henry James's estimation, proofs that in the purpose of the lecturer and the writer, the agrarian movement was only the means towards the great end of independence. In the lecture Mr. Davitt was reported to have said that "selfishness was the mainspring of all human action," the selfish appeal in this case being an appeal to the cupidity of the tenant farmers; while Mr. Devoy, in his letter to *The Freeman*, advocated the severance of the political connection with England, declared that "the physical strength of the nation must be put into the effort," but recommended the adoption of some kind of compromise until the leaders of the agitation should feel themselves sufficiently strong. Here followed one of Sir Henry James's effective passages. "Mr. Davitt says that his 'new departure' was not the same as Devoy's, but I say that the two departures were as the two wings of the same army." Devoy, said Sir Henry, took the physical force wing; Mr. Davitt appealed to agrarian "selfishness"; but their action was combined. In December, 1878, continued Sir Henry James, Mr. Davitt and Mr. John Devoy came to Ireland, and Devoy came for one purpose only—to strengthen, to arm all who were willing to fight against England; Devoy came on a "treasonable" business, and the report which he produced in America in August, 1879, soon after his return from Ireland, proved it. Here Sir Henry James read Devoy's report of his inspection of Fenian military stores in Ireland, of importations of arms, and generally of his tour among the seven "provinces" into which the Fenians divided the United Kingdom. Mr. Davitt, Sir Henry James went on, refused to say what Devoy's mission to Ireland was. In 1879, General Millen and Dr. Carroll came to Ireland, but Mr. Davitt would not tell why they came. "Eloquent silence," exclaimed Sir Henry. General Millen came, like Devoy, for "treasonable" purposes. Mr. Davitt, the speaker continued, was equally reticent about Carroll's mission. And then Sir Henry James finished this part of his speech with an emphatic declaration that at that time Mr. Davitt's open agitation was "a mere ingredient in a treasonable conspiracy."

Put in another way, Sir Henry James's main position amounted to this:— That the establishment of the Land League only proved that Mr. Davitt and Devoy had captured Mr. Parnell's constitutional organization. The objects of the Land League, said Sir Henry James, were not to be found in the written articles of that body, but in the actions of Mr. Davitt and Mr. John Devoy, and in speeches by Brennan, Boyton, Sheridan, and others, including Mr. Parnell, who said that he would not "put off his coat" for the constitutional movement if he did not think it led to the "legislative independence of Ireland." Sir Henry, quoting a few expressions from the speeches, contented himself with giving their dates, places, and names. Then he quoted Mr. Matt. Harris's remark that it was necessary to do something to rouse up the "dormant peasantry" of Ireland. They did need rousing up, Sir Henry James thought, for he proceeded to argue (from statistics) that just before Mr. Davitt started the Mayo Land League, the Mayo peasants were more comfortably off than they had been for many years. Sir Henry James repudiated the stories about Mayo distress about the time of the foundation of the Mayo League. And when the Mayo League was started at Irishtown in the spring of 1879, who conducted it? Fenians: the Irishtown meeting "was a Fenian one," said Sir Henry James, "all the speakers, except one, Mr. John Fergusson, of Glasgow," were Fenians; and the resolutions were so worded as to include the programmes of "both wings" of the "same army."

In a short time the Mayo League was merged in the National Land League of Ireland. This was on the 21st of October, 1879. Sir Henry James repeated the testimony already given by Messrs. Parnell and Davitt themselves—Mr. Parnell was reluctant to found a central organization; Mr. Parnell was apprehensive that the central organization might be held responsible for the acts of local and distant bodies; Mr. Parnell had in mind the warning of Mr.

Isaac Butt, that such responsibility would be sure to arise. But "the man of strong will," as Sir Henry James called him, Mr. Davitt, forced his will upon the parliamentarians, and "secured" them. Once more, Mr. Davitt, who had no means of his own, wanted money for his League agitations, and continued Sir Henry James, a letter, enclosing money, came from Devoy. Mr. Davitt received £480 in all, and he received it from the Skirmishing Fund. "It has been argued," said Sir Henry, "that the League did not receive this money; but the question is, what connection had it with the events out of which the Land League grew; the money went to the movement."

Sir Henry James made some satirical remarks on what he called the "soup delivery" view of the Land League, as set forth by Sir Charles Russell and Mr. Reid, by Archbishop Walsh and the clerical witnesses. The Land League was not an organization for the relief of distress, for the liberation of tenants from landlord oppression. It was valued by its founders only as a means to the end of complete national independence. "Mr. Davitt must have been laughing at my friend," said Sir Henry James; "I give Mr. Davitt the credit that his views are broad enough, and we may think them wrong; but be they right or wrong, he is a man of different character, and of a different style and mode of action to those who will cloak their design under the pretence, and the miserable pretence, of doing an act of charity, when their whole object was of a different, and far different, description."

Sir Henry James concentrated his main effort upon the attempt to establish an identity of thought and feeling between Mr. Davitt and Mr. John Devoy. The Devoy cablegram was, Sir Henry James held, in complete harmony with Mr. Davitt's American utterances, to the effect that the Home Rule party of 1878 did not represent the Irish popular feeling, that "not one of the 103 representatives in Parliament from Ireland ever hints that he represents a people who desire a separate national existence." To prepare for the attainment of this end by physical means was, Sir Henry maintained, the reason why John Devoy accompanied Mr. Davitt to Ireland in December, 1888. And here he made use of the evidence of Mr. John O'Connor, maintaining that Devoy, in spite of his public denunciation of "rat holes of conspiracy," must have secretly advised Mr. O'Connor and other Fenians to remain in them. And in the report which Devoy presented to the United Brethren, or Clan-na-Gaël on his return to America, and to which we have already alluded, he said that as soon as Leinster and Munster were "thoroughly organized" there would be fifty thousand "good members" of the I. R. B. in Ireland.

Mr. Justin McCarthy, having heard glowing accounts of Sir Henry James's oratory, came to hear. He listened for about an hour: he then left, as if he had had enough of it. The only other accused member present was Mr. Biggar. Captain O'Shea sat on the solicitor's bench. So did Mr. Arthur Walter, Mr. Buckle, Mr. Soames. Mr. Reid, Q.C., M.P., appeared for the first time since the great secession. He was in wig and gown. In front of him sat Mr. Lockwood. It seemed as if Sir Henry's eloquence passed by Mr. Lockwood's ears like the idle wind. More caricatures for the collectors of the twenty-first century? Mr. Lockwood was industriously scratching away at something—not jottings of the speech. After a time he picked up his bits of paper and walked out.

ONE HUNDRED AND NINETEENTH DAY.

NOVEMBER 5.

SIR HENRY JAMES began his day's work with a brief recapitulation of Mr. Davitt's career soon after his release from prison. Mr. Davitt returned from America, put himself into personal communication with the Fenian brethren of the western districts, through which he was making a tour, and, according to Mr. Davitt's own statement, John Devoy was going about those same regions at the same time. But Mr. Davitt refused to tell what Devoy was there for. Devoy, the skirmisher and the Clan-na-Gael revolutionist, and Mr. Davitt, still a Fenian—these, in Sir Henry's estimation, were the joint authors of the organizations soon to arise in Ireland and America. As for the Land League organization founded on the 21st of October, 1879, its real object was, not agrarian relief, but political separation; and all that the League leaders did for the relief of distress and the reduction of rents was done, not for these purposes as ends in themselves, but to unite classes in an attempt to secure another end—that of Irish independence and political separation. Such was the general drift of Sir Henry James's argument.

And now he proceeded to give his reasons and illustrations. In the first place, he observed, the central office of the Land League did not publish its Constitution until the 27th of November, 1880—more than twelve months after the establishment of that body. There were, however, very soon after the establishment of the League, certain injunctions issued to the tenant farmers, and in one of them, grabbers, (to use a short title) were named as traitors. These injunctions, or regulations, appeared to have been issued on the 30th of December, 1879. But in the Constitution of November, 1880, proclaimed with all the authority of the League, there was, he said, nothing about traitors, although, according to the injunctions already named, and distributed among the League branches, grabbers would be treated as such. The League leaders, said Sir Henry James, regarded the rules of the Constitution as "a sham, to get the timid" into the new organization. That was the only importance he attached to the League rules. They were framed "for purposes of concealment;" they were silent on the real object of the League; they were devised for the purpose of enlisting all classes "in the common army." This, said he, disposed of Sir Charles Russell's contention that a conspiracy should be tried by its avowed object. If the "public statement" of League rules was "a sham," what was the real "principle" of the organization? To show what this was, Sir Henry James first quoted a letter from Mr. Davitt to *The Irish World*, and reproduced in *United Ireland* on May 21, 1884. In this letter Mr. Davitt, commenting on the differences of opinion about the true character of the Land League [then no longer in existence] observed that in 1879 self-government was not included in its programme; that the programme had to be framed in such a way as not to "scare timid reformers," and with a view to enabling members of the Parnellite party to deny in Parliament that political independence was the goal of the Land League. Sir Henry James next quoted Alexander Sullivan as having said that the "first plank" of the American Land League [a body founded by Messrs. Devoy and Davitt] was "self-government," and the second plank peasant proprietorship. This same word "self-government" occurs, said Sir Henry James, in Mr. Davitt's Boston speech and in Devoy's famous letter quoted in *The Freeman*.

A portion of Mr. Sullivan's letter, as quoted by Sir Henry James, may be given here:—

Contrary to the belief of many, the Land League was of American origin. Its platform was drawn in the city of New York by Irish Nationalists residing in America, of whom the best known is Mr. John Devoy, in consultation with Mr. Michael Davitt on his first visit to the United States in 1878. The first plank of the platform was a declaration for self-government. The second advocated vigorous agitation of the land question on the basis of a peasant proprietary, while accepting concessions tending to abolish arbitrary eviction. After the platform drawn up in New York had been thoroughly discussed by the Irish Parliamentary party, it was agreed to by them, and the Land League was organized in Dublin, October 21, 1879.

Sir Henry James's third point was elaborated at considerable length. It was a denial of Sir Charles Russell's argument that distress produced the Land League. The Land League took advantage of distress, was Sir Henry's counter-proposition. The dexterity with which he argued this proposition was generally admired. There was no distress, he said, when the Land League was being formed. Nor was there distress in 1878 ; that year was, in fact, an average year as regards prosperity. [In a previous part of his speech he called it a more than average year.] Not until late in the year 1879 was there, he affirmed, any reason to expect serious distress. In the address issued at the foundation of the Land League, October 21, 1879, and signed by Messrs. Parnell, Egan, and Davitt, it was not said that relief of distress was an object of the new organization. The relief certainly was given when the distress became acute, but Sir Henry James denied that the contingency had been present to the "minds of the agitators." Not until the last days of December, 1879, did Mr. Parnell say that the League associated itself with relief work ; and that was in his interview with Mr. Ives, of *The New York Herald*, who on that date embarked with him for America. Even on the 4th of January, 1880, the date of his first speech in America, Mr. Parnell still spoke of distress as only being "imminent." Mr. Ives himself, who had seen the condition of things in Western Ireland, said that not until December, 1879, had there been "much talk of distress." The testimony of Dr. McCormack, Bishop of Galway, was to the same effect.

Mr. Parnell, Sir Henry James continued, did send relief money from America ; but relief was not the purpose of his mission. Mr. Parnell went to America "to enlist the sympathies of a certain class of men." "By that time he must have known them full well," for had not Mr. Davitt already laid the League foundations in America, and secured the support of the Irish "Nationalists" (as the Fenians were called up to 1879)? The "combination," exclaimed Sir Henry James, in his most emphatic manner, "had been made," the army had its "two camps" (the open and the secret), and Mr. Parnell went to America to see the chiefs of this, the New Departure. Mr. Parnell went to America "to do the best he could for the new organization," which, up to the time of his departure from Ireland, had held only sixty-eight meetings and founded thirty local branches. According to Mr. Ives's narrative, Mr. Parnell had said, "We cannot prevent all tenants from paying ;" some of them are "cowards." Here Sir Henry James, suddenly stopping, exclaimed with a gesture of indignation, "Cowards if they discharged the duties of their contract !" "Pressure must be brought to bear on such people," was the next expression quoted from the interview ; "that was how crime came," was Sir Henry's comment. Still drawing upon the Ives-Parnell interview, he cited Mr. Parnell's statement that, as the aim of the League was revolutionary, secret conspiracy was no less useful than open agitation. "Did not all this point to the influence of Devoy and the others who were admittedly forming a treasonable conspiracy?" And who were the persons whom Mr. Parnell met in America ? John Devoy, an ex-convict ; Augustine Ford, a skirmisher ; Breslin, Carroll, and O'Meagher Condon, who has already been described in the evidence as "one of the released prisoners in connection with the murder of Sergeant Brett." Mr. Parnell's tour through America was, added Sir Henry James, arranged by those men or men of their stamp.

Upon this Sir Henry James mentioned Major Le Caron, *alias* Dr. Beach, who in his evidence stated that Mr. Parnell's tour was arranged by the Clan-na-Gael chiefs. Major Le Caron, seated in his quiet corner near the door, must have been agreeably surprised at the eloquent defence of him which Sir Henry James now poured forth with all his abundant resource of speech, tone, and gesture. Making a passing reference to the hard things that had been said about Le Caron in court and outside it, he said it was only due to Le Caron that he should say something in his defence.

Here are some passages from Sir Henry's apology for Major Le Caron :—

> It is due, I think, to that man, after what has occurred, that something should be said of him, and I say it openly on his behalf. My lords, who is this man, on whose evidence much depends in this case, on whom I have to ask you to rely, whose word I ask you to accept? As far as I know, that man's character, apart from anything that took place in America in connection with his conduct towards the Clan-na-Gael, is unimpeached. . . . Mr. Davitt used some language which to those who did not follow him closely would appear to impute that Le Caron had been drummed out of his regiment. Those words have been misunderstood. . . . He joined in the American war between the North and the South. He attained distinction whilst serving in the army, in which he attained the rank of major. Shortly after the war came to an end he learnt, by communication with a Fenian, of the intended attack upon Canada. It was a treasonable attack upon an outlying portion of the Queen's dominions, and against men who had taken no part in the misrule, if there had been misrule according to the view of any man, in Ireland. And Le Caron, who was true to his allegiance to this country, naturally communicated what he learnt. . . . And for twenty years that man has held his life in his own hand. He never could have had one moment's security, one moment of certain repose. One letter miscarried, one person unfaithful to his trust in the Post Office, one accident any hour occurring, and that man's death in a moment was as certain as any person's death must be as the ultimate result of life. An attack has been made upon him by those who personally have appeared in this case, and I suppose that the attack must be concentrated upon this, that he took a promissory oath of secrecy. I ask, on whose behalf is it that complaint is made? Is it made on behalf of the men who were thus plotting, those assassins who had not the courage to disclose themselves and who required the secrecy only for the purpose of avoiding the punishment which they knew would follow detection, those men who, as enemies of the human race, as the lowest and most degraded beings that could exist, were plotting destruction of human life by dynamite—are these the men on whose behalf the appeal is to be made that honour has not been maintained between them and the man who was pledged to secrecy? . . . What has he been? Merely a detective acting on behalf of his country with a view to secure the safety of innocent, unprotected subjects of the Queen—unprotected, that is to say, in any other way against the machinations of these assassins. If a detective brings a criminal to justice, the community applaud him; they praise the exertions of a man who apprehends the criminal after the crime has been committed. Why, then, should the conduct of this man be condemned? . . . There are some observations made by my learned friend Sir Charles Russell to which I must refer. I do not suppose, however, that my learned friend meant exactly what he said. If he did, I am sure he had not the facts of the case fully in his mind. He said : "Here we have a man about whose odious profession I will not waste breath in talking. Surely the state of society has something faulty in it when the employment of such a man as Le Caron can be defended or can be necessary. His life was a living lie. He was worming himself into the confidence of men presumably honest, however mistaken in their views, only to make money and to betray them." My learned friend says that the state of society must be faulty that excuses the employment of such men. Well, I first ask who employed Le Caron? He has been employed since 1867. Twenty years have run since he has been engaged in this employment, during which period he has sent home statements of what he has learnt by way of warning to the representatives of the English Government. If he has been paid it has been with the acquiescence, if not by the very hands, of English statesmen. During those twenty years, Ministers of State, men of high honour, unblemished reputation, acting up to the best of their judgment, and seeking to protect their country, were asking from him and receiving from him the results of his inquiries in America. Does my learned friend attack these men, some of whom have been his colleagues and associates in the administration of the country's affairs? What would be said of a statesman, indeed of any human being, who, being told, "Through such a man you can obtain information as to how a contemplated raid upon Canada is to be carried out, and as to a plan for blowing up the public buildings of London, including the House of Commons itself when the representatives of the nation are actually in session"—I wonder what would be said of a statesman who should reply, "No ; we will run the risk of the execution of these acts, involving, as they must, a deplorable loss of life, and we will run the risk because honour must be kept with the gentry who are devising them." Men who should give such a reply would be accomplices, almost participators, in the dreadful deeds that would be perpetrated.

Devoy, Breslin, Carroll, and the rest who were alleged to have arranged Mr.

Parnell's tour, were, said Sir Henry, Clan-na-Gael members. And the Clan was identical with or associated with the I. R. B. Devoy, Breslin, and Carroll were Skirmishers, and from the Skirmishers', or murder, Fund came, said Sir Henry James, the £480 to Mr. Davitt, which Mr. Davitt subsequently repaid out of his own pocket. The payment, said Sir Henry, was published in *The Irish World's* published statement of accounts. There were three results from Mr. Parnell's tour, said Sir Henry James: League funds, *The Irish World* alliance, and the foundation of the American branch of the Land League. In discussing these three results Sir Henry James traversed familiar and well-trodden ground. Sir Henry James made much of the Troy meeting, at which somebody, mounting the platform, gave Mr. Parnell a subscription of "five dollars for bread" and "twenty for lead." Sir Henry James insisted upon it that the words were meant literally, and that the cheers of the American audience in which they were first uttered, and of the Irish audiences where they were repeated, showed they were accepted literally. This view of them was rejected contemptuously by Mr. Parnell himself when in the witness-box. Mr. Parnell explained that the word "lead" was meant as a figure of speech; that the five dollars were given to the distress fund, and the twenty dollars to the political organization fund, both which funds had just been started by Mr. Parnell in the States.

ONE HUNDRED AND TWENTIETH DAY.

NOVEMBER 6.

MOST of to-day's instalment of Sir Henry James's speech dealt with the action of the Land League in Ireland during the year 1880. But before coming to this important subject Sir Henry James had a little more to say about Mr. Davitt's tour in America. In Kansas, September, 1880, said Sir Henry James, Mr. Davitt had spoken to the effect that Ireland must be kept in a state of unsettlement until landlordism was done away with. "This speech," said Sir Henry James, "I have always regarded as one of great importance." Here is a portion of it, quoted by Sir Henry James:—

> We have, as you have already been told, declared an unceasing war against landlordism—not a war to call on our people to shoulder the rifle and go out in open field and settle the question that is now agitating Ireland, although I am not opposed to a settlement of that nature providing I could see a chance of success.

And just before he returned to Ireland from this American visit, Mr. Davitt had declared that Irish lands must run to waste sooner than that grabbers should have them. This was said in a speech at Virginia City. From this speech Sir Henry James quoted the following extract :—

> In 1847 there was no public sentiment, such as now exists, and many well-to-do Irish farmers and tradesmen, as well as English speculators, aided the landlords by bidding for the land from which tenants were evicted. There is none of this competition for land this time. There are not four cases in Ireland to-day where a farm has been occupied by a neighbour when the tenant was turned out. The bye-laws of the Irish Land League declare that no person who bids for the land or cattle of a tenant evicted for inability to pay rent shall be admitted to the League, and that no matter how many farmers are evicted, the land shall remain untenanted until the system shall be abolished. No sale of goods shall be effected and no land tenanted after eviction.

War upon the landgrabber as a means of starving out the landlord garrison—that was the implication in this part of Sir Henry's address.

Throughout this American tour, said Sir Henry, Mr. Davitt was in touch with the Extremists. Part of this time, too, Mr. Parnell was in America. He returned to Ireland in March, 1880. So that from October, 1879, to March, 1880, the chief League leaders were not very active in Ireland. A little later in his speech Sir Henry showed that neither the leaders nor the League itself became active until the autumn of 1880. As for the earlier months—the last months of 1879—and the first of 1880, they were, to summarize Sir Henry's statement as briefly as possible, spent in preparation for the combined action of Leaguers, I. R. B.'s, and American revolutionists. The I. R. B., said Sir Henry James, was still at work in these earlier months. Mr. Matt. Harris had said in his evidence that in 1879 the Irish peasants were supplied with the arms which Mr. James O'Kelly and others had procured for distribution throughout the country. "So that in 1879-80" we find "a dormant peasant class in possession of guns and sword bayonets; and "all this was known to Mr. Davitt, to Patrick Egan, and to Brennan." It was in these circumstances, continued Sir Henry James, that the O'Donoghue gave one or two addresses at Killarney. The district, according to Mr. Leonard's testimony, had been peaceful up to that date. But after it, the district became disturbed.

Mr. Parnell returned to Ireland on the 20th of March, 1880. He landed at Cork, and there, said Sir Henry James, he was received by a deputation of Fenians, who memorialized him to the effect that it was hopeless to look for redress of Irish grievances from Parliamentary action. The members of the deputation intimated that this being the case, they would take no part in the impending Parliamentary elections. And for the first time, said Sir Henry James, Land League money was spent upon electioneering purposes. This use of Land League money was a contravention of the seventh rule of the Land League. Yet a sum of two thousand pounds was given by Mr. Egan for electioneering work. Mr. Parnell had said that he thought the seventh rule had been rescinded; but Sir Henry James had been unable to discover any trace of such change in the constitution of the League. This showed that the direction of the League was left to a large extent in Mr. Egan's hands—a point to which Sir Henry James attached considerable importance.

The League, said Sir Henry James, was left in the hands of Egan and Brennan when in May of that year (1880) Mr. Davitt went back again to America. And how did the Leaguers conduct the agitation during those months of May, June, July, August? Sir Henry James proceeded to show how, by giving extracts from, or otherwise indicating speeches by Brennan, Boyton, Quinn, Sheridan, and the renowned "Scrab." All these speeches, said Sir Henry James, were "eminently suited" for the promotion of Mr. Davitt's policy of keeping Ireland in a state of "unsettlement." Political separation and destruction of landlordism were the themes of these speeches.

In the month of August, 1880, there came about the Fenian raid for arms upon a vessel near Cork. From this vessel, named the *Juno*, about forty cases of firearms, and a large number of cutlasses, were stolen by the raiders. Said Sir Henry James:—

The incident which I wish to mention is the action of the Cork Land League. These gentlemen, I have no doubt, had read the open programme, and they had listened to words which no doubt from time to time were used by the Land League leaders as to the policy of constitutional action. The Cork Land League, therefore, thought raiding for arms did not exactly come within their idea of constitutional action, not finding any mention of any such action in the open programme. Believing that they would be acting in accordance with the wishes of the Land League by condemning such raiding for arms, they passed the following resolution:—

"That we deeply regret that a robbery of useless old firearms has taken place, that we condemn lawlessness in any shape, and that we believe the occurrence in Passage must have been effected by those who desire to see a renewal of the Coercion Acts inflicted upon this country, and who wish to give the Government good value for their secret service money."

But, said Sir Henry James, this resolution was followed by a meeting of the central body at Dublin. At this meeting Mr. Dillon presided, and Mr.

Brennan made a speech to the effect that the Cork branch had meddled with matters "outside its sphere." "We do not want," said Mr. Brennan, "to put ourselves in antagonism to other bodies in Ireland," and "We disclaim the action of the Cork branch." The chairman, said Sir Henry James, approved this speech. If this, said Sir Henry James, was the attitude of the central branch towards the lawbreakers in County Cork, "what must have been its attitude towards the crimes with which we shall have to deal?" Mr. Dillon, he continued, went to Cork, and there Mr. Dillon declared that the League could entertain "no hostility to other bodies who had the good of Ireland at heart."

There was then, said Sir Henry James, an entire reorganization of this unfortunate body, the Cork branch of the League. In a minute or two Sir Henry James made dexterous use of this incident. He was criticizing Mr. Parnell's account of the attack made upon him and his party by alleged Fenians, near Blarney, in October, 1880, two months after the raid. The assailants took two of Mr. Parnell's party as hostages. Mr. Parnell, it will be remembered, gave this as an instance of Fenian hostility to the Parliamentary movement. But, said Sir Henry James, the two men taken as hostages were Mr. Cronin and Mr. O'Brien, the Cork leaguers whose denunciation of the arms exploit was repudiated by Mr. Dillon and Mr. Brennan.

Sir Henry James now came to consider the state of Western Ireland in the last three months of 1880. In the first nine months, he said, the Land League had made but little progress. But after the return of the Irish Parliamentary members to Ireland, in September, the League "spread like wildfire," and crime advanced with it. Sir Charles Russell had argued that "distress" produced crime, observed Sir Henry James. (A little later the President remarked that Sir Charles Russell had used the word "eviction.") Sir Henry James now declared that he would prove that distress did not produce crime, and "even at the risk" of boring those who had come into court "only for amusement," he would do it with statistics. He undertook to show that no crime broke out in localities where distress was present and the League non-existent; but that it did break out in the very localities where prosperity and the League coexisted. He rapidly summarized the Irish Poor Law Board reports of four unions in each of the four counties—Mayo, Galway, Kerry, Cork—for 1879-80, sixteen unions in all, and in doing this he handed their lordships a map of distressed Ireland, showing that the distress was most acute along the narrow fringe of coast, and that it gradually diminished towards a line drawn from north to south, and separating nineteen western counties from the rest of the island. Within the narrow fringe, said Sir Henry James, crimelessness and distress co-existed, according to the reports of the local inspectors.

To show that crime was provoked by Land League activity, Sir Henry James quoted, first, the case of the murder of the land agent, Mr. Feerick, near Ballinrobe, in Mayo, June, 1880. Shot in June, Mr. Feerick lingered until August, when he died. Mr. Feerick was shot on the 29th of June; and it was only nine days before the murder that P. J. Gordon made, in the neighbourhood, a speech in which he said "Away with land-robbers," "it will be better for you (the tenants) to lose your blood, like Allen, Larkin, and O'Brien." And this same Gordon, while Mr. Feerick was still lingering, made a speech in which he said that Feerick had "evicted a poor widow and her orphans." There was not," said Sir Henry James, "one word of regret for Feerick."

Scrab Nally, also, five or six days after the murder, remarked at a meeting that "more good had been done that week than by all the speeches," for "a landlord had been shot in Ballinrobe." Sir Henry James next instanced the case of young Mr. Boyd, of Wexford, who had been murdered, it was said, because his father had been harsh to his tenants. The murder was perpetrated in August, 1880. What, asked Sir Henry James, had Mr. Parnell publicly said in condemnation of this crime? Only that shooting was "entirely unnecessary and prejudicial where there was a suitable organization among the tenants themselves." Was it to be understood, Sir Henry James asked, that where there was no sufficient organization murder was allowable? "Call that speech a denunciation of crime!" Sir Henry James exclaimed; "from that time forward crime spread like wildfire."

Sir Henry James next referred to the murder of Lord Mountmorres, whom, after the murder, and at a public meeting attended by prominent leaguers, James Redpath described as "an infamous rascal." Messrs. Sexton, Sheridan, Boyton, Egan, were present, said Sir Henry James; all that Mr. Sexton, in the witness-box, said about Redpath's speech was that he scarcely thought it constitutional. And lastly, in July, 1880, there was the case of Downey, who received the death wound intended for Mr. Hutchins, and in respect to which Mr. Biggar was reported as having, in a public speech, objected to firing shots that missed their mark.

And now Sir Henry James came to his most striking piece of statistics. Even the idlers who came to be "amused," and who, as Sir Henry James observed in his politely ironical way, might prefer something rather more sensational—even they were interested in the recital. He gave figures about what he called "ripe" counties—*i.e.*, the counties in which the League first took root, and in which its influence was soonest and most widely felt. They were Mayo, Galway, Roscommon, Sligo. In Mayo, crimes rose from 25 in 1878 to 178 in 1879; in Galway, from 22 to 179; in Roscommon, from 12 to 35; in Sligo, from 15 to 53. (The Land League was formally established in Dublin on the 21st of October, 1879.) Then he took four "unripe" counties, Kerry, Limerick, Wexford, Tipperary. In Kerry the advance was from 5 in 1878 to 13 in 1879; in Limerick, from 22 to 27; in Wexford there was a decrease from 5 to 4; in Tipperary an increase, from 12 in 1878 to 28 in 1879. In these "unripe" counties the League did not take root until dates more or less late in 1880. Having thus compared 1878 with 1879, Sir Henry James proceeded to compare 1879 with 1880. He followed the order already given: and he said that the increments in the "ripe" counties were from 178 to 343; from 179 to 402; from 35 to 43; from 53 to 71. In other words, the four "ripe" counties produced 445 outrages in 1879, and 859 in 1880. Now for the "unripe" ones. Their crime list rose, in Kerry from 13 in 1879 to 298 in 1880; in Limerick, from 27 to 186; in Wexford, from 4 to 56; in Tipperary, from 28 to 106. In other words, the total for the four "unripe" counties rose from 72 in 1879 to 646 in 1880. Then came what Sir Henry James clearly regarded as a decisive argument, namely, that the vast bulk of the increase in crime in the unripe counties took place after September—that is, in the last three months of 1880. He had already dated the full activity of the League, and the rapid increase in crime, from the return of the Irish members to Ireland in September from their Parliamentary duties. For instance, said Sir Henry James, there were only eight crimes in Wexford during the first nine months of 1880, but in the next three there were 48—making the total of 56 for the whole year. Taking the whole four "unripe" counties, there were only 148 crimes in them during the first nine months of 1880, and 498 during the last three, making 646, the total for the year. But for the "ripe" counties in 1880, the proportions were 395 for the first nine months, and 464 for the last three, making the total of 859 for the whole year. What produced this crop of crime? Sir Henry asked. "It was not distress;" "and it was not eviction;" "the politicians were at work."

ONE HUNDRED AND TWENTY-FIRST DAY.

NOVEMBER 7.

ON the previous day Sir Henry James claimed to have shown that after the return of the Irish members in September, 1880, from Parliament, crime and League influence increased simultaneously. He now tried to illustrate this proposition by the history of the boycott—"a new procedure," which Mr. Parnell first advocated seriously on the 19th of September, 1880, but which Sir Henry James maintained, was advocated by Mr. Davitt in the beginning of the year. Mr. Davitt had at that date denounced as "traitors" to their country persons who took farms from which others had been evicted for non-payment of just rent. And in this speech of September 19, 1880, Mr. Parnell had called such persons "moral lepers," and said that to leave grabbers "severely alone" was "a more Christian and charitable way" than to "shoot" them. Mr. Sexton had said that boycotting, being at first a purely local growth, was subsequently recommended, under limitations, by the League chiefs.

But Sir Henry James had failed to discover any limitations. He found no "limitation" in Mr. Harris's partridge speech, nor in a speech of Mr. Dillon's in October, 1880, which meant, according to Sir Henry James, that the only limitation was the fear of detection. Mr. Parnell's speech was, as already said, delivered on the 19th of September. On the 22nd, Captain Boycott was subjected to the "new procedure," with one result—among others—that a new verb (or substantive) was added to the English vocabulary. I wish, said Sir Henry James, that I could accept Archbishop Walsh's definition of boycotting as "exclusive dealing." There were in the Irish movement persons more influential than the Archbishop. Mr. Biggar was more influential than his Grace. Sir Henry refused to take Mr. Biggar at Mr. Biggar's modest self-estimate; and Mr. Biggar had said that every kind of boycotting which stopped short of personal violence was allowable. Here Sir Henry James made the objection that Mr. Biggar's boycotting implied the effects of physical violence; and he enumerated, though not at great length, the dreary list of species of the boycott—refusing to sell provisions, refusing coffins, boycotting schools, &c.—with which readers of the Commission's proceedings were only too familiar months ago.

Mr. Parnell, he continued, had attributed to the Lords' rejection of the Compensation Bill the "wild-fire" like spread of crime at and from the last months of 1880; but Sir Henry James had failed to discover in the popular League speeches of the period more than nine instances in which the rejection was even referred to. If that was not the cause, what was it? Sir Henry James asked. He answered his own question by giving a summary of the utterances of the four Land League organizers, Messrs. Harris, Sheridan, Boyton, and O'Kelly, all of whom, with the exception of Boyton, were Fenians. "Well did they do their work of unsettling Ireland!" he exclaimed. Then he paused to deliver a eulogium upon Mr. Matt. Harris. He believed that Mr. Harris had been depreciated by Sir Charles Russell, as "not intellectually a strong man." But, after what had been heard from Mr. Harris in the witness-box, after "the beautiful composition" which Mr. Harris wrote in praise of his dead friend, "some of us," said Sir Henry James, must have thought that Mr. Matt. Harris "was a man of rare ability." Yet even a man of Mr. Harris's character—fine as it was in many respects—did not hesitate to speak of shooting landlords like partridges in September. Sir Henry James admitted that Mr. Harris had explained this speech of his; but Mr. Harris, in a subsequent speech, compared landlords to man-eating tigers—and that at a time when Boyton was denouncing "grabbers" as "double-dyed traitors," no less odious than informers.

Sir Henry maintained that the circular issued in December, 1880, by Mr. Parnell and the Land League leaders was in itself a proof that they were not honestly desirous that crime should cease. Writing threatening letters and mutilating cattle were the only crimes condemned in the circular. Yet, according to his own admission, said the learned counsel, Mr. Parnell had confessed that he was appalled when, late in 1880, he was made aware of the prevalence of crime in Ireland. "I wonder," said Sir Henry, "what the organizers inferred when they read this document?"

Still, Sir Henry James expressed his surprise at Mr. Parnell's ignorance, in 1880, of the state of things in Ireland. Mr. Parnell's colleagues were all about the country; how was it, Sir Henry asked, that the first intimation of the progress of crime was first made known to him by Mr. Davitt, who was all the while, not in Ireland, but in America? "I submit to you," said Sir Henry James, referring to the December circular—"I submit to you that a more wicked document, one more inciting to crime than this circular, could never have been drawn up by any one. Mr. Davitt says he drafted it, and I venture to think that it must have been drawn up by him in somewhat different language, and that it was settled by some one else. There are two descriptions of crime, one of which has never been found to be affected by Irish agitators, and the other of which has been condemned, and could not help being condemned, by every class, so far as I know, of those who belonged to the Fenian body. The first description of crime is that of threatening letters, which go to swell the records of crime, and frequently do not produce any effect. The second description of crime is one which a generous race must hold in abhorrence, and which alienated the sympathies of persons in England—that of maiming cattle. These two crimes are useless, and worse than useless, to those who desire that the movement in which they are engaged shall stand well in public opinion. This circular, so far as Mr. Parnell is concerned, is the only step he took to stop crime." Sir Henry quoted the circular, but it is too long for reproduction here.

Throughout a large portion of the day's instalment of his speech Sir Henry James was insisting that the leaders of the Land League must have known how crime was progressing. On the 28th of January, 1881, Mr. Gladstone virtually accused them in the House of Commons, for had he not said that "crime dogged the footsteps of the Land League" with "fatal precision"? Sir Henry seized hold of an expression of Mr. Davitt's. Mr. Davitt had said in the box that in all his denunciations of grabbing he had never "named" anybody: that he would be sorry if ever he had done anything of the kind. But "why should he be sorry," exclaimed Sir Henry James, if at that time the "naming" of persons was not an unsafe thing to do? Sir Henry James had present to his mind a state of public irritation, of readiness for outrage, which the Land Leaguers should have tried to allay.

It will have been seen that Mr. Harris is one of the two or three Nationalist witnesses who have produced the most favourable—or least unfavourable; which?—impression upon Sir Henry James's mind. Sir Henry James's eulogium of Mr. Harris has been referred to above. It will be remembered that Sir Charles Russell qualified his observations on Mr. Harris's comparative lack of intellectual strength by saying that in recent years, and owing to severe illness, Mr. Harris's faculties had been somewhat impaired, but that at one time he was a man of considerable, not to say remarkable, ability, considering his education and absence of facilities in life. Here, then, is a portion of Sir Henry James's estimate of Mr. Harris :—

That was the view Sir Charles Russell, upon the instructions of his clients, presented to you in relation to Mr. Matthew Harris. Well, of course, I know nothing of Mr. Matthew

Harris, or very little, except that view of my learned friend Sir C. Russell. But Mr. Matthew Harris came into the witness-box, and I cannot tell how far anything I am saying will meet with your lordships' sanction, but some of us who saw Mr. Matthew Harris, an old man now, struggling with a severe illness, standing in that witness-box, and—may I use the term?—bravely giving his evidence, when we heard him express his views as he did, when we read his writings, my lords, some of us thought that the views expressed by Sir Charles Russell never could have been the views of men who knew him well. I am sure Mr. Harris's friends would not object to my referring to the fact that his life has been a life without much opportunity of acquiring knowledge, and yet when we heard him express himself as he did, and when we read that beautiful composition, the speech which he intended to deliver over the grave of a dead Fenian, there were some of us who thought, at least, that he must have been a man of rare ability, and that he had been endowed with such a manner of thought and such a power of expression that the truest thinking man, and even the most polished scholar, might have regarded him as a man of singular faculties. He stood before us here and gave his evidence in a way that was calculated to evoke a sympathetic feeling; and it was with some such feeling that I have tried to find some excuse for Mr. Harris's utterances.

ONE HUNDRED AND TWENTY-SECOND DAY.

NOVEMBER 12.

SIR HENRY JAMES spent most of the day in combating Sir Charles Russell's proposition that Irish agrarian crime sprang from three causes—distress, secret association, and eviction. But in the first place he disposed of the remaining portion of his own argument that the Irish Fenians, the American United Brethren (or Clan-na-Gael), and the Skirmishers were correlated bodies of one and the same organization. O'Donovan Rossa's connection with the Skirmishing Fund came to an early end; but that, said Sir Henry, was because his fellow-Skirmishers objected to his lack of reticence. "So they got rid of him." "But the dynamite policy remained." That was all that Sir Henry James would concede to Mr. Davitt's outspoken and uncomplimentary description of O'Donovan Rossa as "a blatant ass" and "a cowardly ruffian." Though Rossa was the founder of the Skirmishing Fund (1876), Ford was, in Sir Henry James's estimation, the man most responsible for the "hideous policy" which it supported. It was Ford who, in December, 1883, founded the Emergency Fund for plaguing England "with all the plagues of Egypt," for "scourging her by day," and "terrorizing her by night." Patrick Ford, said Sir Henry James, asked for God's blessing on Mr. Davitt, on Mr. Parnell, on Archbishop Croke, and the rest, but declared that their efforts would be unavailing without force. Then Sir Henry drew a pathetic picture of dynamitards trembling in the dock while the man most responsible for their crimes was safe in New York. Sir Henry James was astonished at Mr. Davitt's description of Mr. Ford as a Christian and a philanthropist.

As proof, or illustration, of his position that the American U.B., and the Irish I.R.B., were practically identical, Sir Henry James cited the programme of the U.B., and mentioned that the fact of Mr. Davitt's being a Fenian Supreme Councillor was Mr. Davitt's passport to U.B. secret meetings. The U.B. amended programme of 1877 contained these heads—(1) Total separation of Ireland from Great Britain. (2) Establishment of an Irish Republic. (3) Unceasing preparation for an armed Irish insurrection. (4) Non-interference in parliamentary politics. Besides his inability to hold his tongue there was, according to Sir Henry James, another reason for cutting Rossa's connection with the Skirmishing Fund: O'Donovan Rossa would destroy all vessels under the British flag, even if there were Americans and American-Irish on board them. Once more, though Patrick Ford had no official connection with the

Skirmishing Fund [it was Augustine Ford who had] he subscribed fifty dollars to it, and expended three hundred more in circulars.

Having dealt last week with the first of Sir Charles Russell's explanations of Irish outrages—distress; Sir Henry James now came to the second—secret association. From secret societies he excluded the Fenian body, which, he held, was only an advanced wing of the revolutionary army. What was the meaning, he asked, of Mr. Davitt's intimation to Mr. Parnell, some nine years ago, that the commission of outrages in Ireland was alienating the Americans from the Land League? Why should that be so, if the outrages were the work of the League's enemies? Sir Henry James then declared that in all the speeches and resolutions of the Land Leaguers there was not a word attributing the commission of outrages to secret societies. The speeches, he even maintained, proceeded upon "an entirely different theory." Sir Henry James declined to regard as secret societies the sporadic gangs of young men who committed moonlighting outrages. But he considered that Mr. Dillon's appeals to the young men of Ireland might render them none the less dangerous. And then Sir Henry James turned to the evidence of one of Sir Charles Russell's own witnesses, namely, Father O'Donovan, of Tulla, in Clare, to show that these outrage-mongering young men were the "secret police" of the Land League. Father O'Donovan had taken the unique course of communicating with the police; and, according to Sir Henry James's reading of the priest's evidence, the priest required policemen to protect him against possibly his own parishioners. The gist of Sir Henry James's argument was this :—All the heads of families in the parish were leaguers; with these heads of families lived the sons—in the ordinary one or two-roomed cabins of rural Ireland; "the coming in and going out" (the priest's phrase) of these young men "would certainly be known" to their fathers, and "the moonlighters were mostly the sons" of those small farmers. Father O'Donovan, said Sir Henry James, did not blame secret societies; "but with the full knowledge of the district and his parishioners, he dissolved the League. He knew what was taking place, and it was this reverend gentleman who stands amongst his fellows as a bright example of bravery." Father O'Donovan was President of the Tulla branch of the Land League. Sir Henry James also quoted Mr. Matt. Harris's evidence in the witness-box, to the effect that there were no secret societies during the period under discussion.

Coming to Sir Charles Russell's third explanation of crime—evictions, Sir Henry James said that in the four years of distress from 1849 to 1852 there were 58,423 evictions and 4,245 agrarian crimes. In the four years from 1879 to 1882 there were 12,000 evictions and 9,000 agrarian crimes. How was it that it took about fourteen times as many evictions to produce one agrarian crime in the former period as in the latter?

Sir Henry James's statistics were detailed, but the above brief summary and question will explain the general drift of them. Sir Henry James next struck out a new line of argument, to the effect that the evictions of the Land League period were unlike those of preceding periods, inasmuch as they were the work, not merely of landlords, but of the Land League itself. Evictions, he said, were forced on the landlords as a means of starving them out. Evictions, coupled with prevention of re-letting, would have that effect. So would the stoppage of rent.

This brought him to the three no-rent manifestoes—Mr. Parnell's from Kilmainham; Mr. Egan's, of October, 1881; and *The Irish World's*. He laid particular stress upon Mr. Egan's, which directed that "the person" who paid rent "should be visited with the severest sentence of social ostracism," and that any person entering the Land Courts should be "cast out" "as a renegade to his country and to the cause of his fellow-men." Sir Henry James admitted that Mr. Parnell in the witness-box described Egan's manifesto as "a condemnable document;" and then he proceeded to quote *The Irish World's*, one sentence of which declared that "he who acts the traitor in the hour of Ireland's trial shall pay the penalty of his villainy."

ONE HUNDRED AND TWENTY-THIRD DAY.

NOVEMBER 13.

SIR HENRY JAMES began to-day by quoting the case of the informer Farragher in proof of his proposition that evictions were artificially brought about by the leaguers—that is forced upon the landlords, even when tenants were willing to pay. Informer Farragher had said that he was advised by Mr. Davitt and Mr. J. W. Walsh, the organizer, not to pay; that he had means of paying; but that he refused; and that he was evicted in consequence. Mr. Davitt himself had said, in the witness-box, "that he had no recollection of ever having exchanged a single word with the man Farragher"; and that, though he occasionally advised the farmers as a body "not to pay except under certain conditions," he had no recollection of ever having advised any single tenant to withhold payment. But now Sir Henry James accepted Mr. Davitt's "becoming caution," as he called it, as a reason for believing that informer. Farragher's story was correct.

Another illustration, as Sir Henry James regarded it, of this policy of non-payment, he found in a letter of Miss Parnell's to *The Freeman* of November, 1881, in which letter it was intimated that no help would be given to evicted tenants who intended to pay as soon as they could. All this, Sir Henry James argued, was corroborated by the testimony of Captain Slack, a *Times* witness, a sentence from whose evidence he quoted thus—"In those large cases where you will see evictions are wholesale I am decidedly of opinion that if it had not been for the National League and for the leaders and Members of Parliament who took the thing in hand, the evictions would not have taken place at all."

Sir Henry James next criticized the conduct of the League leaders, after Mr. Forster's notice of motion (January, 1881) for the suspension of the Habeas Corpus Act, and Mr. Gladstone's words about crime dogging the footsteps of the Land League. Accepting this declaration as a warning, Mr. Egan went off to Paris with the League books. Messrs. Harris, Sexton, T. D. Sullivan, Dillon, Kettle, Louden, Brennan, O'Kelly, Healy, and Biggar, followed; when, according to Sir Henry James, they would have been much better employed in keeping Ireland quiet. For, said he, this single year, 1881, was more fruitful of crime than even the four famine years put together (1849-1852). Even when they did speak, Sir Henry complained, they did not utter a single denunciation of crime during that year.

"But if they were silent for good, they were not silent for evil," upon which observation Sir Henry James proceeded at great length to examine the 1881 oratory of Mr. Harris and Mr. Dillon, and to show how close it was, in point of time, to the series of murders which followed its delivery. At a time when, according to his own account, it was extremely dangerous to "name" anybody, Mr. Harris was telling his hearers to keep away from "the wretch" Kennedy, though, as he said in the witness-box, Mr. Harris did not think he called Kennedy a "demon from hell"; and he was also using some ungallant language, as Sir Henry James called it, about Mrs. Blake, of Connemara. "She-devil" was the ungallant expression, quoted by Sir Henry James, who in his own use of language is a model of propriety. Sir Henry James scoffed at the notion that crime was produced by distress. Then he fell foul of his brother Q.C., Sir Charles Russell, for cutting down Shakespeare, and taking liberties with the bard's punctuation. In his opening address Sir Charles Russell quoted the first four lines of Romeo's little speech :—

> Famine is in thy cheeks,
> Need and oppression starveth in thine eyes,
> Contempt and beggary hangs upon thy back ;
> The world is not thy friend nor the world's law ;
> The world affords no law to make thee rich ;
> Then be not poor, but break it.

Sir Henry James, sticking up for Shakespeare and *The Times*, complained that the leader of the English Bar had put a full stop after " law," and forgotten to quote the last two lines. These last two lines, Sir Henry maintained, were precisely applicable to the leaguers and all their works: and Sir Charles Russell had missed the point of his own quotation.

We need not follow Sir Henry James's repetition of the threadbare, wretched history of Galway murders in 1881 ; except to say that he contended strongly for the truth of the informer Mannion's story about the peculiarly cold-blooded, savage crime, the murder of the Lydens, in April, 1881. The Land League, said Sir Henry James, was established in the Lydens' parish in November, 1880. In the first week of April, 1881, Mr. Harris delivered his violent speeches there : and on the 24th day of the month, Lyden the father was killed, and Lyden the son wounded so grievously that he died in a month. The fact that the local leaguers never held a meeting signified nothing to Sir Henry James. It was enough for him that there were in the branch, besides twelve committeemen, twenty collectors, or persons authorized to collect subscriptions, that all the leaguers round about paid their subscription, and that several of them used to assemble in the house of a widow Walsh, whose two young sons were punished for the Lyden murder, the one on the scaffold, the other by penal servitude for life. It will be remembered that Mr. Davitt, when in the witness-box, said that if Mrs. Walsh, knowing her son's innocence, preferred his death to a pardon as the reward of informing, Mrs. Walsh did a noble deed. What was this, Sir Henry James asked, but paying homage to assassins ? It was that kind of homage which led to the spread of crime. It was not necessary, he said, to attribute this or that crime to this or that speech or expression. It was the general encouragement to outrage which he denounced. This general encouragement, he said, amounted to " direct proof of a conspiracy among the persons who made violent speeches so to work up the people that crime should be committed."

The next question upon which Sir Henry James asked the Court to come to a conclusion favourable to the prosecution was the question of Mr. Parnell's alleged message through Le Caron to the Clan-na-Gael in America. Sir Henry James concentrated all his strength and ingenuity on the Le Caron episodes. He recapitulated the old story of the Lobby interview between Le Caron and Mr. Parnell, at which interview Mr. Parnell was reported to have said that he had ceased to believe in anything except force as a cure for Ireland's wrongs ; that he did not see why a successful revolution could not be got up in Ireland ; and that the Irish Fenians could be forced into line with the Parliamentary party by the Irish-Americans threatening to withhold supplies.

Sir Henry James maintained that Mr. Parnell's evidence on this question fell short of a denial. He then answered two arguments of Sir Charles Russell's. As for the argument that Le Caron never afterwards communicated with Mr. Parnell, he reminded their lordships that Le Caron had said that he had been requested to communicate with Egan. And as for the criticism that

Le Caron had never sought "to draw Mr. Parnell and Mr. Egan on," Sir Henry James pointed out that Le Caron only tried to detect crime, not to tempt others to commit it in order that he might expose them. Sir Henry James regarded Le Caron as a meritorious person, who only tried to undermine plotters against the safety of England.

ONE HUNDRED AND TWENTY-FOURTH DAY.

NOVEMBER 14.

ANOTHER witness has interrupted for a few minutes the steady flow of Sir Henry James's interpretation of Anglo-American-Irish history. He is the only witness who has appeared during the speech-making and concluding portion of the inquiry; and it seems certain he is the last, for it is not supposed the judges will call any witnesses on their own account. It has been a long journey from the first witness, Bernard O'Malley, to the last (as he most probably is), Mr. W. G. Simm, of the Old Broad Street centre of the National Bank. Mr. Simm was questioned, not by Sir Henry James, but by the Attorney-General, who has been seldom heard of late. Mr. Simm informed the Court that all the branches of the National Bank, of which there were eighty-six, sent in to the head office at Dublin, brief abstracts of all their accounts. He could not give any particulars just then about the accounts of the persons charged, but he promised to procure them. Exit Mr. Simm.

But Mr. Biggar was up on the instant, reminding the Court of the understanding that no accounts merely personal should be looked into, because, said Mr. Biggar, "if they were, by some legerdemain on the part of Soames——" But Mr. Biggar was not allowed to finish his sentence. Sir James Hannen quickly interrupted him. "No, no, Mr. Biggar; don't use that word. You must state your case without making offensive personal observations." Mr. Biggar then declared that accounts of a purely private character had been examined. Sir Richard Webster quietly observed that he had never heard of any such attempt. The President remarked that he thought that in that respect Mr. Biggar's side had been treated with great liberality. It was arranged that Mr. Biggar should be present with Mr. Soames while Mr. Cunynghame examined the accounts. And then Sir Henry James resumed the thread of his interesting historico-critical review of the leaguers and all their organizations, and all their newspapers, and all their works.

He began with the Parnellite Press. A "new weapon," he called it, with which the League, as soon as it had money enough, armed itself. It was a triple weapon—*The Irishman*, *United Ireland*, and *The Irish World*. To be precise, the League supplied itself with the first two; the third lent its aid, or, as Sir Henry James would say, it took the League captive. Poor, old, wretched Pigott. His name came up again, in connection with the sale of his miserable *Irishman*, in July, 1881. Sir Henry James's description of the position of *The Irishman* in the League organization was little more than a repetition of what the Attorney-General said long ago. Sir H. James ran off a string of specimens of its "abominable language"; but he was careful to remind their lordships, as also the journalists, that the adjective was not his, but Archbishop Walsh's. The particular abominations which Sir Henry James dwelt upon were *The Irishman's* commendatory references to the murderers Joe Brady and Dan Curley. He refused to accept Mr. Parnell's explanation that Pigott's *Irishman* was bought up in order that it might "die a natural death." The purchasers of *The Irishman*, said Sir Henry James, had announced that there would be no deviation from its old principles. He was equally severe upon *United Ireland*. Mr. O'Brien, the editor, had published in it letters in which the Phœnix Park murderers were described as "honest" though "stern patriots"; and yet, said Sir Henry James, Mr. O'Brien himself, when in the witness-box, admitted that the evidence against those accused of the murders was overwhelming. There were, Sir Henry admitted, moderately expressed articles in *United Ireland:* but there were also articles of an entirely opposite character. In other words, there were two sets of articles because there was a moderate wing and an extreme wing of the Nationalist army. Remembering that in his youth he had read a paper bearing the symbol of an open eye, Sir Henry James suggested that *United Ireland* might appropriately have adopted the symbol of two eyes, one shut, the other open—but winking. How could it do that on paper?

Having done with the newspapers, Sir Henry criticized the manner in which the land legislation of 1881 had been received by the Irish leaders. The policy of the Land Act was, said Sir Henry James, a reconciliation between landlord and tenant; but the purpose of the League was to destroy landlordism, and the new Act was used by the League leaders to bring about that very result. That was the second head of the day's discourse. Under the third head he criticized the manner in which, as he said, the leaguers impeded the administration of justice—and especially their systematic defence of prisoners. The League undertook, without making any preliminary inquiry, to defend all prisoners accused of agrarian outrage; and they did it in such a way, Sir Henry James insisted, as to encourage the tenants to commit crime. If, as he said, it was the case that secret societies committed the crimes, and if these societies were hostile to the Land League, why should the League have defended them? He also quoted Mr. Parnell's evidence, to the effect that in August, 1881, he found it the common practice to defend all prisoners accused of agrarian crime; and deeming such a practice objectionable, Mr. Parnell discouraged it, but, said Sir Henry James, he did not stop it. Not only did the leaguers refuse to assist the authorities in the detection of crime, but they even attempted to corrupt the police. Sir Henry James then quoted Mr. Harris, to illustrate the systematic refusal of information to the police:—

If you were to assist in the smallest degree in the detection of criminals connected with this agrarian crime, you would cease then and there to have the slightest public influence in Ireland. If Mr. Parnell himself were to give information against the humblest peasant in the county of Galway he would cease to be a leader of the Irish people to-morrow.

This led Sir Henry James to comment upon the disappearance of the Land League books and documents. Between the central office in Dublin and the branches throughout the country there was, Sir Henry James said, regular communication. In these communications their lordships would have found a complete record of the doings of the League. But, he continued, with the exception of one or two documents from Farragher and Phillips, four books were all that the accused produced in court. Sir Henry James could understand such a thing as the total destruction of the League books when certainty of suppression became manifest; but the books were not destroyed, they were only carried off. We know, he added, about the League's receipts, but what of its expenditure? Mr. Egan, as treasurer of the Land League, had received £248,000. Deducting the amounts spent on relief, and on State trials, and a sum of £27,000 stated to be balance in hand, there remained, said Sir Henry James, £153,000 unaccounted for.

ONE HUNDRED AND TWENTY-FIFTH DAY.

NOVEMBER 19.

SIR HENRY JAMES opened yesterday's instalment of his long speech with some criticism of the Land League accounts. As the details have so frequently been repeated, only the general result need be given here. Mr. Egan, as Land League treasurer, received, said Sir Henry James, £246,000 in all. Elsewhere it had been put at £248,000. Of this amount, a sum of £72,470 had been sent from Paris, by Mr. Egan, to the Ladies' Land League. But, he said, no account was given of the way in which the second sum had been expended. There was a balance remaining of £27,000. A comparatively small sum had been spent on relief. But as to what became of the vast bulk of nearly a quarter of a million, no explanation whatever was offered. Sir Henry having alluded to a sum of £2,000 spent for parliamentary purposes in 1880, the President called Sir Henry's attention to what Mr. Parnell had said regarding the suppression of the League's original rule against the employment of League money for political purposes. Mr. Davitt followed up the President's observation by saying that the rule had been rescinded. But Sir Henry James contended that no public record of its withdrawal existed, and that Mr. Parnell spoke only of his "impression," not his certainty that the rule had been rescinded.

The four books produced before the Commission were not, said Sir Henry James, the books wanted. They had never, he said, been out of Mr. Moloney's possession. Consequently, they could not have been among the books for the conveyance of which from Dublin to Liverpool and Liverpool to London, arrangements had been made by Mr. Campbell, M.P., Mr. Parnell's secretary in October, 1887. These books, mentioned in Mr. Campbell's letter, were "specially guarded." Why, Sir Henry James asked, has not Mr. Campbell been called? Upon this Mr. Davitt remarked that Mr. Campbell had attended the court for many days under subpœna by *The Times*. "No, no, no," quickly interrupted Sir James Hannen, "he ought to have been called by the respondents." Land League clerks, Sir Henry James added, have spoken of "sackfulls" of books that had been removed to Mrs. Moloney's house. But, he continued, a few of these Land League documents, kept by the Land League clerk, Phillips, accidentally came into the possession of *The Times:* and these documents, though most of them were comparatively unimportant, showed conclusively that League money had been spent by League officials for criminal purposes. Sir Henry James contended that these papers were a revelation of the character of the books and documents that were missing. He read some of them in order to prove that evictions were really forced upon tenants, not so much by the landlords as by the Land League.

As the documents in question were addressed by local branch secretaries, to the central office in Dublin, Sir Henry James made the central branch responsible for some at least of the actions advocated in them. The most interesting of these documents was, of course, the letter from Tim Horan, Secretary of the Castleisland branch of the Land League. Upon the Tim Horan letter, a familiar and favourite theme, Sir Henry James harangued vigorously for about half an hour. Here is the letter:—

"I beg to direct your attention to a matter of private character which I attempted to explain to you when I was in Dublin at the Convention. The fact is that one of the men from a shot lost the use of his eye. It cost him £4 to go to Cork. . . . No one knows the patients but the doctor and myself, and the members of that society. I may inform you that the said parties cannot afford to suffer. If it were a public affair a subscription list would be opened at once for them, as they proved to be heroes. One other man escaped a shot but got his jaw grazed. Hoping you will, at your discretion, see your way to making a grant, which you can send through me or the Rev. John Hallagan, C.C.

"Yours truly,
"TIMOTHY HORAN.'

In the letter the priest's name was mis-spelled. Mr. John Ferguson, of Glasgow, who signed the order for the payment of six pounds to the League branch secretary, Tim Horan, on account of the medical expenses of the two men wounded in a moonlighting (?) affair, had said in his evidence that he would gladly relieve any sufferer, even if the sufferer were a criminal. But, exclaimed Sir Henry James, loudly slapping his mountain of books, the money was paid after the two men had been treated medically; it was not a case of relieving suffering, for the suffering had passed away. It was a case of recouping certain other persons for their expenditure upon two men engaged in a criminal enterprise. The secret of the enterprise in which the wounded men had been engaged was, according to Sir Henry James, known only to Mr. Quinn, acting secretary of the Land League; Tim Horan (who had talked over the matter with Quinn), the doctor who attended the wounded men, Father O'Callaghan, of the Land League branch of which Horan was secretary. Mr. Quinn, said Sir Henry, has been in this court; "why has he not appeared in the witness-box? And why has not Father O'Callaghan come to explain the serious charges against his conduct in the Tim Horan affair?." The non-appearance of these and other witnesses was not, Sir Henry James said, to be accounted for by the withdrawal of Sir Charles Russell and his colleagues, for before that withdrawal it was announced what remaining witnesses were to be called by the respondents. Sir Henry James regarded the Horan-Quinn correspondence as a proof of informer O'Connor's and Inspector Davis's statement that there was an "inner circle" among the Land Leaguers—a "secret police," as the accusers have called them. All this while Sir Henry James had been dealing with the year 1881. In that year Ireland—according to his reading of history—had reached her lowest point of degradation. And this was Mr. Parnell's doing. The Ireland which he found in 1879 was different from the Ireland upon which, when he entered Kilmainham, he turned his back for a time. Mr. Parnell convert Fenianism into Constitutionalism, forsooth! Why, all that Mr. Parnell had done was to convert Fenianism into "Moonlighting!" Here Sir Henry James again banged his pile of books, and Mr. Davitt laughed.

Sir Henry James finished his description of 1881 with a rapid account of the Chicago Convention of that year, from which he dated what he regarded as the Clan-na-Gael's gradual acquisition of complete control over the American Land and National Leagues. Then he came to the year 1882 and the Phœnix Park murders, in his account of which he relied greatly upon the informer and convict Delaney, whose evidence he again corroborated in some parts by the evidence of another informer, Major Le Caron, *alias* Dr. Beach. He read acknowledged letters from Mr. Egan in Paris to "My dear James"—Carey the informer. Who were the Invincibles, he asked. Sheridan, Walsh, Brennan, Egan, Byrne, Mrs. Byrne, Tynan (Number One) were in the first rank; and in the second were Carey, Molloy, Brady, Mullett, Kelly, Dan Delaney, Curley, Fagan. Now, said Sir Henry James, Sheridan and Walsh were leaguers, Brennan was a secretary, and Egan treasurer of the Land League; and all the persons named, with only a single exception, had "either suffered at the hands of justice or fled from it. Not one of them has dared to put his foot in the country again." At this point Mr. Davitt rose to remark that no warrant of arrest had ever been issued, and no charge ever preferred against Messrs. Brennan and Egan.

ONE HUNDRED AND TWENTY-SIXTH DAY.

NOVEMBER 20.

HAVING on the previous day given his list of Invincibles, and placed Egan among the "first division" of them, Sir Henry James began to-day's instalment of his speech with a denial of the respondents' statement that Egan went away from Dublin for business reasons. He went, Sir Henry James repeated, to escape from justice, and in such haste that he left his wife dangerously ill at the time, with none to take care of her. Egan, he continued, must have been the man from whom came the money which Delaney swore he saw paid over in the presence of Byrne in August, 1882, to the men who three months before had perpetrated the Phœnix Park murders. Delaney had also sworn that it was arranged that Egan must be consulted before other murders were undertaken. These "Invincibles" were "needy" men; and there was only one man from whom they could have received their large sums of money, namely, Egan, who had power to spend as much as he pleased, and in any way he pleased.

Our case, said Sir Henry James, has been called "a thing of shreds and patches," but Sir Henry claimed that he was piecing them together; and he called Sir Charles's case a thing of "rents and tears." In Sir Henry James's view Egan's utterances in the United States were significant. At Chicago Egan had said that "a more sterling patriot" than Dan Curley (one of the Phœnix Park murderers) "had never died for Ireland." In March, 1883, Egan made a speech in which he said of Mullett that he had "known him personally as a man of sound business principles and integrity of character," and, Egan added, "I do not believe he has turned informer." Egan did not say, remarked Sir Henry James, "that he believed in Mullett's innocence." And why was it, he asked, that "the families of those who pleaded guilty" got nothing from the Martyrs' Relief Fund, but only the families of those who were condemned? Sir Henry James contended that the theory of the perpetration of the murders by American strangers was inconsistent with Egan's opposition to the proposal that the League should contribute five thousand pounds towards the detection of the criminals. Then he came to the story about Mr. Parnell's payment of a hundred pound cheque to Frank Byrne immediately before Byrne's departure for Paris. Of this story he remarked that the explanation of it given by Mr. McCarthy and others might have been given earlier.

Then Sir Henry James came to the question of the Pigott letters. He took the responsibility, he said, of refraining from discussing the course *The Times* took before it published the letters; and he refrained because that very question would be considered in the pending libel action which Mr. Parnell has brought against *The Times*. But one thing he would say, and that was that the stories about Mr. Buckle's disagreement with his colleagues on the subject of the letters were unfounded.

Sir Henry James now addressed himself to the next chief head of his address—the National League. The chief difference, in Sir Henry's estimation, between it and the Land League was that the boycotting methods of the National League were more perfect than those of its predecessor. He admitted that in 1883-1884 there was a great diminution of disturbance throughout Ireland; but he ascribed that partly to the effect of coercive legislation, and partly to the fact that the peasantry had learned how to use their political organization. In discussing the influence of the Catholic clergy under the National League, Sir Henry James was hard on the curates, who, being young men, were prone to agitation, while their elders, the parish priests, preferred a quiet life. To illustrate the position of the "R.C.C."—Roman

Catholic Curate—in modern Ireland, Sir Henry read the refrain of a poem by the Nationalist bard, Mr. T. D. Sullivan :—

> We all revere the great Arch B.,
> We much admire the deep D.D.,
> We know the worth of the good P.P.,
> But the man we love is the R.C.C.
>
> The kindly, friendly R.C.C.,
> The Church's bravest soldier he;
> The hope of Ireland, bond or free,
> The fearless patriot, R.C.C.

ONE HUNDRED AND TWENTY-SEVENTH DAY.

NOVEMBER 21.

WITH " the fearless patriot R.C.C." Sir Henry James began to-day's discourse. Sir Henry James believes that the new generation of R.C.C.'s are a Church Militant in the unfavourable sense. He spoke of the Rev. Mr. Rowan, who was strong on guncotton, and made a speech about " blowing up London into fragments no bigger than grains of sand; " and Sir Henry quoted the "three cheers" exclamation with which somebody in the crowd signified his approval of the warlike priest. This, said Sir Henry, might be regarded as merely foolish, stupid speech, but, he said, it was uttered about the beginning of the dynamite scares, and it would be accepted by the crowd as the serious teaching of their spiritual instructors.

Some specimens of priestly oratory, quoted by Sir Henry James, betrayed a defective sense of literary restraint. One reverend gentleman classified grabbers as he would classify dogs. There were mongrels among them—the grabbers—and "curs of low degree," but presently he passed on to another division of the animal kingdom, and he likened the grabber unto "a poisonous reptile that drives its fangs " into something or other—we forget what. And this sort of talk was going on, said Sir Henry James, eight or nine years ago, when Sheridan and Number One (Tynan), Boyton, and Brennan were in their own way stirring up the peasantry. Sir Henry James was severe upon two priests in particular—Father Egan and Father Considine. Father Egan, one of the Woodford men, was at first " C. C." in the neighbouring parish of Loughrea. " Crime followed the footsteps of Father Egan," said Sir Henry James. Loughrea was peaceful before Father Egan became its C. C. Murders broke out during his incumbency; and they ceased when he left. Father Considine's dismissal of all grabbers to " the cold, deep damnation of disgrace " about finished Sir Henry James's review of " the fearless patriot, R.C.C.'s " political oratory.

As to moonlighting, Sir Henry James said that the true nature of the practice had "in an unthoughtful moment " been disclosed by one of the clerical witnesses, Father O'Connor, who testified that " the new men " used moonlighting for robbery—" petty larceny " as Sir Henry James called it— whereas the original intention of moonlighting was to " intimidate grabbers." Sir Henry James maintained that even Mr. Davitt, in his denunciations of moonlighting, referred more to robbery than to the general system of intimidation—an interpretation of his words to which Mr. Davitt, addressing their lordships, briefly objected.

There came a time, said Sir Henry James, when crimes were denounced by the League. That was in February, 1886, when the Liberal Government came into power, and when, said Sir Henry, the Irish deemed it necessary to satisfy their Liberal friends' demands that no outrages must be committed. He quoted, in proof of this, a resolution of the central office in Dublin, issued on on the 5th of February, 1886. But, said Sir Henry James, your lordships will find no similar resolution in the years 1880–81. Sir Henry James next entered into a long statement about the great difficulties with which the Attorney-General had to contend in his conduct of the case. From first to last, said Sir Henry, obstacles had been placed against the efforts of the counsel for the prosecution to present their case as completely as possible. He referred to the conduct of Molloy and Coffey as an illustration of these difficulties. But he affirmed that, in spite of all these obstacles, the accusers had succeeded in getting at the truth, particularly through informers who had been in the secret work of the League. Excluding the most important informers, such as Le Caron, Delaney, and Mulqueeney, the prosecution had produced fourteen minor informers. The fourteen had named ninety-six persons; but of the ninety-six, said Sir Henry James, only four had been called by the respondents. Again, Sir Charles Russell promised to place all the sixty-five members of Parliament in the witness-box. But, said Sir Henry, "only thirty-three have been called; where are the others?" Here Sir James Hannen remarked that what Sir Charles Russell promised was that all the sixty-five would appear if his friend the Attorney-General or their lordships desired it.

ONE HUNDRED AND TWENTY-EIGHTH DAY.

NOVEMBER 22.

BOTH during the morning and afternoon sittings the court was crowded to its utmost capacity. People came to hear Sir Henry James's peroration; and evidently they expected it would be delivered before half-past one o'clock. Not so many would have come had it been known that Sir Henry James would speak till four o'clock.

In this last day's instalment of his speech there was nothing of any special interest. It was wholly occupied with that portion of the hundred and twenty-eight days' history for which the public have cared least, namely, the portion about the American Conventions. Major Le Caron, alias Dr. Beach, made the American case interesting, but nobody else has. However, the densely-packed assemblage sat patiently all day long, waiting for Sir Henry's peroration. Lord Randolph Churchill came in about half-past eleven o'clock, and sat down on the solicitors' bench beside Mr. Soames, whispering into his ear now and then, as if he wanted to be coached up. Mr. Walter, jun., also came in and sat down beside Mr. Davitt. The pair nodded and smiled at each other in a friendly way. Perhaps it was at the prospect of approaching release. Not for the first time have curious spectators in court been struck by the cheery affability towards each other of men who, especially since the beginning of 1886, have been abusing each other on platforms and in the Press. "No man is a fiend," said "Murty Hynes," in his hearty way, when he was in the witness box, and to see the combatants smiling at each other on the last day of their set-to, one might fancy they were beginning to agree with the bard. Even Le Caron looked happy as he craned his neck (being a short man) to see over the shoulders of the people in front of him.

Sir Henry James argued that from the time of the Washington Convention of 1882 the Clan-na-Gael grew in influence over the entire Irish-American movement until, in three or four years more, they "captured" it altogether. As an illustration of this, he quoted an expression from one of Mr. Davitt's American speeches of that period—"I neither condemn nor repudiate those who rely solely upon physical force for the redemption of Ireland." But Mr. Egan's arrival in America in 1883, and his subsequent activity in the physical force party, were, in Sir Henry James's estimation, of much greater significance even than Mr. Davitt's declarations. Sir Henry James pointed out that the ascendancy of the Clan-na-Gael influence in America was contemporaneous with the dynamite attempts on London Bridge and the Local Government Board Offices. Egan, said Sir Henry James, associated with men who, like Finerty, regretted that the dynamite attempts were unsuccessful. Discussing the Philadelphia Convention of 1883, he quoted the words of one of its leading members, that for any "means of retaliation to which the Irish in their despair might be driven, the cruelty of the English Government would alone be responsible." It was at the Philadelphia Convention, said Sir Henry James, that the "conservative" section of the American-Irish movement, having become numerically weak, merged itself in the more numerous and revolutionary party. And then the entire management fell into the hands of the Clan-na-Gael Committee of seven members, of whom Sullivan was the head. In the same year, the supreme control of the revolutionary body was vested in three persons, of whom Sullivan was the chief. This was the régime of "the triangle," in the revolutionary slang. The next Convention was that of Boston, 1884. At this Convention the Parliamentary Fund was started, with Alexander Sullivan as one of its originators, and a committee of Clan-na-Gael people to supervise it. According to Sir Henry James, this transaction completed the "capture" of the Irish League in America by the physical force men. From the Parliamentary fund established at the Boston Convention, £7,556 were, said Sir Henry James, paid to the Irish members in 1886, and £10,500 in the following year. It was with the source of the money, not with its payment, that Sir Henry James found fault.

Long before four o'clock, Sir Henry's listeners—we mean the laity—were tired of all this ancient history. It had been told months ago by Major Le Caron. It was almost enough to make Sir Henry's hearers groan when he went back to the dismal story of the Curtins and the Fitzmaurices. But they were waiting for the peroration. It came at last. Here are the concluding sentences :

My Lords,—Long as I have occupied your attention, and, badly as the thread of my tale has been told, I have now placed before you, in some sort of sequence, I hope, a history of the past ten years—a sad history to affect any people. It has been a history full of crime, springing from a hasty assumption of power. It is a period of shame, and sad shame, and it is a period that surely Irishmen—patriotic Irishmen—must now be and ever will be bitterly regretting. My Lords, Ireland has had dark and bitter days in her past. She has sent her strong men to fight upon the open field, and they have fought. Even her statesmen—her eloquent statesmen—have been silent in their sadness, in the days when, we are told, Grattan and Charlemont wept in their sorrow. But I know not that ever until now they had cause to be ashamed of the history of their country. It is said, "Happy is the country that has no history." and so it might be true of Ireland that such would be the case. This I know, if men doubt the application of that trite statement to Ireland, happy would it have been for this people, happy would it have been for those who acted and for those who suffered, if the events of the last ten years could be blotted out. No human hand can do so—the annihilation of events is impossible, and all that remains, my Lords, to do is that faithful record shall be made of those acts that have occurred. Such, my Lords, will be your duty. It may be, and probably will be, that all who have taken part in this inquiry, from your lordships to the humblest officer of this Court, will receive some condemnation, some attack, and some obloquy. But let that pass. The effect of the truth being told must be great, for then the people, stirred by an awakened conscience, will be aroused from the dreams of a long night, and, when awake, they will despise their dreams, and finding at length new modes of action of a higher character, and led by truer men, then it will be—and God grant it may be !—that blessings will be poured upon a happy and contented people.

It was thought that after the speeches, the Commissioners would, on their account, call some witnesses—especially with a view to eliciting further information about the League funds. But Sir James Hannen, addressing Counsel as soon as Sir Henry James sat down, intimated that, in the judgment of the Court, the "exceptional circumstances" that would have justified such a step had not arisen. And now, he added, I have to congratulate counsel who are still before us on the completion of their arduous task, and to thank them and those others to whom such thanks are due, for the untiring industry and conspicuous ability which they have placed at our service, and for the great assistance we have derived from their labours. Our labours, however, are not concluded. We must bear our burden yet a little longer. One hope supports us. Conscious throughout this great inquest that we have sought only the truth, we trust that we shall be guided to find it, and set it forth plainly in the sight of all men.

The judges then withdrew; Sir Henry James received the congratulations of his learned brethren, and of not a few among the unlearned crowd; and the Parnell Commission, as far as the public inquiry was concerned, was at an end.

NOTES.

I.

As stated in page 172, the news of Pigott's death reached London on Saturday, the 2nd of March, eight days after his last appearance in the witness-box. Having on Saturday morning, the 23rd of February, relieved his conscience by making a full confession before Mr. Labouchere and Mr. G. A. Sala, he rewarded himself with a visit to the Alhambra in the evening. With the price of some books which he sold at Messrs. Sotheby's, he started some time after 4 p.m. on Monday afternoon for the Continent; and he was rushing at express speed through France at the very time, Tuesday morning, the 26th of February, when Sir Charles Russell was waiting for him in court with a bag full of unpleasant proofs and illustrations of Pigott's past career as a forger and dealer in obscene photographs. On Thursday morning, the 28th of February, the English-speaking interpreter of the Hotel des Ambassadeurs, Madrid, accosted a passenger who had just alighted from the Paris express. This was Pigott. Pigott accompanied the interpreter to the hotel. Having breakfasted, he took the interpreter with him to visit the churches and museums. Judging from the meagre accounts of his two days in Madrid, he appears to have been easy enough in mind, but for one thing—the non-arrival of a reply to his telegraphic request, from Madrid, to Shannon for the money which "you promised." It was this telegram which put the detectives on his track. The accounts of his death vary slightly. But the facts appear to be, that at 5 o'clock on the afternoon of Friday, the 1st of March, the hotel interpreter informed Pigott that a police officer wanted to see him; that on learning from the police officer what he had come for, Pigott re-entered his room; that the report of a pistol-shot immediately followed; and that on rushing in, the interpreter and the police found that Pigott had shot himself through the brain.

II.

At the beginning of last September, the Irish Loyal and Patriotic Union replied to the "foul conspiracy" charge of Sir Charles Russell, by passing the following resolution at a meeting of its general council held in Dublin:—

That this council desires to convey to the subscribers and friends of the association the absolute assurance that no portion of the funds of the association have been applied directly or indirectly, by payment or loan, to or through the late Dr. Maguire, Mr. Houston, or any other person, or in any other way towards the purchase or procurement of the letters in controversy at the Special Commission known as the Pigott letters.

III.

On the 8th of this month, November last, Mr. Campbell-Bannerman made a public statement which adds to the surprise that the accusers should ever have ventured to put Pigott into the witness-box. He says that when he was Chief Secretary for Ireland, Pigott's bad character was a topic of " common gossip " in Dublin. Said Mr. Bannerman's private secretary one day—" Whatever you do, let me answer the letter (one of Pigott's) and upon no account answer in your own handwriting." Some further light upon Pigott's history, including his relations with influential politicians in London, may soon be afforded by the publication of certain papers of Pigott's which were secured some time since by a colleague of Mr. Parnell's.

INDEX.

[*T. W.* means *Times* witness : *P. W.* means Parnell witness.]

ADMISSIONS of *Times*' witnesses favourable to Parnellites—Constable Irwin reports Mr. O'Halloran's condemnation of outrages, 9 ; Captain O'Shea describes effect of Phœnix Park murders on Mr. Parnell, 12 ; Constable Irwin describes reckless despair produced by evictions, 12 ; Many League speeches enjoin patience, 13 ; Secret society men try to break up League meetings, 13 ; Constable Irwin has heard Mr. Davitt warn people against crime and denounce moonlighters, 14 ; Constable Bernard O'Malley describes landlords' indifference to their tenants' distress, 14 ; John Rafferty does not think the League is responsible for outrage upon him, 16 ; Mr. Ives, of *New York Herald*, on starving condition of people and indifference of landlords, 20 ; Mr. Ives' impression of Scrab, 20 ; Mr. Botterill's notions of his duties as a landlord, 23 ; Heagley's evidence, 23 ; Tom Connair "never said his was burnt because he paid his rent," 24 ; Mike Hoarty blesses instead of cursing League, 30 ; Sub-Inspector Murphy says constabulary subscribed to help tenants, 32 ; A blacksmith believes in the League, 34 ; Sullivan says, "The League took my part," 34 ; Farmer Conway declares League denounced outrage upon him, 34 ; Mrs. Leahy says all her neighbours sympathize with her, 37 ; Kerry farmer O'Connor declares he and his friends all members of League, 37 ; Dowling says moonlighters not leaguers, 37 ; Young Curtin asserts he had no reason to believe League had anything to do with his father's murder, 39 ; Mr. Leonard, Lord Kenmare's agent, relates eviction of the Duggans, 42 ; Issues a distress warrant against the Curtins, 42 ; Inspector Huggins admits outrages increase after the suppression of the League, 44 ; Mr. Teahan was boycotted from private jealousy, 45 ; District Inspector Davis says threatening letters often written by those who received them, 48 ; Head-Constable Gilhooly says League contained almost all respectable people, 49 ; Tom Galvin attributes outrage upon him to a family quarrel, 50 ; Brown's failure to give any information, 51 ; John Kennedy doesn't "blame the League," 52 ; Murphy admits he may have been a victim of private vengeance, 55 ; *Kerry Sentinel* denounces outrage on Macauliffe, 55 ; Eugene Sheehy does not blame League, 58 ; Mr. Hussey admits destroying his tenants' houses, but does not consider his unpopularity a result, 60 ; Mr. Hegarty's letter to Mr. Davitt, 61 ; Cornelius Regan says League denounced outrage upon him, 66 ; Character of boy-informer J. Walsh, 67 ; Jeremiah Buckley had never suggested the League was connected with outrage upon him, 68 ; Mike Burke's confused evidence, 71 ; Mr. Kelleher's evidence concerning Mr. Hussey's treatment of his tenants, 72 ; Pat Molloy's story of how he humbugged *The Times*, 74 ; District Inspector M'Ardle says outrages increased after League leaders were imprisoned, 75 ; League denounced murder of young Freeney and father declares he believes it had nothing to do with it, 76 ; Pressed by Sir J. Hannen, District Inspector Gambell admits that he does not *know* any moonlighters who are leaguers, 81 ; Mr. E. Smith, Lord Sligo's land-agent, admits that for years before League agents went about armed, 83 ; Informer Buckley admits no one in Kerry would believe his uncorroborated oath, 85 ;

Worth of Tom O'Connor's evidence, 90; Character of Iago, *Times* witness, 95; Pat Delaney, highway-robber and murderer, 97; Mr. John Barrett admits a tenant evicted by him died in a ditch, 103; Mr. O'Donnell, landlord, himself carries out the wife of one of his tenants having dragged her from her bed, 103; Mr. Studdert, agent to Mr. Vandeleur, admits distress of tenants and landlords' delay in granting relief, 106; No agrarian murders in Tipperary since establishment of League, 106; Rents reduced by Land Courts on Mr. Sandy's estate, 108; Informer Dennis Tobin knows nothing of League, 110; Captain Slack has to admit that no agrarian crime in Tipperary since the League, 112; Mr. Hanley and his battering-ram, 117; Beach (Le Caron) admits O'Donovan Rossa was "hounded out" of Chicago Convention, 133; Mr. Macdonald's reasons for trusting the letters were genuine, 144; Articles written "in the ordinary course of business," 145; Mr. Houston deliberately destroys "the clue to original sources," 146; Mr. Houston's story of the black bag, 147; Of the people downstairs, 148; Mr. Pigott's oath to the Clan-na-Gael, 151; Pigott's account of interview with Mr. Labouchere, Mr. Parnell, and Mr. Lewis, 153; Pigott's correspondence with Archbishop Walsh, 155; "It has flown out of my bosom," 155; Sir Charles Russell consults Pigott on best way of forging and on orthography of hesitancy, 159; Pigott's correspondence with Mr. Forster, 160; Pigott's confession, 166; Sheridan and Fitzpatrick admitted by Mr. Loftus to be enemies of League, 176; Informer Colman's ignorance of matters connected with League, 178; Colman's character, 179; Coffey denies all his evidence, 183; Character of Leavy, 187; Mulqueeny admits Mr. Parnell's cheque of £100 may have been for League and not to assist Mr. Byrne's escape, 189.

Barrett (one of men hanged for murder of Farmer Brown), 51, 52
Barrett, John, land agent, Cork (*Times* witness), 103
Barry, Dominic, Sub-Inspector of Police, Loughrea (*T. W.*), 16–19
Beach, Thomas Miller (called Le Caron); Evidence-in-chief, 120–129; Cross-examined by Sir C. Russell, Messrs. Reid, and Lockwood, 129–136; Evidence concerning Mr. Parnell, 123, 125, 127, 129, 134; W. M. Lomasny, 124, 127; Messrs. Sexton and Brennan, 128, 135; Dr. Gallagher, 128; Houston, 131; "I always voted on the side of the majority," 135; Sir Charles Russell upon Beach, 208, 209; Mr. Parnell denies Beach's story, 215, 217; Mr. Michael Davitt upon Beach, 277, 311, 313; Sir Henry James upon, 331, 340
Beattie, Constable (*T. W.*), evidence on Finlay's murder, 18
Bell, District Inspector, Loughrea (*T. W.*), 19, 20
Bermingham, man evicted from farm taken first by Murty Hynes, then by Dempsey, 16
Bermingham, James, process-server and tenant of evicted farm, boycotted for six years (*T. W.*), 33
Biggar, M. P., Attorney-General upon, 4, 8; Mr. Biggar and Mrs. Blake of Connemara, 26; and Mr. Hussey, 58; and Mr. Hegarty, 62; Mr. Biggar's speech, 307; Mr. Biggar and his accounts, 341; Sir Henry James upon, 334
Blake, Mrs., of Connemara, landowner (*T. W.*), 25; Cross-examined by Mr. Biggar, 26; Father O'Connell upon, 230; Mr. Matt. Harris, 300; Father Finneran upon, 243; Sir H. James quotes an ungallant observation of Matt. Harris, 339
Blake, Mrs., widow of J. H. Blake, Lord Clanricarde's agent (*T. W.*), 27; Father Egan, priest of Dunivy, on murder, 237
Bodkin, Father, priest of Mullagh (*P. W.*), 242
Botterill, Galway landlord (*T. W.*), 23, 234
Bourke, Constable, murdered near Craughwell, Galway, 1882, 21; Father Considine and Stephen Tarpey deny police evidence that people trod in the blood of murdered constables, 232
Burke, Charles, farmer of Kiltimagh, denies T. Walsh's evidence, 274
Boycott, Captain (*T. W.*), 80
Boycotting, Archbishop Walsh's view of, 230; Dr. McCormack's Bishop of Galway, 233; Mr. Roche of Woodford, 240; Mr. W. O'Brien, 246; Rev. Mr. Anderson, 256; Mr. Arthur O'Connor, 259; Mr. Justin M'Carthy, 259; Mr. E. Harrington, 262; Father Godley, 263; Father Lawler, 264; Mr. Sexton, 271; Mr. Thomas Mayne, 287; Sir H. James gives history of Boycott, 335
Boyton, 48, 205, 225; Delaney's evidence that Boyton showed Brady Mr. Burke, 100
Brown, of Castleisland (*T. W.*), 50

Index. 353

Brown, *Mrs. Johanna* (*T. W.*), widow of man for whose murder Poff and Barrett were hanged, 51
Brady, *Joe*, hanged for murder of Mr. Burke in Phœnix Park ; Delaney's evidence concerning, 8, 99
Buckley, *James*, Informer, Kerry (*T. W.*), admits attempts to murder Sheehy and Roche, 83-86 ; Mike Roche's account of Buckley's attempt, 117 ; Mr. H. O'Connor describes Buckley as worst character in Kerry, 268
Buckley, *Jeremiah* (*T. W.*), peasant : ear cut off by moonlighters, 68
Burke, of Woodford (*T. W.*), boycotted ; accuses Father Egan and Mr. John Roche of boycott, 21
Burke, *Mike*, Informer (*T. W.*), evidence on murder of Lord Mountmorres, 70-72
Byrne, M.P. for Wicklow, 287
Byrne, *Mr. Frank*, Le Caron's evidence concerning, 125 ; Mulqueeny's evidence, 188, 189 ; Sir C. Russell, 205 ; Mr. T. Harrington, 275 ; Delaney says an Invincible, 98 ; Mrs. F. Byrne and Phœnix Park knives — Delaney's account of Byrne's presence at murder councils, 99

Cahill, R. I. C. (*T. W.*), examined, 63
Canavan, Relieving-officer, Tuam (*P. W.*), 235
Carey, *T.*, Informer, 5
Casey, *Dick*, see Buckley's evidence, 53
Cawley (*P. W.*), evidence, 233
Charleton, Police-officer (*T. W.*), 21
Clancy (*P. W.*), denies evidence of Connell, 254
Clancy, M.P., examined by Sir H. James
Clanricarde, *Lord*, murder of his agent, Mr. Blake, 27 ; Chief Baron Palles quoted by Sir C. Russell, 204 ; Mr. Reid produces Sir M. Hicks-Beach ; Correspondence with, 240 ; Father Egan on state of tenants, 237
Clare, County, 3, 5
Coffey, *Timothy*, of Limerick (*T. W.*), entirely denies his evidence taken by Mr. Shannon, 180-183; President commits him for contempt, 184
Colman, American informer and spy (*T. W.*), joined I. R. B. 1886, and gave information of proposed outrages to police, 177, 178; Mr. Davitt cross-examines Colman as to his character, 179
Commins, *Dr.*, Member for South Roscommon, examined, 275
Conners, *James*, murder of, 17 ; story contradicted, 242
Condon, *Thomas*, Member for East Tipperary, a prisoner under Coercion Act ; Denies story that he boycotted Mitchell,

293 ; Mitchell's story about Condon, 138
Conolly, Mayor of Sligo, testifies to beneficial influence of the Land League, 291
Connair, *Tom* (*T. W.*), Galway peasant, 24
Connell, *Dan*, man who stated League paid him £10 for moonlighting, 63
Connell, *James*, man boycotted and intimidated, 254
Connell, *Hannah*, boycotted by her own account, 91 ; Story contradicted by Father White, 241
Considine, *Father*, Mr. Hughes' evidence about the Father and the gift of £15, 26 ; Father Considine on Hughes' episode, 231; the Father's strong speeches, 231 ; His views on boycotting, 232 ; He denies police story of people treading in Constable Bourke's blood (*see* p. 21), 232
Conway, farmer, Kerry (*T. W.*), shot at by moonlighters, 34
Coursey, of Loughrea (*T. W.*), evidence about Finlay's murder, 18
Coyle, Mayor of Kilkenny (*P. W.*), on League, 291
Crane, District Inspector, Kerry (*T. W.*), on Land League, 55, 56
Crawford, Mrs. *Emily*, *Daily News* Paris correspondent, on Egan, 314
Creagh, Constable (*T. W.*), arrests moonlighter with League ticket, 30
Crilly, *Mr. Daniel*, of *The Nation* newspaper, states he has constantly denounced crime, 291
Culloty, *John* (*T. W.*), farmer from Castleisland ; Process - server ; Leg broken ; Cannot obtain coffin for child, 36
Curtin, murdered in 1885 ; Miss Curtin's evidence, 38, 39 ; Son's evidence, 39 ; Constable Meehan attempts to implicate leaguers in murder, 39 ; Distress warrant against Curtins by Lord Kenmare, 42 ; Mr. Davitt's sympathy with Curtins, 49 ; Sir Charles Russell up'on, 204 ; Father O'Connor and the Curtins, 267 ; Mr. John O'Connor visits them, 288

Davis, District Inspector (*T. W.*), examined by Sir H. James on Land League and "inner circle"; Murder of Mr. Herbert, terror of people, 45, 46 ; Cross-examined by Messrs. Reid and Asquith, 47, 48 ; by Mr. Davitt, 49
Davis, *Eugene*, Houston upon Lausanne communication to Pigott, 149, 150 ; Pigott's account, 151 ; Pigott's last story, 167

24

Davitt, Michael, 2, 6, 8, 11; Cross-examines Constable Irwin, 14; Informer Flanagan, 29; District Inspector Davis, 49; Pat Molloy, 74; Policeman Feeley's mistake, 81; Cross-examines Pat Delaney, 101; Mr. Studdert, 106; Sir H. James's and Mr. Davitt's extracts from *New York World*, 139; Sir Charles Russell and, 196; Pigott confesses forging Mr. Davitt's writing, 200; Mr. Davitt and Curtin family, 204, 205; Mr. Davitt's reply to Philadelphian Convention, 1883, 209; "Dynamiters don't represent us," 210; Examined by Sir Charles Russell, 276–278; Cross-examination by Attorney-General, 278–284; Early experiences, 276; On Mr. Parnell and Phœnix Park murders, 277; Mr. Davitt's letters, 278; On Egan, 278; On "Scrab," 281; On Ladies' Land League, 281; Young Walsh, 283; on Finerty and Patrick Ford, 283; No connection with Phœnix Park murders, 284; Mr. Davitt's examination of Mr. J. Lowden, 285, 286; Mr. Davitt and the dynamite "hoax," 291; Mr. Davitt's speech, 307-322; Land League "offspring of thoughts that lightened the burden of penal servitude," 308; only the "crime inevitably associated with popular movements against injustice," 308; On Delaney's evidence, 309; Forrester letter, 309; "Nothing is more foreign to my nature than the idea of assassination," 309; Causes of Irish-American animosity, evictions and miseries remembered by emigrants, "America lost through Irish emigrants," 310; General Sheridan, 310; O'Donovan Rossa, thirty years ago a genial, kindhearted young man, 310; Source of Land League funds, 310; Beach and Houston, 311–313; Ford's enmity to Mr. Parnell, 311; Devoy's proposals disapproved by Mr. Parnell and Mr. Davitt, 313; He rejects with scorn *Times'* statement that dynamiters controlled open movement, 312; "It has come to my knowledge through Pigott's servant," 312; Mr. Davitt on Egan's horror at Phœnix Park murder, 313; on "Parnellism and Crime," "that liar's and forger's catechism," 314; *Times* blunder between Mr. Patrick Egan and Mr. P. B. Egan, 315; Because Clan-na-Gael members may have joined League, it is not responsible for Clan-na-Gael, 315; Clan-na-Gael a revolutionary club but not a murder club, 316; Tenants' League origin of Land League, 316; Mr. Davitt's childish memory of eviction and famine, 317; no grosser injustice than *Times'* suppression of conciliatory speeches invariably made at League meetings, 319; Hundreds and thousands of speeches denouncing crime, 319; Mr. Davitt and Ladies' Land League, 319; Farragher, Delaney, Pigott, "three exquisite scoundrels," 320; Delaney's letter — Mr. Davitt interrupted by Attorney-General, 321; Names shall be made public before long, 321; Apology of *Times* "characteristically mean," 322; Conclusion of speech, Sir J. Hannen's graceful compliment, 323; Sir H. James upon, 324, 325, 326, 327, 331, 332, 338, 339

Delahunt, Mrs. (*Miss Reynolds*) (*P. W.*), "whose career will be traced through the country by the deeds which followed her agitation; Attorney - General's speech; Sir Charles Russell upon, 201; Mrs. Delahunt's encounter with Attorney-General, 301

Delaney, Patrick (*T. W.*), Informer, Phœnix Park criminal, undergoing life-sentence at Maryborough Prison; Queen's County; Examination-in-chief, 97–99; Cross-examined by Sir Charles Russell, 99, 100; By Mr. Davitt, 101; Re-examined by Attorney-General, 101, 102; Pat Delaney's early days—five years for highway robbery, 97; he joins Fenians, 1876, and names Patrick Egan amongst Fenian leaders, 97; Delaney says Fenian circles invited to first Land League meeting held in Rotunda, Dublin, 1879, 98; After meeting Fenians ordered not to oppose League, 98; Mr. Matt. Harris, Fenian centre for Galway, 98; Invincible sworn to assist the cause of assassination; Pat Egan, Brennan, Sheridan, Frank Byrne, Pat Molloy, according to Delaney, Invincibles; Mrs. Frank Byrne and Phœnix Park knives; Tynan, No. 1; Delaney told off to murder Mr. Forster, 98; Invincibles got money through Land League, 98; Account of Phœnix Park murder, 99; Delaney recognizes Egan's signature; Mr. Davitt on, 309

Dempsey, Mrs. (*T. W.*), widow of man murdered by moonlighters for taking Bermingham's farm after Murty Hynes, 16; Evidence of Patrick Hughes that torches were lighted on night of Dempsey's funeral, 16; Father John Hanneffy, of Riverside, Galway, denies that torches were lighted or widow boycotted, 242

Devoy, John, Beach's evidence, 121,

Index.

123; Delaney, 98; Sir Henry James upon, 325, 327, 328
Devereux, Mayor of Waterford (*P. W.*), 291
Dillon, John, 32
Dowling (*T. W.*), Kerry man, shot at by moonlighters; Dowling says leaguers not moonlighters, 37

Egan, Father, parish priest of Dunivy, near Loughrea, president of Loughrea branch of Land League; Mr. Burke of Woodford and Father Egan, 21; On murder of Lord Clanricarde's agent Blake (*see* Mrs. Blake's account, 27), 237; On story of Finlay's murder as told by Coursey, &c., 18; Father Egan explains that he thought police inquiries about a coffin a trap, he was in favour of a passive resistance of Lord Clanricarde's tenants to eviction, 238; Sir H. James upon Father Egan, 348
Egan, Patrick, secretary of Land League; Alleged letter to Carey, 5; Delaney says an Invincible, 98; Le Caron's evidence, Egan, treasurer of Land League in Paris, 122; Egan tells Le Caron Fenians had helped the Boers, 122; At Philadelphia Convention, 125; Le Caron's account of Egan's confidences about his escape after Carey's disclosures, 127, 128; Mr. Soames and Egan's letters, 141; Pigott's account of Eugene Davis and Egan, 150; Pigott's attempt in 1881 to blackmail Egan, 157; Sir Charles Russell upon, 208; Mr. Parnell, 226; Dr. Kenny on Egan and League books, 268; Mr. Davitt on, 278; Informer Farragher on, 106-139; Mr. Foley, M.P., and, 292; Sir Charles Russell on, 206; Mr. Davitt's account of effect made on him by Phœnix Park murders, 312, 313; Account by *Daily News* correspondent of his reception of news, 314; Sir Henry James upon, 332, 345

Farragher, Informer (*T. W.*), from Mayo, accuses Mr. Davitt of bribing him not to pay rent, 106; On Egan, 106, 107; Cross-examined by Sir C. Russell, 108; On *Irish World* and Egan, 139; Farragher's character by Dr. Kenny, 268; Sir H. James on, 339
Farrell, Constable (*T. W.*), evidence on Lord Mountmorres, 117
Feeley, Police-sergeant from Sligo (*T. W.*), on Mr. Davitt, 82
Feenicks, *see* Informer Buckley's evidence, 83

Ferguson, of Glasgow (*P. W.*), Land League secretary, 255
Finerty, Irish-American, 246; Mr. Davitt on, 283
Finlay, process-server, murdered March, 1886; Mrs. Finlay's evidence, 18; Constable's evidence, 18; Father Egan upon, 237, 238; Mr. Keary on, 240
Fitzgerald, mother and daughter (*T. W.*), because they worked for Hegarty hurt by moonlighters, 62
Fitzmaurice, man murdered in Kerry by moonlighters; Evidence of Norah Fitzmaurice (*T. W.*), 39; Sir Charles Russell upon, 204
Fitzpatrick, Martin, 275
Flaherty, Peter, Informer (*T. W.*), 29
Flanagan, American Informer (*T. W.*), 29, 30
Flood, chairman of Longford Town Commissioners (*P. W.*), 292
Foley, M.P. (*P. W.*), on Mr. Egan's cheque, 292
Ford, Patrick, of *Irish World*, Attorney-General upon, 6; Mr. Parnell and, 226; Mr. Davitt and, 297; Sir H. James on, 338
Ford (*T. W.*), and moonlighters, 21
Forrester, Mr. Davitt's letter to, 278
Forster, Mr., and Pigott, 160, 161
Freely (*T. W.*), son killed by moonlighters, 75

Gallagher, man threatened in Mayo by moonlighters. Ann Gallagher's (*T. W.*) evidence, 75
Gallagher, Dr., (*see* Le Caron's evidence), 128
Gallagher, Poor Law Guardian of Strahane (*P. W.*), 291
Galvin, Tom (*T. W.*), 50
Gambell, District Inspector of Tralee (*T. W.*), 81
Gilhooly, Sergeant (*T. W.*), evidence on League, 45
Godley, Father, parish priest in Kerry (*P. W.*), 263
Greany, John, Kerry (*P. W.*), 264

Hannen, Sir James, President, and Patrick Molloy, 69; Protests against unnecessary evidence, 79, 221, 243; And Mr. O'Brien, 96, 247; Osman Digna not "very relevant," 115; And Sir C. Russell, 170; About *Irish World*, 179; Commits Coffey, 184; On forged letters, 190; Message to Sir C. Russell, 213; On League documents, 228; The President and Mr. Harrington, 262, 272; And Mr. Sexton, 291; Mr. John O'Connor, 288,

289, 290; Compliments Mr. Davitt at close of his speech, 323; Speech at close of proceedings, 349

Hanneffy, Father (*P. W.*), priest of Riverside, contradicts story of Dempsey's murder (*see* p. 16), 242

Hanley, landlord (*T. W.*), from Tipperary, "Battering-ram on premises," 116

Hammond, Mr. John (*P. W.*), 292

Harris, Matt., Attorney-General on, 3, 4; "Partridge" speech, 3, 115; Delaney on, 98; Letters read, 102; Sir Charles Russell on, 209; Mr. Matt. Harris criticizes Mr. Davitt, 299; Cross-examined by Sir Henry James, 300; Sir Henry James upon Mr. Matt. Harris, 326, 336, 337

Heagley (*T. W.*), evidence favourable to Land League, 23

Healy, M., 8; Le Caron's evidence about, 124; Examined, 257

Heanne (*T. W.*), gives evidence concerning Lyden's murder and meeting at Mrs. Walsh's, 138

Hegarty, Jeremiah (*T. W.*), from Cork, man boycotted for seven years, 61, 66

Herbert (*T. W.*), Kerry, process-server, says he has been shot at; Mr. Harrington's account of incident, 262

Herbert, Mr., land agent, near Castleisland, Kerry, March 30, 1882; District Inspector Davis's evidence, 46; Mr. Reid quotes Mr. O'Riordan's speech, 48

Herds' League, *see* Mr. Lowden's evidence concerning Secret Murder Society at enmity with Land League), 286

Hickey, farmer; Murder denounced by *Kerry Sentinel*, 37

Hoarty, Mike (*T. W.*); Evidence favourable to Land League, 30

Hobbins, Constable (*T. W.*); Evidence concerning Dr. Tanner, 66

Hogg, Mr. John Matner, member of committee of I. L. P. U.; Houston borrows from Mr. Hogg, 294

Horan, Tim, secretary of Castleisland branch of Land League; District Inspector Huggins's evidence about, 43; District Inspector Davis's evidence as to letter of September 30, 1881, from T. Horan, 46; Horan's letter to Mr. Herbert, 47; Horan convicted of keeping firearms, 48; Informer O'Connor's evidence against Horan, 65; Mr. Parnell explains payment claimed by Tim Horan, 217; Mr. J. Ferguson upon, 255; Mr. O'Connor upon, 259; Dr. Kenny upon, 268; Sir H. James on, 343

Horan, Pat (*T. W.*), young witness, 50

Houston (*T. W.*), Secretary of the Irish Loyal and Patriotic Union; Mr. Soames relates payments £1,042 to, 140; Mr. Soames' transactions with Houston, 141; Mr. Macdonald and Houston, 143, 144; Houston's examination by Attorney-General, 145, 146; Cross-examined by Sir C. Russell, Houston admits he deliberately destroyed all clue to original sources of letters, 146; Houston's story of the black bag, 147; the men downstairs, 148; Houston consults Lord Hartington and makes an offer to Mr. Stead, 149; Houston's faith in Pigott a little shaken, 149; Davis-Pigott letter, 149, 150; Mr. Pigott's evidence relating to Houston, 151, 152, 154, 157; behind Houston and Pigott there is a foul conspiracy, 162-169; Pigott's indignation at Houston's breach of faith, 168; Mr. Houston is not allowed to make a statement, 169; Mr. Soames cross-examined by Sir C. Russell upon his dealings with Houston, 171; Mr. Houston professes himself ready for cross-examination, and is honoured by the President with an expression of approbation, 171; Sir Charles Russell's criticism upon, 211; Mr. Hogg, of I. L. P. U., examined by Sir C. Russell, states that he lent Houston money without knowing his object, 294; Mr. Houston and "Parnellism and Crime," 295; Houston and Dr. Macguire, 295; Union books and Houston, 296

Huggins, District-Inspector (*T. W.*), evidence of outrages, 43

Hughes, Patrick, Constable (*T. W.*), evidence about Dempsey outrage, 16; Story contradicted, 23

Hussey, Kerry landlord (*T. W.*), peaceful condition of Kerry by Mr. Hussey's account before League, 58, 59; Mr. Hussey does not think that he became unpopular through demolishing his tenants' houses, 60; Mr. Kelleher's account of Mr. Hussey, 72; Mr. Hussey's treatment of Costelloe, 204

Hynes, Murty, man who took farm from which Bermingham was evicted, but left it in obedience to League, 16

Informers—James Mannion, ex-Fenian, gives evidence about Lyden murder planned at Mrs. Walsh's, 29; Peter Flaherty, ex-Moonlighter, 30; Flanergan, American, 31; Thomas O'Connor, 65; boy-informer Walsh, 67; Mike Burke of Ballyrouen, 69; Buckley James, 84; Iago of Longford, 95; Pat

Delaney, 100 ; Farragher, 105 ; Tobin, 108 ; Colman, 176 ; Leahy, 187
Inglis, expert in handwriting, 141
Irwin, *Constable* (*T. W.*), evidence to League speeches, 12, 13; Cross-examined by Michael Davitt, 14
Irish World, Attorney-General's extracts from, 171-173 ; Mr. Parnell and, 217, 218 ; Attorney-General cross-examines Mr. Parnell concerning, 219, 220
Irishman, Mr. W. O'Brien upon, 245
Ives, of *New York Herald*, 15-20

James, Sir Henry, speech, from 323 to 348 ; Contradicts Sir C. Russell that *Times* has shown itself consistently hostile to Irish, 323 ; Causes of Irish misery removed before 1879, therefore distress did not cause disturbances, 324 ; Mr. Davitt a prisoner during changes in Ireland, remained unconscious of improvements, 324 ; Fenian organization joined by Mr. Davitt, after his release, still party of violence, 325 ; Cablegram to Parnell from trustees of Skirmishing Fund result of Davitt's intercourse with revolutionists, 325 ; Devoy took physical force wing ; Davitt appealed to agrarian selfishness—Davitt's open agitation an ingredient in a treasonable conspiracy, 326 ; Mr. Matt. Harris, 326 ; Mr. Davitt, man of strong will, forced his will upon Mr. Parnell, parliamentarian, 327 ; Devoy sends Davitt £480 from Skirmishing Fund, 327 ; Land League not an organization for relief of tenants, but a means for end of national independence, 327 ; Devoy, of Clan-na-Gael, revolutionist, goes about Ireland at same time as Davitt, 328 ; quotes Alexander Sullivan's remark—first plank "self-government," second, "peasant proprietorship"; Land League took advantage of distress, 329 ; Mr. Parnell sent relief money from America to engage sympathies of a class, 329 ; Mr. Parnell's American tour arranged by revolutionists, 329 ; Apology for Le Caron, 331 ; Results of Mr. Parnell's tour, League funds, *Irish World* alliance, and foundation of American branch of League, 331 ; Literal meaning of "bread and lead" donations (see 221), 331 ; Mr. Davitt's speech at Kansas against landlordism, 331 ; Davitt, Egan, and Brennan know that peasants have been given arms, 332 ; Land League money spent on electioneering purposes a proof of Egan's power to rule matters as he chose, 332 ; League under Egan's control whilst Davitt in America, 1880, a time of violent speeches and outrages, 332 ; Cork branch condemning a raid for arms is condemned by central body for meddling with matters outside its sphere, 333 ; Land League activity and not distress produced crime, 333 ; Ferrick's murder near Ballinrobe occasion for inflammatory speeches, 333 ; Mr. Parnell's condemnation only that shooting was entirely unnecessary and prejudicial where there was a suitable organization amongst tenants, 334 ; Murders of Lord Mountmorres and Downey, and Mr. Biggar's objection to "shots that missed their mark," 334 ; History of Boycott told by Sir H. James, 335 ; Sir H. James on Mr. Matt. Harris, 335, 336, 337 ; O'Donovan Rossa's want of reticence not his crimes cause of his expulsion from Skirmishing Fund, 337 ; Ford (Patrick) real author of dynamite outrages—on secret societies and Father O'Donovan's action in dissolving his branch of League, 338 ; on informer Farragher and Mr. Davitt, 339 ; Mr. Matt. Harris and Kennedy, also on Mrs. Blake of Connemara, 339 ; blames Sir Charles Russell for curtailing his quotation from Shakespeare, 340 ; on Lyden murder, and Mrs. Walsh's preference of death for her sons rather than that they should become informers ; homage to crime, 340 ; Sir H. James supports Le Caron's account of Mr. Parnell's message to Clan-na-Gael, 340 ; on *Irishman* and its abominable language, 341 ; *United Ireland*, 342 ; by undertaking to defend prisoners accused of agrarian outrage League encouraged tenants to commit crime, 342 ; on League books and funds, £153,000 unaccounted for, 342 ; "Where were the books showing payments?" Tim Horan's letter again, 343 ; "Mr. Parnell convert Fenianism into Constitutionalism ? All he had done was to convert Fenianism into moonlighting," 344 ; Egan paymaster to Invincibles, 345 ; alludes slightly to Pigott's letters, 345 ; "The fearless patriot R.C.C.," Fathers Egan and Considine especially, 346 ; Sir H. James's peroration, 348
Jennings (*P. W.*), Secretary of Land League, Clonbur, 235
Joyce, *Mike* (*T. W.*), boycotted for taking a farm after tenant's eviction, 24

Keagh, *Pat* (*P. W.*), evidence, 242
Keary, *Mr.*, Woodford merchant ; Denies

Index.

story of Finlay's mock funeral, and explains declining to provide coffin, 242 (see story as told by constables, 18)

Kelleher, Cornelius (T. II.), whistled at because he works for Hegarty, 62

Kelly, Father, "Get the hot water ready," 274

Kenmare, Lord, evidence of Mr. Lennard, his agent, 40

Kennedy, Mike, America, hands Mr. Parnell "five dollars for bread, twenty for lead," 221

Kennedy, Pat (T. W.), 27

Kennedy, Mr. John, Town Councillor of Loughrea (P. W.); States murder of Sergeant Linton not an agrarian crime, 234

Kennedy, Father (T. W.), 32

Kennedy, John (T. W.), Kerry farmer, 52, 53

Kelly, Father, priest of Moygarna "Get the hot water ready," 274

Kenny, Dr., President of Castleisland; branch of Land League fined for keeping firearms, 48; Sir Charles Russell upon letter from Horan to Kenny, 206; As treasurer of Land League from February to October, 1881, he signed Tim Horan's cheque but does not recollect incident, 263–266; Thinks Mr. Egan has taken books with him, 268; Dr. Kenny on Farragher, 268; Dr. Kenny persists Egan was not in Dublin, 1881; Dr. Kenny and Le Caron, 269

Kerrigan and wife (Times witnesses), on Bailiff Huddy's murder, 22

Kerry Sentinel, Mr. Harrington's paper; Contempt of court, 35, 38; Condemns Fitzmaurice murder, 39; Macauliffe's outrage, 55, 56; Sir Charles Russell on, 206

Killeen, Mike, from Miltown, Clare (P. W.), denies Connell's evidence, 254

Kilmainham Treaty, Captain O'Shea upon, 9

Labouchere, Henry, Pigott's account of first interview with, 152; Last confession of Pigott, 163; Mr. Labouchere examined, 170

Lambert, Galway landlord (T. W.), 17

Landgrabbers, Mr. Dillon upon, 3; Mr. Harrington upon, 4; Mr. Biggar, 4; Scrab upon Landgrabber, "a louse," a "rapacious beast," a "low-life cur," a "putrid companion," 4

Land League—Attorney-General upon, 2, 3; League speeches are followed by outrages; Never denounce outrage; League books prove money paid to assassins, 4; American influence, 6; Constables O'Malley and Irwin on League speeches, 7; Speech of Martin O'Halloran condemns outrages, 7; League attacked by secret societies, 13; Rafferty does not attribute outrage upon him to League, 16'; Heagley speaks of respectability of members, 23; Leonard, Lord Kenmare's agent, considers League has caused outrages, 41; Secret inner circle, 47; District Inspector Crane says League introduced resistance to evictions, 55; District Inspector Wright of same opinion, 57; Hussey says Kerry peaceful Arcadia before League, 59; Canon Griffin, 63; Informer O'Connor on inner circle, 64; Informer Mike Burke connects murder of Lord Mountmorres with League, 71; David Freely says murder of his son not due to League, 76; Miss Thompson, landowner, Mr. Richards, 78; Informer Iago against League, 95; Pat Delaney incriminates League, 98, 99; Fenians denounce League, 99; Captain Plunkett against League, 105; Dennis Tobin, informer, 109; Captain Slacke, 111; Sir Charles Russell on foundation of, 197–200; League circular warning people against crime, 1880, 216; Mr. Parnell on disorganization at League office when Mr. Davitt and he were in prison, 217; Archbishop Walsh says League denounce and put down crime, 229; League makes crime less frequent, says Mr. Cawley, 232; Father O'Donovan says League denounces crime, 241; Mr. Nolan says League prevents crime, 243; Mr. W. O'Brien says there would have been famine and civil war without League, 245; Mr. Harrington quotes League denunciations of crime, 262; D. F. O'Connor shows denunciatory documents, 263; Greany's evidence, 264; Father Harrington, 265; Father Lawler's evidence in favour of League, 264; Condition of Mayo before League, 273; Rules and principles, 277; Mr. Lowden on Herds' League and its opposition to Land League, 285; Mr. Gallager, Poor Law guardian of Strabane, Mr. O'Hagan, chairman of Monoghan Commissioners, Mr. Ryan, Mayor of Cork, Mayor of Limerick, Mayor of Waterford, Mayor of Kilkenny, Mayor of Wexford, Mayor of Sligo, Chairman of Maryborough Commissioners, Chairman of Tullamore Commissioners, Mr. Delahunt of Wexford, all give evidence of services rendered by League,

291 ; Mr. Moloney denies that any money was paid through him out of League funds to those who committed crimes, 305 ; Sir Henry James on, 327, 329, 331, 332, 333
Larkin, Tom, one of the defenders of Saunders' "fort"—a boy of fifteen—who died in prison of hardship, 240
Lawler, Father, P. P. of Killoughlin (P. W.), considers boycotting justifiable, 264
League Books—Mr. Moloney's evidence about books, 305 ; Mr. Miller, manager of Charing Cross branch of National Bank, 305 ; Mr. Tyrrell, Mr. Phillips, Sir Henry James on books, 343
Letters, Times—3, 4, 7; Attorney-General hands President facsimile letter, 5 ; shown to Captain O'Shea, 10 ; Sir Charles Russell complains advertisement of facsimile letter as Mr. Parnell's, 15 ; Convict Delaney professes to recognize Egan's signature, 100 ; Mr. Soames's evidence about, 140 ; Pigott's evidence about, 151, 152, 153 ; Pigott's confession that letters are his forgeries, 167 ; Mr. Parnell denies letters, 169 ; Mr. O'Kelly denies letter to Egan, 170 ; Mr. Campbell denies letter, 190 ; Sir Charles Russell asks for special report, 171 ; Mr. Davitt, 167 ; Sir Charles Russell, 211 ; Mr. Davitt upon, 321, 322 ; Sir Henry James upon, 345
Leahy—man murdered for taking an evicted farm—Mrs. Leahy's evidence, 36 ; District-Inspector Craig's evidence, 37 ; *Kerry Sentinel* denounces murder, 37 ; Mr. Lynes's evidence, 263
Leavy, informer (T. W.), ex-member of Fenian Supreme Council, 186–187
Lennard, Matthew, put in a coffin by moonlighters, and told to pray for his soul, 24
Leonard, Maurice, Lord Kenmare's agent, evidence, 40 ; Considers he knows Ireland better than Mr. Balfour or General Gordon, 41, 42 ; Doesn't think much of General Buller, 42
Lewis, Mr., of Woodford (T. W.), evidence, 17 ; Mr. Roche upon, 239
Lewis, Mr. G. H., Pigott's interview with, 152 ; Mr. Lewis's account of Pigott, 170
Loftus, Tipperary farmer (T. W.), 175
Lyden—man murdered by moonlighters—Mrs. Lyden's (T. W.) evidence, 24 ; James Mannion, informer, says murder planned at Mrs. Walsh's, 28 ; Mr. Davitt, 283 ; Sir H. James on, 340
Lynes, Mr. (P. W.), of Killarney, evidence of Davitt's and Healey's denunciation of crime ; also that Leahy's murder was deplored by leaguers who attended his funeral, 263

Macauliffe (T. W.), Kerry man, brother of a process-server, shot in the arm by moonlighters, 55 ; *Kerry Sentinel's* condemnation of outrage, 55
Macdonald, Mr. J. C., manager of *The Times*, examination by Attorney-General, 142 ; Agreement with Houston, 143 ; "Every journalist must choose his opportunity," 143 ; "I particularly avoided the subject of origins," 144 ; Articles written "in the ordinary course of business," 145 ; Mr. Davitt on Mr. Macdonald
Macdonald, name mentioned by Informer Flaherty as one belonging to a leaguer who took part in outrages, 29
McArdle, District-Inspector, Mayo (T. W.), 75
Macaulay, Informer Colman's charge against him, 177–178 ; Mr. Reid quotes Macaulay's denial in *Freeman's Journal* that he belonged to League, 180
McCarthy (T. W.), "a few grains of powther," 37
McCarthy, Mr. Justin, M.P., examined, 259
McCormack, Dr., Bishop of Galway (P. W.), League destroyed criminal societies, 232
McHale, Father P. W.), from Crossmalina, "People's misery convinced me a tenants' combination necessary," 274
Maloney, Father (P. W.), president of local branch of League, 233 ; Cross-examined by Sir H. James, Father Maloney gives his views of strong speech and boycotting, 234
Mannion, James, informer (T. W.), evidence as to outrages in which he shared, 28
Martin, on landgrabbers, 3
Mayne, Mr., M.P. for Tipperary, 287
Meehan, Constable (T. W.), evidence concerning Curtin's murder, 39
Miller, Mr., manager of Charing Cross branch of National Bank, on League books, 305
Meehan, chairman of Maryborough Commissioners (P. W.), evidence in favour of League, 291
Mitchell, Mary (T. W.), boycotted, 137
Milcarren, evidence of Informer Flaherty, 29
Molloy, Pat (T. W.), sent to prison for not obeying subpœna, 69 ; Molloy's evidence consists in denying first statement, 73–74 ; Delaney names Molloy as one of the Invincibles, 98
Moloney, Mr. Parnell states last person in

whose possession League books were seen, 224-255; In witness-box, 305; Mr. Maloney did not order destruction of books, 305; Sir H. James on Mr. Maloney's supposed possession of books, 343
Monoghan, farmer, Connemara (*P. W.*), weeps whilst describing famine scenes, 236
Morgan (*T. W.*), Bermingham's herd boycotted, 34
Moroney, Constable (*T. W.*), evidence concerning Dr. Tanner's description of Hegarty, 66
Moroney, man murdered by moonlighters, *see* Father Stewart's evidence, 255
Moriarty, Dr., Kerry, Mr. Huggins, inspector, reports Doctor's "ferocious utterances," 43-44
Mountmorres, Lord, Galway landlord murdered, September, 1880. Evidence of Lady Mountmorres, 32; Constable's evidence, 33; Evidence of Constable Farrell, 117; of Informer Burke, 70-72; Sir C. Russell upon, 204; Sir H. James on, 334
Mulcarren, named by Informer Flaherty as one who joined in outrages, 29
Mullett, see Informer Farragher's evidence, 106
Mulqueeny, George, Captain O'Shea's evidence. 11; Mulqueeny's evidence concerning F. Byrne after and before Phœnix Park murders, 188-189; Mr. Parnell's cheque, 11, 189
Murphy, Sub-Inspector (*T. W.*), 32
Murphy, Father, *see* Brown's evidence concerning, 51, 256
Murphy, Pat (*T. W.*), his experiences with moonlighters, 55

Nally, "*Scrab*," vehement abuse of land-grabbers, 3, 4, 7, 8; Constable Irwin's opinion of, 13; O'Malley calls "a sort of drunkard," 14; Mr. Ives' opinion, 21; Mr. Parnell upon, 220-227; Mr. Davitt, 284; Sir H. James on, 333
"*Nation*," *The*, Mr. T. D. Sullivan's paper, 254
National League, "only Land League re-christened," 3, 26; Sir H. James on, 345
New York Herald, Mr. Ives, special correspondent of, 15
Nolan, Mr. John, of Ballynoonan, Galway (*P. W.*), evidence for League, 242

O'Brien, William, United Ireland, 87; Mr. O'Brien's speech in Court, 93; Sir James Hannen upon, 96; Mr. O'Brien examined by Mr. Reid, 243; States that League prevented famine and civil war in 1880, 245; Views on boycotting, 245; League meeting called to check outrages, 246; American tour, 246; Cross-examined by Attorney-General, 246; "The Woodford spirit has made England what it is," 246
O'Brien, J. F. Xavier, M.P., condemned twenty-two years ago to be hung, drawn, and quartered, evidence, 275
O'Connell, Hannah, old woman, boycotted, 91
O'Connell, Father (*P. W.*), priest from Connemara, evidence concerning the servants of Mrs. Blake of Connemara—their misery and her exactions, 230; On Lyden's murder, denies meetings of League at Mrs. Walsh's, as stated by Informer Mannion (see 28), 231
O'Connor, D. F., secretary of Abbeydorney branch of League (*P. W.*), produces League books and documents showing how League denounced crime, 263
O'Connor, T. P., 2; *see* Le Caron's evidence, 124; examined by Mr. Lockwood, 265
O'Connor, Father, P. P. of Firies, Kerry, Constable's evidence concerning, 28; Father O'Connor, president of local branch of League, gives evidence concerning Curtins, 267; unsatisfactory explanation of his coldness after murder, 267
O'Connor, Kerry farmer (*T. W.*), "clears his character," 37
O'Connor, Arthur (*P. W.*), in America, 258; Evidence on Horan's letter, 260
O'Connor, John, M.P., police witnesses accuse Mr. J. O'Connor of cheering Poff and Barrett, accused of Brown's murder, 51, 52; Mr. Harrington's view of Poff's innocence, 61; Examination of Mr. J. O'Connor, 287-290; Mr. J. O'Connor's account of Poff and Barrett incident, 288; He visits Curtins in their trouble, 288; President's reproof, 290; Mr. J. O'Connor explains speech on Prince of Wales visit, 292
O'Connor, Thomas, informer (*T. W.*), evidence, 64, 65; Cross-examined, 88-90; letter to his brother about swearing "quare things," 90
O'Connor, Henry, secretary of Causeway branch of League (*P. W.*), produces books to prove outrage-mongers not members as stated by *Times*, 268
O'Donovan, Father, priest of Corrofin, Clare, president of branch of League (*P. W.*), evidence concerning misery of Major Moloney's tenants, 241; Cross-examined by Sir H. James, Father O'Donovan says he denounced outrages

Index. 361

forty Sundays running, 242; Sir H. James on, 338
O'*Donovan Rossa*, Mr. Davitt on, 310; Sir H. James on, 337
O'*Donnell*, *Dominic*, landlord, Mayo (*T. W.*), when bailiffs hestitate to evict he himself drags a tenant's wife out of bed, 103
O'*Hagan* (*P. W.*), evidence favourable to League, 291
O'*Keefe*, Mayor of Limerick (*P. W.*), 291
O'*Kelly*, M.P., *see* Le Caron's evidence, 121; Denies letter to Egan, 298
O'*Malley*, *Bernard*, Constable (*T. W.*), evidence, 8-14
O'*Riordan*, 48
O'*Shea*, *Captain* (*T. W.*), evidence of, 12; Mulqueeny's information, 11; Captain O'Shea says he destroyed all memoranda of Kilmainham treaty at Sir William Harcourt's advice, 11; Mulqueeny's account of the information he gave Captain O'Shea, 189; Sir Charles Russell on Captain O'Shea and Mr. Parnell, 201

Parnell, *Mr. Charles*, M.P., Attorney-General quotes Mr. Parnell's speech at Ennis advising avoidance of landgrabbers, 4; Allusion to *Times* letters, 4; Mr. Parnell could have stopped outrage, 5; Attorney-General describes Captain O'Shea's evidence, 5; Mr. Parnell felt bound to satisfy American paymasters, 7; Captain O'Shea's evidence, 9-12; Le Caron states Mr. Parnell's American tour under direction of Clan-na-Gael, 122; Le Caron's account of interview with Mr. Parnell April, 1881, 123; Had ceased to believe that anything but force would bring about redemption of Ireland, 123; Le Caron modifies statement about American tour, 133; Mr. Parnell's views as a revolutionist see on Le Caron, 134; Mr. Parnell's photograph, Le Caron alleges given by him, 136; How Mr. Soames verified Mr. Parnell's signature, 140; Firm belief of Mr. Soames upon the genuineness of Mr Parnell's signature, 141; Pigott's grievance against Mr. Parnell, 142; Mr. Macdonald's view of Mr. Parnell's alleged letters, 143; Mr. Macdonald thinks the absence of envelopes suspicious, 144, 145; Mr. Houston does not consider Mr. Parnell entitled to any consideration, 146; Pigott states how he first hears of Mr. Parnell's letter, 151; Pigott's account of his interview with Mr. Parnell, 152; Pigott wishes to save Mr. Parnell and his associates, 155; Mr. Parnell's genuine letters to Pigott about *Irishman*, 157; Mr. Parnell after Pigott's flight, 166; He goes into witness-box and denies letters, 167; Mulqueeny's evidence about Mr. Parnell's cheque to F. Byrne, 187; Sir C. Russell on Mr. Parnell, 197, 201, 202, 203, 208; Mr. Parnell's examination-in-chief, 214-218; Cross-examination by Attorney-General, 218-226; Re-examined by Sir C. Russell, 226-228; Mr. Parnell contradicts Le Caron's statement about American tour, 215; About interview and photograph, 217; Mr. Parnell on Phœnix Park murders, 217; on Tim Horan's letter, 219; on Clan-na-Gael, 219; on John Devoy, 221; on Mr. Redmond, 222; on the *Irishman*, 223; "I have always thought physical force useless and criminal," 224; "I was trying to mislead the House," 224; Explanation of this statement, 225; League books, 224, 225, 227; Mr. Davitt describes Parnell as too conservative, 277; Mr. Parnell withdraws his defence, 296; Mr. Parnell cross-examined about League books by Attorney-General, 296; Mr. Parnell's correspondence examined by Mr. Campbell, Mr. Arthur O'Connor, Mr. Graham, and Mr. Asquith, 306; Mr. Davitt's speech, allusion to Mr. Parnell's, 311-313; Sir Henry James on, 325, 327, 329, 331, 334, 340, 344
Phillips, ex-Land League clerk and wife about Land League books, state Mrs. Moloney took them away
Pigott, *Richard*, ordered to withdraw during Mr. Soames' evidence, 141; Mr. Soames' evidence concerning, 142; Mr. Macdonald's, 144; Houston's, 146, 147; Pigott enters witness-box, 150; Story about Eugene Davis, 151; Meeting with Maurice Murphy and story of black bag, 151; Pigott's oath, 151; Pigott's story of interview with Messrs. Parnell, Lewis, and Labouchere, 152, 153; Pigott and Archbishop Walsh, 154, 155; "Hesitency," 154-159; Mr. Pigott "warns" Mr. Egan in 1887, 159; Pigott and Mr. Forster, 159, 160; Pigott's disappearance, 161; Mr. Labouchere receives Pigott's confession, 163, 164; Letter from Pigott's housemaid "all is consumed," 163; Confession read by Mr. Cunninghame, 166, 169; Mr. Davitt upon future revelations concerning his correspondence, 321

Rafferty, *John*, Galway peasant (*T. W.*), "corded" by moonlighters, 16

Reagh (*T. IV.*), ear cut off by moonlighters, 35
Redmond, Mr. W., M.P., Sir C. Russell on, 207; Mr. Parnell, 222; Evidence of Constable Webb of Mr. Redmond's proceedings as Mr. Mondred, 176
Reynolds, Miss (Mrs. Delahunt), president of Ladies Land League (*P. W.*), Sir C. Russell condemns Attorney-General's statement that outrages followed her, 201; Mrs. Delahunt examined by Attorney-General, 301
Rice, District Inspector (*T. IV.*), Evidence concerning Mr. John O'Connor's cheering Poff and Barrett, 52
Richards, Mr., of Wexford, landlord, 79
Roche, W., Buckley's account of his attempt to murder Roche, 84; Roche's own account, 118
Roche, Mr. John, of Woodford (*P. W.*), on "Doctor" Tully and Vandeleur evictions, 238; denies constable's story, (see p. 18, of Finlay's mock funeral, 238; Mr. Roche's idea of justifiable resistance, 239; On Tom Larkin, 240
"*Roosters*," 53
Ross, Mahon, landlord and agent (*T. W.*), house blown up, 23
Ruane, named by Informer Mannion as an instigator of outrages, 29, 177
Russell, Sir Charles, cross-examines Lady Mountmorres, 33; Colletty, 36; Mr. Hussey, 59; boy-informer Walsh, 67; Mike Burke, 71; Pat Molloy, 74; Miss Thompson, 77-79; protests against unnecessary evidence, and a slight difference with Mr. Justice Smith, 80; cross-examines Informer Buckley, 84; Informer O'Connor, 89; Informer Jago, 93-97; Informer Delany, 99; Informer Farragher, 107; Captain Slack, 112; Constable Farrell, 117; Mike Roche, 118; Le Caron, 129-135; Houston, 146-149; Pigott, 154-161; "Behind Houston and Pigott there is a foul conspiracy," 162; examines Mr. Parnell, 169; cross-examines Mr. Soames, 171; Asks for special report on letters, 171; Cross-examines Informer Colman, 178; Speech for the defence, 190-213; "Attempt to indict a whole nation," 191: *The Times* methods of collecting evidence, 191; Ireland before 1879, 192; Irish agrarian system condemned by Swift, Berkeley, Lord Townshend, Arthur Young, Lord Clare, General Gordon, 193; Landlords did nothing but eject, 195; Foundation of League and Mr. Parnell, 127; Free and open programme, 198; "A grave scandal," 199; On boycotting, 198; "What a wretched thing of sheds and patches," 199; Work of the League relief and organization, 200; on Captain O'Shea, 201-202; National League, 202; On murders of Luke Dillon and Lord Mountmorres, 203; In not a single case has murder or complicity in it been brought home to the League, 203; Curtin and Fitzmaurice outrages, 204; Delaney's evidence and Le Caron's, 205; On Egan, Mr. Sexton, Mr. Davitt, Mr. O'Kelly, Dr. Kenny, 206; "Infamy," 206; Mr. Mat. Harris, Mr. Harrington, and T. D. Sullivan, 207; Irish emigrants, 208; Le Caron "a living lie," 209; The Letters, 211; Peroration, "a great speech worthy of a great occasion," 213; Discussion with President on League financial documents, 228; claims to see books of Irish Loyal Patriot Association, and upon President's decision withdraws from case, 297
Ryan, Mayor of Cork (*P. IV.*), gives evidence in favour of League, 291

Sala, G. A., witness to Pigott's confession, 163
Sanders, agent (*T. IV.*), 108
Saunders, Woodford man who defends his house, 240; *see* Tom Larkin's boy who dies from hardship, sent to prison for defending Saunders' "fort," 240
Scanlon, Patrick (*P. W.*), from Kerry, witness to distress before League, 275
"*Scrab*," *see* Nally
Scully, Mr. Vincent (*P. W.*), landlord and magistrate, resigns because of Coercion Acts, 276
Sexton, Mr. M.P., Lord Mayor of Dublin, Le Caron's evidence, 135; Sir Charles Russell on, 206; says Le Caron's story an absolute fabrication, 270; scene with Attorney-General, 291; cross-examines Mr. Soames, 306
Sheehy, Informer Buckley's story concerning intended murder of, 83
Sheridan, Loftus states he visited him in disguise, 175; Sir Charles Russell, upon, 205
Slacke, Captain (*T. W.*), commissioner for eight counties; evidence against League, 111-113
Slayne (*T. W.*), money-lender, beaten by moonlighters, 75
Smith (*T. W.*), Lord Sligo's agent shoots intending murderer, 82
Soames, Mr., solicitor of *The Times*, enters witness-box, 134; evidence concerning "facsimile letter," 140; money transactions with Houston, 140; Satis-

fies himself the Parnell, Davitt, and Egan letters are genuine, 141; detects Pigott's interview with Mr. Labouchere, 142; cross-examined by Sir Charles Russell, 142; Admits he "made no inquiries into Pigott's character," 164; examined upon his connection with Pigott and Houston, 171; Relates the story of his intercourse with Timothy Coffey, 185; cross-examined by Mr. Sexton upon money paid by *Times* to witnesses, 307

Sullivan, T. D., M.P., ex-Mayor of Dublin, evidence in chief, 252; cross-examined by Mr. Murphy, 252–254; "No man is a fiend," 254

Sullivan (T. W.), Kerry bog-ranger "League took my part," 34

Sullivan, Jeremiah (T. W.), Kerry man assaulted by moonlighters, 54

Sullivan, of Meath (brother of T. D. Sullivan), examined, 275

Tanner, Dr., M.P., evidence of two constables concerning Dr. Tanner's picturesque abuse of Hegarty, 66; Dr. Tanner's examination; admits that to the "best of his abilities" he has denounced landgrabbers, 301; specimens of Dr. Tanner's oratory, 302

Tanner, Major (T. W.), brother of Dr. Tanner, land-agent in Tipperary, evidence against League, 94

Tarpey (P. W.), from Ballyglass, Galway, denies evidence given by Charleton (see 21) of brutal conduct of people after murder of Constable Burke, 23

Teahan (T. W.), hotel-keeper and cattle-dealer of Tralee, says he was boycotted through private jealousy, and not by direction of the League, 94

Thompson, Miss (T. W.), owner of land in Kerry, evidence against League, 78

Times (*Witnesses* see *Witnesses*), Attorney-General says *The Times* has made every possible inquiry into the genuineness of letters, 5; Mr. Soames of (*see* Soames); Mr. Macdonald of (*see* Macdonald); Pat Molloy tricks on, 73; Houston and, 143; Pigott and "Parnellism and Crime," 145; Sir Charles Russell upon, 191; Sir Henry James upon, 323; Mr. Davitt upon, 319

Tobin, Dennis (T. W.), informer, ex-moonlighter from Limerick, 108–110

Toole, Mayor of Waterford

Tunbridge, Inspector, evidence concerning a bank-note traced from Byrne to Walsh, 119

Tynan, No. 1, Delaney's evidence, 98; portrait recognized, 102; Le Caron's evidence, 128; Tynan seen in Miss Reynolds' company by two constables, 137

Wallace, Constable, murdered at Ardraghan, county Galway (*see* police evidence, 21); Mr. Roche's evidence, 232

Walker, Mr., agent for *The Times* (see Pat Molloy's evidence), 74

Walsh, James (T. W.), boy-informer, 67

Walsh, Mrs. (*see* Mannion's evidence that Mrs. Walsh's house was League meeting-place for planning outrages, 28); Young Walsh hanged for Lyden's murder; Heanne's evidence, 138; Davitt's evidence, 283; Father O'Connell's evidence, 231

Walsh, John (*see* Inspector Tunbridge's evidence, 119); Head-constable Wilkinson's, 119

Walsh, Dublin, solicitor, proves money paid to relations of the men executed and imprisoned for Phœnix Park murders, 138

Walsh, Thomas, ex-convict employed by Mr. Soames to hunt for documents damaging to Mr. Parnell, 179

Walsh, Dr., Archbishop of Dublin, Pigott's correspondence with, 154-155; evidence, 228; views on boycotting, 230

Witnesses for *The Times*—Head-Constable Bernard O'Malley, 7-14; Constable Irwin, 9-13; Captain O'Shea, 9-12; Mr. Ives of *New York Herald*, 15; John Rafferty, Galway peasant, 16; Sub-Inspector Dominic Barry, 16; Mrs. Dempsey, widow of man murdered, 16; Mrs. Conners, 17; Mr. Lewis, landlord, Woodford, 17; Mr. Lambert, landlord, Galway, 17; Thomas White, peasant, Galway, 17; Coursey of Loughrea, 18; Constables Beattie, Nally, and Gibbon, 18; District Inspector Bell, 19; Police-officer Charleton, 21; Mr. Burke, landlord, Woodford, 21; Kerrigan and wife, Mayo peasants, 22; Constable Hugh Kelly, 23; Constable Patrick Bolger, 23; Mr. Botterill, Galway landlord, 23; Heagley, peasant, 23; Matt. Lennard, steward, 23; Tom Connair, peasant, 24; Mrs. Lyden, widow of man murdered, 24; Mike Joyce, 24; Mrs. Blake of Connemara, 25; Mr. Hughes, car proprietor, 26; Mrs. J. H. Blake, widow of Lord Clanricarde's agent, 27; Pat Kennedy, peasant, 28; Farmer James Mannion, ex-Fenian, 28; Peter Flaherty, ex-Fenian, 29 ; Edward Flanagan, Informer, 30 ; Mike Hoarty, ex-Fenian, 30 ; Constable Creagh, 30 ; Ford, 31 ; Sub - Inspector Murphy, Woodford district, 32 ; Farmer Kennedy, Galway, 32 ; Lady Mountmorres, 33 ; Constable O'Connor, 33 ; James Bermingham, process-server, 33 ; Morgan, Bermingham's herd, 34 ; Sullivan, bog-ranger, 35 ; Reagh, peasant, 35 ; Culoty, farmer and process-server, 36 ; Mrs. Leahy, widow of man murdered, 36 ; District Inspector Craig, 37 ; O'Connor, Kerry farmer, 37 ; M'Carthy, peasant, 37 ; Mrs. Hickey, widow of man murdered, 37 ; Dowling, peasant, 38 ; Miss Curtin and brother, 39 ; Constable Meehan, 39 ; Norah Fitzmaurice, daughter of murdered man, 39 ; Mr. Leonard, agent of Lord Kenmare, 40-42 ; District Inspector Huggins, 43, 44 ; Mr. Teahan, hotel-keeper and cattle dealer, Tralee, 45 ; Sergeant Gilhooly, 45, 46 ; District Inspector Davis, 47-49 ; Mr. Tom Galvin, farmer, 50 ; Mr. Brown, farmer, 51 ; Mrs. Johanna Brown, widow of man murdered, 51 ; District Inspector, W. H. Rice, 52 ; Farmer John Kennedy, 52 ; Coonahan, blacksmith, 53 ; Griffin, carter, 54 ; Farmer Jeremiah Sullivan, 54 ; Pat Murphy, "land-grabber," 55 ; John Macauliffe, process-server, 55 ; District Inspector Crane, 55, 56 ; District Inspector Wright, 57 ; Eugene Sheehy, 58 ; Mr. Hussey, Kerry landlord, 59 ; Mr. Jeremiah Hegarty, merchant and farmer, 61-62 ; Cornelius Kelleher, Cork, labourer, 62 ; Mr. Jeremiah O'Connor, 62 ; Mary Fitzgerald, Mrs. Fitzgerald, 62 ; Constable Thomas Cahill, 63 ; Canon Griffin of Killarney, 63 ; Thomas O'Connor, Informer, 64-88 ; Constables Moroney and Hobbins, 66 ; Williams, from Cork, 66 ; Cornelius Regan, Cork, 66 ; James Walsh, boy informer, 67, 68 ; Jeremiah Buckley, peasant, 68 ; Mike Burke, Informer, 70-72 ; Mr. Kelleher of Cork, 72 ; Patrick Molloy, 72-74 ; M'Ardle, police-officer, 75 ; Ann Gallagher, 75 ; Sloyne, gombeen man, 75 ; David Freely, 76 ; Dillon, peasant, 76 ; Pensioner Fahy, peasant, 76 ; Moloney, 76 ; Mr. Carter, landlord, 77 ; Miss Thompson, landowner, 77, 78 ; Mr. E. M. Richards, landlord, 78, 79 ; Captain Boycott, 80 ; District Inspector Gambell, 81 ; Denis Feeley, police sergeant, 81 ; Mr. E. Smith, Lord Sligo's agent 82 ; Hugh Macauliffe, herd, 82 ; James Buckley, Informer, 83-86 ; Moroney, 91 ;

Hannah Connell, 91 ; Major Tanner, landlord, 94 ; Iago, Informer, 95 ; Patrick Delancy, Informer, 97-102 ; Mr. J. Digby, land agent, 102 ; Mr. Hewson, land agent, 102 ; Mr. Young, land agent, 102 ; Mr. Garrett Tyrrell, 103 ; Robert Powell, 103 ; Verriker, 103 ; Mr. John Barrett of Cork, 103 ; Mr. Dominick O'Donnell, landlord, 104 ; Captain Plunkett, 104 ; Mr. Studdert, agent of Mr. Vandeleur, 105 ; Farragher, Informer, 106, 107 ; Mr. Robert Sandy's, agent, 108 ; Denis Tobin, Informer, 109-111 ; Captain Slacke, 111 ; Mr. Hanley, landlord, 116 ; Constable Farrell, 117 ; Mike Roche, 117 ; Sheehy, 118 ; Head-Constable Wilkinson, 119 ; Inspector Tunbridge of Scotland Yard, 119 ; Sergeant Sheridan, 119 ; Mr. W. Jackman, 119 ; Constable Couslton, 119 ; Le Caron, or T. M. Beach, 120-136 ; Mr. Mitchell, machine maker, 137 ; Mr. Kreagh, solicitor, Kerry, 138 ; Mr. Walsh, solicitor, Dublin, 138 ; Heanne, peasant, 138 ; Mr. Soames, solicitor for *The Times*, 139-142 ; Mr. J. C. Macdonald, manager of, 142-145 ; Mr. Houston, 145-150 ; Mr. Pigott, 150-161 ; Police - constable Ough, 175 ; Detective Inspector Peel, 175 ; Mr. Loftus, Tipperary farmer, 175 ; Sergeant Caulfield, 176 ; Mr. John Webb, 176 ; Colman, Informer, 176-179 ; Constable Francis Connor, 179 ; Timothy Coffey, 180-184 ; John Leavy, Informer, 186 ; Mr. George Mulqueeny, ex - Fenian, 187-189.

Witnesses for Parnellites—Mr. Parnell, 214-228 ; Archbishop Walsh of Dublin, 228 ; Father Q'Connell, 230 ; Father Considine, 231 ; Stephen Tarpey of Ballyglass, Galway, 232 ; Mr. Patrick Cawley of Craughwell, 232 ; Dr. McCormack, Bishop of Galway, 233 ; Father Fahy of Gort, Galway, 233 ; Father Maloney, Galway, 234 ; Mr. Kennedy, Town Councillor, Loughrea, 234 ; Mr. Bartholomew Canavan, relieving-officer, 235 ; Mr. E. Jennings, secretary of League at Clonbur, 235 ; Mr. John Monaghan, farmer, 236 ; Father Egan of Dunivy, near Loughrea, 236 - 238 ; Mr. McInerney, solicitor, Woodford, 238 ; Mr. John Roche, merchant, Woodford, 238-240 ; Mr. Keary, 239 ; Father White, 241 ; Rev. Michael O'Donovan of Corrofin, 241 ; Father John Hanneny of Riverside, Galway, 242 ; Patrick Keogh of Kiltullagh, 242 ; Father Bodkin of Mullagh, 242 ; Father Finneran of Ballinasloe, 243 ;

Mr. William O'Brien, Ballinasloe, 243-252; Mr. T. D. Sullivan, ex-Mayor of Dublin, 252-254; Father Stewart, 254; Mike Killeen, secretary of local branch, 254; James Clancy, 254; Mr. John Ferguson of Glasgow, 254; Mr. Mackay, journalist, 255; Canon Shinkwin of Bantry, 255; Father Malley of Drimoleague, 255; Rev. Mr. Anderson, Protestant rector of Drinagh, 256; Father Morissey of Ballinteer, 256; Canon Ryan of Aghada, 256; Father Murphy, Skull, 256; Mr. Edward Raycroft, 256; Mr. Maurice Healy, 257; Mr. Biggar, 257, 258; Mr. Arthur O'Connor, 258; Mr. E. Harrington, 260; Mr. Patrick Kenny of Castleisland, 263; Father Godley, 263; Mr. D. F. O'Connor, 263; Mr. Lyne of Killarney, 263; John Greany, Kerry, 264; Father Lawler of Killoughlin, 264; Father Daniel Harrington, 264; Thomas J. O'Connor, 265; Mr. John Shea, hotel-keeper of Glenbeigh, 265; Mr. T. P. O'Connor, 265; Father O'Connor of Firies, Kerry, 267; Mr. Foley, 268; Mr. Henry O'Connor, 268; Dr. Kenny, M.P., 268; Mr. Sexton, M.P., Lord Mayor of Dublin, 270, 271; Mr. T. Harrington, M.P., 271; Father Hewson of Belmullet, 272; Father Kelly of Moygarna, 273; Mr. Waldron of Ballyhaunis, 274; Charles Burke of Kiltimagh, 274; Father McHale, 274; Mr. Thomas Harrington, 275; Dr. Commins, M.P., 275; Mr. J. F. Xavier O'Brien, M.P., 275; Mr. Sullivan of Meath, 275; Mr. Clancy, M.P., 275; Patrick Scanlon of Kerry, 275; Martin Fitzpatrick, Mayo, 275; Mr. Power, M.P., 275; Mr. Vincent Scully, Tipperary landlord, 275; Mr. Michael Davitt, 276-284; Mr. J. J. Lowden, barrister, 285; Mr. Garrett Byrne, M.P. for Wicklow, 287; Mr. Jeremiah Jordan, M.P. for West Clare, 287; Mr. T. Mayne, M.P. for Mid-Tipperary, 287; Mr. John O'Connor, 287-291; Mr. Daniel Crilly, M.P., of *The Nation*, 291; Mr. Gallagher, Poor Law Guardian of Strahane, 291; Mr. O'Hagan, chairman of Commissioners, 291; Mr. Ryan, Mayor of Cork, 291; Mr. O'Keefe, Mayor of Limerick; Mr. Toole, Mayor of Waterford, 291; Mr. Cayle, Mayor of Kilkenny, 291; Mr. Devereux, Mayor of Wexford, 291; Mr. Conolly, Mayor of Sligo, 291; Mr. Meehan, chairman Maryborough Commissioners, 291; Mr. William Adams, chairman Tullamore Commissioners, 291; Mr. Delahunt of Wexford, 291; Mr. Foley, M.P., 292; Mr. George Shrubsole, 292; Mr. Flood, chairman of Longford Commissioners, 292; Mr. John Hammond of the Carlow Town Commission, 292; Mr. Robinson of Kingstown Commission, 293; Mr. Thomas Condon, M.P., East Tipperary, 293; Mr. T. Berrane, 293; Mr. Kelly, general merchant, 293; Mr. McCarthy, League branch president, 293; Mr. Hogg, member of committee of I. L. P. U., 294; Mr. O'Kelly, 298; Mr. Matt. Harris, 299; Mrs. Delahunt (Miss Reynolds), 301; Dr. Tanner, 301

Webster, Sir Richard, Attorney-General. — Opening Speech, 3-7; League speeches followed by outrages that are not denounced by leaders of movement, 3; Open organization a screen for underground movement, 3; Messrs. Harrington and Biggar, 4; Every possible inquiry into genuineness of letters made by *The Times*, 5; Facsimile letter produced, 5; Mr. Parnell could have stopped outrages, 6; Patrick Ford, real father of League, 6; Irish Americans, paymasters of League, 7; Insinuates witness Sullivan has been influenced by Mr. Harrington, 38; On part of *The Times* states he begs to withdraw the question of the genuineness of letters, 168; Cross-examines Mr. Parnell, 218-226; Cross-examines Mr. O'Brien, 246-252; Cross-examines Mr. Sexton, 270, 271; Cross-examines Father Kelly, 273, 274; Cross-examines Mr. Davitt, 278-284; Cross-examines Mrs. Delahunt, 301; Cross-examines Mr. Parnell about League books, 303

www.ingramcontent.com/pod-product-compliance
Lightning Source LLC
Chambersburg PA
CBHW051248300426
44114CB00011B/935